Betty
SHABAZZ

A REMARKABLE STORY OF SURVIVAL AND FAITH BEFORE AND AFTER MALCOLM X

RUSSELL J. RICKFORD
Foreword by Myrlie Evers-Williams

SOURCEBOOKS, INC.
NAPERVILLE, ILLINOIS

Published by Sourcebooks, Inc.

P.O. Box 4410, Naperville, Illinois 60567-4410

(630) 961-3900

FAX: (630) 961-2168

www.sourcebooks.com

Library of Congress Cataloging-in-Publication Data

Rickford, Russell John.

Betty Shabazz: a remarkable story of survival and faith before and after Malcolm X / by Russell J. Rickford.

p. cm.

ISBN 1-4022-0171-0 (alk. paper)

1. Shabazz, Betty. 2. African American Muslims—Biography. 3. Black Muslims—Biography. I. Title.

BP223.Z8R53 2003

320.54'092–dc21

[B]

2002003447

Printed and bound in the United States of America

QW 10 9 8 7 6 5 4 3 2 1

For single mothers…
and for my own mother,
Angela E. Rickford

ACKNOWLEDGMENTS

A s always, all praises to the Lord and to the ancestors. Respect and gratitude to one of the more formidable of those ancestors, Dr. Betty Shabazz, whose spirit has graciously permitted a young artist to craft this portrait. My deepest appreciation to Aisha al-Adawiya, Laura Ross Brown, Herman Fulton, and Gamilah Shabazz, who have been patient, kindred spirits during this difficult but rewarding quest.

I am also grateful for the guidance and assistance of the following souls: Alice Adamcyzk, Abdul Alkalimat, Zaharazed Amin, Margie J. Anderson, Norma Jean Anderson, Sam Anderson, Maya Angelou, A. Peter Bailey, Safiya Bandele, Carol Banks, Amina Baraka, Amiri Baraka, Marge Battle, Yosef ben-Jochannan, Saba P. Bireda, Velma Blackwell, J. Herman Blake, Cora Eaves Braynon, Herb Boyd, Elombé Brath, Ethel Brown, James Campbell, Zerrie Campbell, Juollie Carroll, (Sonny Carson), Janice Cave, Zala Chandler, Vernice Chenault-Williams, Ruth Clark, Steve Clark, Sybil Williams Clarke, James H. Cone, Vette T. Crane, Larry Dais, Ron Daniels, Ernest Davis, Ruby Dee, David N. Dinkins, Richard Dixon, Howard Dodson, Beth English, Myrlie Evers-Williams, Johnnie Fairchild, Muriel Feelings, Herman Ferguson, Badi Foster, Elizabeth P. Fox, Jacqueline Gay, Bertie Gilmore, Peter Goldman, Esther Gordy-Edwards, Dick Gregory, Robert L. Haggins, Linda Harvey, Dorothy Height, Alexis Herman, Milton Henry, Lydia Hibbert, Eleanor Holmes-Norton, Aubrey Holder, Lynsyd Holder, Charles Hurst, Annette Hutchins, Heshaam Jaaber, Edison O. Jackson, Leonard Jeffries, Herman Johnson, Maxine Prince Johnson, Norma Johnson, Ingrid S. Jones, Louis E. Jones, Wardell Jones, A'aliyah Abdul Karim, Kareema Abdul Karim, Osman Karriem, Charles Kenyatta, Sister Khadiyyah, Grace Killens, Yuri Kochiyama, Ali Lamont, Paul Lee, Claude Lewis, Sue MacCree, Haki

Madhubuthi, Manning Marable, Miles McAfee, Andree N. McLaughlin, Natalie Mendoza, Michael Mowatt-Wynn, E. Ethelbert Miller, Sara Mitchell, James Briggs Murray, Evelyn Neal, Altamese Nelson, Novella Nelson, Gil Noble, Eleanor Holmes Norton, Imari Obadele, Ameenah Omar, Ahmed Osman, Andi Owens, Jean Y. Owensby, Rose Perkins, Juanita Poitier, Dorothy Pleas, Abdullah Abdur-Razzaq, Arnold Rampersad, Mary D. Redd, Socorro Relova, Jean Reynolds, Hilda Richards, Eugenia Rucker, William Sales, Sonia Sanchez, Madeline Sandlin, Shelmon Sandlin, Jr., Stanley Sandlin, Attallah Shabazz, Ilyasah Shabazz, Imajean Simpson, Elinor Sinnette, Barbara Skinner, James Smalls, Cynthia Smith, James Spady, William Strickland, Barbara M. Strong, Jones Stukes, Niara Sudarkasa, Ruth Summerford, Percy Sutton, Leida I. Torres, Halima Toure, James Turner, Marta Vega, Preston Wilcox, Vernice Williams, Cynthia Wilson, Sylvia Woods, and Lloyd Yearwood.

My thanks to the Institute for Research in African-American Studies at Columbia University, the Department of Linguistics at Stanford University, and the librarians, archivists, and staff at the Burton Historical Collection; Bentley Historical Library; Moorland-Spingarn Research Center; Blockson Collection; Philadelphia Public Library; Schomburg Center for Research in Black Culture; Hoskins Library, University of Tennessee–Knoxville; Tuskegee University; Library of Congress; and Vianna Historical Society.

I am indebted to Hillel Black and Peter Lynch of Sourcebooks, for able stewardship and editing; to my folks, John and Angela Rickford, for indispensable feedback and encouragement; to my siblings Shiyama, Anakela, and Luke, for support; and to my "boys," especially Ali Roberts, Todd Triplett, and Christopher Tyson, for camaraderie.

CONTENTS

Foreword

By Myrlie Evers-Williams

I am honored that I was asked to introduce this tome chronicling the life of my friend, Dr. Betty Shabazz. Dr. Betty had a cornucopia of friends, each having their special memory, yet sharing the common knowledge of this highly unusual woman of strength and courage.

This memoir reads like a historical suspense novel, even though the outcome is known. It is apparent that the author has thoroughly researched and documented his book, and *Betty Shabazz: A Remarkable Story of Survival and Faith before and after Malcolm X* strikes at the very depth of the reader's emotions. One feels the joy, pain, growth, love, and challenges of all its characters. It is a passionate portrait of Betty Shabazz from her many childhood experiences that shaped the very evolving adult woman that she became and was still evolving to be up to her untimely demise.

One will find that this biographical rendering of her life embarks on a journey of a woman who had a definite public persona, but also a relatively mysterious and undefined private personality. It gives a moving account of a loving, intelligent, fascinating, and complicated woman who had a wonderful sense of humor and enjoyed having a good time—someone with whom many will feel a kinship. In that way, she is not much different from many other housewives and mothers, except that she shared the life of one of the most dynamic black revolutionaries of his time.

This is a story that almost any woman who has felt the loss of a man in her life would be able to understand, to grasp strength from the meaning of it all. Perhaps most importantly, she could see that as a single parent, she is not alone. This is not a book only for women, though; all readers can gain wisdom and strength from reading this book because it clearly provides a historical yet personal outline on how to survive heartache, self-doubt, anger, bitterness, and personal growth.

The pace in which I read this book echoed its intensity, particularly as I approached the passage detailing the firebombing of the Shabazz home. Particularly haunting was Betty freezing for a moment when that fire engulfed their home, and realizing that fear was a luxury she couldn't afford—that she would never have that luxury again. The pace of the book quickened and reached a crescendo until the retelling of the actual assassination. I realized that of the three widows, as we were known, Betty's nightmare was the most terrifying of all. I had thought until reading this book that my experience was the worst, witnessing my husband being shot down and my children and I witnessing the blood and life drain from his body. Yet when I reached those passages that were told in such a vivid way—of Betty hearing the commotion, seeing the men dash toward her husband, firing bullets into him, of actually seeing him fall, measuring minute by minute—I realized that her horror was worse than mine. But who has the right to determine the worst pain?

Ironically, although a distant admirer of Coretta Scott King and Betty Shabazz, I had never met either woman in person until after their husbands were assassinated. We were all young women raising families without husbands and fathers. It is not surprising that we became close friends. We knew too well this type of tragedy and what challenges we faced as a result of our husbands' deaths.

The public tends to compartmentalize "us"—the widows—or, at least the three of us: Betty Shabazz, Coretta Scott King, and me. We had been grouped together as widows whose husbands were sacrificed to the civil rights struggle in this country. It is a private club, but open to new members—if one is willing to pay the price. It is a club, as my daughter, Reena, puts it, "that no one wishes to join." That price begins with marriage to men who are thrust willingly or not into the public arena. It starts with a desire to do something good, an objective to change the status quo, an effort to make a difference in other people's lives. And then along comes love.

Malcolm lovingly referred to Betty as "his brown sugar." Betty once said, "My children think my persona is me, when actually it is their father's." And so it was, two people loving life and living it in the midst of public opinion and private pain.

I wish that words would flow from me effortlessly, with substance and eloquence. I wish that Betty were here. Since Betty was always a private woman, the few times that we shared as friends are precious and treasured. It is difficult to describe a woman who was complex and yet simple in her wisdom.

Her strict upbringing by her adoptive mother and what one could consider secretive ways she had from her Muslim teaching made her at times appear to be tough beyond reason. My catharsis was in the spoken word—the more I verbally relived the experience, the freer I was from the pain. I was able to express my rage without any idea of holding back, sometimes being chastised by the NAACP leadership for being too honest. Betty was different. I remember how the question of reliving each moment of those last moments would serve as a mechanism to shut her down emotionally in an instant.

You could sense Betty's anguish and growing displeasure at those surrounding who were friends, those who surrounded her that she questioned their sincerity, and those she knew she couldn't trust. Public opinion dictates that you must not express your feelings openly because of your image. Even then I remember thinking, "Damn the image." The image wasn't going to bring our husbands back, but they would expect us to conduct ourselves in a way appropriate to their work.

That carries over into a time that this country and the world had never witnessed before. Once you and the public have defined that image, it is almost impossible to break away from it. You find yourself asking, "What would my husband want and expect of me? What would my friends expect of me? What do the enemies expect of me? What obligation do I owe to my children? And, most of all, What do I expect, of myself?"

At times, there was a tendency to want to please everyone. In Betty's case, I would suspect that she had an extra burden on her because so many people, black and white, had seen Malcolm as a radical troublemaker. I did not have to suffer that kind of hurt, although I knew that there were people of my own race who wished to see Medgar silenced, and of course white people who were overjoyed when he was silenced. But there was no one knowingly in the Civil Rights Movement who wished Medgar dead. Perhaps I am trying to say that the more I read of this story leading up to the time of the assassination of Malcolm X, the more the love and respect that I had for Betty continued to grow until it now knows no bounds.

My most vivid memory of Betty is that she was first and foremost a woman who cherished her family. A wife and mother, she was extremely protective of her children. Mothers instinctively protect those they love, even more so in the face of danger. And, when you are the wife of a civil rights activist whose philosophy is perceived equally by blacks and whites as caustic, you become the shield that wards off the evil spears of hatred. You place yourself in harm's way.

Many of the personal conversations we shared tended to lean toward concern for her children after Malcolm's death. It was a common theme, and one that allowed us to ease the pain and encourage the healing process. Our children often became a reflection of their father's spirit, as well as symbols of the future generations who would benefit from this ultimate sacrifice. So, thusly, we endured whatever the public perception was during that historical moment so that our children could live as freely as they chose in the future.

I recall my visit to Betty's hospital bed a week before she slipped into eternity. I looked at her and said aloud, "OK, girl, let's get it on." Through my tears, I spoke in a lighthearted, joking way, for we always said something similar when we felt we were too tired to go on. And I remember having the urge to put my arms around her and say, as I did, "I love you, Betty." And in reading this book, I felt the urge to reach out to embrace her and say over and over, "We love you."

This book provides you with an even deeper understanding of this time in America's history: of Malcolm's journey; of Muslim belief and practices; of a real marriage; of those true friends who were there for Betty and Malcolm throughout it all; and, most of all, of this wonderfully loving, complicated woman and how blessed all of us are that she walked this path and continues to inspire us.

Introduction

A MIRACLE IN THE DESERT

—

*"And sometimes, of course, black women
have just argued for the right to be tired."*
—Angela Yvonne Davis

Hajar the Egyptian hunts for water in the valley as her infant son writhes with thirst. She is a handmaid to Sarah, Prophet Abraham's wife. Sarah has cast her out for lying with Abraham and bearing him a son. Sarah, who is barren, had given Hajar to her husband so that he might have a child. But when Ismael was born, Sarah grew jealous and ordered mother and child abandoned in a wasteland. Today this is part of Mecca, the sacred Arabian city and the center of the Muslim World.

Hajar prays for deliverance, staggering over the parched earth. Surely God will not abandon her. She presses on. The child is near death. She sprints between the hills of Safa and Marwah. She flings her legs before her. The sand is scorching. She runs on the bulbs of her feet. Her lungs are fingers of flame. She sucks air from her belly. The child is still. Hajar collapses, weeping for her half-dead boy. Miraculously, where her feet have tattooed the land, a spring gushes. The water of Zamzam is cool, sweet redemption in the wilderness.

Betty Shabazz loved this story. In the Muslim tradition, brown-skinned Hajar symbolizes the virtue of perseverance and faith amid suffering. But for Betty there was something more personal and poignant; a sisterhood with this woman who had been stranded with a child, bereft but for her trust in God. When Betty made her *Hajj*, or pilgrimage, in the spring of 1965, she reenacted Hajar's quest, running seven times between Safa and Marwah, as do all Muslim pilgrims. Already the mother of four little girls, Betty performed the ritual while pregnant with twins. Only weeks earlier she had become a young and destitute widow, and her life had seemed unsalvageable.

As she sat with her daughters in an Upper Manhattan ballroom, she saw sheets of bullets topple her husband, notorious Black Muslim fire-eater Malcolm X turned international human-rights crusader El-Hajj Malik El-Shabazz. The Civil Rights establishment and the American mainstream would embrace Reverend Martin Luther King Jr.'s widow, Coretta, after her husband's assassination in 1968, but aside from a conscientious ad hoc committee of black elites and some tattered loyalists from the ranks of black nationalism, America largely ignored or shunned Betty.

Her pilgrimage to Mecca, however, was "the Amen to a very long prayer." She returned to New York, retreated to the suburbs, and began toiling toward the future. She raised six girls alone, earned a master's degree and a doctorate, and rose to a top administrative post at Brooklyn's Medgar Evers College. Ultimately, she emerged as an educator, heroine, lecturer, "queen mother," custodian of Malcolm's legacy, informal ambassador, radio personality, symbol of grace and survival, healer, grandmother, counselor, fund-raiser, socialite, corporate board member, mediator, and internationally embraced traveler.

Betty was a twenty-three-year-old nurse fresh out of school when she married Malcolm. She stood by him for seven exhilarating, harrowing years and remained a potent and complex symbol of his life and legacy for three decades thereafter. Considering all she endured, both as Mrs. Malcolm X and as the evolving Dr. Shabazz, one imagines that a lesser woman would not have made it. "A lot of people say, 'The guy gave me the chills when I saw him,'" Betty's fourth daughter, Gamilah, once said of her father. "But it was my mother who kept everything together, who maintained a sense of reality. My father's loyalty sort of gave him tunnel vision. But my mother was on the real side."

Recognizing the widow's stature and ambassadorial éclat, one Medgar Evers College president in the late 1980s garnished her already lavish job title with the phrase "cultural attaché." By then, "Dr. Betty" (as she was known to students) had become a celebrated figure in her own right, a seemingly unflappable "diva" and icon of black woman-hood from whom strangers begged hugs in theaters or on sidewalks, as if her mere embrace bestowed fortitude. But for all Mrs. Malcolm X's durability, one had only to mention Hajar to demolish her. "Just like that she would weep," said a close Muslim friend who delighted her with gifts of Zamzam water whenever she returned from Mecca.

Betty was not given to maudlin displays. In her childhood, she had adopted a "don't-look-back" strategy for coping with calamity. (Malcolm would later urge her to use the same philosophy to survive his death.) Nor was she ceremonious or outwardly religious, though she lived by a modern woman's reading of the Qur'an and quietly observed some Sunni (orthodox) Muslim traditions up to her death. So it is difficult to imagine allegory overwhelming her. When one thinks of the steely Madame Shabazz, one thinks instead of a woman like Hajar, a woman who tapped a spiritual reservoir while navigating the bleakest landscape. Someone once asked author Maya Angelou, herself a survivor of some consequence, how her friend Betty had developed such a reservoir. For a moment, Angelou only smiled tolerantly. Then, with that aristocratic growl that seems to encrust one's ears, she replied, "It is always in you, you know."

I must acknowledge up front that attempts to psychoanalyze the dead can only send us down a perilous path. "When ya die, niggas lie on ya," hissed one of my sources. Another cautioned that as a black man, my efforts to interpret Betty would be tantamount to "performing surgery on a family member." It is a good tradition that leads many blacks to avoid excavating the suffering of the dead, or rummaging through their earthly affairs. A healthy regard for the spirits and great sympathy for my subject notwithstanding, I was compelled to search, however vainly, for Betty's spirit, mostly because I suspected that I would discover something indispensable about black women.

The woman whom I met only through my research had many faces, each flawed and compelling. Her vitality charmed me; her volatility rattled me. Like much of the American public, I knew next to nothing about the widow (aside from the fact of her existence) when I began conducting interviews. But I came to understand why ghetto girls, boardroom empresses, single moms, church ladies, and so many other sisters admired her. Betty gave them the gift of "sticking in," and she gave generously. I once asked a teenaged girl in a beauty salon why she was wearing a Betty Shabazz T-shirt (the widow as a living symbol never spawned the iconography that her dead husband did). "If she can make it," the girl replied, "I can, too."

As dynamic and inspiring as Betty was as a public figure, she was exceedingly secretive, even among dear friends. This in itself should surprise no one. A sensible celebrity does not array her past on her front lawn. And a minor celebrity is what Betty finally became, with more than the typical strain and isolation of that station. ("I ain't bringin' no dirt to a mountain," activist-comedian Dick Gregory once said, describing the predicament of the widow's fame. "I'm takin' it away.")

Before her celebrity, she endured many seasons of terror and betrayal, so her obsession with privacy was hardly unfounded. "She had lived in a real world that a paranoid might dream of," said Peter Goldman, one of the many Malcolm biographers whose interview requests she summarily denied. Still, the deepening stealth of her latter years hid some of her torment from those who might have helped deliver her. "She did not want nobody to know too much," said her longtime secretary.

Betty's eldest daughter, Attallah, has said that we, the interloping public, robbed her parents in death and life of "the simplicity they yearned for." That is probably true, especially of Black America, which can be rougher on its heroes (often for the wrong reasons) than anybody. But Malcolm and Betty were deeply complex souls, and their union became equally so. "The ones who know about Malcolm and Sister Betty will never tell," Sister Sybil, widow of the late black historian John Henrik Clarke, once said. "There's too much pain." A

Muslim woman who had known Betty since the late 1950s echoed the sentiment, invoking one of Black Islam's stock expressions: "Those who know ain't talkin'," she said. "Those who talkin' do not know."

The Betty Shabazz story does contain in character and plot even more paradox and enigma than one would expect of the wife of a man whose memory still inspires growling accusations at conferences and still leaves grown black men and women cursing or crying. Indeed, her life hints at more layers of suffering and darkness and triumph and strength than history will ever dissect. "Her life defies clarity of diagnosis," said Gil Noble, host of New York television's *Like It Is*, who befriended the widow in the early 1970s (after he recognized that her slain husband had been the emissary of his manhood). It was Betty's often inscrutable and gruff persona, as well as the heartache that still swirls about her memory, that led a Malcolm researcher, after I had announced that I was working on a life of Betty, to reply, "You have my regrets."

Perhaps it was Betty's bottled-up suffering that Malcolm's brother Robert Little was trying to spare her daughters when he handed all six women—nieces he barely knew—identical letters at their mother's June 1997 memorial service. "I understand grief, loss, fear, and suspicion, since I too have lived with such feelings for most of my life," Robert Little wrote. "Let me just say that you should embrace these feelings, rather than pretend to yourself or others that they are not real, strong, and true." His words would have rung as true for Betty as they did for her daughters. Betty and most of her in-laws had by then long stopped talking, so Robert Little may not have known the grief the widow's friends gave her for refusing to the end to see a therapist. He may not have known about the mornings when she called them painfully early, sometimes before dawn, her girlish voice chasing away loneliness and something more menacing.

One of Betty's friends with whom she unburdened late in life remembered that the widow occasionally talked in riddles. Another companion sometimes caught the normally composed, even stoic matriarch locked in a far-off stare and mumbling a kind of "gibberish," though the woman could not be sure the soliloquies were not interwoven with Arabic, which Betty had studied. The friend who heard Betty's riddles confessed that she did not understand them. "Eventually you will," the widow would say, promising to explain later. More often than not, she never did. When an interviewer later asked Dick Gregory what he made of Betty's riddles, he replied with one of his own. "Swamps do not create mosquitoes and mosquitoes do not create swamps," he said. "But if you get rid of the swamps the mosquitoes will leave. Everything I knew of Betty she was trying to get rid of the swamps. That was her life."

After her heartrending death in the summer of 1997, journalists and friends eulogized Betty as a phenomenon of resilience—as one who had conquered betrayal, violence, grief, and fear. "That she survived at all is miraculous," Angelou said. "And she survived whole." But whether they served on the battlefield or by the hearth, none of the black-liberation struggle's veterans escaped undamaged. Nobody that drew close to Malcolm and survived—and none drew closer than Betty—escaped the vortex of his death and life. "There are a lot of people who went back into the grave," said Jean Reynolds, one of Malcolm's former disciples, describing the despair that followed the minister's 1965 slaying. "People lost their mind, committed suicide little by little every day."

In many ways, Betty not only survived in the post-assassination years, but thrived. She fought with quiet conscience for education and human-rights causes, exhausting herself in far too many campaigns for dignity, often on behalf of black women and children. She was not an ideologue. She never lifted Malcolm's sword to slash white supremacy. She preferred to think of herself as a moral booster for Black America. Some black nationalists dismissed her as a bourgeois integrationist. But throughout her life, her defiance against the power structure's disposal of her husband surfaced in subtle shades of resistance.

She believed in womanpower, yet she never considered herself a "libber," and often sent young women home to boyfriends and husbands after dispensing earthy advice about communicating with men and choosing the right lipstick. She was queenly and eruptive, aristocratic but touchable to the rootsy folk in Brooklyn or Harlem. She demanded respect and deference always, whether holding forth at an international women's conference or bargain shopping. She was gracious and cantankerous, soulful and uncouth, fantastically generous and nosy. She was almost always disgracefully late. And she could cuss like twenty men, a genius she discovered after fielding too many threatening phone calls from her husband's enemies in the months before and after his death.

Betty was charming and coy, and knew just when and how to sling the javelins of her eyes. "That lady had the prettiest eyes," gushed a Harlem nationalist who had secretly served as her bodyguard in the late 1960s on behalf of her domineering sister-in-law and rival, Ella Collins. "Yeah, I know that was Malcolm's wife," he said, "but I still flirted with her." Her femininity, one friend said, "just oozed. And she knew it. And she enjoyed it." Betty was afflicted with neither fits of dullness nor brilliance. But she was divinely practical and sensible when discussing education, Malcolm, and other beloved topics. She saw through hypocrisy and pretension, and had no compunction about telling it like it was. "The sister did not play," said a friend. "If it was bullshit, she stopped you right there and told you it was bullshit." Few of her comrades ever saw her crumble, not even when the men began tossing fistfuls of dirt on her husband's coffin. Royalty never weeps in the streets. Besides, Malcolm had warned that the salt in her tears would only embitter her.

To Niara Sudarkasa, a friend and former president of Lincoln University, the historically black school in Pennsylvania, Betty was "a tireless traveler and resolute voice on behalf of economic, political, and social justice for the dispossessed and downtrodden from Selma to Soweto." To an academic colleague, she was a "rock steady" homegirl. To a travel companion who helped nudge her relationship with Coretta Scott King from rivalry to tolerance to genuine affection, she was "a flawed, lovely human being." To her eldest daughter, she was a heroine who dwells "amongst the spirit of women."

Yet the widow's life was also an epic tragedy. In her latter twenty-five years, she shrugged off the nostalgic "Mrs. Malcolm X" cape and clad herself in a distinguished new identity. But she may never have fully come to terms with the past. In the end, she was no more indomitable than countless other long-suffering black women whose names history has ignored. She longed for the privilege of fragility as often as they surely did, but there was her children's survival to consider, and her own. Only in recent years has African-America begun to properly recognize the women who stayed alive and upright through the convulsions of the black-liberation struggle. But to ignore the cost of their endurance is no less than abuse.

Despite having led a life of amazing fortitude, Betty in her final weeks sometimes seemed near collapse. Less than a year before, she had fallen ill and barely out-danced death. Looking after the bright but rootless and deeply troubled grandson she had cared for in recent months had exhausted her. Ironically, the adolescent was reeling with much of the anguish, rage, and confusion that Betty had sought to submerge in her own soul.

A couple of years earlier, the widow had gone to war against federal prosecutors who charged her thirty-four-year-old daughter Qubilah with plotting an assassination of Nation of Islam chief Louis Farrakhan in vengeance for his rumored entanglement with Malcolm's assassination three decades before. Though Betty herself had long believed that Farrakhan—once Malcolm's protégé and "little brother"—had been among the conspirators in her husband's death, and though the sham grated her conscience, she agreed to a choreographed public "reconciliation" with the Nation of Islam chief for Qubilah's sake. She was simultaneously struggling to institutionalize Malcolm's legacy, protect her daughters, and hold herself together. "I'm worn out," she told a friend in her final weeks; "I'm tired of being strong." This rather shocked her friend. If anyone deserved to be worn out it was the widow, but she never *said* as much.

She had taken to shuttling between hotels, though she had homes in the New York suburbs and could even have escaped comfortably to Hilton Head Island, South Carolina. "She was in flight," said a man close to the family. There were whispers that she was working on an autobiography, but few of her friends knew anything about a book deal. Some said she had mellowed in recent months. But she hardly seemed serene slaloming through the halls at Medgar Evers College, her papers cascading from a pull-cart. In her apocalyptic office, uncashed checks and unopened letters floated in the eddy of awards, mementos, and lecture requests. Betty was notoriously disorganized (her secretary routinely filed five copies of all her documents, knowing Betty would inevitably misplace the first two), but some of her friends swore they had never seen her in such a tailspin.

In early 1997, she posed for an *Upscale* magazine cover story on the "Mothers of the Civil Rights Movement." It was a flattering piece sequined with quotes from her third daughter, Ilyasah, who had most closely been her understudy in polite society. But though she was impeccably made-up as always in the accompanying photo, her eyes were swimming and sad, her lips taut. During the shoot, Myrlie Evers-Williams, widow of Civil Rights martyr Medgar Evers, glanced over at her friend and knew instantly that she was suffering. "We were so worried about her when she took that picture," she later remembered.

That Malcolm also began unraveling in his last frazzled days is but one of the many ironies of Betty's story. It is no coincidence that both husband and wife in their latter years heard endlessly from friends and family that they were working too hard. They fought on different fronts and in vastly different fashions. While he chose history, she herself acknowledged that history had chosen her. Both paid to the debt of freedom more pieces of body and spirit than anyone in a sane country could. And few such men or women die quietly in their sleep.

Betty died horrifically at age sixty-three, canvassed with burns from a fire her grandson set in her suburban New York apartment, having long ago endured more psychological and emotional pain than most of us can imagine. Nobody called her a victim. "God is good," she reminded us in her last radio interview. "It was rough, but I made it." Yet in many ways she was haunted to the end. Some of those haunts tormented her long before Malcolm's body thudded to a scuffed-up ballroom stage amid the bloodstained 1960s.

This book, then, is less about triumph than it is about sticking in. It is not a book about a superwoman, for despite the extraordinary circumstances of her life, Betty was eminently ordinary in many ways. In confronting and overcoming personal disaster, she could be as volatile as she was regal, as harsh as she was heroic. Her formidable strength of spirit, tempered more by an almost mystically unfurling chain of tragedies than by any single event, never supplanted her deep vulnerability.

Indeed, chasing the widow's story has taught me that the trope of the "strong black woman"—a figure of fantastic physical and emotional endurance—obscures far more than it illuminates. Black women (like all women, I presume) are capable of astonishing feats of survival when circumstances demand. They are also marvelously, maddeningly intricate by virtue of their humanity.

If there is a grand essentiality to be drawn from the life of Betty Shabazz, I hope that it is somehow enclosed in the following pages. I must admit that I have reached no such profound conclusion. In fact, much of what I found in the widow was surprisingly familiar: a fierce resolve that I first encountered in my mother; a passion for living that I recognize in my blood sisters; a hunt, as it were, for water in the wilderness.

Chapter One

A BRASS VALENTINE

—

"Very seldom did I think of myself in relationship to the world."
—Betty Shabazz

Shelman Sandlin, Betty's birth father, had hands like bassinets. He passed them to Betty, but not his three boys. Malcolm would kid Betty about those mannish hands, and her six daughters would inherit them because she would have no sons.

For most of his life, Shelman tied steel, and by the time he died at seventy-three, friends had taken to calling him the oldest steel-rod man in the country. He went by "Juju" (as a child his first son had set his mouth to say "Dada," and that's what came out instead). The 265-pounder helped reinforce dozens of Philadelphia buildings during a career in construction. Though he was perfectly at ease fourteen stories up on a steel girder, his massive hands could also tantalize a piano.

For Juju, two-fisted jazz was a breeze. His fingers would shed their weight, splaying over the jumping keys as "Sweet Georgia Brown" unfurled. People thought he even looked like a swarthier Duke Ellington. He had trained at a conservatory, and during World War II played for the USO, but there were many years when work did not come to a piano man. By the early 1950s, he had a wife and sons, and construction was paying. So he joined the steel union and found himself on Philadelphia's naval shipyard.

Years later, Juju's eldest son, Shelman Jr., remembered the man who "took no tea for no fever," who even as he aged could wear slats in your behind with a belt. In discipline and love, Juju believed in plain talk and action, though his piano highjinks belied a prankster's soul. They bragged in parts of North Philly that he "could work steel like a monkey," but he longed to work the ivories. He had come from a powerful line of southerners—willful, big-boned people. So he persevered, a church pianist and laborer until a fall in a freighter's hull wrecked his hip.

Juju was born around 1913 in Pinehurst, a miniscule town near the heart of Georgia. He grew up shooting rabbits and squirrels, wheeling through clay, and dodging his mother Mathilda's switch. From her side of the family he had gotten Negro–Blackfoot Indian blood. From his father's side he had gotten Black Baptist preacher's blood, which might have explained his appetite for musical flourish.

As far back as anyone could remember, Pinehurst's citizens had numbered about five hundred: 250 black and 250 white, the two tribes split neatly by the railroad. Many of the blacks had come upon Pinehurst while following the road elsewhere and had stayed, seduced by the bouquet of crops its spongy topsoil surrendered. They were destined to lead coarse lives as dayworkers and sharecroppers of peanuts, corn, watermelon, wheat, and cotton. (The town's nineteenth-century founders were also wayfarers who, having gotten their wagon stuck, had decided to stay and settled on that very plot.)

Juju met Betty's mother, Ollie Mae, on this gopher-pocked landscape. Betty seldom discussed the woman, even with her daughters. Ollie Mae conceived and probably bore Betty in Pinehurst, though all her life Betty maintained that she had been born in Detroit. Most of her adult documents, including her nursing license and marriage certificate, list the Motor City as her birthplace. Yet some of her earlier records, including high-school and college transcripts, identify her as a Pinehurst native, born May 28, 1934.

Juju was twenty-one and Ollie was likely a teenager when Betty was born out of wedlock. At the time, the families of young, unwed girls who got pregnant often sent the expectant mothers away to give birth. According to family lore, this is how Betty wound up in Detroit, where she grew up. Betty's precise birthplace remains one of the many

Shabazz mysteries, for neither Georgia nor Michigan could find her birth certificate.

—

The origins of Helen Lowe, who became the truest mother Betty ever knew, are much more certain. Born in Huntsville, Alabama, on October 7, 1898, Helen, at the age of four, moved with her parents and three siblings to Birmingham, where as a young woman she taught grammar school for thirteen years. After graduating from Alabama State Teacher's College, she married and moved to Detroit in 1932, the bride of willowy and distinguished Lorenzo Don Malloy, maker of orthopedic and conventional shoes.

More than a dozen years her senior, Lorenzo had courted her in Birmingham and gallantly asked Helen's mother for her hand. But Helen, not expecting that one could make much of a living from shoes (her own earning power having leapt to a tolerable $125 a month), had at first demurred. Those were Depression years, after all, and romance would not buy bread. "I told him I wasn't ready," she later recalled with some pleasure.

How Lorenzo ultimately won her has been lost, but since 1926 he had operated a spacious repair shop on Detroit's Chene Street, and this success could not have hurt his case. Helen need not have worried—her husband turned out to be a splendid provider. In the mid 1930s, he moved the business to a modest storefront on Hastings Street in the Brewster Project, and there, a boot-shaped sign cresting its threshold, Malloy's Shoe Service moored for several years.

Hastings ran through Paradise Valley, a swath of Negro businesses and nightclubs just east of downtown. The place was a collision of Negroes. They were there suffocating in tenements, hauling clothes to tailors or cleaners, buying face powder or furniture, crowing in blues joints, running elevators and numbers, gossiping in beauty salons, spinning lies in barbershops, jazzing, porting, praying, riveting, bootlegging, peddling, and preaching. Merchants lorded over the district by day, doing their damnedest for the rent. At dusk, the resident prostitutes, stickup men, and other creeping elements took their turn at the hustle.

Hope and irony built Paradise Valley. The Negro mecca had formed in the crush as throngs of blacks migrated out of the South in the early half of the twentieth century. They glutted northern metropolises such as Philadelphia, New York, and Chicago, chasing dignity, honest wages, and freedom. "I have never wanted to be a boy in my life," said one pilgrim. "I wanted to be a man." After 1916, many of these sojourners ended up poor and desperate in Detroit, caged in wretched homes and neighborhoods, servants to the whims of racist bosses, banks, cops, and landlords.

Over the years, as industry boomed and war and car manufacturing brought many white Detroiters decent jobs, thousands of the city's blacks strained on mop-and-broom crews, in blazing foundries and furnace rooms, or as threadbare domestics. Meanwhile, race relations curdled. As whites fought to hem blacks out of neighborhoods and workplaces, frustration and hatred ruptured in bloody skirmishes, brawls, and race riots, the most deadly of which unfolded in 1942 and 1943 against the backdrop of World War II. For many blacks who had traveled "from field to factory," Detroit at times felt like nothing more than a new hell in the North.

But the Malloys were among the lucky and industrious who managed to scratch a good living from an emerging Paradise Valley during the Depression. Declaring service his "motto and brand," Lorenzo Malloy sold half-soles and heels for as much as three dollars and made a handsome-enough profit to hire at least one employee. Meanwhile, Helen Malloy cinched a reputation as a stalwart deliverywoman. She shuttled about endlessly with a carload of mended galoshes, wingtips, and pumps—and Malloy's Shoe Service grew.

The couple settled into a yellow house at 313 Hague Street on the North End, a tony black neighborhood of well-kept homes on Detroit's east side, and eventually bought a second car. These were no small feats at a time when one in every fifty of the city's retail merchants was black, and life for most Negro Detroiters was so tattered that "Room for Rent" signs appeared in the windows of even the most congested homes.

———

Lorenzo Malloy had learned his trade during World War I at what was then the Tuskegee Normal and Industrial Institute, the Alabama school established to offer the Negro a practical education and uphold the "dignity and worthiness of productive labor." He had come to Tuskegee from his hometown of Cotton Plant, Arkansas, where he had earned forty dollars a month in a veneer factory. Upon arriving at the Institute in 1911, he signed up for shoemaking, machinery, and foundry work, and got himself a job driving the school's mail truck.

Lorenzo Malloy was a Tuskegee man in the truest sense, for he walked the campus in the time of its legendary founder, Booker T. Washington, and even had an encounter with the patriarch. As Malloy loafed in the dining hall one day, his seat cocked back just so, Washington had come along and discovered him. "That chair has four legs!" the elder had thundered as the hapless student clicked to the floor in a fright. This was to become a favorite story of Malloy's. He held Washington below no mortal, except perhaps African Methodist Episcopal (AME) Church founder Richard Allen, who, like Washington, had once been a slave. The philosophies of both leaders—as marked by faith, education, thrift, enterprise, labor, and self-help—steered Helen and Lorenzo Malloy's lives and shaped their approach to race matters.

The Malloys were church folk, so first came faith. They belonged to Bethel AME, a palatial worship house at Frederick Avenue and St. Antoine Street, where one found them between pews as many as three or four days a week. "They must have been there every time the doors opened," one congregant recalled. Lorenzo Malloy served as a church officer, a member of the men's "brotherhood," and superintendent of the Sunday school. Helen Malloy, a member of the women's trustee auxiliary and a class leader, taught both Sunday school and vacation Bible school.

Though they had no children of their own, the Malloys became aunt and uncle to a generation of the Bethel faithful. They were that sort of people, and Bethel was that sort of place. "Bethel people married Bethel people," a former member later recalled. Another described the church as her social cosmos. "Our parents believed you didn't go to the shows on Sunday," she said. "After Sunday school you attended church, and in the evening you were probably back there again. It was church or nothing." Indeed, for many Bethel children, love of God and fear of parents were indistinguishable.

The church in the 1930s and 1940s posed a "mighty challenge" not just to evil (as solemnly advertised in a 1941 pamphlet), but to apathy. Its congregation, one of the city's oldest and largest, evolved from a band of free black Methodists that had gathered in 1839, decades before the Reconstruction era and the great northerly black migration. Under the pastorate of William H. Peck, the church followed a dizzying curriculum of self-help, operating a credit union, missionary society, Girl Scout troop, and its own mutual-benefit association.

Bethel helped clothe and feed the city's poor during the Depression, and in 1940 established a club for the study and distribution of black history. It became a magnet for visiting blacks of big affairs, largely because many of Detroit's downtown hotels and other venues refused Negroes. It regularly hosted such immortals as NAACP attorney Thurgood Marshall, who became the first black Supreme Court justice, and Paul Robeson, humans rights activist and giant of stage and screen. Bethel was a bastion of pride. In its sanctuary, little girls learned from the fanning, humming ladies to sport fancy hats and gloves, and to love Jesus and their black selves with their whole hearts. It was within this stronghold that Betty Dean Sanders studied her Bible, sang her hymns, and at age thirteen vowed soberly that she would die a Methodist.

⌁

None of Betty's church peers learned much about her early childhood. "In those days they didn't tell children what was going on," one later remembered. "Whatever was known stayed among the adults. We simply understood that she hadn't been treated right." Sue MacCree, a teenage neighbor the Malloys drove to Bethel every Sunday morning, recalled that Betty simply showed up with the older couple one Sunday morning before church. The Malloys introduced the younger girl, then about eleven, with no explanation of whence she had come or how she had wound up in their care. MacCree believed that Betty had once lived just east of their block. But Betty never discussed the life she had led before arriving in Helen and Lorenzo Malloy's orderly, well-furnished home around 1944 or 1945.

MacCree did not think that her new friend's abrupt arrival was especially odd. Adults in many black communities of the time were known to take in children whose own parents could not care for them. Indeed, the Malloys sheltered and looked after the needy on three other occasions: raising a four-month-old boy for eight years, caring for a paralyzed elderly woman, and boarding a young woman while she attended Wayne State University to become a teacher. Many years later, when Betty sent for a severely emotionally disturbed grandson who was fascinated with fire, she was only heeding the cultural wisdom that said, "Let no child grow like a weed."

How Betty herself was treated as a small child is unclear, though there is some hearsay and legend in the Shabazz family. According to an elderly family member who spoke as authoritatively on the subject as any living soul could have, Ollie Mae raised Betty almost from infancy in Detroit. But in the child's first year, her paternal grandmother, Matilda Greene, spotted an ugly sore on her neck. Suspecting that she had been neglected, the elder took custody of Betty, raising her for a time in Pinehurst. Greene died when Betty was six, and the child landed back in Detroit with Ollie Mae (who had married Arthur Burks, with whom she would have three more daughters).

Betty was about nine when she began knocking around the Malloys' shoe store. The couple took to the dark-skinned girl with the raven plaits. They began letting her think she was working at the shop, allowing her to rearrange items on the shelves and do other chores. She lived nearby on Erskine and began dropping by their place and occasionally spending the night. "She got attached to us," Helen Malloy later said.

Mrs. Malloy added that Betty's mother was "mean" to the girl, but never elaborated. She told one interviewer that she had not known for sure what the source of the mistreatment was. The situation was serious enough for the Malloys to invite Ollie Mae over one night and plead with her to allow them to keep the girl. The woman refused. "You are not going to take her," she told them bluntly.

A couple years later, an innocent slip forced Betty from her mother's house for good. Betty was a studious child. Because Ollie forbade her to burn light well beyond nightfall, Betty often stopped by a neighborhood friend's place to finish her homework. One night, according to Helen Malloy, Betty came home late—about 10:30 or 11 P.M. Furious, Ollie Mae put her out, forcing her to spend the night at a friend's place. "The next day she came to me," Helen recalled. Years later, Betty told her daughter Gamilah that she sat and witnessed "the transaction" that landed her informally in the Malloys' custody.

Betty had only limited contact with her birth mother after moving in with the Malloys. The abandonment transformed her life, whatever trauma it wreaked. She had entered the embrace of a kind, childless couple ready to nurture a discarded little girl with elfish eyes. They would love her, she later said, "with or without cause."

———

A popular joke circulated black Detroit about this time:

> A black man and a white man are selling ice. A Negro spots the pair and starts toward them. "Will you buy from the black fellow?" his companion asks. "No," replies the Negro, "the white man's ice is colder."

It was the kind of easy self-mockery that had always been good for a chuckle. But when black businesses began withering for lack of Negro patronage, the joke dried up, too. Looking to boost Negro business and destroy the mentality that made ice colder, milk fresher, and suits sharper when procured from white hands, Reverend Peck established the Booker T. Washington Trade Association in April 1930. That June, his wife, Fannie B. Peck, formed the Housewives League of Detroit, a sister organization dedicated to urging black homemakers to buy within their race.

Mrs. Peck and a progressive band of Bethel women quickly recruited Mrs. Malloy, whom they knew as a congregant and the popular, capable wife of a prominent businessman. Over the next sixty-four years, Helen Malloy would serve the League as secretary, historian, and president, and hold top offices with the National Housewives League. The Detroit Leaguers, who modeled themselves after the first Housewives League (organized in Harlem the same year), had discovered that women spent the lion's share of income in most households, and could thus be black trade's enemies or saviors. Rallying behind the motto "Build, Boost, Buy" and vowing to "stabilize the economic status of the Negro," they organized campaigns supporting black accounting firms, restaurants, drug stores, florists, insurance companies, car dealerships, and funeral homes.

The League also championed boycotts of white shops that refused to hire black clerks or carry black products. During one protracted fight, its members regularly marched into neighborhood grocery stores and placed large orders—about ten dollars worth of food—before demanding Parker House Sausage, a black brand. If the owner did not stock the product, they left without spending a dime. Mrs. Malloy herself waged a similar battle on behalf of Pure Gold Syrup. During one shopping trip, she repeatedly demanded the brand, which a white grocer claimed was unavailable. When she pointedly advised him that she and her "sisters" would go wherever they could get what they needed, he produced the Pure Gold. In the 1930s and 1940s, such audacity was not expected from the mouths of black women, who had traditionally served as domestics. But as many a rueful shopkeeper learned, the Leaguers did not retreat.

For years they marched through black neighborhoods with circulars and coupons, rapping on doors on the west and east sides, in Highland Park, Conant Garden, and other areas, and urging those who emerged blinking and bothered to patronize black businesses.

The response was often confused or hostile. "People would shut the door in our faces," Helen Malloy recalled. "We had a hard way to go. They didn't want to hear about Negroes. They didn't want to do nothing." Christina Fuqua, a founding Leaguer, would remember that "in those days it was more than a trade campaign. It was an educational experience."

On one door-to-door romp to drum up business for a neighborhood physician, the "boosters" came across an adamant Negro mother. "I ain't going to no black doctor!" she told them. When her visitors asked what her children wished to become, she mentioned that one of her sons talked about going into medicine. "Well," the Leaguer replied, "if you don't believe in Negroes, you don't believe in yourself." The woman had not thought of it that way. In the end, she became one of the doctor's most faithful patients.

Thanks in no small part to Helen Malloy, who worked "like a madwoman" for the organization for the rest of her ninety-six years, the Detroit Housewives League burgeoned into a thriving movement with sixteen neighborhood units, five hundred members, and twelve thousand pledges of support from local black housewives. Its "directed spending" strategy channeled thousands of dollars into black businesses during the World War II era, and never truly went obsolete, even after the organization flagged in later decades. "In many ways the plight of black business in Detroit might be worse today than it was in the 1940s," Mrs. Malloy told the *Detroit Free Press* in 1980, her fiftieth anniversary as a booster.

Betty would remember that though her foster mother was a great believer in prayer, "she always said that when you finished praying, you've got to work." A Bethel parishioner would recall that Helen Malloy "did not know how to say no to anything." Betty would inherit the vice. In her fifties and early sixties, she would wave off warnings that she was exhausting herself trying to satisfy the world's new appetite for Malcolm. Her friends would insist that if she maintained the whiplash pace, she would land in the emergency room or the asylum. But industry was in her bones.

As a junior member of the League's educational group, Betty had idolized women who toiled for their cause in fur-fringed overcoats, rakishly tilted hats, and leather attaché cases. Less chic in her saddle oxfords and skirts, Betty presented short speeches and compositions before the membership at biscuit-and-tea affairs in the Malloys' living room. As an eleventh grader, she represented Acme Flowers in the League's Business Queen Contest. The League essay and scrapbook competitions Mrs. Malloy created (and oversaw for the National Housewives League for years) provided her first doses of black history.

The League was not the only society for black uplift to which Betty was exposed. Mrs. Malloy also belonged to the National Council of Negro Women and the NAACP—mainstream groups to which Betty would return after her husband's death. In her late thirties, Betty would also rejoin the League, then as a member at large of its trustee board. It was a foreseeable homecoming, for her loyalty to middle-class, Christian organizations would lie dormant—not dead—during her prolonged adventure with black nationalism.

Betty later declared that Malcolm had taught her far more about life and living than her adoptive mother did. The impertinence would spark more than a few rows between the two women. "When I say that she just goes ape!" Betty once said. What she meant, she explained, was that her husband had been her most important spiritual and intellectual tutor, the first adult who had convinced her that her rightful station transcended whatever gutter some "wicked racist mind" could assign. "I'm talking about understanding one's self and where you are and where you fit," she said.

But the Malloys had wanted the best for their foster daughter. And for them that meant nurturing in her not worldliness but talent, grace, book smarts, and Christian ethics. Mrs. Malloy, as an original Leaguer, had helped launch one of black Detroit's early struggles for self-determination and economic empowerment. She and her husband belonged to a church that celebrated black history and a denomination that embraced African heritage. But the couple never discussed racism or race relations at home.

If there was irony in this, it may not have occurred to many of the Leaguers. As the organization recognized explicitly in an early mission statement, its purpose was not "to right the many injustices we have forced upon us or as a result of discrimination within the field of civil and property rights." The League's primary goals were financial prosperity and economic independence, not political power or racial pride. Few if any blue-collar workers belonged to the organization. According to one historian, some blacks considered the League "merely a reflection of the class interests of the black bourgeoisie."

So, Betty's teenage years, while steeped in the ideals of black self-help, unfolded with little acknowledgment or confrontation of racism. "Anyone who openly discussed race relations was quickly viewed as a 'troublemaker,'" she later remembered. She had often heard Mr. Malloy brag about how he had scrimped to buy the house at the height of the Depression, or lecture about how public housing should be a temporary fix for families down on their luck. Why, if an Arkansas bumpkin like himself could become an entrepreneur and homeowner, he insisted, surely Booker T. Washington's program of modest economic enterprise could deliver other blacks.

Thus education and elbow grease became Betty's yin-yang. She knew nothing of black nationalism or Pan-Africanism, having never encountered the aging Detroit followers of back-to-Africa czar Marcus Garvey, who had built a massive black-pride movement before his 1927 deportation. And she knew nothing of Islam and black separatism, having never happened upon Temple Number One and its parishioners, the local disciples of Elijah Muhammad. Since the 1930s, the self-proclaimed Messenger of Allah had been building his congregation among indigent "so-called Negroes"—descendants, he said, of a "tribe of Shabazz" lost in antiquity. No such exoticism colored Betty's world. Even the words "radical" and "militant" were taboo in the Malloy household.

Betty later confessed that she was a "typical lil' African-American girl" whose most daunting burden was schoolwork. The Malloys pampered her with a spacious room of her own and a frilly "sweet sixteen" party. "Their one agenda for me was that I should be happy," she said. "If I wanted a new dress or whatever, I got it." Every now and then there was a Saturday-night house party with her Bethel mates or a splash party at the pool. Otherwise, she was in church, class, or the cinema, or behind the cash register in her foster parents' shoe store. "Pick a week out of my life," she later told journalists. "If you understood that week, you understood my life."

Meanwhile, in a Charleston, Massachusetts, lockup, a hard-timer named Malcolm Little, son of a fearsome Garveyite preacher and a West Indian mulatto; a rawboned man-child who had grown up quick slumming in the back alleys of Boston and Harlem; an ex-numbers runner and low-life; a self-inflated "bad nigger" who had hustled, pimped, and thieved his way to a seventy-seven-month prison term, was feeding a rapacious appetite for books and bopping around the jail yard "pulling the coats" of other black inmates. "My man! You ever heard about somebody named Mr. Elijah Muhammad?"

Malcolm swam an "ocean of blackness" before the law—then the Prophet—overtook him. Born Malcolm Little on May 19, 1925, in Omaha, Nebraska, the fourth of Earl and Louise Little's seven children, his childhood near Lansing, Michigan, was poor and calamitous. Earl Little was a boot-black country preacher from Georgia. Louise Little was a slender, Grenada-born immigrant who could almost have passed for white. Both were disciples of Marcus Garvey, a Jamaican native and the president general of the United Negro Improvement Association (UNIA) and self-appointed provisional president of Africa.

Garvey's nationalist UNIA, rejected by more mainstream black leaders such as Booker T. Washington and union leader A. Philip Randolph, swelled internationally with one million or more mostly working-class blacks by the early 1920s. Earl Little evangelized ably for the UNIA, preaching a gospel of self-determination and African pride as he roamed rural Michigan. Louise Little was a prolific journalist for the movement.

Internal strife battered the marriage, and Malcolm and his siblings sometimes endured severe beatings. Betty later remembered Malcolm talking about his father's bearish frame, but if the minister discussed those whippings with her, she never mentioned it. That Earl had built the Littles' Lansing home with his own powerful hands became a point of pride for Betty. In her latter years, she acknowledged that Malcolm's beginnings had been "absolutely poor" and "troubled." But she also insisted that he had been "a very happy child until he was six." (Betty may tacitly have linked the childhood thrashings, which Malcolm said his mother often meted out, to the minister's repressiveness as a husband. She declared in a 1972 interview that a boy's relationship with his mother and sisters determines how he will treat women as an adult. Was she suggesting that if women raised their sons properly there would be no need for women's liberation? Betty smiled at the reporter's question. "Right on," she replied, with a wave of her hand.)

The Littles suffered through a series of hostilities at the hands of whites who resented Earl and Louise's activism and defiant spirit. Malcolm later claimed that rifle-wielding Ku Klux Klansmen had once galloped out of the night, surrounding the family home and menacing his terrified mother while she was pregnant with him. He believed that Christian whites had run his family out of Omaha, torched their Lansing home, and—thinking that the minister had gotten above his place—finally killed Earl Little, shoving his battered body beneath a trolley car in 1931.

A proud but embittered matriarch, Louise Little wilted in the years after the mysterious slaying despite her will to survive and shore up the family. As the Depression deepened, hunger clawed Malcolm and his siblings. State authorities finally committed Louise Little to a mental hospital and parceled the children out to foster homes. A bright, unruly adolescent, Malcolm shuttled between a reform school and foster homes. He fled the eighth grade and landed by 1941 in Boston with his half-sister Ella (one of Earl's three children by a previous marriage). He idolized her for her inky skin, business smarts, and brassy spirit. Like Earl and Louise Little, she was a staunch believer in Negro self-determination. But Malcolm, who by his mid-teens had grown ganglier and more incorrigible than ever, drifted inexorably toward the Roxbury ghetto.

In the early 1940s, Malcolm reinvented himself, swapping his yokel costume for blaring zoot suits, roasting his naps with conk paste, copping the juke slang, and lindy-hopping like a madman in dance halls and dives. Mean jobs came for a few years in staccato succession—shoe shining, busing tables, busting suds in kitchens, peddling sandwiches in railcars—as he bumped around the urban Northeast. Greedy for action and the slick scene, he took up the petty hustler's lifestyle.

Over the next few years, he moonshined, peddled reefer, ran numbers, steered johns to hookers, smoked pot, sniffed cocaine, swilled liquor, gambled, stole, scored a street alias (the felonious crowd knew him as "Detroit Red"), and descended into cool nihilism on the edge of Harlem's underworld, a ghetto-hopping white girl with looks draping his arm. "My mind and my soul were in chains," he later said. A December 1945 burglary spree ended the odyssey. Caught and arrested, he spent the next seven years in three Massachusetts penitentiaries.

Malcolm's fellow inmates thought him so impious that they called him "Satan." But he devoted himself to intellectual rebirth, and, despite a noxious temperament, read, studied, and debated hungrily. His siblings eventually recruited him to the Nation of Islam, which they claimed represented the black man's "true religion." He thus began a blinding resurrection, studying the sect's demonology and sacraments while corresponding with its leader. Malcolm Little, in all matters psychological and spiritual, died. From the ashes rose Malcolm X. He had learned his purpose: waking so-called Negroes. And in the bargain he had discovered his savior, a "spotless little lamb" named Elijah.

Elijah Muhammad was not much for the eyes. Squint and you might have missed him. He was a severe bronchial asthmatic, and coughing fits regularly wracked his body. His breathing by the late 1950s sounded at times like he was trying to inflate a zeppelin with a straw. But the idea that the frail, amber-hued Elijah Muhammad had studied at the feet of Allah, had indeed been divinely appointed to lead His children to Zion, lent him a mystique among the "Original People"—the Nation's flock—that made even Garvey seem prosaic.

Muhammad, son of a Baptist minister, was born Elijah Poole in Sandersville, Georgia, on October 7, 1897. His followers believe that he met and apprenticed himself to Master Farad), Allah's earthly, olive-skinned manifestation, before founding Temple Number One in 1931. After tangling with religious rivals, he fled to Chicago to preach his quasi-Islamic gospel and build his empire. The law sent him briefly upstate for urging his disciples to duck the World War II draft. He later won a little populace for his Nation of ex-cons and malcontents.

Even corralled by an honor guard and crowned with an emblazoned pillbox cap, Muhammad seemed a dainty deity. His clattering lungs often betrayed him. With his fourth-grade education, he might have been just another Great Migration pilgrim from the rural South. But his seemingly ancient wisdom, scriptural knowledge, fatherly disposition, charisma, and genius for parables made him a shrewd, imposing monarch. As scholar C. Eric Lincoln noted:

> The characteristic mood of the Muslim laity is simply a blind faith—a complete confidence in Elijah Muhammad, who "has a plan for all of us" and is considered well-nigh infallible. The Muslim brotherhood has a sense of manifest destiny, an awareness of some kind of impending social cataclysm in which they will figure prominently. They are not certain what this cataclysm will be or when it will take place, but they are unshakably convinced that Messenger Muhammad knows. And they are prepared to lay down their lives at a signal from their leader if dying will forward the goal he has in mind.

Journalist Louis Lomax reported that Muhammad was for the Nation "the meaning around which everything else occurs and orbits." Malcolm absolutely worshipped the elder. He once acknowledged that the so-called Messenger was "the first man whom I had ever feared—not fear such of a man with a gun, but the fear such as one has of the power of the sun." Malcolm lieutenant Charles Kenyatta later recalled that "Elijah had Malcolm by the throat." He might more accurately have said that the Old Man had him by the heart.

—

Betty would remember having had "not a very ethnic kind of upbringing." Yet she insisted that the realities of post–World War II Detroit prevented a clean escape from racism. She fraternized with a few whites at Northern High School, whose student body had gone almost solid black by the time she arrived in 1948, as white homeowners fled the expansion of Negro neighborhoods. But she also recalled that "small instances of direct racial hostility" peppered her adolescence. Betty's black classmates remembered whites shrinking from them in streetcars "as if you were going to plant some dread disease on them." They faced overt discrimination in the downtown restaurants and other businesses that refused to serve blacks. "People said things were totally better," one classmate would recall. "They weren't."

Indeed, Betty and her peers' race consciousness had begun to crystallize as early as grade school, when riots twice shattered the city. On February 28, 1942, a mob rallying for the "right" to keep "white tenants in our white community" clashed with black families moving into the ironically christened Sojourner Truth housing project on the city's northeast side. The ensuing melee was "ungodly," Mr. Malloy later told a teenage Betty. Crosses were torched, bricks were flung, and within hours more than one thousand blacks and whites were scuffling in the streets. Police brutally corralled the blacks. Of the 220 rioters arrested, 109 stood trial. All but three were black.

The following year, an even bloodier riot flared on a sweltering summer day in Belle Isle, the city's largest park. Skirmishes between young blacks and whites throughout the day escalated into a virtual race war. Before the rioting subsided, thirty-four people were dead, twenty-five of them black. Police had killed seventeen blacks and no whites. One survivor later remembered the carnage: "I went down on Alfred and Hastings Street, picked up a man down there that the police just took an automatic gun and, he was lying on the ground, cut him in two," he said. "You had to pick up one part of him and then pick up the other part. I shipped him back to his home in Mississippi."

Quite simply, Detroit during Betty's formative years was a racial minefield. Not even Northern High's largely white faculty knew what to make of the Negro. There was little overt racism at the school, but the students understood without having to be told that they must somehow establish their singularity, prove themselves a credit to their race, or risk damnation as common objects of contempt, suspicion, or charity. Few of the teachers were willing to discuss career goals with students, several of Betty's classmates later remembered. "You were there to sort of be watched," one alumna said. Northern High taught practically no black history, though teachers mentioned black botanist and agricultural chemist George Washington Carver parenthetically during Negro History Week.

Despite Detroit's crackling racial climate and the drought of Negro studies in the classroom, many Northern High students were unaware of collective black consciousness. "We just sort of regarded ourselves as human," one later confessed. "We knew what we had to do," said another. "There was nothing to talk about." Few if any of the students openly debated color politics. Nobody questioned why light-skinned girls were treated like fine porcelain. One simply took for granted that the most popular and athletic boys went after the "high yellows."

If you were stuck up and high yellow, moneyed, "quite the quite," or part of a certain clique, the crowd at Northern High branded you an "E-Light." Color conferred real privilege and power at the school. Light skin gave you a shot at the "most desirable" crown in the semi-annual yearbook, and might even have landed you a job beside a white man after graduation (which meant more prestige and money).

If you were dark-skinned, you were unlikely even to win "most likely to succeed."

The message was hard to miss. One local newspaper advertisement of the day warned women not to let their romance "hit the rocks because of rough, harsh, uneven, and too dark skin." Betty's earth-brown complexion conferred upon her an invisibility that she rarely discussed in later years. But vindication was coming, for her skin would suit the tastes—political and esthetic—of her high-yellow husband, who preached "black is beautiful" before the slogan was *en vogue*.

Betty's Northern High classmates remembered her as mannerly, even-tempered, and quiet. She was studious without being bookish. She joined the orchestra, the Russell Scholarship Committee, and the French Club, whose members were forever conjugating verbs in a rambling chorus. Aside from her melange of extracurricular activities and a grin brandished like a two-by-four, she did not especially stand out. "Not very many negative things were said about her," reported one of her classmates.

She was tall, wide-eyed, and so uninitiated in affairs of the world that each alien encounter was the start of a love affair. So it was with pork. One Friday night, Betty stopped by her friend Peggy's and spotted a steaming platter of chops on the dining table. "What on earth are those?" she asked. (Mrs. Malloy so avoided cooking pork and other foods that aggravated Lorenzo's severe indigestion and high blood pressure that her foster daughter had not recognized the soul-food favorite.) Betty and her girlfriend sat on the back steps, balanced their plates on their knees, and attacked the slabs of meat like wildebeests.

Betty went weak for shrimp, too. During one visit to Dot and Etta's Shrimp Hut, her date made the mistake of eating some of her meal before he had returned to the car. When she noticed the missing shrimp, she advised the boy indelicately that he had had his last mouthful of the evening. Within a few years, amid a conversion that might more precisely be called reincarnation, she would abandon shellfish and "filthy swine," but as a teenager she relished both these delicacies.

Her true love, of course, was Billy Eckstine. Before and after choir rehearsals, she and her friend Sue MacCree spun Eckstine and Sarah Vaughn records and baked Tollhouse cookies, talking fashion between gooey mouthfuls as Vaughn moaned over some lover man she had misplaced. Sometimes Betty performed a dance that looked like a compromise between a pirouette and what they later called the slop. Her body became a tentacled mass, as she dangled as if from a string. Betty had rhythm. She handled the snare drums for Northern High. She even walked with her own cadence. "Girl, you can strut!" one of her high-school mates often said.

Her girlfriends would always envy the tom-tom in her strut. But as a teenager, Betty shunned the girls who sashayed immodestly at sock hops. "She was always the lady," one of her fellow students later recalled. Back then, "ladies" avoided garish displays. They smiled often and never gave their families trouble. They did not smoke—at least not in the street. At one high-school house party, someone passed Betty a Parliament cigarette. She later told her daughters that she "just about died" (whether from inhalation or indignation she never said).

Home-economics class imparted the other duties of womanhood: sewing, cooking, and polishing pans. The course taught Betty some of the techniques the Black Muslim men later dismissed as women's "trickery," such as how to avoid licking one's fingers while preparing meals (one instead tested the aroma to determine whether the meal was done). According to several alumnae, Northern High expected its girls to make good marks, pay attention, and avoid speaking up too much in class. Even less attractive than a slouchy or boisterous girl was a show-off.

At the height of Betty's rascality, she fell in with a crowd who crank-called strangers when they got bored, picking numbers at random from the telephone book. But mostly she ran with the cultured girls. If some in her group suspected that she wasn't as high born as others, they never let on. She wasn't particularly newsy. "She didn't do a lot of talking except when it was just the two of us," one of her girlfriends recalled.

She believed in keeping the right company, and belonged to the Del Sprites, a social club for East Side teens who planned to pledge the elite black sorority Delta Sigma Theta in college.

Membership in the Del Sprites was by invitation only. One had to be the type who stayed out of trouble. "It didn't have much to do with looks," a member from Betty's time later said. "But the girls were very pretty." It helped if one's father was a professional, though a former Del Sprite president remembered that the membership was not overly class-conscious. "Some of the girls were poor, but they didn't know they were poor," she said. "They just knew what was expected of them."

Delta sisters oversaw the club and managed its intake ritual, shooting fidgety aspirants with questions to reveal their breeding. Those fortunate few who escaped the blacklist entered a swirl of dances, variety shows, and debutante balls, many of which benefited children's foundations. The girls occasionally volunteered at foster homes, but the Del Sprites' favorite affairs were the dinner parties in which they toasted each other with "cocktails" of colored lemonade. Betty would years later array socialites with conscience about her, inhabiting a world of gowns, good dinners, and charity fundraisers once again.

In the early 1950s, black women who did not intend to scrub linoleum or take dictation had rather few professional options other than nursing and teaching. Though she had joined her high-school nursing club, Betty chose the latter, planning to follow Mrs. Malloy into the classroom. After she graduated from Northern High in 1952, it was only natural that she attend Mr. Malloy's alma mater. Lorenzo had always dreamed of sending a son to Tuskegee. "It was clear that I wasn't a son," Betty later said, "so he changed the rules in the middle of the day."

The Malloys had taught Betty that education meant security and happiness, and she had rarely defied them. When she did so a few years later, the insubordination would rock her relationship with the aging couple. But Betty remained grateful to her folks to the end. Some years after Lorenzo Malloy's death in 1960, she began wiring Helen Malloy money every Christmas and Mother's Day, and calling dutifully almost every Sunday. "Mother!" her shrill voice would come jangling over the line. "How *are* you, Mother?" Helen Malloy would laugh. "You'd think I was her real mother!" she once exclaimed.

Early in the spring of 1952, the Malloys took up a collection at Bethel to help cover Betty's tuition, and sent her off to study elementary education at Tuskegee Institute. At the train station, Mrs. Malloy looked upon the girl she had grown to love, trying to muster a few reassuring words to salve the wounds she knew Betty would soon suffer. (Her own childhood had taught her what hospitality Alabama afforded its Negroes.) Betty looked at the plain, wiry woman in horn-rimmed glasses who had become her "Ma' dear," the foster parent who had rocked her through measles and mumps and delivered her from a brambly relationship with her birth mother. Mrs. Malloy had always known how to comport herself. She had defied Negroes and white shopkeepers who pooh-poohed black women's buying power. Now she looked like a schoolgirl called to the blackboard to work a tricky equation. "Whatever she was trying to tell me she was not very good at it, and I laughed to myself," Betty later recalled. The two women parted with a squeeze. Before she had long been in the South, Betty would realize that her foster mother "was trying to tell me in ten words or less about racism."

Chapter Two

A VELVET GLOVE

—

"Alabama's got me so upset..."
—Nina Simone, *Mississippi Goddam!*

Five academic quarters at Tuskegee Institute was time enough for Betty to taste hate and love. She arrived at the historic black school in central Alabama just ahead of her eighteenth birthday, having not seen the Deep South since her infancy. But exhilaration delayed the jolt of returning to "the sticks," for like Paradise Valley, the school encapsulated black life. With its recreation room, boutiques, lunch counters, hospital, chapel, pep rallies, and sock hops, there was little need for students to hike to the shops and other diversions downtown. "You could live on campus and feel like the world was black and controlled by blacks," one of Betty's classmates later said.

On weekends, students headed into town in expeditions of at least two or three. If they tired of films screened in a lecture hall or at the gym, they tromped to a local movie house, took the side door, and packed the balcony. (The front entrance and first-floor seats were reserved for whites). Now and then, the Tuskeegeeites shopped the town's "dry goods" stores, and at times they even rode the back of the bus to Montgomery to escape the country scene. But for meals and snacks they looked no farther than the campus canteens or the "last-call men," work-study students who rambled through the dormitories after hours hawking light fare. The hub of student life was the "rec" room. Here Betty filled idle hours with chatter and bid whist after history of civilization or human biology.

Like Mr. Malloy before her, Betty had come to Tuskegee on a five-year plan that allowed for part-time work. She spent many afternoons toiling in the laundry room and later at the switchboard and reception desk of the school's John A. Andrew Memorial Hospital. "Whenever we came in she was right there at the front door with a smile," a former nursing student remembered. Betty was not crazy about having to help offset her expenses. "She thought we were able to pay her way," remembered Mrs. Malloy. A Tuskegee education was costly relative to that of many black schools of the day. Tuition was one hundred dollars per quarter, and room and board ran another forty-two dollars. So Mr. Malloy had leaned on one of his old friends at the Institute to get Betty a job.

If Betty was sore about the work, it did not show. To her classmates she seemed neat and pleasant—"well-preserved," one thought. You could count on her pageboy hairstyle and quick grin. The girls envied her thick, glossy bangs, which she swooshed to the side. She never really abandoned that old-fashioned, pin-curled hairdo. It would elicit groans from her daughters, and as the look went out in later years, someone would occasionally wonder aloud if it were a wig. But Malcolm had always liked her hair that way, and that was how it would stay.

As an undergraduate, Betty was less reticent than she had been in high school. Despite her demureness, she could talk a person flat. "She was never loud," one of her classmates recalled, "just warm and chit-chatty." For a time, she was dating a fair-skinned man from Atlanta who played defensive tackle for the football squad. The two went strolling across campus on double dates, and she proclaimed him her first love. Another classmate remembered him as tall and "kind of reddish." It seems this was Betty's type.

Betty herself was a long-boned five feet, seven inches tall. By her college years, she was also stunning. "Any man who wasn't blind deaf and dumb would have wanted her," writer Maya Angelou thought upon meeting her several years later at a house party. She had a slender waist and the sort of figure that sent men scrambling to hold doors. Yet in 1952 and 1953, as servicemen returning from the Korean War surged onto Tuskegee's campus to learn bricklaying or plumbing or dairying, even less-fetching coeds were said to have easily won suitors. By one facetious count, every female student was entitled to seven veterans.

Even with its social hum, Tuskegee had a backwoods feel. Pastures quilted its acres. Montgomery, the closest city worth speaking of, was a good drive from campus. Yet the school was an enchanting province for a "colored girl" taking her first steps toward womanhood. Sunday mornings brought the "line of march," a procession to the campus chapel led by the ROTC band, the trailing students arrayed by academic school and costumed smartly in navy blue and white. Townsfolk often gathered just to watch the cavalcade.

Some of the day's majestic preachers spoke in the chapel, including "Daddy King," Martin Luther King Jr.'s father. During Sunday services, which like Wednesday vespers were compulsory, women sat on the right of the sanctuary, men on the left. (Betty later learned that the Nation of Islam favored a similar segregation.) After the service, Betty and the other women went high-heeled into the dining hall for Sunday-evening suppers, where a dean ensured "becoming conduct."

In 1952 and early 1953, Betty's lords were Tuskegee protocol, Tuskegee tradition, and the 10 P.M. curfew at White Hall girls' dormitory. She could not afford frequent trips home, and rarely left campus for more than a day. But for Christmas and Easter, she begged a ride to Atlanta from a classmate and there boarded a train back to Detroit. Other vacations and some weekends she frittered away at the home of a girlhood friend's sister, where she seamed her skirts on a prattling sewing machine. These were innocent, disciplined days. The camaraderie was strong among her fellow students, for "Mother Tuskegee" had convinced them that they were the golden few that would ennoble the race. "Finishing from Tuskegee opened the door," they were told. And despite the bigotry twisting about them, they

believed it. "We were happy among ourselves," one of Betty's classmates recalled.

The serenity was fleeting. Within three years, the Montgomery Bus
Boycott would flare. During the 1955–56 school year, Tuskegee students would turn the campus's ten-cent Coca-Cola machines to face
the wall, a jab at the white establishment and a gesture of solidarity
with Montgomery blacks who were battling segregation. The boycott
of Montgomery's public transit system would kindle Negro self-respect
and determination and anoint a precocious young leader named King.

But no such rebellion roiled the Tuskegee of the early 1950s. "We
were not ready to go to war" against discrimination, one of Betty's
classmates remembered. Mother Tuskegee taught her students that bigotry was immaterial. They would prevail because they were good and
smart, and there could be no excuses. For Betty, it was a familiar
refrain.

The town tested this aura of invulnerability. Some area whites
complained about those "uppity niggers" at the Institute, while the students privately dismissed the locals as "rednecks." Downtown clerks
would tend to every white customer in the store before they served
Betty and her classmates—if they served them at all. But she would not
confront this and other Southern injuries until she met Malcolm, for
the Malloys still refused to discuss racism, insisting that "if you're just
quiet it will go away."

Betty found silence a poor inoculation against reality. She saw
no outright racial violence as an undergraduate. No Alabama lynch-
ings were reported in 1952 and 1953, according to Tuskegee's own
annual survey. But she was less accustomed to the tapestry of segregation and discrimination than many of her southern-bred classmates were. "The whole atmosphere at Tuskegee wiped me out," she
later remembered.

Perhaps partly as a consequence of what she called the "mental
irritations" of race, she only drifted through her classes, showing
none of the fierce scholarship that during more desperate years
would earn stellar reports from Jersey City State College and the
University of Massachusetts at Amherst. She got only one A at

Tuskegee—in physical education. During one quarter, she logged a 1.4 grade point average, a stumble from her almost solid string of Cs. Among the courses she struggled with that period was child psychology.

One could hardly have imagined that she would become an icon of black motherhood and a champion of children's causes. In the late sixties and early seventies, black and white audiences who knew little of Betty other than a vague media composite of her late husband often expected her to be incendiary, dramatic, or eloquent. Many looked for her to chasten white America. So her rambling early lectures and interviews often disappointed. The widow Shabazz was not Malcolmesque in the least. But if there was a topic that moved Betty, and that revealed her own keen intellect, it was early childhood development. She would preach about society's responsibility to children through the tumult of her life and times.

Betty embarked on yet another romance at Tuskegee when she switched her major from education to nursing. Perhaps working the front desk of the 175-bed campus hospital lured her back to the profession that she had dreamed of in high school. Tuskegee's segregated hospital had long overcome skimpy funding and mediocre facilities to serve mostly poor, country blacks, many of whom would have been turned away elsewhere. Surrounded by professionals and students that nobly attended to the most impoverished people, Betty pondered a nursing career. Before long she was seeking the counsel of Lillian Harvey, Tuskegee's pioneering dean of nursing.

Harvey's voice was like a screwdriver in the small of the back. "Whenever she said your name you would freeze," said one alumna. Articulate and pretty, she was known among nursing students as "the iron fist in a velvet glove," though they never uttered the alias outside a giggling huddle. The first dean of the School of Nursing, she had arrived at Tuskegee in 1944 and had played a central role in establishing its bachelor of science degree in nursing, the first baccalaureate program in Alabama. She was unrelenting—a taskmaster who demanded perfection from her students, molding them in her own image with a stern tongue and heavy hand.

At a time when many nursing societies and academic programs excluded blacks, Harvey regularly traveled forty miles to integrate the Montgomery meetings of the Alabama Nurses' Association. The other members ostracized her, forcing her to sit by herself. "I wasn't welcome," she told her students. "And they didn't care about me raising my hand. But I attended anyway." Though some white colleagues sneered at her efforts, she would pave the way for many of the state's black nurses.

Her tomahawk style reminded Betty of the Housewives Leaguers. But Harvey was rather more candid than the Leaguers in preparing her apprentices for the white man's world. She taught them the subtleties of discrimination—"When you're white, you're 'Miss'; when you're black, you're 'Nurse' "—and they grew to love her, as few surprises awaited them after graduation.

Harvey regularly arranged clinical experiences for her students in northern cities where Jim Crow would not encumber them, especially New York, where she herself had studied. Aware that she was also creating cultural emissaries, she tended to choose the prettiest girls for the journey. "You didn't see any unattractive nurses from Tuskegee," remembered one of Harvey's former pupils. The dean eventually recommended that Betty attend a three-year school in Brooklyn with a Tuskegee-affiliated psychiatric nursing program. "Don't let the grass grow under your feet," Harvey had always warned her pupils. Perhaps she sensed that Betty, who had continued to flounder academically, needed a change of scene.

So against her foster parents' wishes, Betty struck out for New York City. As a small child she had rebounded between the urban North and the rural South. Now she was headed for an earth unto itself. "New York is the place that my husband loved," she told an audience years later. "It is dear to my heart." In the city she would come fully to womanhood. And in one of its desperate neighborhoods she would climb out of the grave.

Almost a dozen years after Betty left Tuskegee, Malcolm swooped onto the campus and delivered his searing gospel, quite forgetting, according to one of Betty's confidantes, that he was crunching across the ground his wife had roamed as an undergraduate. Betty could only chuckle at the oversight. By the time the minister had galloped into her life, she was well educated by the standards both of Black Islam and Negro women. Malcolm, it seems, chose her largely because she was so sharp and well spoken. But in their early marriage, he refused to take her desire to work outside the home seriously.

An eighth-grade dropout, he secretly admired the lettered blacks he so often lampooned. For him, the academy always held a special allure. In his last days, he faced an opponent in an Oxford University debate, and though the worshipful audience was almost solidly white, he basked in its applause at least as sublimely as he had reveled in Harlem ovations. He told his photographer Robert Haggins that he regretted having missed out on attending college. "That's where the white man locks up his knowledge," the minister said.

While the street bestowed Malcolm's sensibility, Betty's adoptive parents and the African Methodist Episcopal Church furnished hers. Malcolm got much of his book smarts from the prison library; she gleaned hers from the sociology and chemistry texts she hugged while strolling Tuskegee's leafy campus. Betty's education was genteel and strict. Her Tuskegee experience, she later said, reinforced the "worldview of a middle-class young woman."

Though Betty had left Tuskegee for New York City before 1954, when the Supreme Court ordered public schools desegregated, Lillian Harvey and other influential blacks in her life had for years embraced integration as a means of ensuring equal access and quality education for blacks. With its solidly Negro student body, Tuskegee was hardly an archetype of integration, but cultural assimilation as an ideal undergirded the campus in Betty's time, as it had from the start.

Begun by Booker T. Washington in a shanty near African Methodist Episcopal Zion Church, Tuskegee emerged piecemeal from the Alabama farmland in the late nineteenth century. Washington dreamed of its annual tide of educators and craftsmen forming a strong black working-class base. Tuskegee stood for compromise and cooperation between ex-slaves and a white world comprised substantially of ex-slavers; a harmonious if paternal relationship that her sponsors hoped would help convince the republic of the worthiness of the darker brother and his labor.

"Cast down your bucket where you are—cast it down in making friends in every manly way of the people of all races by whom we are surrounded," Washington charged blacks at the Atlanta Expedition in 1895. "Cast it down in agriculture, mechanics, in commerce, in domestic service, and in the professions." For the leader, the way to freedom and prosperity was modest economic enterprise rather than racial confrontation. The Negro would overcome by dint of his perspiration in the factories and fields, but along the way he must court white benefactors.

By the mid-twentieth century, catering to white liberal patronage remained a Tuskegee mindset. A 1950 leaflet about the school's history prepared by its public relations office diplomatically credited blacks, southern whites, the government, and northern philanthropy with helping to nurture the school in its infancy. "As is true today it was true then that substantial elements in all these groups wanted to advance the cause of Negro education," the leaflet read. Thus Betty left the Deep South a pupil not just of elementary education, but of a sensibility that juxtaposed white benevolence and black progress, a sensibility that in the logic of Black Islam made her a lost sheep. She was nevertheless to discover, in the movement and in one of its dashing ministers, what she later described as "the turning point in my life and racial consciousness."

———

Betty enrolled at Brooklyn State College School of Nursing in 1953. Brooklyn State was known mainly for its mental health facilities, so she drew some funny looks when she told New Yorkers that she was studying there. Her new classmates gawked when they learned that she had transferred from rustic Alabama. "They thought we lived in boxes under the railroad tracks," another Tuskegee transfer later remembered.

Searching for roots, Betty looked up Ruth Summerford—a distant cousin on her birth father's side—shortly after arriving in the city. Summerford, who was also studying nursing in Brooklyn, was several years Betty's senior. Later, as "Aunt Ruth," her slightly crotchety veneer would never fool Betty's daughters, whom she would love and tangle with almost as much as Betty did. Summerford became a maternity-ward nurse, and was present at each of the girls' births.

Upon meeting her cousin, Summerford thought Betty "ordinary" and rather green. But having come up in a large, southern family, she knew the thickness of blood. She decided to look out for Betty, and the two became fast friends. "We bonded pretty good," Summerford later remembered. Betty's bond with New York was less immediate. She eventually warmed to her surroundings, and was soon running with Summerford and her classmates to Radio City Music Hall shows or private "rent parties." At these pay-at-the-door soirees (thrown by tenants to ward off evictions), she bought hot homemade dinners, played cards, and scarred improvised dance floors. "She was social," Summerford recalled. "She met quite a few of my friends who she got along with very well and they'd say, 'Well look, is your cousin coming over tonight? Can she go out?'"

Betty and her new partners haunted the movie houses and the amateur talent contests at a Brooklyn church. They caught performances by touring gospel choirs from black colleges such as Fisk, Hampton, Howard, and Morgan State. Sometimes they broke out their good skirts and blouses and took the Manhattan train to the Savoy or wherever Duke Ellington or Tito Puente was headlining. If Small's

Paradise (where Malcolm had waited tables years earlier) was hosting a cocktail sip, they went jitterbugging with men who moved like marionettes.

Betty adored Harlem. Even Paradise Valley seemed Lilliputian by comparison. But she visited the Upper Manhattan community for its nightlife, not its seething racial politics. Race for her was hardly a pre-occupation. She had not even discussed with her cousin the indignities she had suffered in Alabama. ("I didn't get into that race thing," Summerford later explained. "Being a Southerner you knew sometimes to stay away from that stuff.") So despite her weekend romps in New York's black mecca, it was some time before she met the minister.

In later years, Betty's relationship with Harlem would be laced with ambiguity. I walked 125th Street with one of its radical sons, City College of New York Black Studies Professor Leonard Jeffries while he praised the Pan-African consciousness he believed Betty had developed late in her post-Malcolm era. "She wore Malcolm's mantle with dignity and grace," he said. "So the African ancestors looked after her." Later I sat in a shoebox apartment paces from 22 West, the 135th Street diner Malcolm had favored, and listened to elderly Egyptologist and black nationalist Dr. Yosef ben-Jochannan ("Dr. Ben") lament what he con-sidered Betty's abandonment of the grassroots. "She became elite and middle class," he said. "She was going towards the upper class. She wasn't at all associated with the poor black folks that Malcolm had asso-ciated with. She didn't live a life commensurate with Malcolm's."

Finally, I sat in Harlem's Morningside Park and listened, as dusk fell, to Betty's fourth daughter tell a story about love, betrayal, pain, and bitterness; about suspicion, sacrifice, and confusion; about loss, regret, fear, and a redemption that was maybe still coming; about a dead dad she never knew and a dead mom she was desperate to under-stand. Gamilah (a down-to-earth artist who lived nearby) smoked and talked for more than an hour, her fingers trembling slightly, her eyes grown prematurely weary. And I realized then the truth of something a Malcolm disciple once told me: "The assassination of Malcolm was not an assassination of an individual."

Sooner or later, all Harlem visitors discover its number-one racket. In 1958, the *New York Post* noted that race matters dominated the community's newspapers. "Its bookstores sell racial books almost exclusively," the paper said. "Its politicians run year after year on the single issue of race. Its people grumble about race, joke about race, get hopeful about race, and despair about race."

The other Harlem surplus was despair. Every day its zombies chased needles or hooch; its painted mistresses courted sidewalk traffic on spindly heels; its cops glowered and patted their holsters; its absentee landlords swooped in to collect their booty and pile more families into dingy tenements. Far too many were busy forgetting who, what, and why with drink or dope or skin-lightening creams. Black writer John Killens saw the community as a plantation. "You'll see lawyers in three-piece suits, real-estate brokers in mink coats, pimps in white Cadillacs," he said. "But they're all sharecropping. Sharecropping on a mean plantation."

A New York senator in 1956 declared Harlem a "rebuke to the north." "I have sympathy for those long-suffering individuals—Americans like you and me—who, for all their lives, have endured the whiplash of discrimination and segregation," Herbert H. Lehman, a white Democrat, told the city's Urban League. Yet despite Harlem's decay, its streets coursed with Negritude. (In 1958, one of its Chinese merchants hung a "Me Colored Too" sign outside his shop.) Betty and Summerford in 1954 and 1955 only sampled its cabarets. But had they joined the human current along 125th Street, they might have come upon one of the most colloquial uptown Negroes: the Harlem nationalist.

A Black Jew or Moor or Garveyite or "Buy Black!" crusader of the rather more militant sort than Betty was accustomed to from her days as a junior Housewives Leaguer, he would have mounted a rickety pine platform and rained fire on the white man. He would not have proclaimed humbly that "We shall overcome." His line would have been harsher: "To hell with the future—I'll take mine now!"

Some Negroes shunned the stepladder evangelists, but their diatribes exhilarated others. Indeed, for a people trained to accept under penalty of death or disfigurement that whites rule this life and probably the next, and that their own natural condition was to squirm forever underfoot, the idea of returning to Africa or of getting even with "the Man" was, if not catharsis, at least a delicious diversion. As James Baldwin noticed, "the speakers had an air of utter dedication, and the people looked toward them with a kind of intelligence of hope on their faces—not as though they were being consoled or drugged but as though they were being jolted."

Malcolm peddled his street gospel, too, casing the fringes of Harlem's pro-black crowds and trolling for converts outside storefront churches, pool halls, bars, barbershops, and even YMCAs, often with a somber detachment from the Nation of Islam's local Temple Seven. Massachusetts had paroled him in 1952 into Elijah Muhammad's embrace. After proving himself a faithful and prodigious missionary in Detroit, he had landed at the helm of the startup mosque on Harlem's 116th Street in 1954. A precocious fisher of men, he had begun reeling in souls. "You're lost, but you can be found," he assured passersby on uptown street corners. He dared them to:

> Join unto your own. Get that old devil off your back.
> Return to the father. Hear the teachings of the
> Honorable Elijah Muhammad. Come help build this
> black nation.

Had Betty dawdled at Lenox Avenue and West 125th, or elsewhere on Malcolm's turf, the beguiling young minister might have pounced. He might have hailed her as "my sister" and assured her that she was nothing less than the mother of civilization and the "field" from which a mighty nation would grow. "*Beautiful* black woman!" he might have crooned. "The Honorable Elijah Muhammad teaches us that the black man is going around saying he wants respect; well, the black man will never get anybody's respect until he first learns to respect his own women!"

But until Betty earned her undergraduate degree in 1956, she spent most of her time in Brooklyn poring over textbooks and dreaming about her nursing career. She was serious about her studies. "We wanted to do something to help others," Summerford later said. And, as was the case at Northern High, ambitious blacks at Brooklyn State had to make a special effort to distinguish themselves. Nursing was a coveted profession for a black woman, and integrated hospitals hired only so many Negroes. Betty did not intend to miss this shot at respectability.

She let the dorm mother know whenever she planned to spend the night at Summerford's. Otherwise she returned to the nurse's residence well before the 10 P.M. weeknight curfew. Brooklyn State was strict, and students too fond of revelry risked a one-way ticket home. Betty did not have time to act out. Her schoolwork precluded a love life. She was too busy even to attend church regularly. By 1956, when she began her clinical training at Montefiore Hospital in the hardscrabble Bronx, she was seeing less of Summerford and the old crowd. She was also reckoning again with racism.

Betty discovered that she and the other black nurses inevitably got the tough assignments on the floors with the curmudgeonly patients. "Even if you were the best, they put a white nurse as your supervisor," Summerford remembered. White male patients were more inclined to take liberties with the Negro attendants, sometimes trying to grope them, or suggestively calling them "Sunshine." So rampant were the offenses that the black nurses began consorting before their shifts. "Watch Mr. so-and-so," they whispered. "He's fresh."

On the whole, Betty found New York's racial climate less sweltering than Alabama's, but she often wondered whether she had not simply swapped Jim Crow for a fancier prejudice "Up South." She could not yet articulate a clear vision of racial justice, but she was sick of pretending that race did not matter.

She later claimed that Malcolm introduced her to the word "racism." "It makes me nervous thinking of the narrowness in which I formerly perceived and projected, and a little apprehensive because a lot of people still think as I thought and still operate as I operated before I met my husband," she said. She did not plummet from the clouds to racial awareness. ("Only a stone would not have had a race consciousness in Detroit," Maya Angelou once said.) Yet Betty would learn among the Black Muslims that any black person clever or lucky enough to reach adulthood must choose between slumber and struggle. She had survived racial trauma and had grown impatient with slumber. By the time she began turning up at Temple Seven, an obligated visitor and then an improbable enlistee, she was ready to hear the Original People's gospel. By the time she had taken an uncertain first step toward Allah, she was ready for Malcolm's Harlem.

Betty needed a break from cafeteria food. She was earning no more than sixty dollars a month as a nurse and could afford nothing but the hospital cafeteria's "waterlogged" fare. So she was delighted when an older nurse's aide, a Black Muslim, invited her to a Friday-night dinner party. When she saw the food, she could have just cried. There was a sumptuous array of dishes laid upon with corn oil, margarine, onions, garlic, celery, green pepper, and chives. (The Nation enjoyed its women's reputation as proud cooks who labored to outdo each other in the kitchen.) There might have been as many as four or five courses that night. Betty had never tasted anything so delicious.

After dinner, the hostess invited Betty and her date to a Temple Seven lecture. "Now, how are you going to sit and eat all that food and say 'no'?" Betty thought. She went to the mosque, hoping the talk would not be boring. The nurse's aide had wanted her to meet Malcolm, but he was not there. So, drowsy from the feast, Betty sat bewilderedly among the chastely robed women and staid men in the belly of the Harlem ghetto. As one of Malcolm's sidemen preached the plight and salvation of the "so-called Negro," she tried to digest Black Islam's dogma.

Betty left the lecture dizzy, the rhetoric ricocheting in her skull. Her hostess asked at once why she did not join up (Muslims were not for puttering around). Betty explained that she knew nothing of Islam and its philosophies. "I was not under the impression that you brought me here to join," she added indignantly. She could only imagine what the Malloys might do if they learned she had sampled another god. "Just wait until you hear my minister talk," her hostess said confidently. "He's very disciplined, he's good-looking, and all the sisters want him."

Betty decided that if she were to have another go at the women's cuisine, she would have to give this so-called Brother Minister an ear. The Muslims had an illicit appeal, but they coiled their daring blackness around a dark and alien philosophy. Plus, the congregation hardly seemed like her crowd. The temple by 1956 had enrolled a smattering of professionals and college students, but the flock still hailed overwhelmingly from the submerged classes. Many of the faithful were sobered-up cons and hustlers who had dropped the dice, the cards, the dope, the wine, the pork, the "gray chicks," and the Bible. To theology professor C. Eric Lincoln, these were the dispossessed who "wake up to society's kick-in-the-teeth each morning and fall exhausted with a parting kick each night."

No matter, Betty thought; she would go back. She told herself that she would not discard years of Sunday school and Bible study for this murky paganism, but she would give the Muslims another listen. Then maybe she would shoot over to that sister's house and feast again. The next time Betty made her way to Harlem for a Muslim meeting, her hostess leaned forward and hissed, "The minister is here!" *Very big deal,* Betty thought, slackening in her folding chair inside the scoured temple. But then she glanced over and saw a rangy man hustling up the far right aisle toward the stage.

———

Today, decades after his death, irony still fuels Malcolm's fire. Though his memory may warm those who did not walk with him, it often consumes those who did. So mythical has his aura become that he now inspires far more idolatry than the living man ever did. The danger of revisionism continues to grow with the legend of his death and life, but nothing can dim the intensity of the Malcolm the world encountered in the flesh—an amazing talent who struggled toward truth.

To experience the minister's intensity, one need only talk to his disciples and devotees. When she confronted Malcolm in the early 1960s, poet and activist Sonia Sanchez was working for the New York branch of the Civil Rights outfit CORE (Congress of Racial Equality):

> And Malcolm got up on that stage, and you could see the redness in his face. The people I was with decided to leave; they said they didn't want to listen to that racist. And I stayed and listened. I was mesmerized. I remember jumping down from that island when he came down from that stage with the FOI [Fruit of Islam, the Nation of Islam's paramilitary guard]. And I cut through the crowd, because I'm so small, and got up in his face and extended my hand and said, "Mr. Malcolm X, I thank you for that, although I don't agree with everything you said." And he said, "That's all right, my sister. One day you will."

Jean Reynolds joined Temple Seven after meeting Malcolm at a lecture in 1957 or early 1958:

> I knew that I did not die and go to heaven. But to me, he in my time was the Christ that I hear everybody talkin' 'bout. Like, he's my everything. "Take your burden to the Lord and leave it"—that's what he represented to me. And I could not wait to get away from there to go tell my family and my friends. And they just knew that I was a case for Bellevue. I was never dissuaded from my first impression of him. I never let nobody tell me that he was a hoodlum. He gave me a gut and a backbone. He took the fear out of me. He said, "Sister, when you talkin to this devil, you look him straight in the eye. And as long as you're presenting facts, he'll have to turn his eye down."

Malcolm hurtled into Betty's life, too. In the years after his death, she sometimes reminisced about him or invoked his wisdom in the present tense: "My husband *says*...." Even in her final years, she talked about meeting him as if it had happened the day before. She often referred to him as "our brother" or "your brother," but she made sure you understood that he was *her* sweetheart and hers alone. "She was wrapped in his love, even though he wasn't there," Myrlie Evers-Williams once said.

When Malcolm was on Betty's mind with especial gravity—perhaps on February 21 (the anniversary of his death) or May 19 (his birthday) when Black America dusted off his autobiography and recycled his sermons and rethought him endlessly—something within her would slip. Her face would become gossamer. You almost expected the man she had both revived and synthesized over the years—the black-liberation crusader who simultaneously managed to be an almost ideal husband—to bust through the door, grin askew, bending for a kiss before rifling off to another lecture or press conference. And you expected that when he showed, she would simply swivel one of those dangerous shoulders, slit her eyes, and ask, "Baby, where you been?"

Betty sat up. There was something about the way the minister had galloped onto the temple stage, each limb vaulting over the last. "It looked as though he was going someplace much more important," she later remembered. He was soberly uniformed in a roomy suit and skinny tie. His eyes bored through horn-rimmed glasses. His hair was burnt umber. He was long-muscled, and colored like pulled taffy and tree sap.

The minister paused at the lectern to clean his glasses. "My God, this man is totally malnourished!" Betty thought. "He needs some liver, some spinach, some beets, and broccoli. You know what I'm saying?" Surely no one was at home cooking for this man, and she knew from the scalloped spaces beneath his eyes that he was working himself ragged. "I wanted to hold something in front of him so no one could see what I saw," she later recalled. But his augustness captured her. She wondered when it had slipped this man's mind that he was just a

Negro. What did he mean by drawing himself up like that? Somehow she could not shake the feeling that she had known him or his regal energy in some ancient past. "Isn't that strange?" she asked more than three decades later, just as amazed as ever. Betty, in her last years, increasingly sought spiritual explanations for her fate, adding scholar and Santeria priestess Marta M. Vega to her circle of standby Muslim and Christian counselors. But only in those years had she grown to appreciate "vibrations, spiritual connections, and chemistry." As a twenty-two-year-old Methodist, such ethereal phenomena spooked her.

She never recalled the precise sermon Malcolm preached that first night, though she always believed it was about finding the strength to do what is right. The message may not instantly have won her soul, but the minister won her heart. Sitting there among the faithful, she decided that he would be the father of her children. "I'd better not get close to him," she thought, "in case he can read minds, too."

Chapter Three

LEAVING THE GRAVE

—

"They say that only the people who have been trampled upon become Muslims.
Well, in that case we should be twenty million strong because
there isn't a Negro in America who hasn't been trampled on!"
—Malcolm X

Betty, who with the Bethel AME choir had sung "Guide Me, O Thou Great Jehovah" and "Just a Closer Walk with Thee," whose foster parents had tried to shutter out the ugly with scriptures and aphorisms, who long ago had accepted Jesus Christ and by all signs had found him an agreeable companion, finally met Minister Malcolm in Allah's temple and fell utterly in love. It was a necessarily durable love, or so it became. Betty, a confessed romantic, always fancied it an unbeaten love, despite its vulnerabilities and stresses, and held fast to its schoolyard innocence long after everything grew complicated. She smiled when a friend called it a "virgin love" (meaning it had never been betrayed). But like most love affairs, it began as fascination. "Sister," Betty reminded a friend in later years, "your brother was fine!"

A parishioner introduced Betty to the minister after she had absorbed the lecture. "My reaction was somewhat akin to respect or maybe even fear," she later remembered. She had expected him to be as soldierly in person as he was on stage and was startled to find him friendly, even charming. He wore an ingratiatingly oversized grin paneled with far too many teeth and interrupted at the center by a substantial gap.

Some took his formal pleasance for shyness. But in his presence, you knew he meant business. And for all his warmth, you somehow felt that he was parrying, holding you at a distance, trying to get a fix on you. It was a manner that Betty herself later adopted. "She smiled, but she didn't let you penetrate," remembered attorney, politician, businessman, and longtime friend Percy Sutton. "That big smile came only when you touched upon something she was interested in. It wasn't a concert smile."

During her second visit to the temple, Betty admired the masculinity of the well-barbered brothers and the sisters' modesty and grace. "But I was willing to leave it right there," she later recalled. "Will you be back?" Malcolm asked as the meeting adjourned. Then, as if she had attended a Sunday tea, he added, "We'd love to have you." Whatever Betty's reservations about the religion, the invitation flattered her.

In the days and weeks that followed, the nurse's aide who had first dragged her to the mosque hunted her in the hospital halls like a suitor. "Are you going to the temple?" she would ask. "No, I'm on duty," Betty would reply, or she offered some other excuse. She told herself that the flirtation was over; she had had enough of this Muslim business. Brother Malcolm, though quite the intellectual heavy, was surely dangerous.

Before long, though, Betty attended another dinner affair. When she showed up at the Brooklyn address, full in the cheek, almond-eyed, and all lips and inky hair, who was there but that "X" fellow? "Sister, how are you doing?" She was fine, thanks. "Are you sure?" he asked. "Because you look worried." Betty assured the minister that everything was all right, but soon the two were chatting about school and life and Alabama and her foster parents' refusal to discuss the racism she had encountered there. "They thought it was my fault," she told Malcolm.

He insisted that her foster parents were mistaken. "I really had a lot of pent-up anxiety about my experience in the South," she later recalled. "And Malcolm reassured me that it was understandable how I felt." Ever the evangelist, he then plunged into a sermon. If she could discard all that she had learned about her people's condition and its proper solution, he said, she might soon discover a passage out of America's racial wilderness. Betty did not find her first impromptu Malcolm lesson overly preachy. "I began to see myself from a different perspective," she later remembered.

Malcolm was almost nine years her senior. Though he was not half as formally educated as she was, he spoke with the ease of a man utterly in command of himself and his convictions. "Some people teach well, but at the same time that they're teaching they're trying to impress the student with the distance between the two," one of his aides later said. "Malcolm didn't do that. He met you on your ground and spoke your language, and not in a condescending manner."

Betty was drawn inexorably back to Harlem, Temple Seven, and Malcolm. She attended more of his lectures with a young couple she had befriended, finding herself in the ghetto and among the proletariat with whom she had never fraternized back in Paradise Valley. She did not write home about her budding fascination with the Muslims just yet. "My parents would kill me," she reasoned. Nor did she mention her flirtation with Black Islam to her cousin Ruth, who swore that quite unlike "them Moo-slims," she "just couldn't stay upset all the time." Still, Betty looked forward to fleeting tête-à-têtes with Malcolm after his marathon sermons. He was refreshing, intellectually and otherwise. And, as she later recalled, he brimmed with "worldly maturity that women my age at the time just dreamed about."

She had found the temple sisters locked in fearsome combat for the minister's attention. "The brother projected a majestic strength that black women don't generally find among us," his pupil Osman Karriem (née Archie Robinson) would remember. Betty was not happy about having to share Malcolm with his admirers. "I was not about to be in line, ever," she later said. Nor did she intend to join the mesmerized throngs of women. "She was never a hanger-on," Sutton would remember.

To Betty, some of the faithful seemed strung out on Malcolm, as if his fearless mystique were a narcotic. The men idolized him. The women—even those with no romantic designs—were spellbound. "Malcolm was everything a man could be to you other than lover," remembered his former parishioner Jean Reynolds. "All the divine things. All the wholesome, manhood things." Abdullah Abdur Razzaq, who as James 67X was one of the minister's most trusted lieutenants, decided in retrospect that many of the women had eyes for Malcolm simply because he was "tall, light-skinned, spoke and dressed well, took a bath everyday, shoes shined, wearing shirt and tie, carrying a brief-case, wasn't on no drugs or alcohol. These sisters had been surrounded by junkies, bums, pimps, ne'er-do-wells, rapscallions, rogues, and vagabonds. Next to them he was shining like silver and grinning like gold!"

For Charles Kenyatta, who as Charles 37X was an early Temple Seven recruit, Malcolm's appeal lay in how he "burned" the micro-phone. "They like a man who can, as the boys say in the street, 'run down murder one,'" he said. "It haven't been one before him, and there haven't been one after him, could absolutely paint this picture about being in bondage like Malcolm X. On any given Sunday afternoon, Malcolm would have all of us ready to jump out that window and kill the first cracker we seen."

Karriem slipped onstage once during a college lecture to pass Malcolm a note, and spotted several young women in the front row vying for the minister's eyes. "It was like a movie audition," he later said. Even at the mosque, where women draped themselves in hospital white and sat demurely with their hands knitted in their laps, a swash of hair might peep out from under a headpiece, or a hem might crawl up just enough to bare an ankle or the upsweep of a calf. The offend-ers faced suspension. "If I see another sister with her hair coming through her head wrap, I'm going to give her thirty days out," Malcolm often growled. Most of the women held higher ambitions, but some risked a month or more "in the wilderness" for half a chance at baiting the minister.

Always aware of her femininity, Betty would herself cheat the dress code slightly as she struggled with the Nation's strictures in later years. Though her hemlines all but scraped the floor, in time she would let more hair swirl from her gauzy white veils than Malcolm preferred. She was not so bold, however, during her early brushes with Temple Seven.

Her first flickers of jealousy for Malcolm would flare into a preoccupation that outlasted his death, but as a proselyte, she soon learned that one did not spar for the minister. "The most you could do was hope he noticed you," she later told a girlfriend.

Some of the temple's older women had begun carrying on loudly that "These young sisters need not have any notions about marrying Brother Minister, because he likes good food, and he likes it cooked in a Muslim way—and if you don't know how to do that, forget it." Betty always believed that the chorus was meant mostly for her, and it pleased her that the women seemed to think her worthy of a dig. But Malcolm tolerated no bickering in his temple. Backbiting and gossip could also earn an indiscreet soul thirty days "in the street." Nor did the thirty-one-year-old minister humor the women who hinted that he ought to take a wife. As he later said, "I always made it clear that marriage had no interest for me whatsoever; I was too busy."

———

Were Malcolm's sermons particularly rough on women? "Listen brother," Razzaq once told an interviewer, "that's an understatement." The minister's rebukes often left women "layin' in the cut," Kenyatta later recalled. Malcolm taught that weakness was a woman's "true nature." She's like a bent rib, he told the men. Later he suggested that "to tell a woman not to talk too much was like telling Jesse James not to carry a gun, or telling a hen not to cackle." For years he preached that Black America was the only matriarchal society under the sun:

> Slavery robbed the Negro man of his masculinity. The American Negro female has been more bold and domineering, since she had to be. Her earning power generally has been greater than that of the man as has her education level....But a woman must be taught her role. And the man must be sufficiently equipped to create an income for the family, to be given more respect and so respect himself.

He had not authored the philosophy. Until his last evolutions, many of Malcolm's lessons were regurgitated Elijah Muhammadisms. The minister glorified his master-redeemer, casting himself as a mere vessel:

> When you hear Charlie McCarthy speak, you listen and marvel at what he says. What you forget is that Charlie is nothing but a dummy—he is a hunk of wood sitting on Edgar Bergen's lap. If Bergen quits talking, McCarthy is struck dumb; if Bergen turns loose McCarthy will fall to the floor, a plank of sawdust fit for nothing but the fire. This is the way it is with the Messenger and me.

Still, Malcolm seemed to his flock especially zealous when he preached that women were sexually and emotionally "receivers" while men were "providers," or when he trammeled women who—dressed garishly or immodestly, their faces slathered with makeup—looked like they could have "walked the banana boat." As one aide saw it, Malcolm "would attack anything that he saw that did not enhance the spiritual dimension of females." The minister had also developed a rabid distrust of women.

He confessed that he had long considered them "tricky, deceitful, untrustworthy flesh," and reminded his followers that, "even Samson, the world's strongest man, was destroyed by the woman who slept in his arms." In later years, even admiring critics would marvel at Malcolm's misogyny. Prominent black feminist bell hooks would observe that readers of the minister's autobiography inevitably confront the "hatred and contempt he felt toward women for much of his life." James H. Cone, author of a comparative study of Malcolm and Martin Luther King Jr., later noted that both leaders embodied the patriarchy of the time, living as they did "at the threshold of the rise of feminism in the 1960s and not during its flowering in the 1970s and 1980s."

Malcolm was molting at a spectacular pace at the end of his life. His attitude toward women and their place in the movement would evolve almost as dramatically as many of his other beliefs did. By 1964, his deeds more closely matched his declaration that "no nation can rise higher than its women." But on the matter of gender, Black Islam had always been schizophrenic, for while proclaiming their frailty and backwardness, the sect glorified black women, especially those in its ranks, acknowledging their sacredness with litanies about the primacy of "mother tongue, mother culture, mother country, and mother wit." Elijah Muhammad himself hailed the black mother as mankind's first nurse and teacher. "My beloved brothers in America," he declared, "you have lost the respect for your woman and therefore you have lost the respect for yourself."

Muhammad insisted that the black man must protect and control his woman in order to recover himself. Black men were to wean black women from "white women's vices" by keeping them under cloth and curfew. Black women were to shun coed swimming pools and never be alone in a room with any man but their husbands. "Our women are allowed to walk or ride the streets all night long, with any strange men they desire," Muhammad lamented. "They are allowed to frequent any tavern or dance hall that they like, whenever they like." Restoring the black woman's honor also meant ending the oppressor's rascality. "Our women...cannot go without being winked at, whistled at, yelled at, slapped, patted, kicked, and driven around in the streets by your devil enemies," he charged.

At times, Malcolm championed black women even more emphatically. Years after his death, his widow and grown daughters armed themselves with one of his adages: "If you educate a man, you educate an individual; if you educate a woman, you educate a family." Black women, he said, were the "backbone of civilization." Even in his early ministry, he taught that "a man should never be ashamed to say he loves a woman, for this is the highest act he can perform. None of us are going to the hereafter by ourselves."

He also counseled men against violating their wives' rights. It is said that a certain man at Number Seven had taken to carousing on payday. When the man's wife complained, Malcolm dispatched some enforcers to the errant brother's door. "Look," they said, "we heard you ain't been taking your paycheck home to your wife." The man tried to act tough, as the story goes, but soon found himself lying in the dirt. "Brother," the men asked politely as they dusted him off, "did you fall down?"

Malcolm also had gentler methods of suasion. He was fond of an allegory about a man who crawled into the earth's bowels to grub for a ruby. The prospector delivered the stone to another man, who symmetrically cleaved it and sent it to a third man, who crafted it for the next man, who put it in the window for the final man, who worked hard to buy it for his lady. The moral, Malcolm explained, was that through all this labor, the woman herself was the jewel.

So it went in the temple. Women were precious objects, but objects nevertheless. "Every brother at that time was looking for a 'producer,'" Kenyatta later said, slipping into the Nation's old parlance. "Men was looking for what they called 'earth.' Some rich earth that could help bring about this nation."

The women were to busy themselves educating and civilizing the children. (Elijah Muhammad taught that infants leave the womb as savage animals.) In MGT (Muslim Girls Training), the women's corps and finishing laboratory, they learned to cook, sew, and keep fastidious households; to carry themselves modestly at home and abroad; and to honor and defer to their husbands, often addressing them as "sir." They studied English, penmanship, refinement, beauty, hygiene, and art. According to Malcolm, such graces spared black women from Western corruption. He said that Western civilization had destroyed women's femininity. "It is oriented to make her what she is not," he explained. "Western society has lost touch with home and family...marriage is deglamorized. We want to restore femininity to woman, which automatically makes her more beautiful."

Restoration was not enough. Black Islam also sought to preserve femininity with a menu of fundamentalist rules. In Betty's time, Muslim women could travel only in the back seats of cars. The movement was so patriarchal that many of the men began referring to themselves in the divine third person. "A lot of them was going home talkin' 'bout, 'Will you bring god his shoes?'" Kenyatta later recalled. "And the sisters wasn't going for that."

Still, women such as Jean Reynolds never felt repressed. The idea that the men were sworn to defend her, she later said, filled her with what Christians call the Holy Spirit. Few of the women considered the movement overly prohibiting, Sister Khadiyyah insisted. They, too, performed some of the tasks that fell to the Fruit of Islam, such as serving as sentries at meetings, a privilege known as "standing on post." "If the brothers took karate, we took karate," Sister Khadiyyah insisted. ("The only time Malcolm really came down on sisters," she added, "is when he said 'there's a rooster in the hen house'"—an allusion to a lesbian.) Muhammad taught that men and women were equal in the eyes of Allah, and granted each their spheres of influence. But a woman's authority seldom transcended the household. The black man was to uplift his sister—just so long as she did not forget her place.

———

The rigid gender roles did not put Betty off. Indeed, none of the Muslim laws seemed unbearable. She had submitted to strict proscriptions with the Malloys, at Tuskegee and again in nursing school. She was not a boozer or a smoker, nor was she given to fast living or loose dressing. She would miss the cards, dancing, and pork chops. But Betty did what she had a mind to do, and as she began appearing more regularly at Muslim bazaars and meetings, Malcolm increased the pressure for her to convert.

She waited for him to raise the issue whenever they ran into each other, and he always did. Malcolm was towing the Nation out of the back alley more powerfully than all its other catechists combined. A poised, well-spoken young nurse would be a valuable conscript in Muhammad's battle not just for souls, but power and respectability. Yet Betty was neither weak minded nor impulsive. Though she was smitten with Malcolm, she still had qualms about signing up.

"I knew I wanted *him*," she later said. "That was about the only thing I knew I wanted. But I had gone to college, and I pretty much had a sense of right and wrong." She noticed that the minister, always attentive to his entire congregation, seemed especially to seek her out at temple affairs, where the two made small talk. But during these early brushes, Betty never suspected "that he thought of me in any way other than as a sister who was interested in the Movement."

She and Malcolm soon discovered their commonalities. (He had fished souls for Muhammad in Detroit, and still had family there.) In coming years, they found kinship in other circumstances. Like her, he had grown up largely without his biological parents. He had lost his father as a young boy—he always blamed white supremacists for Earl Little's grisly death under a trolley car—and as a seventh-grader had gone adrift emotionally when his slowly unraveling mother was institutionalized. While the shared experience of childhood trauma may have helped unite Betty and Malcolm, in the end (especially the minister's final, tortured year) the old wounds may also have exacerbated a badly strained relationship.

Such revelations were years away in the latter months of 1956, as Betty fell in step with the temple rhythms. There was no dalliance between her and Malcolm. The Nation prohibited the coed "winking and blinking" it said was rampant in Christian churches. Besides, the movement was Malcolm's mistress. "His whole mind was hooked up to revolution," Kenyatta later said. Yet the minister, a monkish bachelor at thirty-two, encouraged marriage and often chided women who claimed they needed no mate. "You're lying," he told them. "You're saying you don't need a *black* man. You better go out there and get you one."

Malcolm was no more immune to beautiful women than any other well-formed, charismatic leader. He had developed a singular self-restraint. There was something about the minister that forbade vulgarity, intimacy, or intrusion. To his congregation, he sometimes seemed almost asexually upright. But he had eyes. He later confessed that he "just noticed" Betty, though "not with the slightest interest." He was sure that "you couldn't have convinced her I knew her name."

That name, by late summer or fall 1956, was Sister Betty X. In the Nation's mysteries, "X"—the unknown—supplanted the "slave name" that had been forced on the convert's ancestors. One agreed to renounce that European name, which Muhammad would ultimately replace with an "original" Arabic name. Betty was one of few believers who actually received one of the coveted aliases, and then only by marriage. (Malcolm had taken the surname Shabazz—after the ancient African tribe from which the Original People believed "so-called Negroes" had descended—by the mid 1950s.) Betty's formal conversion began in the final minutes of a Temple Seven lecture, when the minister asked those whom the gospel had convinced to please stand. The Nation brothers then ushered the risen forward to declare their intention to accept the faith.

Ruth Summerford did not know precisely when her cousin fell in with the Muslims, but she noticed that the proselyte began wearing her nursing uniform longer on the leg. Indeed, Betty insisted in September 1956 that her entire graduating class at Brooklyn State lengthen their gowns to a more modest hem. She finally told Summerford, whom she had already dragged to at least one Muslim bazaar, that she had met somebody special. It was not long before Malcolm, in an unusually intimate disclosure, told his friend and counselor Percy Sutton that he was sweet on a young convert with a killer smile. "He had a crush on this lady," Sutton later recalled. "He was smitten. And she was beautiful. Very beautiful."

Betty X's conversion inspired great speculation among her friends and family. Her childhood mate Sue MacCree figured that Malcolm was sponsoring her. "I guess being in New York was expensive," she later said. "That's probably how she hooked up with the Muslims." Summerford had another explanation. "Maybe it was their discipline," she offered. Yet Laura Ross Brown, a Northern Virginia realtor whom Betty befriended years later, said the widow admitted to having been utterly proselytized by Malcolm. "She believed the philosophy," Brown insisted. "She believed everything he said."

Until Betty encountered the minister and his flock, she had believed and obeyed the Malloys, almost without question. When, with some apprehension, she phoned to tell them that now she was

Muslim, it was as if she had announced that she had taken up with Lucifer. Betty later recalled that "members of my family were opposed to what they thought Malcolm was saying." More precisely, the Malloys feared that a doomsday cult they did not understand was wrenching away their darling.

Lorenzo and Helen Malloy may have known of Malcolm. His assistant-minister stint at Temple One afforded him some name recognition in Paradise Valley. Yet the couple had only hazy notions about him and this possibly communist, certainly pagan order for which he spoke. Though mystery shrouded their foster daughter's new god, they feared that the consequence of her apostasy would surely be the loss of her soul.

Back in Detroit, Bethel AME whirred with the news that its own Betty Dean had "gone Moo-slim." "Of course a lot of people wondered why she'd switched her faith," remembered Lydia Hibbert, a Housewives Leaguer. The very question sent the Malloys to their knees. Feeling betrayed, and believing that drastic measures were in order, the aging couple threatened to quit paying their foster daughter's tuition unless she left the sect.

It was the Nation's masculinity that first enticed Betty. Years later, she told a friend that she just could not spurn the idea of "a man being a man." Long before she understood the sect's theology, she gravitated toward the chivalry of its fearless-looking brothers. Though empowered, assertive black women had shaped her girlhood, the middle-class Leaguers had never won the prestige and regard that Muslim women enjoyed in exchange for their submission. Betty now felt utterly protected among black men, perhaps for the first time. The congregation also radiated the sense of collective purpose and responsibility for which she yearned. Though the Malloys' economic activism and Christian charity had strongly influenced her early years, she had begun to reject their political isolationism. "My folks' philosophy was everybody for themselves," she later said.

The Muslims affirmed in raw terms a truth she could no longer dismiss as her own paranoia: that America was an organically racist society. She had begun to doubt the authenticity of the racial indignities that the Old South and even the Liberal North had subjected her to. "People don't behave like this," she thought. "Something must be wrong with you." But as she began mingling with the Muslims and acknowledging racism's omnipresence, her belief in the need for a liberation struggle broadened.

This very awareness had flared in the South she had just departed, as the Montgomery Bus Boycott ground away at Jim Crow, popularizing some of the integrationist strategies that would fuel the Civil Rights movement for years. Had Betty stayed at Tuskegee, the boycott would have coincided with her senior year. Its churchly style of resistance might have seized her. She might have studied Gandhi and volunteered for sit-ins or marches, or gotten arrested alongside Martin Luther King Jr.

However, to many blacks in the northern slums, a community to which Betty now belonged (by virtue of her Muslim association if not her dormitory address), integration was a hollow ambition. The war for freedom was vividly cast and easily defined in the South; there it was a contest of the segregationists and the oppressed. Up north, the Negro faced a matrix of crises, including ramshackle housing, shoddy schools, police brutality, and labor discrimination. When viewed from a rat-chewed tenement in Detroit, an integrated swimming pool or library in Dixie could seem a measly conquest indeed.

The Muslim doctrines of self-determination and separation, on the other hand, struck many urban blacks as a sensible solution to their misery. Black Islam hardly needed to explain its fixation with self-defense. The 1955 lynching of Emmett Till was one of many cases of white savagery that had singed the Negro psyche. Till, a fourteen-year-old from the south side of Chicago, was visiting relatives near Money, Mississippi, when, on a dare, he called a white woman "Baby." A few days later, his nude, bloated body was found twisting in the Tallahatchie River. The barbed wire that tethered a seventy-five-pound cotton-gin fan to his neck had snagged on a gnarled root. Till's killers had shot him in the head, gouged out one of his eyes, and crushed his forehead.

In the face of this and other atrocities, "A guy like this Muslim leader makes a lot more sense than I do to the man in the street who's getting his teeth kicked out," Chicago Urban Leaguer Edwin C. Berry said of Elijah Muhammad in 1959. "I have a sinking feeling that Elijah Muhammad is very significant." For twenty-two-year-old Betty, his racial outlook certainly was. She now framed black consciousness in terms of reality and fantasy—the tangible threat of white supremacy versus her foster parents' illusions about its irrelevance. "Most people can't deal with reality, but indulge heavily in fantasy and fear," she later said.

Betty did not choose separatism over integration as a guiding philosophy so much as she simply wandered into the Muslim camp starving for consciousness and uncompromising black identity. Now she was blinking awake to Malcolm's revelations. A slow transformation from parochialism to globalism had begun.

Betty's conversion marked her first open defiance of her foster parents. She was "hanging on to Islam," Malcolm proudly recalled years later. Around the time Betty earned her "X," he told his growing congregation that "Islam poses a challenge and a threat. Thousands of so-called Negroes are beginning for the first time to think for themselves, and are turning daily away from the segregated Christian churches and rejoining the ranks of our darker brothers and sisters of the East, whose ancestral faith is the age-old religion of Islam, the true religion of our fore parents."

For Betty, embracing true religion meant migrating to a distant planet, or so it seemed during her early months among the Original People. She was to abandon most of what she had always considered proper and holy and accept Muhammad's theories about the history of civilization, the origin of the species, and the very nature of the universe. While the AME church had once urged her to embrace all of humanity in Christ, she now was taught that whites were a depraved race hybridized ages ago by a wicked "big-head" scientist bent on the destruction of the "so-called Negro," Allah's chosen people.

She learned that integration equaled death. (The demise would be psychological if not physical.) She learned that nonviolence as a tactic and philosophy was a swindle designed to unman the Negro and leave him open to attack. And the Bible that had governed Bethel and the Malloys? According to Black Islam, the devil had twisted the once prophetic book to keep the Negro ignorant and servile.

Indeed, the Nation taught that Christianity itself was a scheme— an anesthetic fed to the "deaf, dumb, and blind" Negro. America coursed irredeemably with hypocrisy, immorality, and racism, and no Negro with "knowledge of self" whimpered for integration. The only salvation for blacks was Islam and separatism. The only prophet was the Honorable Elijah Muhammad, supreme ruler of the "Lost-Found Nation" and harbinger of Allah, who in 1930 had Himself come to earth—Detroit, of all places—in the person of a mysterious silk peddler named Master Farad, only to vanish four years later.

The dogma was addling—an "intellectual 'Fantasia,'" one critic later scoffed—that rivaled "in its fabulous loopiness, the racial anthropology of *Mein Kampf*." Betty may have struggled for a time to scour Christianity and integrationism from her mind, or she may simply have mothballed them. It is unclear whether she ever fully subscribed to the Nation's eccentric theology, though she later acknowledged that she probably would have remained a Methodist were it not for Malcolm. "Betty fit her Christian beliefs under the Muslim dress," one of her husband's aides later said.

Whatever the depth of her spiritual conversion, Betty's rupture from the world she had always known had begun. She now belonged to a ghetto movement comprised largely of young men, a movement that boasted its own demonology, ontology, eschatology, and jurisprudence; its own politicized, hybrid Islam; and, in the tradition of Marcus Garvey, its own demand for an independent black homeland (though the Muslims wanted their bit of earth in the United States if the republic would not finance their return to Africa).

The Nation was in many ways a conservative society. Its emphasis on economic independence mirrored that of the Housewives League. In a sense, Betty, as a former African Methodist Episcopalian, had inherited a tradition of self-determination almost as radical as Black Islam, for AME Bishop Henry McNeal Turner, an eloquent black spokesman and racial separatist of the late 1800s, had himself declared God "a Negro" several generations earlier. Still, most of Betty's Detroit neighbors and old AME parishioners would have simply dismissed the Nation's philosophy as "black supremacy."

Even stripped of its foreign theology and culture, the sect for her—and for more and more urban blacks—meant political, psychological, and spiritual transmutation. Betty Dean Sanders had been satisfied with the narrow confines of her world. Sister Betty X was becoming the malcontent who in a few years would wish for her children "a better life than I have had, than any Negro in America has had, and an earth of our own."

Betty neglected to tell Malcolm how her conversion had shaken her relationship with her foster parents. (Malcolm was surprised and impressed when he later discovered this bit of independence.) Mrs. Malloy would guess that the minister had subsidized Betty once the tuition checks ran dry. But showing new resourcefulness, Betty was in fact earning extra cash baby-sitting for doctors at the hospital. She was as close to poverty as she had ever been. Yet the greatest challenge of those days was her inability to share her exotic new life with her "Ma' dear."

As far as Sue MacCree could tell, Betty never fell out with the Malloys over her conversion. Whatever animosity Mrs. Malloy felt eventually thawed, according to Lydia Hibbert, a family friend from Bethel AME. In fact, for years after Betty was widowed, Mrs. Malloy boasted that her foster daughter "was like Jackie Kennedy" (though this insistence on measuring grace with a white yardstick would have infuriated Malcolm). Betty, however, later acknowledged that she had resented the Malloys' efforts to pry her away from Islam. "I think that was really a lot of time wasted," she said, "because eventually they accepted my way of life without compromise. And I think that life could have been better not only for my parents but for Malcolm and me and the children if they...had accepted then rather than later."

By 1957, Betty had little time to mend her relationship with the Malloys; she was building a nation. The Muslims believed idleness led to backsliding. So, like her fellow proselytes, Betty went straight to work. While many of the women at Number Seven were domestics or clerks with a high-school education at best, she was a nurse apprentice who had begun her clinical training. Before long, she was teaching women's health and basic hygiene at the temple. ("Some of us didn't know how to do certain things that we needed to do under our clothes," Sister Khadiyyah remembered.)

Betty relished the role. It allowed her to share her new expertise and commune with Malcolm, whose pastoral duties called for him to drop in occasionally on the temple's Thursday-night MGT and GCC (General Civilization Classes). Every now and then, he would pause to ask Betty how the sisters' lessons were coming along. "Fine, Brother Minister," she replied. Malcolm would thank her, and little more was said. From time to time, Betty also gave brief talks on basic medicine to the unconverted who stopped by the temple on Saturdays. The visitors studied speech, posture, manners, arts and crafts, and even some Arabic alongside the believers.

Betty's academic background granted her status. It was not long before she had risen to a higher social stratum in the temple, one occupied mostly by the wives of the ranking men under Malcolm, such as lieutenants and assistant ministers. "She was in that clique," Sister Khadiyyah said. Inevitably, the position and its perceived privileges aroused the envy of some of the women.

Betty's bourgeois credentials had already generated some friction among the believers. Though they professed to shun white society's aspirations and the Negro establishment's pretensions, "the pervasiveness of the middle-class spirit and aspirations among the Muslims cannot escape the attention of a keen observer," a Nigerian scholar noted in 1962. The congregation's acquisitive flavor resonated with Betty's past. But while she as a future nurse was "arriving," most of the Original People had only just embarked.

———

Despite its stern ethics, the Nation of the 1950s bred all the petty jealousies and suspicions that afflict the Christian church and every other human institution. One imagines that it was both Betty's snobbery (as several of Malcolm's former aides remembered) and sour grapes (as the widow herself insisted) that sparked antagonism between her and some Harlem parishioners even before she wed the minister.

Still, Betty was not a terribly conspicuous figure at the temple as a neophyte. She rarely if ever "stood on post." She was comely, but so were many of the other women. She was better educated and more authentically bourgeois, but as Kenyatta put it, there were "no big 'I's'" in the ranks. "You don't come in talkin' 'bout where you came from," he later said. Was Betty not an exceptionally gifted recruit? "Brother," the aide told an interviewer, "no woman was noticeable." Indeed, if any of the women came down with a case of ego, the local sister captain or Ethel Sharieff, Muhammad's daughter and national captain of the women's corps, would put them straight. Muhammad himself warned the flock against the "middle-class" renegades among them who clung to "worldly learning and high positions" rather than bowing to his divine authority.

Conformity could not dim the exhilaration of Betty's new identity. Though she had become an MGT instructor, she remained an eager student of Black Islam. "It was a whole new way of living and learning and eating and being," she later said. Returning from "the dead" is not a feat accomplished in a matter of months. Leaving the grave to achieve finer womanhood requires an even more drastic re-education.

So while studying a black god called Allah and a white devil that needed no other name, Betty learned to correctly wash vegetables, brown rice, and cook certain squashes and greens (but

absolutely no collards). She learned to prepare staples such as cab-
bage, candied carrots, and potato, bean, and cheese pies. Her old
"slave" diet, she learned, would ultimately have proven fatal. Now
she was eating to live. Fresh, well-cooked lamb, chicken, fish, and
beef would do, but "scavengers of the sea" (shellfish), yams, sweet
potatoes, black-eyed peas, white bread, liquor, and the "vile, filthy
hog" were contraband.

Cleanliness was sacred and overeating was forbidden. Soon Betty
noticed a new luster and clarity in her skin and eyes. "We were looking like angels," Sister Khadiyyah later remembered. Betty began ton-
ing down her makeup. "Food is your cosmetics," she later said. "We
don't believe in covering our pores with greasy creams." Though the
Nation never explicitly banned makeup, it discouraged the faithful
from layering themselves with paint. Yet Betty accented her eyes and
lips tastefully throughout her Black Muslim years. "She refused to look
anything but beautiful," Ameenah Omar, the wife of Malcolm's older
brother Philbert, would recall.

Black Islam left cosmetics to the believer's discretion. There was
no alternative, however, to divine cuisine. Nostalgic for soul food,
Betty considered cheating the Muslim diet. "Oh, they will never
know," she told herself. But she found she could no longer stomach
impiety. After that momentary weakness, she did her best to submit
fully to Allah.

Betty spent her days at Montefiore Hospital. Weekends and most
weeknights belonged to the Nation. She learned to move gracefully in
silk headpieces and snowy robes during Sunday services and other formal affairs. (Malcolm had no use for black women who let themselves
go simply because they could no longer dress like the "devil's kind.")
With the minister approving and guiding her curriculum, she continued teaching the women that cleanliness *is* godliness.

At the temple, she learned why blacks should never call themselves "Negroes"—the term signified death and failed to link the race
to a homeland—how Allah in her lifetime would smite whites, and
why the black man and woman must respect each other's "true
natures." She learned to pray and fast and grieve and recreate in the

Muslim style. She memorized snatches of Arabic and those Qur'anic passages Muhammad ordered his phalanx of ministers to teach the body. On Sundays, Malcolm sermonized on heady topics such as the holy city "in the East" that he swore no white man could enter. As the believers bore witness (*Go 'head, sir! Run it down! Preach!*), Betty sat as still as a sapling and let him stretch her twenty feet tall.

By the time Betty ventured into Harlem, Malcolm was forever ripping down highways, anchoring in urban wildernesses only long enough to open a temple or thunder for Allah's Messenger in the local mosque. The right hand of the man with God in his ear *had* to roam. Malcolm was Muhammad's national spokesman, indefatigable deputy, subject, and beloved son by any measure but blood. Already jealous grumbles could be heard among the society's upper echelons. His efforts had also piqued the attention of the white man's agents. The FBI had begun monitoring him in 1953 as a possible communist sympathizer but was soon focusing on his role within the sect.

The intelligence community's reach did not seem to hinder Malcolm. Only one question consumed him: "How we gonna build this black nation?" Harlem in April 1957 handed him her answer. Black Muslim Johnson X Hinton came across a pair of white police officers billy-clubbing a black suspect one evening. When Johnson protested angrily, the sticks fell on him, and the officers hauled him away. Harlem conducts bad news swiftly, and soon Malcolm had his unsmiling parishioners in formation outside the 123rd Street police station where Johnson X was oozing life.

Expecting a showdown, hundreds, perhaps thousands, of Harlemites materialized. Malcolm confronted the police, demanding to see Johnson. Eager to avoid a race riot, they took him to Johnson, who was in terrible shape. Malcolm had him rushed to the hospital. Only after his congregant had received medical attention did the minister step into the street and, with a single gesture, disperse his legion.

The face-off catapulted Malcolm to fame among area blacks. With its headman now something of a folk hero in Harlem, Temple Seven's congregation burgeoned to more than one thousand members. Meanwhile, the minister's schedule had him careening. He huddled monthly with Muhammad and other Muslim ministers and dignitaries in Chicago. He was dispatching a widely read newspaper column and otherwise propelling the movement with amazing success. But he was exhausted. Malcolm observed the order's ritual of one daily meal, and often snatched only four hours of sleep. In October 1957, he was hospitalized with another episode of the heart palpitations that had plagued him in prison. "He was all-giving, all-helping, and it didn't look like anybody was helping him," Betty later remembered.

It was just as plain to Malcolm's older half-sister, Ella Collins, that he needed a caretaker. One of the few women Malcolm ever trusted, the wily Collins had boarded him in Boston during much of his teens. A mother figure and advisor to Malcolm, her will would provoke epic feuds with the equally intractable Betty. Collins may inadvertently have prodded Malcolm toward Betty by pressuring him to get married. She even talked about finding the minister an African wife, knowing that he'd never consent to an arranged marriage.

Malcolm may have had his own indefinite plan. It came to him that Betty, who had helped type some of his papers, would do well to visit the Museum of Natural History. Malcolm regularly led his congregation on field trips to libraries, cultural centers, and other temples, sometimes in great caravans. If he were to escort Betty to the museum, he told himself, he could point out the evolutionary displays that would edify her as an instructor. He mentioned the idea to Betty in the offhand manner to which she would grow accustomed, stressing that the outing would be strictly pedagogical. "I had even convinced myself," he later recalled.

When the agreed-upon hour arrived, however, Malcolm backpedaled. He telephoned Betty and announced brusquely that something had come up. "Well," came the reply, "you sure waited long enough to tell me, Brother Minister. I was just getting ready to walk out the door." All right, then—it was back on, he said. But he warned her that he did not have much time.

———

Betty would insist that Malcolm pursued her "persistently and correctly." Perhaps he did, for no matter how oblique the advance, a woman knows when she is pursued. But as Betty acknowledged, the Nation forbade "fraternizing" among single brothers and sisters. Malcolm could not have courted Betty, at least not in the Hollywood fashion he so disdained. He himself all but bragged that "there had never been one personal word" between him and his future wife.

He did pelt her with questions during their museum visit to gauge her attitude and reasoning skills. Later he admitted that her responses and overall intelligence had "halfway" impressed him. Shortly after the outing, when an older woman at the temple told him that Betty's foster parents had revoked her college funding, he again found himself pondering Sister Betty X. (Betty later told a friend that a kindly older sister at the temple had helped match her and the minister.)

Soon Betty was meeting Malcolm for sweet cake and tea, or occasional Sunday suppers at the temple restaurant, near 116th and Lenox Avenue in Harlem. The other guests who often bookended him during the meals became mere chaperones in Betty's mind. She and Malcolm were, in her estimation, "just friends." However, she always felt crumpled after dining with the minister. Some of the parishioners had grown even more watchful of her and Malcolm's exchanges. She felt the stab of their eyes, but seemed to enjoy the attention. At times she entered the restaurant and "every man and woman—old, young, fat, whatever—would offer me a seat to prevent Malcolm and me from sitting together," she later remembered. The men, Betty figured, resented even the possibility that some "heifer" was out to domesticate their warrior. And the women? "Just plain jealous," she concluded.

Only later did Betty get the first inkling that Malcolm fancied her. She noticed that she was always among those herded along on temple field trips, but she could not understand why Malcolm always maneuvered her into the seat directly behind his. Then, during one expedition, she glanced up in mid-sentence and caught his eyes in the rearview mirror. He smiled. She smiled back. "That," she once remembered, "was as much as we could do."

Betty seized every chance to win Malcolm's eyes. Whenever she got word that he'd returned to New York from one of his ecclesiastical trips, she begged her hospital supervisor for time off. "Did that man come into town again?" the woman would ask.

Malcolm took to interrogating her. He was always finding excuses to ask about her background, future plans, and outlook on the movement. She had learned from experience to respond carefully. She once mentioned that she had some serious partying planned for after graduation, and instantly regretted the comment when Malcolm's face clouded.

The minister was always apologizing for plying her with personal questions, and she was always assuring him that she knew his interest in her was purely ministerial—"brotherly," as she put it. She had heard him complain that "there were so many women who, if you opened the door for them or bought them dinner or sent them a card, before you know it they'd have their wedding dress all ready." She would have died before she came off so "fickle-hearted." She and Malcolm had a subtle magic, but they were far from familiar. He was her pastor, and an exacting one at that. "You can't play with this guy—he's serious," she thought. Yet his intensity never eclipsed what Betty called his "high civility." "A lot of girls took it to mean that he was interested in them," she later recalled.

"If he said he was going to call," Betty later said of Malcolm, "you could bank on it." They had known one another for months, and he seemed content with their parlor game of feigned nonchalance. She had begun to suspect that he was mulling a proposal. "I was onto something," she later recalled. But when would it come?

Malcolm was rigid on the matter of wedlock. He once asked Betty whether she had ever been married. At first she replied truthfully. Later, teasingly, she told him that she had lied and had been married. "I'll never forget the way he looked at me!" she later exclaimed. She quickly assured him that she was only kidding, but Malcolm was obviously angry. "That is something you never kid about," he said dryly.

If one was contemplating marriage, "the worst person to come to was Malcolm, because he didn't play that," aide Osman Karriem remembered. Officially, engagements in the temple were brokered by the brother captain—a notorious tough named Joseph—and the sister captain. One was obliged, however, to seek Malcolm's blessing, and that meant taking heat:

> Excuse me, you're going to do what? You know her? How you know her? Have y'all been out? Y'all live together? Y'all used to hang in the streets? Look, brother, what's her background? Has she been married? Have you? Have you been to prison? She comes from a strict upbringing. What bearing would your having been to prison have on the marriage? Why are you attracted to her? What you bringing to the game, brother?

That was just the start of it. "How much time between the two of you?" Malcolm would demand. A proper Muslim bride was half a man's age plus seven. (Betty was twenty-three when she married the thirty-two-year-old minister.) "Anything under five years, you could forget it," Karriem later recalled. "And you better not come talkin' about nothing with no woman if you were younger than she."

Malcolm invoked no lesser wisdom than that of Allah's Messenger when he declared that "no marriage could succeed where the woman did not look up with respect to the man." The wife was to lean on her husband for "psychological security," and the husband was to be capable of "handling" his mate. "Responsibility and authority go hand in hand," Malcolm told Karriem. "If you're going to take responsibility for someone, you must have authority to deal with them."

—

Betty later remembered drifting away from Malcolm before joining the Nation. "I thought I was strong enough to do that," she said. After attending a Sunday meeting at the temple in 1956, she returned to Detroit for summer vacation. Malcolm had suggested that she look up one of his siblings there, but had made her promise to "leave my brother as you found him." "I sure will, sir," Betty had chimed innocently. She wound up spending a memorable summer of movies and dinners with Wesley, Malcolm's youngest brother. Wesley scolded her for always talking about the minister. "I wasn't even aware of it," she later said.

While home that summer, Betty succumbed to the familiar rhythms at Bethel AME. Again she asked herself why she was fooling with Islam. But after the break, she was back among the faithful, studying Black Islam and cavorting with trouble. Shortly after she had returned to New York, Malcolm told her that Wesley was planning a visit to the city. "I wonder why he's coming," the minister said, shooting her a look. Betty had no idea. She later ran into Wesley at the Muslim restaurant, not knowing that he was in town. "Why didn't you tell me you were going to marry my brother?" Wesley sputtered. Betty froze. (She later recalled that Malcolm had posted himself nearby to gauge her reaction.)

Malcolm may have been contemplating marriage, not as a consummation of romance so much as an obligation of his station. "Brother, a minister *has* to be married," he later told Razzaq. He badly wanted sons to inherit the movement. Sister Betty X, he reasoned, just happened to be precisely the right height and age. (Though he later reflected, with an almost forced nonchalance, that it could have been "any sister in any temple.") Betty was quick-witted and carried herself well—a must for any man with an appetite for elegance. Her skin was brown, so the children, Allah willing, would have some color. Her complexion would complement his ferocious preaching on the deficiency of white blood.

She had few relatives, or so Malcolm thought. "My feeling about in-laws was that they were outlaws," he later said. Her nurse's training also increased her currency with the minister, who had a vitamin imbalance and a fluttering heart.

But Malcolm was ambivalent. He hardly lifted a finger without considering the Nation as a whole. How would the insular sect respond to the marriage of one of its cardinals? With his maniacal travel and work schedule, how could he sustain a marriage in the first place? How could he possibly expect to tell a woman where he was every minute of the day? And what if the relationship fell apart? Though permitted under extreme circumstances, Muslim divorces were discouraged.

The minister dreaded choosing the wrong woman. He told Betty he still associated marriage with his parents' riotous arguments. She later assured him that "the one thing I won't do is argue." He explained that he intended to devote his life to the cause. "He felt that marriage was a responsibility, and he didn't know if he could live up to it," Betty later remembered.

Betty might have wondered whether Malcolm had taken a vow of chastity as well as poverty. "Malcolm didn't have no feelings for a woman," Kenyatta later declared. The aide said that he had always believed that Muhammad himself had ordered Malcolm wed, despite the minister's insistence that he would marry at his will. Kenyatta had labored in Malcolm's ministry well before Betty hit the scene, and never accepted that anything besides black nationhood and Armageddon might enthrall him. "They thought that Malcolm was weak, that he was looking for a very high-profile, attractive woman," Kenyatta said. "That was far from the case."

Yet it was Malcolm who in 1957 proclaimed family life "the backbone of Islam," and declared that "a righteous wife and children is one of Allah's greatest blessings to man." Though some of the faithful had not detected his and Betty's compatibility and mutual affection, at least one outsider had. Dr. Yosef ben-Jochannan, the history professor who first encountered Malcolm as Big Red and later "fed him many books," remembered meeting Betty—probably at the Muslim restaurant—as the minister's "wife-to-be." The title could not have been official; there would be no engagement. Dr. Ben nevertheless got the impression that the two were bound for matrimony.

Still, Malcolm was spooked. The more he thought about marrying Betty, the more he found himself avoiding her. Whenever she turned up at the restaurant, he would leave. "I was glad I knew that she had no idea what I had been thinking about," he later admitted. It's difficult to imagine any woman unnerving the minister, so fearless did he seem with a microphone at his chin. But the prospect of rejection terrified him. He later admitted that he had simply heard too many women brag about having told some man, "Get lost!"

Betty may have captured Malcolm long before he began to squirm. He wondered years later whether she hadn't feigned ignorance about his intentions. She had, of course, but he was oblivious in late 1957. He reasoned that she wouldn't grow suspicious if he sent her to Chicago to attend the Headquarters Temple Two women's classes and meet Muhammad in person. By then it was customary for instructor sisters from temples throughout the country to make the pilgrimage. And so it was that barely a year after she'd earned her X, Betty learned that she was to receive one of the highest honors of her new society; she was to be a house guest of Elijah Muhammad and his wife, Sister Clara.

In the years after Malcolm's death, Betty never forgave Muhammad and his men for the crimes she believed they had committed against history—the first being the slaughter of her husband. She never tried to erase the Nation from Malcolm's story; he had spent more than a quarter of his apoplectic life defending and expanding the organization. But Betty would be damned if anyone forgot that ultimately his intellect and awareness outgrew Black Islam and its fanciful program for black liberation. "Your speech was very beautiful," she would tell scholars and authors after they encapsulated Malcolm's life at commemorative affairs. "But you left my husband in the Nation."

An unlikely odyssey unfurled between the hour Betty addressed her Nation of Islam application letter to Master Farad in lilting script ("I bear witness that there is no God but thee") and the months in which she began to pointedly suspect, then despise, his apostle Muhammad. But perhaps the doubt stirred first during her stay at the Messenger's home. She may have been as eager as Malcolm had been in 1952 to confront his savior, or as impressed as writer James Baldwin was years later when he met the "Prophet":

> the man who came into the room was small and slender, really very delicately put together, with a thin face, large, warm eyes, and a most winning smile. Something came into the room with him—his disciples' joy at seeing him, his joy at seeing them. It was the kind of encounter one watches with a smile simply because it is so rare that people enjoy one another. He teased the women, like a father, with no hint of that ugly and unctuous flirtatiousness I knew so well from other churches, and they responded like that, with great freedom, and yet from a great and loving distance.

Betty learned firsthand during her visit that Muhammad was beguiling. But there was something else, something darker. She later told her mentor and confidante Norma Johnson that she "had a feeling that Elijah wanted me for himself." Whatever prompted the suspicion, Betty may not have shared it directly with Malcolm until very late in the game, if at all. Still, according to Kenyatta, there were whispers in the Chicago dynasty and beyond that "the Old Man had eyes for Betty."

Yet it was as a son might seek his father's blessing that Malcolm had gone to Muhammad with the news that he was contemplating "a very serious step." Muhammad had smiled when he learned what his de facto second-in-command was brooding. (Muhammad offered to make Betty one of his personal secretaries, but Malcolm—who may even then have harbored suspicions of his own—declined.) Upon making

Betty's acquaintance, the Apostle of Allah declared her "a fine sister." Having received God's consent, Malcolm prepared to close the deal.

———

Coretta Scott King often maintained as a widow that fate brought to her a stubby young minister named Marty King, the future emblem of the Civil Rights movement. "While my husband was being prepared for the job he was to do, I feel that I was being prepared also to be his helpmate," she once mused. "When I think back over my life experience, I feel very strongly that it was meant to be this way."

Coretta and Betty were more dissimilar than the public generally supposes. But the latter never allowed that her marriage was accidental, either. Four years after his death, Betty reflected on the distinctly human quality that may finally have bound her and Malcolm. "I guess he got lonely," she said. But as time passed, she began insisting more frequently that providence itself made the match, that she was destined to be with Malcolm.

Overall, though, Betty saw her role opposite Malcolm as more necessary than divine. "You know, he just kind of, I felt, needed me," she said once. "I thought he'd be a much better 'whatever' if I were in his life." She had on first sight thought him rather pasty and hungry-looking— "rhiny," as she put it—and had never quit wondering whether maybe she should be the one to rescue him. "I didn't know exactly if Malcolm was the right person for me," she recalled, "but I was willing to try."

So when he phoned her Clarkson Avenue, Brooklyn, nurse's residence around ten o'clock on a Sunday morning, January 12, 1958, she hustled to take his call. "Oh, hello, Brother Minister," she said, trying to sound casual. Malcolm had left New York the night before to visit his older brother Wilfred, minister of Temple One. Once inside Detroit, he had stopped to call Betty from a filling-station pay phone. He had made a point of not memorizing her number, and had to dial information for the exchange. When she came on the line, he put it to her like Big Red would have: "Are you ready to make that move?"

Betty screamed. The receiver was squawking faintly; she realized that she had dropped the phone. She spooled the cord and found the lungs to say "yes." (Later she recalled that she had instantly understood Malcolm's colloquial proposal.) A few forgettable courtesies were exchanged (Black Muslims were tediously polite), and it struck her to hang up. A giddy haze began enveloping her. The squeal had drawn her fellow nurses from their rooms, and they now stood staring at the normally subdued girl. Betty thought she ought to call that pleasant older sister from the temple who had always talked her up in Malcolm's presence. She dialed, and listened to the phone's trill. Then the sister was on the other end. "Hello?" And despite her best intentions, Betty screamed again.

Chapter Four

WINDOWS OF THE HEART

—

"None of us knew Malcolm like Betty. None of us knew him as a wife."
—Dick Gregory

Betty steadied herself as the other resident nurses filtered back to their dorm rooms. She packed a bag, caught a plane to Detroit, and was soon beside Malcolm. Perhaps the two embraced, but a kiss would have been unlikely, and not just because the minister abhorred exhibition, as Betty would discover. The relationship, however charming, had been that of pastor and parishioner, and no proposal could instantly bridge that divide. Besides, time was short. She drew herself upright and collected her nerves; she and Malcolm were off to face the Malloys.

It seemed to Malcolm that Betty and her foster parents must have made up since their quarrel over her conversion. The couple appeared "happily surprised" to greet the minister that Betty had so carried on about. "At least they acted that way," Malcolm remembered. Months earlier, when Betty told them that she had managed to meet somebody worthwhile, Mrs. Malloy had quite benignly asked, "And what does he do?"

Standing now before them, armed only with a slack suit and a boyish smile, Malcolm more resembled a broker than an "extremist." Excusing themselves, the Malloys led their foster daughter out back and did their best to sound enthused. "A marvelous young man...clean-cut and he *knows* so much," they said. "The one thing we can say about you is that you've always had nice friends. We've never had to worry about you." Betty seized the moment. "So," she asked, "how would you like to have him for a son-in-law?"

Mrs. Malloy nearly collapsed. Betty was not ready for marriage, she wailed. He was too old, and he was not even Christian. "She wept on and on," Betty remembered. Mr. Malloy tried to console his wife. "See what you're doing to your mother?" he demanded. "What have we done to make you hate us so?" Soon Betty, too, was sobbing. She rushed to her old room and flung herself onto her bed. She had expected friction, not hysteria. The Malloys had been convinced that sooner or later she would simply outgrow Islam. (In fact, Mrs. Malloy never fully abandoned the idea that her foster daughter would come around.)

Mrs. Malloy always believed that Malcolm had meant to ask her and her husband for Betty's hand during that surprise visit on January 13, 1958, but had thought better of it when the family withdrew into the house and quarreled. "He got cold feet," she said. She later confessed that she had not wanted Betty to get married, "especially to him, because he was a Muslim or something." As it happened, she saw the minister on only three or four occasions before his death. (Some years later, Malcolm traveled to Detroit to give a talk and spotted his mother-in-law in the audience. "You be sure to go," Betty had admonished her well before the event. Upon making her out in the crowd, Malcolm strode over to the uncomfortable-looking woman. "You here?" he teased, his face elasticized in a lopsided grin. "I know the world's coming to an end!" "No," Mrs. Malloy replied in her understated clip. "Betty told me to come.")

Whatever resentment Mrs. Malloy had once felt, she conceded in later years that her son-in-law ultimately became "very powerful and interesting to people." But by the time she and Mr. Malloy met the minister, they had already picked a husband for Betty. Even the parents of the young man—a Christian—had approved of the match. So when Betty sprung her marriage plans on the Malloys not long after she announced her conversion, they fretted anew that she was ruined.

Though the Malloys might have seemed uptight, they were proud of having done right by Betty. From the time she had entered their home she had, through no small effort, been superbly brought up, quite unlike the many foster children who were simply yanked up. They had always drawn comfort from this knowledge. Never had they counted on Malcolm's interference.

Betty in later years told a friend that her foster mother and Malcolm "fussed over who did the most for me." The two seem to have kept a cool distance. Other relatives were more embracing. When Betty as a newlywed took her husband to Philadelphia to introduce him to her birth father, the Sandlins received Malcolm rather openly. "I'm not sure Juju expected this tall, well-dressed businessman," Betty's half-brother, Stanley Sandlin, later recalled. After Betty appeared in Muslim garb, however, Juju's wife, Madeline, drew the line. "My mother told them that when she was coming up, anybody wearing a sheet was Klan, and wasn't no Klan coming in her house," Shelmon Sandlin Jr. remembered. "Malcolm might have won a whole lot of debates. But that was not one of them."

Nor did Betty win her foster parents' blessing after she and Malcolm showed up on January 13, 1958 to announce their betrothal. She spent a miserable night at home, and early the next morning Malcolm phoned from a store around the way and announced that if she intended to come with him, she'd better get moving. Betty tried to stay calm, but two more calls from her betrothed had her in a flurry, trying to make ready without arousing the Malloys' suspicions. She was to be married within hours, and they could not even know.

With a frantic good-bye, Betty bolted out the door and into Malcolm's Oldsmobile, which she had asked him not to park directly in front of the house. (Mrs. Malloy later insisted that her foster daughter and the minister had "slipped off.") Betty's tears blurred the old neighborhood as they pulled away. For years, the pale yellow house at 313 Hague had been her sanctuary. Though she had left many times, she sensed that this would be the first departure. "Drive quick!" she said.

The two wasted no time getting blood tests and a pair of rings in Lansing, Malcolm's hometown. According to the Nation's strictures, "the sun could not set with us together and not married," Betty later explained. (They had planned to get married in Indiana, but the state had recently rescinded a law permitting marriages without a waiting period.) Traveling alone with her intended, Betty discovered that she had unconsciously mashed herself against the passenger-side window. She felt like a fugitive. Her foster parents had always wanted a gorgeous wedding for their only child. Now here she was eloping, her wedding dress balled in a suitcase behind her. Yet she had resolved not to look back, and would never regret the getaway. She believed she was fleeing a "backyard mentality." Tomorrow, she told herself, she would embrace the world.

A justice of the peace whom Malcolm would remember as "an old hunchbacked white man" performed the civil ceremony later that afternoon before white witnesses and Philbert X and Wilfred X, Malcolm's blood brothers and the ministers of Temple Sixteen (Lansing) and Temple One (Detroit), respectively. The official pronounced Malcolm and Betty "man and wife" by an authority Malcolm disdained, on behalf of a government he rebuked, then directed Malcolm to kiss his bride. The minister did so without pageantry—perhaps the couple's last public intimacy. "All of that Hollywood stuff!" he later scoffed. But Betty would recall that he grinned when she got on tiptoes in the white man's courthouse and pressed her lips to his cheek.

Wilfred had invited the couple to spend the night with him and his wife in Detroit, but Malcolm wouldn't hear of it. Later at the hotel, Betty pulled out her rumpled, unused wedding dress, complete with headgear, and she and her husband laughed until they wheezed. She undressed in the bathroom, wormed into a modest nightgown, and scooted into bed beside him. "Don't hurt yourself," Malcolm said. From where he was sprawled, his eyes had chased her across the room. Betty later recalled that he had tried to pretend that he was not looking. But as she observed, "A hotel room is just so large."

———

Betty flew home the next day to complete her nursing classes, then rejoined Malcolm in Detroit. The couple worshipped that Sunday at the city's Temple Number One, where Elijah Muhammad announced their wedding, jolting the congregation. (Betty "claims she didn't tell anybody in Temple Seven that we had married," Malcolm later said.) By the following week, when the couple returned to New York and moved into three rooms of a two-story building in East Elmhurst, Queens, the Harlem mosque and the entire Nation were abuzz with the news that Brother Minister had gotten hitched.

"I didn't even know he was courting," Jean Reynolds later remembered. "Malcolm X Wed; It's a Surprise," exclaimed one black newspaper. (Malcolm told the *Amsterdam News* that only Allah and His Messenger had advance knowledge of his "carefully laid" plans.) It was a surprise indeed to the many Muslim sisters (and not a few Christians) who were in love with Malcolm, and particularly to the two or more women that Malcolm's sidemen, and some of the laity, knew he was considering for a wife.

There were whispers that Malcolm intended to marry Sister Lucille Rosary or Sister Evelyn Williams. Nation officials and some of his close former associates later insisted that he had actually been quietly engaged to Williams, a claim he confirmed in a 1959 letter to Muhammad that also acknowledged his proposal to—and rejection of—a third Muslim woman, Betty Sue. (He later recommended both Rosary and Williams for Muhammad's corps of fetching young secretaries.) The minister may indeed have been mulling a proposal to any one of several women. The only certainty is that just about every parishioner had a notion about whom he should wed.

Sister Khadiyyah, for one, loved Sister Winnifred for Malcolm, though she later insisted that because of his fanatical self-discipline and allegiance to Muhammad, "the brother could have went his lifetime without marrying." She decided, therefore, that marriage was foisted on him. When an interviewer later asked what she thought Betty and

Malcolm had in common, she replied without pause: "Elijah Muhammad, that's what! The Nation had a lot of control over what you did as a human being. If you were in a particular echelon, you had to marry who they picked out for you." Charles Kenyatta echoed the sentiment, perhaps overstating Betty's status as a single woman. "In the heart of the movement," he said, "big stars only came to big stars."

Abdullah Razzaq also suspected the Old Man of having pressured or commanded Malcolm to the altar. "If Mr. Muhammad told Malcolm to stand on his head, he'd do it," Razzaq said. Most of the parishioners agreed that Muhammad was the only soul who could have forced Malcolm to do anything; not even Ella Collins could harry her brother into marriage. But for a time, Muhammad had actually encouraged his top evangelist to stay single so that he could, as Kenyatta put it, "be about his father's business" without distraction.

Despite the ban on gossip, the laity murmured about Malcolm's marriage for some time. While the news left some believers indifferent ("I wasn't concerned with anything other than going to hear the Minister," Jean Reynolds said), others wondered whether Betty was right for their beloved brother and teacher. Some complained that she was little more than a schoolgirl. If the whispers shook Betty, it did not show. "She stood her ground," Sister Khadiyyah remembered. Betty's indifference inflamed those who privately accused her of haughtiness. But she was now Temple Seven's first lady, and the faultfinders, as her cousin Ruth put it, could "walk by the wayside."

Still, Betty was to learn that first ladies can inhabit psychological prisons quite as real as their privilege. Enduring veiled hostility was just one burden of a reign that felt at times like captivity. She was with the juggernaut temple's number-one man and would have to bear the scrutiny, for despite its mythology of spaceships and big-headed scientists, the Nation clung to a strict pragmatism in matrimony. There was, for instance, the Temple Seven man who confessed his love for a woman in the congregation. His marriage request was summarily denied on the grounds that he, a sidewalk vendor, had not sufficiently established himself. "You can't take care of no family sellin' fish," he was told. In questions of conjugality, love had little to do with it.

Of course, Betty never suggested that Malcolm married purely for love, though she acknowledged that she had. ("I sometimes had to tell him that he was my hero," she once recalled. "But I married him because I loved him.") Nor did she entertain the theory that he had wed for convenience, or simply to please leaders in Chicago. Malcolm later assured Muhammad that his proposal had been pragmatic. "I deliberated long and selected carefully," he confided. "Betty is physically strong, near my height, looked something like me, and seemed to be able to produce children that would be strong and resemble us both. Plus, she seemed intelligent and had qualifications that would be helpful to me in my work." Betty, however, would acknowledge no such calculation, insisting that she and Malcolm were simply meant to be, and that they'd both known it.

She developed during the marriage a powerful sense of duty as the minister's wife. By the end, disillusionment had confounded this awareness, but she always insisted that she had loved him like crazy and had been loved in return. "He loved his parents, he loved his people, and later he loved me with the same passion," she declared.

Malcolm's professions of amour were more equivocal. "I guess by now I will say I love Betty," the minister, in his final year, told Alex Haley, the collaborating writer of his autobiography. "She's the only woman I ever even thought about loving." (One biographer thought the minister had Haley insert this declaration into an earlier chapter of his memoirs after a series of transforming experiences revealed how the myopia of his Black Muslim years had tormented his family.) On another occasion, Malcolm exclaimed that "all she's put up with—man I've *got* to love this woman!"

Despite the tensions that streaked his marriage, Malcolm grew to deeply appreciate Betty, who he realized had sacrificed far more at his side than any spouse should have to. "Awakening this brainwashed black man and telling this arrogant, devilish white man the truth about himself, Betty understands, is a full-time job," he once declared.

Malcolm dismissed Western notions of love as superficial. "You take it apart," he said, "it really is lust." But Islam "teaches us to look into the woman and teaches her to look into us," he taught. "Betty does this, so she understands me." The minister's scorn for Yankee romance was clearly evangelical. Still, his utilitarian attitude toward love and marriage seems to support the theory that at least initially, he saw in Betty more a dutiful partner than a soulmate.

Whatever finally drew Malcolm into a lonesome phone booth in the chill of a Detroit winter to ask Sister Betty for her hand, their lives from that moment were forever entwined. And whatever genuine affection Malcolm felt for his bride, there was an enduring sentiment among many of the believers that their Brother Minister had been captured.

Betty remembered her marriage as "hectic, beautiful, and unforgettable—the greatest thing in my life." She described those years with superlatives not because she associated them with power, but because her time with Malcolm, as harried as it often was, taught her what it meant to live. He had propelled her on a journey, a search for what she described in her final years—with stream-of-consciousness scribbles in the margins of envelopes—as "God and truth."

But on January 14, 1958 when she became his bride, she was a callow twenty-three-year-old still trying to balance the Nation's strictures with a longing for the world she had forsaken. Though a collision was inevitable, she never got a chance to brace. "Betty didn't understand the life she had been pressed into," Kenyatta later declared. "She didn't know how powerful a man she had."

She was nevertheless proud to be Mrs. Malcolm X; so thought Sutton, who found her suitably reserved but confident when the minister accompanied her on a social call early in 1958. "I knew she was a strong woman," he recalled. Ruth Summerford remembered that upon returning from her honeymoon, her cousin fluttered over to her Brooklyn pad brandishing her marriage certificate. Betty and Malcolm were settling into a humble parsonage at the time. They were to share the second story of a small, 99th Street building with a young couple from the mosque. With another Muslim family below, the place was a sort of mini commune.

Malcolm and his movement had captivated Betty for almost a year and a half. Now she was his wife. Her mind wheeled at the idea. She had dutifully camouflaged her affection for him as long as had been necessary. "I was always holding back," she remembered. She knew that she had not won the minister with sultry design. (She later confessed that she had "always wished and dreamed that I could be that smooth.") Quite the opposite, really. In his company, she had been soft and poised—a good instructor and an apt pupil. She had not come off flimsy or vacuous, either. She was not such a woman, and she was quite sure that Malcolm would not have wanted her if she were. "Betty was never invisible," Sister Khadiyyah later said.

Now that Malcolm was her husband, she resolved to become the attentive caregiver conjured in the women's classes at the mosque. The first great challenge would be the kitchen. Mrs. Malloy had never taught her how to cook. Betty had arrived in New York able to prepare little besides "a great salad and delicious toast." And though she had been coming along, fixing homemade beef sausages or chicken dishes and practicing the endless bean recipes, she soon discovered that Malcolm counted on his daily meal to fuel him through twenty or more grueling work hours. She also learned that he had taken to gulping vitamin cocktails to correct the dietary imbalance he had developed in prison shunning pork and other foods tainted by "swine." Betty had suspected that the minister needed proper nourishment, but never had she imagined that his condition was so serious.

She later told a friend that she was "preoccupied with keeping the brother healthy." To satisfy Malcolm's appetite and cure his deficiencies, she learned, after not a few missteps, to cook like a Muslim wife and a nutritionist. Drawing on knowledge she had gleaned as a temple neophyte, nurse, and Tuskegee home economics student, she squeezed her husband fresh orange, grapefruit, and vegetable juice in the morning, blending in milk, egg yolks, honey, brown sugar, and flavoring. Malcolm, however, seemed to want nothing but coffee "integrated" with cream. Betty remembered that later in the marriage, when she failed one morning to push the fruit and vegetable purée on her

husband, he asked whether she was feeling all right, and even wandered downstairs from his study looking for the libation. "The next
morning I went back to the old routine and received no more resistance," she recalled.

She fussed over dinner, too. There was usually grapefruit and vegetables, light soup, wild rice, wheat bread, no more than a sliver of lean
meat, and a quart of milk. Sometimes Betty prepared as many as six
courses, with braised lamb shank or another favorite for the entree.
"All the basic essentials," she liked to say. The gourmet treatments
worked; Malcolm's nutritional deficiency disappeared.

Fixing those meals often fatigued Betty, though she later boasted
that Malcolm never cooked during their marriage. After Betty had prepared an especially savory dish, Malcolm sometimes volunteered for a
turn at the stove. "If necessary, I'll cook in a minute," he would say. She
would hush him, knowing this was more an ovation than a genuine
offer. Malcolm was complimentary "in an offhand way," she later
remembered. Betty, who admitted that she had once considered her
own ineptitude in the kitchen "disgraceful," longed for explicit praise.
When Haley, during a visit with Malcolm, fawned over her cinnamon
apple pie with buttery crust, she practically wafted out the door. "It was
important to me to have someone say, 'Hey, this is delicious, how on
earth did you make it?'" she later said.

In her later years, when the mood was right, Betty occasionally
charmed friends with trivia about the domestic Malcolm. But though
she had been a housewife for years, she seldom mentioned the endless
household chores. She liked to reminisce about nurturing her husband.
She wanted to remember and share the Malcolm who had been the
center of her energy. "I was not hypnotized or mesmerized," she told a
friend. "I was just…wow!"

Betty baked loaf after loaf and bragged that the minister never
broke store-bought bread. She discovered and indulged his weakness
for cling peaches, chocolate pound cake ("Think of the calories!" she
later exclaimed), banana splits, cookies baked from scratch, milk
guzzled from the bottle, and strawberry, chocolate, or vanilla ice cream
by the quart. In later years, she always reminded interviewers how lean

he had kept himself. "But he loved ice cream," she told television journalist Gil Noble. "And I of course tried to follow him."

Later she chuckled about her techniques for demilitarizing her man
after he returned from preaching the doomsday gospel. There were
times when she managed only to hurry something simple onto the fire
as he was heading home. Tossed into the pot at the right moment, a
fistful of onions and green peppers produced a garland of odors. "Oh
man, Betty!" Malcolm would exclaim as he strode through the door. To
his young wife, the words were an aria.

Betty was startled to discover the dimensions of Malcolm's asceticism. "Initially," she said, "I was overwhelmed by the breadth of his
commitment." He rose at 5 A.M. without fail for exercise and prayer,
a ritual she later cited as the "source of his strength." By dawn, he
had encircled himself with newspapers and read each at a pace that
astonished Betty. "He was informally educated," she said, "but educated."

Muhammad taught his minions to "seek knowledge from the cra-
dle to the grave," to pursue an education that would "benefit their
own." Malcolm enthusiastically obeyed, breezing through books on
history, philosophy, the arts, religion, and other subjects ("anything by
or about black people," Betty would remember) in a matter of hours.
In spare moments, he read articles to his rapt wife, lending the home a
cerebral feel that intoxicated her. She understood this craving for
enlightenment and self-possession in time, just as she ultimately understood many of her husband's obsessions. Malcolm, she later realized,
was "forever compensating" for his crooked years. "He had a lot of
catching up to do," she explained.

Malcolm was fiercely private, as one would expect of a man who
risked attack from so many sides. His friends and associates would ask
about his wife, and later the children, and he would smile and reply
warmly that they were fine, thank you. He rarely went further, unless
to moralize about family in general. "A black man ought to be willing

to give his life so that his children can be free," he told newspaperman Claude Lewis. Few people ever got "familiar" with the minister, and fewer still got close to his family. Bedroom peeping was especially bad form in the Nation. As Razzaq explained:

> You don't be in a man's house and focus on what he says to his wife. You black it out. You could see or hear something, but you still don't see or hear. You were like a ghost. You didn't have nothin' to do with that.

There was also the irony that the wives of the most visible Muslims felt the greatest pressure to be invisible. An outsider who mingled with the believers may not even have known who the bureaucrats' wives were. Dr. Ben, the scholar who had assigned Malcolm a black-history syllabus, recognized and quite respected this isolationism, or inviolability. "You didn't meet with Sister Betty," he said. "You may meet with the minister and he may say, 'This is my wife,' and you respectfully say hello and continue your business. You don't go behind that."

So it was in the East, whence the Nation borrowed its patriarchy. Orthodox Muslim wives were often retreating domestics. "You don't have tea with a Muslim's wife," Malcolm later declared. So the desultory accounts Betty gave in the years after his death offer the most intimate glimpses at their marriage. These were sweetheart recollections. Betty intended them to help humanize a figure the establishment had cast as a bogeyman of racial hatred and violence. She predicted that those who knew Malcolm only from his fiery speeches would have trouble picturing him as a family man. But she insisted that he had been a loving, devoted husband and father who treated his wife and daughters tenderly, even as the Movement consumed him.

Some of her anecdotes read like whimsical diary entries. One got the sense that they were therapeutic; in recounting enchanting episodes and rituals, she got the fawning attention from her husband that he could never have provided consistently in life. So though Malcolm traveled constantly, even in the early months of their marriage, and worked continuously for the cause, as she acknowledged, she remembered fondly that he treated her to weekly restaurant dinners when possible. She recalled taking in two operas with him, *La Traviata* and *La Bohème*, and even accompanying him to Duke Ellington concerts. "All work and no play makes Jack a dull boy," she said, praising the sense of "equilibrium" that led the minister to clear fleeting but cherished moments for his wife. "He was really a balanced person."

Betty ascribed to Malcolm a boyish romanticism. She said he displayed throughout the marriage the tenderness "that every woman looks for in a husband." (In the dedication to her 1975 doctoral dissertation, she declared that he'd "opened the windows of my mind and heart.") The minister recited original poetry to her. "He'd give a verse off the top of his head to suit the particular occasion," she later recalled. Though his weekly ministerial allowance at the time was a relatively scant $125 (later $150 or $175), he often returned from trips bearing gifts, including a strand or two of what Betty called "good jewelry."

Sometimes he would call from out of town and tell her to go look in the back of the third dresser drawer or in some nook, and she would discover a love letter, a photograph, an original poem, or a small wad of cash. It got so she nearly tore the place apart hunting for stashed tokens the moment he left for a long business trip. But there was a new hiding place every time.

Despite the occasional sport, Malcolm was not demonstratively affectionate. He did not go for the white man's frivolous rituals or make much of Valentine's Day. "Love must not be a one-day affair" but rather "twenty-four hours a day, seven days a week," he told Betty. So it was up to her to finagle the February 14 observations. When the holiday arrived, she would suggest that he treat her to dinner, or bring some flowers home for the table. The morning after, she recalled, he would say very casually, "Did you know that yesterday was Valentine's Day?" "No, sweetheart," she would reply. "Was it?"

Betty saw one movie with Malcolm in seven years, and then only in his final months. She never forgot the exhilaration of sitting beside him in the shadows as they watched *Nothing But a Man*. Betty hadn't had any particular interest in the low-budget, black detective picture. But when, upon passing the theater, he'd asked, "Hey, Girl, would you like to see this?" she had jumped at the chance to unwind with her man.

The couple always planned to see more films, but never got the chance. What private moments they shared, however, delivered the memories that linger in one's heart. "I couldn't be so enamored of my mother today if I hadn't watched my father adore her first," said Malcolm and Betty's eldest daughter, Attallah, who was six when her father died. She recalled that her parents:

> were silly and giggly and whimpery. They'd go off on long walks alone, and when he was traveling, he'd leave her treasure maps with love letters at the end. I know now how extraordinary their love affair was. At the time, I thought it was mushy; they embarrassed me. I mean, yecch, this is cor-ny!

Attallah remembered her dad as the jaunty "dude-guy" who rapped to her old lady. She reminisced about them dancing together at home— Big Red and Miss Goody Two Shoes swaying in the den. Perhaps they did the Horse, the Roach, the Mashed Potato, the Lindy—him popping his fingers and scatting as she twirled. Malcolm commanded the *lingua franca* and swagger of the street. He had been born again in Islam, but anyone who had heard him harangue Harlem from a scaffold knew he had retained the vernacular genius. Betty may have seemed prissy to some of the Original People, but she was more than conversant with the Detroit swing that the world was then coming to know as "Motown." She and the minister may have enjoyed a soulful if short-lived courtship that began in earnest only after they swapped vows.

Malcolm's lady was his "Apple Brown Betty" or "Brown Sugar," though he often called her "Girl" (the pet name she loved). She bristled when he joshed her about her anemic singing voice. Years later, she embarrassed girlfriends with graphic tales of his attentiveness in the bedroom. When the two wed, she had had far less experience with intimacy than he did, she said. The marriage's early months, she remembered, were a crash course in "the male."

She later told her closest cronies that Malcolm taught her about lovemaking, often adding some torrid footnote about his prowess. Her friends knew when she was cranking up for an especially racy dish; she would let off a lilting "*Girrrl....*" "He was my husband, my hero, my best friend, the father of my children," she declared in one television interview, "and my children don't like for me to say it, but he was my lover."

Betty said her inkwell eyes and lustrous skin had dazzled Malcolm. She talked about how sublimely beautiful he had made her feel. "I was very thin then," she said, "and he liked my black beauty, my mind. He just liked me." Even a quarter-century after his death, one thought one glimpsed traces of Malcolm's affection in her sleepy chuckle or sway. "I thank God I had someone who loved me for me," she proclaimed. "She knew she was his sweetheart, his baby," Myrlie Evers-Williams remembered. "She would kind of move her head like that." Betty's daughters watched this side of their mother first squeamishly then admiringly, awed that the widow's love affair could so long outlast her lover. "What they had together must have been so intense that she kept him around," said Gamilah, who was an infant when her father died.

Among close friends, Betty expressed only quiet endearment for Malcolm. Etiquette prohibited all but tepid displays of public affection. When the newlyweds joined Sutton and his wife for supper, all four would linger at the dining table, and as Malcolm talked politics or religion or history or music, Betty's hand would float over and land gently on his. "She loved him very much and expressed it often," Sutton said. Betty later declared that she and Malcolm were so close that "sometimes it's hard to fathom."

But she also acknowledged that at first, "Malcolm was still a little apprehensive about marriage." The minister dreaded even the prospect of a wife lording over him. "He didn't know where that fear of a woman having control came from," Betty said. In his autobiography, Malcolm bemoaned domineering, complaining, demanding wives who "psychologically castrated their husbands." He remembered steering the beaus of many such women to the arms of prostitutes in his hustling days. "More wives could keep their husbands if they realized their greatest urge is to be men," he declared.

Conscious of the minister's distaste for bossy women, Betty said she stepped gingerly in her first months as Mrs. Malcolm X. But before long, she said, Malcolm warmed to his spousal role and began volunteering details about his comings and goings. As he was dashing out the door in the morning, he would announce that she could find him at such-and-such a place from 10:00 until 11:30, or jot down several numbers where she could leave messages. While crisscrossing the country, he called as often as twice a day. Later he "made it practically a fetish never to stop without telephoning his Betty," Haley would recall. Eventually, Malcolm's anxieties about sharing his life with a woman became fodder for her gentle taunts. "What's all this?" she would tease when he phoned to share his schedule.

Still, Malcolm took love seriously. "So get yourself together, Girl," he often commanded with a grin. Betty knew he was only half-kidding. "He'd waited a long time for marriage," she recalled, "and he wanted it to last." He began sermonizing early in the marriage about his expectations of a good wife. Though he did not think to ask what she required in a husband, Betty later said that she had appreciated the "family talks." "Malcolm domesticated me into feeling and believing that a woman is supposed to be able to give to a marriage," she said. By her account, the minister generously supported and guided his younger wife. "I certainly needed it," she said, insisting that he was "sensitive and understanding of my shortcomings—and my strengths."

But Betty was no geisha. She decided early in the marriage that Malcolm would not run the household with the incontestable authority that he ran the temple. "The first time I told him what I expected of him as a husband, it came as a shock," she remembered. Malcolm, she said, came to respect her input. "Here I've been going along having our little workshops with me doing all the talking and you doing all the listening," he once exclaimed.

According to Betty, this easy harmony prevailed in the minister's home. Even trust and communication came naturally. "He said it was the only civilized thing to do in a committed relationship," she said. In her reminiscences, the minister was sensitive and understanding and she doting and deferential. Although he "encouraged me to express my own ideas, I preferred to listen to him," she recalled. She minded his admonitions and settled into a marriage that she would remember as one long, endearing lesson. "I haven't had a romantic experience like that since," she said in 1987. "But I'm delighted that I had it once."

Though Betty embroidered her memories of life with Malcolm, one should not doubt that the marriage was intense. Clearly it was rooted in obligation, if not devotion. Malcolm's last decade was a tempest of almost ceaseless travel, and some of his devotees have wondered aloud whether he was still long enough to develop a relationship as deep as the one his widow described. But among the hordes that have laid posthumous claim to the minister's comradeship, Betty's title remains the least controvertible. She was at his side when his fledgling ministry was maturing, and there she stayed long after many of his comrades had scattered. "None of us knew Malcolm like Betty," Dick Gregory later insisted. "None of us knew him as a wife."

Betty's vignettes may be less apocryphal than incomplete. "Find the good and praise it" wasn't just her personal motto; it was an unwritten rule among the "movement widows" for memorializing their men. The slogan's obverse, of course, is "omit the bad and the ugly." (Myrlie Evers-Williams told me that after she had revealed in her memoirs that she and Medgar Evers once had a spat that briefly turned physical, Betty and Coretta Scott King gasped like schoolmarms at her candor.)

In the years after Malcolm's death, Betty often fed the public from her grab bag of happy Malcolm memories. She brushed over the marriage's excruciating intervals with the same determination that she tried to blot from her own mind the terror she and the minister had experienced. ("We're not going to get into that," she told reporters who tried to probe the nightmarish episodes of her past.) It is natural to want to remember only the warmth of a relationship. When society thinks your late husband had horns, it may indeed be obligatory.

So Betty retold that story about Malcolm stashing love letters about the house many more times than it likely ever happened. But she seldom directly acknowledged one painful truth—that she had married a movement more than a man. The notion of a Betty-Malcolm romance is enchanting, and probably necessary in a society where black love is under siege. Yet without dismissing or belittling the love affair, such as it was, one must acknowledge that life with the minister was crisis-ridden, restrictive, and often harrowing.

Chapter Five

SINEWS OF INDEPENDENCE

—

"No nation can gain its full measure of enlightenment and
happiness if one half of it is free and the other half is fettered."
—Frances Ellen Watkins Harper

A s magnetic as Malcolm was, Betty knew from the start that she
would be taking on more than the typical wifely burdens. Mrs.
Malcolm X's role had already been scripted when she agreed to play the
part, Percy Sutton later observed. What she may not have suspected in
the marriage's early months is that her husband would never truly be
hers. By 1958, Malcolm had been Elijah Muhammad's spiritual property for almost a decade. Thereafter, in the final, transitive years of his
life and beyond, he would belong to the masses straining against white
supremacy and oppression around the world. For Betty, only time
would bear out this truth, and it would not be an easy realization. (In
the early 1990s, Maya Angelou was with her in Washington, D.C.
when a woman approached and volunteered her counsel. "You know,
you have to let go of Malcolm," she told Betty. "I let go of him when I
married him!" the widow snarled. "It was you [expletives] that never
knew how to receive him!")

Betty had indeed surrendered the minister. At Temple Number
Seven, Jean Reynolds recalled, Malcolm "was family to the whole congregation." After handling an exhausting array of official duties and dol-
ing out brotherly advice to this woman with marital problems or that
man with legal woes or embittered Christian relatives, the minister

often trudged home to his wife in the dead of night. And that was when he was in town.

In the late 1950s, Malcolm's treks around the country lecturing, recruiting, inaugurating temples, training ministers, and otherwise tending the Nation's pastoral and public affairs quickened from an already delirious pace. At times he saw his home no more than twice a month. "Betty wasn't getting that attention from him," Charles Kenyatta remembered. "He was always on the go. His job was to put the fires out." Betty later maintained that though it rarely was possible, Malcolm liked her to travel with him. But considering Black Muslim protocol, it is unlikely that the minister would even have considered taking her on most business trips.

Nevertheless, Dr. Yosef ben-Jochannan in 1966 would eulogize Malcolm as the husband that every black woman wants but few get—"a man who could speak up for his race in the face of oppression by the whites." Betty liked the appraisal. She relished the fact that *her* black man was America's most outspoken, and one of very few willing to call for black women's defense by any means necessary. Yet a wife wants her husband not just gallant, but around. The widow privately acknowledged in later years that though Malcolm had captured her heart, the marriage often left her yearning for someone "to cuddle with and take her out." Malcolm himself confessed near the end that, "I never get much chance to take her anywhere, and I know she likes to be with her husband."

Even on the rare occasions that the couple ventured out after hours, Malcolm was less than affectionate. He was not "touchy-feely," Betty complained privately. The minister tisk-tisked her hankerings for dime-novel romance. During one outing, Betty spotted a pair of lovers in each other's arms. "I want that," she whispered to Malcolm, gesturing toward the duo. The minister stiffly flung an arm about his wife's shoulders. "You happy now?" he asked.

If Malcolm did not always deliver the affection his young wife wanted, he certainly dispatched the austerity he felt she needed. Betty sampled an array of serious nonfiction during the marriage, including such ponderous race studies as Lorenzo Turner's *Africanisms in the*

Gullah Dialect. But with the Nation devouring her husband's time and with her often home, she turned to paperbacks and television between household chores. The indulgences rankled Malcolm, especially since Muhammad discouraged idle forms of recreation (the faithful shunned ballgames and most forms of popular music). Malcolm "stayed on her to stay out of that TV," Kenyatta later remembered. Never one to fold easily, Betty demanded a new television. When the minister, a biblio-phile, asked why she needed another television, she fell to her wiles. "You know," she said, "you never know when you're away on all these trips....At least I have my TV." A new set straightaway appeared in the living room.

Other constraints she tested with less success. Though she was known for her whole-wheat rolls and other healthy, homemade snacks, she struggled to resist grape soda. During one pregnancy, she succumbed. When Malcolm caught her at the kitchen sink gulping from a can, he snatched it, poured it down the drain, and strode off. Grape soda and pulp novels, of course, were lesser prohibitions; like her shrimp cravings, they were not so hard to suppress early into the marriage. And even though she missed bid whist and the jitterbug, Betty had embraced the Black Muslim ethic for a year and one half before she became Mrs. Malcolm X. Still, the reality that she had subscribed to a way of life and not merely a man was often con-stricting to her.

Malcolm's zealotry and her heightened visibility required a new asceticism. It was not enough that she fasted regularly (except when menstruating or pregnant). It was not enough that a scarf always bound her hair, or that she sometimes wore prim white gloves in public. It was not enough that her buttoned-up cotton dresses, some of which she sewed herself, came in plain gray or off-white tones, with hems that grazed her flat-heeled shoes. She was only too familiar with Malcolm's rants against women who flounced around in clothes so tight that you could see their freckles. But Betty's demeanor was also to be as gracious and demure as her look was modest. Here, ironically, her upbringing paid off; Malcolm often seemed proud of the way she carried herself socially.

Of course, the minister was scrupulous himself. One biographer noted that he "wouldn't even say 'hell' unless powerfully moved." A stickler for exactitude, Malcolm bristled whenever someone referred to his daughters as "kids." "A 'kid' is a baby goat," he would scold. This was a man "clothed in words," Charles Kenyatta later declared. Malcolm was also famously prompt. "Precise," some thought. "Obsessive," others decided. "I drive by my watch, not my speedometer," he declared. "Time is more important to me than distance." (Betty's tardiness later in the marriage exasperated him, though she told a friend that he never seemed to consider the time and effort needed to prepare small children to go outdoors.)

To support her claim that he was actually quite balanced, Betty would point out that Malcolm enjoyed jazz and soul music at home. His taste for Miriam Makeba notwithstanding, though, the minister was "a purely organizational man." He had consigned himself utterly to the Black Muslim mission. He was convinced that the Movement had saved his life, and he believed with a singular depth of spirit that it could redeem his people.

Betty also developed a passion for black redemption. She later acknowledged that she admired and respected the drive, dedication, and selflessness of Malcolm's ministry. She described his approach to his work, in complete flattery, as "obsession." But an obsessive personality can form its own maelstrom, sucking in any nearby object and subjecting it to the same furious purpose. Indeed, Malcolm at times seemed almost as demanding of Betty as he was of himself, even though he privately counseled the Muslim brothers against expecting as much from women as men. When her behavior offended his code, he would say quietly, "I certainly wouldn't recommend that." She knew instinctively what this meant: stop! "I thought Malcolm was a little too strict with me," she later confessed.

Yet she bore the discipline, and years later she still accepted the wisdom of his bidding. "I was moving into his space and, after all, he was the minister and if he didn't correct me, the parishioners certainly would," she recalled. She acknowledged, however, that submitting had not been easy. "I didn't know it was going to be that difficult," she said.

"I was, you know, with the romance, you know—just to be with him....So, if you really want to know something about a person, live with them."

~

Malcolm awed Betty. His insight and wisdom "boggled my mind," she said. She later insisted (after earning three degrees) that "my husband is brighter than I ever will be." She told a confidant that her love for him was not "worshipful." She did confess that she had surrendered to his "thorough indoctrination." She felt safe with him—enveloped. And she believed that he would hold her face to Allah. "You will hear a lot of Malcolm in me," she once said. "I admired him, adored him, trusted him, respected him, believed in him, and had confidence in him."

She was in many ways a devoted helpmate. While he was in the field, she was forever answering phone calls and jotting messages, especially after white society discovered the minister and sent journalists to chronicle him and the dark movement he championed. She responded to the jangling phone in those days with a formality at once queenly and secretarial, addressing black and white callers as "Mister" and "Miss," and offering neither warmth nor aloofness. When Malcolm returned, he would spend a few minutes scribbling her messages into his pocket notebook.

She also pressed his white shirts and creased the trousers of his roomy suits to razor-blade perfection. Even the Nation brothers wondered how Malcolm always managed to look so sharp. She kept a suitcase packed with his "burnin'" uniform—dark suit, high-buffed shoes, slender tie with his favorite arching sailfish clip—for when he galloped in from out of town and had to go blazing back out. He would exchange a bag of soiled clothes for a freshly packed one, and lunge again into the street. Meanwhile, she would do the laundry and load another case.

She entertained royalty, too. Louis X, Malcolm's apprentice and one of the movement's most beguiling young ministers ("he could charm the spots off a leopard," Abdullah Abdur Razzaq later said), often came calling from Boston. She would cook Louis's favorite dishes and hand him the lessons that Malcolm had left for him, and he would descend into the basement to study. All the Chicago theocrats visited her and Malcolm's home when they were in New York, including Elijah Muhammad himself, whom she had her suspicions about (though she probably was not yet letting on to Malcolm). Her home in those days served as a vault for tithes and much of the kingdom's other spoils, and Muslim officials were always waiting at her door to collect more bounty for the Nation's coffers.

The hosting sometimes frazzled Betty. After Malcolm's long Sunday lessons at Temple Number Seven, he occasionally had his assistant ministers by for dinner. Betty and some of the other women would suddenly have a living room full of ravenous men. Benjamin Karim, who joined Malcolm's cadre of sidemen in 1958, later recalled that Betty "made sure that we didn't leave the table in any way unsatisfied." As the men sat guzzling homemade ginger beer or milk, Betty and the women whirled about the kitchen. Finally, they would surface in a caravan of casseroles, bean soup, and barbecued chicken. Four, five, six, seven courses might emerge, depending on the crowd's size and temperament.

Thus Betty helped run Malcolm's operation, enduring his tyranny all the while. "I handled it, and I handled it well," she later declared. The hardship and modest triumphs of those days convinced her that women are obliged to "give more, help more, and do more," for she declared in 1971 that "no marriage can exist on a 50/50 basis." Her role opposite Malcolm was not so distant from that of any Christian minister's spouse, for the Nation, despite the news media's exotic portrayals, was in its soul a benevolent organization. The Muslims had their peculiarities, but insular, secretive societies governed by charismatic leaders and liberation gospels were hardly anomalies in Black America.

Betty must have anticipated her aide-de-camp function as the minister's wife. Though Malcolm did not submit his articles and speeches to her for substantive content edits, he relied on her to type and correct certain communiqués and papers, particularly as he drafted *Muhammad Speaks* copy and otherwise assembled the tabloid's early issues in his basement. She was more formally educated, after all, than perhaps 90 percent of his parishioners. "This woman's grammar was hooked up!" Ella Collins's bodyguard James Smalls later exclaimed.

Betty's wifely duties, however, did not end with cooking, washing, ironing, and proofing prose. If Malcolm defended the most trampled blacks of the urban north, then she at times defended the defender, even from himself. She harangued him to get enough food and rest (which pleased Ella Collins, despite the bad blood simmering between the two women even then). And she tried to keep the sanctity of the home, for in the Muslim tradition, a wife guards her husband's house. It was a tenet, she later told Angelou, that she embraced. "She wouldn't take her home life into the street," Angelou said. Yet Malcolm wanted reassurance. When he overheard women from the mosque gossiping about their husbands, he would ask, "Girl, do you talk like that?" Betty invariably answered no. "Well, I certainly hope not," he would mutter.

Betty was often so discreet that visitors hardly noticed her after she had ushered them into her home to await an audience with the minister. Whenever Claude Lewis, a *Newsweek* reporter who met Malcolm in 1958, came calling, she greeted him at the door, shaking his hand with gentle elegance and tendering just enough small talk to lighten the occasion and put him at ease. He noticed that Betty would never offer refreshment unless her husband first gave the command. Then it was water or juice, never liquor. "She was very polite," Lewis recalled. "But some people you meet and they're kind of intimate and close, and she was always at a respectful distance." She held herself in the same manner with many women. After their first meeting in 1963, journalist Ann Geracimos wrote that Betty acknowledged her, "the way a queen might greet a subject."

That Muslim women were to hold their peace in public and avoid henpecking at home was hardly a congregational secret. Journalist Louis Lomax observed in 1963 that the women of Black Islam "almost never talk to strangers—non-Muslims, that is—and maintain a general silence that is unnerving." The Nation praised the virtues of silent, docile women. "A woman who speaks loudly or forcibly or in a demanding voice to her husband is cursed with unhappiness because she destroys her man and his respect for her," a 1961 *Muhammad Speaks* declared. Malcolm's almost paranoid mistrust of women also inspired Betty's reticence. The minister insisted that proper communication would assure that neither spouse "violate the trust of the other," she later recalled. Betty believed that the approach paid off, for she would proclaim herself "the first woman he'd ever really loved and trusted." Malcolm indeed declared his faith in Betty on several occasions. But he said in his autobiography that she was in fact one of *four* women—including his mother and his half-sister Ella—whom he had ever trusted.

Betty always bridled at this disclosure, and even suggested once that Alex Haley had fabricated it after Malcolm's death. "I don't know who the four—who the other three were supposed to be," she snipped. Yet in the autobiography's moving epilogue, Haley also recounted the minister's confession that he actually trusted his wife "seventy-five percent," and that he had told her as much. Of course, this was a deep confidence by Malcolm's standards. "You never can fully trust any woman," he told Haley. "Whatever else a woman is, I don't care who the woman is, it starts with her being vain."

It seemed to Lewis that Malcolm often shuffled Betty into a separate, sacred category when he decried women's sins and frailties. The minister readily admitted that as a hustler he had sold black women. But he told Lewis that streetwalkers and the artificially noble women he concocted in the pulpit were of different species ("women of the night," he called the former, or "women who did business"). On other occasions, he told Lewis that black men owed black women—all black women—unqualified respect and homage. "Through all our trials and tribulations," the minister said, "our women have been there."

Yet even in his final days, he linked womanhood with weakness, suggesting that masculine black men should force Uncle Tom Civil Rights leaders to "stand up and fight like men instead of running around here nonviolently acting like women." Betty, who may have understood her husband's contradictions better than anyone, accepted on faith that his mistrust of women did not lessen the sincerity with which he exalted them. Still, she soon found herself smothered under double layers of chauvinism—Malcolm's and the Movement's.

It was not that she wanted the pulpit or the limelight. Betty was generally content with her place in the pews and enjoyed the untouchable status of a Muslim wife—Brother Minister's wife, no less. Though her husband's words lathered audiences, she did not long for his power. "She didn't seek to become the minister," Sutton later said. "She sought to be the helpmate, the friend, the colleague."

Muslim women were not to seek or receive publicity, and Betty rarely granted media interviews. When she did, her husband chaperoned, steering and often answering questions. She deferred to him constantly, taking pains not to project herself as an authority. She was reticent about her past, and often parried reporters' queries. She never mentioned that she had studied at Tuskegee, and refused to name the New York City hospital in which she had worked, revealing only that she had grown up in Detroit. Her duty as Mrs. Malcolm X, she said, was to master herself and obey the feminine protocols emanating from the Muslim command post in Chicago. Her model in this regard was Elijah Muhammad's daughter and national MGT captain Ethel Sharief. "All of us try in some ways to copy her," Betty said.

Mrs. Malcolm X's public demureness complemented her husband's message that women were innately needful and brittle, and thus "attracted to the male in whom they see strength." The minister taught that the rigors of movement leadership belonged to men. He quoted First Corinthians—"Let your women keep silence in the churches"— telling his sidemen that even the Bible, whose coded truths the Messenger had dredged from its morass of lies, banned women from the priesthood and, by extension, the frontlines of liberation struggle. The minister generally avoided strategizing, deliberating politics, or otherwise talking shop with his wife. His home was his refuge. And after eighteen or more nonstop hours "waking the dead," even the dogged evangelist needed a breather.

The same was true, of course, of other warriors along the Civil Rights front. Myrlie Evers would remember that her husband, the NAACP's Mississippi field secretary Medgar Evers, was by 1963:

> like a man possessed, up by six in the morning, at the office by seven. It was a rare night now that he was home by eleven. When he did come home, he would want something to eat....I would ask what had happened that day, and, after filling me in briefly, he would stop my next question. "Let's not talk about it, Myrlie. I've been up to my ears in it all day."

Betty would reminisce fondly about her soothing influence on Malcolm, recalling that he seemed to appreciate having a home to return to for rest and renewal. Her Muslim training had taught her to receive him serenely and resist peppering him with questions. She longed to discuss his pastoral life more extensively, but she had her own duties to attend to. Before the obligations of motherhood largely removed her from the scene, worship services, rallies, bazaars, and weekly civilization and women's classes packed her weeks. During those fleeting hours when she found herself alone with Malcolm—after he had put aside his papers and the phone had quit bleating—she was often just as eager as her husband to forget the movement.

She later maintained that though she did not participate directly in the minister's work, she understood and backed his mission, and accepted her wifely role. "She knew her place," Lewis later said. Officially, Muslim ministers never discussed policy with their wives for fear of burdening or unsettling them. Lewis noticed that whenever he hunkered down to talk current affairs with Malcolm, Betty vanished. To the journalist, her thinking seemed clear: "This is men's business. Time to go."

Yet Malcolm shared some revelations about his work, philosophies, and evolving spiritual life with Betty, particularly in later years, as he questioned the empire he had helped build and asked her to embrace new visions and shoulder new burdens. "I was a good Muslim wife," she once declared, "and you don't go out and say, you know, 'He talked to me about this' or 'He did that.'" But of course he confided in her, she added, "because my job was to support him."

—————

Privately she volunteered her opinions, too. When Malcolm returned at night, hurled homeward from the day's centrifuge, it was in her lap that he laid his head. When he discussed his day, when he pondered the movement and his family's future and wondered aloud how the two would intersect, in the hush of hopes and fears, only Betty was there. "She didn't just say, 'Good evening, sir,' and fix him a meal and go to bed," former bodyguard James Smalls later said. Smalls told an interviewer that Betty shared Malcolm's life. "You can't lead without sharing in your bedroom," he insisted. "So I don't care what he had to say, okay? I know what the rules of an organization are. But I know what reality is when you roll upside that woman at night who you want to get into and who want to get into you."

Muslim machismo notwithstanding, Malcolm sooner or later discussed some elements of the movement at home. How explicitly or often is immaterial; Betty was a sympathizer, not a sounding board. She was never effusive, but neither was she an arm prop. When she and Malcolm went by Percy Sutton's for dinner, she joined in conversations about international affairs, segregation, and civil rights. "Sister Betty was no different five years after she married him than she was the day he first brought her to our house, so far as sophistication was concerned," Sutton later recalled. "She was very well read and well spoken." Even Kenyatta, who feuded with her, would acknowledge that "you had to be top cotton to be in her range." Malcolm acknowledged that his wife spoke her mind around the house. He later confessed to civil rights leader James Farmer that Betty was a staunch Farmer fan, and that she had told Malcolm that he had better stop debating Farmer because in her opinion, Malcolm kept losing.

Though Betty had her own mind, she never dissented publicly with her husband, even when she disagreed with him. Except for views on children and education that were distinctly hers, the opinions she expressed around company were the minister's, Sutton remembered. Never did it occur to Malcolm's aides and confidants that she harbored distinct political views. If she did, she was loath to embarrass or contradict Malcolm by airing them. Like his other congregants, she had tailored her thinking to his (and thus to Elijah Muhammad's) to earn her "X" in the first place.

But Betty discovered that her man could be as domineering at home as he was with his underlings in the field. "I shared Malcolm," she later said, "but I don't know if he could have shared me to the same extent. He was possessive from the beginning to the end, though I think he learned to control it." The minister regimented her social life, allowing her to mingle only with the parishioners he approved of. "He just wanted me to be for him," Betty remembered. "He didn't even want me to have women friends."

At first she believed that his motives were noble. He must have been trying to spare her from confrontations with the temple sisters who disliked her or who were sweet on him, she reasoned. She later concluded that Malcolm's own phobias were leading him to restrain her. She knew he was obsessed with secrecy, and that he detested idle chatter. She knew that he believed men must forever guard against women's guile, and that he wondered still whether she would not succumb to her "womanish nature" and start whispering in the pews. ("When you return from out of town," the minister once told Razzaq wryly, "never ask a man what has gone on. Find yourself a woman and you'll get the whole story.")

In the end, Betty decided that Malcolm wanted nothing competing with his influence and authority as her husband. She had begun drifting from some of her old confidantes, including Ruth Summerford. Occasionally she invited her cousin to weekend bazaars or stopped by her Brooklyn flat when the minister was away, but the bond between the two was dissolving. Betty began to feel sequestered, a prisoner to Black Islam's strictures and her husband's paranoia. "I was not accessible to a great number of people on a personal level," she later said, recalling that she had had to withdraw from anyone who wandered within a certain psychic perimeter.

Occasional visits from non-Muslims reminded her how far she had withdrawn into Black Islam's veil. Her childhood neighbor Sue

MacCree visited from Detroit in 1962 and smirked at the portraits of Muhammad that spangled the walls. When MacCree spotted the Messenger's face gazing upon her from a washroom wall, she cracked up. Her hostess did, too. For Betty, the social call was a welcome escape. "I could send someone to get you," she had told her friend beforehand. "But I want this to be our visit. And if they came for you everybody would know and would ask questions."

Malcolm was away during the visit. Even when home, he rarely entertained non-Muslims alongside Betty. Summerford later remembered that during her visits he would sometimes streak through the door, offer a grinning hello—"we didn't get into a whole lot of politics," she said—and bound upstairs to the converted attic study in which he often roosted for hours on end. "He was in and out," she recalled. When Summerford stayed into the evening for Betty's four-course lamb or beef suppers, the minister hardly ever materialized; she seldom saw him and Betty together at all.

If Betty was lonely, her cousin didn't know. "That she probably didn't discuss with me," Summerford later said. Nor did Betty complain to Sutton about her husband's absences. Though the counselor later acknowledged that he and Betty were close "from the day she married 'til the day she died," he said he sidestepped her private life in those early days. "In my home I didn't discuss that," he said. "I respected her relationship to her husband."

Betty occasionally rang her mother for comfort and counsel as she struggled with marital pressures. Yet her relationship with the Malloys was still rickety at best. "Loving my husband was leaving them, instead of having their lives enriched by my differences," she later said. And neither Helen nor Lorenzo could have eased what would become one of the most chafing conflicts of her marriage: Malcolm's refusal to let her work outside the home. Betty begged him constantly, but to no avail. "You want to do what?" he would ask. "Here, read these three books and give me a report. I'll need the first one tonight." Or he would take her pining for a job to mean that she was unhappy and did not love him, she later remembered.

She believed in the Muslim cause. As a proselyte, she had enjoyed serving the Harlem mosque by tutoring the sisters and helping to fund-raise. Now consigned to the household, her desire to wield her talents and intellect became a dull but constant throb. (It did not help when Malcolm came home praising the talents of career women such as Evelyn Cunningham, a New York correspondent for the *Pittsburgh Courier*.) Betty decided one evening early in the marriage that she was going to accompany Malcolm to one of his lectures. She began dressing as he was preparing to leave. He looked at her but said nothing. "Where are you going?" he finally asked. She said she was going to the talk. "No, you're not," he replied. Betty was as furious as she was powerless to disobey. She plopped down on the front steps, fully dressed, and sat there fuming until the minister returned that night. Malcolm "did not believe that a woman's role was just in the home and in the bed," she insisted in 1969. But in later years she acknowledged that "all my stress was over the fact that I wanted to work, and he wouldn't even entertain the idea."

Coretta Scott King could have empathized. Her husband, Martin Luther King Jr., also believed that "biologically and aesthetically, women are more suitable than men for keeping house," according to biographer L. D. Reddick. Biographer James H. Cone later observed that both Malcolm and King "believed that the woman's place was in the home, the private sphere, and the man's place was in society, the public arena, fighting for justice on behalf of women and children." But that sort of "chivalry" troubled Mrs. Malloy, who imagined her foster daughter shut away in a kitchen toiling over Muslim delicacies. "She saw my being relegated to having babies as oppression," Betty later said.

Summerford knew her cousin was unfulfilled. Betty told her that she missed the challenges of nursing, especially caring for surgical patients. The state of New York had issued Betty's professional license on January 14, 1958, the very day she married Malcolm. Yet Betty had never done a single rotation as a registered nurse.

Malcolm should have anticipated the conflict. Like his father, he had chosen a bride with much more formal schooling than himself. He never beat his wife, as he said Earl Little did when Louise Little "put those smooth words" on her husband. ("An educated woman,"

Malcolm once declared, "can't resist the temptation to correct an une-
ducated man.") But the minister was taken aback when some of the
qualities that had drawn him to Betty hindered his efforts to keep her
homebound.

Despite the evidence that she outwardly conformed to many of the
Nation's rules, Betty decided early in the marriage that she was not
going to live under anybody's thumb. She began to resist in the great
and small ways that she could. She resisted when the opportunities
arose, in the not inconsiderable manner of a Muslim wife. She
remained Malcolm's helpmate, still seeing to her wifely duties. But she
reserved the right to get thistly or go cold, and she knew when and how
to do so.

Malcolm himself had sensed her pluck as early as 1956 or 1957.
Indeed, despite his many expositions on the virtue of accommodating
wives, his reluctant admiration for willful women surfaced now and
then. He later bragged that the manner in which his domineering half-
sister Ella "sat, moved, talked, did everything, bespoke somebody who
did and got exactly what she wanted."

Yet the minister was dumbfounded when Betty's "mellow thunder,"
as one black scholar later described it, began to sound. In the beginning, her protests were subtle but "continuous," Abdullah Razzaq, one
of the few Malcolm aides with more than peripheral knowledge of the
minister's home life, would remember. Betty later told a friend that
though her husband's word was final, the meekness she fronted publicly
"just didn't go in the home." She began chipping out a measure of independence in the marriage's first year. She did so, she later told Maya
Angelou, "without having to be rude."

Her efforts were not totally isolated. One often felt a faint pulse of
resistance among the women of the Nation, Razzaq would recall. "No
woman who has been brought up under the devil can accept this," he
said of the sect's patriarchy. Kenyatta later remembered that the
women were "put to shame if they tried to rebel" openly, for Malcolm

did not brook dissension. "When he came down on you it was like a ton of bricks," Razzaq said.

But Betty persisted. Though Lewis never heard Malcolm criticize her, the two men joked about her having protested his long absences. "I'm sure it's the same with you," Malcolm once said with a chuckle. "Your wife would like you to be home more." Betty was even more outspoken among women at the mosque. Malcolm occasionally mentioned her recalcitrance in Muslim Girls' Training classes to his older brother Philbert. "Betty was out at MGT," he would complain.

Though flippancy from most of the other women would have drawn swift rebukes from the temple hierarchy, Betty enjoyed some immunity as the parish's first lady. Yet her brass often frustrated the minister. Kenyatta thought he could tell when she and Malcolm had argued, for Malcolm's next sermon would be especially rough on women. "He would really get into showin' the life of a woman and how they was," the aide would remember. "He'd use the line of Solomon, saying, 'there's nothing worse than an arrogant woman.'"

Though the couple's sparring was generally benign, it almost got nasty one Sunday early in the marriage. Benjamin Karim, who that evening had joined several other associate ministers at Malcolm's place for supper, later recounted the episode:

> Betty came in from the kitchen with the milk and glass as usual, but you could tell something was ruffling her by the weighty silence that accompanied her, and her face was somber. We were between courses, so Malcolm was talking, and he continued talking without looking up at Betty when she set the glass down in front of him....Malcolm continued talking and Betty started to leave the room. She was about to step across the threshold into the kitchen when Malcolm, without even a glance toward her, said, "Pour it." Betty stopped dead in her tracks. She seemed to be considering some alternative. Then she walked back to the table. She picked up the pitcher. And she poured it....Malcolm was still talking when she left the room.

Though such face-offs were rare in front of company, Malcolm's aides thought Betty often smoldered with unspoken tensions. Some of her later acquaintances got the same impression. Sister Sybil Williams-Clarke, widow of John Henrik Clarke, remembered meeting Betty in the mid 1960s and discovering that she had been a victim of "the religiosity of the Nation and the backwardness of their ideas about women." Television journalist Gil Noble later marveled at how utterly Betty had revered Malcolm. "But there were flashbacks," he said. "She would feel the tug of her upbringing."

The constraints, zealotry, and other tensions overwhelmed Betty at times, for she briefly left Malcolm after the birth of each of their first three daughters. She first took flight in 1959, bundling up Attallah and shooting over to Ruth Summerford's via subway. In 1961, she fled again, alighting in her biological father's North Philadelphia rowhouse with Attallah and Qubilah. Finally, in 1962 or early 1963, she escaped to Detroit with her two toddlers and baby Ilyasah.

These were not breakups so much as distress signals; she later insisted that she never stayed away more than forty-eight hours, and Summerford remembered that she rarely left carrying more than a single change of clothes. After Betty and his eldest first went missing, Malcolm cruised over to Summerford's, told his wife it was time to leave, calmly packed her and the child into the Oldsmobile, and within minutes was homeward bound. The Philadelphia retrieval was almost identical, though Malcolm was forced to spend two unhappy hours on the New Jersey Turnpike. Years later, Summerford dismissed both departures with a wave of her hand. "When you get tired of people, you got to get out and get some air, honey!" she said. By "hook or crook," she remembered, her cousin always let the minister know where she had gone.

By the Detroit flight, however, Malcolm had had it. He returned from a ministerial trip to find Betty and the babies missing. By then they were holed up at the Malloys'. When a day or two passed without word from Malcolm, Betty got nervous. "What have I done?" she thought. She was beside herself and ready to rush home when Malcolm finally turned up. "I don't have a job where I can leave at a certain time and come home at a certain time," he told her. "You knew that when you married me. If you leave again, I'm not coming after you."

Betty later recalled the defections lightly. "Each time I left he found me," she said, "and I was always so happy to see him." Few if any of Malcolm's aides knew about the first lady's departures. Had it leaked, the story would surely have embarrassed the minister. But the couple's reconciliations were amicable enough. "Girl, every time I came back I got pregnant!" Betty later told Myrlie Evers-Williams. She never seriously considered running off a fourth time, though, for Malcolm had given notice. "And sister," she told another friend, "I knew the brother meant it!"

Malcolm eventually made small concessions. He allowed his wife to do occasional volunteer work for the Nation, and she began organizing women's classes and developing curriculum for the sect's parochial schools. As time passed, she recalled, the minister let her shoulder duties that he felt she was "gifted" enough to bear, "whether it was tradition or not."

Betty compromised, too. She accepted much of Malcolm's paternalism and for awhile maintained a façade of wifely obedience among the laity. "In that movement you could not have a woman who obviously led you around," she later remembered. She began to see housewifery as part of her contribution to Malcolm's work. "It was necessary for him that I was stable and at home," she said. In later years, she acknowledged that she had generally been content to let the minister shelter her. But she also confessed that naïveté helped her survive the marriage. "I don't think that what I would look for in a man today would be what I looked for in a man then," she said thirty years later. "I was very accepting. I just wanted love."

Despite their periods of rapprochement, Betty and Malcolm's relationship was probably more strained than either ever publicly acknowledged. An extraordinary letter that surfaced in 2002, fewer than five years after Betty's death, indicated that her defiance and Malcolm's almost draconian views on women may have nearly dissolved the marriage far earlier than most observers had previously suspected. In the seemingly authentic March 25, 1959 letter, which Malcolm appears to have sent Muhammad a year and two months after he and Betty wed, Malcolm portrayed his wife as insubordinate and cantankerous, and complained that she had continuously tormented him with sexual demands.

"The main source of our trouble was based on sex," Malcolm confided to his leader in the four-page, typewritten missive. He said that Betty's complaints about her lack of satisfaction had grown increasingly hostile, and that she had accused him of inadequacy. Malcolm assured Muhammad that he had tried to appease Betty, but said her frequent carping had left him resentful and cold. His domestic life had grown so intolerable, he declared, that at times he lingered on the road to avoid coming home. He said that Betty often cursed him and spoke of leaving him, and added that she had only abandoned the topic of separation after he agreed that perhaps it would be best.

The minister cited his wife's "luxurious tastes" ("I really did keep her in jail financially," he confessed) and the cramped quarters of their home as additional sources of conflict. He accepted some responsibility for the domestic turmoil, suggesting that he had been too indulgent of Betty and conceding that circumstances in his past had left him suspicious of women and sensitive to his wife's affronts. He acknowledged that he was not without his own faults as a spouse, and declared that he still thought Betty a better match than any of the other young Muslim women he had considered marrying. "She has stood up longer and better with me than most of the others who may be quick to condemn her or me," he said.

Yet he described her mood swings—from conciliatory and "lovey-dovey" to petulant—as heartbreaking, and implored Muhammad to talk to her during her upcoming trip to Chicago. "It was not that I did not have love and compassion for her," Malcolm said, "but that she was driving me just as crazy as she was acting."

The letter, which administrators of Muhammad's estate offered for sale through an auction house about four decades after it was written, caused some buzzing among Malcolm scholars and devotees, many of whom believed that the document was consistent with Malcolm's language, writing style, and signature. Other experts were more suspicious, especially in light of the FBI and other intelligence agencies' documented history of falsifying letters to disrupt or tarnish the Nation.

However, the chronology of the missive, which coincided with one of Betty's visits to Black Muslim headquarters in 1959, appears accurate, as does Malcolm's mention of the large financial debts Betty had amassed at the time of their marriage. His acknowledgement that he often slept apart from his wife, and his admission that he was tightfisted with her allowance, are also consistent with anecdotal and other reports. (In a later communiqué with Betty, the authenticity of which scholars have not contested, the minister instructed his wife to use the twenty dollars he had sent her from abroad "sparingly.")

If the Malcolm-Muhammad letter casts a shadow of doubt over any accounts of Betty's soothing effects on her husband and her role as dutiful helper, it also offers more insight into Malcolm's early chauvinism.

In the letter, the minister depicts women as naturally guileful, manipulative, and childish creatures who use tantrums and other antics to gain dominion over men. "She could sense that she was losing her hold over me," Malcolm wrote of Betty, "which by nature made her begin to resort to various female tricks to try and get around the barrier that was becoming between us." She was "only doing what all other Sisters would do...under the same circumstances," he declared.

Of course, Malcolm wrote the letter just after Betty's twenty-fifth birthday, when both his wife and the marriage were still quite young. As time passed, Betty would both adjust to and more effectively challenge the constrictions of her wifely role.

Betty embarked on her most enduring mission at age twenty-four. Though being Mrs. Malcolm X was an awesome experience, and no role would more inspire or change her, or bring deeper joy or anguish, than that of mother.

More than Malcolm or the Nation's patriarchy, it was motherhood that kept Betty home throughout her seven-year marriage. The sect shunned contraception, and she and Malcolm—who wanted a brood of six or seven—did not tarry in the work of making babies.

As her first pregnancy began to show in the summer of 1958, Malcolm took to pampering her. He ferried her to and from the hospital for routine appointments with Dr. Josephine English, the obstetrician who would deliver each of their children. (The minister wanted no man touching his wife, not even a physician.) He had Betty reschedule any prenatal visits that coincided with his travels so that he could personally escort her to the doctor's office. (English arranged special 7 A.M. office hours to accommodate the couple.) Malcolm quoted Qur'anic passages that glorified motherhood and preached that a man must always remember the womb whence he came and the woman whose suffering gave him life. "The black woman," he proclaimed, "is the sustainer of life."

Then, not one year into the marriage, Betty's birth pangs hit. Hours later, she labored as English and Summerford attended. She declined painkillers (Black Muslims embraced natural living). Meanwhile, flanked by his aides in a hospital waiting room, Malcolm paced, tapped, and trembled. He talked temple minutiae with Benjamin Karim and Captain Joseph X as his third cup of coffee went cold. He stepped outside for a walk in the brisk air, and quickly returned to chat some more. He announced abruptly that he had come up with only one name—a masculine one—for the imminent arrival.

Finally, Attallah appeared, beige and bawling, an uncanny miniature of Malcolm. "It looked like somebody had taken Malcolm and shrunk him," the minister's eldest blood brother, Wilfred, later said. Betty had wanted a boy, for the minister's sake. Yet gazing upon her daughter, she could not remember being happier. Her freshman year as Mrs. Malcolm X had at times seemed a Sisyphean task. But her reward had come.

Moments later, Malcolm stood in the maternity ward gaping at the child in his hands. "I don't think he really accepted the fact that I was going to have a baby until she arrived," Betty later said. His firstborn's tawny complexion alarmed him. "We both wondered what in the world we'd done wrong for this little girl to come out looking like that," Betty remembered. But in Baby Attallah—whose name Malcolm had borrowed from Attila the Hun, who invaded Rome in the fifth century—the minister saw himself more starkly than he ever could have imagined. The freckled skin, full mouth, and cindery eyes all were his. Soon the firebrand was cuddling and cooing. "The gentleness he showed was really quite profound," Betty recalled.

At the time, though, Betty's strongest emotion was panic. Allah had entrusted her with the well-being of a miniature human being. Despite her nurse's training, it was her husband who offered sound advice in the coming weeks for handling the newborn. Malcolm expounded upon the essential nutrients of human milk. A suckling infant hears its mother's soothing heartbeat and feels her nurturing embrace, he said.

Attallah was hardy and alert, and most of Betty's anxieties melted in the coming weeks. Only one worry remained: would her marriage change? During her pregnancy, the minister had doted over her like never before. "One of the happiest times of my life was when I was pregnant and pampered and catered to," she later said. Now here was this curling pout and these smoldering eyes, this tiny intruder come to teach her more about sharing and giving and selfless sacrifice than she had imagined one could learn.

—

Some years later, Betty summed up the overwhelming sentiment of her early marriage. "I was Malcolm's choice," she said, "and I thank God for that." Malcolm often seemed equally pleased with his lady. In his autobiography, he proclaimed Betty "a good Muslim woman and wife." He told comrades in his final months that he loved her for her loyalty, and that he could count on her regardless of the circumstances. "She's there for me," he said. He also acknowledged her sacrifices, which he thought noble. "I don't imagine many other women would put up with the way I am," he declared. He was moved when Betty told him once that she understood and accepted his absences, assuring him that, "You are present when you are away."

Malcolm also defended his wife on several occasions. In the early 1960s, when black women with natural hairstyles began appearing at Nation of Islam bazaars and in *Muhammad Speaks*, a few emboldened women wondered aloud why Mrs. Malcolm X was still pressing her hair. "You should be more concerned with what's in her head than what's on it!" Malcolm snapped. On another occasion, the first lady learned that a certain parishioner had confronted the minister, alleging that Betty had committed some insubordination. To her delight, Malcolm had shushed the informer. "Don't you see that everything she does is for me?" he asked calmly.

Some of the faithful never warmed to Betty. "She didn't want to be a regular sister," Kenyatta later said. "You'd be around her, she'd want to show you how 'classical' she were." Razzaq concurred. "She never had the common touch," he said. Karim described her as "cool," and recalled that she had an attitude. Some of the Original People branded her a social climber, even though her people back in Detroit whispered that she had "married down." Enough Temple Number Seven women had experienced her attitude, however, for the rest to know to steer clear. "You couldn't be rough on Sister Betty," Sister Khadiyyah remembered. "Betty was Betty, right or wrong."

Jealousy—both the congregation's and Betty's—inspired some of the ill will. Of the women who carried a torch for the minister, several were "determined to see how close they could get," Betty later told a girlfriend. She could not believe their gall. Some would even drop by the house, she later told one of her daughters. "As-salaam alaikum, Sister," they would twitter. "I just came to bring you and the family this pie."

Betty knew that Malcolm never went for the chicanery, and the women generally acknowledged her right to guard her territory. But some of the parishioners believed that her perhaps once-understandable suspicions were giving way to paranoia. Sister Khadiyyah later recalled one late-night phone call in which Betty accused her of carrying a torch for the minister. "I know you love my husband just like the rest of them!" Betty snapped. "Yeah," the sister returned, "I love your husband's dirty drawers. But not like you think!"

Jean Reynolds, another former congregant, later remembered that most of the women, like the men, loved and respected Malcolm utterly and honorably. "I would have given anything if that was my blood brother," she said. Few of the minister's disciples understood why Betty so often misread their affection. After all, Sister Khadiyyah said, "We went to war with that brother." What some of the parishioners could not see then, and did not necessarily care to acknowledge in coming years, was that Betty's anxieties and insecurities deepened as her crises mounted.

There was pressure enough within the ranks, but Betty also weathered external attacks in her early years as Mrs. Malcolm X. The most traumatic occurred in mid-May 1958, just four months into her marriage. She had just entered her second trimester, and her pregnancy (with Attallah) was showing. She and Malcolm were comfortably ensconced in the two-family upstairs apartment they were sharing with Temple Number Seven Secretary John X and his wife, Minnie. (Later granted the surname "Ali," John became the sect's national secretary and one of Malcolm's archenemies.) Muslims John and Yvonne X Mollette and family lived below.

One morning, while Malcolm was in Boston on Muslim business, two white detectives arrived at the 99th Street building. They told Yvonne that they were seeking Margaret Dorsey, a mail fraud suspect. When Yvonne informed them that nobody by that name lived in the building, the officers asked if they might come in and have a look around. Many urban blacks distrusted police, from whom they had known more intimidation than protection. Yvonne, a Muslim woman home with her children while her mechanic husband was at work, charged by tradition with guarding her husband's house, was doubly suspicious of the sleuths at her door. When she told the officers they could not enter without a warrant, they got curt and possibly rough with her and two of her daughters. They were furious when they left.

The officers returned shortly after with a federal search warrant and a postal inspector and made their way to a back door. John X Mollette, who by this time had rushed home, stepped outside and confronted the trio, asking to read the warrant. After an exchange, one enraged officer barged inside. (Mollette later claimed that the officer cuffed him in the eye and kicked him in the groin.) Another detective mounted a rear stairwell leading to the second floor and began firing into Malcolm and Betty's home. Meanwhile, Mollette tangled with an investigator below. Within minutes, a knot of neighboring Muslims swarmed the building and fell on the police. By the time police backup units arrived on the scene, doors had been kicked in, windows had been shattered, soda bottles had been flung, and several shots had been fired (one, allegedly, at a thirteen-year-old girl). The battered detectives were carted off to St. John's Hospital, and Betty; Yvonne; Minnie, a pregnant seventeen-year-old; and the Mollettes and their adolescent daughter were hauled away to face charges, such as assault and resisting arrest. (Betty later told her husband that an arresting officer had threatened to throw her down the back stairs because she "wasn't moving fast enough.")

Betty and Malcolm's home was left glinting with glass shards and pocked with bullets. Malcolm would maintain that the police had fired through a door into the hallway of the home. The detectives contended that the Muslims had started the violence by dropping a bottle from a second-floor window onto their heads. By the afternoon of the incident, throngs of spookily silent Muslims had materialized in front of the Astoria station where their comrades were being held. The Muslim outcry escalated in the coming weeks and months, and the trial drew nearly one thousand members of the congregation.

White newsmen ignored the story; the Muslim "peril" had not yet seized mainstream America's imagination, or even appeared as more than a distant flicker in the constellation of white fear. But Malcolm made characteristically good use of the black press, declaring in their pages that though Muhammad's followers obeyed the law, the officers in question had invaded a "religious home," threatening the lives of women and children and forcing the Muslims to defend themselves. He condemned the "Gestapo tactics of white police who patrol the black belts," describing the black ghetto as occupied territory. "Where else and under what circumstance could you find situations where police can freely invade private homes, bust up furniture, break down doors, threaten to beat pregnant women, and even try to shoot a thirteen-year-old girl…but right here in American Negro neighborhoods, where the occupying army is in the disguise of police officers," he said.

The case tied up a Long Island court for three weeks—an eternity by assault-trial standards. A judge finally acquitted Betty and the other suspects, and the Nation chalked up a win. The City of New York felt it was in some hot water over the affair and eventually forked up a negligible sum to settle a lawsuit Betty had filed. At 25-46 99th Street, Muslims replastered the walls, rehung doors, and replaced windows.

Malcolm was soon back on the road, sparing no energy in rousing the "blind, deaf, and dumb," though the attack on his home had been among the most harrowing of the sporadic skirmishes between the sect and the law in recent memory.

For Betty, however, a kind of shell shock set in. She was a college graduate, an expecting mother, a former choirgirl who had never handled a "piece" or run the mean streets, as had her husband and a good portion of the brethren. The talk at the mosque was of Armageddon and white annihilation almost as often as it was of frugality and table manners. But she had trained to dress wounds, not suffer them. One imagines that she had never contemplated dying in the service of Allah's Messenger.

Indeed, the minutes in which she had crouched with several Muslim women and children in the locked bedroom of her and Malcolm's apartment as a door frame ripped, a glass pane smashed, and slugs tore into the walls may have been the most horrifying of her twenty-four years. Her pregnancy only heightened the trauma. She knew now that this war her husband was fighting was for real. Malcolm was a growing power in the urban northeast. Every Negro he drafted into Muhammad's army was a soul that traditional institutions within and beyond the black community no longer controlled. And control is not a commodity surrendered lightly in restless times.

Several months earlier, President Dwight Eisenhower had federalized the Arkansas National Guard to escort nine black students through a shrieking white mob, thus integrating Little Rock's Central High School. Now an upstart Southerner named King, whose popularity in the black South was growing nearly mystical, was peddling his subversive notions about shaming a barbaric nation into racial reform with the moral force of nonviolence. A collective cry of discontent was building. And one of its harshest voices, the world would shortly discover, belonged to Malcolm.

Chapter Six

A PERILOUS ORBIT

—

"It's much easier to fight to get at a lunch counter
than to say that we have rights as human beings."
—Betty Shabazz

Sugar killed him, or so Mrs. Malloy always thought. For all his diges-
tive troubles and high blood pressure, Lorenzo Malloy loved sweets.
He was always ducking out of the family store to grab handfuls of cookies from a confectioner next door. In February 1960, the bonbons, or
fate, caught up with him, and a vessel in his brain hemorrhaged. Thus
Bethel AME lost a pillar, Mrs. Malloy lost her beloved, and Betty lost
her only constant father.

Though Betty and her foster father never fully reconciled after her
marriage, his death stunned her. This was the even-keeled man who
had sent her to the land of Booker T. Washington and insisted that she
begin making her own way. He was the first black man she had seen rise
early and return late, his face embossed with fatigue. But bereavement
was not the Muslim way. "Let the dead bury the dead," Malcolm
preached.

The believers were not to wallow in the past, but stride toward an
age in which Black Islam would reign on high, preparing its subjects for
Allah's return and the laying low of the "blue-eyed Willies." For years,
Malcolm was utterly convinced of the inevitability of this new order. If
Muhammad said Armageddon was coming, it was so. Indeed, the
Messenger taught that the final power shift from white to black, wicked

to divine, Christianity to Islam, had already begun. So when a pair of newsmen finally introduced the Muslims to middle America, the Faithful saw another sign that their great getting-up morning was near.

One might consider "The Hate That Hate Produced" the beginning of Malcolm's fall as the Nation's envoy and Muhammad's darling. There is some irony in that, for the television series anointed him as *the* Black Muslim in the public imagination. But jealousies were already stirring within the cloister. The 1957 Johnson X Hinton affair—the police brutality riot that almost happened—had lifted the minister to new fame in Harlem. His columns in the black press and platform harangues in the street had further hoisted his name and swelled the Nation's ranks.

Between Malcolm's ordination in the early 1950s and 1960, the Nation had burgeoned from an isolated flock of several hundred to a truly national congregation of fifty thousand in dozens of cities. "When the brother started out," Charles Kenyatta remembered, "you could put all Elijah Muhammad's followers in a station wagon and still have some room left." There can be no doubt that Malcolm was the catalyst. In the era of hostilities, the Chicago pooh-bahs would get collective amnesia about the labors of their kingdom's most valuable architect; but it was Malcolm who, finding recruitment trickling in 1952, had proselytized legions of Muslims in a decade-long crusade.

He had launched scores of temples nationwide, trained dozens of ministers, and served as the official Muslim presence in legal matters. For a time, before he married Betty, he had simultaneously pastored the New York, Philadelphia, and Boston mosques while serving as the movement's propagandist, ambassador, constable, and missionary. Malcolm was Black Islam's mouth and wit. He had also become its most recognizable face, which even then vexed some of its bureaucrats. "There were others striving to be the spokesperson," Kenyatta later recalled.

Then came the summer of 1959. That July, a bolt of black fury struck New Yorkers as they switched on their televisions. During a five-part series on the Muslims, Channel 13's *Newsbeat* broadcast the documentary "The Hate That Hate Produced," which flashed scenes of Minister Louis X reciting the soliloquy that had consummated his rise as one of the Movement's precocious lieutenants:

> I charge the white man with being the greatest liar on earth. I charge the white man with being the greatest drunkard on earth. I charge the white man with being the greatest swine-eater on earth. Yet, the Bible forbids it. I charge the white man with being the greatest gambler on earth. I charge the white man, ladies and gentlemen of the jury, with being the greatest murderer on earth. I charge the white man with being the greatest peace-breaker on earth.

The series contained footage of Muhammad saluting his minions and preaching in a stilted pidgin:

> The Christian religion has failed. Now the government of America has failed you. You have no justice coming from no one. It is written that we are like sheep among wolves…every wolf taking a bite at you. You want justice. You want freedom. You want equality…but get none.

But with his nearly shorn scalp and laser eyes, Malcolm was the telecast's leading villain. He hit the sect's classic themes: the evil white man had built the divine black man's hell on Earth, but his time was nearly up, and he would soon cook in a fiery lake. Calmly, the minister explained that the serpent in the Garden of Eden—the instigator of original sin—was actually a Biblical symbol of the Caucasian.

"The Hate That Hate Produced" stunned the public. Whites blanched, scared that Negroes were saying this sort of thing. Blacks recoiled, shocked that these "crazy niggers" were saying it out loud (though the rebuke itself privately thrilled many of them). The white press instantly descended on the Nation. *Time* warned of a surge in "cold black hatred." *Life, Newsweek, U.S.News & World Report,* major newspapers, and radio stations joined the frenzy, blazing the Muslim "menace" on the white psyche. Newsman Alex Haley did a widely read piece for *Reader's Digest*. Three books on the sect appeared within four years, including C. Eric Lincoln's seminal 1961 study, *The Black Muslims in America*.

Muhammad had bristled at the foreboding tone of "The Hate That Hate Produced." But now droves of Negro malcontents were making for their local mosques and signing up. During the broadcast, Malcolm himself was overseas touring newly independent Ghana and several other African and Arab nations as Muhammad's emissary. Already he was looking to internationalize the struggle. He wrote from Khartoum, Sudan, that:

> The African finds it difficult to understand why in a land
> that advocates equality, twenty million Black Americans
> are without equality. Why, in a land classing itself as
> leader of the free world, twenty million black Americans
> are not free; why in a land of schools, colleges, and all
> forms of educational opportunities, twenty million
> Negroes need Army escorts to accompany them to many
> of these institutions.

The media seized Malcolm upon his return to the United States, and they held on until well after his body was in the ground more than five years later. Some of Malcolm's disciples in the mourning years complained bitterly that the media had killed their man. They argued that the avaricious and slanted coverage had made him a public specter, and that the press had not sufficiently raised the alarm when it grew clear that his stalkers would prevail. But if Malcolm became a victim of international media, it was only after he became its master.

By mid 1959, Betty's life was as serene as could be with a feisty infant on the crawl. Aside from temple functions and occasional treks to her Muslim grocer in Brooklyn, she spent much of her time minding Attallah, keeping the house, and fixing dishes such as "Egyptian style" string beans with sauce, lamb or beef meat loaf, and bean soup with garlic and sage. Even the temple sisters acknowledged how far she had come from her toast-burning days. She later remembered their concession that "she might be educated and she might be this, that, and the other, but she does know how to cook."

Betty had withdrawn into the Muslim cloister. Her phone number was unlisted, and she tendered her address only to a few intimates. She was pregnant again, so Malcolm hovered over her when home. Sporadic quarrels still flared between the two, but often the jostling was affectionate. And though his authoritarianism lingered, he was slowly embracing her presence in his world. Indeed, the two may have just been striking a delicate balance when television catapulted him to infamy.

For Betty, it was another jarring reveille. It had been three years since her surrender to Black Islam. Despite her husband's modest celebrity in the black belts of the North, her world had always been domestic. She had grown numb to the order's shrillest rhetoric, and even to the flak from family members and old friends who misunderstood her lifestyle and reviled her faith. She was leading a quiet, churchly life.

Now, suddenly, her man was a hobgoblin of the white media. His ministry would hereafter spiral toward more perilous orbits, but her faith in his mission would endure. His rejection of integration as distracting fantasy and dangerous hoodwink alienated many blacks. ("It's much easier to fight to get at a lunch counter than to say that we have rights as human beings," Betty later said.) Yet Malcolm's genius was to unveil whatever frivolity lay in singing one's way into a "whites only" café. "An integrated cup of coffee is not sufficient pay for four hundred years of slave labor," he insisted.

—

Betty was wife before pupil. The minister had little time or inclination to tutor her in black-liberation theory, a science he was refining in the university of Harlem's streets and beyond. He did introduce her by Socratic method to Pan-Africanism and militant self-defense. "He was so cool with this stuff," his photographer Robert Haggins later remembered. "He would tell you to go and look this stuff up. He never gave you the answer."

Betty occasionally prepared book reports for the minister to pore over during his travels, plucking titles such as *The World's Great Men of Color* and *The Destruction of Black Civilization* from the bowed shelves of his study. Slowly she internalized the merits of collective struggle over individual prosperity. Before she met Malcolm, she had planned to hoist herself first and then look back if she could find the time. "I guess my feeling was that who else should you be concerned with other than yourself?" she later said. But the minister re-sorted her priorities, convincing her that a victorious liberation movement would benefit the entire race.

She struggled in turn to plant grains of prudence in his life, as at least one partner in every marriage must. Now that the white media had come calling, however, her clerical duties consumed her. "Betty would put down the phone after taking one message, and it was ringing again," Malcolm later remembered.

Allah must have a sense of irony, for in 1960 he sent Betty and Malcolm a Christmas gift; daughter number two arrived on December 25. Malcolm named her Qubilah, after the thirteenth-century Mongol emperor Kubla Khan. In later years, she became the most visibly wounded of the Shabazz daughters. And though she shunned the family fame, the public came to know her troubles most intimately.

If Attallah was Malcolm mimeographed, Qubilah was Betty's facsimile. The young mother proudly dressed her two small girls in matching smocks, scarves, knee socks, and darling play clothes. They always seemed more nearly costumed for Catholic school than Black Islam's nursery. They grew gorgeous, their faces melding Malcolm's angularity and Betty's curling features.

Daughter number three arrived in July 1962 and was equally fetch-ing. Malcolm named her Ilyasah in honor of Elijah. She grew bronze like Qubilah and tall like Attallah. In later years, she flirted with a modeling career, an ambition her mother was not crazy about. What Betty did approve of was Ilyasah's eagerness to please, which may have led her to follow her mother into a public-affairs career.

Betty adored her girls and found motherhood fulfilling and challeng-ing. As late as 1963, she was still occasionally lecturing to civilization and women's classes at the mosque. But she was laden with babies and house-work, and could only watch as women across the country flowed into the workforce. Despite Mrs. Malcolm X's insulation, however, shifting gender roles outside the sect were creating subtle tensions within.

Muhammad Speaks continued to exalt motherhood and homemak-ing as women's essential roles. The tabloid still offered tips on how to properly iron doilies and wipe grease from pots, advising women to sea-son their homemade vegetable soup with cracked beef knucklebones, and reminding them to monitor their posture, carriage, and "voice modulation." However, the Muslim organ was increasingly profiling "busy career girls" and heralding "the drive by Negro women for more active roles in the vital field of education." Quiet acknowledgments that the movement needed "men and women of science, of the med-ical professions, those learned in economics, business administration, and jurisprudence" were creeping into the text.

Though times were changing, Betty remained rather the same. She kept on pressing and waving her hair in the style she had worn since high school, even as more black women in the early 1960s began sport-ing natural hairdos such as "the Zulu." And it was not just the day's esthetic that was passing her by.

The Negro Left and the African revolution were in some ways con-verging. Black demonstrators in early 1961 disrupted United Nations Security Council proceedings in New York City, decrying U.S. imperi-alism and complicity in the assassination of Congo Premier Patrice Lumumba. Malcolm, who had met Lumumba and Fidel Castro, Cuba's revolutionary leader, in Harlem, was also cultivating ties to the Dark World, brushing with Ghanaian President Kwame Nkrumah, Sékou

Touré of Guinea, and other African dignitaries stateside. Betty was proud of her husband's ambassadorial feats. "He should have been a foreign policy advisor," she later joked. But as his international circles widened, her world inside their Queens bungalow shrunk.

———

With her husband a virtual transient and a trio of girls to mind, Betty came to expect frustrations and learned to live with diminished expectations. Still, she loved Malcolm and the girls fiercely. She experienced some of her happiest moments when he was home in the early 1960s, with she and the babies arrayed about him. In those days, the Oldsmobile trundled up to the narrow house under a crescendo of squeals: "Daddy's home!"

Malcolm would stride through the door and fall on the paisley couch, sweeping his daughters onto his knees. By then Betty had swabbed, frocked, and bereted the girls for his arrival. The smell of fresh-baked bread would hang thick and sweet, as a meal warmed in the oven. Betty, perfumed, her hair parted above her right eyebrow and swirled about the nape of her neck, would put supper out, but not before Malcolm had peeked impatiently inside the fridge.

"Whenever Daddy was home, the whole house was happy," Betty later said. "It wasn't a time for a lot of big, knock-down, drag-out fights." She always cooked something special and added cosmetic touches to the already tidy house. After the minister telephoned to say he was on the way, Ilyasah would dodder over to the door to sit and wait. Before long, her giant would burst in, a bedlam of laughter never far behind. "Just his presence was so very calming for us kids," Attallah later remembered. Sometimes the mood was giddy. As Malcolm watched himself on television, his confused toddlers would swivel between his gangly frame and the screen, trying to reconcile Daddy's simultaneous appearance in three and two dimensions while he and Betty chuckled quietly.

Malcolm arrived without entourages or drumrolls. Though his wife and children often welcomed him like a war hero, he was not a celebrity at 23-11 97th Street. He was rather a masculine presence in a feminine hive, a warm current that blew indoors, delighted, and often left just as swiftly. He was "big fun," Attallah remembered. "As grand a nationalist as Malcolm X was," she said, "he was an even grander parent."

Every May 19, Betty baked Malcolm a chocolate cake, and the children sang "Happy Birthday," hanging about his neck like a writhing lavaliere. He would protest: "Oh, you don't have to do this." But as Betty later recalled, that cake and vanilla ice cream always vanished. There were other sublime memories: Betty and baby Attallah romping at the beach as the minister scribbled his speeches nearby; Attallah and Qubilah in the ivy-dappled backyard, jockeying for position in Daddy's lap.

Betty later insisted that Malcolm spent as much family time as any man, "in terms of quality." He was a devoted father, she said, who whenever possible had tender little talks with each of their daughters and took time to read to them. Yet Betty was the constant nurturer. The girls' universe swelled and shrank according to her ministrations, so it was her with whom they first fell in love. "My mother set the rhythm in our household," Attallah later said.

Malcolm relished fatherhood. Were it not for racism's stranglehold, many of his friends later insisted, the minister would have happily lived out his days frolicking with his daughters. Malcolm "liked the idea that God had allowed us to create these new human beings that were a part of both of us," Betty said. He wanted his daughters to honor authority, think independently, behave civilly, respect and accept themselves, and fulfill their spiritual and moral duty to oppressed people.

Betty was to see to all of it. When members of the Nation coddled the girls, the minister intervened, declaring that "other people will spoil your children and be the first to criticize them for their apparent lack of training." Yet it was Betty who dealt with the children's daily mischief. It was she who adorned them with bonnets and white cassocks, plaited their hair, fed, bathed, entertained, and punished them. Despite his daughters' rascality, Malcolm returned from the Muslim front bestowing not discipline but oatmeal cookies and tickles like a rangy Father Christmas.

"You were never a bad girl," Attallah later remembered. "And if you came in with mud on your face, you didn't feel like you were dirty. He'd say, 'Well, let's go wash it off and start again.'" Though the minister could be soft when it came to the girls, he urged Betty to be firm, especially with Attallah, who was rebellious even as a toddler. "He saw in her a lot of traits that he himself had possessed," Betty later said. Percy Sutton thought the girl inquisitive and "delightfully bright." Young Attallah had a rough road to walk, though. Betty later acknowledged that her early struggles with child rearing were hardest on her eldest.

Although Betty was a strict and protective young mom, she was not dogmatic about her daughter's upbringing. Despite the faults she had found in recent years with her own parochial breeding, she provided a middle-class backdrop for her children that in some ways mirrored her past. She signed Attallah and Qubilah up for tonette and recorder lessons because she and Malcolm wished them to learn "precision, poise, timing, and coordination." When Attallah was of age, she sent her to a predominantly white public school in Queens.

The girls learned subconsciously to straddle two worlds. Attallah would never forget the hand wringing that her father's arrival one afternoon to pick her up from the first grade inspired among the grownups. Yet she would remember her early years as quaint and "wholesome." Her desire to become a doctor never troubled Malcolm, though he often accused Negro professionals of selling out. As Betty later explained, he insisted only that his children remember their heritage, regardless of what paths their lives took.

Of course, cultural nationalism shaped even the girls' early childhood. Betty proclaimed in 1963 that, with proper training, her daughters—then ages one through four—would never marry outside their race or faith. The black history she read to them nightly, though, never taught disdain for whites. The bedtime lessons were reminiscent of the old Negro heritage scrapbooks she had once composed for the Housewives League. So were the girls' coloring books, which bore etchings of Benjamin Banneker, Ida B. Wells, and other black heroes.

"When I went to school and parts of me were omitted from history books," Attallah later recalled, "I knew the hole wasn't in me, it was in the books."

Betty and Malcolm were determined not to shelter their daughters from racial realities. As the Civil Rights struggle and its backlash stunned national television audiences, the couple let the girls watch stark images of the liberation campaigns flicker across the living-room set. Attallah later recalled that her folks never "candy coated what was ugly" or hesitated to steep their daughters in African heritage. "The black woman has the chief responsibility for passing along black cultural traditions to the children," Betty later declared.

Sometimes she preened the girls and carted them to the mosque to watch their father lecture. Gradually they learned that he was a focus. Despite his objections, they continued to win the congregation's fawning attention. A cherubic Attallah appeared in the September 1960 *Muhammad Speaks,* and the organ named Qubilah a "natural beauty" two years later.

The children found their father's attention much more finite than the laity's. He delighted them with gifts when he returned from his travels, yet he was always retreating upstairs to his office to handle paperwork or snooze. Betty hushed them and herded them into the playroom when he was working (he later acknowledged the pains she took to give him the peace he needed).

Every now and then, Betty raised the matter of a son. "I wanted a son for him more than he wanted one for himself," she later said. Malcolm confessed that he was praying for a boy, but he never discussed the subject unless Betty brought it up. He always insisted that they should be grateful for the healthy children they already had. Besides, he said, they could always have more children—and more.

Malcolm burst into the 1960s a restless dissenter and heckler, railing for self-defense, self-determination, and separation. As many blacks rested their hopes on the Civil Rights establishment, with its integrated ranks and "redeem-with-love, turn-the-cheek" gospel, Malcolm hawked his eye-for-an-eye doctrine. "Never be the aggressor, never look for trouble," he commanded. "But if any man molests you, may Allah bless you!"

Though he won untold sympathizers among the black elite and intelligentsia, the minister's staunchest following lay in the northern ghettos. "We don't want to integrate with that ole pale thing!" he cried to Harlem's throngs. He sliced through the American "wilderness," alighting any place with a mosque or meeting hall to receive him and his bad news for "the slavemaster." As Elijah Muhammad's health failed, the elder often ducked out of appearances at the final hour, leaving his top man to give the word. Malcolm did so stunningly time after time, blending the Nation's dogma with his own smarting rebuffs of white hypocrisy and "responsible" Negro leadership.

It was not lost on the Muslims that their prince's eloquence eclipsed their king's, whose speech was halting and crude. In the summer of 1961, an audience of seven thousand turned out for Muhammad in Washington, D.C., expecting to drink from the "Living Fountain." After two hours of filler, the crowd learned that coughing fits the night before had kept the elder in Chicago. A couple of his family members spoke on his behalf, but the show clearly belonged to Malcolm. He seemed impossibly tall as he took the podium, bow tie gleaming white against a starched shirt. To uproarious applause and chants, he trounced his boss's many detractors, defending the sect's call for immediate separation from the oppressor and a few fertile states for the black man. Minutes after he announced the collection, the crowd had filled the baskets several times over.

Malcolm hardly caught his breath in those years, ranting night after night to smitten or stunned overflow audiences in cities as far flung as Boston, Cleveland, Detroit, Seattle, San Francisco, Los Angeles, Atlanta, and Miami. The liberal colleges discovered him as a menace to the status quo, and soon he was trotting the academic lecture circuit. He spoke at Harvard, Brown, Yale, and Columbia and on major national and local television stations and in various radio forums, appearing more frequently as he hopscotched the nation than a U.S. president during a White House term. He lamented that, "Blacks are still knocking on the door begging for civil rights....Do you mean to tell me that in a powerful country like this, a so-called Christian country, that a handful of men from the South can prevent the North, the West, the Central States, and the East from giving Negroes the rights the Constitution says they already have? No! I don't believe that and neither do you."

Drawn to his ominous quotability, reporters bathed him in ink, casting him as the chief apologist for "the most sinister of all Negro cults in the United States." Though its spokesmen privately envied the hold he had over ghetto crowds, the Civil Rights vanguard accused him of fueling bitterness and mongering hatred. Malcolm only rained more lava on their cause, arguing in 1961 that:

> It is not a case of integration into the American way of life, nor is it a question of not integrating. The question is one of human dignity, and integration is only a method or tactic or role that many of the so-called Negroes are using to get recognition and respect as human beings. And many of these Negroes have gotten lost on the road. They're confusing the objective with the method.

During the same televised forum, he proclaimed that:

> Now you have twenty million black people in America who are begging for some kind of recognition as human beings, and the average white man today thinks that we're making progress. He cannot justify the fact that he made us slaves in the first place, which was contrary not only to man's law, contrary not only to God's law, but also contrary to nature's law. I don't call that progress until we have gotten everything we originally had. If a man robs a bank he can't jump up and say: "Well, I'm sorry I've been a robber." He has to make restitution. Here you have twenty million black people who have worked for nothing for 310 years

and then for the past hundred years we have been deprived
of practically everything a human being needs to exist and
keep his morale up. I just can't bring myself to accept the
few strides that we've made as any kind of progress.

Betty held up half the sky in those days, keeping the minister
groomed and fed when he popped in, and running behind their vivacious daughters while he was away. Telephones sustained their relationship. "If my work won't let me be there," he later declared, "at least
she can always know where I am."

If Betty did not wonder about her husband's whereabouts, she certainly worried about his welfare. She agonized over the pace of his
labors, and hoped to slow him down. She might have had more luck
trying to lasso a comet. Malcolm was always hoarse and beat. The dark
crescents under his eyes often looked pitifully hollow. He took no sab-
baticals and had never vacationed with his wife. Though she fretted
that he was going to work himself into the ground, this was the
Movement's golden era, and she knew he was happy.

The Nation was growing. While still on the fringe concern, the
sect was gaining legitimacy in some pockets of Black America.
Students and professionals were mingling with blue-collar workers, ex-
cons, and others in the ranks. In the streets, the Fruit of Islam were
moving stacks of Muhammad Speaks, each edition thick with news of
Malcolm's exploits. Seeing Malcolm and his church's momentum,
prominent New York politicos such as Congressman Adam Clayton
Powell and Manhattan Borough President Hulan Jack looked to curry
favor with the sect, even though its faithful were forbidden to vote.

Max Roach, Abbey Lincoln, actors Ruby Dee and Ossie Davis,
drummer Babatunde Olatunji, comedian Dick Gregory, and other popular entertainers had begun appearing at Muslim bazaars. Dee recognized the sect as a "positive organization," and described Muhammad
and Malcolm as "dramatic personalities."

If the Nation was arriving, Malcolm had in many respects arrived. Never had he seemed more ensconced as Muhammad's lieutenant. During rallies, the servant sat at the elder's elbow, grinning toothily as warm currents flowed between the two. Muhammad seemed a proud father, often proclaiming his affection for his protégé and boasting about the minister's unflagging loyalty.

The love was mutual. Everywhere Malcolm went, he trumpeted his savior, garnishing almost every utterance with "the Honorable Elijah Muhammad teaches us...." Every thought, deed, and triumph of his ministry and the Movement he attributed to the guru with a cascade of hosannas. Betty accepted that her husband's spiritual marriage to Muhammad in some ways transcended their legal union. She recognized that Malcolm, robbed of his parents in childhood, had found a surrogate father in him. Later she proposed that Muhammad treated the minister like a son because "he realized the potential that Malcolm had for the Movement."

Betty swallowed some of her protests about Malcolm's absences and frenetic pace, less because she thought the complaints counterrevolutionary than because she had come to accept their futility. "Woman who cries all the time is only because she knows she can get away with it," Malcolm once scrawled on a cocktail napkin in Alex Haley's studio, perhaps revealing his attitude toward the dissension at home. Yet on another occasion the minister scribbled, "I have a wife who understands, or even if she doesn't she at least pretends." Betty certainly understood sacrifice and devotion. Though Malcolm occupied much of her waking reality, she had her own sense of duty in Islam.

She had joined Allah's army and watched the troops amass. She had discovered that she was the "Mother of Civilization" and that her detachment from the world was natural, proper, and revolutionary. The Nation glorified the feminine role in the "Great Battle" at hand. There were men to prop up, babies to civilize. And though she'd never been a zealot, Betty was as convinced as any of the Muslim sisters that the force of her grace and modest virtue would help bring down Babylon.

One cannot know whether she took the whole body of her husband's rhetoric literally while under Muhammad's mystical sway. She understood that Malcolm's main purpose in demonizing whites was to loosen blacks from psychological inferiority. And though she never questioned his sincerity, she suggested many years later that he occasionally hyperbolized. "Sometimes you have to exaggerate in order to get people to see," she said. Yet Malcolm was "absolutely properly focused," she always said. She understood that he was doing something powerful, that he was seizing black men and women who all their lives had cowered in the face of white power, and snatching them up off their knees.

The media fixed not on the redemptive qualities of his ministry, however, but his searing condemnation of whites and America itself. His blanket indictments and broadside assaults on Negro leadership made him a pariah even in some progressive black circles. At the time, poet Sonia Sanchez was with New York's Congress of Racial Equality (CORE), which was veering to the left of some of the statelier Civil Rights outfits, such as the Urban League and the NAACP.

CORE's was a young, hip crowd that often partied as much as it protested. One weekend the race work spilled over into a house jam on Riverside Drive. As Sanchez later recalled, she was mamboing with a man when she happened to mention the minister, whom she had just met and been rather impressed by, despite her leanings toward nonviolent confrontation as a liberation strategy. "Malcolm said..." Sanchez began, but hesitated after her partner shot her a look. She kept on mamboing. "And Malcolm said..." she continued, smoothly executing a spin. When she turned back around, the man had split. "He left me on the floor by myself!" she later remembered with a chuckle.

Despite the concerns of the established Movement, the inner city considered Malcolm one of its own. Sylvia Woods was among those urbanites who thought from a religious, if not ideological, distance that the minister was righteous, an affable street statesman who told white folks off and pressed black men and women to do right. In 1962, Woods took over the luncheonette that became "Sylvia's," now a bustling Harlem landmark. At the time, Malcolm haunted a small office above the establishment, occasionally dashing downstairs for coffee or, rarely, a non-Muslim-cooked meal. Woods, one of the well-wired women who helped throw Betty and her daughters a lifeline after his death, later said of Malcolm, "It's so sad that so many didn't know him the way he should have been known."

Betty knew him. She knew him like she knew Helen Malloy's worry lines, like she knew how to double stitch a seam or remove a suture. She always said that if you knew Malcolm you understood where he was coming from. "He used to say that people, especially white people, had pompous gall to insist that he change before white people themselves changed their treatment of black people," she later said. She remembered him telling her that, "when a people have oppressed your great-grandfather, your grandfather, your father, and yourself, it is sheer gall for these same people to call you a racist when you tell them that you have had enough."

Yet it was not white audacity that most galled Malcolm. Though he had preached for a decade that whites were devils, Negro attacks on Muhammad's gospel also incensed him. He summarily dismissed or sparred publicly with every Civil Rights titan, including the NAACP's Roy Wilkins, CORE's James Farmer, the Urban League's Whitney Young, professional baseball's Jackie Robinson, diplomat Ralph Bunche, and the elder of Negro protest, union man A. Philip Randolph himself.

Martin Luther King Jr. particularly disgusted Malcolm, who had taken to publicly calling him a "chump." "Any Negro who teaches Negroes to turn the other cheek in the face of attack is disarming that Negro of his God-given right, of his moral right, of his natural right, of his intelligent right to defend himself," Malcolm fumed. To him, King was nothing but a barbiturate the oppressor had fed a righteously angry people. "For years Malcolm said if he ever meet King he was gonna slap him to see how nonviolent he was," Kenyatta later recalled.

In the meantime, Malcolm would have to settle for slashing the reverend and his cause in the media. As "race-mixers" in Greensboro, North Carolina, perched at white lunch counters smeared in goop ignoring the reflex to sock their tormentors; as white college kids clambered onto interstate buses in the North to take perilous Freedom Rides; as the federal government muscled James Meredith through the doors of the milk-white University of Mississippi; as blacks queued up

134 - BETTY SHABAZZ

in Birmingham, Alabama, sacrificing themselves to Bull Connor's water jets and German Shepherds; Malcolm sneered that the self-deluded integrationists were bleeding and dying for "coffee with a cracker."

The Civil Rights establishment lashed back. They dismissed the minister and his master as supremacists whose rhetoric inverted white bigotry without winning tangible victories for blacks. No one understood better than Betty how deeply the charge cut Malcolm. How many times had he come home after some Negro with the ear of the masses had invoked the image of the bloodthirsty Muslims? The "unbelievers'" hypocrisy angered her, too. She later recalled that some of the black spokesmen who demonized Malcolm publicly, privately sympathized with his philosophy or acknowledged the political leverage he afforded them. "You're right, absolutely right," she remembered them conceding, "but we would get nowhere if you were not out there."

The Muslims' refrain was "Don't tread on me." For some time, the word on ghetto streets was that the Original People were bad enough to whip any white man who messed with them. In its show of dint, the Johnson X Hinton affair seemed to justify the reputation. But as the Civil Rights movement gathered steam and spilled onto the streets in gallant showdowns with white power, the Nation and its noninvolvement policy began to seem shamefully detached. People were starting to talk. Even in the northern slums, they were saying that Black Islam cocked its fist but never threw a punch. The charge smarted, but never did it stick like after April 27, 1962.

Late that night, a couple of Los Angeles patrolmen spotted some Black Muslims near the city's mosque hauling clothes from the trunk of a car. It was a dry-cleaning delivery, but suspecting a burglary, the officers moved in. They questioned and searched the men. One cop wrenched Temple secretary Ronald Stokes's arm viciously behind his back. A quarrel flared, and in the fuss a throng of men came hustling from the temple, apparently managing to disarm one of the patrolmen.

Meanwhile, a call went out from a squad-car radio, and within minutes a battalion of police swarmed the worship house.

By the end of the debacle, one police officer and seven Muslims had been shot, many in the back. Several of the Muslims had been beaten, and one was paralyzed for life. Police had ransacked the mosque, systematically ripping the clothes off unarmed worshippers and marching them into the street. Stokes lay on the pavement, blood coursing from a bullet hole in his head. Within days, a coroner's jury would rule his death a justifiable homicide.

Malcolm wept. He had launched the Los Angeles temple and knew the deceased well. Stokes had been a good brother, a *clean* brother, Kenyatta later recalled, amid not a few ex-hustlers and racketeers. Now he had been brutally killed. The Muslims were fired up and hungry for revenge, and the minister was ready to give the order. This would be the hour of reckoning. With retribution and death in his heart, he flew to the coast to preach the funeral and preside over the counterstrike.

Then the command came from Chicago: "Hold fast to Islam." Allah alone would punish the devil. As for the believers, they were to sell more newspapers. Malcolm fumed, but as always, he obeyed. In the coming days, a furious outcry rose from the black community and Civil Rights groups over the temple invasion and Stokes's death. The minister himself roved the pulpit in a masterful rally, berating the Los Angeles mayor and police force. When a jet full of white Americans later plunged from the sky over France, a seemingly gleeful Malcolm called it a tooth for a tooth. But it was hollow, bitter rhetoric, and everybody knew it.

Betty had never seen Malcolm in such a rage, yet her thoughts also leapt to Stokes's widow Delores and the couple's baby girl, Saudi. Pregnant with Ilyasah, Betty was not among the two thousand who attended Stokes's moving funeral. Yet she knew of the woman who stood shrouded in white at the last rites, clutching her composure, gripped on both sides by gloved women. "Sister Delores" had lingered dolefully in the courtroom where fourteen of the Los Angeles mosque's survivors faced assault charges. The Muslims were calling her a hero's widow.

The image of Sister Delores clutching her fatherless child chilled Betty, who wanted a husband, not a martyr. Being a good Muslim wife and mother could shield her husband from danger no more than it could reverse the black protest's mounting body count.

———

Patrice Lumumba was dead. An idol to America's Black Left, he had emerged as premier of the Congo after the former Belgian colony won its bloody independence in 1960. But in a grotesque coup, puppet troops answering to a political rival clandestinely supported by the U.S. and propped up by Belgium had tortured and slain the African leader, long an immutable foe of colonialism. After the assassination, Egyptian President Gamal Abdel Nasser had sent for Lumumba's twenty-nine-year-old widow and presented her with a furnished villa in Cairo's diplomatic district, a chauffeured car, and a complement of servants. Egyptian officials had offered to educate her four children so they could someday return to the Congo and serve their country. But the royal treatment could not ease the widow's anguish.

By June 1963, Medgar Evers was dead. A white rifleman's slug had hurtled out of the darkness and toppled the dogged NAACP organizer as he approached his Jackson, Mississippi, home. Hearing the blast, his wife Myrlie had flown to the door, switched on the light, and found him sprawled face down just paces away, drenched in blood. He'd dropped a trail of papers and some sweatshirts inscribed with the slogan "Jim Crow Must Go."

Myrlie Evers had lived on the edge with Medgar. In those last months, they had jumped at phantom noises in the dark. One night, a rustle in the house had startled her husband from bed. Moments later, she had found him clutching his head, a rifle dangling by his side as their eldest son obliviously used the bathroom across the hall. Two weeks before his death, she had scrambled outside in a nightgown to douse a plume of flames with a garden hose after a Molotov cocktail had sailed onto their carport. Now Medgar was gone. Soon she would gather her courage and speak before a Baptist church brimming with supporters and journalists:

> I come to you tonight with a broken heart. I have lost my husband. No one really knew how hard he worked, how much he sacrificed over the years to help his people. No one but me. I knew. I know.

In the minutes after she watched the life run out of him, she had managed only to dial the police and sob and pray and call comrades and screech the splintering phrase that Betty herself would echo within two years: "They've killed my husband!"

Chapter Seven

FORESIGHT

—

"Imagine how you would feel if you woke up one
morning to find the sun shining and all the stars aflame."
—James Baldwin

She was discreet among the unconverted, but Betty could gossip. Maybe the occasional whisper eased the pressures of her station in the ascetic society, or helped stave off a sense of isolation. Perhaps an old passion was resurfacing. Whatever the case, her idle talk drew frowns in Temple Number Seven, where anything worth saying was to be said to your sister's face.

When the sect's Upstate New York women's retreat erupted with bickering, parishioners named Betty as a source of the commotion. Malcolm got wind of the affair—"somebody must have brought his attention to it," Sister Khadiyyah later remembered—and flushed a deep crimson. "I thought his heart would pop," Abdullah Razzaq later recalled. "I said, 'This man gon' put his wife out of the mosque!'" It was not a wild notion. Malcolm had already stood by the excommunication of his brother Reginald and half-sister Ella (the first having been booted for heresy, the second for insubordination). As it turned out, the minister did not suspend or oust his wife, but he surely upbraided her upon returning to East Elmhurst.

Of course, Betty was not the only Muslim woman—or man—guilty of rumor mongering. The rank and file would soon spread slimy tales about the minister himself. In the years when mumbling about

Malcolm was considered blasphemy, however, Betty bore much of the congregation's spite. Some of the laymen had never quit scrutinizing her. She probably could not have expected otherwise. "Who likes the first lady?" Razzaq later asked rhetorically. "They are tied to power." But Black Muslim patriarchy encouraged the faithful to humble "uppity" women. Betty might have quieted her detractors by staying low, yet she had consistently struggled to escape her constrictions; "Tryin' her level best to break out," as Charles Kenyatta put it.

Though at times she had concealed her resistance from the congregation, the men knew that she was far from meek. By her third daughter's arrival, a more or less accepted theory was circulating among some of the temple operatives: Allah, the men said, was punishing Betty's disobedience. Until she submitted to staying "wrapped up" and homebound, she would bear Malcolm no sons.

The men's clucking never bridled Betty. Invisibility did not suit her, and she continued to sharpen the intransigence that would shape her reputation. Her fondness for gossip flourished, too. In later years, she meddled notoriously, and it was not just a trivial pursuit. She had learned as Mrs. Malcolm X that one ought never close one's eyes and ears at once.

———

Betty later insisted that parenthood never eclipsed her and her husband's love affair. "He loved the children—but you know, I was still his Betty," she remembered. The babies gobbled her time, though. During those days, when the minister rang from out of town and hinted that she ought to scour the house for a hidden trifle, she sometimes brushed him off. "Well," he would bristle, "I can see you're not much in the mood for talking, so I'll call tonight." But she would discover the gift and phone him back excitedly. "Now tell me," he would tease, "do you love *me* or my money?"

It was an ironic question. Malcolm had no wealth to speak of. Their "ninety-eight" Oldsmobile belonged to the Nation, as did their modestly furnished 97th Street East Elmhurst parsonage, which Muhammad practically had to order Malcolm into after he, Betty, and baby Attallah outgrew their original 99th Street apartment. "I own nothing except a record player," Malcolm told an interviewer in 1959. While many of the sect's hierarchs had begun sporting tailored suits, Betty and other Muslim women sewed many of the minister's clothes. "Frequently a very sincere leader becomes trapped by material possessions and consequently becomes alienated from the aspirations of his followers," he explained.

Chicago meted out his living wage and covered his expenses. These were pittances, and the minister was so committed to the cause that he routinely funneled his college lecture fees and other outside earnings into Muslim coffers. He was careful not to give the impression of privilege, moored as he was in the common man's plight and given as he was to dismissing Civil Rights leaders as charlatans. Malcolm "had no use for schemes designed to enrich certain individuals," Betty later said.

She came to believe, however, that he was dedicated to a fault. His zealotry "left him with practically nothing of his own." While propagating the Nation handsomely in the 1950s and early 1960s, Malcolm salted away no nest egg. Even in the days when his home bulged with tithes awaiting transport to Chicago, his family lived humbly. "Malcolm, like all spiritual men, had a higher calling," Kenyatta observed. According to Betty, the minister was so earnest about his mission, so trusting of Muhammad, that he often declined the elder's offers to transfer the title of the East Elmhurst house to him. "No, sir, dear Holy Apostle," she would recall Malcolm protesting. "If anything ever happened to me, I know the Nation will take care of my family."

Malcolm's self-deprivation seemed almost contrary, for the Nation encouraged entrepreneurs and economic independence, and bragged about its mom-and-pop shop owners. In this sense, the Muslims clung to the very Booker T. Washington model that the Malloys had embraced. "Islam is mathematics," one Muslim dictum held, "learn to use it and secure some benefit while you are living, that is luxury, money [and] good income." But Betty did the math, and she found, to her growing displeasure, that her family was coming up short.

By 1960, Muhammad and his Nation controlled a pyramid of businesses. There were restaurants, bakeries, grocery and butcher stores, and clothing plants. Muhammad had bought farmland, Chicago apartment buildings, and other properties, including his tightly guarded eighteen-room Victorian mansion on the city's south side. He later bought a second estate in Phoenix, where the winters were easier on his worsening bronchial asthma.

The businesses upheld his and his extended family's increasingly lavish lifestyles, and rallies, plays, records, and tithes further padded the treasury. "The money was big," Kenyatta later said. The laity were soon sagging under the load. Forced to regularly buy parcels of *Muhammad Speaks* at street prices, each Fruit of Islam legionnaire had to hawk all of his allotted copies just to break even. The brethren would haunt ghetto sidewalks for hours, sweating through funeral-parlor suits and conservative ties, pushing the tabloid purported to "tell it like it is."

While the men often took crippling losses, the Nation profited, urging its people toward frugality while forcing them to give generously to the cause (which by 1961 included building a proposed twenty-million-dollar Islamic Center in Chicago). The believers generally surrendered their hard-won money willingly, but the taxes were getting outrageous. Chicago often ordered the Fruit of Islam to show up for rallies and other major gatherings with pockets full of cash. "In any community," Kenyatta later recalled, "brothers would be sticking up brothers because everybody wanted to walk up and put one-hundred dollars on that table."

Malcolm's congregants suffered, too. On Monday nights, the men met at the Harlem mosque, filing before Captain Joseph as he looked over their latest contributions. "Brother, what's your problem?" the official would ask any laggards. "Why you ain't sold these papers? And look, you're down in your dues. How you think the royal family gonna have their soup?"

Malcolm was not stone blind. He recognized the sect's "creeping capitalism," as one writer later called it. Rather than try to justify the abuses, the minister for a time simply tightened his blinders and pressed on with Allah's mission. He was convinced that Black Islam was the solution. It had spared him from wretchedness and salvaged thousands of others. It had its blemishes, but he was sworn to its service. And in those astigmatic days he may have trusted Muhammad more emphatically than the Prophet trusted himself.

Betty was less indoctrinated. She was watching the religious order become an oligarchy. She knew the kingdom and the court well. She had hosted the pooh-bahs and compared notes with their wives. She saw money and privilege drenching Muhammad's kin and the nobles in his entourage. Greed, she later declared, had begun to cloud a "noble vision." She and Malcolm had the car and the neat seven-room house at their disposal, but next to some of the Chicago courtiers, they seemed almost threadbare.

The disparity chafed her. Her husband was the Nation's prince, after all—Muhammad's number-two man. Yet Malcolm had his rewards, and she knew it. The steady march of Muhammad's Islam electrified him. The idea that he was stripping away Negro shame, paralysis, vice, and mental servitude and slashing the tentacles of white power, exhilarated him. Of course, some of the minister's emotional returns were more egocentric. He enjoyed his demagogic role as Black Islam's apologist, a role that armed him with a doting congregation and dressed him in power.

For years he reigned like a prizefighter, the smitten crowds roaring as he threw haymakers at the white man. As he preached in Temple Number Seven and in mosques across the country, lieutenants stalked the aisles rousing brothers who appeared too sedate. *Bear witness! Bear witness!* At rallies, lectures, forums, news conferences, and debates, blacks and whites teetered breathlessly on his words. Malcolm, Kenyatta later remembered, was "in his moment."

Betty was not immune to the thrill of confrontation and the promise of black nationhood, but she had perks and prerogatives of her own. While many of the Muslim sisters rode the buses and the subways, the Fruit of Islam chauffeured her. At banquets and other formal affairs, she dined with Malcolm beside Muslim luminaries and the occasional dignitary from the black and brown world. She enjoyed front-row seats at Nation bazaars. The laity deferred to her as Brother Minister's wife. And though she may not have welcomed the honor, Muhammad himself was often a guest in her home. "Every woman would have liked to be in her position," Razzaq later insisted.

It was a position Malcolm defended. Once, while chatting with the minister, Razzaq happened to refer to her as "Sister Betty." Malcolm immediately interjected: "My wife," he said quietly. Unheeding, the aide kept on talking. A few minutes later, Razzaq again referred to "Sister Betty," the name she'd held since joining the temple. Malcolm again interrupted: "My wife," he said. This time Razzaq took the hint. From then on, when talking to Malcolm, he referred to Betty only as "your wife."

Betty relished the status. "She made sure that you appreciated the fact that she appreciated the distance between you and her," Razzaq later said. "She wanted you to know that she knew that because of her relationship with Malcolm, you and her were not equals." In the end, the token privileges could not offset the burdens. Though she was not immune to the materialism trickling through the Nation, she was more concerned with ensuring her family's welfare. The Malloys had always stressed home ownership and financial autonomy. Now Betty meant to introduce an ounce of their pragmatism for every pound of Malcolm's zealotry. Sister Khadiyyah later recalled that:

> She tried to explain to him—as we all did at one time or another—that you can't live off the crumbs. You makin' millions of dollars for this man. You don't own the house you live in. You don't own the car. You barely own the clothes on your back. But he loved Elijah so much he couldn't see the forest for the trees.

Betty's hints became pleas. "We need to have some money for the future," she pleaded. She was farsighted; already there were three children, and she and Malcolm planned on several more. But Malcolm hushed her. Allah would provide. And faith in His Messenger, Malcolm said, was the only safety net they needed. (The Movement even forbade him from buying life insurance, Betty later said.)

The couple had their arguments, but nothing would cause more friction between the two than his refusal to tuck something away for the family. According to Malcolm, the couple warred over the issue—"the only domestic quarrel that I have ever had with my beloved wife"—so furiously that it almost wrecked the marriage. "We nearly broke up," he later recalled. But he never budged. "I knew I had in Betty a wife who would sacrifice her life for me," he later said. He insisted, however, that "too many organizations had been destroyed by leaders who tried to benefit personally, often goaded into it by their wives." Malcolm claimed to have convinced Betty that the Nation would look after her for life and provide for the children until they were grown, should he fall in combat. She later told a confidante, though, that the debate smoldered on. In the coming months, life only grew more complicated for her and Malcolm, and more clashes lay ahead.

One argument may have flared in spring 1963, when Elijah Muhammad sent Malcolm to Washington, D.C., to assume the ministry of the city's floundering mosque. Malcolm was still heading the Harlem parish, but he declined to move his family to the capital, where he was spending a good deal of time. Betty was not happy about her husband's increased absences and burden. (His Harlem pastorate and national duties had already overtaxed him and the family.) However, the great source of unrest in their home at the time was not Malcolm's short-lived Washington assignment; it was his general myopia.

Malcolm's intuitive powers dazzled his aides. "Sometimes he was so perceptive I'd say, 'Damn, how did he figure this out?'" Razzaq would recall. Malcolm often described how he had exploited his "quick picking up" talents on the street and honed them in jail. "Girl," he once told Betty, "when I was in prison, there was so much time that if a fly flew through a window, you would not say, 'the fly flew through the window,' you would say, 'the fly flew through the lower right-hand quadrant and landed on its front legs.'"

Betty wondered how a man so keen could be so maddeningly daft. In the years that devotion blinded him most powerfully to Black Islam's deformity, she realized better than anyone that he was missing the clues, that he was simply making too little of his growing disfavor among the Chicago elite. Malcolm's shortsightedness was not unfathomable. A confluence of forces finally knocked the minister from his pulpit, and his own success doomed him. Betty had long recognized the kingdom's jealousies and corruption, but a thin line separated counsel from sedition in Malcolm's household.

Observers within and outside the sect, however, had begun to detect in the Chicago palace a growing resentment toward the minister. Malcolm's celebrity in the media and the college lecture halls had overshadowed Muhammad and his golden theocrats. A major publisher had contracted Malcolm to produce an "as-told-to" autobiography with Alex Haley. At a time when Muhammad's health was withering, Malcolm's status as the elder's logical successor also fanned the pyre of envy. "He had got to a place where he was more high profile," Kenyatta later remembered. "And all the old crows wanted that front row."

There were further strains on Malcolm's ministry. The Nation was hemorrhaging. Some of the defectors were quitting the Spartan lifestyle, but others were fleeing in the face of profiteering, corruption, and even fratricide. What's more, the gulch between the tactical accommodationism of the movement's old guard and the militant ambitions of its new generation was expanding.

To make matters worse, the press reported that American Nazi Party leader George Lincoln Rockwell had attended Muslim rallies. Despite Malcolm's halfhearted "at-least-he-practices-what-he-preaches" defense, many blacks saw a treasonous willingness to sit down with professed white racists. (After his schism with Muhammad, Malcolm revealed that he had traveled into the South in 1961 to parley with the Ku Klux Klan, seeking cooperation and aid for the Nation's goal of a separate black republic.)

Meanwhile, the minister's own doubts and aggravations festered. Though he had long recognized some of the glaring incongruities between orthodox Islam and the religion Muhammad had midwifed, disguising or explaining away the discrepancies was an increasingly awkward task. Then there were the spies. Agents from the FBI and New York City Police Department routinely monitored the Nation, mounting counter-intelligence campaigns to try to fracture or neutralize the movement and discredit Muhammad and his cadre.

Malcolm's pulpit might have survived these and other stresses, had the dark revolution not overtaken him. By 1963, the freedom struggle had permanently damaged America's institutions of oppression, and young blacks were swelling with audacity. Negroes were promising to become something infinitely greater than they had been just yesterday—or certainly more militant—and Malcolm wanted desperately to help conduct the transformation.

The problem, of course, was that he had always fulminated from the margins of black protest. He was a genius when it came to undressing the hypocrisy and pretensions of black leadership and spotlighting the vanities in their liberation strategies and visions. He was brilliant as an incendiary, a tom-tom to rouse the people. But he was weak on workable solutions.

The Civil Rights leaders, on the other hand, were handing their people victories, piecemeal and symbolic as they might have been. Though his nonviolent soldiers had been bloodied and jailed in droves, King was toppling segregation in Birmingham. The Muslim demands had always seemed rather metaphorical. Now there was new action in the streets, and the zeitgeist threatened to doom to irrelevance any Negro who would be satisfied to call for Uncle Sam to surrender a chunk of earth and a quarter century worth of cash and technical support so that they could go it on their own.

Malcolm still sang strains of that song. He was still demanding land, regurgitating the Muslim dogma and revelations as if by rote, and exalting Muhammad. He still sneered at nonviolence as a tactic and integration as an aim, dismissing the Negro establishment and Civil Rights legislation as disingenuous and flimsy. But he was evolving. Black protest was moving him more powerfully than Black Islam. He was engaging the integrationists without joining them and coming to see himself as an unofficial actor in the Civil Rights melo-drama. In his labor to convert the freedom fight to "true" revolu-tion—one seeking land and sovereignty by any means—he was politicizing his church.

Malcolm flayed John F. Kennedy for bungling Birmingham. "President Kennedy did not send troops to Alabama when dogs were biting black babies," he charged. "He waited three weeks until the sit-uation exploded...then sent troops after the Negroes had demon-strated their ability to defend themselves." He made fragile gestures toward a united black front. That summer he organized a morality rally on a Harlem turf notorious for dope, gambling, and prostitution, invit-ing Roy Wilkins, Martin Luther King Jr., James Farmer, and Whitney Young to see "the real mood of the black masses and get back in touch with their own people before it is too late." A couple of weeks later, he called for an internal caucus of black leaders, suggesting that they could foil the white man's divisive schemes by huddling in a backroom and hammering out their disagreements.

Then, one quarter million protesters marched on Washington, D.C., for jobs and freedom. For King and the Civil Rights struggle, it was a glittering and transcendent moment; for Malcolm, it was a fiasco. Malcolm forbade his people from attending the "picnic," but went to the National Mall himself and bristled at its edges. Later he jeered. "What is this so-called Negro revolution?" he demanded. "Is that what you call Uncle Tommin' in Washington...walkin' up and down between two dead presidents [the Lincoln and Washington Memorials] while the live president sits up there behind closed doors rockin' in his chair?...The white man told you what time to be there...where to march...and then told you to get out of town by sundown!"

Brooklyn activist Herman Ferguson, who met Malcolm that year, later came to accept the minister's charge that the whole affair had been a farce, that the White House and a gentrified lineup of Negro leaders had controlled what might have been a gnashing deluge of revolutionaries. As Ferguson mingled with the grassroots in Queens hours before the march, the mood had been decidedly militant. "Some wanted to take their pistols down to Washington," he later recalled. But when he and his comrades reached the capital, they met a tranquil salt-and-pepper sea and a poignant but safely scripted pageant. "The bus we had chartered told us, 'You got to be out of here at six o'clock,'" he remembered. "At five o'clock everybody made toward the bus. At six everybody disappeared, like a huge vacuum cleaner had sucked all those people out."

Malcolm hissed at the march. But he had shown up, he confessed, because he wanted to be—*had* to be—wherever black people were moving. He kept making overtures toward solidarity with the Civil Rights generals, though he could not strategize with them from behind Muhammad's psychological barracks. Muhammad, sticking to the creed of nonengagement that kept the laity even from casting ballots, had prohibited his ministers from joining or backing Civil Rights demonstrations. And though he had earlier marched brazenly through Times Square against police harassment and brutality, Malcolm submitted.

Malcolm had taken to stalking the peripheries of picket lines, powerless to do anything but heckle while his men peddled newspapers. Even then his rhetoric and secular advances were chafing the temple foundations. Even then the noose was drawing tight. But Malcolm would no longer be content to sit and wait for the fall of the West.

Few outsiders could have appreciated the complexity of Betty's predicaments. She had been the society darling and obedient schoolgirl before passing into the subterranean world of Black Islam. She had lost her heart to an evangelist and become wife and first lady. She had been dutifully mute and reserved on many occasions, and self-willed, defiant, or downright ornery on others. She had struggled to carve a niche for her personality and talents within a demanding marriage and a society so ironclad that it cast at least one woman back into the "wilderness" for the sin of cooking with fatback meat.

Along the way she had shown signs of loneliness. Her daughters had kept her company while her husband was away, but one yearns for and needs adult communion. Former congregant Jean Reynolds remembered that Betty, often cool to the Nation sisters in the austere setting of the temple, once spotted Reynolds and her husband at a restaurant and just about "broke her neck coming over to speak." Later, an unescorted Betty asked Reynolds to join her car in a Muslim funeral procession.

There had been blissful moments with Malcolm and the girls, but there had been moments of terror, too. And even as Malcolm's celebrity had risen, his rhetoric and reputation had quarantined Betty from whatever constituted respectability in the outside world. "You got to appreciate that in those days very few people wanted to identify with Betty and Minister Malcolm," Percy Sutton later said. "They were frightened."

By 1963, mounting pressures were tearing new fissures in the marriage. Malcolm had taken to sleeping more frequently in his attic office, and some of his aides thought Betty often seemed "hot" with him. A lanyard of challenges had left the twenty-nine-year-old acutely more aware of danger, deceit, and the harsh realities of liberation struggle than she had been at twenty-three. She watched warily from home as an insistent world tugged Malcolm away from Black Islam.

Malcolm was a champion of the grassroots. He spoke about the house and field Negroes of the Antebellum South—the first privileged and servile, the second tattered and subversive—and suggested that the quest for freedom and manhood was still a bout between the two. He painted the black bourgeoisie as shot through with turncoats. Yet by the early 1960s, his outreach to the more progressive thinkers of the black establishment (and vice versa) had yielded a web of relationships.

He met and befriended writers John Killens and James Baldwin; Harlem Congressman Adam Clayton Powell; historian John Henrik Clarke; actors Ossie Davis, Ruby Dee, and Sidney Poitier; psychologist

Kenneth B. Clark; Civil Rights leader James Farmer; and a host of distinguished others. He disarmed them with his enameled gash of a grin and his charm and roving mind; he drew them into intellectual jousts over black or integrated coffee in apartments and cafés and on platforms; he sampled their societies of ideas and coalitions.

Some of them winked at his genuflection to Muhammad. But until the late hours of the hostilities, Malcolm never so much as paused during his private odes to the man who had resurrected him. Comedian Dick Gregory, who generally cleaned up his cussing and woman talk when the minister came around, once suggested backstage at Harlem's Apollo Theater that Muhammad was nothing but a pimp. Malcolm, who in his soul had never been a violent man, instantly clenched to unleash on his friend. "He was smokin'," Kenyatta recalled. The "blasphemy" went unpunished; too much doubt had already crept into the minister's head.

Malcolm had actually been venturing beyond Black Islam's tent for years to whet his mind among intellectuals and artists. The cross-fertilization seldom nurtured Betty, though. By late 1963, she was pregnant again and consumed with her trio of girls, to say nothing of the anxieties pressing her and Malcolm. She could no more accompany the minister on his ecumenical rounds than she could join the rap sessions about black resistance that often held him into the late evening. She "wanted to meet all of Malcolm's contacts," Kenyatta later said. Betty would in coming months mingle superficially with such personalities as Clarke and Lewis Michaux, the grandfather of Harlem nationalists and owner of the National Memorial African Bookstore. Even this glancing exposure to some of the minister's cronies exhilarated her.

One such comrade was Cassius Clay. In 1962, Malcolm came home talking about a young fighter who had turned up at Muslim meetings in various cities. The minister saw a glorious destiny for the kid, as he had for Minister Louis X, and had adopted Clay as a pupil and friend. "Malcolm accepted Cassius and loved him like a younger brother," Betty later recalled. "He felt his job was to get this young man to believe in himself and stand squarely on both feet with his shoulders back." Malcolm "did not have an intimate relationship with that many people," Betty would insist. Malcolm later acknowledged that "some contagious quality" about Clay made him "one of the very few people I ever invited to my home." The ebullient heavyweight enchanted Betty and the children, and she was pleased to learn later that he had joined their Nation.

She was equally delighted when Alex Haley entered the scene. He had a few articles about the Nation already under his belt, including an interview with Malcolm for *Playboy* that had fueled the minister's fame, especially on college campuses. In 1963, the journalist was commissioned to write Malcolm's life and found himself sitting across from the granite-faced leader in a Greenwich Village studio, trying less than fruitfully to win his confidence.

Betty shared some of her husband's early suspicions of Haley, but to her the newsman also seemed splendidly cosmopolitan. He blew in and out of town on writing assignments, booking hotel rooms for what she imagined were weeks on end. He regularly fraternized with society blacks. He was the sort of black man, she later recalled, that white people seemed to consider benign. His sheer access fascinated her. He was much closer to the type with whom she had hobnobbed in college than the Muslims who now comprised her social pool. "I thought, 'God, you know, this is a man of the world,'" she later remembered.

Though less dazzled than his wife, Malcolm also warmed to Haley as the weeks passed. Their frequent meetings were soon yielding the meandering soliloquies and narratives from which the autobiography would evolve. Eventually Betty and the journalist established a "telephone acquaintance." He became her periscope to an urbane, secular scene; she, bright and inquisitive as ever, charmed him. Haley later recalled with admiration how Betty "ran a home with, then, three small daughters, and still managed to take all of the calls which came for Malcolm X, surely as many calls as would provide a job for an average switchboard operator." In time, he became one of the few souls in whom she confided some of her frustrations with Malcolm. During one of their conversations, she exclaimed abruptly, "The man never gets any *sleep!*"

Betty and Haley would telephone one another for more than a year before they met face to face. When she first told her husband that she and the journalist had begun chatting regularly, the minister bristled. "What are you talking about?" he demanded. "Well," Betty replied, "we talk about you." After she explained the nature of her and Haley's relationship, Malcolm consented to the conversations. When he ventured overseas in 1964, he asked Haley as a personal favor to call and check on her regularly, Betty later said. Malcolm rarely granted such liberties, and Haley must have considered the request a vindication. As Betty herself would observe, the writer "would never have been around me if my husband felt that he was in any way hostile."

———

Brushing with her husband's comrades seasoned Betty's intellectual and social life, but hardly sweetened the time. Malcolm's ministry was crumbling, his faith was slowly unraveling, and confusion was overtaking the couple's once ordered world.

In late 1962, the minister had gotten hard evidence that something was amiss—a possibility that Betty had tried to nudge him toward even earlier—when he discovered that Herbert, one of Muhammad's sons, had commanded *Muhammad Speaks* staff writers to start pruning him from the tabloid's pages. "Them songs wasn't being sung no more," Kenyatta later remembered. Malcolm had long sensed envy from the royal court. He knew that some of his colleagues had been quietly accusing him of empire building; it was an eventuality Muhammad had himself anticipated years before when he prophesied the minister's fame.

Malcolm later claimed that he tried to quell the envy by dimming his own star. He began refusing the sort of high-profile interviews that had made him a media fixture. Still he felt a chill from some of the Chicago courtiers. The taut faces and whispers baffled him. He had given his life to Muhammad. Once the kingdom had begun to thrive, he'd even seen that the elder's eight children—most of whom were languishing or toiling humbly for white society—were arrayed in high positions around the throne. None of this had spared him from the gnawing gears of Nation politics.

Betty later suggested that her husband had misjudged the royal sons. "Perhaps these men were in menial jobs because they didn't have the ability to do anything else," she said. "Malcolm used to say one of the worst things to do is to give an ignorant man power, but he never applied the rule to Elijah Muhammad's family." The minister had indeed gotten close to Wallace Muhammad, one of the elder's most gifted sons and a man similarly conflicted by the sins of the Movement and its despot. Wallace, internally the Movement's heir apparent, confided in and sympathized with Malcolm. He would soon renounce the cult. But he returned to Muhammad in the end, and Betty never forgot it.

Royal blood was not the only type souring. Malcolm had come to suspect that National Secretary John Ali, Fruit of Islam Supreme Captain Raymond Sharrieff, Captain Joseph of his own parish, his favorite understudy Minister Louis X, and other well-placed clerics and functionaries—many of whom he himself had recruited—had forsaken him. "He didn't see it at the time," Betty would recall. "But he had a hand in setting up his own doom through the very people he helped."

One's own doom is always difficult to forecast, especially when one is a zealot. Muhammad anointed Malcolm his first national minister in 1963, expanding his duties and praising him publicly as he had none of his other servants. Goaded by members of his family and entourage, however, the elder even then fretted privately that Malcolm's celebrity was ballooning out of control and that his activism was imperiling the kingdom.

Betty later recalled that informers had told her husband as early as 1962 that Chicago was out to unseat him. Malcolm would hear none of it. He was no Brutus, no Doubting Thomas. He convinced himself that white men or black stooges out to sabotage the movement were behind the heretical voices. Meanwhile, Betty was facing a crisis of influence. She had always queued up for Malcolm's attention and affection. Now that their universe seemed to be coming unhinged, she would have to vie even more frantically for his ear.

The ultimate contender was Muhammad, who still had a vice grip on Malcolm; the runner-up was also powerful. Malcolm bragged that his half-sister Ella Collins had "broken the spirits of three husbands." She was "more driving and dynamic than all of them combined," he insisted. Despite his misgivings about the feminine condition, he regularly sought Collins's counsel. "No other woman ever was strong enough to point me in directions; I pointed women in directions," he said.

Not surprisingly, Betty and Collins clashed from the start. The minister entrusted his half-sister with his deepest hopes and fears. Collins later acknowledged that he regularly confided in Betty, too, especially during trying times. But Betty did not have the influence over him that the older woman did. "Betty felt that Ella was leading Malcolm," Kenyatta later said. Both women wanted the minister to take better care of himself physically and financially. Yet in coming months, their visions for Malcolm's future would collide even more thunderously.

The Muslims' puritanism had won a solid street reputation. Once, a certain Harlem woman took it upon herself to test their restraint. She approached a parishioner hawking newspapers on the corner one afternoon and struck up a conversation. He managed only feeble protests when she invited him back to her place. Some time had passed when the telephone at the Muslim restaurant rang. It was the woman. "You all talkin' bout you 'gods,'" she whispered triumphantly. "Come up here and look—I got one of you gods in my bed." As the story goes, the man awoke to the sight of Captain Joseph's forbidding mug. "As-salaam alaikum, Brother!" he cried pitifully.

Malcolm always fended off such come-ons. "I must be purer than Caesar's wife," he often said. Ferguson swore years later that he had never met another man with Malcolm's looks, charm, and incorruptibility. The minister would simply pour more hellfire into his gospel when women tried to bait him, his disciple Osman Karriem later remembered. "That was his way of dealing with temptation," Karriem said.

For years, Malcolm could not conceive of his idol violating the moral code he stuck to so earnestly. Amid the tensions of 1963, however, tales of Muhammad's philandering began to quicken, and Malcolm began to listen. The rumble was that Muhammad had made a harem of his personal coterie of young Muslim secretaries. After several of them had gotten pregnant, they had been brought individually before an internal court, charged with adultery, and sentenced to isolation.

In late 1962, Malcolm discovered that the scandal had driven waves of believers from the Chicago mosque. He later sought out the secretaries and then Wallace Muhammad, all of whom confirmed the stories. Then, in April 1963, he flew to Phoenix and confronted Muhammad. The elder confessed. But the misdeeds, he told Malcolm, were the fulfillment of prophecy. The Bible had chronicled David's adultery, Noah's drunkenness, and Lot's incest, Muhammad said. He, too, must sin before fulfilling his divine purpose.

Malcolm was shattered. He telephoned Betty from Chicago after encountering some of Muhammad's mistresses and illegitimate children outside the royal mansion. "The foundation of my life seems to be coming apart," he told her. "Why are you saying that?" she asked. "I'm all right—the children are all right." The minister only sighed. "Oh, honey," he said. "I'll talk to you when I see you."

Betty probably had a good idea what was tormenting her husband. As early as 1957, she had suspected that Muhammad was less than self-denying. She had come to believe, in fact, that the "Dear Holy Apostle" was keeping a lascivious eye on her. By the early 1960s, she was well-connected to the Chicago scene, and as Sister Khadiyyah remembered, close to women "who would have known" about the bacchanalia.

Malcolm himself had heard murmurs since 1955, but entertaining even the possibility of a chink in Muhammad's character had been unspeakable. For a decade, he had considered Muhammad a "little lamb without spots or blemishes." He had taught and believed that Allah had overhauled the elder's heart. Only when the prospect of Muhammad's susceptibility finally struck him, Betty later recalled, did

Malcolm begin to heed years of innuendo that he had simply "put out of his mind." The minister joked in his last year about having once considered Muhammad's purity his own moral keel. "Elijah Muhammad really did have him fooled," Betty remembered. The revelation was far from laughable in the closing months of 1963. This was the start of the nightmare, and there were moments when Malcolm thought he might be cracking.

For a time, he discussed Muhammad's indecorum only with his wife. He soon decided that to save the kingdom and its monarch from a possibly deadly epidemic, he would have to immunize his colleagues. He was still in a haze when he gave a handful of east coast ministers and officials the sordid details, explaining that he was only sharing the information to keep them from a blindsiding once word got out. Within the loop were Captain Joseph and Minister Louis X, who, according to Malcolm, announced that he had known for some time about Muhammad's improprieties.

Passing the news about the royal philandering turned out to be a ruinous blunder for Malcolm. When Malcolm earlier began vaccinating his flock against the scandal, Razzaq remembered clearly how the minister reworked his message:

> The Nation had always taught that no prophet can do anything wrong. The prophet is imbued with the spirit of God. And he cannot do criminal things, immoral things. They said the Bible had prophets doing all kinds of crazy things that are wrong. They said that was put into the Bible. But they said the Qur'an is purified. Then lo and behold, Malcolm started teaching the opposite. He said, "Oh, the way you measure a man is in the balance. If he is a good man that does some bad but does more good, then he is good in the balance." I said, "This is not what he was teaching before. He must be trying to protect somebody. But who?"

Black Islam was unambiguous. It arrayed its fraternal wisdom in numbered catechisms for the faithful to memorize. It dazzled converts with the promise of divine retribution raining from outer space at a black god's command. Kenyatta later remembered sitting around for hours sucking down black coffee and pondering the "End of Days." "Brothers' minds would shoot up to the sky!" he said.

The flip side of that mysticism was cold discipline and militancy; Malcolm's lay photographer, Robert Haggins, was amazed to learn how quickly a few phone calls could summon five hundred or one thousand believers to the street. Nationally, however, the movement tended more toward internal terrorism than race war. It trained men to take heads. But when all was said and done, they mostly manhandled each other.

Well before Malcolm's slide from grace, there were signs that the laity had gotten crowded with toughs who were willing to uphold Muhammad's mandates with fists or lengths of pipe. "The story has never been told how many brothers lost they life," Kenyatta later declared. The aide remembered one would-be defector who privately acknowledged that he was too scared to leave. "You think I'm gon' fight against God?" the man once exclaimed. "I'm not gon' let nobody put my feet up on the sidewalk and break my legs!"

Betty knew that the Nation did not deal gently with apostates. Malcolm himself had enforced absolute obedience to Muhammad and his laws, sometimes with the help of tough six-footers. None of the minister's close subordinates were tenderhearted. ("Don't be tryin' to play me for no damn fool," Razzaq told him during one tense hour. "Don't chump me once, 'cause I'll kill you.") Now that Malcolm's pulpit was skidding and Chicago seemed to be turning against him, Betty began mulling the possibility that one or more of the believers might someday do him bodily harm.

For the moment, though, it was his spiritual and emotional health that most worried her. In the months after he had discovered Muhammad's ungodliness, Malcolm had grown increasingly haggard and heartsick. He told Kenyatta that he was "losing his religion." Knowing the profundity of Malcolm's devotion, the aide was stunned. Betty may have understood the depth of the minister's anguish better than anyone. But for all her psychiatric nurse's training, she could not console him.

As dark waters buffeted the Muslims, Black America took a gruesome hit. That September, a bomb exploded in Birmingham's Sixteenth Street Baptist Church, obliterating four black girls as they prepared for Sunday school. The carnage touched off bloody rioting, sapping the afterglow of the March on Washington and Negro support for nonviolence in general.

Malcolm would soon suffer a spiritual blast of his own. Louis X had relayed tidings of the minister's scandal-mongering to headquarters. The Chicago hierarchs, having disowned Malcolm, were moving to upend him. Fearing that he might be losing control of the kingdom, Muhammad furiously rebuked the minister whom he had only months earlier hailed as his beloved servant.

Thus Malcolm was already reeling when Muhammad ducked out of an early December rally at New York's Manhattan Center and authorized him to speak in his stead. Razzaq watched the minister carefully script his remarks for the occasion. He could see Malcolm's relationship with his idol unraveling. "I'm writing this down," the minister told Razzaq. "Because I'm not speaking for me; I'm speaking for the man." On the day of the rally, a few white reporters showed up. Malcolm told Razzaq to admit them but to turn away any others, as Muhammad had recently banned whites from Muslim meetings. Then the occasion was underway, and the minister was prophesizing America's doom in a typical harangue. When Malcolm opened the floor for questions, however, someone asked for his reaction to the death of President Kennedy, who had been assassinated in Dallas a week before.

Malcolm had always denounced Kennedy as a hypocrite. This day was to be no exception. He accused the fallen president of "twiddling his thumbs" at the killing of the South Vietnamese President Ngo Dinh Diem, the Congo's Patrice Lumumba, Medgar Evers, and the four casualties of the Birmingham church bombing. Kennedy's death, he said, was a case of the "chickens coming home to roost." The minister continued amid the believers' laughter and applause: "Being an old farm boy myself, chickens coming home to roost never did make me sad; they've always made me glad."

The "chickens" crack made a *New York Times* headline the next day. Malcolm would complain that the newsmen had taken the remark out of context. He had not meant to dance on the president's grave, he later explained, only to illustrate that as you sow so shall you reap— that America had nurtured the very climate of hate and violence that had finally claimed its chief commander.

Chicago was irate; Muhammad had forbidden his ministers to discuss Kennedy's death. Now the elder summoned his national spokesman to headquarters and scolded him. The president was well loved, Muhammad said. Malcolm's comment had been ill timed and had hurt the kingdom. To avoid further damage and to distance the organization from the gaffe, Muhammad announced, he would have to silence the minister for ninety days. Malcolm could continue to take the rostrum in Temple Number Seven and run the mosque's daily affairs, but public speaking was out until early March.

—◆—

Malcolm returned to Betty in a daze. The couple concluded that the suspension was inevitable; she may have been convinced almost immediately and he certainly suspected within days. Betty later insisted that had the gag order not followed the Kennedy quip, it would have resulted from some other triviality. However, in the minutes after Malcolm first came through the door—weary, confused, and nearly blind with disbelief—neither he nor his wife could manage any such clarity.

One can only guess what mood dominated the home. Perhaps Betty and the minister prayed or held each other as the children slept. Perhaps they argued. She had tried for years to show him some of the dangers of Muhammad's hypnosis. Now he had submitted humbly to a muzzling; he had not even had the good sense to get angry! But she must also have tried to soothe him, and he to reassure her. And tears were shed; Betty sounded choked up when—after several rings—she finally answered Haley's phone call around nine the following morning.

Before long, the telephone was ringing nonstop and the minister was telling reporters contritely that he should never have run his mouth about Kennedy's death. "Anything Mr. Muhammad does is all right with me," he said. "I believe absolutely in his wisdom and author-ity." Meanwhile, Muhammad, who had never offered America and her politicians anything but spite, was backing away from the "chickens" remark. "We are very shocked at the assassination of our president," he told the press, adding that he had rebuked the minister because "he has not followed the way of Islam."

Malcolm was confused and heartsick, but his devotion to the church and its head endured. Betty's churchly loyalty, however, was dying fast. Her thoughts kept returning to the darkest clues Malcolm had ignored and to the insiders who had told him that they had over-heard noxious whispers in recent years: *We are going to get rid of him whenever we can.* Every day, Betty's fears seemed more valid. Within a week, speculation about Malcolm's ouster as the Harlem minister hit the daily newspapers. Malcolm denied the rumors. "I shall be carrying out my responsibilities for the mosque whatever they may entail," he said. But when he learned that he had been forbidden to teach even in his own temple, he could no longer ignore the feeling that he had been hustled.

The whole affair seemed wrong to Razzaq, too. Muhammad had always taught that the white man was Satan. How could he now swat his spokesman for acknowledging that the West was minus one more devil, and that it was its own wicked fault? "That's weird," Razzaq thought. But he didn't dwell on it; the suspension was only temporary. Then the gossip among the Original People got ugly. "The brothers started talking about 'you have to watch Malcolm,'" Kenyatta would remember. "They said 'he's like [the Biblical] Aaron—he's going to set up the golden calf.'" The tales multiplied. "A lie was being spread that Malcolm had put his hands under the table to feel on a sister in the restaurant," Kenyatta later said. The talk appalled Razzaq. "Brothers who had been almost worshipping him started talking 'bout, 'Kill Red—he never was with the Messenger," he recalled.

One evening in that time of disintegration, Betty answered the telephone and heard Razzaq's familiar voice. She greeted him, "As-salaam alaikum, Brother," and started to fetch the minister. But the aide spoke directly to her. "Tell my big brother I said be careful," he said. She suspected by then what this meant. "Do you want to speak to him?" she asked anxiously. Razzaq said he did not; Muslim law precluded the faithful from talking to isolated congregants. It was as if those Black Islam had convicted dangled between paradise and the grave.

Something vile was rising. Razzaq called and warned Betty a second time days later, again declining to speak to Malcolm. By the third call, the aide's voice was tinseled with stress. He named the Muslims who had been openly damning the minister. "This is serious," he told Betty. Malcolm grabbed the phone. "Listen, Brother," he growled, "if you got something to say to me, say it. What you mean, 'Be careful?'" There was a pause. Finally the reply came: "They talkin' 'bout killin' you, Brother."

Chapter Eight

REVELATIONS

—

"I never had a moment's question that Betty,
after initial amazement, would change her thinking to join mine."
—Malcolm X

M alcolm played down some of the omens in the early days of his suspension. "I'm no Sunday Muslim," he scoffed during Razzaq's last panicked telephone call. He had spent a dozen years following Allah and His Prophet, he told the sideman. He had given his heart and soul to the Movement, and he was not going to backslide now. Later, he and Razzaq met in Morningside Park and talked for two or three hours in the shadows. The minister seemed unsettled but far from distraught. "I don't think he had given up," Razzaq remembered.

Betty saw a more frantic Malcolm. He was "always under a great deal of stress," she later said. Muhammad upbraided him for meddling in royal affairs and accused him of seeking the throne. "How could you take this poison and pour it all over my people?" the elder erupted during one phone conversation. "Messenger," Malcolm meekly replied, "I'd rather be dead than say anything against you." The minister later appeared at the winter manor in Phoenix for an irregular, closed-door hearing before a panel of Muhammad's courtiers. Among them were his known foes John Ali and Raymond Sharrieff. "Son," Muhammad told him that evening, "I want you to go back and put out that fire you started."

Meanwhile, Betty continued to worship at the Harlem temple, probably as a show of loyalty and perhaps at her husband's behest.

Mosque officials were soon alluding to Malcolm's heresy and teaching that hypocrites must perish. The parishioners could not have openly shunned Betty simply because her husband was now *persona non grata*; she remained officially in good standing. This did not stifle the whispers. Once the locus of her spiritual and social life, Temple Number Seven now crackled with hostility.

Her attendance eventually petered off, but she found no relief at home. Under the strain of enforced idleness, Malcolm was as testy as a snared mink by January 1964. He brooded and bristled, the color of his neck betraying his torment. Though Betty was three months pregnant with her fourth child, he had yet to begin his usual coddling. Alex Haley sensed that the minister was suffering. "Knowing his temperament, my sympathies went out to Sister Betty," he later remembered.

The nightmare burgeoned. Chicago announced to the body that it would unmuzzle Malcolm once he had submitted. "But I *already* submitted," he complained privately. The spies wanted him to bow, too. In mid January, two FBI agents visited him at home and tried to recruit him as an informant. (The FBI had secretly aggravated the Muslim schism that had led to his disfavor among the Original People.) After the agents suggested that his cooperation would yield a lucrative *quid pro quo*, the minister tossed them out. "A lot of money and other things were offered to him," Betty would remember, "and he felt that was not what he was about."

Then came the word that one of his underlings at the mosque had been telling believers that, "If you knew what the minister did, you'd go out and kill him yourself." It struck Malcolm that such talk would be impossible without the knowledge and consent of Muhammad himself. The realization nearly wrecked him; he began to suspect that his brain was literally bleeding. "He was being punished because somebody else had been discovered to be living wrong—not for one or two years, but for the span of the Movement," Betty later said. The minister began weighing the possibility that his almost sixteen-year relationship with his master had been symbiotic. "I was going downhill before he picked me up," he scribbled in Haley's flat, "but the more I think of it, we picked each other up." He had a distance to stagger yet, however, before he would outright deny Muhammad's divinity. "He was still willing to do his bidding," Betty recalled.

The lingering loyalty might have sparked more feuds at home, and the minister's nerves might have frayed irreparably were it not for the Louisville Lip. As a sixth wedding anniversary present to Malcolm and Betty, Cassius Clay invited the family to visit him in Miami, where he was training for his upcoming heavyweight championship bout with Sonny Liston. Glad to escape the clamoring telephones and tensions of the New York scene, Malcolm accepted. On January 16, he, Betty, and the girls went to Florida on Clay's dime.

Betty had not traveled with Malcolm in some time, much less with the entire family. This was to be the couple's first vacation; they called it their "honeymoon." The plane touched down, and the children were soon tumbling against the slabs Clay passed off as arms. Despite the trouble brewing back in New York, Betty slackened as she stepped onto the tarmac and tasted the moist air, her head draped in a scarf. For months she had felt powerless to ease Malcolm's strain. Maybe he would now get the rest she and his doctor had prescribed. Maybe he would even regroup and discuss their growing family's future.

During the vacation, the girls romped in and around the Negro-clientele Hampton House Motel. The older two had lately sensed a pall over their Long Island home and welcomed this chance for revelry. Betty glided with the usual Muslim decorum, spending easy hours on the fringe of the fight-camp crowd and time alone with Malcolm. Perhaps she joined him on his walks, hustling to keep up as he pistoned past ficus trees and palms, smiling at his exuberance as he snapped photos, popped peppermints, and freckled under the sun. She might have snickered at the white golfers and tourists who gawked and craned to see "if he had horns."

Spiritually, though, he was elsewhere, and she knew it. He chatted with her, but he was only mouthing words. His mind was in Chicago. His heart was with the Old Man. Even in sun-drenched South Florida, he felt like an expatriate, a son in exile. Publicly he had insisted that Muhammad could switch him off and on as he pleased, like a radio. But he was struggling even then to confront what his soul already knew:

the Messenger had discarded him. "I was like someone who for twelve years had had an inseparable, beautiful marriage—and then suddenly one morning at breakfast the marriage partner had thrust across the table some divorce papers," he later remembered.

Malcolm abruptly ended the Miami "honeymoon," sending Betty and the girls back to New York three days after they had arrived. He spent much of the next few weeks at Clay's side, a presence newsmen duly footnoted, one writer would remember, as "some black Svengali filling Cassius's ingenuous young head with Allah-knows-what." Before the press and his admirers, the fighter inevitably did his crazed burlesque, mugging and clowning and bellowing and strutting. He was the greatest, he bawled—the prettiest. And he was gonna whup that old Liston, that ugly bear. Privately Clay was hysterical with fear. Only Malcolm shored him up, convincing him that Allah was in his corner. "They talked constantly about how David slew Goliath, and how God would not allow someone who believed in him to fail, regardless of how powerful the opponent was," Betty later said.

Malcolm was ringside on February 25, 1964, when Clay defeated the heavily favored Liston. Though Clay had joined the Muslim fold much earlier, the Chicago theocrats had refrained from openly embracing him; like virtually everyone else, they figured that the loudmouth would be soundly defeated. When Clay took the belt, they flipped the script. "All of a sudden," Betty remembered acidly, "they were breaking their necks trying to get close to the heavyweight champion."

Within days, Clay announced that he had converted to Black Islam. Soon he was singing his new name: Muhammad Ali. The kid from Louisville idolized and adored Malcolm, but he belonged to the Messenger now, and his relationship with the minister could only wither. Ali would snub Malcolm several times in coming months, ultimately joining the Muslim chorus by cursing him publicly. "Mr. Muhammad will destroy him through Allah," he predicted later that year. "You just don't buck Mr. Muhammad and get away with it." In early 1965, he told a two thousand–strong Muslim audience that, "Malcolm believed the white press which referred to him as the 'number two man' and became disillusioned."

The most stinging rebuke occurred in Ghana in May 1964. Ali and his entourage happened upon the minister and a clique of his supporters in a hotel parking lot. When Malcolm, full of boyish exuberance, hailed Ali, with whom he had originally planned to tour Africa, the fighter shunned him. In early February 1965, as hostilities between Black Muslims and the ousted evangelist boiled, Betty herself ran into Ali inside the door of Harlem's Hotel Theresa. "You see what you're doing to my husband, don't you?" she demanded. Ali put up his hands. "I haven't done anything," he said. "I'm not doing anything to him."

For more than a dozen years, Malcolm's *raison d'être* had been black freedom. That much would not change. But by February 1964, even a casual observer could see that his bedrock was melting. Chicago headquarters delivered a smarting backhand by barring him from the Savior's Day festivities, the highlight of the Black Muslim calendar. At the Chicago convention, an effulgent Louis X introduced Elijah Muhammad and seemed to settle into Malcolm's seat beside the throne. (Years after he had succeeded Malcolm as the sect's spokesman, the world came to know the artful orator as Louis Farrakhan.) Burning for a chance to answer the false charges against him, Malcolm had demanded a hearing in his home mosque before the congregation, a right of any accused Muslim. Yet Chicago kept putting him off.

As word of the sect's internal "power struggle" spilled onto the pages of the *New York Times* and other newspapers, the minister learned from a close former aide that a Temple Number Seven official had ordered his car wired with a bomb. The aide defied the command and later defected with other would-be assassins, including members of a planned "death squad" that Malcolm managed to convert to his camp. The foiled plot marked the first direct order on the minister's life. He later discovered that temple functionaries had sought a pistol silencer in connection with another assassination scheme. Malcolm also learned that Captain Joseph and other mosque officials were fueling rumors that he had finally succumbed to the psychosis that had afflicted his mother and brother Reginald. "Hating me was going to become the cause for people of shattered faith to rally around," he later recalled.

Malcolm thought the talk about a power struggle between him and Muhammad inane—one does not pull a power move on Allah's Messenger. The minister's struggle was actually for his own equilibrium and future. Everywhere he went he saw old comrades, Muslims who had once saluted him as their warrior-prince. They now glowered or dropped their eyes and hustled off. Since December, he had showered Muhammad with letters, bargaining and begging for reinstatement like a scorned lover. Finally, in the crescendo of murder plots and smears, he sunk to a more reckless tactic.

Looking to publicly expose the root of his undoing, Malcolm dialed up his stable of newsmen and told them about Muhammad's illegitimate children. "I thought it was an imposter on the phone," Claude Lewis later recalled. "It was such an about-face." When the reporters told Malcolm that they could not run the story without hard evidence, Kenyatta remembered, "he had a fit." The orders for his head had staggered him, but it was Chicago's sheer betrayal that threatened to knock him down. Nightmares tormented him; he could feel himself being edged out of paradise. His enemies had convinced Muhammad and a good portion of the body of his treason, and all his thrashings to the contrary had been for naught.

One of the outsiders who intervened on his behalf was Harlem nationalist Lewis Michaux. Michaux begged Muhammad to grant Malcolm a fair hearing, reminding the elder that it was Pontius Pilate's inaction that had enabled the crucifixion. "Minister Malcolm X will have to be judged before he can be condemned, otherwise the condemnation will fall upon his accusers," Michaux proclaimed. But neither biblical appeals for due process nor the minister's maneuvers could seal the abyss yawning at his heels. With what seemed to Malcolm Muhammad's cold indifference or consent, Muslim conspirators continued backing him toward the brink.

As the omens multiplied, Malcolm began hinting publicly at the move he had been discussing with Betty and other intimates. Until recently, leaving Muhammad had been an unspeakable proposition. But as he mulled his predicament and searched for a way to stay on the frontlines of black protest, independence seemed the only option. He was tentatively embracing the "psychological divorce" he had begun to feel viscerally years ago. Without Betty, he acknowledged in his autobiography, the effort might have been wasted. "I never would have dreamed that I would ever depend so much upon any woman for strength as I now leaned upon Betty," he said. "There was no exchange between us; Betty said nothing, being the caliber of wife that she is, with the depth of understanding that she has—but I could feel the envelopment of her comfort. I knew that she was as faithful a servant of Allah as I was, and I knew that whatever happened, she was with me."

Betty never doubted that her husband would return to the struggle. She knew that everything he did publicly and privately was for the cause of black freedom. His gut was echoing what his advisors had told him: "the Old Man ain't gonna let you up on the mountain no more." Then a letter from Chicago all but confirmed just that. There were no tears, Betty later remembered. "He had already begun to set other things in motion," she said. Betty would portray the minister's defection as the culmination of his disgust with Elijah Muhammad's debauchery and the kingdom's corruption. "He wanted no part of it," she said. She admired the courage her husband demonstrated by leaving a world he had helped create. "Whenever he was wrong he would always admit it and go from there," she said. "It never stopped him."

In truth, Malcolm's flight from the Nation was rather less composed. Betty left out how he had pleaded for reinstatement, then snarled that "niggers" had ruined the best organization blacks ever had; or how he had drooped when he learned Muhammad Ali was sticking with Muhammad. She never described how, addled and wounded and mourning the loss of something at least as profound as a father's love, he had sunk into despair. The minister would acknowledge that only his wife knew the depth of his anguish in those days of purgatory. She recalled the time as one of "confusion and reassessment," but she would omit the bitter conversations they had had as he found himself convicted without trial by brothers and sisters they had once known as neighbors, colleagues, and allies, and shoved out of the cloister that they had labored for.

Under different circumstances, the prospect of independence might have thrilled her. Here was her chance to shed the Black Muslim straitjacket. In the early spring of 1964, though, she was far too pregnant and practical for reverie. She knew her husband must escape Black Islam to make his full contribution to the race. She also knew that for her family, apostasy would mean no less uncertainty, and quite possibly more. So she passed the last days of the minister's penance big with child and ambivalence, trying to prepare herself to accompany him beyond the Nation's mystical curtain. She was home waiting on the future when Malcolm, in a March 8 press conference, announced his split with the man he believed had seen God.

In the next few frenetic weeks, the minister tried to both re-create and preserve himself. He assured the world that he was still Muslim and that he still backed Muhammad. He said envy and narrow minds had dislodged him from the Nation, and that he could best spread Muhammad's message working outside the sect and among the masses. He said he would fight *by any means necessary* —a slogan that precluded neither ballots nor bullets—for fair education, housing, and jobs for blacks, but that his priority was human rights, which belonged inalienably to every mortal on the planet.

He wanted to broaden the Civil Rights movement. He still considered integration and bloodless revolution pipe dreams, and vowed to continue converting blacks from nonviolence to active self-defense. But he now called the aims of African repatriation or establishing a separate black territory within the U.S. "long-range," and announced that he would gladly join the racial struggle wherever he was needed. "I am prepared to cooperate in local Civil Rights actions in the South and elsewhere and shall do so because every campaign for specific objectives can only heighten the political consciousness of the Negroes and intensify their identification against white society," he proclaimed.

Malcolm said America's slow racial progress had roiled the black masses, and he predicted a long, hot summer of bloodshed. The coming tumult, he declared, would doom the mainstream Civil Rights struggle and usher in an age of black nationalism. He described himself as an evangelist who would spread the gospel of nationalism across the country, winning black souls for local activist groups. Yet he had already formed his own spiritual base. He announced that his Harlem-headquartered Muslim Mosque, Inc. would practice what the Nation had preached, mobilizing a wide spectrum of blacks under the canopy of Islam. He stressed that the new temple would complement Muhammad's movement, and urged existing Muslims to stay with the Messenger.

Betty eyed Malcolm's transition anxiously, unable to fully share his fervor. Attallah now was five, Qubilah was three, and Ilyasah was almost two. By July, there would be a fourth arrival. The family was limping along on lecture fees, donations, and collections. "The Nation had paid the gas, the car note, the mortgage," Razzaq later said. "What the hell was this man to do with four children?"

Betty had other questions. How could she manage with an even more fatigued husband? How much more lifeblood could he pump into the cause? How would the establishment and the government agents who were forever casing her block respond to this potentially more threatening Malcolm? Then there was the Black Muslim peril. Would the minister's lingering devotion to Muhammad continue to scale his eyes? Days after the split, Malcolm was still exalting Muhammad for "teaching me everything I know and making me what I am," and addressing his former boss in a conciliatory letter as "leader and teacher." "The final cord had yet to be broken," Betty later acknowledged.

Muhammad cried when he learned of the minister's defection, and the next day told reporters he had "never dreamed this man would deviate from the Nation of Islam." The elder was soon condemning his former lieutenant as a mutineer. "There is no weeping or moaning over anyone who leaves Islam," he declared, "as such a man is a deviate or hypocrite, who does not want to live under the guidance of God's

Messenger." Within days, the Muslim Mosque had siphoned off dozens of Temple Number Seven congregants, despite Malcolm's promise not to filch souls from his former church. Meanwhile, Muhammad rejected Malcolm's public testimonies of loyalty. "Whenever a brother walks away from us, all is gone," Muhammad said. "Malcolm's doing more running off at the mouth than he can back up."

The words wounded Malcolm, but never deterred him. "It's hard to make a rooster stop crowing once the sun has risen," he said. He booked a flurry of appearances and again flung himself into the chore that his actor friend Ossie Davis called "twisting the white man's tail." He struck some familiar chords, applying the logic of reciprocal bleeding to police dogs and Klansmen: "Any Negro who is attacked should fight back; if necessary he should be prepared to die like a man, like Patrick Henry." He also escalated his rhetoric of armed self-defense, calling on blacks to form rifle clubs in areas where white brutality threatened life, limb, and property. He had taken to plucking from his breast pocket a card bearing Article II of the Bill of Rights and reciting passages to reporters: "The right of the people to keep and bear arms shall not be infringed." He swore before a gathering of black Methodist clerics that he would get results in 1964, whether it took a political party or an army.

He was growing more politically engaged, lending himself to black Civil Rights causes and courting community leaders such as Harlem rent-strike leader Jesse Gray; Cambridge, Maryland, activist Gloria Richardson; and New York City school boycott organizer Rev. Milton Galamison. He talked about convening a black nationalist convention, launching a black political party, and even organizing a new march on Washington composed of African-America's "uncontrollable elements." (None of these plans materialized, but they signaled a stark departure from Black Muslim noninvolvement.) "We can't awaken the moral consciousness of America," he said, dismissing Martin Luther King Jr.'s popular appeal. "America has lost all moral consciousness."

The minister encouraged voter-registration drives and extolled the might of the ballot, declaring that, "Negro voters have it in their power to decide next November whether Johnson stays in the White House or goes back to his Texas cotton patch." He even visited the U.S. Senate to observe proceedings on the Civil Rights Bill that Southern Dixiecrats were filibustering. Afterward, he ran into King near the Capitol halls and good-naturedly ambushed him, unfurling a grin as he pumped the reverend's hand. "Now you're going to get investigated," Malcolm teased before the two men parted, never to meet again.

Malcolm hoped to convince the black struggle that he had shed the Nation's manacles, but the Civil Rights warriors looked askance at his emancipation. Said the NAACP's Roy Wilkins, "We do not know whether he intends to help American Negro citizens in their Civil Rights campaign, or whether he really is serious in wooing them to some kind of a Black Nationalist separate state." CORE's James Farmer, whose own fond relationship with the minister was often strained, called the very notion of armed, black self-defense "ultimately suicidal."

King himself scolded Malcolm's "unfortunate" prophecies of bloodshed, declaring that, "In the past the constant prediction of violence had been a conscious or unconscious invitation to it." (Yet in the same statement he issued a caveat of his own, proclaiming that lawmakers who sought to dilute the Civil Rights Bill risked a "dark night of social disruption.") Some Civil Rights supporters understood that Malcolm had as large a role to play in the "Negro Revolt" as did writer James Baldwin or Harlem Congressman Adam Clayton Powell. "A lot of people are saying that we should let Malcolm scare the masses and Baldwin scare the intellectuals and Adam scare the politicians," one well-known leader told the *Times*. There were signs that Malcolm was nursing a Black Muslim hangover. Peopled by a motley band of Nation deserters, his upstart Muslim Mosque was already weaving schizophrenically between Muhammad's cultic theology and secular black nationalism.

Though Malcolm's militancy, contradictions, and reputation were largely to blame for tethering him to the margin of black protest, many of his new dimensions simply went unremarked. In those pell-mell weeks, he addressed urban ills in a manner that would have been impossible as an evangelist of Black Islam. He touted community control, arguing that "the tax dollars that we are sending to Poland and Russia and Chiang Kai-shek…should be directed into Harlem to build better schools staffed by better teachers." He also conceded the heterogeneity, if not humanity, of white men. He said his lectures before white college students were worthwhile because many of the students were more aware of America's racial crisis than their parents.

He was not preaching integration. "I do not say there are no sincere white people," he declared, "but rather that I haven't met any." He explained that he and his ideological brethren were anti-exploitation, anti-degradation, and anti-oppression, "and if the white man doesn't want us to be anti-him, let him stop exploiting, degrading, and oppressing us." The mainstream media did not rush to renovate Malcolm's image. Reporters fixed not on his ideological shifts, but on his call for armament, and his name was thereafter linked with rifles. "When people would say 'violence' they would automatically think of my husband," Betty said years later. "And yet he never committed any violence in his life; in his own death he did not either."

America was unsure what to make of Malcolm the activist-at-large, having never quite recovered from meeting Malcolm the Black Muslim bishop. Betty understood her husband's frustrations with the media pigeonhole. "I tell you as I live and breathe," she later said, "he was sensitive to the public view." She saw both his projected confidence and his private doubts. She sensed that he was inventing and reinventing himself extempore. She assured him that Muslim defamation and media distortion notwithstanding, her regard for him was incorruptible. "I don't think anyone really understood him the way I understood him," she later said. Self-evaluation kept him sane in the months after he bolted the Nation, she said. "But of course," she added, "I was there."

She always believed that Malcolm needed her more than she needed him—to "support his life mission." But she refused to support a death mission. He was always telling her that any black leader worth his or her salt must prepare for prison, the hospital, or the cemetery.

She knew he was not kidding when the threats began. Days after his defection, carloads of Muslims began cruising ominously by the house. "They were very, very vicious," Betty later said. Malcolm, who as a Muslim evangelist had never worn a weapon or urged violence, got an automatic carbine rifle with a full double clip of ammunition for his home and kept it loaded by the door. Betty felt the weapon's cold heft as he taught her to use it and told her not to hesitate to shoot "if anybody tries to come through that door, black, white, green, or blue."

Meanwhile, the propaganda war between the minister and his old church escalated. *Muhammad Speaks* had begun rebuking him as a hypocrite in a series of columns. Feeding the enmity was the defection of Wallace Muhammad, Muhammad's son, and Hassan Sharrieff, favorite son of bitter Malcolm rival and Fruit of Islam Supreme Captain Raymond Sharrieff. The Nation blamed Malcolm for both departures. On March 26, the sect called a Chicago press conference starring Malcolm's older brother Philbert, minister of the Lansing, Michigan, mosque, and the sibling who had introduced him to Black Islam.

Reading from a script that Muslim hierarchs had shoved into his hands moments before the event, Philbert denounced his brother as a turncoat who had betrayed Muhammad. In a grim monotone, he declared Malcolm insane; likened him to Judas, Brutus, and Benedict Arnold; and warned ominously that his recklessness would "cause many of our unsuspecting people who listen and follow him unnecessary loss of blood and life." Two weeks later, *Muhammad Speaks* ran a cartoon depicting Malcolm's severed head sprouting horns and jabbering, "I split because no man wants to be number 2 man in nothing!" as it bounded down a path toward a gravestone cluttered with skulls and bearing the names of famous traitors.

Though he dismissed it publicly, Philbert's betrayal gored Malcolm. Betty etched it in the ledger of her heart. Her poise was unraveling. At times she was short with the minister's cohorts. Malcolm had asked Haley to help him reword his literary contract so that proceeds from his forthcoming autobiography would benefit the Muslim Mosque, or, in the event of his death, Betty. "How is it possible to write one's autobiography in a world so fast-changing as this?" he wondered aloud.

Still, the noxious climate did not paralyze the minister. He had begun arguing that blacks would never find justice on American soil, and that they ought accordingly charge the United States before the United Nations' World Court with violating their human rights. It was a brazen (though not unprecedented) move to internationalize the struggle at a time when most race leaders were embroiled in local crusades or the pending federal Civil Rights Bill.

Malcolm was locked in a territorial battle of his own. Just two days after he had announced his independence, the Nation had sent him a dispassionate letter declaring the East Elmhurst home that he and his family occupied the legal property of Black Islam and demanding that they kindly clear out forthwith, since they no longer were affiliated with the kingdom.

The house was the only possession of real value Malcolm had ever been able to offer Betty. "And they want to take that away," he complained bitterly. He knew he was overburdening his wife, and the guilt tormented him. "I can't keep on putting her through changes—all she's put up with," he told Haley. In early April, Malcolm learned that the Nation had filed suit in Queens civil court to recover the residence. Though he and Betty might have predicted the move, he went nearly mad with rage.

Since the estrangement, he had kept quiet publicly about his erstwhile idol's failings. In coming months, he would spew venom at Muhammad's ministry, church, and prolific love life. He told Haley that he was not frightened for himself, "Just as long as my family doesn't get hurt." Now Chicago was threatening to turn his children and pregnant wife out into the street. This was a declaration of war. So Betty had to swallow her distress when, amid the psychological siege, her husband jetted off to Africa and the Middle East to embrace the Mother Continent and touch the House of God.

~

For years, Betty had found permanence in Black Islam. Though the temple's strictures had stifled her, the parish had also offered psychic shelter from a volatile society. Now that she and her man had wrenched away from the cloister, her need for sanctuary had deepened. Malcolm was searching for a spiritual and ideological port. She was looking to dock where the babies would be safe. Shielding them from fear had meant drawing inward and bearing up.

The girls had not yet sensed the panic. They watched Mommy's middle bulge and tighten, and they waited for another sister. "For me," Attallah later remembered of those months, "the continuity and the image and the energy in my house was very much the same." But life had changed. Betty and the minister were always starting at street noises and rustlings in the hedge. "There were places we couldn't go or be," Attallah recalled. "People who once were around weren't."

Sometime in those inauspicious days, Malcolm and Betty discussed the minister's desire to make the *Hajj*, the pilgrimage to Mecca required of all able Muslims at least once in a lifetime. "He wanted to clear up certain unanswered questions about Islam and see if it held any solution to the black man's problem," she later remembered. The ambition was born well before his 1959 trip to the Middle East as Muhammad's envoy, and had grown with his awareness of the elder's contortions of Islam. Over the years, Malcolm had met orthodox Muslims of all colors who had urged him to make the pilgrimage, knowing that it would expose him to the brotherhood of the faith. Ella Collins; Muhammad's son Wallace; and Dr. Mahmoud Youssef Shawarbi, distinguished Egyptian Muslim and director of New York's Islamic Center, had also encouraged the minister to explore the international religion then practiced by some 750 million believers.

In the weeks following his secession from the Nation, Malcolm visited Collins in Boston, deliberated his future with the beloved half-sister, and borrowed the money he needed for the *Hajj*. Back on Long Island, Betty was conflicted. She understood that the pilgrimage was the culmination of her husband's advance toward Eastern Islam and psychological detachment from the Nation. She would have welcomed almost anything that promised to loosen his heart from Muhammad's grip. Yet as much as she hoped Mecca would renew her husband, she desperately wanted him around in the days ahead.

An old rivalry also fueled her ambivalence. Though Collins's $1,500 loan would enable Malcolm's spiritual growth—she "never once really wavered from my corner," he later said—Betty's resentment of the sibling only deepened. Again the half-sister's influence had eclipsed her own during one of Malcolm's critical turns. "Why, he can't even move unless he gets permission from you!" Betty once exclaimed.

As the minister studied orthodoxy with Shawarbi in the weeks before the pilgrimage, he might have brought home revelations about Islam's colorblindness. For him, some of the news about the diversity of Allah's chosen was redundant. Though for years he had been too blinkered to acknowledge them, shafts of doubt had been piercing his faith for some time.

Ahmed Osman sensed as much. A Sudanese Muslim then studying at Dartmouth, Osman began sending Malcolm orthodox Islamic literature in 1962. The minister responded graciously to the graduate student, but only in a note invoking Nation dogma, printed on the sect's stationery, and embroidered with homages to Muhammad. In 1963, however, the minister wrote Osman asking for further explanation of a Qur'anic passage that the two had previously debated. This time the note came bearing no obeisance to Muhammad, and it arrived on plain paper. "That second letter really meant a lot," Osman later said. "It showed that he had started to question."

Perhaps Betty, too, had begun to question. Perhaps she had begun to realize how jarringly Muhammad's racial demonology clashed with the reality of the Muslim World. But Malcolm was her only periscope to Eastern Islam, for she had only a crude understanding of the Qur'an. In fact, she had woven her own image of the Holy Land he was preparing to visit largely from Black Muslim mythology, which painted all Mecca's pilgrims black. For a more authentic picture, she would have to wait on her husband's report.

In the meantime, she was again to play the dutiful, patient wife, the quiet-suffering Madonna of black nationalism. Though the role had never quite fit, she knew it well. So on April 13, not a week after the Nation had filed eviction proceedings against her family, she packed three weeks' worth of the minister's summer clothes, quietly accompanied him and a handful of his followers to John F. Kennedy International Airport, and saw him onto a 7 P.M. Lufthansa Airlines flight to Frankfurt, Germany.

Traveling under his Arabic name, Malik Shabazz, Malcolm continued from Frankfurt on a United Arab Airlines jet to Cairo. As the Muslim throngs swept him through the Egyptian airport, a strange elation overtook him: *there is no color problem here.* The realization, he said later, caught him unaware, as though he had abruptly been paroled from some phantom prison. After two happy days of sightseeing in Cairo, he returned to the airport, shucking his Western raiment, swathing his loins and shoulders in snowy cloth, and poking his copper feet into sandals. Thus uniformed, he and thousands of the faithful declared their intent to perform the *Hajj*, crying, "I come, O Lord!"

On the plane to Jeddah, the prismatic mass of pilgrims dizzied him. The sense of warmth and fraternity was enveloping. He passed a few awkward days in the port city as *Hajj* authorities scrutinized his credentials. He mumbled gibberish sheepishly as his companions droned Arabic prayers. He struggled to collapse his gangling self into the proper prostration, and managed only a sort of unfurled lotus. An eminent white Saudi finally rescued him from the airport hostel, lodged him in a posh hotel suite, and helped squire his passport out of customs. The sincere hospitality overwhelmed the minister, who, feeling safe and secure thousands of miles from the turmoil back home, prayed that Allah would bless his wife and children for their many sacrifices.

That very morning, he later told Haley, he began rethinking the nature of whiteness. "I began to perceive that 'white man,' as commonly used, means complexion only secondarily; primarily it described attitudes and actions," he said. "In America, 'white man,' meant specific attitudes and actions toward the black man, and toward all other non-white men. But in the Muslim world, I had seen that men with white complexions were more genuinely brotherly than anyone else had ever been."

In ancient Mecca, the minister basked in the *Hajj's* community. He ate from a common plate "with fellow Muslims, whose eyes were the bluest of blue, whose hair was the blondest of blond, and whose skin was the whitest of white." He slept and worshipped with believers of all hues. "Why, the men acted as if they were brothers of mine!" he later exclaimed. He made the ritual seven revolutions about Ka'ba, the imposing black stone house within the Great Mosque. Unable to touch the sacred monument for the awesome press of bodies, he settled for reciting the traditional declaration: "God is Great!" He prostrated with the legions, drank from the Zamzam well, and dashed between the Safa and Marwah hills. Finally, he supplicated on Mount Arafat and cast seven stones at a colorless devil. The *Hajj* had ended.

Some of his fellow pilgrims sheared their hair and beards. Malcolm decided to keep his briery growth. He wondered what Betty would think. In a letter from the Holy Land, he reminded Alex Haley to "please phone my wife if you have time. It keeps her morale up, and without *her* high morale I could never take my place in history." Below the request was an orderly signature: "El-Hajj Malik El-Shabazz."

While the minister communed with Allah and His pilgrims, Betty was battened down at home with the girls, awaiting tidings from the East. She made daily calls to Haley, Percy Sutton, and other confidants, wondering and worrying about Malcolm. Was he all right? Would he be safe rambling the Arab world without a bodyguard? Were U.S. agents on his trail? When would she next hear from him? According to Sutton, Malcolm telephoned his wife whenever possible while overseas, and the minister later mentioned that he had cabled her regularly while touring Mecca and the African continent. "I could always expect a call," Betty would remember. She had grown accustomed to having the minister no more than a phone message away, even as he traversed the country. Not since his first visit to the Dark World in 1959 had an ocean separated the couple.

There were other aggravations. Malcolm had ordered Charles Kenyatta to guard her and the children. "Wasn't nobody allowed into that house but Charles 37X," he later remembered, using his Black Muslim name, Kenyatta belonged to the hardcore clique of lieutenants who had always comprised her husband's inner council and who had risked much to follow him out the Nation. One or more of them routinely shadowed the minister through most of his waking hours, alternately serving as bodyguards, secretaries, and assistants. In their ranks were the men he trusted most, the loyalists who, though he had never dispatched them for aggressive acts of violence, would not have hesitated to take or give a bullet on his behalf.

They represented the old ways, though; they reeked of the Black Muslim fanaticism Betty was eager to move beyond. She trusted few of them and had grown to despise several. "She hated me with a passion," Kenyatta later said. "She didn't like the role I was playing." Craving conversation and news about the minister's progress, Betty phoned Razzaq almost nightly while Malcolm was abroad, though as a rule her husband never communicated with her through his sidemen. Still, Razzaq would recall, "she had a particular aversion to me."

Malcolm's time was one source of the rancor. The more hours the minister spent in the field with his followers, the fewer he spent at home with his wife and children. New conflicts between the first lady and the henchmen flared once Malcolm left for the Middle East. In his absence, a bad case of cabin fever struck Betty and her trio of girls. Yet the security-minded men practically barricaded the family at home. Betty understood the need for caution better than anyone. She had watched the Muslim "zombies" vilify her husband by day and stalk him by night. But having just been liberated from Black Islam's brig, she refused to go gently into black nationalism's dungeon.

At least once during that first of Malcolm's two 1964 excursions, she packed up the children and took them to Sutton's home without a bodyguard. The counselor, who was preparing the minister's defense for the upcoming eviction trial, in turn looked in on her at home. "We'd talk about his travels," Sutton later remembered. "She was very pleased. She was proud." Betty taped a world map to the living room wall, and in a ritual that developed over the next month, began tracing with the girls Malcolm's trek through the Middle East and Africa. "Anytime you got a little lonesome and wondered where Daddy was, we'd run over to that map," Attallah, then a coltish five-year-old, would recall. "Where is he now? He's in Cairo, he's over here with Nkrumah. When he came back, we were connecting the dots."

Betty had always assured Malcolm that his presence warmed her even while he was away. Attallah would echo the sentiment. "The more he traveled," she said, "the freer he became, the freer we became." But even as the minister was in the East awakening to mankind's capacity for brotherhood, newspapermen in the West were chronicling his potential for inspiring white terror. Citing an unnamed source, the New York Times in early May 1964 uncovered what it fancied was a four hundred–strong Harlem "hate gang" known darkly as the "Blood Brothers." Police were linking the youngsters to the fatal stabbing of a white woman. The Times reported that Black Muslim dissidents under Malcolm's command were reputed to have trained the platoon of dope pushers, thieves, and numbers runners to battle police and whites in the community.

Unaware of the absurd allegations swirling stateside, Malcolm busied himself unveiling his new racial insights in a flurry of dispatches from the Holy Land. Among the family members, comrades, and newsmen who received his breathless letters was M. S. Handler of the Times, whom Malcolm had grown to trust. "There are Muslims of all colors and ranks here in Mecca from all parts of this earth," the minister said. The goodwill of the white pilgrims he encountered had astonished him. "I could look into their faces and see that these men didn't regard themselves as 'white,'" he said. "Their belief in the Oneness of God (Allah) had actually removed the 'white' from their minds, which automatically changed their attitude and behavior toward people of other colors...[and] made them so different from American whites, their outer physical characteristics played no part at all in my mind."

Witnessing this, he wrote, demolished some of his old thought patterns and conclusions. In the missive, which the New York Times published early that May, he insisted that white Americans were guilty of "conscious racism." But he suggested that if they embraced Islam "they could also sincerely accept the Oneness of Man" and scour bigotry from their hearts. "As America's insane obsession with racism leads her up the suicidal path," he said, "I do believe that whites of the younger generation, in the colleges and universities, through their own young, less hampered intellect, will see the handwriting on the wall and turn for spiritual salvation to the religion of Islam and force the older generation of American whites to turn with them."

It was hardly a pardon. Malcolm had neither embraced integration nor forgiven whites for their crimes against the Dark World. As biographer Peter Goldman later observed, the minister in his communiqués had simply imagined "an entire nation now lost in sin being led to Allah by its own children." Acknowledging even this dim possibility, however, had meant ditching his universal indictment of whites as irredeemable souls, a turnaround that caused a minor stir back home.

While the headlines of Malcolm's transition heartened some white liberals, many of his staunch disciples felt betrayed. Some of his followers wondered whether their intrepid leader had not gone soft (or soft-headed), and several of them began drifting emotionally from his side. A stream of critics, sympathetic and otherwise, detected a certain calculation in Malcolm's "reversal." He had been angling toward the protest establishment in recent months; perhaps this latest shift was a bid for respectability or a larger share of the Civil Rights market. Perhaps he hoped that shedding a stance many blacks found unpalatable would thrust him into the echelons of the Movement, which he hoped to convert to black nationalism.

Betty thought she understood better than most what her husband was unbosoming. "His attitude and ideas changed immensely on a lot of things after he left the Black Muslims," she said less than a year later, "and with travel his whole outlook broadened." She was too insulated to fathom his evolving vision of racial justice, but she knew his heart. She knew his rage at white supremacy had not blinded him utterly to the prospect of white humanity, a prospect that had widened in the latter days of his Black Muslim epic. "Malcolm didn't hate whites as individuals," she chorused in later years. "He hated what whites had done to blacks." (The minister's cousin and disciple, Hakim A. Jamal, later declared that Betty was one of the few figures who realized just how far from racism Malcolm had swerved.)

Even in the days when the original sin of the "blue-eyed devils" had anchored Malcolm's gospel, Betty had seen him treat his loop of favorite reporters and other white familiars with genuine respect and, in a few cases, something approaching affection. (She herself had enjoyed a "tele-phone friendship" with a handful of whites, including *New York Amsterdam News* columnist Gertrude Wilson.) In recent months, she had felt at least reverberations of the inner debate that led Malcolm to start painting whites with finer nuance. Actor Sidney Poitier's wife, Juanita, was another woman with whom the minister had lately bandied the notion that complexion was in fact a poor gauge of human character.

Malcolm in his correspondence from Mecca nevertheless portrayed his new philosophy as a thunderbolt revelation. And that's how he said Betty received it. "The first letter was, of course, to my wife," he remembered in his autobiography. "I never had a moment's question that Betty, after initial amazement, would change her thinking to join mine," he said. "I had known a thousand reassurances that Betty's faith in me was total. I knew that she would see what I had seen—that in the land of Muhammad and the land of Abraham, I had been blessed by Allah with a new insight into the true religion of Islam, and a bet-ter understanding of America's entire racial dilemma."

Whatever the depth of her surprise, Betty never questioned the sincerity of her husband's proclamation or agonized over her response. "Whatever Malcolm did and wherever he went," she later said, "he always knew that I loved him and that whatever he said I would do— not blindly, but because over the years he had proven that he had my best interests at heart." She cringed forever after, however, whenever anyone interpreted her husband's pilgrimage as an about-face. "A lot of people said that Malcolm had the capacity to change," she said. "I think he had the capacity to expand."

Malcolm shifted tactics, Betty conceded, but his mission was eter-nal. "He was totally committed to freedom for oppressed people," she said. She attributed much of his broadened scope to the spectacle of the *Hajj*, the exhilaration of seeing believers of all colors advancing under a common conviction and toward a common God. She suspected that the treachery of recent months had deepened the experience, for strangers in Mecca had embraced him while black brothers and sisters he had devoted himself to for years rebuked him.

"Many people fail to see that Malcolm was only reporting what he saw," she later said. "It was an observation." But by the time he had left the Middle East for the African continent (after a sojourn in Saudi Arabia, where Prince Faisal honored him as a guest of the state), it was clear that Malcolm had embarked on an inner journey, as well. Though he had not entered their tent, he began wooing black integrationist leaders more candidly, ordering Razzaq to send them letters expressing his new position—"we pray that it will be attractive to you," he said—and proposing a united front.

In coming months, the minister would find himself explaining his evolving ideology to the Civil Rights mainstream and his own watchful ranks. Having become a Sunni Muslim by virtue of her husband's conversion, Betty would meanwhile adapt fractionally to the ways of traditional Islam's largest denomination, which Malcolm assured her offered blacks the "soundest spiritual base." She began reciting Islamic prayers in Arabic, chanting beside the minister as they faced east: "I perform the morning prayer to Allah, the Most High, Allah is the greatest. Glory to Thee Oh Allah, Thine is the praise, Blessed is Thy Name, and Exalted is Thy Majesty. I bear witness that nothing deserves to be served or worshipped besides Thee."

Within a year, Betty would experience firsthand the rhapsody of the *Hajj*, thereby grasping Malcolm's awakening more fully and arriving at her own enlightenment. For the moment she could only pray that his pilgrimage heralded a more stable era for her family, though she might have suspected otherwise. She must have known that his Holy Land message would deepen his heresy in the Black Muslim world, but she was powerless to slow the wheel of events. Some of the men grumbled that their once unyielding champion had compromised. Other Malcolm sympathizers, while glad that he seemed to have finally shrugged off Elijah Muhammad's mystical cloak, worried that the minister had lunged for a fresh philosophy before coming home to suitably prepare his partisans. It was this thought that chilled Juanita Poitier as she watched Malcolm in a newscast recall his revelation about the potential for white redemption. "Oh my God," she thought. "He just signed his death warrant."

❧

Maya Angelou, who was in Ghana among a troupe of black American intellectuals at the time, would remember Malcolm arriving in the land of Nkrumah that spring and setting their tiny expatriate colony aflame. "He was like a burning spear," she said. The minister sparked conversations about liberation struggle that blazed through the African night. But when he began talking about his wife, his voice and face softened like candle wax. "He metamorphosed," Angelou recalled.

It struck Julian Mayfield, Alice Windom, and some of the roughly three dozen other émigrés that Betty and the children never strayed far from Malcolm's mind as he gulped Africa's vistas, culture, and revolutionary zeal. "Betty is the sweetest woman in the world," he said during one afterhours chat. Then he fished out his wallet. "Did I show you these pictures?" he asked Angelou. Each time, the writer denied that she had seen the photographs, and Malcolm repeated his daughters' names.

The sentimental moments followed searing indictments of America. The minister told the expatriates that the black nation back home would never escape oppression until it convinced the world to consider its cause. Once the dirty linen had been hauled out of the closet, he said, blacks could start getting results and stop courting white liberals and enduring the indignity and bloodshed of street protests. Malcolm had arrived in Ghana after trips to Egypt and Nigeria. There he had conferred with politicians and intellectuals, looking to cull support for his plan to take the Black American case before the United Nations General Assembly.

The quest would send him bounding across Africa for three weeks. He rumbled through Liberia, Senegal, Morocco, and Algeria, denouncing

U.S. racism and urging African solidarity with the struggle back home. Africans, he charged, could not justify their indictments of racism in South Africa and Angola while ignoring the plight of twenty-two million Black Americans. He had come as an informal ambassador for the marooned black men and women of the West, hoping to forge a bond between Black Africa and Black America, not unlike the psychological, economic, and cultural link to Israel with which he believed American Jewry had climbed from oppression to power.

Africa adored him. A handful of the statesmen he met were too wary of jeopardizing American funding for their emerging nations to fawn over a notorious black dissident. But most of the high officials, intellectuals, luminaries, journalists, and young people that Malcolm met fêted him wildly. A Nigerian student association named him Omowale ("the child has come home" in Yoruba). In Ghana, revered President Kwame Nkrumah granted him an audience (it was the greatest honor, he said, of his African trek). The minister passed his final days on the continent dazzling its elders and its revolutionary children, swooning at its natural beauty and snapping photos. In letters home, he proclaimed Africa "the land of tomorrow." He insisted that its masses, upon learning the scope of America's racial atrocities, had been deeply moved by the troubles of their distant brothers and sisters in the West, despite U.S. State Department efforts to shroud the truth. "Africans in general and Muslims in particular, everywhere, love militancy," he declared.

With renewed purpose and rekindled spirit, having spent his thirty-ninth birthday in Africa, Malcolm returned to the United States a confirmed orthodox Muslim. The tour of Africa and the Middle East had been his most triumphant hour. It had spurred his personal and political evolution beyond the glare of Western scrutiny. He had grown worldlier. Having shed much of his Black Muslim scar tissue, he now dreamed of embarking on a broadened human-rights campaign, with the black protest establishment and independent Africa in tow.

Betty had remained stateside. Travel had not widened her vistas. She had not rendezvoused with the Dark World, or spent several weeks in a distant hemisphere having grand revelations about the freedom struggle and her particular role in its unfolding. Years later she explained to an unschooled public how Malcolm had linked Diasporic African struggles and connected Muslims in the West with believers abroad. But in late May 1964, she was a parochial, care-worn housewife whose wayfaring husband had stayed away two weeks longer than scheduled.

She sensed that this latest expedition was essential for his ministry and soul. But now the threatening phone calls had begun. Each taunting voice that rippled over the line thrust another skiver through her chest. She had gotten the minister's stream of letters, and soared inwardly with his every coup. (She later recalled that a new communiqué arrived almost every day.) Yet the strain of hunkering down in a house she feared the family might soon lose as her relationship with her husband's aides frayed and her pregnancy neared its term had begun to grind her patience. Her two older children had asked repeatedly when Daddy was coming home. She had missed him desperately herself, but she had not known precisely when or—considering the political climate and the audacity of his mission—*if* he would return at all.

Nor had she recuperated from the blows of recent months: the suspension, the banishment from Black Islam, the death threats. Malcolm's absence had not allayed the siege. While the daily newspapers had proclaimed him the "hate gang" mastermind, the Nation had continued to curse his name. Louis X, whom she and Malcolm had treated like kin, denounced the minister as a phony who had tried to fracture the Original People and smear Elijah Muhammad in the white press. "I knew, perhaps more than any, what the Messenger of Allah had done for this man," Louis wrote in *Muhammad Speaks*, "and I, too, was shocked by his almost unbelievable treachery and defection."

Even amid the blizzard of crises, Betty took heart. Malcolm was coming home. She was jubilant when she phoned Alex Haley with the news. On the afternoon of May 21, she spruced up the children and accompanied the welcoming committee to the airport. When she caught sight of Malcolm, draped with bags and video cameras, all the resentment of the recent weeks evaporated. Her beloved was safe!

But where was the old Malcolm? This new man had sprouted a feathery beard, and his hair was crying out for a barber. "He looked brand new," Attallah later remembered. Something else had changed, too; something less tangible but just as obvious in his countenance. Betty did not dwell on it. The clump of grass in the family's skinny backyard needed at least as much attention as Malcolm's mane. There would be time to pick at those whiskers later, and to discover the voyager's expanded soul.

She held herself with the usual restraint, emerging from the tangle of men and approaching the minister. She had layered baby Ilyasah in a white bonnet and tunic. Now beaming, Malcolm hoisted the sleepy child, brandishing a handsome African walking stick in the other hand. Ilyasah stretched for a moment, hoping to glimpse her father behind this tall man's reddish-blond bristles. Then, having satisfied herself of his authenticity, she dozed off. A throng of reporters engulfed the weary minister in the terminal and began pitching questions as Betty waited off to one side with his aides.

Two hours later, Malcolm drove to 135th and Lenox Avenue in his midnight-blue Oldsmobile. Alex Haley hopped inside and laid eyes on Betty for the first time after more than a year of telephone conversations. She was chic in her dark glasses and blue maternity suit, and her skin and hair gleamed. The writer and the first lady grinned at each other. That evening at the Hotel Theresa news conference, Malcolm escorted Betty gently through the doors of the Skyline Ballroom and into a conflagration of camera flashes and floodlights. As the minister squared himself before the throng, she glided to the rear, smiling proudly.

Yes, Malcolm explained to reporters in the days ahead, he had undergone a "spiritual rebirth" overseas. "No longer do I subscribe to a sweeping indictment of any race," he said. But though he conceded the possibility of white goodness, he was more emphatic than ever that the American scene was a panorama of racism. Within the stifling climate of oppression, he said, blacks would only waste time searching for right-eous whites. Sympathetic whites could back his cause if they wished, but they could not join his movement, and he certainly was not count-ing on their patronage. "If whites want to help, good," he said. "If they don't want to help, that's good, too." He sneered at reports that he had spawned the Blood Brothers. If the enemy could stoop to such defama-tion, he said, "perhaps we need some blood brothers." Besides, as far as he was concerned, everybody who had caught the kind of hell that he had was his blood brother.

He said his travels had heightened his awareness of the provincial-ism of the Negro Revolt. Though he still fiercely rejected integration and nonviolence as philosophies and liberation strategies, he insisted that he was absolutely committed to a united front of all African-American leaders, and announced that he would soon convene a closed-door summit to create such a loose confederation. He said he had won African pledges of support for a stand at the UN against the United States, which he accused of preaching integration while prac-ticing racism. America, he insisted, had colonized blacks, and should have to defend itself before the world against the same human-rights charges that other corrupt nations had faced.

Malcolm wanted to see this happen by autumn. To that end, and to promote black unity, he announced that he would form an organi-zation that was open to all blacks and that would transcend petty ide-ological differences. He swore that he would no longer yoke himself to any particular dogma or philosophy. He was devoted to neither separa-tion nor integration, but self-rule and freedom. "My position," he said, "is flexible."

During a debate with Malcolm in those days, black author Louis Lomax suggested wryly that the minister was becoming a moderate. Malcolm had actually raised the retaliatory pitch of his rhetoric. "Unless the race issue is quickly settled," he said during the Lomax encounter, "the twenty-two million American Negroes could easily adopt the guerrilla tactics of other deprived revolutionaries around the world." In Betty's mind, Malcolm was courting not moderation but global struggle. After his return from Africa that May, she later said, he came to believe that leaders of all denominations and ideologies in the First and Third Worlds would have to act collectively to end the universal injustice of white supremacy. "It was primarily a non-white problem," she said, "but it was the white man's problem, too."

Betty may have overstated Malcolm's faith in working alliances with non-blacks both in the states and abroad. Though Islam's pluralism had enchanted him, he was too shrewd a champion of black self-determination to be taken in by the spectacle of multicultural harmony. Yet even his willingness to work with the black establishment became fodder for Black Islam's cannons. There was no "new" Malcolm, Louis X said in an early June edition of *Muhammad Speaks*, "It's the same old Malcolm who is trying desperately to recover from a monumental blunder." In seceding from the Nation, the Boston minister said, Malcolm had lost "the only solid ground he's ever had."

Betty argued later that Malcolm never would have begun airing Elijah Muhammad's moral transgressions "if the Black Muslims had been intelligent enough to let things lie." Muhammad's men had just the opposite in mind that June of 1964. Some of them had glowered at the minister from the audience during the Lomax debate. Everywhere he went he saw their shadows. The kingdom of Allah as revealed to Muhammad was at war against an infidel. Now it wanted back its little Long Island rectory. In order to get it—and perhaps humiliate its famous deserter—it would even enter the white man's courts.

Malcolm had not wanted to let the "enemy" sort out their differences. He later claimed that he had offered to settle the matter "internally," asking Temple Number Seven officials for permission to address the body and defend himself against the charges spiraling in *Muhammad Speaks*. If the congregation still wanted him out of the East Elmhurst home after that, he told his one-time brethren, he would pack up his family and leave graciously. The Nation had turned him down, of course. It was far too late for an exit interview, and Malcolm knew it.

The Muslims had kept on bruising him in their gazette and stalking him on the streets, and finally, desperately, he had struck back. Whether for revenge or to protect himself, as he later insisted, he broke the news about Muhammad's harem for the first time on June 12 in a Boston interview. The disclosure made a quiet splash and hardly any ripples; the media still needed a public record before they would print such damning allegations. The counterstrike, though, was swift.

Within hours, a car full of Black Muslims bearing knives tried to ambush a group of Malcolm's followers in the city's Callahan Tunnel, believing that he was among them. "You're not going to get out of here alive!" they yelled as they converged on the Malcolmites, retreating only when they saw a shotgun muzzle poke out of the car's window. Several newspapers had received anonymous telephone tips that Malcolm would be gunned down. When the minister, wreathed by his men, appeared outside Queens Civil Court for the eviction suit hearing the following week, twenty uniformed police officers and twelve detectives waited to usher him inside.

Betty handled herself beautifully during the two harrowing days of the trial. "I saw how strong she was," Percy Sutton later said. The courtroom scene was far too hot for her to attend. (Authorities kept the shades drawn throughout the proceedings to thwart any snipers.) The climate even spooked some of Malcolm's loyalists. "The brothers claimed they was going to testify for him," Kenyatta later said. "But when I looked around in the courtroom, wasn't nobody but me and him and Percy." Sutton discussed the goings on with Betty. "I told her the difficulties and prejudices I saw on the part of the judge," he recalled.

The defense had to prove that the neat, sixteen-thousand-dollar brick bungalow belonged to Malcolm (though the Nation held the deed) and that he had not been dismissed with due process, so he should not now be forced out of the place. (Betty always insisted that Muhammad himself had given her and her husband the house as "a wedding gift.") Black Islam's argument—that Malcolm and kin were squatting in the Harlem parsonage months after he had deserted the pulpit—was rather less convoluted, and in the end proved irrefutable. "The judge really favored the other side strongly," Sutton later said.

Malcolm dealt his forsaken church another counterpunch on the stand. Replying to an innocuous question from Sutton, the minister abruptly announced that Black Islam had in fact muzzled him that last December because he had too much dirt on Muhammad, that Chicago and its stooges had poisoned the believers' minds against him, and that Muhammad had fathered several illegitimate children by six mistresses. The outburst did not shift the weight of evidence. Judge Maurice E. Wahl ruled that Malcolm and family could remain in the home for another month, pending submission of legal briefs. He finally ordered the eviction that September, but stayed its execution until February 1965.

As their case had begun to unravel, Sutton brought the bad tidings to Betty. She, the attorney, and Malcolm discussed the court proceedings at length. (Even the old Black Muslim veneer of sparing women emotional strain had disintegrated.) She understood that an eviction order was likely. Though she was now eight-and-one-half months pregnant, she did not seem to despair. More than ever before, Sutton recalled, she gathered her children and courage about her. "It wasn't 'Poor me,'" he said. "I don't remember any special complaint that she had."

Yet she was as scared as the minister, who had personally trained scores of Black Muslim soldiers and knew precisely what they were capable of. His desperation began to surface in uncharacteristically clumsy statements. "Muhammad was nobody until I came to New York as his emissary," he blurted on one occasion. There were times, however, when he seemed preternaturally cool. Sutton sat wedged between two of Malcolm's husky convoys as the minister's car left the courthouse one afternoon. Each man had a pistol in his lap and a shotgun at his side. They traveled about twenty blocks in frosty silence before Sutton spoke. "Minister Malcolm," he asked, "don't all these guns disturb you?" Malcolm smiled humorlessly. "I'm not disturbed," he said. "The brothers think they'll protect me. But the truth, counselor, is that there's a destiny for each of us. And nothing can keep you from that destiny."

Chapter Nine

THE DEATH CARD

"The price of freedom is death."
—Malcolm X

By June 1964, newspapers were reporting that police considered Malcolm a marked man and were surveilling him around the clock. "The vigilance extends to his home in Queens, his office in Harlem, and wherever he travels in this area," the *New York World Telegram* announced.

Had Betty read the piece, she might have laughed out loud. She had seen the lawmen. Police officers and intelligence agents had plagued her almost from the first day she had wandered into Temple Number Seven. In 1958, they had nearly shot her and unborn Attallah through the door of the family's apartment during a raid ostensibly designed to nab a mail-fraud suspect. They had shadowed the minister, bugged his phones, and tried to draft him as a snitch. Never had she gotten the impression that they were out to save her husband, and she doubted that they were genuinely trying to do so now. Malcolm had in any case assured her that they could not. Every day, there were omens that he was right.

On the evening the eviction hearing wrapped up, Betty discovered that her telephone line had gone dead. She suffered in silence until the minister returned from Harlem. The phone company told Malcolm that a "Mrs. Small" had requested the cut-off because the minister was preparing to leave town for an extended vacation. To Malcolm, it stunk of the Nation—"Small" sounded like a play on "Little," his

196 — BETTY SHABAZZ

"slave name." Meanwhile, one of his men called the house and got the recorded "disconnect" message. Alarmed, the lieutenant and a small posse raced over to their leader's place. It was about 9:30 P.M. when they found him and Betty safe at home.

The men then proceeded to 116th Street and Lenox Avenue, near the Black Muslim restaurant in Harlem. There they spotted several members of the Nation and some bystanders gathered in the street watching a noisy row between a white john and a black prostitute. The Malcolmites tumbled from the car in a rumbling mood. A squat Black Muslim punched one of Malcolm's disciples in the jaw. Brandishing a knife and a semiautomatic rifle, the Malcolmites surged toward the lunchroom and a clot of Elijah Muhammad's faithful, who had taken up broomsticks and other improvised weapons. "Get in the restaurant!" a Malcolm disciple hollered.

Police broke up the fracas, and the next day Malcolm sat at home granting interviews. He bristled when he learned that the Nation had accused him of manufacturing the incident. "I've gotten all the public- ity I needed," he snapped. "The thing that has Elijah Muhammad insane with rage is that his followers are leaving in droves." Again he told the newsmen that the sect was trying to kill him. "I have a rifle here in my home," he added ominously, "and I can take care of myself."

Privately he was furious with his men. "There was a time bomb in Harlem," Malcolmite James Campbell would recall, and the minister was desperate to defuse it. After another tense Temple Number Seven showdown, he summoned the guilty men into his nook of an office at the Theresa Hotel and chewed them out one by one. Malcolm was not a man who raised his voice—he did not need to—but that day his anger scalded the offenders' ears. "When they came out they were chastened," Campbell later said.

Back at home, Betty brooded. The Malcolmites had learned from the street that her husband was to die violently by the June 28 Harlem rally that Muhammad was headlining. She and the minister were nearly broke. No insurance company would sell a policy on his life—he was too "hot." The family was maybe a month away from losing the house, and within two weeks she would bring her fourth child into the world.

"It was a terror-filled time for her," one of her colleagues later said. "And sometime during those days she said she'd never go back to terror."

—

On July 1, 1964, Gamilah Lumumba Shabazz arrived. Malcolm named his fourth daughter for yet another intrepid man: Patrice Lumumba, the slain revolutionary leader of the Congo. The minister would never truly get to know the child. He had not coddled her mother while she was in the womb. Now that she had entered the world, he was, in a sense, already making his exit.

Betty's labor with Gamilah was not extraordinarily strenuous. None of her children had taken their time emerging. But this time there were complications. The baby, she was told, needed a transfusion. Malcolm had never trusted the white man to preserve *any* black life, much less that of his progeny. (Betty had had to vaccinate their first three girls on the sly.) The violent political climate only deepened his unease. He mellowed somewhat after Betty's cousin Ruth Summerford, herself a maternity-ward nurse, assured him that the procedure was legitimate.

After the delivery, Malcolm and Betty shared a brief respite—one of their last. She propped herself up in the Brookdale Hospital bed. He scooted his chair to the edge of the cot, and there was a soft exchange. Later he ushered her to the nursery, and the two gazed through the glass at their new daughter. At home that night while Betty recovered in the hospital, Attallah, Qubilah, and two-year-old Ilyasah huddled quietly around their father, who sat beside a large portrait of Nkrumah. Against the glow of a nearby lamp, the Redeemer's stark features glimmered.

—

Malcolm kept pleading for détente. In an open letter to Muhammad, he argued that he, Muhammad, and other black leaders should unite against the atrocities blacks were suffering down South instead of squandering their energy in a spiral of hostilities. Still, the minister could not resist another jab at his former boss. How could Muhammad now resort to internecine violence, he demanded, when white racists had in the past attacked Black Muslims without reprisal? That same day, a reporter asked what the minister made of the Nation's claim that he and his men were plotting a hit on Muhammad. Malcolm's lips curled. "We don't have to kill him," he said. "What he has done will bring him to his grave."

Despite his rhetorical war with Black Islam, the minister had plunged ahead with plans for a dream organization to align Africa and African-America against racial injustice—a nationalist group so transcendent that no black person could ignore it. He had been fishing among the protest Movement's malcontents since his return from Africa. The recruits brought expertise from the university, the professional world, and the street. They had formed a planning group, and from several meetings in Harlem haunts such as the Dawn Café, the Organization of Afro-American Unity (OAAU) sprang.

On June 28, Malcolm stood draped in seersucker on the dingy stage of the Audubon Ballroom, a once-swank dance hall just north of Harlem, and unveiled his OAAU. Modeled after the Organization of African Unity, a year-old confederation of Africa's newly independent nations, the nonsectarian group hoped to submerge black organizational and ideological differences in the struggle for human rights. Its panoramic mission statement encompassed the political, economic, social, educational, and cultural spheres, and touched on such initiatives as housing self-improvement, pro-black school curriculums, and voting-education drives. Its base, however, was pure Malcolm: staunch self-defense, political and economic self-determination, and brotherhood with Africa.

Brotherhood with defectors was hardly the order of business at the Harlem armory, where Muhammad was rallying his faithful. Edgy police and dour men sporting WE ARE WITH MUHAMMAD armbands patrolled the sidewalk outside. The Fruit of Islam in separate incidents took two men for Malcolmites or gatecrashers and roundly thrashed both in the street before police came running. Inside the armory, Muhammad gasped through his speech with only an oblique reference to Malcolm. "There is some person who wants to be what I am," he declared, "but that person is not able to be what I am."

The next week, *Muhammad Speaks* rotated another columnist into the Malcolm firing squad. "If it were not for the Messenger," wrote John Shabazz, "you would still be just another unheard-of penny-ante Harlem hustler. Now that you have defected, you are a FAMOUS penny-ante Harlem hustler. The Bible accurately describes you as 'a dog returning to his own vomit.' You've even grown shaggy like a dog."

The only mutts that concerned Malcolm were the German shepherds and the "two-legged dogs" that had bloodied black demonstrators throughout the Civil Rights movement. He promised that if the horrors continued, he would lead guerrilla-trained squads into the South to battle Ku Klux Klansmen and other hostile whites. Yet even though the Mississippi Freedom Summer had opened with bombings and the murders of three volunteers—a local black youth and two white collegians—the minister never made good on the threats to reinforce the nonviolent troops with his own detachments. Indeed, considering his own combative record with the black establishment, the most radical southern trip he made that June was a dip into Washington, D.C., to amicably observe an NAACP convention.

He made less conciliatory moves, too. While in Mecca, he had vowed before Allah to atone for having embalmed so many minds with what he now considered phony dogma. He was determined to expose the hypocrisies of the elder he had once sworn to defend with his life. It was with his urging and affidavit that former Muhammad secretaries Lucille Rosary and Evelyn Williams in early July filed paternity suits against Muhammad with Los Angeles Superior Court, alleging that the elder had fathered four children between them.

That night, Malcolm stayed home with his daughters and a young baby-sitter. Betty was still in the hospital convalescing from the recent delivery. Around 10 P.M., the minister decided to move his car. Anticipating Muslim retaliation for his role in the paternity suit, he'd parked the Oldsmobile down the street earlier that evening. Asking the baby-sitter to keep an eye on him, he ventured outside, leaving the door ajar.

Instantly, he spotted four men streaking toward him with blades flashing. He sprinted to his car, leapt in, and peeled off, gunning around the block. When he careened into his driveway moments later, the would-be assailants had vanished. Breathing hard, he dashed back into the house and called the police, who later collected statements from him and the baby-sitter. After the officers had gone, the minister paced miserably in the living room, his "talking stick" at the ready. Every so often he brushed aside the diaphanous curtains, cracked the blinds, and peered into the corners of the night.

Betty, an old soul with a knack for understatement more typical of her parents' generation, told a television audience a quarter century later that those days "were not as pleasant as they could have been." The summer of 1964 was indeed a harrowing time, as much for the nationals Malcolm now called Afro-Americans as for the republic. But there was no alternative to the forward course. "If you're in the middle of the Atlantic Ocean, what are you going to do?" Betty later asked rhetorically. "If you don't go in either direction, you're going to drown."

The maelstrom only quickened. That June 8, a voice on the telephone asked for Malcolm. Betty demanded that the caller identify himself. "Just give him this message," the man replied. "Just tell him that he's as good as dead." Each threat claimed another strand of Betty's already tattered composure. "It was constant," remembered Muriel Feelings (then Gray), a charter OAAU member. "She got sick and tired of it."

The calls came in clusters, building to sundering crescendos before subsiding. The culprits were and, to a lesser degree, FBI agents. A former Temple Number Seven parishioner later told biographer Karl Evanzz that "soldiers" from the mosque obeyed orders to telephone the minister's house every five minutes. The idea was to unnerve both Malcolm and Betty. "Sometimes we would say something threatening," the man remembered, "sometimes we would just hold the phone and hang up."

The voices tormented Betty while the minister was away. "You'll never see your husband again," they declared. "We got him. We cut his throat." Sometimes they threatened her daughters. In the early days of the hostilities, Betty would simply drop the receiver and walk away. In time she learned to "curse that phone until they hung up," she later told Maya Angelou.

It was years before the children saw that eruptive streak. A photograph from the era showing Malcolm clutching a rifle while peeking out the living-room window was among the welter of images that helped convert him posthumously into a champion of armed aggression rather than militant self-defense. The photo fueled the notion that his was a militaristic home. But this charged atmosphere existed mostly in the public imagination, Attallah would insist. "It wasn't like 'Everybody duck!'" she said years later, remembering the scene. "My parents just calmly called each of us, 'Honey, come on over here.' Then Daddy looked out the window."

The couple's cool veneer could not fully insulate their daughters. "You have to remember that the three oldest girls can recall three different times when someone tried to kill their father," Betty later said. She kept the girls close, struggling to shield them from the sense of warfare that had seized her and Malcolm. She trusted only a few women with them. One was Feelings, a recent college graduate with a sincere heart and a gentle disposition. The elegance with which Mrs. Malcolm X shepherded the children impressed Feelings. In coming weeks, she visited Betty and the minister's home, which she would remember as orderly and "semi-suburban."

She later baby-sat for the couple, granting Betty a few rare hours to herself. A Christian woman's presence in the home was still novel for Attallah. The five-year-old greeted Feelings with wide-eyed curiosity. "Muriel," she asked, "do you like white people?" An even more wondrous possibility struck the child: "Muriel, do you eat pork?" The Shabazz girls were polite and mischievous. (Attallah led her sisters in a campaign to convince Feelings that they routinely enjoyed the privileges in which they reveled the night that Feelings baby-sat them.), and they lacked the hollow-eyed look typical of traumatized children.

Still, fear that the girls were in jeopardy further embittered Betty and the minister. "Her concern was not just in losing him, but losing the children," Sutton later recalled. "She was frightened not of Malcolm's fate but of the children's—not of her own, but of the children's." Of course, imagining life without Malcolm was awful enough. Sutton believed that Betty shared Malcolm's philosophy about the indelibility of destiny. Yet the minister's fatalism terrified her. For months she walked away whenever he tried to talk to her about the possibility of his death. "I couldn't bring myself to listen," she later said.

What she did not hesitate to discuss were finances. Malcolm kept a blistering speaking schedule; he needed honoraria and platforms for his evolving gospel. Though he was scratching to support Betty, the children, and at least one full-time OAAU staffer, he still funneled much what he earned on the road back into the infant organization. This inevitably provoked Betty, who was more concerned about money than ever. Later that year, Haley passed the minister a large advance check from Doubleday, the forthcoming autobiography's publisher. Malcolm, laughing wryly, soon after told the writer, "It's *evaporated*. I don't know where!"

The minister's burdens were manifold, as he told an orthodox Muslim audience in Cairo later that year. His war, he explained, consisted of battles "material as well as spiritual, political as well as religious, racial as well as non-racial." Betty had embraced that multidimensionality, but continuing to do so meant greater risks. She knew that for all its nobility, Malcolm's mission was deadly. "She saw her husband being destroyed," OAAU organizer Herman Ferguson later said.

With four children now at home, the stakes had never been higher. She trusted her husband to guide the family. "Despite the stresses that came in her life and that marriage because of all the hell they were living through," Feelings later said, "they were companions." But when the minister again departed for what he intended as a six-week African tour less than two months after returning from his first journey, Betty's frustrations finally overflowed.

———

Ironically, Betty's constrictions coincided with her husband's most sincere efforts to conquer his chauvinism. As a hustler, he had peddled women in Harlem's streets. As a Black Muslim minister, he had glorified and repressed them. Now, seeking truth before dogma, and struggling to imagine a society free of degradation, Malcolm rediscovered black women.

He began to see them less as sacred wombs or chaste symbols or capricious children needing men's guiding hands and more as essential engineers in the struggle. By late 1964, he had swapped revolutionary wisdom with activists such as the Mississippi Freedom Democratic Party's Fannie Lou Hamer; Gloria Richardson of Cambridge, Maryland; and Maya Angelou of the American expatriate colony in Ghana. It was during his second African expedition of that late summer and fall, however, that he truly recognized women's power. In a November 1964 interview in Paris, the minister declared that:

> In every country you got to, usually the degree of progress can never be separated from the woman. If you're in a country that's progressive, the woman is progressive. If you're in a country that reflects the consciousness toward the importance of education, it's because the woman is aware of the importance of education. But in every backward country you'll find the women are backward, and in every country where education is not stressed it's because the women don't have education. So one of the things I became thoroughly convinced of in my recent travels is the importance of giving freedom to the woman.

Even before his return to Africa, he had enlisted a handful of educated, strong-headed women to help organize and operate his OAAU. Among them were Muriel Feelings, journalist Alice Mitchell, and Lynne Shifflett, whom he placed nominally in charge of the organization while overseas. The minister had actually formed the secular OAAU partly to transcend patriarchy. There had already been ugly exchanges after Black Muslim apostates in his Muslim Mosque tried to subjugate some of the new black nationalist women. "He needed another kind of organization where women would be allowed to flourish," Ferguson later remembered. Angelou herself would declare that, "Malcolm valued women's opinions, which is why he and I were brother and sister." Betty concurred. "In the movement, he felt that a woman's role should be determined by her qualifications," she later said.

But Malcolm never deputized his wife. Though he occasionally asked her to relay simple messages to his corps while he was overseas, she belonged to neither the OAAU nor the Muslim Mosque. "You don't have to be a man to fight for freedom," Malcolm told a Harlem audience that December. "All you have to do is be an intelligent human being." Yet even as he awakened to women's revolutionary potential, he did not invite Betty to join in organizing efforts. For her to transcend her symbolic role by volunteering part-time with local OAAU efforts, she would have had to dramatically alter her role as mother and wife. That was nearly impossible with an infant, three frisky little girls, and a harried husband on her hands. Besides, Malcolm would not hear of it.

Betty was as educated and bright as any of the women he had entrusted with OAAU chairmanships and other duties. Her inability to join her husband's corps now that women were in its vanguard demoralized her. Most of the men never sensed the ambition. Ferguson had met Betty a year earlier as Temple Number Seven's first lady, and expected nothing but the usual demureness from her now that Malcolm had quit the Nation. But to Mitchell, it was clear that she longed to participate in the movement.

There was no dearth of projects needing Betty's hands, and no end to the tasks that might have restored her sense of dignity. Late that summer, the OAAU's Harlem-based Liberation School began offering children and adults one-hour Saturday classes on subjects such as black history and international affairs. Despite her passion for education, Betty never got involved; by then, security concerns bound her to the hearth as powerfully as her domestic duties did. "I can't even go to the store to get a quart of milk," she once complained. She also missed social and cultural affairs (such as a Tanzanian independence reception at the United Nations that several OAAU members later attended with Malcolm) that might have helped replenish her spirit and boost her morale.

She did retain her secretarial role, clipping and mailing her husband pertinent articles and fielding media inquiries. One of her tasks in those days was helping Malcolm review rough chapters of his autobiography as Alex Haley delivered them. The minister actively edited and furnished new material for the book well into his final months, though outside pressures increasingly diverted him from the project. Betty acknowledged in later years that he had revised the manuscript heavily, but refused to reveal his amendments. (The original manuscript bearing Haley's and Malcolm's handwritten edits would surface after the author's death almost three decades later.) In the end, she declared the book an important but incomplete portrait. "Alex wasn't told everything and I don't think he would expect that," she said in 1989. "Haley didn't get any big secrets."

The "secrets" revealed in the vignettes of Malcolm's seedy early years, however, were enough to roil some of the Muslim authorities in the East who had lately certified his orthodoxy and embraced him as a legitimate spiritual leader. After the Saturday Evening Post published an abridged version of the autobiography during the minister's second African tour that summer, his spiritual mentor, Mahmoud Shawarbi, phoned Betty to complain that the narratives had troubled some Islamic World ambassadors. Betty defended her husband, explaining that in his Black Muslim days, "he told bad things about himself to make Elijah Muhammad look good and give himself no credit for anything." Her ambivalence toward the autobiography resurfaced in later years. In 1989, she suggested that the work—published the autumn after her husband's death—diluted Malcolm because Haley tended to glean "safe passages" from the minister's dictations.

Malcolm, however, could find few safe passages anywhere in the frazzled fall and winter of 1964, and Betty's constrictions intensified with his desperation. By his second African voyage, the minister had forbidden her to leave the house unless absolutely necessary, and then only with a bodyguard. The tightening security threatened even her modest liberties. Earlier that summer, she had managed a couple of unescorted visits to the home of Japanese-American Yuri Kochiyama, a Harlem activist who had met and befriended Malcolm in late 1963. "She wasn't afraid to walk the streets," Kochiyama later remembered. Betty had perched at the edges of Kochiama's multicultural affairs, enjoying polite conversation and talking proudly about her children while other guests hovered respectfully. 'Everybody's talking to her because it's their one opportunity," Kochiama recalled.

The streets had since grown too treacherous for cameos with the progressives. Now Betty mingled mostly with the Muslim Mosque or OAAU women who stopped by the house. Her earthiness whole-wheat rolls were what Feelings would remember most. The minister's wife was only a couple of years older than her husband's latest recruits, yet some of the women found practical wisdom in her soft admonishments. "She felt a responsibility to be brave for us," Feelings recalled. "None of us had been through anything like this before."

It was during these conversations that Feelings discovered Betty's facade. She learned that Betty sometimes feigned naïveté around outsiders. "She had to play the traditional role," Feelings later said. "And because of this a lot of people underestimated her." Betty was much savvier—and better informed—than she let on, for the desperation of those days forced Malcolm to entrust her with more inside information than ever before. He shared the names of those Muslim Mosque and OAAU newcomers he believed were sincerely with the cause, and those he suspected were double agents for the government.

Even as he confided certain executive secrets, however, he continued to cocoon Betty from the inner workings of his ministry, and expected her to remain literally and figuratively beneath the veil. He even forbade her to watch television coverage of Muhammad, fearing that any exposure to the elder might weaken her resolve. "He knew how charming, how slick Elijah was," Charles Kenyatta later remembered. Yet in the inferno of the minister's final days, as Betty faced the prospect of his death, he demanded of her a consciousness and commitment that only the struggle's most "liberated" women had developed. "He wanted her to stay home and have the meals ready and take care of the children," Mitchell later said, "and then he wanted her to drop some of that."

After Malcolm traveled abroad on July 9 to attend the second Organization of African Unity Summit Conference, what Betty dropped (or what began sliding from her grasp) were the vestiges of her restraint. Frictions with her husband's aides flared. The minister had again commanded Kenyatta to guard her and the children at home. She quarreled constantly with the sideman and routinely escaped his supervision by ordering him into her airless basement. She also clashed with Abdullah Razzaq. "Malcolm had said 'Anything that Betty wants please get it for her,'" Razzaq later said. Eager to exercise new freedoms, the sister demanded carryout shrimp, a food Black Muslims shunned. Razzaq dispatched a man for the shrimp, but thought the request an indulgence unbefitting Mrs. Malcolm X.

Indeed, some of Malcolm's inside people had come to see Betty as a spoiled, incorrigible egoist. "Betty—God rest her soul and damn mine if I'm saying this unjustly—had a way of causing confusion," Razzaq later declared. The first lady had grown accustomed to high status during her Black Muslim years. She was relieved that her family had escaped the order's fanaticism and corruption. Her husband's breakaway cadre treated her with deference, but she struggled after the defection to adapt to a more common station, especially after the *Hajj* deepened Malcolm's humility. "He came back saying, 'Look, just call me brother,'" Mitchell later recalled. "He did not want to have people bowing to him."

That self-sacrificing impulse and devotion to the cause led the minister to register even his 1963 Oldsmobile to the Muslim Mosque. Betty knew her family owned nothing. It was the financial and other uncertainties that inspired much of her discomfort with her husband's shifting role vis-à-vis his followers, a role that increasingly left him open to posers and traitors. Yet some Malcolmites thought she was clinging to the trappings of prestige. Organizational strains only deepened the resentment. A "benign jealousy" over Malcolm erupted between the Nation of Islam apostates in the Muslim Mosque and the OAAU's young intellectuals. Internal squabbling beset both camps as funds dwindled. The organizations were ostensibly self-governing, but the minister's charisma and energy had been their mortar, and they crumbled as his African sojourn stretched from weeks to months.

Distrust fueled the bickering. Malcolm's people knew that intelligence agents had infiltrated the ranks, and suspicion—rational and otherwise—curdled the camaraderie. "There were rumors and counter-rumors and charges and counter-charges," Ferguson later said. Meanwhile, the stream of supporters who seemed intent on basking in the minister's celebrity or compromising his agenda worried the old guard. The veterans were just as leery of the professionals and black establishment figures in his inner cabinet and other circles.

Cynicism alone might have shredded Betty's composure. "There was a culture of confusion," the OAAU's James Campbell remembered. There was also a communication breakdown. "Malcolm wasn't telling nobody what was going on," Kenyatta later said. Though the minister wrote his wife and lieutenants regularly while in Africa, he was too busy selling his United Nations campaign to the continent's statesmen to do his own housekeeping. His international chores precluded even the close dialogue with his congregation that had always girded his ministry. Betty was without meaningful access to her husband now that she needed him most. "I don't know why you can hear from him and I can't!" she told Kenyatta.

The minister's aides were tight-lipped. They knew how obsessively Malcolm sheltered Betty. When she asked for bulletins about her husband or his troupes, they suggested that she ask the minister herself. "If she's a member of the OAAU she ain't got nothing to do with the Muslim Mosque," thought Razzaq, heeding Malcolm's separation of church and state. "If she's a member of the Muslim Mosque, she ain't got nothing to do with the OAAU. So the safest thing for me to do is don't tell her nothing." The sideman later explained his reticence. "Suppose, for interest, Malcolm had an interview with Gertrude Samuels from the *New York Times*," he said. "Now, suppose Malcolm told me I'm going over to Gertrude Samuels's. What I'm supposed to do, tell his wife? Even if I knew what he was doing was absolutely legitimate, his wife might not think so. So the best thing for me to do was keep my mouth shut."

Considering the rampant chauvinism of many of Malcolm's top men, it is no mystery that the women in his retinue were more sensitive to Betty's predicaments. Yet it was with some of these women that she fought most ferociously. The young women of the OAAU worked closely with Malcolm, with none of the inhibitions of their Muslim counterparts. Their familiarity fanned Betty's already smoldering jealousies, especially in her state of isolation.

"You were one of the few women who weren't in love with my husband," she later told Feelings. Some of the women, like those in Temple Number Seven, resented her possessiveness. "Nobody was trying to be with him," Mitchell later said. "But Betty was making that her whole world." Other Malcolmites acknowledged that the first lady's suspicions, while extreme, were far from groundless. Razzaq would remember that up to the end "there were women after Malcolm like flies to honey."

Since his defection from Black Islam, the minister had taken pains to assure his wife that he was tolerating no more coquetry now than he had as the sect's most admired evangelist. When he occasionally got desirous calls at home, he motioned for her to pick up the other line so she could hear him reject the admirers, she later told an OAAU veteran. She suspected that the FBI was also trying to lure him into a tryst. "Of course they paid money to some ladies to try to entrap him," she told a radio station years later. "He would share it with me. I mean, we could do better with taxpayers' money."

Whether or not government agents were hoping to bait him, Malcolm was just as abstemious overseas. "When we were in Cairo together there were so many pretty girls," attorney Milton Henry later recalled, "but he acted like they weren't even there. He never even noticed them. He only spoke of his wife." The minister was conscious of Betty's tensions and frustrations, even while abroad. He tried to calm her, as he did his beleaguered cadre. In one letter from Egypt, he reminded her to make her five daily prayers—one of the "pillars" of orthodox Islam. She wrote back that very day. If he did his job, she declared, she would not have to pray at all.

Some of the minister's disciples resented what they considered Betty's efforts to recapture Malcolm the Husband at the expense of Malcolm the Revolutionary. "You can't be married to a world renowned figure and want him to be like he's a minister at First Baptist Church," Mitchell later said. It was a point Betty conceded, but only obliquely, and long after her husband's death.

Reminiscing about old days with Feelings years later, she declared that, "Sometimes you have to watch what you say to men." Feelings thought the remark was an acknowledgment of the widow's own past indiscretions, especially her occasional unruliness during Malcolm's last months. Yet Betty morally supported her husband's overseas missions, even as his long absences frazzled her, and even as his efforts chafed powerful forces in the United States. She also faced greater perils than most of his lieutenants—perils that in the end nearly cost her and her children their lives.

"Our problems are your problems," Malcolm told the thirty-three heads of independent states at the Organization of African Unity's second meeting in Cairo, Egypt, that summer. An accredited observer at the mid-July gathering, the minister appealed in an eight-page memo for the leaders' help in his crusade to take the United States to task before the UN. America was unable or unwilling to defend its black citizens against the murderous onslaught of racists, he told the assembled dignitaries. Yankee oppression was worse even than that of South Africa, he said, for Uncle Sam exalted himself as the paragon of liberty.

The minister argued that if South African apartheid was not a domestic matter, then black Africa's leaders should also treat African-America's plight as an outrage of global dimensions. "Your problems will never be fully solved until and unless ours are solved," he said. "You will never be fully respected until and unless we are also respected. You will never be recognized as free human beings until and unless we are also recognized and treated as human beings."

Malcolm glided among the conference delegates, enchanting premiers, presidents, and kings and frustrating the U.S. State Department emissaries who hoped to curry favor with the fledgling nations. The OAU granted him a floor pass and a berth on the yacht *Isis*, which meandered down the Nile, bristling with revolutionary Africa's dignitaries. He knew many of the states represented at the summit received substantial U.S. aid, and that few of their rulers were eager to bite Uncle Sam's hand. "We pray that our African brothers have not freed themselves of European colonialism only to be overcome and held in check by American dollarism," he declared. "Don't let American racism be 'legalized' by American dollarism."

The minister's elegant efforts ultimately fell short. There would be no African-sponsored inquiry into America's racial horrors. On the summit's opening day, Egyptian President Gamal Abdel Nasser, a Malcolm ally, applauded the Civil Rights Act that President Lyndon B. Johnson had inked just two weeks before. It was a bleak omen for the minister, who had rejected the bill as a "rubber check" whose empty promise would embitter blacks and provoke violence. He later insisted that several statesmen and high officials at the conference "relieved and delighted" him with their private assurance that they recognized the historic American legislation as little more than an election-year maneuver. But the African leaders were facing their own political woes and entanglements that summer, and in the end they refused to make war on American imperialism.

Malcolm nevertheless left with some spoils. Conference delegates finally penned a cautious resolution praising the Civil Rights Act on one hand while challenging the U.S. government to expand its efforts against racism on the other. Malcolm's ambassadorship had broadened the consciousness of independent Africa's leaders. He had firmed his and Black America's ties to Africa while sabotaging U.S. efforts to portray race relations on its soil as a mending wound. The most compelling evidence of the mission's impact surfaced later that winter when African statesmen launched a concerted attack on American racism during a UN debate on the crisis in the Congo, drawing on political strategies Malcolm had championed in their capitals.

Columnist Charles Bartlett, however, granted the minister not even ancillary victory. Like other American pundits, he drubbed Malcolm as a bitter extremist who had done nothing but stir African antagonism while chasing his own disturbing notions of liberty. In a late July 1964 commentary, he said that the minister and his "terrorist" loyalists' hatred for their native land had rightfully attracted the FBI's continuing scrutiny. Back in Queens, Betty fumed as she heard a radio commentator give an equally unflattering appraisal of her husband's lobbying. Whatever her awareness of the diplomatic implications of Malcolm's mission, she understood the hypocrisy of those who accused him of threatening America's racial progress.

It riled her further that the Civil Rights establishment ignored or spurned his presence on the continent. "Some leaders felt that Malcolm had no business in Africa, that the African problem was not our problem, that he should be in Mississippi and Alabama," she later said. Betty would insist that independent Africa had embraced the minister's appeal, though "a lot of people could not read between the lines and understand that." Washington could, and did. The *Times* reported in August 1964 that Malcolm's campaign had drawn the attention of the State and Justice Departments. Government officials privately acknowledged their fear that the minister's efforts could undermine the nation's status as a global leader in human-rights advocacy, and furnish Communists and other foes with ideological ammunition.

Malcolm knew he was vexing Uncle Sam. He discovered early in his African trek that CIA agents were shadowing him. He told Betty that he had confronted the men on his trail. One explained apologetically that he was only doing his job, adding that as far as he was concerned, Malcolm's crusade was both legal and noble, Betty later said. But she and her husband also suspected the agents of sinister designs. During the OAU summit, Malcolm got violently sick one night after dinner at the Nile Hilton. He awoke in agony, vomited until he dry heaved, then dragged himself to a sink in his room and let the water run down his throat.

His friends came running and whisked him to a hospital, where doctors pumped his stomach. He guessed that Western agents had poisoned him, and Betty never doubted it. The minister worried that American operatives were looking to do him in throughout the eighteen-week African epic, but he never quit. He trundled through fourteen nations and sat with seven heads of state, including Kenyan Prime Minister Jomo Kenyatta, Ugandan Prime Minister Milton Obote, and Guinean President Sékou Touré. And finally, as he navigated the continent that had cradled civilization, he came as close as he ever would to outrunning his past.

"I am no longer in Elijah Muhammad's 'straight-jacket,' and I don't intend to replace his with one woven by someone else," he said in a letter to a journalist back home that read like a proclamation of spiritual and intellectual independence. Malcolm branded Muhammad a religious "faker" and reaffirmed his allegiance to orthodox Islam, a faith he said embraced "all human beings as equals before God." He denied being un-American, seditious, subversive, "anti-capitalist or anti-communist," and explained that he was still seeking a whole vision of justice:

> I'm trying to weigh everything objectively and of its own merit....I need no one anymore to tell me who to hate. I'm searching for truth and justice, not someone else's propaganda. I've had enough of that. I'm for truth, no matter who tells it. I'm for justice, no matter who it is for or against. I'm a human being first and foremost, and as such I'm for whoever and whatever benefits humanity....

Ella Collins and Betty wanted to greet him at home. "We shared a concern about his safety and would have preferred that he return quietly and get out of that airport terminal as quickly as possible," Collins later said. Both women feared that John F. Kennedy International Airport would be writhing with FBI and CIA agents and Black Muslims for Malcolm's November 24 arrival. The scene had never been hotter. Earlier that July, a white police officer's slaying of fifteen-year-old James Powell had unleashed shock waves of unrest. During the rebellion—one of several that wasted inner cities that summer—moderate black leaders had been powerless to cool enraged Harlemites, many of whom chanted "We want Malcolm" as they spilled into the streets. Again the media had charged the minister in absentia with stoking the flames. Meanwhile, the Nation maintained its cyanide commentary. "Is Malcolm bold enough to return and face the music?" Louis X demanded in *Muhammad Speaks*. "Only those who wish to be led to hell, or to their doom, will follow Malcolm," he wrote. "The die is set and Malcolm shall not escape....Such a man as Malcolm is worthy of death."

Betty swabbed the stress of recent months from her eyes as she waited in a Kennedy terminal, fingering the line of pearls at her neck. Journalist Louis Lomax was among the comrades who had phoned her in recent weeks, worrying about the dangers that awaited the minister stateside. "But she remained firm in the faith that all would be well once Malcolm returned home," Lomax later said.

Betty gleamed as she stood in her fur-fringed topcoat, black gloves, and a sheer black scarf, grinning bashfully among the crush of supporters and WELCOME BACK BROTHER MALCOLM signs as her husband strode toward her. Though she had begun forgoing the scarf, she had slipped on an especially fetching one that evening, perhaps for his benefit. The minister was in no condition to notice the gesture. He was spent and harried. Pouches hung beneath his eyes. He looked like a man who was walking on his coffin.

His organizations were no better off. Membership had bled down to only the most hardcore loyalists, and many of them were halfway out the door. The weeks ahead were wintry. The minister complained that journalists who had exaggerated every scuffle between his people and the Nation now downplayed his declarations that the Black Muslims wanted him dead, that they had already tried to kill him several times, and that they would soon succeed. "The press gives the impression that I'm jiving about this thing," he said bitterly. Then there was the more clandestine but no less ominous threat of the intelligence community and the white power structure, which the Malcolmites called the "Old Ones." "They all wanted to jump him," Kenyatta later remembered. "We expected that any minute the bullets would start flying."

Everyone around Malcolm foresaw the end. "These brothers gonna put you on a cross!" his photographer Robert Haggins warned. As 1964 rattled to a close, the asylum offers began pouring in. Friends—rich and poor, eminent and unknown—offered summer homes, guestrooms, and furloughs with relatives. Actress Ruby Dee even considered harboring Malcolm in a secret wall of her home before her husband Ossie Davis vetoed the suggestion. "No, no, no," he said. "Malcolm could never hide behind a wall. Please, don't mention such a thing."

Many of the minister's sympathizers in Africa had begged him to stay. "Let that jazz cool off," the expatriates in Ghana had pleaded. "Bring Betty and the children." Malcolm told Claude Lewis that Saudi Arabia had invited him and his family to live in its capital as guests of state. Ethiopia offered sanctuary, and several other African and Middle-Eastern nations and universities made lucrative job offers. "He could have stayed," Alice Mitchell later said ruefully. "They were crazy about him."

Malcolm believed his destiny was in New York. "I'd be a coward to stir up all this trouble and just run away," he told Lewis. "There's a lot I want to get done, because I don't know how long I'm going to be here." In a letter to Julian Mayfield, he said he was prepared for the worst. He hoped that if he were killed, his wife and children would find asylum in some African country. "He had purged himself of fear," Ferguson later said. Some of the Malcolmites thought their leader even welcomed the stillness of the grave. "Malcolm wanted to die," Kenyatta remembered.

The minister discussed the possibility of moving to Africa with several of his close advisors, including Razzaq and Ella. His obligation to continue the struggle on American soil seemed to tether him. Black protest was entering a restive new phase, and he hoped to harness its young radicals. There was another obstacle to an African move. "Brother," he told Razzaq, "my wife will not go."

———

Betty desperately wanted to save her husband. "I was among those close to Malcolm, including Betty, who wanted him to take a breather from the struggle and focus for a while on himself and his family," Collins later said. Malcolm would not slow down. He would not stop attacking Muhammad or whirling from one lecture to the next or granting media interviews or booking appearances and tearing about the country like a haunted gypsy. Betty thought she might reason with him during the fleeting minutes at home when she held his attention, but all the intercession in the world could not have tempered the minister. She loved him dearly and resented him bitterly, and in the end did not know whether to leave him or consign him to the grave.

She knew she did not want to move to Africa. She had a network of friends and family in the United States. What awaited her and the children in Ghana or Egypt or Guinea? She was also pregnant again, and could not fathom giving birth overseas. "In the sixties, Africa wasn't just another continent," Angelou later said. "It was another universe." A new universe free of Western perils was precisely what many Malcolmites wished for Malcolm. Some of them boiled when they discovered Betty's refusal to go abroad.

Mitchell could not understand why Betty insisted on "pulling him back into the fire." Razzaq, one of the many apostles who had grown disillusioned with Malcolm's risk taking and shifting ideologies, only shook his head. "We are addicted to America," he thought glumly. Never one to surrender gently, Collins badgered her brother. "Betty is much stronger than she appears," she said after the minister suggested that his pregnant wife was too frail for the journey. "You should tell her straight out that we are going to pack some suitcases, get the children ready, and move on."

Betty and Collins were even then on the verge of a calamitous falling-out. The latter had for years sought to mold Malcolm—first as a man-child, then as a revolutionary. The former was fed up with her domineering in-law's interference. James Smalls, who became Collins's bodyguard and an *imam* (spiritual leader) of the Muslim Mosque in later years, would describe the women's relationship:

> Theirs was a rift over a "momma" having one aspiration for her child and a wife having another aspiration for her husband. They were unable to reconcile. Ella wanted Malcolm to be the greatest leader in the world. And she felt that you can't do that if you are hamstrung by a woman. She felt that Betty should have come to Boston and just help her run her business and let Malcolm go out in the world and do his thing. Ella wanted to control the marriage. And Betty didn't go for it.

Betty had in fact grown to loathe many of her husband's confidants. She was certain that some of them were out to betray him, and nobody—least of all the minister—could say for sure that she was mistaken. "Malcolm had no friends in the last ninety days," Kenyatta later said. Some of the minister's comrades believed Betty was an exception. Malcolm told Percy Sutton and Lewis that she was a loyal soldier. "She's the only person I'd trust with my life," he told Alex Haley. "That means I trust her more than I trust myself."

In those final jangled weeks, the minister shrunk from shadows, jumped at innocent noises, and dreaded turning his back to the door. Yet Lewis found he could always soothe him by asking about the wife and children. To some, Betty and their daughters and unborn child— "This one will be the boy!" he sang—seemed the last sunbeams in his life. But other disciples thought Betty was compounding the strain with demands for his time. "He was always trying to pacify her," Mitchell later said.

In the end, Betty's clamoring, Malcolm's obsessions, and the bitterness and uncertainty of those days all seemed to corrode the marriage. One afternoon, the minister tramped through the door with a sideman and ordered her to fix him and his companion a meal. When she refused, he spun on his heel and wordlessly marched out. The Malcolmites began whispering about an impending divorce, and Collins later maintained that Betty was considering an annulment. Malcolm himself confessed to his men during a drive back from the Poitier estate that he and his wife were having problems. "She didn't want to stay in the house," Kenyatta later recalled. "She didn't want to stay wrapped up. But it was his law."

It's not surprising that Malcolm couched his marital woes in terms of Betty's intransigence. Yet the truth may have been more intricate. The bread-and-butter concerns had always fallen to Betty. She had seen that the children were clothed and fed, that the household functioned, and that the minister did not run himself into the ground. He in turn had ventured forth to seek dignity and self-determination with the promise that tonight or tomorrow night or the following night he would return.

Now that delicate balance had collapsed. He was desperate to transcend street-corner ideology and unearth a philosophy of struggle that would outlast him and deliver his children's generation. She was desperate to preserve the family in a tolerable state. These may have been reconcilable ambitions in the greater scheme, but under the circumstances, they were doomed to collide.

Malcolm never believed he would die of old age. Now he was certain he would not last the winter. "Everybody was sure that he was going to get it," Lewis later said. "And nobody wanted to be there when he did." Not even Betty could ignore the inevitable. "Malcolm tried to prepare me for it," she later said, "but I'll never say that I was totally prepared." She stopped walking away, though, when he discussed the end. "Don't look back and don't cry," he told her. "Remember, Lot's wife turned into a pillar of salt." Betty wept privately but held herself together in front of her husband. "I just closed my eyes and hung onto everything he said," she later remembered.

Malcolm's courage moved Ahmed Osman, the orthodox Muslim graduate student with whom he had once debated theology. "He knew he was to be martyred," Osman later said. "He never flinched." Inwardly, though, the minister was wielding all the weapons at his disposal against the crushing fear. In his anguish, even his humor grew callous. He told his wife with a joyless smile that after he was gone, "no man will want you with all these children."

Meanwhile Betty made a volley of frantic calls to practically everyone she remotely trusted, seeking the solace that she knew in her heart they could not provide. "The situation is getting desperate," she told Lewis. "I don't know what's going to happen, but I don't have a good feeling." The journalist asked her who she thought might make an attempt on her husband's life. "Somebody's going to do something," she repeated, insisting that she had no idea who. "I really think she knew," Lewis later recalled, "but didn't want to say."

She may have had no lineup of specific suspects in mind, no faces within the menacing ranks of the Original People and the Old Ones whom she felt she could finger. Considering her isolation, she may in fact have known less than the minister's apostles until the final hours. All that many of them knew was that Malcolm had testified endlessly before the public, press, and police that the Nation was going to kill him, and that he had lately begun to privately suspect that the conspiracy's perimeters were actually far wider than Black Islam. Sometime near the end, though, Malcolm compiled a list of five Muslim men who he suspected would do the deed. Betty saw the names just before the bullets flew, but never publicly revealed them.

In later years, she complained that "identifiable" members of the sect were "running my husband all over the country" in the months before his death. Who did she suppose arranged the murder? "I believe what Malcolm told me," she repeated throughout her widowhood. She said the minister predicted after "careful analysis" that forces in Washington, D.C., would order his death, but would capitalize on his open war with the Nation by colluding with or abetting Black Muslim assassins. "He learned some things the government did not want him to know," she once said cryptically.

Malcolm was dodging death as 1965 whirred to life. In a year-end speech, he had suggested that blacks needed a Mau Mau—a guerrilla society—to "even the score" with white aggressors, drawing fresh ripples of condemnation from the press and black moderates. His rhetoric now revolved around black unity while blending strains of nationalism, African socialism, and Pan-Africanism. He was transcending the black-white dialectic, speaking increasingly of global, non-white revolution against imperialist oppression. Meanwhile, he was cementing relationships with such Dark World revolutionaries as Abdulrahman Mohamed Babu, the radical Tanzanian government minister.

The minister began practicing the solidarity with the Civil Rights struggle that he had been preaching. He went to Selma, Alabama—Martin Luther King Jr.'s turf—to talk with some of black protest's young lions, whipping the audience at a Civil Rights rally into a frenzy. King was in prison in connection with a local march, so his colleagues hustled his wife, Coretta, to the pulpit after Malcolm's speech to cool the crowd and preach nonviolence. Despite the vigor of his speech, Malcolm was on a peace mission. Overseas appointments prohibited a meeting with King, but he left his regards with the reverend's wife. "Mrs. King," he said, "will you tell Dr. King that I had planned to visit with him in jail?...I want Dr. King to know that I didn't come to Selma to make his job difficult. I really did come thinking that I could make it easier. If the white people realize what the alternative is, perhaps they will be more willing to hear Dr. King."

Malcolm was still groping for a core ideology and strategy. His organizations were still disintegrating. The Civil Rights establishment was still recoiling from him. Baleful Black Muslims still prowled everywhere he appeared, trying clumsily to rush him on several occasions, and once chasing him down a Los Angeles freeway. Bodyguards and police kept him cordoned. When he dipped into North Philadelphia for a mid-January address, sixty uniformed officers, thirty detectives, forty teams of highway patrolmen, and two police buses kept vigil.

The blue line offered little comfort. Malcolm believed that the New York constabulary was sympathetic to the conspiracy against him, if not one of its agents. He thought that the police only intensified the militaristic aura that had started thinning his crowds. Fearing that the tense atmosphere was also fueling the firebrand image he had struggled to shed, Malcolm ordered his men to stop frisking spectators at the door before his lectures. He later forbade them to wear weapons of any sort—either visibly or under their clothes—at OAAU events. The media had portrayed him and his followers as heavily armed warhawks, he explained, and guns only reinforced the stereotype. Under the circumstances, however, the ban seemed suicidal. After the explosive meeting in which he announced it, some of his most loyal men stalked off in disgust.

Meanwhile, other crises festered. Malcolm's insistence that only armed self-defense could deter violent white aggression continued to repel liberal whites and many of the black audiences he wished to capture. Yet his new talk of human "brotherhood" alienated much of his base constituency in Harlem. "For the Muslims, I'm too worldly, for other groups, I'm too religious; for militants, I'm too moderate; and for moderates, I'm too militant," he complained. "I feel like I'm on a tightrope."

Then the tightrope shuddered. Malcolm flew to London for a lecture before the First Congress of the Council of African Organizations then made the short hop to Paris on February 9 to address a rally of black Africans and Americans. When he arrived at Orly Airport, customs officers informed him that the French government was barring him as an undesirable. A ring of gendarmes ushered the furious minister onto a return flight to London, where he landed four hours after he had left. Before officials hustled him out of Paris, he flipped them a British one-cent piece and told them to "give that to de Gaulle, because the French government is worth less than a penny."

Betty panicked when she got the news. She knew all the high authorities in Black Islam could not have kept her husband out of

France. "Some very powerful forces were beginning to move against him," she later said. After a rambling tour of a racially embroiled corner of England, Malcolm returned to New York. A band of his followers engulfed him at the airport and shuttled him to the Hotel Theresa. He tromped up the stairs to his office and slumped into a chair. "You know, brothers," he told his huddled men, wincing as if it hurt to speak, "I've been making a serious mistake. I've been focusing on [the Black Muslim headquarters in] Chicago, thinking all my problems were coming from Chicago. And they're not." The men asked where he thought the trouble originated. The minister pointed south. "From Washington," he said.

On February 14, 1965, Betty and Malcolm were sleeping soundly. He had flown in from London worn and edgy, and had gulped a sedative. She had tucked in the children and gone to bed, slipping beneath sheets and layers of fear. (Malcolm was slumbering upstairs in his study that night, as he often did.) She had gotten so many threatening calls that day that she wondered whether she was having a nervous breakdown. More horrors lay ahead. At 2:45 A.M., fracturing glass and an explosion shattered the night as the first Molotov cocktail hit.

Within seconds, black smoke was churning and orange tentacles of flame were skimming along the floor and flitting up the walls. Malcolm was vaulting out of bed and pounding through the house toward the children as the second firebomb struck. Betty, leaden with pregnancy, staggered into the hallway and found herself near the kitchen door. She heard the thud as a third Molotov cocktail glanced off a rear window and fizzled. "Get the girls!" she thought, but the linoleum seemed to have swallowed her up to the shins.

Then Malcolm was flinging open the back door and barking at her—"Stay here!" He plunged into the clotting smoke, scooping up shrieking children, the older three from a bedroom beside his and Betty's and Gamilah from her crib nearby. In an instant he returned and deposited them at Betty's side. Their incandescent faces jolted her from her trance. Still in her nightgown, she hustled the bawling girls into the yard. Again Malcolm bounded into the house, now for some of their belongings. Soon he reemerged in his underclothes and a singed overcoat, joining his wife and children in the frigid darkness.

They stood there coughing and shivering, their eyes stinging as firemen battled the leaping blaze. The flames would incinerate almost half of the uninsured house. But its occupants were alive. Qubilah, who had been the first child awake and whose screams may have roused her parents, sobbed beside her sisters. She was four, the age Malcolm had been when white men torched his family's Omaha, Nebraska, home in 1929, an episode he described in his autobiography:

> I remember being suddenly snatched awake into a fright-
> ening confusion of pistol shots and shouting and smoke and
> flames. My father had shouted and shot at the two white
> men who had set the fire and were running away. Our home
> was burning down around us. We were lunging and bump-
> ing and tumbling all over each other trying to escape. My
> mother, with the baby in her arms, just made it into the
> yard before the house crashed in, showering sparks.

Now, thirty-six years later, it was Betty who struggled to comfort her children as flames swallowed the home they had only just escaped. "I was almost frightened by his courage and efficiency in a time of ter-ror," she later said of Malcolm. "I always knew he was strong. But at that hour I learned how great his strength was." The minister was so composed that even his eldest daughter had not fully grasped the dan-ger. "My mother's like that, too," Attallah later said. "Together." But Betty never forgot her own paralysis. She had been useless as a corpse in the few precious moments that might have meant her children's lives, and she vowed never again to freeze in the face of danger.

Numbness, however, yielded swiftly to rage. "I couldn't imagine any-body being that cruel," she said later. "I couldn't imagine that anyone who claimed to love black people could do something like that." She wondered how an order that preached love for God, race, and family could so despise a man who honored all three with body and soul. Malcolm thought it was the Muslims, too. When a reporter screeched onto the scene and asked whom he thought had torched the place, his only reply was a peal of bitter, half-crazed laughter.

The Malcolmites ushered a distraught Betty and her daughters to the house of Ruby Dee's brother, Tom Wallace, a dear friend and OAAU member who lived nearby in Queens. Malcolm did not accompany them; he was scheduled to speak in Detroit later that day and spent the next few hours preparing to catch a morning flight. He could almost hear the countdown to his death, but he was determined not to bow to his enemies. There was still much to say and do.

Having barely escaped death by fire alongside her husband and daughters, Betty discovered that Malcolm planned to keep his out-of-town speaking date, and flew into a rage. This last injustice charred whatever sliver of her composure had survived the flames. Later that Valentine's Day, a fatigued and tormented Malcolm stood before a Detroit audience in clothes that reeked of smoke and proclaimed that the bombing had not sapped his resolve, "because my wife understands and I have children from this size on down [gesturing] and even in their young age, they understand." But neither Betty's fear nor her fury had kept the minister in New York.

The Nation said Malcolm bombed the place himself—as a publicity stunt. The suggestion riled Malcolm. "I have no compassion or mercy or forgiveness for anyone who attacks sleeping babies," the minister told an audience of five hundred at the Audubon Ballroom that Monday. Investigators fueled the arson theory with the left-handed mention to reporters that firemen had discovered an upright bottle of gasoline on a dresser in the scorched home. Betty had come across the whisky bottle in the fire's aftermath and had shown it to investigators.

"We knew it didn't belong there," Malcolm later said. "We don't have whisky in our home." He suggested that it was a plant, that perhaps a crooked firefighter was out to frame him. Betty was equally suspicious.

"Only someone in the uniform of a fireman or policeman could have planted the bottle of gasoline on my baby's dresser," she said.

Malcolm, however, charged Black Islam with the firebombing. Ridiculous, said his former Temple Number Seven underling and nemesis, Captain Joseph. "We own the place man," he told journalists. "We have money tied up here." Besides, Joseph said, the minister had been facing certain eviction.

Judge Wahl had ordered the family out of the house by the end of the month. Percy Sutton had filed a last-minute appeal, and Wahl had set a final hearing for that Monday, February 15. Powerless to grant any further stays, Wahl upheld the displacement order that week. Malcolm and his men returned to the ruins on 97th Street early one morning to collect whatever belongings they could salvage.

Malcolm may have been trying to salvage his marriage, too. The following Saturday, he took Betty house shopping. A real-estate agent showed the couple a modest property in an integrated, predominantly Jewish Long Island neighborhood. Betty liked the place. As the minister drove her back to the Wallace home (where she and the children were staying), they planned for the future. Where would they find the three thousand dollars for a down payment on the house? What about the estimated one thousand dollars in moving costs? Malcolm had only a fraction of that left in savings.

To avoid the trouble that using his name would invite, he and Betty decided to buy the house under Ella Collins's name. They agreed that eventually they would transfer the title to Betty or Attallah. Malcolm had begun clearing his calendar of appearances and had made an appointment with Sutton for the next week to draw up a will. In recent days, he had brought Betty and the bonneted, bundled-up children to the Hotel Theresa with him, and she had sat up front bottle-feeding Gamilah as he addressed the OAAU body. He was finally slowing down long enough to handle domestic matters. His relationship with Betty had nearly dissolved. Perhaps it now had a fighting chance.

The couple arrived at the Wallaces' and talked quietly for a few hours. Then the minister retrieved his hat and prepared to leave for the

New York Hilton, where he was to pull together his notes and rest for a rally at the Audubon Ballroom the following afternoon. In the hallway, he turned and faced Betty. He said he understood what he had put her through. He apologized for the hardship and vowed that change was coming. "We'll all be together," he said. "I want my family with me. Families shouldn't be separated." He promised that there would be no more long trips without her —they would get somebody to keep the children if necessary. "I'll never leave you so long again," he said. Betty had not smiled like that in months.

Later that evening, Malcolm huddled with James Campbell in a stall behind the Theresa office chalkboard. Campbell discussed the progress of the OAAU's Liberation School, reporting that another set of diplomas awaited the minister's signature. Malcolm was tense but managed a flash of levity, telling his comrade that Betty was expecting again. "Every time I look at her she gets pregnant!" he exclaimed. Campbell had never before heard him mention his wife. When Malcolm spoke again, his tone was sober. "I'd like for her to stay in touch with brothers like you," he told Campbell, jotting down the phone number where Betty was staying. His companion nodded.

Malcolm telephoned Betty at nine in the morning on February 21, 1965, and asked if it would not be too much trouble for her to collect the girls and ferry them to the Audubon for the two o'clock lecture. "Of course it won't!" Betty said. The request surprised her. Earlier he had forbidden her to attend, insisting that the scene was too risky. Why the change of heart? Betty would never know whether he had had a premonition. "But it was a very warm conversation," she later remembered. Before the minister hung up, he told her that someone—it had sounded like a white man—had phoned his hotel room an hour earlier and said, "Wake up, brother."

Betty and the girls were late arriving at the Audubon. She had spent the early afternoon encasing them in snowsuits and preparing for the drive to Manhattan, pin-curling her hair and sheathing her hands and forearms in long black gloves. The children were fidgety. A trek uptown was a departure from the tenor of recent days. "It was still an exciting adventure to get ready and go see Daddy," Attallah (then six) later remembered.

By the time Betty marched the girls up to the second-floor ballroom, the flecks of sunlight that had stolen into the musty room were starting to skitter back out. It was shortly before 3 P.M. (Malcolm had been checking for her in the audience and had asked someone to call the Wallaces to see if she had left.) The four hundred seats were filling fast. On stage, a blue-green landscape mural loomed behind a plywood lectern, a white grand piano, a drum set, and a row of eight brown chairs. Betty steered her daughters up one of two side aisles, past the rows of wooden chairs in the center of the room and the restaurant-style booths along the walls.

She ushered the girls into the second booth near the stage (on Malcolm's left as he took the podium) and started peeling off their snowsuits. "We were seated near the front on one of those old-fashioned benches with a drop front—it was like a box with a back," she later recalled. She might have wanted to go see Malcolm in the cramped offstage anteroom in which he was waiting for the crowd to reach critical mass. The trauma of the firebombing was fresh, and the night before had been fitful. But she never disturbed the minister before his lectures. Besides, she expected to see more of him in the days ahead. She could wait; she always had.

So she sat minding the children, too preoccupied to spot some of the nuances of the scene. If on the way into the building she had noticed that the solitary policeman manning the front entrance was a flimsier presence than the queue of patrolmen that typically covered her husband's Audubon rallies, she never mentioned it. (With the exception of two uniformed officers in an adjoining room, the rest of the men in the police detail were out of sight in a hospital across the street.) The lone sentinel did strike Kenyatta as odd. When the aide discovered that none of the Malcolmites were frisking spectators upstairs, he realized how brittle the minister's line of defense would be that Sunday. He asked the men what was going on. Malcolm's bodyguard, Reuben

Francis, told him that Malcolm had forbidden body searches. Kenyatta flared. "Y'all poppin' game!" he said. "That's bullshit! You know he don't know what he's sayin' or doin'. Y'all know better."

Meanwhile, Malcolm sat in the wings brooding. He had a bad feeling about the rally, and it showed. His people had never seen him so spooked or jumpy. In the last hour, he had blown his cool with one after another of them. He had invited several prominent guests to the rally, and had grown testier as each one phoned in a no-show. Now he paced and muttered and scowled, the last wisps of his princely aura melting away. When Razzaq walked in and passed the news that Reverend Milton Galamison, the militant Brooklyn Presbyterian and scheduled co-speaker, was not going to make it either, Malcolm lit into his sideman. "Why haven't you told me he wasn't coming?" he snarled. Razzaq explained that he had called and given Betty the message earlier. The minister berated the aide for talking business with his wife and for entrusting a woman with such information. "And then he calmed down right away," Razzaq later remembered.

Benjamin Karim was on stage delivering the thirty-minute warm-up speech. Malcolm emerged from the wings and sat behind his assistant minister. "Make it plain," he murmured. Taking the cue, Karim wrapped up. "I present to you...one who is willing to put himself on the line for you...a man who would give his life for you...." The sideman turned to take a seat in one of the chairs lining the stage. As he was passing the minister, Malcolm clasped his arm gently and whispered for him to return to the offstage cubicle. Now alone on stage, the minister loped across the scarred planks to his lectern. He stood there for a moment in the muted glow of the hall, his smile widening under the applause. Finally he gave the greeting: "As-salaam alaikum." The crowd roared its response: "Wa-alaikum salaam."

Suddenly, seven rows deep in the audience, came a scuffle and a growl—"Take your hand out of my pocket!"—and the crowd was swinging to look as two men leapt to their feet, their chairs scraping the floor. Betty saw the jostling in her peripheral vision and felt a surge of panic. The two rostrum guards were jogging up the side aisles toward the skirmish. Betty glimpsed the back and side profile of one of the tussling men only long enough to notice the rusty hue of his jacket. "Let's cool it, brothers," Malcolm said. He stepped around to the side of the lectern, leaned over slightly, and raised his hands in a calming gesture. It is entirely possible that he never spotted the three men down front who leapt to their feet and whipped guns from their overcoats. If he did get a look at the young black men lunging at him, Mitchell later said, "they did not have to touch him because he died of a broken heart."

Betty heard the blast of a shotgun and swiveled back toward the stage. "I knew there was no one else in there they'd be shooting at," she later remembered. She heard someone say, "Oh my God, oh my God," and she saw Malcolm stiffen, his hands flying up halfway, his face and white dress shirt speckled with blood. Then there was the *clak! clak!* of pistols and his eyes were rolling back, his mouth dropping open. "If he would only fall," Ferguson thought frantically, "maybe he'd survive."

Then suddenly, finally, he did—floating backward, straight as a gymnast, his palms turned out. Betty saw him keel over and crash through the chairs behind him. She heard the thud as his head slammed into the dusty stage—"Must've smashed his brains," one onlooker thought—and then she was snatching her children, sweeping them to the floor beneath the booth's wooden bench, shielding them with her body and coat. Attallah would insist as an adult that she had watched the slaughter. Betty believed otherwise; she had pinned the girls with all her might. "They never actually saw it," she later said.

Betty lay there atop her daughters with her head bowed. She held them down to protect them as much as to calm them; the assassins might have wanted the wife and daughters, too. But the gunmen were busy guaranteeing their hit. They stood before the sprawled minister and squeezed shot after shot into his jerking body, the bullets sizzling into his calves and thighs. "They're killing my husband!" Betty heard herself scream.

There was an eerie hush, as if the room had plunged into a vacuum. Everyone had hit the floor when the fusillade began. They lay there now, splayed about like cadavers. The killers stood frozen in their topcoats, their guns smoking at their sides. "It was almost like they were posing for a picture," Ferguson remembered. Suddenly they turned and ran, heading for the rear, bounding over chairs and people. Betty felt their footfalls like a mallet in her throat.

The place erupted. Everybody was screaming, colliding, ducking, skidding, hurdling chairs, and dashing for the exit. Beneath Betty, one of the Shabazz girls wailed that she could not breathe. "Are they going to kill everyone?" another daughter sobbed. Betty tried to scramble through the stampede toward the stage, but somebody seized her from behind and yanked her back down. At the back of the room, a homemade flare fashioned out of a gasoline-soaked sock sputtered and smoked. "It's a bomb!" someone yelled as a man tried to stamp it out.

The man with the shotgun vanished into the churning melee. One or more Malcolmites had worn guns, despite the minister's order. They now drew their weapons and tried to fire through the blur of bodies at the pair of pistol-wielding assassins who were squeezing off rounds as they fled. Stray bullets wounded a couple of bystanders. Reuben Francis shot one of the gunmen—a man later identified as Talmadge Hayer— in the thigh. Hobbling over to the staircase, Hayer spilled down the steps toward the main ballroom entrance, where the horde seized him. "They were trying to pull him apart the way you pull a drumstick off a turkey," Ferguson later said. A couple of patrolmen finally rescued Hayer from the crowd with a warning shot and flung him into a squad car. Several people saw a second man they assumed was a suspect ushered into another police cruiser and whisked away.

Back inside the ballroom, a handful of Malcolmites leapt onto the stage. One woman hurled herself over a prone figure, believing she was shielding Malcolm from another volley. But the minister lay graying nearby, his goatee a bloody clump, his eyes half-closed behind his glasses, and his face a ghastly leer. Six or seven of his disciples surrounded him and began the futile ministrations. One propped up his legs. Another loosened his tie and tore open his shirt to reveal a platter-sized ring of craters—the buckshot pellets' damage.

"His chest looks like the moon," Sister Khadiyyah thought. A woman bent over him, and whether or not she heard the faint rattling of his last gasps, said, "He's still alive. His heart's beating." Gene

Roberts, an undercover police officer who had infiltrated the minister's corps in recent months, crouched over Malcolm and appeared to try mouth-to-mouth resuscitation. A woman took over for Roberts, straddling the minister. "You gonna blow up his lungs," a man told her.

Betty, who had been frantically wheeling about somewhere in the eddy of overturned chairs, now sliced through the clot of onlookers. She was hysterical. A woman grabbed and slapped her. "He can't see you like this!" she said. Finally the ring of aides parted. Still sobbing, Betty knelt by her husband and knew instantly that he was gone. She had wanted to perform mouth-to-mouth resuscitation, but now started on CPR. Then she seized his hands and pumped his arms uselessly, her face a mask of anguish. Suddenly she was rifling frenziedly through his clothes. Malcolm's people watched incredulously. A detective saw her remove a bloodstained note, and later told the *New York Post* that she "seemed very interested in getting papers out of his pocket."

The rest was denouement. Somebody pulled Betty off of her husband and led her into the wings. "Oh, Muriel," she said to Feelings, "he's gone! And I'm *pregnant!*" Feelings glanced down from the stage and saw Attallah's tiny, crimson face burst into a shriek that still ricochets in both women's hearts. A dozen or more policemen finally sauntered into the dance hall. Yuri Kochiyama, who had cradled Malcolm's head in her lap while the others tried to revive him, drifted over to the stage's side door. Someone thrust seven-month-old Gamilah into her hands and she stood there numbly, feeding the infant milk from a bottle. The women had ushered the other Shabazz girls into the green room. Betty now drew the terrified and confused children near. "Suddenly I feel too old to be sitting on that lady's lap," Attallah later recalled.

The Malcomites and the police got Malcolm onto a stretcher and hauled him out of the dance hall, across Broadway and one block up to Columbia Presbyterian Medical Center. Mitchell and another woman wrapped the Shabazz daughters in coats and prepared to shuttle them back to the Wallace home. Attallah, unsure what had happened, later handed one of the women a penny "for keeps." Betty found herself outside the Audubon entrance, out in the bitter chill. "Jean!" she cried to one of her husband's disciples. "Don't leave me!" Jean Reynolds stood by the widow, her face creased in torment. "I had to be strong for her," she later remembered. "I was just about ready to break. I wanted to just be out of it."

Betty had wept hysterically as she followed her husband's body across Broadway. Now she calmed down. Her eyes closed, and her breathing grew shallow. She spent twenty minutes in the stifling emergency clinic among the press, the faithful, and the curious. Finally, a man appeared before the throng and made a terse announcement: "The gentleman you know as Malcolm X is dead." Minutes later, the men would half-carry the screeching widow from Columbia Presbyterian, but for the moment her only thought was that she had to see for herself.

Reuben Francis and some of the others escorted her into a brimming elevator and onto the hospital's third floor. When they got to the operating room, two of the men started through the door ahead of her. A woman objected. "That's his *wife!*" Betty entered the room. Somebody flung back the curtain, and there was Malcolm. Betty saw the freshly sutured seam where doctors had opened his chest and massaged his heart in a final, desperate attempt to revive him. "They took his heart out," whispered Sister Khadiyyah. She turned in horror. "Betty," she said, "remember this, okay?" The long-time Malcolm devotee believed her leader's body had been desecrated, and wanted to ensure that the widow could bear witness in the event of a future effort for retribution or revenge. "But she was just not there," Sister Khadiyyah later said. "I don't know what happened after that. I was too through."

By 7:15 P.M., the police had left the Audubon with their chalk and sandwich bags of scrapings and spent shells. Three cleaning women began scrubbing the darkening blood off the stage. A crew arrived to clear away the overturned chairs and set up musical instruments. Within hours, the guests of the Metro Associates of Brooklyn would start trickling in for the club's annual dance. Meanwhile, Louis Lomax was desperately ringing the Wallace residence from Los Angeles. Again and again he dialed before finally getting through. Someone put the widow on the line. "The niggers *did it*, Lomax," she cried. "The niggers *did it!* I didn't believe they would; but the niggers *did it*."

Chapter Ten

AFTER THE WINTER

———

"[The black woman] had nothing to fall back on:
not maleness, not whiteness, not ladyhood, not anything."
—Toni Morrison

The night before Malcolm's assassination, Juanita Poitier had a visitor. The estranged wife of actor Sidney Poitier and mother of four girls had gone to bed in her Pleasantville, New York, home and was drifting off to sleep when she heard a faint voice calling to her. She looked up and saw a stringy child standing near the bedroom door, which she always left cracked with the hall light on. Poitier thought it was her youngest daughter, and in some fragment of consciousness threw back the covers and said, "Come get in bed with Mommy." But the girl's hair looked curiously light, almost phosphorescent. After she glided across the room and put one knee on the bed, she disappeared.

The following afternoon, not long after Malcolm fell, the wife of jazz hand-drummer Michael Olatunji telephoned Poitier and said, "Let's go and see about Betty." The two women arrived at the Wallaces' later that evening. Malcolm disciples and devotees—mostly young, black men—milled about inside, wearing the jolted expression one gets when somebody beloved has died suddenly and awfully. Somewhere amid the nationalists and assorted others, the pair of new arrivals found Betty. Attached to her was Attallah—the child Poitier swore she had seen in her bedroom the night before.

Attallah had never met the society wife. Yet, she lifted her damp face to the woman and said, "I'm glad you're here." Taken aback, Poitier extended her condolences to Betty, with whom she had had almost no contact. Then she turned to Attallah. "I don't know you and your mother," she told the six-year-old gently. "But I knew your father, and I'm so sorry."

"Oh yes you *do* know me," Attallah said, taking Poitier's hand. The two spent the next several minutes together among the bereaved. At one point the little girl spotted legendary Nigerian drummer Babatunde Olatunji weeping. She recoiled, having never seen a man cry. "He's just upset about your father," Poitier assured her. Nearby, Tom Wallace's wife, Antoinette, comforted an anguished Betty. Before Poitier rose to leave, she invited the widow to come to her guesthouse with the girls and stay as long as she needed.

—❦—

At the Wallaces', the smell of fresh coffee wafted from the kitchen, where women were fixing drinks for the mob of visitors and the evening meal for Malcolm's family. A woman crouched with three of the Shabazz daughters in the dining room, quietly helping them practice the alphabet. Attallah ventured into the living room and found a newswoman. Settling by her side, the intent child showed the grown-up how to teach her children the alphabet. The reporter obligingly printed her name. With finicky block letters, the girl did the same. "This is for you to keep for your own," Attallah announced. "Don't forget to teach the children."

The phone jangled, puncturing the children's susurrations and the grown-ups' staring silence. A small TV set blathered. On the couch, surrounded by the survivors—including four of the men who had sworn to defend her husband with their lives—sat Betty. She looked at a journalist friend nearby. "They've taken him away from me, Mrs. Wilson," she said, her eyes wide as wounds.

Later that evening, with a cordon of her husband's stunned disciples behind her and her two eldest girls nestled at her side, Betty watched a television review of the minister's stormy life. Malcolm glinted on the screen, excoriating his enemy, unconquerable again. It was too much for the widow. She found her feet and wandered into the kitchen. A strapping man nearby whispered, "Tell 'em like it is, Brother Malcolm, tell 'em like it is."

Betty stood staring at the wall. "Is Daddy coming back after his speech, Momma?" Attallah asked. The widow wrapped her arms around the child as her head dropped near the refrigerator. Four-year-old Qubilah tugged at her mother's skirt. "Please don't go out, Momma." Betty guided the girl's head into her lap. "I won't go, Baby," she said softly. Ella Collins eyed her sister-in-law—a woman almost twenty years her junior—from somewhere nearby. Suddenly she was proud of Betty and the grace with which she soothed the children.

Qubilah was the only Shabazz daughter who seemed to realize that her father was not coming home. Attallah had expected Malcolm to spring to his feet after he toppled onto the Audubon stage. He had once assured her that the gunned-down cowboys on television's *Bonanza* were only pretending to be dead. But Attallah was starting to understand. Before sleep overtook her, she plopped down with her marker and scrawled a note: "Dear Daddy, I love you so. O Dear, O Dear, I wish you wasn't dead." Meanwhile, Betty huddled with pho-tographer and writer Gordon Parks in the kitchen. She told him that she'd been ready for her husband's death. She was ashamed that she had cried over him "when he was lying there all shot up."

"He was always away," the widow said, "but I knew he would always come back. We loved each other. He was honest—too honest for his own good, I think sometimes." Parks started to wander off. "I only hope the child I'm carrying is just like his father," Betty added. "I hope you get your wish," Parks said.

Earlier, Betty had shown the photographer the bloodstained list of names that she had plucked from Malcolm's jacket. Parks jotted down the names, thinking he would do a *Life* magazine piece some-day. The article did not materialize. Like Assemblyman Percy Sutton, who also saw the roll of likely assassins, he never publicly disclosed the men Malcolm believed would take his life.

Late that night, the widow prepared to leave for a meeting with Sutton, who with his brother Oliver would offer solace and legal counsel in the days and years ahead. She gritted against tears, offering a few farewells to the congregated visitors as she headed out the door. "Thank you for coming," she whispered. "Good-bye. I am deeply touched." Sutton was beside her when, swathed in grief, she arrived at nearby George's Supper Club in East Elmhurst. She lingered for a minute or two before the row of reporters, tearfully recounting her husband's ominous wake-up call that morning.

Then Sutton took over. "Malcolm X died broke," he announced. He said the minister had pumped every penny of his outside earnings into Black Islam and into his Muslim and nationalist camps thereafter. The succinct media conference wrapped up, and Betty was moving again. She wanted to surrender to the shadows, to let the creeping paralysis engulf her, but the affairs of the dead and the living demanded for her attention.

❦

Malcolm's corps scattered in the hours after the assassination. A few of the men had wanted to go on a shooting rampage, with Black Muslims as the chief targets, but most were too numb for revenge. The minister's security detail had spotted and removed a few of the Original People who had trickled into the Audubon audience before the rally. Yet some of the loyalists seriously doubted whether the Nation was the killer.

For many, the despair set in even before they bore Malcolm off the stage. "The whole room was a wailing woman," writer Larry Neal later recalled. "Oh, Lord, oh Lord, goddamn it!" one man cursed as he paced near his fallen leader. "There ain't no goddamn hope for us any more," another said to no one in particular. "Not in this goddamn country. You gotta fight the lousy whites and then you gotta fight the stupid niggers, too." An elder touched an onlooker's arm. "What are we gonna do, brother?" he whispered. "What are we gonna do now?"

Benjamin Karim pocketed the onyx ring inscribed with "*Allah*" in Arabic that a bullet had knocked off Malcolm's finger. He later gave it to Betty. Several of the disciples finally picked themselves up and headed home. "There was no longer any reason to jump when the phone rang or to sleep with a loaded gun," the minister's lieutenant, Earl Grant, later remembered. "The best year of my life was at an end."

A throng of distraught Malcolmites gathered outside the Theresa Hotel, where they stood looking blankly at one another. One man blinked away tears as he listened to an account of the murder on a transistor radio. Harlemites swarmed before the House of Proper Propaganda, the black nationalist bookstore across the street, buzzing about the slaying, police deception, and the certain culpability of "the man downtown." A middle-aged woman spoke up. "I'll tell you this," she said. "We're going to get another Malcolm X." Her companion nodded. "For every one they get we've got ten more," she said. Inside the locked OAAU office across the street, a telephone rang on and on unanswered.

Harlem grieved, but it was not paralyzed or overwrought. It loved Malcolm for telling off "the Man" and refusing to sell out. But his ideology had lately grown too polymorphous, too conciliatory to black moderates and white liberals for much of the uptown crowd. Even in the minutes after his death, as the news flashed from one Harlem household to the next, not everyone wept. After all, the noose that finally claimed Malcolm had been tightening for months. The police prepared for street war. Two tactical force buses trundled into Harlem, patrolmen dispersed the crowd outside the Theresa, and the Black Muslim restaurant and mosque closed. But all was quiet.

Twenty hours after the assassination, there was still no private mourning for Mrs. Malcolm X. Authorities had listed the minister's body as "John Doe" and handed it over to the medical examiner's office for autopsy and formal identification. The postmortem would confirm that the sawed-off shotgun blast had shredded his heart and that a flurry of .38 and .45 caliber bullets had burrowed into his legs, hands, and chin. But before investigators began chiseling lead out of him, they laid him on an icy table to await his widow.

She arrived at the Bellevue Hospital morgue shortly before noon on Monday with a small party that included Sutton, Unity Funeral Home director Joseph Hall, and Ella Collins. Though Collins and Betty had not reconciled during Malcolm's life, the women would unite, however briefly, to handle the grim chores of his death. Betty leaned against the men as they squired her through Bellevue's double doors. A detective greeted her with crisp formality and led her to her slain husband.

He looked pasty and synthetic against the stainless steel. Betty almost crumpled, but Collins had ordained that there would be no weeping before the white officials, and the widow was equally determined to remain intact. Again she stretched the membrane of composure over her tearful face. As a row of officials looked on, she said yes, this was Malcolm. Minutes later, Sutton led her outside into the uneasy semicircle of reporters waiting in the piercing cold. Her bangs jutted from a scarf, canopying her full face. Daggers rimmed her eyes as the clump of white reporters pelted her with questions.

Did her husband fear for his life? "No," she said, "but he was concerned." Now darkening, she lashed out. "The police and press were unfair," she said. "No one believed what he said. They never took him seriously. Even after the bombing of our home, they said he did it himself. Now what are they going to do—say that he shot himself?"

Throughout the convulsions of recent days he had refused to "fold up his arms and cry," she said, flashing with defiance. She said she had always known that his enemies would kill him. Someone asked what would become of his infant organizations. Betty could not say, but she straightened when she proclaimed that "the magnitude of his work will be felt around the world." A quickly waning sob escaped. Finally a newsman asked if she knew who had murdered her husband. The widow did not flinch. "You'll have to talk to my attorney," she replied.

—

The police did not know—or were not saying—whether they had caught one of the killers. Talmadge Hayer lay writhing in Jewish Memorial Hospital hours after the assassination, his leg shattered by the stomping, howling crowd outside the Audubon and a bullet in his left thigh courtesy of Malcolm's bodyguard. A sergeant told the press that he had discovered a cartridge clip with .45 caliber bullets in Hayer's pockets. Police had not booked anybody for the slaying by that Sunday night, and they were refusing to acknowledge whether the twenty-two-year-old was a suspect. Later, based on ballistics and other evidence, they tentatively determined that there had been three shooters and at least two additional accomplices at the Audubon, and that Hayer was indeed one of the gunmen.

Hayer was not talking. Officers hauled him to Bellevue's prison ward and fingerprinted him. They learned from the FBI that he lived in Paterson, New Jersey, and that he had a "sheet"; he had been arrested in 1963 for warehousing a cache of stolen guns in his basement.

Yet Hayer was still a mystery. Like everybody else, the police had their suppositions about what had happened at the Audubon. Hours after Malcolm's death, an assistant chief inspector had declared that the homicide seemed to be the culmination of "a long-standing feud between the followers of Elijah Muhammad and the people who broke away from him, headed by Malcolm X." But police still had not linked Hayer to the Nation. They were drawing little substantive information from the gaggle of terrified witnesses. By 7:30 that evening, a chief detective was predicting an intricate, drawn-out investigation. The sense of intrigue swelled when Sutton told reporters that Malcolm had planned to disclose at the rally the identities of the men who were out to kill him. Investigators now had the names, the counselor said. Meanwhile, police brass stressed that the department had done everything possible in recent days and months to protect Malcolm.

Malcolm had been a bayonet in the side of the Civil Rights movement, even in his post-*Hajj* incarnation. But now the black protest generals rushed to condemn the violence that had cut him down. NAACP head Roy Wilkins called the slaying "a shocking and ghastly

demonstration of the futility of resorting to violence as a means of settling differences." Martin Luther King, Jr. said the minister had died
amid "a morally inclement climate." He lamented that "our society is
still sick enough to express dissent through murder," and declared that
"we have not yet learned to disagree without being violently disagree-
able."

From Chicago came less sympathetic notes. Police and the Fruit of
Islam had surrounded Elijah Muhammad after the FBI reported that six
Malcolmites might be coming to town to avenge their leader's death.
Under a jeweled fez inside his nineteen-room palace, the elder reigned
comfortably. He was brittle as an autumn leaf and as civil as a maître d'
when he addressed reporters from an armchair on Monday afternoon.
Malcolm "preached violence and violence has taken him away," he
declared. "He has been free to preach whatever he wants since he left
here a year ago," he said. "We don't believe in carrying weapons. He
seems to have taken weapons for his God. We preach peace. He
preaches war."

Muhammad insisted that his legions were innocent of the minister's death. "Not even one of us even knows the man who shot
Malcolm," he said. Though a blaze had gutted Muhammad Ali's
Chicago apartment hours after the assassination, Muhammad dismissed the notion that he himself was in danger. "I don't feel disturbed
in the very least," he said, as a heavy detail of his bodyguards glared at
the assembled newsmen. "We are not afraid in any way. We are not taking any precautions."

Meanwhile Betty had traveled back uptown from the morgue to
the Unity Funeral Home on Eighth Avenue near 126 Street in Harlem.
There she chose a wrought copper, velvet-lined coffin—the show-
room's most expensive model. Collins covered the $2,100 bill, which
included a limousine and hearse. Malcolm had lived humbly right to
the end, but the women he loved would send him off in style.

He was dapper in a dark business suit, nestled in eggshell velvet
and cased in full-length glass as he lay in state Tuesday through Friday,
February 26. Muslim tradition holds that the sun must not rise and set
twice on the body of a believer. In light of her husband's position and

the circumstances of the case, Betty had decided to break the custom. She believed Arab and African dignitaries would attend the funeral, and she told Unity's Joseph Hall that foreign ministers were en route. She never said whom she was expecting.

"Mrs. Shabazz was still pretty well shaken up when I spoke to her, and we weren't able to accomplish very much today," Hall told the press on Monday evening. The mortician took care to stress that he was neither affiliated with nor sympathetic to Malcolm's politics. "To me this is just another funeral," he said, firing up a pipe. "It's my job." The statement may have sounded callous, but in the aftermath of Malcolm's assassination—the bloodiest and most stunning since the November 1963 rifle shots that killed John F. Kennedy—a cloak of hysteria had descended. Harlem understood that men brazen enough to pump a fusillade of bullets into an internationally known figure before four hundred witnesses on a languid Sunday afternoon were hardly the sort with whom one wishes to mix. "They wanted to execute him in public—put fear in the people who were around him," Abdullah Abdur Razzaq later said.

Tensions mounted on Tuesday after firebomb blasts in the predawn gloom charred Temple Number Seven. The media treated the torching as a retaliatory strike by Malcolm's camp, but police made no arrests. Many of the ministers were convinced that the white establishment was looking to cripple the Left by provoking open warfare between Black Muslims and Malcolmites. To them, the revenge arson theory was just another sleight-of-hand. "You could find very few black people that would set their churches on fire," Benjamin Karim later said.

———

Hours after the assassination, Ahmed Osman, Malcolm's Dartmouth friend and orthodox Muslim comrade, squeezed into a car with three other students in Hanover, New Hampshire, and headed south on the turnpike entombed in silence. The car proved less resolute than its occupants. Somewhere in Connecticut, it broke down. When

244 - BETTY SHABAZZ

the nearest mechanic learned that his would-be customers were en route to pay Malcolm last respects, he refused to look under the hood. "I took the Greyhound," Osman later recalled. The graduate student finally arrived at the Wallaces' on Monday night and presented himself to Betty. "I have come to offer whatever I can," he said in the purling accent of his native Sudan. The grateful widow immediately issued her request: she wanted her husband put to rest according to Islam.

It was rather late for that. The funeral home was even then arraying the minister in Western garb, and the six days he was to remain aboveground was an abomination to Islam that Sheik Daoud Ahmed Faisal of New York's Islamic Mission of America would protest. (Even Malcolm's autopsy violated strict Muslim customs proscribing the desecration of believers' bodies.) But Osman suspected that Betty, fresh in the faith, had only a frail grasp of orthodoxy. He promised to aid Sheik Ahmed Hassoun in arranging an authentic burial.

Hassoun, the inky-skinned, white-haired imam (spiritual leader) who had come to New York as the Muslim Mosque's advisor after meeting Malcolm in Mecca, was not the only orthodox believer in the area concerned about how the fallen brother would be lain away. A dozen black Sunni Muslims heretofore unassociated with the minister had swept ceremoniously into a Harlem police station Sunday night and announced that they wished to claim the martyr's body in the name of Islam. Leading the delegation was Heshaam Jaaber, a young imam from North Jersey. He and his companions handed police a note addressed to Betty asking that she confer with them to ensure that Malcolm's last rites were kosher.

The zeal of the Jersey Muslims did not move Betty. She and Malcolm had been orthodox believers for nearly a year, and these newcomers had arrived only after he had gone cold. Besides, there were bigger fish to fry, for it was starting to seem like no Harlem church would funeralize her husband. Fearing violence and reprisal, or looking to preserve their respectability, at least fifteen Protestant churches refused to host the rites in the days after the slaying. Among them was one of Harlem's grandest worship houses, Abyssinian Baptist, which the minister's comrade Congressman Adam Clayton Powell pastored.

Malcolm's loyalists and widow were growing increasingly bitter that the community for which their man had stood was going to shirk the responsibility to lay him down.

Harlem's "mayor," Bishop Alvin A. Childs, finally offered his Faith Temple Church of God in Christ as a "humanitarian gesture." The converted movie theatre at 147 Street and Amsterdam Avenue seated one thousand in its auditorium. It may not have been the ideal final tabernacle for the man who had embodied Black America's defiance and solidified its ties to Africa. But for the man who had expired in a bedlam of gunfire on a shabby dancehall stage, it would have to do.

"I did not agree with all of his philosophy," Childs said of Malcolm, "but this did not affect our friendship." That was blasphemy enough in the eyes of Malcolm's enemies, and Childs and his wife Mildred received a string of bomb threats to their church and home. Yet the reverend never flinched, and Betty was eternally grateful. With all the flourish of the black pulpit, Childs later explained his resolve. "I founded Faith Temple with a five-dollar deposit and a treasury of faith," he said. "It is now a half-million-dollar edifice, and a man doesn't like to see his dreams vanish in an explosion or to lose loved ones in the fires of hatred. But I preach [that] the Fatherhood of God taught us to love our neighbors. And Malcolm X was a neighbor, no matter which way he chose to serve the one God who made us all."

———

The hours dissolved in currents of sympathetic faces and strange and kind embraces. Betty spent disjointed days preparing for the funeral and what lay beyond, and tormented nights coiled about her children in a claustrophobic room. On February 22, the day after the assassination, the traffic at the Wallace residence surged and ebbed. Reporters scuttled in with cameras and notepads and escaped with accounts of suffering. Through it all the television flickered, a porthole to a grotesque world.

"Of course we offered Malcolm X police protection many times—as late as the day his house was bombed—but he always refused it," a ranking police officer said on the television news one evening. Betty did not blink. "That's a lie," she murmured. (Police officials insisted that they had offered to guard the minister no less then seventeen times in recent days and weeks, and that Betty herself had turned down extra protection the day of the Molotov cocktails and of the assassination itself.)

Elijah Muhammad materialized on the screen, echoing his remark about Malcolm having exhorted violence. The widow smothered a cry of exasperated bitterness and darted into the bedroom. Sprawled across a tussled quilt were Atallah, Qubilah, and Ilyasah. Gamilah gurgled in a nearby crib. Betty collected herself, then returned to the living room and the conversation she had abandoned. "The greatest emptiness is that I'll never get a letter again; no letter, no phone call," she said. "The children always ask for him when he's away. How will I tell them he won't come home again?"

Again she flayed the press for entertaining the notion that her husband had torched their home "with our children in it," and for dismissing his proclamations that his life was in danger. "And those stories they told about how he got big sums of money from Red China to carry on his work," she sneered. "Ridiculous." She softened as she recalled his spiritual growth in Mecca. "He told me he now felt that all men were human beings and that we must judge a man on his deeds," she said. "Maybe there are a lot of white people with good hearts and good deeds."

And what of her and the children's future? When a reporter mentioned that there were those who wished to help the family, Betty flashed with indignation. Where were these benefactors when Malcolm's enemies were stalking him? Where was the support when White and Black America were demonizing him? What would she say to those who now offered charity? "They can contact my husband's lawyer," she said.

As the widow searched for self-possession and solace at the Wallaces', a river of mourners flowed past Malcolm. Bomb threats had delayed the viewing at Unity Funeral Home, and a bevy of police sharpshooters crouched on nearby rooftops. The militarized scene did not thin the crowds. By the end of the week, thirty thousand admirers had endured barricades, fastidious searches, spotty rain, and swarms of bluecoats to bid the minister farewell. Bent old women and teenagers wept. An ambulance shuttled a woman to a nearby hospital after she collapsed in hysterics. "I saw that boy speak when he was alive," one white-haired housewife said. "Now he's dead. And I don't know what I feel except mad."

Betty arrived at the chapel Tuesday evening amid a cordon of patrolmen and a ripple of flashbulbs. "She handles herself beautifully," a white newspaperman murmured. The admirer—"ever faithful to his duty of elevating the white archetype," one critic later snipped—hailed the widow as "a black Jacqueline Kennedy." Police cleared the building and shut its double folding doors, and Betty found herself in a dusky mourning room before her husband—the man she could never keep still, now inert forever. Half an hour later she emerged, slumping against the funeral director and a police lieutenant as she made her way back to the car. Her escorts whisked her away, and the trudging file of callers cranked back to life.

The Malcolm eulogies rolled in all that week and in days beyond, spanning from the reverent to the cautious. Bayard Rustin, a chief organizer of the 1963 March on Washington, said the minister had awakened in young blacks a new self-vision. Student Nonviolent Coordinating Committee Chairman John Lewis swore there had been no finer articulator of "the deep feeling of the Negro masses."

The *New York Post* was among the mainstream newspapers that remembered Malcolm as a rough diamond, declaring that "even his sharpest critics recognized his brilliance—often wild, unpredictable and eccentric, but nevertheless possessing promise that now must remain unrealized." Leftist publications described the minister as a victim of imperialism.

James Farmer of CORE declared Malcolm's death "a political killing with international implications" (though he later acknowledged that he himself had not known what the statement meant, and that he had mostly been hoping to ease the fratricidal passions between Malcolmites and the Nation). James Baldwin argued that whoever did the deed evolved "in the crucible of the Western World, of the American Republic." The writer thrust a finger at white journalists who sought his reaction to the slaying. "It is because of you—the men who created this white supremacy—that this man is dead," he cried. "Your mills, your cities, your rape of a continent started all this!"

Newspapers around the world treated Malcolm as a hero of the oppressed. In Cuba, *El Mundo* decried the assassination as "another racist crime to eradicate by violence the struggle against discrimination." The *Daily Times* of Lagos, Nigeria, declared that the minister "will have a place in the palace of martyrs." Writers in Ghana, Pakistan, China, and Algeria hailed the fallen militant. American media scantily reported the Dark World's veneration for Malcolm and outrage at his murder. "There was concern his assassination might build him up as a symbol," the *New York Times* acknowledged.

There was also a cannonade of less flattering words. The *Times* dubbed Malcolm the "Apostle of Hate." Carl T. Rowan, black director of the United States Information Agency, lamented the praise-shouts that were echoing from the Dark World. "All this about an ex-convict, ex-dope peddler who became a racial fanatic," he scoffed.

Urban League Director Whitney Young warned that the minister's spiritual offspring were germinating in the American ghetto. "Take fifteen million seeds, cultivate them with the callused hand of indifference, nurture them with despair, water them with injustice, and another misshapen human flower is certain to bloom," he said.

Meanwhile, *Newsweek* branded the minister a "desperado," insisting that even after his conversion to orthodox Islam, "his own overwhelming talent was still talk; he always followed his agile tongue instead of his wasted mind." The *Philadelphia Daily News* called him bloodthirsty. "His heart filled with hate, he wanted a revolt, he wanted to see blood spilled," it said.

The calumny incensed Betty. The newspapers "continued to fight him, even in death," she protested two weeks after the assassination. The widow lamented that the media "still refuse to believe" the righteousness of Malcolm's mission and the inevitability of his prophecies. Some of the black establishment's dirges galled her, too. She said she felt "a little embarrassed" for the civil righters who for years had dodged her husband's invitations to public debate, and who in recent days had woven careful statements lauding his eloquence and sincerity while disavowing his "bitter" militancy. "They were afraid to match him in life or in death," she said. A Marxist periodical may best have summed up her nausea at the moderates' response to the murder. Liberals "are, of course, opposed to assassination," *Spartacist* declared that summer. "But their mourning at the death of the head of world imperialism [President Kennedy] had a considerably greater ring of sincerity than their regret at the murder of a black militant who wouldn't play their game."

If liberal hypocrisy chafed Betty, Black Muslim hubris maddened her. "We did not want to kill Malcolm and we didn't try to," Elijah Muhammad told 2,500 of his congregation during a Chicago sermon. "It was his foolishness, ignorance, and his preachings that brought him to his death." Despite a spate of threats against Muhammad, the Savior's Day convention opened as scheduled that Friday, February 26. The coliseum crowd was far from capacity, the risk of violence having deterred many of the believers.

Only verbal attacks marked the occasion. Muhammad rasped on for more than an hour, acknowledging that Malcolm had once been his indefatigable apprentice. "In those days he was a *light*," he proclaimed, "he was a star among his people, as long as he was with me. But he criticized the God who brought him salvation and liberation." Under cascading hurrahs and Muhammad Ali's "amens," Muhammad sputtered through a litany of Malcolm's sins. Malcolm turned his back on his master teacher, the elder charged. He even preached that the enemy "has the right to the kingdom of heaven."

Two of Malcolm's blood brothers joined the flogging. Black Muslim ministers Wilfred and Philbert had ducked behind a shroud of silence after the assassination. Now, amid clamorous applause, they openly scolded their younger brother's "recklessness." Philbert told the audience that he had tried to rescue Malcolm from himself: "When he was living, I tried to keep him living; now that he is dead, there is nothing I can do."

Both brothers drew cheers as they vowed to boycott Malcolm's funeral. Then Muhammad's thirty-one-year-old son consummated the melodrama, emerging from the wings for a crowd-pleasing reconciliation. Though Wallace had sided with Malcolm, his friend and confidant, and denounced his father's doctrine and kingdom the previous July, the prodigal now begged and received Muhammad's pardon. The Old Man beamed. "Allah opened my son's heart and caused him to own up to his foolish mistakes," he told his subjects. Philbert and Wilfred's final repudiation embittered Betty, but Wallace's return to the fold astounded her. It would be thirty years before the widow and the heir again broke bread.

———

Saturday, February 27, 1965 saw a schizophrenic funeral. Sheik Hassoun had at the last hour rescued Malcolm's body from Western trimmings. He had thoroughly washed and scented it, wrapping it in a *kafan*, the Islamic burial sheet. Tradition demands that the white winding cloth shroud the entire body, but to accommodate the American fascination with beholding death, Hassoun had left the minister's face peeking out. (The elder would complete the veiling before interment.)

Malcolm was thus swaddled for eternity when the men wheeled him before the altar of Faith Temple. Eight stolid police officers flanked his bier as he lay beneath two murals of Jesus Christ. The funeral home had meant to honor Betty's request to display his Muslim name, El-Hajj Malik El-Shabazz, on the coffin template. Yet, a typographical error attributed the body to one La-Hajj Malik Shabazz.

There were other incongruities. Flowers are not traditional at Muslim funerals, but Betty had arranged for a dazzling floral tribute. An embossed white star and crescent, the symbol of Islam, gleamed against a bank of red carnations below Malcolm's coffin. A card rested against the velvet backdrop: "TO EL-HAJJ MALIK, FROM BETTY." The details were crucial, Ahmed Osman later said, because "the press was trying to strip him even of his religion." Yet the ceremony's most jarring cultural clash lay not in Western ornament, but lamentation.

Muslims are not to weep for their martyrs. ("And say not of those who are slain in the way of Allah 'They are dead,'" the Qur'an commands. "Nay, they are living, though ye perceive it not.") Westerners openly bemoan "martyrs," but to Muslims, martyrdom in a struggle on behalf of Islam is the highest form of bearing witness, the supreme testimony. Scripturally, a martyred Muslim enjoys the superlative pleasures of paradise and expects his loved ones to rejoice.

However, all the sanctimony in Allah's kingdom could not have brightened Malcolm's last rites. The evening papers and downtown officials had worried all week about rioting or a bloody showdown between Malcolmites and Muhammad loyalists. Tensions climbed after rent-strike leader Jesse Gray threatened to organize a boycott of stores along 125th Street that refused to close through the weekend in Malcolm's honor. By Friday afternoon, Gray had marshaled only eleven pickets, four of whom were white, to trudge the sidewalk before Blumenstein's Department Store. Still, whether out of fear or respect, shoppers stayed away.

Civic Harlem had tried to snuff the hysteria. The community's hometown organ, the *Amsterdam News*, had pleaded for order in a front-page editorial titled "Steady, Eddie!" The police relied on their own peacekeeping tactics. Hundreds of bluecoats and plainclothes detectives patrolled Faith Temple and the surrounding blocks on Saturday morning. "It looked like a town under siege," Osman would remember.

Harlem turned out anyway. Police barricades could scarcely hold the masses outside the church. Jittery police had scuttled a plan to seat overflow guests in the basement, and many of the invited wound up listening to the service over the loudspeakers in the street. They stood in billowing silence along with several thousand anonymous people and some of the neighborhood royalty, including sixty-six-year-old Garveyite veteran Audley "Queen Mother" Moore, who was resplendent in her leopard print turban and dancing silver earrings. "It was fourteen degrees out," an onlooker later recalled, " and those little old soul sisters were coming out of the subway and getting in line for a last look at Malcolm."

A thousand mourners crammed into Faith Temple. An elderly woman in a white crocheted scarf sat wringing her mittens with hands worn from years of scrubbing floors. A husky young man covered his eyes and slumped awkwardly, feigning sleep to hide the tears. A corps from the OAAU and Muslim Mosque marched in. There was an army of reporters, photographers, and television cameramen, and a smattering of notables, including John Lewis and James Forman of SNCC, Dick Gregory, James Farmer, Bayard Rustin, and Stanley E. Branch of the Chester (Pennsylvania) Freedom Now Party.

But the absences were conspicuous. Though many sent glittering eulogies, no high-ranking African dignitaries came. First-tier protest spokesmen and artists were also missing. Even Harlem's normally dauntless Adam Clayton Powell stayed away. Malcolm's stigma and the threat of violence had deterred his lay siblings. Collins was the only blood relation accounted for.

Nor were the Shabazz daughters present. Betty could not bear to imagine them seeing Malcolm prone; all that effortless energy arrested. "I had to deal with their psyches afterwards and I thought it was best," she later said. The anonymous telephone warnings—"We'll cremate Malcolm with fire bombs"—must also have influenced her decision to leave the girls with the Wallaces' adolescent daughter. The widow herself arrived at 9:45 A.M. with Collins and a ring of dark-suited men, and sat in the second pew, straight-backed under a torrent of black veiling between two black undercover officers. There she remained through the hour-long service, amid the proletariat, the intelligentsia, the news-gatherers, and the police, looking terribly beautiful and alone.

Broadway actor Ossie Davis and his actress wife Ruby Dee, who had been among the earliest black luminaries to befriend Malcolm, were first into the pulpit. Malcolm's aides had tapped Davis as the funeral emcee for his integrity. "I was a man with whom nobody in this shooting argument could quarrel," he later said. On behalf of Betty, the actor thanked Bishop Childs for the accommodations. Then he and Dee began reading condolences. There were notes and telegrams and cables from revolutionary premiers and college clubs and diplomats and freedom fighters. King and Young sent their regards, as did Ghanaian President Kwame Nkrumah. "The death of Malcolm X shall not have been in vain," Nkrumah swore.

Salutations arrived from the Nigerian Ambassador from Lagos, the Pan-African Congress of South Africa, the African-Pakistan West Indian Society of the London School of Economics, the Michigan Freedom Now Party, the American Muslim Students Association, the Los Angeles NAACP Youth Chapter, and the Freedom Fighters of Ohio. The roster ran on and on, an abridged index of the people and places Malcolm had revolutionized. Slowly the messages filtered through Betty's grief. She began to understand then, and more fully in the years ahead, that despite the white establishment's ongoing campaigns to anathematize him, many of the world's laborers and commoners and intellectuals loved Malcolm. And it was they who now consecrated his remains.

Still cameras clicked, movie cameras whined, and orange light poured through the church's stained glass. Ahmed Osman rose. Speaking on behalf of the Islamic Center of Switzerland, he proclaimed Malcolm a "blood brother" who had refused to bow to tyranny. The highest honor for a Muslim "is to die on the battlefield and not at the bedside," he said amid swelling applause. There were a few more testimonies. Only Ossie Davis's, however, would become immortal:

> Here, at this final hour, in this quiet place, Harlem has come to bid farewell to one of its brightest hopes—extinguished now, and gone from us forever....Many will ask what Harlem finds to honor in this stormy, controversial, and bold young captain—and we will smile....And we will answer and say unto them: Did you ever talk to

Brother Malcolm? Did you ever touch him, or have him smile at you? Did you ever really listen to him?...For if you did you would know him. And if you knew him you would know why we must honor him: Malcolm was our manhood, our living black manhood!...And we will know him then for what he was and is—a prince—our own black shining prince!—who didn't hesitate to die, because he loved us so.

Davis surrendered the ceremony to Islam. Clad in a brown robe and white burnoose, Jaaber recited the traditional prayer. When he chanted "Allahu Akbar"—"God is most great"—the believers in the audience placed their open palms by their earlobes.

Betty had held up marvelously. But now the men led her forward for a last look at Malcolm. It was he—not the revolutionary or the icon or the demagogue, but simply Malcolm. She bit her lip, fighting to control herself as she swept back her veil and bent forward to kiss the glass shield over him. Finally she broke, her sobs resounding in the sanctuary and mingling with a chorus of wails and moans.

Minutes later she was trailing the men as they bore the casket from Faith Temple and loaded it onto the silver-blue hearse waiting outside. (There had been no glut of volunteers brave enough to serve as Malcolm's pall bearers.) She glanced up and saw the Harlemites clotted on fire escapes and leaning out tenement windows and straining against police barriers, the loss glistening in their eyes. "I was genuinely impressed and grateful to see so many people from Harlem turn out to show their last farewell," the widow said days later. "I was deeply touched when I walked out of the church and saw the thousands on the sidewalks, and I am positive he was worthy of their tribute."

Under a thick police guard and a scowling sky, two or three dozen cars followed the hearse out of Manhattan to Ferncliff Cemetery in nearby Westchester County. More than twenty-five thousand onlookers jammed the route in twenty-eight-degree weather. At the graveyard, the two hundred mourners and newsmen circled the fresh plot marked with a modest bronze plaque: EL-HAJJ MALIK EL-SHABAZZ

("The *Hajj* pilgrim Malik Shabazz"). Betty clutched her handbag in gloved hands, her veil sweeping over her face. She did not stir as the last prayers echoed and the casket descended into the two feet of murky water at the grave bottom.

The cemetery's men had been idling in the background, waiting to seal the cavity, but the Malcolmites refused to let white men throw dirt on Malcolm. The cortege was starting back to the city, and the undertaker warned the Malcolmites that they would be left behind. "We'll bury him first, man," one man said. "We'll walk." They crouched in the rain and began tossing handfuls of dirt into the grave. Finally the gravediggers surrendered their shovels, and Malcolm's men scooped the earth over their leader.

Betty did not sleep for two weeks. Every time her eyes drooped, she would see Malcolm falling like lumber. What is it about the human mind that misplaces license plate numbers and anniversaries but records in precision the cruelest minutes of lives? The widow did not dare dream; she could not bear to relive the sickening thud of his head against the hardwood. So she lay awake, shrouded in withering silence until Poitier anesthetized her with diluted brandy and honey.

Betty shunned the media in the miserable days following the funeral. One exception was her talk with the *Amsterdam News*, whose senior staff Malcolm had known and trusted. Published in mid-March, the interview allowed the widow to speak directly to her husband's people, particularly his core constituents in Harlem.

"He was obsessed with the idea that his children and upcoming generations should not have to face the kind of conditions that his generation faced," she told the *Amsterdam News*. It was this obsession that fueled his crusade to make the black revolt a human-rights struggle, she explained. She offered personal notes about the minister as husband and father, recalling the "devoted family man." She confessed that she did not know precisely what she was going to do next and added that the recent media speculation about her future amazed her.

She said she was determined to follow Islamic custom by mourning no more than three months.

The widow said that she and Percy Sutton were discussing plans to shelter her family, and acknowledged that she was still considering the Queens home she and Malcolm had agreed to buy. She thanked those who had grieved with her, as well as the hundreds of sympathizers who had sent condolences and small sums of cash. She insisted that the masses could best honor her husband's memory by upholding the resistance. "He tried to impress on his children that they should never forget their Afro-American heritage like some of our professional people do, or try to sweep it under the rug," she said.

Yet before she could ponder her own role in the struggle, or even contemplate the bread-and-butter matters of survival, she had to go meet "the Man." The police had been advertising how busy they were. They said Manhattan North detectives were missing sleep, going all out. They had worked through dozens of witnesses, though rather fruitlessly. Some of the attendees of the Audubon rally had glimpsed the black triggermen. But most of the spectators believed the white establishment had given the order. Several clammed up or spouted diatribes when investigators reeled them into the stationhouse for questioning.

Malcolm's cadre was even warier. When the police came asking questions, the disciples' more or less uniform response was, "I ain't seen nothing." So it was mostly detective legwork that yielded the second arrest. The day before the funeral, police booked Norman 3X Butler, a twenty-six-year-old tough from the Bronx whom they described as a Black Muslim "enforcer" (police parlance, it seemed, for any beefy Fruit of Islam legionnaire). Butler was already facing charges in connection with the shooting of Benjamin Brown, a local corrections officer who had earned a bullet in the shoulder that January after leaving Temple Number Seven to organize a mosque in the Bronx.

Arrests or no arrests, Betty did not trust the law, either. She had promised to present herself as an on-scene witness the day after the slaying, but almost forty-eight hours had elapsed before her first contact with investigators. They shoved a jumble of suspect photos under her nose on Tuesday, February 23. Oozing hostility, she said she recognized no one.

Detectives got another sit-down with the widow on the Monday after the funeral. She insisted on neutral ground, so Jimmy Rushin, a black homicide cop, cruised to Frank's Restaurant in Harlem and met her at a back table. As Percy Sutton looked on, Betty told Rushin that though she did not fear for her life, she did not care to reveal where she and the girls were staying. She told the officer that investigators could contact Sutton if they needed to reach her.

As she explained to Rushin, she really hadn't seen much that Sunday at the ballroom. She had walked into the place and sat down, she said. When the shots rang out, she had shoved the children beneath her. She had not gotten a good look at the killers, and she certainly was not willing to volunteer any other information about trouble within Black Islam or her husband's camp. And no, she knew nothing about Malcolm's list of likely hitmen other than what she'd read in the papers. The interview lasted no more than a few minutes. When Rushin rose from the table, the most memorable tidbit he had coaxed from Malcolm's widow was that she genuinely suspected that the CIA had helped kill her husband.

Earlier, on March 3, thirty-year-old Thomas 15X Johnson, another Fruit of Islam heavy from the Bronx, had become the third and last man arrested for Malcolm's murder. He was also among the Muslim suspects indicted in the January corrections-officer shooting.

If Betty thought then, ten days after the assassination, that justice was arriving, she certainly did not believe it was coming from downtown. Oliver Sutton assured investigators that she would cooperate fully with the probe. "It is my understanding that she was not herself deeply involved in the movement, but was a typical Muslim housewife without great awareness of her husband's activity," he said. "However, she is anxious that the true assassin of her husband be known."

A week later, when the widow appeared before a grand jury impaneled to hear witnesses in the case, she was only slightly more forthcoming than she had been with Rushin. Again she droned through the details of the dreadful day. Brother Benjamin had finished his intro and her husband had given the greeting. The scuffling had begun. She had swiveled and spotted one of the decoy men standing—"I could see his back, sandy jacket on, more rust color"—and heard the salvo—"I thought it was the men that were, organizing you know, in the middle." She had turned and saw Malcolm fall, and had swept her children under the bench as everybody hit the floor.

She had not made out the face of the man with the sandy jacket, and she could not say for sure whether any of the men in the three grand-jury exhibit photos now before her were he. She did not know the men in the photos by name, but she remembered the man in exhibit No. 1 from her Black Muslim days.

Betty's testimony was flowing as freely as could be expected, though she was not wasting words. Then Assistant District Attorney Herbert Stern restated a question she had ducked earlier. "Mrs. Shabazz," he asked, "whom did you go to the Audubon Ballroom with that day?" Betty said she would rather not say, but Stern insisted. He reminded her that Oliver Sutton was just outside if she needed a word with him. Betty stayed silent. Was Stern now to understand that she refused to respond? "I said I'd rather not say," Betty snapped. "You can put it in whatever language you'd like." Stern said she was legally bound to reply and again suggested that she confer with her attorney. Then the foreman spoke up: "Mrs. Shabazz, the purpose of the grand jury is to see that justice is done in this case or any other case. Please think very carefully about it before you decide not to answer it." Betty believed that the white establishment had demonized, haunted, wiretapped, and poisoned her man, then conspired to have him killed—even if the Nation's thugs had actually done the job. She would be damned if she was now going to allow these white men to pester one of the men she knew for sure had nothing to do with Malcolm's death. But the prosecutor kept needling, and after stepping into the hallway to huddle with Oliver Sutton, the widow returned and acknowledged that Tom Wallace had ferried her to the Audubon that Sunday, February 21.

Stern asked a few more questions. Did her name have any religious or other significance? "Well, it goes back to—supposedly to a tribe of Shabazz that was a group of black people," she said, "supposedly the oldest and the first." Then the interview was over. It would be nearly a year before prosecutors called her back to the witness stand. "Thank you very much, ma'am," Stern said. "Thank you, Mrs. Shabazz," the foreman echoed, "very much." Betty nodded. She was thankful, too.

—

"So there we were," Malcolm recalls in the opening pages of his autobiography, describing the aftermath of his father's 1931 lynching. "My mother was thirty-four years old now, with no husband, no provider or protector to take care of her eight children." Betty, herself a month shy of her thirty-first birthday, began to feel the weight of her similar predicament after the funeral. "I didn't know how I was going to live without Malcolm," she later remembered.

She was broke, grief-stricken, and two months pregnant with twins. (She still thought she was carrying only one child, and for whatever reason, perhaps her husband's sheer will, believed it was a son.) There was no house, no savings, and no inheritance. She had become the executor of Malcolm's "estate," such as it was. When his autobiography entered its third printing late that year, checks would start trickling in. (She was to split the royalties with Alex Haley.) But for the moment, the widow wondered how her babies would eat.

That may not have constituted as severe a crisis in the Muslim World, where societies and states traditionally offer their martyrs' families long-term aid, but Western culture has no equivalent safety net. The institutions of black protest, which the American mainstream viewed with anxiety, had few resources from which to parcel out survivor's benefits. Myrlie Evers, the decade's first civil rights widow, had survived. As she had discovered in the summer of 1963, Americans find weeping widows and fatherless kids infinitely easier to embrace—and finance—than defiant freedom fighter.

In the months after a white rifleman blew away Myrlie's husband Medgar, the NAACP's man in Mississippi, a menagerie of liberals had anted up. The Civil Rights establishment had led the relief drive; King had announced a Medgar Evers Memorial Fund to buoy desegregation efforts, and the NAACP had launched a Medgar Evers Scholarship

Fund to cover future educational expenses for the fallen leader's three children, two of whom were gradeschoolers at the time. Movie stars, schoolchildren, churches, Jewish organizations, civic groups, and sympathizers of all colors from every state had also chipped in. "One by one," Myrlie Evers later remembered, "my financial problems had been solved."

But Malcolm was no NAACP man. Since his defection from Black Islam, he had represented no established, national institution. He had been the black protest's miscreant, the one that "responsible" race men debunked if they did not wish their political clout and liberal funding to run dry. Malcolm had always argued that it is the *invisible* roots that nourish the tree. But his aboveground following had shriveled. The Organization of Afro-American Unity had bled from several hundred to a few hardcore members, with a ragtag of hangers-on. Those who stayed had shallow pockets. Malcolm's lieutenants had had to pass the bucket two or three times at the last meetings to cover the Audubon's $150 rental fee. "They ain't even payin' 50 cents a week," Razzaq (of the Muslim Mosque) had complained.

Now the minister was gone, and his frazzled disciples found themselves without the means to support his widow and little girls. "Most of us wasn't supporting ourselves," Razzaq would recall. Malcolm's ideological heirs—the radical young intellectuals and artists—were no more solvent. "We had no money," poet Sonia Sanchez later remembered. "We had no books out. We just had the ideas." Indeed, the only nationalist camp with the wherewithal to sustain Malcolm's family was the Nation. "It's not like today," the OAAU's Herman Ferguson said years later, "when the people in the so-called movement have jobs."

It was the gainfully employed, however, that swooped in to lead relief efforts for Betty and the children. Hours after the assassination, Ossie Davis and television actor P. Jay Sidney appealed for funds on behalf of the family on the Barry Gray radio show. Percy Sutton made a similar plea before a cluster of journalists the next day, announcing a fund at Harlem's Freedom National Bank to cover family expenses, including Islamic lessons for the girls. He stressed that the Shabazzes were not begging. "But there are people who might have disagreed with Malcolm but who still feel for humanity," he said. "There were many who admired him; others who are just kind. From all of these we hope to establish a foundation to keep this family together and educate these kids."

On February 24, eight ministers from the Harlem-Upper Manhattan Church Association, a federation of 251 Protestant worship houses, established an educational fund for the slain militant's children with an initial $125 contribution, vowing that their congregants would donate more. Though he was privately friendly with many of them, Malcolm had pilloried black clergymen as "Uncle Toms" throughout his public life, and most of them had treated him like a snake in their wading pool. Ideological and theological differences notwithstanding, the church association's president Rev. W. Sterling Cary said that he and his colleagues admired how Malcolm had "restored manhood to the Negro and taught him how to defend himself."

"The Negro community owes a debt to the children of Malcolm X," Cary declared. But uptown clerics, some of whom had feared losing parishioners to Malcolm after he had repudiated Black Islam and begun courting the Civil Rights mainstream a year earlier, may have had other motives for embracing the milder elements of his legacy. After a local paper identified the Williams Institutional CME Church as one of the places of worship that had refused to host Malcolm's last rites, its pastor hastened to deny the report, touting his trusteeship of the Shabazz educational fund and lauding Malcolm's message of "hope and dignity." The reverend lamented that the misprint had laid his church open to "misunderstanding and possible violence."

Meanwhile a coterie of society women launched the most successful and enduring relief drive for Betty and the girls. Responding to Juanita Poitier's and Ruby Dee's call, a handful of well-heeled women formed the Committee of Concerned Mothers. Poitier chaired the committee, which accepted contributions at her home and a New York City Post Office box. Black feminist Florence Kennedy, a bodacious

Manhattan attorney, oversaw the funds and otherwise helped steer the widow through the trying months ahead.

None of the committee members were close to Betty. Most knew her only as the elegant but retreating housewife of the scythe-tongued radical their husbands or they themselves had befriended in recent years. Dee later explained why the Committee of Concerned Mothers enveloped the widow. "It is something we did out of love and passion for the Movement," she said. "All of us were very much connected to Malcolm, and that's something that he would have done. We moved from the impulse that we wished we were more aware of the dangers he was facing before he died. It was a way of making up for all the efforts we might have made to save him while he was alive."

Killens, Baldwin, and Sutton were among the men who assisted the committee, which set an initial three thousand–dollar goal to help secure a binder on the Queens home Betty and Malcolm had selected. The fund surpassed four thousand dollars in ten days and five thousand dollars within the following week. It topped six thousand dollars days later after Shirley Graham DuBois, widow of W.E.B. DuBois, sent five hundred dollars from Ghana, where she had comforted her husband in his last days and later received the sojourning Malcolm. "It would be ideal if we can buy you a house outright," Poitier told Betty. Yet for a young, pregnant housewife with a small sorority of daughters to clothe, feed, shelter, and educate, even the twelve thousand dollars the group had raised by June was pocket change.

Then the concerts came together. That April, Students against Social Injustice, a high-school group, sponsored a blues and folk concert at a Manhattan church to benefit Betty and the girls, with artists such as Julius Lester and Joe Wilson headlining. The same month, artists and entertainers such as Sammy Davis Jr., Dick Gregory, Nina Simone, Ossie Davis, and Ruby Dee appeared at Harlem's Apollo Theatre for a midnight benefit show to help buy a house for the Shabazz family. Though delayed by bomb threats, the event yielded about five thousand dollars.

The Committee of Concerned Mothers reorganized in June as the Concerned Mothers Mutual Benefit Committee, dedicating themselves to aiding the Shabazz family and others "who have met disaster during the struggle for human rights." The circle of fifteen women began planning an August 8 jazz festival at Poitier's Pleasantville manor.

By July, chanteuse Lena Horne, trumpeter Dizzy Gillespie, drummer Max Roach, singer Abbey Lincoln, comic Scott Mitchell, crooner Billy Frazier, and the Billy Taylor Trio were among the confirmed acts. The Concerned Mothers hoped the concert and individual donations would help raise another twenty-eight thousand dollars to buy Betty a forty thousand–dollar two-family brick home in an upscale neighborhood of Mount Vernon, a suburb thirty minutes north of New York City. Bella Abzug, the outspoken congresswoman known for her ostentatious hats and activism on behalf of women and the environment, had previously owned the house. The Concerned Mothers wanted a brick dwelling for the widow (there would be fewer repairs over the years), and they liked the wooded seclusion of its cul-de-sac. "At the time the family was still getting death threats," Sutton later said.

Betty was not sold. "She had her own ideas," Poitier, herself a former Mount Vernon resident, would remember. "She didn't really want a two-family house." The committee members gently brought the widow around and began making plans to move her and the children into the place by the early fall—before the baby arrived and in time for Attallah and Qubilah to start school in the Westchester County town. Meanwhile the benefit concert's lineup grew. The *New York Herald Tribune* predicted that the "jazz potpourri" would yield a handsome sum.

It did not. Fewer than one thousand guests turned up that August to tromp Poitier's yard; dig the activist bebop, gospel, and soul masters; and aid the widow and children of the era's most reviled black liberation figure. The concert had morphed into a variety show. Art exhibits lined the halls inside, and writer-playwright Amiri Baraka's (LeRoi Jones) stark drama blended with the scatting and crooning acts on a makeshift stage outdoors. Rain preempted some of the performances and chased the crowd into the estate. At the end of the night, Mrs. Malcolm X was only five thousand dollars closer to home ownership.

Though the event was not the boon its organizers had hoped for, it hinted that even six months after his death, Malcolm's name was becoming chic in some liberal circles. Several of Poitier's ritzy white neighbors and a handful of corporate executives and clergymen mingled with college students and Harlemites that Sunday, enjoying chicken dinners, cold cuts, and sodas. A few large companies and department stores even donated equipment and refreshments. Curiosity and the chance to stargaze surely lured some of the businesspeople. Others turned up to help Betty and express admiration for Malcolm, a sentiment rather easier to acknowledge with him safely in the ground. Later that winter, the widow herself would proclaim that her husband's philosophy was gaining ground, "even in circles that don't want to admit it."

Lest anybody get the wrong idea about the concert's sponsors, however, Paule Marshall, author of *Brown Girl, Brownstones*, assured the press that the Concerned Mothers were "strictly nonpolitical." Betty Lomax, on the other hand, stressed that they were earnest. "We'd like to see the white American public show some of the compassion for Mrs. Shabazz that they showed in donating sixty thousand dollars to Lee Harvey Oswald's widow," she declared. "I personally don't consider Malcolm guilty of anything wrong. But nobody, even his detractors, can equate him with Oswald. Yet Marina Oswald is cared for."

Upstairs, Mrs. Malcolm X lounged on a porch in the east wing. She surveyed the scene below blissfully. It seemed to surprise the widow that several hundred people would hike out to the secluded estate to support her and the girls. If she felt a twinge of suspicion or resentment for the white and black professionals who had attended and the many souls of all stripes and castes who had not, it didn't show. "It's wonderful," she exclaimed, looking down at the throngs. "Oh my goodness, I was so excited when I got up this morning, I couldn't eat."

A clique of black notables led the most organized and ongoing fundraisers for Betty and the girls. A few conscientious black entertainers and artists boosted the effort. Yet most of established African-America viewed Mrs. Malcolm X as a pariah's widow, and ignored or shunned her. "A lot of black people were very much afraid of me when Malcolm was assassinated," she later said. So though their quiet efforts garnered almost no press, the little people helped keep Betty and her daughters afloat.

Historian and black nationalist John Henrik Clarke, a Malcolm advisor and ally, coordinated one of the first grassroots drives from his Harlem home. Like the minister, Clarke's circles intersected the literati and the street. In the days after the slaying, men and women from both camps clogged his 137th Street home to drop what they could spare into the pot. "Money wasn't like it is today," Clarke's widow Sister Sybil later recalled. Still neighborhood people dug into shabby purses and put off utility bills, and Clarke eventually raised several thousand toward the widow's new home. "This is a part of the story that people forget," Mrs. Clarke said.

Other sympathizers from the black lumpenproletariat sent Betty rumpled one- and five-dollar bills through a Muslim Mosque Post Office box and the OAAU's headquarters at the Hotel Theresa. "Buy milk for Malcolm's babies," one donor wrote. Razzaq called on the minister's international admirers to pitch in. "Peoples throughout the world who are in some small degree aware of the vast contribution that Brother Malcolm made...are making welcomed contributions for the widow and children of Malcolm X—as was done for the widow of our Congolese brother, Patrice Lumumba," he said. There were firmer appeals. A handful of zealous devotees muscled cash and merchandise "donations" for the Shabazz family from reluctant Harlem merchants.

More than a smattering of white people joined the fundraising. Most of the New Yorkers who responded to radio appeals for cash belonged to the tribe that Malcolm, in the days of his less nuanced rhetoric, had slashed as "blue-eyed devils." Malcolm's lieutenants had refused to let white men seal their leader's grave, but according to Sutton, whites covered a good share of the burial expenses. The irony was not lost on Betty. "Had it not been for some of the white people who were friendly with Malcolm, I might not even be here today," she later said.

Egyptologist Dr. ben-Jochannan was among the Harlem national-ists who escorted Betty to Poitier's place within days of the minister's funeral. She and the children would stay in guest quarters at the manor for several weeks, until they could move temporarily to a hotel and a Jackson Heights, Queens, apartment. "Everybody met Betty with respect," Dr. Ben later remembered. Though uptown ideologues like himself, Clarke, and bookstore owner Lewis Michaux helped comfort the widow, only an elite few surrounded her.

At the time, the voices that would demand black power were still forming. The young lions of the New Left were still in the margins. Malcolm's death would draw them to the brink of history. (Within a year, Baraka abandoned Greenwich Village's beatnik scene and moved uptown to found the Black Arts Movement—BAM—from a Harlem brownstone.) But when the minister fell, they lacked the institutions to embrace Betty in any organized manner. Plus they could not find her. After she had recovered from the trauma of Malcolm's death, Sonia Sanchez's thoughts flew to the widow. She began poking around New York's activist and artist circles. "You know where Betty is?" she asked. "You know where she's gone? Can we get some money to her?" She called the young writers and nation-alists. No luck. Finally somebody told her that Ossie and Ruby's crowd had spirited Betty away.

Future BAM poet Haki Madhubuti (Don L. Lee) did not know what had become of the widow, either. He was a twenty-two-year-old bibliophile fresh out of military service, living in a basement apartment and going to school on the GI bill. He'd fallen in love with the pitiless candor of Malcolm's rhetoric. "What bothered me just as much as the assassination was what's happening with the family," he later remem-bered. "When Malcolm was hit, immediately I said, 'What's happening with Betty and the children?'" Madhubuti inquired with writer Hoyt Fuller and other emerging black intellectuals. The woman who had been invisible to the world as a first lady was no more tangible as the emblem of martyrdom.

"We wanted to offer our help," Sanchez would recall. "And when we found out where she was, we had no entrée to that, because there was very obvious division between what we were saying and what the middle class was saying at the time." Baraka, who became a close friend of Betty's, later noted that the black elite's political cadre understood far better than the grassroots the symbolic importance of ushering Mrs. Malcolm X into its fold. "I began to lament the fact that it was always the middle class Negroes that had come to her aid in any sort of substantial way," he said. "She began more or less to be shepherded rather than just gravitate toward the Civil Rights, institutional path. I think she came to feel that she had been abandoned by the [nationalist] Movement."

"Nobody abandoned her," Sara Mitchell later said. Mitchell was among the OAAU women who helped baby-sit the Shabazz daughters in the weeks after the assassination. A few men from the corps ran errands for Betty in those early days. Later that fall, the loyalists she trusted most, including OAAU charter members Muriel Feelings and Peter Bailey, helped move her into Mount Vernon. "We got closer to her," Feelings later remembered. "We came in and did whatever she needed done."

Still, for many Malcolmites it was as if the widow had vanished. Few knew precisely where she was or how to contact her. "I remember trying to reach her once," Sister Khadiyyah later said, "but she was at Antoinette's house. Then she went with that elite group. The Poitiers, Jackie Robinson's wife—they got together and helped the sister." Ferguson and a few of the men helped boost funds for the Concerned Mothers. "But in terms of a call for the OAAU to help Betty," he later recalled, "if it existed it never got beyond the talk stage."

It hardly could have. The disciples that spring were embroiled in crises. Their movement was rudderless. The police were sniffing around, hauling Malcolmites into the station for harrowing interviews.

The faithful guessed the white establishment, having doused the flame, were looking to smother the embers. "There was so much fear," Ferguson remembered. Nobody knew who was legitimate and who was a double agent for the police or the federal government. It seemed probable that the men who killed Malcolm had inside knowledge of the thinness of his security detail that day at the Audubon. Many of his people were convinced that a Judas had delivered him to the slaughter.

Then there were the legal woes—Reuben Francis was facing serious jail time for shooting Hayer—and the looming questions of succession and continuity. Was the cadre to join the Civil Rights mainstream or remain stringently nationalist? Should they try to avenge their leader? And if so, who should die? They laid plots for counterstrikes, most of them ending in Black Muslim bloodbaths. But the minister had forbidden retaliation in the event of his slaying, and his retinue was loath to play into the power structure's hands, deciding that "Malcolm would have preferred justice."

Despair may have been the disciples' gravest problem. "I lived for weeks inside the cloud of my own grief," Benjamin Karim later recalled. The aide could barely eat or sleep. "I'd stay awake most of the night, then at five or six in the morning, just before sunrise, I'd find my way home and fall into bed," he said. "For an hour or so I'd drift in and out of shallow sleep while time, it seemed, unraveled inside my head."

The slaying's aftershocks widened the gulch between Betty and the corps. A series of conflicts that spring amplified the resentment and foreshadowed a lasting alienation. One of the first encounters involved Razzaq. The Malcolm confidant and longtime deputy had continued to handle many of the Muslim Mosque's and OAAU's administrative affairs in the days after the minister's death. He had been opening mail, forwarding Betty the checks and condolences directed to her and keeping correspondence addressed to the organizations.

Under Betty's orders, another Muslim Mosque official approached Razzaq shortly after the assassination and demanded that he turn over all the mail and transfer the post office box to the widow. Razzaq refused. Like some of the other veterans, he believed he had a greater claim to Malcolm's intellectual legacy and the custodianship of the movement than the minister's uninitiated young wife, whom the Malcolmites knew only as a homemaker. "She was a grieving widow, a hero's widow," Razzaq later said. Yet the difference of opinion flared into an argument, and Betty never talked to him again.

The bad blood between Mrs. Malcolm X and the disciples had boiled even earlier. Hours after her husband's funeral, a distraught and embittered Betty had ordered a pair of OAAU men to dump the minister's papers into trash cans outside the Wallace residence. (Malcolm had moved the documents to the basement of the nearby home after the Valentine's Day firebombing.) The command appalled the men. While some understood the widow's disillusionment, others complained that she had hurt their prospects for fulfilling the minister's program. Betty soon realized the intellectual value of Malcolm's effects, but there were more clashes as she tried to gather materials from the aides. She fell out with the same man who had demanded the mail from Razzaq when he left for Ghana that spring with several of the minister's tape recordings and speeches.

The estrangement deepened in coming months as it grew clear that Betty was abandoning some of the strictures of her first-lady role. She had tested modest liberties throughout her husband's final year. "She said the first thing she did after leaving the Nation was undo the top button of her shirt," Gamilah later recalled. Now that liberated, Christian career women had enveloped her, she began shrugging off some of the constraints that had followed her out of the Nation.

It was a humble transition that in that first year consisted of little more than dangling jewelry and colorful dresses, a slow emergence from the veil and a less bashful deportment. Nevertheless, some of the women who had fled the Nation for the Muslim Mosque clucked that, "she grew up overnight." The cadre's more fundamentalist brothers also disapproved. "Men are predators and women are prey," one cautioned. "And a woman that has lost her husband is particularly ripe prey."

A more universal lament among Malcolmites was that Betty was quitting her husband's grassroots circles. "The classes moved in on her," Kenyatta would complain. Some of the disciples saw omens of a return to her pre-Malcolm sensibility. "She fell back on what she knew," Ferguson later said. "She moved from the field slaves to the house slaves."

Yet for a time she was just as wary of the elite crowd. "Betty wasn't an easy person to get to know," Poitier would remember. "She was used to being very secretive, and she wasn't very trusting. Her attitude was, 'Why would you do this for me?'" Quite apart from fleeing Malcolm's camp, the widow made frail attempts to organize it in the groping weeks after his death, summoning a handful of the men and women she thought she could trust for a couple of wandering meetings. When the troops arrived, she stuck Malcolm's Astrakhan hat on her head and tried to rally them. "She was saying what this was to do and what that was to do," Mitchell later recalled.

But Betty had no real political agenda. As the aides who showed up quickly realized, she had called the meetings out of a need to connect with her husband's loyalists and ministry. The widow could not have led anybody or anything—her first concern was feeding and sheltering the children. Yet she felt a proprietorship for the OAAU, then the most palpable evidence of the minister's final labors. It was this impulse, along with an old enmity, that led to war with her in-law.

Days after her half-brother's death, Ella Collins proclaimed herself the OAAU's interim leader. While she acknowledged that Malcolm was irreplaceable, she said she intended to serve as the organization's custodian until the body could choose a successor. In mid-March she announced that she was taking over for good. She explained that the minister had named her sole heir to his movement's political arm in a private conversation the night before the assassination (a story Betty never believed). "We will carry out my brother's program to the letter," Ella told the press. To the bewilderment of some of the OAAU loyalists who had been struggling to form a provisional council, she promptly hired a white lawyer and began pulling together incorporation papers.

The organization desperately needed leadership. "I called a meeting of all those interested in the OAAU, because I wanted to turn in these papers," Razzaq later remembered. "And none of the people who was rah, rah, rah Malcolm showed up." Drawn to Ella's commanding persona, a few of the minister's lieutenants clustered around her and tried to revive their movement. Yet the troupe floundered without Malcolm's charisma and keen articulation of the racial crisis. "They say his infant nationalist group never really got an initial spanking," a reporter said a year later, "and its current mewings go unnoticed."

Ella and the brothers managed to organize a tribute for the slain leader on May 19, 1965—his fortieth birthday. In what would become an annual ritual, a quiet file of devotees made the pilgrimage to his grave that Wednesday afternoon. Hours later, a modest crowd trickled into Harlem's Rockland Palace and paid two dollars to hear speeches by Collins, Razzaq, and Jesse Gray. The attendees enjoyed regional jazz artists and rededicated themselves to Malcolm's mission. Betty, who had said earlier that she knew nothing of the affair and that its sponsors had not bothered to consult her, was conspicuously absent. She had already announced her intentions to shun all OAAU affairs.

The Rockland hosted another Malcolm tribute a week later. A second faction had formed a memorial committee and planned the more ecumenical affair, with a lineup that included Baldwin, Davis, Fannie Lou Hamer, and John Lewis. Michaux, Clarke, and Sutton also appeared, as did African diplomats and local orthodox Muslim officials. Making her first public address before the reverent audience was Mrs. Malcolm X, who did not mention her husband, but gently thanked the attendees "on behalf of my four babies and myself."

Betty had a coterie of sympathizers among her husband's nationalist comrades. A splinter group of OAAU veterans who rejected Collins's vision (or refused to take orders from a woman) maintained loose ties with the widow. But the press soon discovered that the OAAU was hopelessly balkanized, and that Betty and Collins were at odds. "She was just a ruthlessly dominating leader," bodyguard James

Smalls later said of Collins. "And Sister Betty in her own way was very domineering. So there wasn't gonna be no partnership unless it was on an equal footing."

After their collaboration to arrange the funeral, the two never even managed another armistice. Betty believed Collins's counsel had drawn Malcolm away from her while he was alive, and Collins believed Betty's refusal to leave the country with him had left him open to attack. Each woman felt she had a uniquely authentic perspective on his life, and their relationship continued to sour.

That December, Betty finally made public her displeasure with Collins's stewardship of the OAAU. "I think of all the work and sacrifice he put into it," she told the *New York Times*, "and it's saddening and disheartening to see people who know nothing about it taking it over." Collins believed it was the widow who was compromising Malcolm's legacy. Later that year, when Betty signed a contract with a socialist publisher to release a collection of the minister's speeches, Collins grumbled privately that her in-law had sold out.

The older woman was objecting to *Malcolm X Speaks*, one of the earlier titles in a body of Malcolm literature that would span several continents and languages. The edited book contained "Message to the Grass Roots," perhaps his greatest oratory, and a melange of speeches and statements from his final year. New York's Pathfinder Press (then Merit Publishers) had written Betty in August to propose the compilation. She responded enthusiastically, and the $5.95 book had appeared in stores that winter.

Pathfinder had not been the first to propose a Malcolm project. Louis Lomax had approached the widow months earlier with a plan for a film that would borrow heavily from his 1963 book about the minister and the Nation, *When the Word Is Given*. Betty had not gotten involved; she was too busy tending the girls and trying to piece her family back together. Scholars, journalists, foreign diplomats, activists, publishers, and producers had also courted Collins with ideas for projects. The sibling had proven less receptive than the widow. Malcolm had fought too hard, she thought, for his survivors to become "tools and fools" for dubious memoirists and profiteers. Betty, however, desperately needed the modest income a collection of Malcolm's speeches would provide.

In later years, Betty was emphatic that her husband had never been a socialist. But despite his discomfort with the White Left, the minister in his post-Nation era had spoken regularly at the Militant Labor Forum, a Trotskyist program with ties to Pathfinder. Many of his later addresses had coursed with socialism's anti-capitalist, anti-imperialist themes. None of this seems to have inspired Betty's decision to give *Malcolm X Speaks* her nod. Aside from the promise of royalties, it was the prospect of reviving Malcolm's words that attracted her. Pathfinder's Steve Clarke later recalled that the widow did not seek to censor or shape the collection's selected extracts or the manner in which the publisher presented them, "as long as she was confident that it was being done with integrity." She was eager to see a public record of her husband's later discourse, much of which his autobiography omits.

Having hastily trashed some of the minister's private materials, she had limited access to the speeches and statements themselves, which Pathfinder editors gleaned from private tapes, radio-station recordings, and other sources. She did not fancy herself an editor, but she was not closemouthed about her visions for the project. "Betty was strong willed," Clarke later remembered. "She was a hard bargainer. She wanted to get as much of Malcolm in print as possible."

Pathfinder released several more Malcolm books in later years, prompting some black nationalists to lament the white socialists' "publishing monopoly" on the minister. Yet from the beginning, Betty had liked the house's forthright recognition of her as legal executor of her husband's literary and spoken legacy. Pathfinder would print Malcolm's speeches when many other publishers and scholars—black and white—were ignoring him. Collins, however, had misgivings about the White Left painting her brother as a late convert to Marxism. She was not alone. "I lose track with them," Dr. Ben later said of the widow and her daughters. "A bunch of the socialists start to get involved, and the people with the magazine—the *Militant*. I went my way, which was a nationalist way."

Collins would suggest that Betty was too heartsick in 1965 to ponder the minister's legacy. The dearth of financial support from the American mainstream, she thought, left the widow especially vulnerable to the "predatory" advances of publishers and other agents. "If we had had more family unity, we would have been able to exercise more control over the way Malcolm was treated in books and movies and documentaries," she later said. "We could have insisted on their presenting the Malcolm that we all knew rather than one they envisioned."

Chapter Eleven

BAHIYAH

—◆—

"Betty, you'll have to speak for yourself."
—Juanita Poitier

Betty churned with rage, grief, and despair in her early widowhood. The beasts had slunk from their pit and robbed her of her hero, provider, and spiritual counselor. They had robbed her babies of their father, her family of its patriarch. They had crushed hope, smeared truth, and destroyed her belief in humankind. "I lost faith in a lot of people," she later said. "Not just white people—black people and people of all colors."

Malcolm had warned that bitterness only debilitates. Wrath, he had counseled, would sap her creativity and devour her joy. But in the month after his death, she could find neither the weapons nor the will with which to fight. She expected her boiling insides to consume her. Or, she imagined, the toxic air itself would do her in. "She was in turmoil," Dr. Ben later remembered.

Much of the brown and black world shared her anguish. In the days after the assassination, Muslims in Indonesia held prayer services in the minister's honor, and a fiery demonstration flared in Guyana. Betty knew vaguely of the international ferment. Despite the slanted press coverage, there were comrades who advised her of the outcry. But she herself had never ventured outside the United States. Besides, Malcolm was dead, and all the hellraising in the Third World would not revive him.

Though pro-Malcolm rallies could not hearten her, the defamation deepened her wounds. "People forget what was being said about Malcolm at the time," journalist Chuck Stone recalled. "They said death was too good for him." The name that Harlem exalted was acid elsewhere. When Amiri Baraka later invoked Malcolm during a Newark speech before alumni of Howard University, one of the nation's leading black schools, the audience blanched. "Some of those Negroes actually booed," he later remembered. Betty herself would proclaim her husband "the most slandered man in America."

The enemy was everywhere, but the widow harbored special malice for the Nation, whose hierarchs she believed had helped arrange the minister's death. "Sometimes she would curse when she talked about Elijah Muhammad and Farrakhan," Ferguson later recalled. She abhorred the white power structure and its agents—the CIA, FBI, and local police—who she was convinced had allowed if not orchestrated the hit. She also detested her husband's blood brothers in the Nation of Islam, for their public betrayal, and many of his lieutenants, whom she suspected of treachery. One OAAU cofounder would remember that after the slaying, she treated even some of the most devoted disciples "like hustlers."

Betty told an OAAU woman that the minister's security detail should have ignored his orders not to frisk spectators on the day of the assassination. At times she seemed as bitter at the men who had failed to intercept the bullets as she was at those who had stood squeezing them into her husband. Both parties, she believed, were guilty. And both were black. In time, her mistrust and volatility antagonized even those Malcolmites who tried to stand by her. "The brothers didn't know what to do, because they wanted to protect her," Mitchell later said. While some of the disciples hoped to soothe her, others were "busy trying to act like they were her critics or advisers," Feelings recalled.

The widow's bitterness and suspicion only intensified when Malcolmites started leaving town. Fleeing fear, disillusionment, the threat of police persecution, and more bloodletting, many of Malcolm's top deputies slipped away in the months after his death. Several landed in the Caribbean or Africa, where they set down for years. "All of them niggers done run out of town," Sister Khadiyyah later remembered.

"Like they got something to lose. Don't nobody want them, but they was takin' planes and trains."

It was hardly idle paranoia that scattered them. Just three weeks after the assassination, a maid discovered the body of Leon Ameer, one of Malcolm's top aides, sprawled in a Boston hotel room. Investigators ruled out foul play. Malcolm's disciples were unconvinced. Even journalists with close ties to the minister had cause to fear. After he revealed in a *Life* magazine piece that Betty had shown him her late husband's list of likely hitmen, Gordon Parks learned from the FBI that four henchmen (presumably Black Muslims) had gotten orders to kill him. Within twenty-four hours, he and his entire family jetted off to a tropical seaside hideaway.

Fear clutched the widow, too, even cloistered in guest accommodations at Poitier's remote manor. But she had never been the cowering sort, and she was too heartsick to dwell on the menace of the Nation's zealots or the white establishment. Instead she sought composure. Donning Malcolm's hat was some comfort. She had first slipped it on after intruders had firebombed their home. Now its powers multiplied. "It was my security blanket," she later said. "When I wore it, I felt spiritually in touch with him."

Betty was groping for serenity and a new role. Poitier soon discovered that her houseguest was totally unprepared for the public and private demands of her widowhood. Through her society contacts, Poitier managed to arrange a conversation between Betty and New York Governor Nelson Rockefeller's people. But as she later recalled, the talk did not go as she had planned:

> I said, "Betty, they want to talk to you. Tell them you want your children's education taken care of." And she said, "Oh no, I can't do it." I said, "You've got to ask them." She said, "No, you ask." And when they came over, she said, "Oh, I don't want nothing."

Poitier gently told Betty that she would have to swallow her pride. "At least you have somebody to protect you," the widow cried. "Betty," the hostess replied, "you'll have to speak for yourself." For seven years, Mrs. Malcolm X had left the speaking out to her husband, at least publicly. Now her pangs of loss were far more powerful than her grasp of his global meaning. "She was not aware of a lot of her African family," Mrs. John Henrik Clarke would remember. Without a sophisticated sense of her husband's legacy, the widow's disillusionment with the struggle deepened. "She saw that Malcolm had given his life for black people," Baraka later said. "And where was the reciprocation?"

＊

Grief could have driven Betty mad. "I could be someplace where somebody would be feeding me or changing my diapers, you know," she later told an interviewer. She had no blueprint for survival without Malcolm. Squinting ahead, all she could see were the contours of more pain. If it were not for her daughters, she genuinely wondered if she would have bothered to pull herself upright every morning.

Her faith had been quitting her. Perhaps she felt its passing. Perhaps she was too numb to know the difference. Some of her brothers in Islam detected it, in any case. Only days after the minister's funeral, Ahmed Osman and Said Ramadan, a young Harvard scholar, asked her to accompany them to Mecca in her husband's stead.

"What I thought best was to take her out of the mood of the country," Osman later remembered. The graduate student suspected that the *Hajj* would be an ideal remedy for the misery that had enveloped Betty. She had been contemplating the pilgrimage for almost a year—since Malcolm had testified to its power in those ebullient letters. His death had dashed her tentative plans to make the journey. Now Poitier, who had marveled at how profoundly the experience had enriched the minister, urged her new friend to go. The widow agreed.

Again Osman hopped on the Greyhound, this time to meet Betty at the Saudi mission in Manhattan. The next few days vanished in a bleary rush about town. They secured a visa and certification of the widow's authenticity from Muslim authorities in the city. Sheik Faisal provided the requisite papers, recognizing her as a true convert to Islam based on her husband's confession of the faith a year before. Saudi officials finalized arrangements with the World Muslim League, which agreed to sponsor the trip.

Osman's fellow Sudanese immigrants saw him dashing about with Betty and thought he had lost his mind. "You crazy?" they said. "Maybe the CIA and FBI are following you." Betty did not share Osman's idealism. She worried about leaving the children for the month-long excursion. Then Antoinette Wallace agreed to help Poitier and another woman baby-sit Attallah, Qubilah, Ilyasah, and Gamilah while the widow was away.

In late March 1965, a month after she had watched assassins topple her husband, Betty kissed her daughters and, traveling under an assumed name, took off for the Holy Land. She hardly blinked during the flight. This was her first trip overseas, and she rippled with excitement as her escorts prepared her for the rituals of the pilgrimage. When the trio touched down in Beirut, Lebanon, where they were to spend the night, a local newspaper editor emerged to greet Betty and conduct an interview. (She refused to talk to correspondents for American news sources.) The Lebanese people knew of Malcolm from his travels through the Middle East and were quite in awe of his widow.

Betty and her companions arrived in Jeddah, Saudi Arabia, the following day. She wore modest, flowing garments and a headpiece in the style of the other female pilgrims, all of whom left their faces unveiled. The men had wound two strips of unsewn white cloth about themselves like towels. Protocol officials met the widow and her escorts at the airport and whisked them to the Jeddah Palace Hotel, where they were to stay as guests of state. The Saudi government provided Betty with a chauffeured car and offered to cover all her expenses while she was in the country.

The following week was exhausting. Betty had entered the state of *ihram*, an abstemious phase that precedes the pilgrimage, but she had to balance the demanding *Hajj* preparations with newfound diplomatic duties. Saudi dignitaries were already queuing up to receive the widow of the Black American revolutionary who had first dazzled them the previous spring. Yet the dual role was a happy burden for Betty, who basked in the bureaucrats' attention.

Here was the veneration for Malcolm that seemed so sparse back home. The Muslim world was especially reverent now that Malcolm had become a *shaheed*, a martyr in a righteous struggle *(jihad)* on behalf of Islam. Among the luminaries that greeted the widow was the secretary general of the World Muslim League, an elegant black Saudi named Saban. His grace so moved her that when her twins were born later that year, she bestowed upon each the middle name Saban in his honor.

There was not enough time to accommodate all the Saudi notables who wished to welcome Mrs. Malcolm X. As the pilgrimage season neared, her fellowship with the faithful ended and her communion with the creator began. She and her companions left Jeddah for the forty-five-mile drive into Mecca among busloads of pilgrims. There were blacks, whites, Asians, and Arabs. All wore the unadorned *Hajj* garb signifying the equality of humankind in Allah's eyes. Along the route, the sojourners chanted the *talbiyah*:

> Here we come, O Allah, here we come! Here we come.
> No partner have You. Here we come! Praise indeed, and
> blessings, are Yours—the Kingdom, too! No partner have
> you!

Malcolm himself had taught Betty the words. Now they awakened a prickling anticipation. Her excitement mounted as her car passed the white pillar marking the sacred territory and approached the outskirts of the holiest city in Islam. She traveled through the barren valley that encloses Mecca, marveling at the walls of craggy hills at its edges. Allah had certainly chosen a harsh landscape upon which to command Prophet Abraham (Ibrahim) to build His house. Finally the widow entered Mecca and beheld the Sacred Mosque.

It was majestic. Rearing from the bustling cityscape, the ornate worship place lofted seven minarets skyward. With the masses swarming its base, the edifice looked like the fusion of a coliseum and a temple. Following her guide, Betty made her way through the Gate of

Peace and into the droning multitude within the temple courtyard. At its center loomed the *Kaaba*, God's house.

Betty for almost a year had joined more than three quarters of a billion believers worldwide in bowing for five daily prayers in the direction of the black cube, the symbolic center of Muslim worship. Now she was making her seven circumambulations about its faces, just as Malcolm had described in his letters. Like the minister, she chanted with the other pilgrims as she performed the revolutions, brimming with a sense of kinship. After making the prescribed circuits, she visited the Well of Zamzam. She had learned that Allah had revealed the oasis to the infant Ismael's mother Hajar as she staggered through the desolate valley centuries ago. Now Betty renewed herself with the rich mineral water.

More than three months pregnant, she did her best to trot seven times between the hills of Safa and Marwah, mimicking Hajar's frantic search for water in the wilderness. During the treks she prayed for mercy, as the forlorn mother once had. No other ritual would bring her more comfort. In the ensuing days, Betty proceeded east from Mecca to nearby Mina with the other women in her *Hajj* party. There she and her companions crowded into one of thousands of tents that blanketed the land like a silken metropolis. The following morning was the day of standing. She rose with the others and advanced upon the Plain of Arafat. By noon the legions had flooded the barren expanse, more than one million believers come to renew their covenant with the Lord.

As she traveled internationally in later years, Betty would realize that Malcolm's frothy accounts of Eastern Islam had wildly overstated the Muslim World's colorblindness. White supremacy, she would discover, infected every head on the planet. Yet in the spring of 1965, as she ventured into the Arabian wasteland among the sea of pilgrims, she experienced the brotherhood that had so profoundly moved her husband. She saw the diversity of Islam, whose adherents hail not only from the Middle East, but Africa (almost 25 percent), the Indian subcontinent (30 percent), and Southeast Asia (17 percent) as well as Latin America, Australia, the Caribbean, and Europe.

The widow worshipped under a wicked sun. She had not known what to expect during the *wuquf*, the pilgrim's day of supplication on the Plain of Arafat. She understood that the rite was the centerpiece of the *Hajj*, and that no pilgrimage was complete without it. She knew that it was here, on the Mount of Mercy, that the Prophet Muhammad had delivered his farewell sermon in the seventh century. But would she experience fear, rage, or euphoria as she stood on the knuckled terrain? Was it possible that unpracticed in her faith and embittered with life, she would feel nothing at all?

The passing hours melted her anxiety. There was no lightning-bolt revelation or shuddering trance for the widow. But as she prayed in the boiling desert heat, whispering into the gloaming with the multitude, a warm tranquility enfolded her. Though Allah did not tell her how she would make it, she knew He was listening. And when she finally turned to make her way back to the tent, she was sure He meant for her to survive.

This certainty buoyed her throughout the final days of the journey as she returned to Mina to rest and pelt Satan's pillars before pressing onward to Mecca for the culminating Festival of Sacrifice. She had been reborn there in the Holy Land. Mecca's camaraderie, climate, and symphony of cultures had enthralled and cleansed her. "The brotherhood that I have heard preached about all my life is here," she wrote in a letter mailed to the *Amsterdam News* but addressed to the people of Harlem. "This ancient city with its beauty and sereness [sic] is indeed something for all men to behold."

Betty did not share with Harlem the pilgrimage's physical strain and humble accommodations. Pregnant and, by the standards of the region, pampered, Betty had struggled to complete many of the rituals, sleeping and sitting on rugs and performing arduous tasks in blistering heat with little refreshment. A year earlier, Malcolm had tried to hide his decidedly Western discomfort with some of the rigors of the *Hajj*. His widow was less subtle. "Why can't we have a little comfort here?" she complained.

There were psychological hardships, too. Betty worried about her daughters. (Telephones were unavailable during much of the trip.) Between rituals she reminisced about her husband, remembering his bubbling accounts of the *Hajj*. But she had not grieved since she had arrived in the sacred territory. Even her despair was dissipating. Now back in Jeddah, she thought about the people everywhere who loved her because they loved Malcolm. She thought about those who had prayed for her and her girls. "I stopped focusing on the people who were trying to tear me and my family apart," she later said. She reflected upon her children and her foster mother and the good souls she had left behind in the United States. Suddenly, she could not get home quick enough.

But a final ceremony lay ahead. Though she had made no diplomatic requests, Betty learned that Prince Faisal, ruler of Saudi Arabia, would grant her and her escorts an audience at the palace. It was a fantastic honor—the prince was one of the most powerful men in the Arab World. Throughout the pilgrimage season, scores of visiting dignitaries would petition unsuccessfully to meet the busy monarch. Yet he had reserved time for the widow of the man he had received a year earlier as Black America's emissary.

Tall and well-formed, the prince strode forward to welcome Betty on an afternoon in late April. He offered his condolences, telling her that he appreciated Malcolm's martyrdom. He uttered a few kind words about the minister. Then he opened his kingdom. "You and your children consider Saudi Arabia your country," he declared. The prince was offering the widow and her daughters citizenship. He was inviting the family to settle permanently in Saudi Arabia as official guests. Osman hoped Betty would accept. To him, it seemed an ideal opportunity for her and the children to escape the venomous climate of the United States. But New York was home, and anxious to get back, the widow declined the prince's offer.

Days later, almost five weeks after they had arrived, she and her companions left the Holy Land. The journey had restored her emotional balance, replenished her sensibility and sense of worth, and deepened her commitment to orthodox Islam. Though she had recited the *shahada*, the confession of belief in one Lord—Allah—months before, in Mecca she had touched His cheek. "I knew, after the pilgrimage, that I was going to do it and that I could do it—with or without help," she later said.

Somehow in the bustle of those weeks she had managed to send postcards to friends back home. One arrived for journalist Claude Lewis bearing the cursive signature of "Mrs. Malcolm X." Upon the greeting card Alex Haley received was the autograph of "Mrs. Betty Malik Shabazz." The widow sent Haley's family her regards and announced that, "I am indeed happy to be making the *Hajj*." In the card's margin she scrawled yet another alias—an Arabic designation meaning "beautiful and radiant" that a female pilgrim had conferred upon her only days before. "My new name," Betty proclaimed, "is Bahiyah."

As the widow was making peace with Allah, the United States was making war with North Vietnam. As American and Vietcong troops bloodied each other in Southeast Asian jungles, the enemies of Civil Rights were bloodying the movement's last grand campaign—the march from Selma to Montgomery—in the racial wilderness of the American South. The violence in Alabama spurred the last great Civil Rights legislation, the Voting Rights Act, even as a black generation's disenchantment with nonviolence swelled. As President Johnson signed the historic bill early that fall—"today we strike away the last major shackle of...fierce and ancient bonds"—and frustration with poverty and oppression exploded in the Watts street rebellions, Betty moved into an upscale Mount Vernon neighborhood known as the Heights.

Mrs. Malcolm X had never been immune to the call of suburbia. Westchester County had enticed her even before the era of ill will with the Nation. "I wanted to move where I would have a nice backyard and all my kids could play," she later said. She was even hungrier for seclusion now, amid the glut of sympathizers, foes, and dubious newcomers. "I just wanted to get away from it all," she recalled. "I was terribly disillusioned."

A mother of four (and counting) does not retreat to the suburbs on the cheap. The Concerned Mothers had grown rather more so after their efforts had garnered only seventeen thousand dollars—twenty-three thousand dollars short of the cost of Congresswoman Abzug's old house, an eight-room colonial on a hill. Poitier and company worried that the jobless widow of a notorious black dissident would be a dim prospect for the mortgage companies. Yet, by September, the Shabazz children were exploring their new place and Betty was shouldering a formidable house note.

Royalties from Malcolm's autobiography helped ease the burden. There were whispers of other cash sources. Charles Kenyatta later insisted that the minister had received funds from abroad in his final days. The speculative Louis Lomax guessed that Malcolm had become a political and financial beneficiary of Algeria's and Ghana's revolutionary leaders, and that this "Ben Bella–Nkrumah axis" had funneled him cash to sustain his family and spotlight American imperialism. The rumors even permeated official circles. A March 3, 1965 telegram to the U.S. Department of State from the American Embassy in Egypt indicated that there had been talk in diplomatic quarters of an infusion of overseas aid for Betty.

Among certain Malcolmites, the folklore has endured that Prince Faisal or other Arab/African dignitaries sent the widow money that spring or summer. (Though some of the disciples reported that Betty's less than gracious displays in Saudi Arabia offended its monarch and withered his magnanimity.) Still, it remains unclear whether Mr. or Mrs. Malcolm X were ever on a foreign dole. The minister once told Ella Collins that there were several nations willing to finance him, but he feared that if he accepted the offers the State Department would nail him for violating federal laws regulating civilian receipt of funds from foreign governments.

Betty later told an academic mentor that the minister in his last months secretly arranged a modest monthly allowance for her that went into effect after his death. She did not reveal the source, and it is possible that she did not know. Nor would she disclose whether the cash arrived from distant lands. All the widow would say was that she understood that the installments would continue as long as she remained single. From this, the mentor inferred that Malcolm did not want her to remarry, a theory Betty refused to comment on.

Money was still tight that autumn of 1965. The widow had no idea how she was going to manage with four girls and a baby on the way.

She had rendezvoused with God, and He had told her she was going to make it. So it seemed a rather mean trick on His part when, on September 30, she gave birth to twin girls at Brooklyn's Brookdale Hospital. "I wonder what was all of that about," she later mused. "I couldn't handle one and then I had two."

Malikah ("queen") emerged first, making Malaak ("angel") the baby of the family. Betty graced both girls with feminine versions of her late husband's Arabic name, Malik. She had expected a son, and here were a couple more ladies to round out her brood at a half dozen. Without Malcolm, the pregnancy had been lonely and the delivery especially harrowing. Yet the babies, whose faces conjured memories of his, signaled a transition from the death and despair of the previous winter.

Betty brought the twins home and their sisters huddled around them. In recent weeks, the widow had garnished the large crib Poitier had loaned her with bunting and a carousel toy. Now she wondered where her new arrivals would sleep. Years later she remembered how she improvised: "I said to Juanita, 'Listen here.' I said, 'Buy an extra bunting and some more blankets, and put the bunting at the foot of the bed.' And you know this was a huge baby bed, so they looked lost in this big bed. So they stayed there until they were about four months."

⎯⎯

In the first, frigid weeks of 1966, Harlem continued to quietly eulogize its "black shining prince." Young men had begun sporting the fur Astrakhan hats Malcolm had favored. "Freedom by Any Means Necessary" buttons dotted lapels. The House of Proper Propaganda and other uptown bookstores could not seem to stock enough Malcolm books and albums (though most of the proceeds did not benefit Betty). "I guess they'll sell as long as the Bible sells," Michaux proclaimed.

Malcolm devotees huddled nightly in The Truth, a local haunt, to talk about self-determination, black identity, and the evils of the white establishment. That December, on the eve of Malcolm's murder trial, Betty herself turned up at the basement coffee shop. She chatted quietly with friends in a corner as her husband's intellectual legacy unfurled about her. It was a rare surfacing for the widow. She had generally eschewed the Harlem scene since withdrawing to Mount Vernon. Her only public statement had been a telegram to the *Amsterdam News* supporting Assemblyman Percy Sutton's efforts to soften New York divorce laws.

She had prayed for inner peace in the seclusion of Mount Vernon, but her grief was still raw. ("A man said to me the other day, 'The void is so deep and the silence is so silent,'" she told one journalist.) And whatever serenity she found was fleeting. A year after she had struggled to revive her husband, pumping his arms while blood seeped through his starched shirt and coagulated on the dusty Audubon stage, she went downtown to face his accused killers.

It was the twenty-sixth day of *People vs. Hayer, Butler, and Johnson*. The trial had begun the first week of December 1965. A jury of nine whites and three blacks had heard a parade of prosecution witnesses give sometimes clashing accounts of a murder as brazen as it was bizarre. A Supreme Court judge presided impassively over the proceedings while a gallery of spectators, including Black Muslims and Malcolmites, looked on with cynical eyes. At the defense table, three young, well-groomed black men watched it all unfold.

Betty did not even glance at the trio of defendants as she took the witness stand. She wore black, the white pearls Malcolm had bought her gleaming at her neck. She sat as stoically as she had at the funeral. The district attorney asked how long she had been married to the deceased. "Seven years and six weeks," she said. Again she recounted for the prosecution what she had seen the day her husband died. "I heard someone, I saw someone stand," she said. "First I heard a voice. They said something to the effect of, 'Get your hands out of my pocket,' or 'Don't go in my pocket'—you know, very loud and demanding…."

The prosecutor asked if the loud and demanding man was white or Negro. "Afro-American," the widow replied. Then she continued. "It was a lot of things happening all at once. There was chairs falling, people hollering…a succession of shots…." She narrated for a few more

minutes. Then the district attorney thanked her. None of the defend-
ers wished to cross-examine, so she rose and started walking out of the
room. But when she reached the defense table she suddenly stopped,
clenched her fists, and yelled, "They killed my husband! They killed
him! They had no right to kill my husband!" She was still hollering as
the court attendants hustled her out the court. The lawyers instantly
moved for a mistrial, but the judge turned them down. "I watched her
very carefully," he said. "She did not point to anyone."

The People's case was firm against Talmadge Hayer, the gunman
whom Malcolm disciples had mobbed outside the Audubon minutes
after the slaying. But the evidence against Norman 3X Butler and
Thomas 15X Johnson was spotty. Both swore their innocence, as did
Hayer initially. The prosecution argued that all three were indeed
Black Muslims who had been in the ballroom on February 21, 1965,
and who had means and motive to do away with Malcolm as a heretic
of their church and a blasphemer of Muhammad. The district attorney
hoped to prove that on the day in question, Hayer and Butler had
feigned a skirmish to distract the crowd while Johnson crept forward
and shotgunned Malcolm. Hayer and Butler had then dashed toward
the stage, blasting the fallen minister with pistols.

A procession of witnesses emerged to swear to some strand of this
scenario. Few of Malcolm's inside men were among them. The motley
cast of eyewitnesses still was good enough to build a decent case, at
least against Hayer. As he confronted the state's strongest corroborat-
ing evidence in the waning days of the eight-week trial, Hayer suddenly and dramatically confessed. Yes, he had done it, he said, but his
codefendants had not been involved at all. Yes, he had lied under oath,
but now he wished to come clean.

"I just want to testify that Butler and Johnson had nothing to do
with this," he declared. "I was there. I know what happened, and I know
the people who were there." Though he would not name his confederates, he insisted that they were not Muslims. He swore that he himself

had not been a Black Muslim on February 21, 1965, and that he had never belonged to Newark's Mosque Number Twenty-Five. Somebody—he would not say who—had approached him in early February and asked him and three other men to do the job, he explained. This somebody had offered cash—he would not divulge how much—but he had never collected. He acknowledged that he and his coconspirators had rehearsed the hit. When or where he would not say.

Hayer claimed he had met the other assassins on the day of the rally in a George Washington Bridge bus terminal and traveled with them to the Audubon. Somebody had shoved a .45-caliber automatic into his hand. Another man had gotten a Luger and a third a twelve-gauge. When they arrived at the ballroom, he and the man with the Luger had sat down in the front row; the man with the shotgun took row four and another man sat in the rear. The man in the back had started the commotion and the rostrum guards had gone for it. Meanwhile, he said, the man with the shotgun had blasted Malcolm, and he and the man with the Luger followed suit.

The jurors did not buy the story—not the part about Butler and Johnson's innocence, at any rate. They seemed to believe, as did the district attorney, that Hayer was simply trying to save his two equally guilty Black Muslim compatriots. The trial ended routinely with a trio of first-degree-murder convictions. On April 14, 1966, a Supreme Court judge sentenced the men to life in state prison. Thus one of the most mysterious and sensational whodunnits of the century drew to an official close. The police were satisfied. The courts were satisfied. And so, it seemed, was Betty.

But the Black Left was not, nor would it ever be. A cyclone of conspiracy theories would spin out of Malcolm's death. At the time of the verdict, the conventional wisdom in Harlem and throughout northern ghettoes was that the white establishment had been in on the hit. In later years, the theory would practically become black orthodoxy.

Malcolmites, for their part, subscribe to a theory of their leader's undoing that goes something like this: when Malcolm quit the Nation, he became infinitely more menacing to the power structure than he had been as a Black Muslim bishop. He was revolutionizing blacks at home, kindling anti-Americanism in the Dark World and prodding African and Arab states to haul the U.S. before the United Nations on human-rights charges. Most disquietingly for his enemies, he and Martin Luther King Jr.'s ideologies and paths were starting to converge, raising the specter of an irrepressible black axis. The CIA almost killed Malcolm by poison in Cairo in the summer of 1964 and was going to try again in Paris in February 1965, but France got wind of the plot and barred his entry. According to this explanation, it was government agents and not Black Muslim arsonists who firebombed his home. Washington ordered the assassination and New York police colluded, leaving Malcolm defenseless that day at the Audubon. Black trigger-men were the marionettes, but the "System" was the puppeteer. Police arrested Hayer only because the mob outside the ballroom seized him first. A patrolman was able to hustle another assassin who had spilled out of the ballroom into a squad car and whisk him away to freedom. All of this may or may not have happened with the connivance of a traitor or traitors inside Malcolm's corps.

Each of the disciples have developed their own hypotheses within this conspiratorial frame. "A man fall the way he was hit," Kenyatta told an interviewer years later. "Malcolm was hit from the back." Razzaq thought Black Islam had joined hands with the state. "Yes, the Nation did the smokescreen," he said. "Make smoke in the east and fire in the west." Malcolm's photographer believed the media did him in. "The press is the one group that could have had Malcolm shot," Robert Haggins said. "The press was against him. And the police was against him."

Black Islam clearly was not Malcolm's only enemy. It is hard *not* to conclude that the government wanted him out of the picture, for its agents monitored, harried, and sabotaged him as an enemy of the state throughout his public life. Malcolmites often cite among the com-pelling evidence of conspiracy the words of their leader, who himself believed at the end that he would become a victim of intrigue. According to Alex Haley, the minister said the day before he died that, "The more I keep thinking about this thing, the things that have been happening lately, I'm not at all that sure it's the Muslims. I know what they can do, and what they can't and they can't do some of the stuff recently going on. Now, I'm going to tell you, the more I keep thinking about what happened to me in France, I think I'm going to quit saying it's the Muslims."

Betty, too, believed that Uncle Sam had colluded in the slaying. But she was convinced that Black Muslims had been the executioners, and that the order had come from the kingdom's highest echelons. Years later, she even accused Haley of inventing the "I'm not at all sure it's the Muslims" quote:

> Malcolm said from the beginning that it would be the Black Muslims in coordination with the government. He never changed. Now, he was a thinker. Why would he at the last minute say he wasn't sure that the Black Muslims were the only ones involved? He knew from the very beginning who it was. He had been told who it was.

The widow's insistence that Black Islam had been the chief conspirator in her husband's murder would frustrate Malcolmites and other nationalists, many of whom believe that the white establishment used the Nation's naked hostilities toward the minister as a smokescreen. It was Betty's testimony in the 1966 murder trial that first piqued the disciples. Many of them falsely assumed that she had fingered the trio of defendants as Malcolm's killers, and thus, according to the conspiratorial assassination theory, perjured herself. "Betty Shabazz knows that neither Norman [3X Butler] nor Thomas [15X Johnson] was involved in shooting her husband because she was sitting right at the stage," Razzaq later said. "And [the assassins] didn't wear no masks."

Much of Malcolm's cadre believed that avowed Black Muslims Butler and Johnson had wrongfully gone to prison, and that the widow, who never questioned the verdict, had helped put them there. "To her, all of them [Black Muslims] was guilty," OAAU veteran Sara Mitchell later said. After the trial, some of the minister's apostles guessed that Betty was lost to them forever. There was no love lost between them and the Nation, but they feared that the widow's overt hatred for the sect would work in the white establishment's favor, deflecting attention from the government's complicity in the death of their hero.

———

To black nationalists, the trial was the masterstroke of a shrewd coverup. To Betty, it was the last great hardship of her first mourning year. Intestinally, she knew that justice had not fully been served. However convinced she might have been of Hayer's, Butler's, and Johnson's guilt, the theocrats she believed had issued the command reigned on in the Nation. But she was the single mother of six children, and she knew her life must begin anew.

In the past twelve months, she had received thousands of telegrams, cards, and letters of sympathy and goodwill, even as Malcolm's enemies had danced on his grave. She would sift through many of the missives in the months ahead. She loved the minister as a husband and father. As she pored over the expressions of devotion, her understanding of his true meaning for the masses would deepen.

Among the early epistles was a February 25, 1965 telegram from Harlem human-rights activist Yuri Kochiyama. "No words can express the profound grief that we share with you," Kochiyama wrote. Malcolm was more than one great man, she declared. He was "an epic." She closed with a wish for endurance: "May his great love for you and your children and your infinite love for him keep his spirit alive forever." It was not until the summer of 1967 that the widow replied. "Just a short note as I dash…" she said. "It has been my honest intention to get in touch with you, but the responsibility of being one parent to six has somewhat hampered me. My very best to your family and of course your kind self. Always Strength, B. Shabazz."

Chapter Twelve

RECONSTRUCTION

"Nothing is insurmountable."
—Betty Shabazz

A year after the bullets rained on Malcolm, a train of mourners trudged through Harlem in his name. The temperature had dipped into the teens, and the streets were bare. Thousands had once queued up to file past Malcolm's bier. But the fear was still fresh, and only seventy-five now ventured into the bone-chill to pay their respects. A mixed bag of uptown nationalists, secular and sectarian, were nonetheless determined to mark the anniversary of what some Harlemites now called "Sacrifice Day." Under the eye of the television networks and the police, the bundled-up lot set off from Lenox and 110th, parading for their fallen champion.

They marched three abreast past Fritz's Bar and Grill and Dunbar Pawnbrokers, winding solemnly along 145th to St. Nicholas to 161st to Broadway. Some men wore black leather caps and high boots. Several of the women were clad in white. Among them were practitioners of Orisha Vudu (Voodoo), the West African faith. A ceremonial drum pounded out the cadence. "Slower, slower," one man cautioned. "If we walk any slower," somebody muttered, "we'll freeze to death."

Finally the devotees huddled before the Audubon in Washington Heights. A man read a resolution calling for the race to cast off "the white man's yoke." Queen Mother Moore stepped forward. "Arise you mighty, captive, non-self-governing nation," she bellowed. "You can move mountains if you dare." The ample woman spiked the air with a fist and cried, "Uhuru!" The onlookers answered heartily, stomping against the chill.

The parade organizers had hoped to culminate the affair in the Audubon, but the ballroom had rejected their application. The marchers insisted that the hall was boycotting black nationalists. The Audubon management said the place was simply overbooked. Betty, in any case, had not turned up. Only four days earlier, she had testified in the trial of her husband's accused killers. The march's leaders explained to the press that it had been "a trying week" for the widow. Still, their cavalcade could have used another body. As the rally ended, cries of "Freedom!" echoed down Broadway, drifting back into Harlem. The marchers soon did the same.

Mount Vernon did not want her—not black bourgeois Mount Vernon, anyway. "When Betty moved there, the community was very, very upset," her cousin Ruth Summerford later said. The city was of mixed caste and color. Most whites lived on the north side; the working-class south side was largely black. But college-bred blacks were displacing whites in the Heights. A few years after the widow led her daughters into a corner house in the posh neighborhood, the local kids, without a hint of irony, took to calling the remaining white families "pilgrims."

Mrs. Malcolm X's new neighbors were dentists, lawyers, clergymen, and celebrities (jazz diva Nina Simone lived two blocks away). Many of them cringed at the prospect of a notorious militant's survivors in their midst. Would the newcomers sully the enclave and its middle-class, integrationist sensibilities? Would Malcolm's daughters radicalize the children? Some of the brown Brahmins did not intend to wait and see. As the word spread in the fall of 1965 that Betty and family were coming to town, there was talk of a petition to stop the sale of Bella Abzug's old place, and one or more gadflies began collecting signatures.

Mount Vernon was no racial haven. As the Shabazzes were settling in, local NAACP pickets marched on city hall, demanding integrated schools and decent housing on the south side. Two weeks later, the rights group again raised the desegregation question. "The Mount Vernon NAACP asks the Board of Education to tell the community in the clearest possible terms where it stands on the issue of racial imbalance in our schools," a black minister proclaimed.

Yet while white resistance to integration was lan irritation for Mount Vernon's African-American middle class, a threat to respectability was a full-blown crisis. Most of the black professionals wanted nothing to do with Malcolm's legacy, Lawrence Otis Graham, a grade-school classmate of Attallah and Qubilah, later remembered. Some of the elites spurned Betty. Others ignored her. "The first people who reached out to me in Mount Vernon were white," the widow later told a mentor.

Black hostility and ignorance simmered throughout that first year. "Qubilah?" said a society wife one afternoon outside the local private school the elder Shabazz daughters attended. "What kind of a name is *that?*" Another mother waiting for her child chimed in. "I think it's Islam or Muslim—something like that," she said. Betty managed a frail smile and steered her girls into their designated seats in the back of the blue Oldsmobile she had inherited from her husband.

There was white animosity, but it was the spite within her race that embittered the widow. Were *these* the Negroes for whom Malcolm had died? Nor was Malcolm's mystique less burdensome than his stigma. Some of the privileged blacks delighted in stunning black cronies with the news that Mrs. Malcolm X and company lived around the way. "But they didn't share this *frisson* with white friends and acquaintances," Graham later said.

Few of the locals were openly malicious; most whispered out of curiosity or anxiety, and the widow maintained a web of black support. (The Malcolmites with whom she was speaking were among the "movers" who had helped lug her possessions up two flights of steps to her front door.) Besides, chattering neighbors could not spoil the neighborhood's charm. Stately colonials squatted on hills and light traffic buzzed on shaded streets. Lawns were lush and rimmed with clouds of shrubbery, and staircases unfurled from porches. Even the garages were airy. The black residents were lettered, and their kids were college bound.

Nestled in foliage and drenched in ivy, the Shabazz house anchored East Fifth and Cedar, which ended in a sprawling, wooded area. Behind the home's foyer were eight tastefully appointed rooms. Here was the upper-middle-classdom that Betty had longed for throughout her marriage, the kind of comfort Malcolm himself had known only during his wandering teen years with Ella Collins, a self-made member of Boston's landed black aristocracy. The widow later recalled that the assassination left her life in "bits and pieces." Mount Vernon seemed an ideal place to mend.

—◆—

The grief did not dissolve so much as slacken, only to constrict every night after the children fell asleep. They drove it away each morning with their clamoring for cereal, but the respites were brief and often joyless. That Malcolm was gone still seemed absurd. It was two years before Betty could bring herself to hang his portraits about the house. "When we did put the pictures up, I thought that we had finally reached the point where we could talk about him without tears," she said in 1969. "But now I doubt this will ever happen."

The children were scarred, too. They knew only that "something terrible had happened," Betty later said. Attallah, Qubilah, and Ilyasah had seen at least two attempts on their father's life—the firebombing and the assassination. The peril had seeped too deep into their consciousness for Betty to absorb. In the early years, the girls cried not just for their father, but out of a shattered sense of security.

During trances that spooked her playmates, Attallah relived the flaming house and the tumult of gunfire. For years she wondered if the army that had executed her father would return for the rest of her family. As a second-grader, she sometimes walked into the classroom and plunked down in her seat with her coat on, staring ahead blankly.

"After a while," she later said, "you get to thinking, 'How dare they? How *dare* they take my father from me?'"

Qubilah would not confront that rage for years. On the fourth anniversary of her father's death, the precocious child, then seven, scrawled an essay titled "Malcolm X. A Black Leader" on a four-by-six card and handed it to her mother. The details and grammar were off, but the sentiment was crushing:

> Malcolm X was a brave leader, he fought for rights for all
> black people. His black preachings were in everybody's
> heart. In 1964 he was at the autobaum preaching. And
> everyone was listening instead of falling asleep. Listening
> to his black word. Then for not long he was shot. He dyed,
> but his black beautiful soul is in every black person's heart.

The twins shared the burden of their father's absence, though they had never felt his caress. Until she was sixteen, Malikah regularly slept in Betty's bed. "I always knew that, OK, they killed my father, they could also kill my mother," she later said. For years she and her sisters saw fatherhood as a mystical institution. They would make a friend and run home to announce, "She has a daddy, Mommy!" One afternoon, a playmate of Malaak's happened to mention her own father. In response, the twin led her into the living room and pointed at a large painting of Malcolm above the sofa. "I felt kind of misty behind that," Betty later said.

Soothing the children became a quiet war that the widow waged as she struggled to heal. For a time she acted like Malcolm was still around. She hid her copy of his autobiography in the linen closet, fearing that the girls might see the ghastly death photo. She set homemade oatmeal cookies out for Ilyasah, breaking off a piece like he had stolen a bite. The smoke and mirrors worked for a while. Each of the girls came to realize that Malcolm was dead, but as Gamilah later remembered, they felt his comfort long thereafter:

> He was there. I guess a person who isn't spiritual might
> not get it. Society, especially this culture, has given you

this impression that you're supposed to see a ghost. But you can feel something guiding you. And if you ask any of my sisters they'll tell you. It wasn't just that [Mom] talked about him. His *presence* was there.

Betty did not formally discuss Malcolm with her children in those years. "They had their private sessions," Ruth Summerford later said. "They had their time to sit and talk." The daughters would recall no lectures; the funny stories and yellowing photos were far more memorable. Betty would reminisce about his favorite meals, or the older girls would talk about the times he romped with them or bought them trinkets. The remembrances were more than consolation; they were life support. At East Fifth and Cedar, Malcolm never truly died. "There is an African proverb that says if someone is no longer living—if they are dead and gone—they live if one person calls their name once every day," the widow later explained.

Because children's memories are ephemeral, even the silly tales were sacred. Attallah as an adult would recall her father's subtleties. "When he was hurting, he showed it," she once said. "If he was in pain, his eyes watered. When it was time to be giddy, he was giddy." But Betty suggested that Attallah's godfather, Alex Haley, was the only father that the eldest daughter knew in any sophisticated sense. "Regardless to what she says," the widow told an interviewer, "she was six years old, you know [when Malcolm died]."

The children were well acquainted with Malcolm's spirit. "Do you think your father would like that?" Betty would scold her little ones. The thought of disappointing Daddy could dampen the twins' eyes even before they were old enough to form complete sentences. But the widow chastised far less than she shielded. She learned never to grieve before her daughters. She tried to avoid exposing them to her depression and occasional hysteria. She knew she could not ward off all the demons. "But I can stress the happy times and put their minds at ease," she said.

Doing so required will, stamina, and discipline. "I had to believe my condition was not cast in stone, that it was fluid, and I would retain

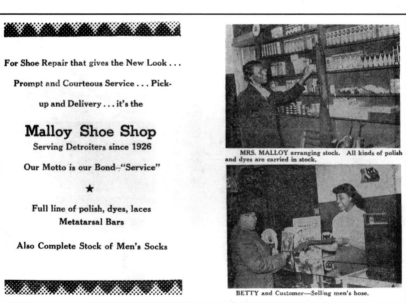
This advertisement shows Lorenzo Malloy (upper left) and Helen Malloy (lower right) at the Malloy Shoe Shop, where Betty (lower right) met and worked for her foster parents.

Betty's *photograph in the 1952 edition of* The
Viking, *the Northern High School yearbook.*

Helen Malloy, Betty's foster mother,
was an activist for black economic
independence and a leader of the
Housewives League of Detroit.

A flyer for the 1951 Fannie B. Peck Day
Business Queen Contest, in which Betty
was a contestant. Her photo appears in
the upper right corner of the flyer.

Malcolm X at the trial of fourteen Black Muslims facing charges from an April 1962 fight with police. The outfits of the women next to Malcolm represent the typical covering required of women in the Nation of Islam.

Charred furniture rests outside the Shabazz home after it was firebombed on February 14, 1965.

Malcolm X's body is carried away from the Audubon Ballroom after
a bloody assassination claimed the life of the controversial leader.

Betty Shabazz is questioned by the press outside Bellevue Hospital
after identifying the body of Malcolm X.

Temple Number Seven burns two days after the assassination of Malcolm X in what many suspected was a retaliatory attack by Malcolm's followers.

The funeral of Malcolm X took place on February 27, 1965, overcast by controversy about the location of the funeral and the preparation of Malcolm's body. Betty Shabazz can be seen to the left of the police officer's shoulder.

Betty Shabazz speaks to Spike Lee at a tribute to Malcolm X in 1992. Although Shabazz and Lee had differences during the making of the film Malcolm X, she was happy with the finished work.

Betty Shabazz poses with Coretta Scott King and two other women at a 1995 event. Betty and Coretta overcame an early rivalry to form a triumvirate of leadership and friendship with Myrlie Evers-Williams.

*Qubilah Shabazz enters a car after leaving
a court appearance for her 1995 trial.*

*Betty Shabazz speaks to reporters outside the trial of her
daughter Qubilah. Betty defended Qubilah's innocence
throughout the trial, and the charges were eventually dropped.*

*Betty Shabazz speaks at an Apollo Theatre fundraiser
for Qubilah's trial costs. The event was touted as a
reconciliation between Betty and Louis Farrakhan.*

Daughters of Malcolm X and Betty Shabazz speak to the press at the Jacobi Medical Center, where Betty Shabazz passed away after sustaining severe burns in a fire set by her grandson.

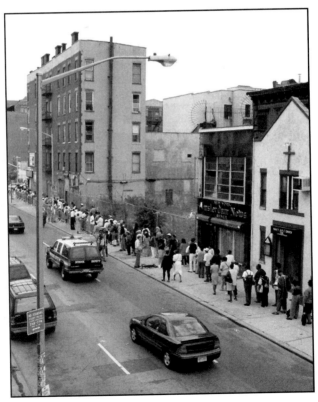

Mourners line the streets of Harlem waiting to view the body of Betty Shabazz.

my sanity," Betty later remembered. She sought to ascribe meaning to her and her children's lives, creating daily schedules to draw the girls out of their gloomy silences. Making short and long-range plans helped everybody cope. "If we had a victory—a whole day—we celebrated," she said. "If we had a day not as fruitful, I would analyze it and see how it could have been amended."

Gradually the girls began to respond. "I would say 'It's time for this' or 'It's time for that' and one of them might say, 'I don't want to do this,'" she recalled. "I would ask, 'What do you want to do?' and we began to talk. I knew I was getting through."

———

Single parenthood exhausted Betty. The girls were vivacious and strong willed. "I often have to wrack my brains to convince my daughters that they have done wrong," the widow said. At times their stubbornness made her lonesome for Malcolm—he had always admired youngsters with pluck. There were joys in single-handedly rearing half a dozen gangly, curious, clever girls. And there were days when she would have traded all the joy under the sun for a few hours of sleep.

Of course, she never truly was alone. In the early days, her stepmother, Madeline Sandlin, came up from Philadelphia to help watch the children. Summerford, who was working nights at the time, would take the train from Brooklyn and baby-sit during the day while Betty ventured out in search of piecemeal nursing work.

Then there were the housekeepers. For years, a good share of the widow's income from Malcolm's autobiography and other sources went toward a succession of maids. Most of them were older black women who lived in and around Mt. Vernon. Some were Caribbean. (Betty wanted her daughters to know their paternal grandmother's culture.) Few stayed more than a couple of years. The girls had a way of tormenting their charges, as children will. And though the widow hired character over competence—"I would often have to come home from a trip and pick up the mop and bucket," she later remembered—she was not an easy boss.

There were other surrogate parents. When the kids jangled Betty's nerves, she sometimes called Haley. "You've got to talk to them," she would complain. "I can't take this." After they returned from school, Uncle Alex would drop by to offer gentle, masculine guidance. But Betty did not hesitate to handle the discipline herself. "It was nothing for her to pick up something and knock Attallah or 'Yasah or whoever needed to be knocked," Jean Owensby, the girls' neighboring playmate, later said. "She had that slow, steady kind of walk. But she was real quick." The household laws were strict. No outside time until you had read a book. No sweets. And years later, no boys. "She kept her hand on them children," Summerford said. "You have to be strict on girls."

It was not until much later that the children discovered the peril behind many of the rules. How long the menacing phone calls continued is unclear, but they certainly did not stop when Malcolm hit the ballroom stage. Gamilah learned as an adult that her mom got several ominous calls in the early Mount Vernon years. The widow would answer the phone while the girls were at a nearby Montessori school and hear a chilling whisper: "Your daughter has a pretty plaid dress on today." Years later, the children remembered their mother occasionally popping up at school to check on them. "We thought she was talking to the principal," Gamilah said.

They never suspected in those days that Betty lived in fear. "She didn't know whether or not she was gonna be next," said Rev. Richard Dixon, a neighbor and one of the black clergymen with whom Malcolm had been friendly. "She didn't know who was out there. But she was a Trojan." The widow did not explicitly warn her daughters about the dangers. "Growing up with our phones tapped, with strangers asking neighbors questions about us, my mother would gradually feed us information to cope in that environment," Malaak later said. The girls had their safety drills, like other children, but never thought much of them. There was a routine in case a stranger was lurking around the house or trying to break in. They were to run inside if they spotted someone snapping photos as they caroused in the backyard.

The scenarios became games. Attallah, of course, played the lookout. One day, five or six years after the assassination, Betty drove into

Harlem to pay the bill for ballet lessons and left the girls in the Oldsmobile. Gamilah recalled that four men, two on each side, approached the car and jiggled the door handles. The children slumped down in their seats. Within seconds, the strangers hustled off and Betty returned. Whoever the men were and whatever their intentions, Attallah had given the signal and her sisters had responded. The game could be great fun. "The CIA is coming!" the eldest child sometimes hissed. "We'd all laugh, you know," Gamilah later said. "But we'd duck."

One wonders how much of a threat Betty's purely symbolic power posed for Black Muslims, the intelligence community, or any of her husband's enemies. There is no question that the FBI kept a keen eye on her as well as Malcolm's disciples and ideological heirs well into the late 1960s and 1970s, launching a campaign, for instance, to keep the minister's fragmented cadre from allying with New York socialists. For its part, the Nation continued to demonize Malcolm throughout his daughters' early childhood. In a 1971 *Muhammad Speaks*, Raymond Sharrieff, Malcolm's old foe, scolded the minister's glorifiers. "You must remember that Malcolm's greatest desire was to get people to think about fighting," Sharrieff said. "We never have learned how much fight Malcolm had in *himself*." [Original emphasis.]

There is no evidence that the Nation ever directly threatened Betty and the girls in the years after Malcolm's death. (Though, the widow later told a close friend that a car full of Black Muslims had tried to "run us off the road" as she was traveling in a car with her daughters shortly after the assassination.) And though the FBI routinely monitored Mrs. Malcolm X as the wife of a dissident in her husband's last year and for a dozen years thereafter (in one missive to his superiors, an agent noted Betty's fading limp and reported that her broken ankle seemed to be healing), there is little evidence that the agency worried seriously about the activities of her widowhood. It may, however, have wondered about her ideology. Betty later told a friend that a woman approached her on an airplane during this era and announced that the FBI had asked her to wear a wire and strike up a conversation with Mrs. Malcolm X.

The widow took no chances in those years. She trusted only close comrades with her telephone number and address. She collected her mail from a post-office box miles from home. For a time, she even kept to herself at the grocery store. Her allies shared her vigilance. During the mid-to-late sixties, male friends "in the movement" served as her security detail during occasional public appearances. The protection was mostly symbolic. "You could have took a paper sword and beat the hell out of them," Ella Collins's one-time bodyguard James Smalls later said.

Whether out of simple loyalty to Malcolm or concern for her sister-in-law and nieces, Collins secretly beefed up Betty's security forces with her own sentries. As early as 1967, her men would show up wherever Mrs. Malcolm X was and melt into the crowd, keeping a sharp eye on her. It was while on assignment at one of Congressman Adam Clayton Powell's rallies on 125th Street that Smalls met her. He approached the widow and introduced himself. "Get away from me!" she exploded. "You with that old Ella Collins!" When Smalls later reported the outburst to Collins, she told him, "That's what you get. You should have asked me before you spoke with her." But ten minutes after cussing the bodyguard out, Betty returned and seized his arm. "You!" she barked. "Take me to Reverend Powell." Smalls could only obey. He plunged through the crowd, the martyr's wife in tow. "I'm proud now, Jack," he later recalled. "I'm knockin' Negroes out of the way." He reached Powell and planted Betty's hand in his.

Aside from her encounter with Smalls, Betty never acknowledged the guards Collins detached. For a while, their work was light. The widow seldom ventured into the public sphere during her first years in Mount Vernon. "I made an unrealistic decision after Malcolm was assassinated," she later confessed. "I said I would never mingle again with society, because I thought there was so much injustice in the world."

Malcolm X Day in 1966 marked one of her early absences. The Organization of Afro American Unity (now a small troupe of men under Collins's command) sponsored the occasion, a pilgrimage to the minister's grave on what would have been his forty-first birthday. About fifty loyalists congregated in Hartsdale to pay tribute to the martyr that May 19. It was an ecumenical affair. Priests intoned in English, Arabic, and Yoruba, asking Malcolm to defend Harlem through eternity.

A six-man chorale sang a dirge to the tune of "Let My People Go." Collins proclaimed in a graveside talk that the slain prophet's birthday should become a national holiday. The commemoration ended at the Hotel Theresa with dinner, speeches, and African dancers. Though Ferncliff Cemetery is near Mount Vernon, the mourners had not expected Betty to show. Harlem activists knew by then that Collins and the widow were at war. What they may not have known is that Betty could not bear to visit her husband's grave.

She never attended the annual Ferncliff pilgrimages, even in the late 1960s, as they grew larger and more elaborate in rough proportion to Malcolm's legend. Yet she grappled with the challenge of honoring and sustaining his political legacy. For a time she thought the Black Brotherhood Improvement Association held the answer. Named after Garvey's Universal Negro Improvement Association, the upstart Brotherhood was a ministry of street-corner nationalism in Queens. In the spring of 1965, it formed a gun club.

Since "Take up arms to defend thyself" had been one of Malcolm's last commandments to the black man, Betty accepted an honorary membership to the organization the following year. She was an active member in the sense that she sometimes went shooting with the troupe. Malcolm had taught her to handle a rifle in his final, harrowing months. Now she routinely met one of the gun club's organizers at a secret spot and caught a ride with him to a firing range near Suffolk County.

The widow's affiliation with the Brotherhood was short lived. She was more concerned with caring for her daughters than with rehearsing for the militant self-defense her late husband had preached. But she

304 — BETTY SHABAZZ

clearly felt a deep loyalty to black nationalism and brimmed with questions about radical struggle. OAAU veteran Herman Ferguson, who helped recruit her to the Brotherhood, sensed that she was groping for an ideological link to Malcolm. "There was at that time no indication that she was interested in getting involved with the integrationists," he later said.

Though black militancy fascinated Betty, it was still a distant and menacing affair. Children and motherhood, on the other hand, were real and immediate. The widow continued to draw inward in 1966 and much of 1967, sheltering herself and her daughters from the outside world. Yet her youngest girls were now toddlers. She sensed that she was smothering them, and she needed relief from the stress of simultaneously raising grade-schoolers and tots. So shortly before Gamilah's third birthday, she drove the fourth child across town to the Mount Vernon Day Care Center.

The school board had launched the experimental center, which emphasized parent involvement, in the city's southeast quarter. The fifty children it cared for were largely black and needy. Betty began taking Gamilah to the center for an hour every day. "She needed to get away from me at the time," the widow later recalled. Eventually she started bringing the twins and mingling with other parents. She did not warm up to the adults right away. She knew that they knew she was Mrs. Malcolm X, and she still mistrusted new faces, regardless of their pigment.

Slowly the social creature within her resurfaced. Though many of the parents at the center were among the working poor, they were not as worshipful of the widow as many Harlemites were. These were humble people struggling to make ends meet and infuse their children with dignity and self-respect. It was a battle Betty knew well. School officials recognized her expertise with early-childhood education, and she accepted their invitation to join the center as a regular administrative volunteer.

The children adored her. She would sashay into the place and they would scrum at her shins. She transfixed them when she read aloud at storytime. No three- or four-year-old could know her as the lady of black nationalism's warrior-king. Still, her aura enchanted them. "She had an easy way of starting a conversation with practically everybody," Dorothy Pleas, then the center's director, later said. Equally striking was the widow's habit of snubbing parents who disapproved of Malcolm or who failed to show proper deference. "She could be so aloof it was like an iceberg," Pleas remembered.

Betty devoted herself to the center. She rewrote its early health-care literature and urged the parents to screen their children for sickle cell anemia, a chronic disease that strikes blacks almost exclusively. She saw that the children got the proper immunization shots. She revamped the breakfast program, boosting its nutritional content. She devised strategies for clothing the neediest children without offending their parents. When she noticed several of the kids behaving errati-cally, she raised the possibility of lead poisoning, an environmental hazard in many old tenements. She later prevailed upon jazz songstress Nancy Wilson to perform a benefit concert on the center's behalf. In time, Betty joined the day care's parent group, then accepted a volun-tary position as its school-board representative.

She remained guarded. "She never would give too much of herself away," Pleas said. But she found the work at the center therapeutic. The experience gradually "built up a trust, a respect, a cooperation, and a willingness to work with adults," the widow later recalled. The vol-unteer position was the closest she had come to an actual job, and the rhythm of getting up and going to work energized her and distracted her from grief. Slowly she was developing the courage to make deci-sions without Malcolm. "I grew and recognized, 'Hey, I can handle this experience,'" she later said. "'I can handle being an adult. I can handle being with other adults.'"

Betty empathized with the housewives at the center. She liked the idea that the day care was helping to draw them out of the home while also supporting working women, some of whom were single moms themselves. She later credited volunteerism with inspiring her first tottery steps back into the world after the assassination. It was the center itself that provided the nudge.

———

The widow was emerging in Mount Vernon, but she was light years away from the new black revolution. She had been settling into suburbia as street uprisings ravaged Watts, the Los Angeles ghetto, in August 1965. She had been grappling with single parenthood in 1966 as the Student Nonviolent Coordinating Committee's Stokely Carmichael (Kwame Ture) called for Black Power during a Mississippi march, blazing the slogan on a rebellious generation.

She was barely older than most of the new radicals, but she had not tasted their scene. Her husband, however, was their patron saint. The day he died, Bobby Seale, future Black Panther Party chairman, dashed into the street to fling half a dozen bricks at white motorists. "I was ready to die that day," he later remembered. Eldridge Cleaver, the Party's someday minister of information, reeled in his California jail cell. "I have, so to speak, washed my hands in the blood of the martyr, Malcolm X," he would declare. Carmichael was a Malcolm scion. So were Amiri Baraka and H. Rap Brown.

Detached though she was from her man's idolaters, Betty relished the idolatry, doubly so because it was hardly universal. In 1967, an activist in black Washington, D.C., distributed three thousand invitations to an affair featuring recordings of the minister's greatest oratories—"Message to the Grassroots" and "Ballot or the Bullet." Only twenty people came. So when a loose coalition of Bay Area nationalists (including members of the Revolutionary Action Movement) invited Betty to be their honored guest at the kick-off of a three-day Malcolm memorial that year, she quickly accepted. Her talk was to culminate a mass meeting in Hunter's Point, San Francisco's black enclave. Organizers had hoped her presence would help galvanize the community.

The widow gleamed with anticipation as she boarded an American Airlines jet on the second anniversary of the assassination and took off for Northern California. This was to be her first major public address. Yet minutes after she landed the misgivings began. As she and Malcolm cousin and devotee Hakim Jamal stepped into San Francisco Airport, twenty bereted, heavily armed black men encircled them and announced that they would be escorting them to the memorial. "Who are these fellows here?" Betty asked. They were Black Panthers. Twenty-five-year-old Huey P. Newton and thirty-year-old Seale had formed the party months earlier in nearby Oakland. They had embraced Malcolm's call for self-defense by taking up weapons in an open challenge to police, who they considered an occupying army in the black city.

The Panthers had rounded up a posse to guard "Sister Betty" amid swirling paranoia that dozens of assassins were lurking to mow her down. "She was the widow of Brother Malcolm, our greatest leader and martyr, and the mother of his beautiful children," Newton later wrote. "We would not allow anything to happen to her after the way the establishment had so treacherously assassinated her husband." Newton and his brethren were especially resolute after hearing that a security detail from the "US" group under cultural nationalist Ron Karenga (later Maulana Karenga) had fled from police, abandoning Betty "in the middle of the street" during an earlier visit to Los Angeles.

At three o'clock, the Panthers had marched into San Francisco Airport bristling with shotguns and pistols, their black boots rapping and waist-length leather jackets swishing. The widow had fallen asleep on the plane. When she entered the terminal and spotted the security detail, she kicked herself for having missed whatever celebrity the granite-faced men had come to protect. Then she realized the detachment was for her. Years later she remembered the scene warmly. "And there was a young man reciting part of the Constitution about carrying firearms," she said. "And it really did something to me. I just said, 'Oh wow. That's just really fantastic.'"

She was less sublime that afternoon. Jumpy airport deputies had asked the battalion to wait out front, promising to usher Mrs. Malcolm X from her gate themselves. The men had simply brushed past them, scattering alarmed passengers from the unloading zone. They led Betty and Jamal to a six-car convoy waiting on the street, and ferried them to the *Ramparts* magazine office in San Francisco's North Beach section. By the time the cortege had arrived, the bodyguard had dwindled to five and the men had relaxed. Their ward had not. Betty liked an article about Malcolm that recent parolee Cleaver had written for the radical monthly. She agreed to sit for an interview with him. But behind dark sunglasses, her face was taut. She said nothing when the men introduced her to Cleaver, who had just met the Panthers himself. "She looked cool enough on the surface," he later recalled, "but it was clear that she felt hard-pressed."

The widow granted a fifteen-minute interview about her husband. Newton, the Panther's minister of defense, stood at a window nearby. In his hands, at port arms, was a shotgun. Sirens whined faintly in the distance as police sped toward the *Ramparts* headquarters. Cleaver left the back room to fetch the widow a glass of water. Panthers, police, and journalists clotted the hallway. Minutes later, Newton arrayed ten of the men around Betty and Jamal and sent an advance guard to clear a path through the throng of spectators and police. "No cameras," the widow said. The men formed a screen, holding magazines aloft as they whisked their charges out the door, past the police, and into a car. Within seconds, they had melted into traffic.

Then Newton and the cops faced off. The police stood poised to shoot as he and Seale started up the sidewalk toward their car. "Don't turn your backs on these back-shooting dogs!" Newton growled to his comrades. "Let's split, Huey!" Seale pleaded. A burly patrolman got in Newton's face, ordering him to lower his weapon. The other officers were urging the patrolman to cool down, but the Panther commander kept needling him. "What's the matter," Newton said, "you got an itchy finger?" The reddening cop made no move. Newton dared him to draw, calling him a "cowardly dog," and jacking a round into the chamber of his own shotgun. Finally the officer backed down. Newton floated past him, laughing triumphantly. "Work out, soul brother!" thought Cleaver, who joined the Panthers shortly thereafter. "You're the baddest motherfucker I've ever seen!"

Betty was less impressed. In her last year with Malcolm, she had experienced enough guns and tense showdowns for several lifetimes.

She tolerated the Panther guard with cool restraint during her visit to Black House, the local den of militancy, but inwardly she seethed. The police encounter had been a coup for the Panthers; for her it had been an all-too-familiar nightmare. The militants had proven that they meant business, that they were serious about armed resistance to white oppression in the spirit of Malcolm. Through Betty, they had won the martyr's blessing by proxy.

That evening the widow addressed a crowd of three hundred at Bayview Community Center. Security guards meticulously searched each spectator. Earlier, the memorial organizers had exalted Malcolm before the press. "He was a man who represented the future, a common Joe Blow from nowhere," Roy Ballard declared. "He was a king. And we have his queen with us." Ballard stressed that the sponsors wanted freedom from repression and second-class citizenship, not trouble with Black Muslims or any other faction. He then kicked the journalists out, citing security concerns. Mrs. Malcolm X, he explained, was in much danger.

It is hard to say which unsettled Betty more, the possibility of ambush by her husband's foes or the grim Panthers and their arsenal. In either case, the San Francisco visit taught her that Black Power's interpretation of Malcolm could be problematic for her. The adulation of the minister pleased her, nonetheless, though it was still coming from the fringe. A day after the Bay Area memorial, Carmichael, Collins, and two hundred other staunch souls commemorated Malcolm, parading from the Audubon to 125th and Seventh Avenue in Harlem. At the corner, once Malcolm's prime "fishing" hole, the marchers displayed a sculpted bust of the minister. Carmichael wore a Malcolm T-shirt as he kindled the crowd, calling on Black America to anoint its own heroes. "No one else will tell us whom to honor," he proclaimed.

Betty now realized that *how* the New Left honored her mister was no less important. That May, on Malcolm's birthday, five hundred people gathered for a memorial service and Black Power rally on Chicago's south side. The occasion turned ugly when two white girls in their early twenties showed up. Someone yelled that the oppressor had arrived, and the pair fell in a tangle of fists and hair-pulling. The girls fled with minor injuries after black undercover police officers drew their weapons. The mob then surged to nearby Washington Park, rechristening it "Malcolm Shabazz Park" and trying to uproot its sign. The melee ended in thirty arrests.

Malcolm had forecasted the generation's unrest. In much of the urban North, black unemployment was twice that of white unemployment. Nationally, 75 percent of working blacks held menial jobs. In New York, the rate of infant mortality among blacks was double that of whites. The inequity glared in Vietnam, too. In early 1967, there were twice as many blacks as whites in combat, and twice as many died in action in proportion to their numbers back home. The outlook was no brighter in the classroom. Black gradeschoolers lagged one to three years behind their white peers, and one-twentieth as many blacks as whites made it to college.

No matter how righteous the rage, however, when it boiled over violently in Malcolm's name, it jeopardized what Betty wished for herself as much as for the minister—respectability. As his icon grew, so did the dilemma. In 1968, a "get guns" chant rattled a Malcolm memorial at Harlem's Intermediate School 201, incensing officials who had bowed to student and community pressure to host the event. During the program, James Baldwin called America "the Fourth Reich," and Herman Ferguson, who was then facing conspiracy charges in an alleged plot to assassinate prominent black moderates, urged the audience to arm themselves for self-defense during that summer's "hunting season" (a reference to street rebellions).

A year later, the widow was on hand for an even rowdier affair. She brought her daughters, then ages three to ten, to Harlem's Cooper Junior High to observe the fourth anniversary of their father's death. Her eyes welled during the ceremony, which included African dancers, a skit dramatizing the power structure's divide-and-conquer schemes, and, to Betty's astonishment, spurts of profanity. Ossie Davis, whom the Shabazz girls knew as "Uncle," also appeared. Earlier he had recited his "Black Shining Prince" eulogy at the legendary Apollo Theatre, where 1,600 schoolchildren had fidgeted through two hours of Bach during a memorial concert by the New York Symphony. It was a glorious day for Betty. Harlem had honored Malcolm in a dozen or more events. His legend and spirit were capturing the hearts of thousands of uptown students, many of whom were too young to remember him.

But the Cooper crowd got carried away. Some of the six hundred students who had gathered for the program marched to 125th and 7th, where the city had cleared ground for a gargantuan new state office building. Grassroots Harlem had fought the edifice as a big-brotherly intrusion. Several of the youngsters converged on a state urban affairs office nearby, smashing a door, shredding drapes, scattering desk drawers, and upending a photocopier. The widow was not amused. "Some people invoke Malcolm's name to justify some highly unorganized, anarchistic ventures that he would never have dreamed of becoming involved in," she later said.

Betty's own involvement in the zeitgeist remained mainly social, and she was cautious even in this domain. She moved among the more established figures in Malcolm's progressive circles, mingling now and then with a crowd of writers, artists, and academics that included Baldwin, Larry and Evelyn Neal, John Henrik Clarke, and John and Grace Killens. She occasionally attended dinner parties and other affairs at the Killens' home, alone or with some of the children. "We enjoyed her company and she enjoyed ours," Grace later said. "She would chat around, but [the betrayals of the past] she would never forget. She sort of withdrew from people. She might have felt, 'Are these people sincere?'"

In time, Betty realized that they were. First, however, the intellectuals had to coax her out of seclusion. They hoped that she would better understand Malcolm's legacy and come to terms with his death as she emerged in the public arena. So when students at historically black

Hampton Institute (now University) in Virginia asked Larry Neal to speak at a February 1968 Malcolm memorial, he immediately thought of Betty. "Glad to see the brothers getting it together at Hampton," he wrote in response to the invitation. "I would like to suggest that you try to have someone like Rap Brown or Stokley. Also try to invite Malik's widow Sister Betty Shabazz."

Betty began to surface. There was the occasional visit to a Harlem boutique to shop for African jewelry with Amina Baraka and Mrs. Neal, or an afternoon tea at the home of the United Nations ambassador from Tanzania. On these occasions, Mrs. Malcolm X was unfailingly chic in contemporary suits. She waved her hair into a soft flip or coiled it inside vibrant scarves, depending on her mood. Some of the Muslims from Malcolm's old retinue were scandalized. For them, the widow's attire and appearances at soirees were the height of immodesty. "I didn't keep up with her movements," Sister Khadiyyah later said. "But I knowed the stories I was getting back. And I shuddered."

One well-known nationalist offered a more brazenly sexist rebuke. After spotting Betty in a skirt, her hair uncovered, he remarked, "That's why the pharaohs took their wives with them to the grave, lest they be left behind to shame them."

The Old Muslims' mutterings fazed Betty not in the least. She relished her new freedoms. (Shortly before the birth of her twin daughters, amid the crises of the time, Betty had puzzled her female Christian friends by marveling at the comfort of wearing a skirt above the shin.) She was grateful whenever baby-sitters granted her a glimpse of the Black-Is-Beautiful scene. It was during one such outing that she finally met Maya Angelou, whom she had spoken to (after the writer had returned to California from Ghana, an apparent candidate for a top OAAU post) but never seen in person. Baldwin had invited the widow to a house party, mentioning that he was going to bring Angelou along. Betty turned up at the affair and perched on a couch, enjoying the artist crowd. "Do you know many people here?" she asked a stylish young woman nearby. "Not really," said the woman, who unbeknownst to Betty was Angelou. The widow said that she was waiting for a friend. Then someone pulled Angelou onto the floor. "You dance so nice," Betty said when Angelou returned. "My friend is a dancer." With a slow grin, Angelou asked her friend's name. "She said, 'Maya Angelou,'" Angelou later remembered. "And I said, '*Girrrrrrl!*'"

Betty also had another clique. This one was younger and saucier. Its members were self-made, well read, and college bred. They were artists, but they were not too artsy. They were heavy, though not as heavy as the old-guard Civil Righters or the New Left. Nor were they as ethereal as the black bourgeoisie. They were, in truth, misfits. Stage and screen actress Novella Nelson was among them, as was poet Nikki Giovanni. At the center of the ring was Ellis Haizlip.

"I think every woman who knew him—straight or gay—loved this man," Nelson later said. Haizlip himself was decidedly in the second category, a flamboyant, free-spirited television producer and host of the variety show "Soul" who seemed wired to practically every young, gifted, and black New Yorker. He had not been a friend of Betty's at the time, and he may not have even formally met her. Yet sometime in the late 1960s, he sent a car around and took her to a show. Afterward he introduced her to the group. Betty was not a trusting soul, so perhaps she sensed that Haizlip was "safe." She enjoyed the company, at any rate. She ran with the artists for a couple years thereafter, surfacing when the children were away at school or camp.

On those evenings, she and her mates ate at elegant nightclubs ("before this Studio 54 silliness") where integration was a reality rather than a polemic. They laughed long and loud as a matter of principle. And they let Betty be Betty. "She didn't have to be the martyr's wife," Nelson later said. "We demanded nothing except for her to find the time to smile and laugh." Betty did lots of both, but little dancing. Though the gang often forgot who she was, she never could. One night everyone spilled into a house party. The sweet stink of marijuana wafted from a back room. "I'm leaving," Betty announced abruptly, and she did. "She could tell a risqué joke," Nelson would recall. "But there was always a weight."

The emergence was not just social. Betty began dealing more forthrightly with her public role and discovering her power to promote Malcolm. One of her earliest efforts involved Hollywood, whose superficiality she had heard her husband deride throughout their marriage. In 1966, she sold the movie rights of his autobiography to Marvin Worth, an independent filmmaker. Worth had begun his career as a jazz promoter. (No doubt he was among the tides of Harlem-hopping white men the minister had flouted in his memoirs.) He remembered Malcolm as a freckly kid in the jazz haunts and had met him again as an evangelist. After the assassination, he had read the minister's story and begun negotiating with Haley and Betty for the screen version.

The widow had backed away from writer and Malcolm friend Louis Lomax's proposed movie less than a year before, saying she was overburdened. She was more self-possessed by the time Worth came along. Plus, the producer had retained James Baldwin to write the script. Malcolm had respected the writer as a bard of the black soul, and his presence greased the negotiations. (When Baldwin later abandoned the project, Worth signed Arnold Perl, author of the musical *Fiddler on the Roof*, to finish the screenplay.) Columbia Pictures agreed to release the picture—conceived as a literal, documentary-style treatment of Malcolm's autobiography—under the auspices of Warner Brothers.

Betty was a consultant for the production and got a presumably generous sum for the rights. She would also receive royalties on the film's net profits to cover her back bills and supplement her daughters' college fund. The bonus was seeing Malcolm on the big screen. She liked the idea that the film would be true to his words. She believed Baldwin's involvement guaranteed integrity, though the scribe himself was jittery about the gig. "This was a difficult assignment," he later said, "since I had known Malcolm, after all, crossed swords with him, worked with him, and held him in that great esteem which is not easily distinguishable, if it is distinguishable at all, from love."

Baldwin was not the only anxious stakeholder. The FBI wondered how Hollywood would portray the Bureau. Collins wondered how it would portray her brother. In the end, the feds were happy and Collins was incensed. *Malcolm X* finally hit cinemas in summer 1972, with Mrs. Malcolm X's participation prominently billed. The FBI may have been relieved that the film did not probe its shady dealings with the minister. Collins, for her part, dismissed the production as a superficial spectacle. An Academy Award committee disagreed—*Malcolm X* received an Oscar nomination—and so did the critics. Malcolm "would have liked the way Hollywood handled his life," one columnist guessed. "He comes through as a hero," sang the *Washington Post*. "For Warner Bros. to make a documentary about Malcolm X seems about as likely as for the D.A.R. to sponsor the Peking Ballet," *Time* said. "That the film should come from such a source is the first surprise. The second is that it is good—a fair forum for Malcolm's fundamental ideas and an exceptional visual chronicle of how those ideas took shape."

With newsreel footage and still photographs (some of which the widow had supplied), the movie traced the minister's evolution from his turbulent boyhood and underworld adventures through his street-corner exhortations for Black Islam. Actor James Earl Jones narrated as the grainy scenes retold Malcolm's quarrel with Muhammad and pilgrimage to Mecca. The documentary suggested that Black Muslims had killed the minister for heresy against the kingdom. But it also showed CORE's James Farmer testifying for the camera that Malcolm had approached the State Department with inside information shortly before his death. Farmer's implication was that the minister had known too much for the federal government's liking.

Hoping to soften some of the suspicion its unlikely midwifery of Malcolm's tale would arouse, Columbia announced that it would distribute the film's opening-night profits among national black organizations. At Betty's behest, the company also funneled a fraction of the proceeds into the health and education program for pregnant Mount Vernon girls that she was then directing. The civic efforts satisfied the widow, and the movie thrilled her. She quibbled at a Detroit screening, insisting that, "his mother didn't look anything like that lady." Yet her mood was light during the luncheon that followed the picture's Washington, D.C., premier. "I think he was a fantastic person," she told the assembled journalists. "Even if I hadn't been his wife, I would think that." Betty paid the film her highest compliment by taking her daughters, then ages six to thirteen, to see it. Afterward, she asked them what they thought. "We felt sorry for you," one of the girls said. "You seemed so helpless. Daddy was everything to you, wasn't he?"

Collins and other students of Malcolm thought the movie short-changed the minister's international impact. Baldwin had quit the project in the late 1960s, declaring that he refused to be a party to "a second assassination." On ghetto streets, where Hollywood was just another arm of the power structure, the critique was no more flattering. Some blacks mistrusted the outside consecration of their martyr. Others grumbled that "whitey" always urged them to venerate their leaders—once they were dead. In Harlem, the sentiment that Uncle Sam had somehow been behind Malcolm's murder had never been stronger.

During the years between her signing of the Warner Brothers contract and the film's premier, Betty began to spend more time memorializing Malcolm. As the Malcolm literary canon evolved, she authorized the publication of various materials in new tomes, including three lectures in the *Speeches of Malcolm X at Harvard* (1968) that were under her legal domain. She also contributed her personal recollections to projects she deemed worthy. Chief among these was John Henrik Clarke's *Malcolm X; the Man and His Times*. The historian in late 1967 had set out with OAAU men Peter Bailey and Earl Grant to collect original articles about the minister for publication by a major house.

Whether or not the widow was speaking to Grant at the time (the bad feelings had lingered between her and many Malcolmites), she had kept up with Bailey, former editor of *Blacklash*, the OAAU organ. Clarke, of course, had been a stalwart comrade to both her and the minister. So in late 1968, she agreed to write an essay for the anthology. By this time, she was growing savvy about copyright matters. Malcolm crony Milton Henry and an associate had released a "Message to the Grassroots" record that became an underground hit in inner cities. They sent Betty a portion of the proceeds—perhaps one hundred dollars a month—before losing control of the production. (The rumor persists that the New York Mafia began distributing the album.) But many of the Malcolm tapes and publications on the market fell under public-domain laws, and thus did not benefit the widow. "Most of the people who have commercialized these speeches have not been considerate enough to give her a portion of the royalties," Percy Sutton told *Jet* magazine. Betty granted Clarke permission to excerpt several of the minister's articles and lectures in *Malcolm X*, so long as the publisher noted her as the proper copyright holder and assured her 25 percent of the royalties.

The book was more than a cash source for the widow. At a time when a menagerie of ideologues were laying claim to Malcolm's legacy, she welcomed the chance to resurrect (if not somewhat revise) the man she loved. Clarke sent her eight seed questions ("How did your children react to the fact that sometimes they saw more of their father on television than at home?"), and she took to her typewriter to tap out "Malcolm X as a Husband and Father."

The anthology appeared in 1969. In Betty's piece, readers glimpsed a romantic who pampered his wife and occasionally taxied his family to the beach. This Malcolm was a strict and tender father, as well as a man utterly devoted to the oppressed. The widow flung a couple of barbs at Elijah Muhammad and kin. She also recounted a marriage that was "short but abundant with experiences more rich than most people enjoy in a lifetime."

She said Malcolm had taught her to shape a better society with her mind and spirit, and to "live and love as a woman, to be true to myself and my responsibilities as a mother." She acknowledged that she still struggled to cope with his absence. She also flared against the system— "any black man today who strives to be a man among men is singled out and accused of everything except what he is trying to do"—and white liberals. "Everyone has used the black problem to get support for their own cause," she proclaimed. "But once they get the support, the black man's freedom has been left at the back door."

Betty was still particular about the Malcolm projects she backed. Peter Goldman, then a senior *Newsweek* staffer, wrote her around 1970 to request an interview for what was to become *The Death and Life of Malcolm X*, one of the most eloquent biographies of the militant. Goldman had covered Malcolm from the early 1960s. He had liked and respected the firebrand and thought the feeling was mutual. He was also a veteran of the "race" beat who had managed to score dozens of interviews with Malcolm lieutenants and confidants. But then he entered the widow's territory.

She never told him no. In fact, she invited him to the house on several occasions. On the first visit, he arrived promptly and found nobody home. He sat on the porch to wait, assuming she was running late. A passing neighbor finally told him that Betty was out of town. He rescheduled. This time he caught the widow hustling out the door. She was heading to a routine doctor's appointment with one of the girls, but she was good enough to offer her caller a lift to the subway. Goldman thought he had cracked her on the third attempt. She appeared in her doorway and whispered for him to meet her out back, explaining that her housekeeper was not keen on white people.

The widow set up two chairs in the backyard. Hers was in the shade; his was in the sun. She listened with half an ear to the pitch, encouraging and aloof in turns. "She could be almost flirty," Goldman would recall, "and in the course of a conversation go stone cold." In one of the frostier moments, she informed the writer that her husband had certainly *not* been a socialist. Goldman had not proposed this, but he sensed that she figured him for a Trotskyite or government informant. "She was essentially gaming me," he later said.

Betty was more forthcoming with a white reporter from *Look* magazine in 1969. This was to be one of her first major interviews. She coordinated the girls' outfits then picked a green knit dress and matching headband for herself. When her visitor arrived, she set a bowl of plums, melons, and grapes before him. "She is the essence of what soul brothers mean when they proclaim, 'Black is beautiful,'" he thought. But he glimpsed a troubled heart beneath the elegance. "There are long, pensive spells, and moods of fleeting sadness, of hurt and yearning, of melancholy," the newsman noted. "Then abruptly comes a sunburst of mirth and a warm shower of smiles."

When the conversation turned to black revolt, however, the widow was resolute. She echoed many of her husband's doctrines. "A lot of political leaders say they won't tolerate violence, but they have tolerated violence to the blacks for more than three centuries," she said. "When white people say they won't tolerate violence, they mean they won't tolerate social change." Black freedom "by whatever means" meant exactly that, she added. Only hypocritical whites would try to criminalize the proclamation. Why, Patrick Henry himself had demanded liberty or death. But *his* liberty was for white, Protestant men. "Every group that has come to these shores has had to fight to be included in the Bill of Rights—even women," Betty said.

Her own interpretations of Malcolmology emerged as she talked. "I tell my friends that we should not let the white man off the hook by calling ourselves 'African,'" she said. American blacks were centuries removed from Africa, she explained. "The white man robbed us of our culture, tore our families apart, and tried to dehumanize us. To that extent we are different, and the term 'Afro-American' stresses both the kinship and the period of enslavement."

Not the Second Amendment hawk her husband had been, the widow acknowledged her support of gun control. She especially favored the control of guns in white hands, and she insisted that it would be insanity for blacks to disarm before their oppressors did. "When the armed white man becomes an enraged beast, he doesn't stop to differentiate between one black man and another," she said. What of the dream of a colorblind society? The reply was classic Malcolm. Integration, she said, had failed. "Now we blacks are going to rule ourselves."

Betty again echoed the minister's logic, if not his searing rhetoric, in an essay for *Ebony* three months later. Peter Bailey, then an editor for the magazine, convinced her to write "The Legacy of My

Husband" and to sit for a photo spread with her daughters as a means of humanizing the icon. The girls bubbled with curiosity as a photo-journalist hauled his equipment up to the house on the day of the shoot. They had never regarded themselves as attractions, and Betty had trained them to shun cameras. Still, the photographer shadowed them all day as they frolicked on the backyard swings and studied their lessons and laughed and raced and warred.

When the article finally appeared, the carefree pictures clashed with some of the prose. The widow's essay contained plenty of Malcolm trivia—his eating habits, approach to fatherhood, and musical tastes. But she interwove the reminiscences with his politics, and some of hers. She began by proclaiming that he had died because powerful interests in this country wished to maintain the status quo. (There was no indictment of Black Islam.) She praised the Black Power generation for embracing his model of self-determination and resistance. "Afro-American youths have totally vindicated Malcolm's faith in them," she said.

Then she flexed her intellect, presenting a cogent argument for black nationalism based on her husband's philosophies. African-America must institutionalize its distinct cultural traditions for the children's sake, she said. Cultural nationalism alone would not guarantee freedom, but political and economic power begins with a love of the land, family, language, and folkways of the African and African-American past. "Call it black awareness, black consciousness, or black pride—it's all nationalism," she said.

The widow answered those who called nationalism a dead end, explaining that the philosophy was necessary to cure "denationalized" blacks who felt more kinship with their oppressor than with their own people. "They will have to be taught what others have taken for granted," she declared. Faithful to her husband's final metamorphoses, she acknowledged that the ultimate phase of revolution was a global, ecumenical struggle of the exploited against the exploiter. "One moves from this form of nationalism to internationalism—dealing effectively with people ideologically, crossing political, racial, and religious lines," she said.

Betty had made occasional appearances for the cause in the short history of her widowhood, emerging around Malcolm's birthday and the anniversary of his death. Organizers often billed her as "guest of honor," expecting her to contribute queenly presence and little else. But she had never imagined herself as a token. "I don't want to live off my husband's reputation," she told a neighbor months after moving to Mount Vernon. At the 1968 Harlem middle school memorial that rang with the "get guns" chant, she towed her bonneted daughters onstage and offered brief reflections not on her husband, but on the growing demand for black studies. "Long before the white man came to this country, when he thought the earth was flat, you gave civilization to the world—your fore-parents," she told the audience. And saying so, she added, had nothing to do with hatred:

> They say, "We don't want Black History taught in the schools. We don't want hate and Black Power in the schools." This is a lot of propaganda. This is to frighten people away. We don't want hate. We want facts taught to our children to let them know that they have contributed more, or, just as much as any other ethnic group, to make America what it is today.

As the widow appeared at more affairs, she grew more conscious of the need to shield her daughters from the celebrity glare. Somewhere in the annual arc of commemorations between the anniversary of the minister's death and birth, she collided with the inevitable self-doubt. Was spreading the good word worth exposing the girls? Did she have anything worthwhile to say? She answered the second question and tabled the first, and in 1969 hit the lecture circuit in earnest. She was no less reticent than before and avoided long absences from the children. Still, the younger generation's beckoning and the need to support her family drove her inexorably into public life. She felt a further sense of duty to promulgate *her* Malcolm—the visionary and family man—while offering youngsters a redeeming image of black womanhood.

Over the next few years, she spoke at Wheelock College in Massachusetts and Capitol University in Ohio. She lectured at Wayne State in Michigan and Morehead State in Kentucky. Wilberforce University, University of Florida, University of West Florida, Penn State, and two State University of New York campuses also made her calendar. Women's groups or black student unions generally sponsored the talks (sometimes over the grumbling of college administrators who anticipated echoes of her husband's rhetoric). Though her focus more than half the time was Malcolm, she often touched upon broad social issues. Her repertoire included the sweepingly titled "Role of Black Women," a topic she explored at such unlikely forums as Bethany College, West Virginia.

"Black Americans want the same things you do—freedom, justice, and equal opportunity," she told a white audience at Morehead State in 1971. "We seek peace and equality, not violence and hatred." She was more insistent before a mixed crowd at Wayne State in 1970. "Until there is peace for the blacks there's going to be no peace for anybody else," she cried. At times her remarks resonated with the swelling feminist movement. "If women had been happy in the home, there would have been no suffrage movement fifty years ago," she said during the Wayne State talk.

She trumpeted woman power again during an address to high schoolers and undergraduates at nearby Highland Park College. A girl in the audience asked if the role of the black woman was not simply to stand by black men while they declared their manhood. "If a burglar comes to a house and the woman can shoot better than the man, it's up to her to protect the home," Betty said to a roar of approval. She had always celebrated black women. During a 1967 appearance at Detroit's Shrine of the Black Madonna, she admired the beauty and spirituality of the holy mother and child depicted in the sanctuary's famous painting, and invoked the great mothers of African and African-American history. Yet she was more apt to stress women and men working side by side against racism than to urge the former to battle chauvinism. She later confessed that she was "no women's libber." The feminist movement, she told a university crowd in 1975, "just doesn't answer my needs."

Regardless of her message, college crowds invariably treated the widow like royalty. Black and white students often hailed her with prolonged applause before she had even opened her mouth. (The audience at a Miss Black America competition in which she appeared as a judge interrupted the contest to grant her a thunderous standing ovation.) She could talk soul like nobody's business among her partners, but enunciated with a formal, almost Elizabethan clip at the lectern (though she slipped into the vernacular when she got excited).

Her softness belied her grit. In interviews, she tolerated white journalists. "Malcolm didn't preach violence," she intoned endlessly, "but self-defense." No, he did not reform in his last months; he refined. "Matter is continually changing," she explained. "Nothing remains the same." But she was short when her interrogators turned to trivial matters or when they dared guess her age. "My goodness, you surely don't think I'm forty, do you?" she asked a reporter in 1969, shortly before her thirty-fifth birthday. She could be dramatic: "And just where do I begin?" she would say slowly. "We have so many problems today." And she could be exacting: "Just what are you doing about it—anything?" she asked one audience after running down the litany of racial crises threatening American children.

Her deportment buoyed the students at a Philadelphia public school that had been fighting to rename itself in her husband's honor. After her 1969 visit, a seventeen-year-old student paid homage in a letter. "Your entrance was so dynamic with your graceful smile that said with its expression, 'I am black and I am proud and will accept no substitute for freedom,'" he wrote. "[Your presence] restored my energy to fight on for justice for the black man. We the students of Malcolm X High will continue to push for the official change of the name, but in event they don't officially change the name, we will hold in our minds that our school is Malcolm X High and no one or anything can change it or make it otherwise, now or forever more."

Betty's lectures, like her husband's, were often laden with history. In 1975, she explained to a largely white crowd at Lawrence University in Appleton, Wisconsin, how the European partition of Africa had devastated Africans and how imperialism continued to ravage the continent. She talked about the price black women had paid for survival, excluded from the wealth of a society that scattered their sons across the globe to die in wars of white domination. She even traced the pattern of prejudice and paternalism to the contemporary Peace Corps, taking to task white volunteers who traipsed into African nations with no knowledge of local culture and heritage. "Most of the white students in America feel that others have to adjust to them," she said. "They go to teach and they get taught."

Often the most striking impression the widow left was that she was a remarkably well read pupil of black nationalism and a fierce guardian of her husband's memory. Such was the case on May 18, 1971, when she visited McClymonds High School in Berkeley, California. McClymonds seethed with Black Power defiance, lying as it did just north of Oakland, the Black Panthers' birthplace. Mysterious fires and "illegal" assemblies had roiled the school in recent years. Students had deemed the former principal overly accomodationist, and had agitated until "a righteous black man" replaced him. This was a tough crowd in a militant community.

But the East Bay was not ready for Betty. She chose a question-and-answer format for the talk, which Oakland's Merrit Community College had sponsored. Merrit's president introduced her as Malcolm's "lifetime partner," and students and community members flocked to the floor microphones. Somebody asked the widow to compare nationalism and Pan-Africanism, the pillars of her husband's ideology. Nationalism, she replied, was a natural "collecting force" that prescribed love for African heritage. Pan-Africanism was simply a "secondary" (and supreme) nationalism that united African people around the world. She illustrated the latter definition by citing George

Padmore, a pre-Nkrumah master of the philosophy who only its serious students would recognize.

Someone asked if she thought the United States would ever honor her husband with a national holiday. "I kinda doubt it," Betty said. The crowd tittered knowingly. "Although I think in a few years history will bear me out that he has done more to defining—pointing the finger at a solution—than any other citizen in this country." She paused. "No, he wasn't a citizen, was he?" (Another ripple of laughter.) "I don't know what they're going to do," she concluded. "I would like to hope that black folks remember Malcolm. Because it is for them that he gave his life."

Someone asked what she made of the ideological war between the political nationalists (who emphasized community control) and the cultural nationalists (who stressed Afrocentric dress, customs, and awareness), a bitter conflict that to the delight of J. Edgar Hoover's FBI had divided the Black Left. "Man without culture is dead," the widow proclaimed, channeling her husband. "Man without politics is also dead." After all, she said, one needs both bread and meat to fix a sandwich. "You know, I was going to wear a real bright regalia tonight," she added. "They said, 'Oh no, don't wear that! They'll consider you a cultural nationalist.' I'm a *black* woman! Period!"

Malcolm, Betty said, had abhorred such factionalism. She went on to scold blacks who refused to support ousted UCLA philosophy professor and leftist icon Angela Davis because she was a communist. (Davis was in a California prison at the time on charges that she had plotted and supplied weapons for a Marin County Courthouse kidnapping of three San Quentin prisoners that had ended in a deadly shootout.) "So if black people don't support Angela Davis because she's a communist, then support her because she's a black woman," Betty said. "If you don't want to support her because she's a black woman, support her because she's a human being. But for God's sake, support her!"

Finally a young woman rose and asked the widow what influence she had had on Malcolm. "I think any other woman who'd been with him would have done equally or more than I did," Betty replied. "I was happy to have just been there when he needed me." What of the proverbial great woman behind the great man? Yes, she thought there was some truth to that. "But it was all Malcolm," she insisted. "I just happen to have been there, that's all." She paused, then conceded with a chuckle that she had probably had a hand in his success. "How did you inspire him?" the audience prodded. The widow grinned. "Sisters know," she said.

Chapter Thirteen

HUMANIST

＿

"All those heads to braid!"
—A neighbor of Betty's

Betty's speeches of the late 1960s struck a bold tone. Her message was never patently radical, but she was openly sympathetic to the ideological warriors whom the American mainstream branded "extremists." She defended the logic of militancy. "Is it really such a bad word if it means to strike out against evil? Or to preserve your own life?" She insisted that Western society itself seethed with "a missionary militancy against African culture." She countered black establishmentarians who vaunted the race's advances in politics and business. "Progress will be realized," she declared, "when the black man can determine his own destiny."

In 1968, she embraced radicalism explicitly, accepting the vice presidency of the Republic of New Africa, one of the separatist groups the FBI routinely monitored as a threat to the state. Detroit's Malcolm X Society, an alliance of nationalists for whom the martyr's teachings were orthodoxy, had convened a national summit of black militants that year to form the Republic. The attendees renounced their American citizenship and proclaimed the autonomy of their "provisional government," demanding for its territory Mississippi, Louisiana, Alabama, Georgia, and South Carolina. "The Republic is all about land—not an illusory black nation where unessential palliatives are offered: *bubas* and *dashikis* made from cotton from Bakersfield and dyed in Los Angeles," one of its patriots later declared. "We feel that to be free you should have a nation and a right to defend it."

The RNA named Robert Williams, the radical, former Monroe, North Carolina, NAACP leader then living in exile, its nominal president. Betty volunteered for a seat in its cabinet. During an inaugural meeting at the Shrine of the Black Madonna, she leaned over and whispered to RNA Minister of Information Imari Obadele that she was willing to serve as an officer. The men and women of the Republic promptly installed her as second vice president. Three years later they honored her husband, consecrating their capital, El Malik, on a farm in Hinds County, Mississippi.

The obligations of single parenthood made the widow's vice presidency an honorary title. Yet she attended occasional RNA planning meetings, including a North Philadelphia affair in 1968. Her ties to the group dissolved by 1970. She said she wanted a more "service-oriented" life. But she never disavowed the RNA or any other separatist camp. Nor did she agonize over whether a "black nation" meant sovereign land or psychological self-government. Blacks "should work for equal opportunity and for a piece of this land," she told the *Detroit Free Press*.

In a 1971 talk, she recognized the long history of black nationhood as an American ideal, insisting that separatism was a perfectly logical ambition in a country that refused to acknowledge black humanity. "If they can get some land and set up a republic, right on!" she said of the RNA. Even Betty's manner fit the nationalist mode. At times she addressed students and professionals of color almost accusingly as "educated blacks," leading onlookers to conclude that she shared her husband's disdain for the bourgeoisie. "Look at some of our leaders today," she told one black audience. "Wealth, position, power…And if it's threatened they'll sell their mother down the river, let alone you."

Black insurgents granted Betty a visible if token station as the martyr's widow. She did not hesitate, though, to veer off the sidelines and join their discourse. In March 1972, she and eight thousand other blacks congregated in Gary, Indiana, for the National Black Political Convention, an ecumenical occasion with a nationalist tenor. Among the attendees were 3,500 delegates from forty-four states who had committed themselves to framing a "Black Agenda." The summit signaled a rejection of white paternalism. It seethed with antiwar passion and disgust with the political elite's "law and order" chorus as a code for racial repression. There was talk of a prisoner's "bill of rights," community control of schools in black neighborhoods, universal health care, and the abolition of the death penalty.

The widow shared the convention platform with a gallery of leaders, including Rev. Jesse Jackson, who called for a black political party. "It's 'nation time' for an exploited nation of people whose political impotence and enslaved mentality has handcuffed us in the dungeon of the Republican Party and shackled us on the plantation of the Democratic Party," he proclaimed. Organizers had barred white media from the proceedings, and controversy tinged the whole affair. But its message of solidarity and self-determination exhilarated Betty. "Some people say it failed," she later said. "No. It didn't fail. Because people came together and crystallized their thinking."

The widow had made overtures of active cooperation with the Left as early as 1967. Before he joined the Black Panthers, Eldridge Cleaver in a private conversation promised her that he would help her "carry out Malcolm's dream." But by the early 1970s, Mrs. Malcolm X began looking and sounding like a moderate. In July 1971, she became a trustee of the Housewives League of America, the national order of the group her foster mother had helped launch in Detroit forty-one years before. In January 1973, she was among a handful of figures who accepted directorships of Operation PUSH (People United to Save Humanity), the moderate, Chicago-based organization Jackson had formed in 1971 after breaking with the Southern Christian Leadership Conference.

Basketball colossus and first black NBA coach Bill Russell also assumed a top PUSH post that year, succeeding Jackie Robinson, the professional baseballer who had broken the sport's color line, as the rights group's vice chairman. (Robinson, who died in 1972, was among the "responsible" black spokesmen Malcolm had spent much of his career debunking.) Betty and other dignitaries appeared in social-action workshops at the July 1973 national PUSH convention, an occasion that heralded a "new" Civil Rights goal—black economic power. Betty's drift into the black establishment continued into 1974, when as a doctoral candidate at the University of Massachusetts Amherst, she entered the New York Alumnae Chapter of Delta Sigma Theta, an elite sorority. She began calling herself a "humanist" and espousing a pacifist, nonsectarian philosophy.

"We're supposed to share the riches of the earth," she told *Newsweek* in 1969, urging blacks to avoid reciprocating white racism. In 1972, she condemned an attempt on the life of presidential candidate and notorious segregationist George C. Wallace. A gunman had shot and seriously wounded the former Alabama governor at a Maryland campaign rally. Though many blacks considered Wallace a sworn enemy, the widow decried the country's culture of violence. "I disagree emphatically with his philosophies," she said of Wallace. "But he has the right to live, just as I have the right to disagree." America, she insisted, would have to start teaching its children by example that only God had the right to take life. "We now spend billions going to the moon," she said, "but the world still is ruled by brute force. How do we expect one generation to rule by brute force and the next not to do the same?"

⎯⌒⎯

Betty was maturing politically. She was expressing opinions—especially on issues crucial to women and children—that spun not from Malcolmology, but from her own sensibilities. She had once aimed her activism at the schools and community her daughters roamed. Now she began broadening, talking as much about education, juvenile delinquency, student unrest, male-female relationships, and Vietnam as she did about the minister. "You know, if their thing is war and our thing is children, then we just push forward, because it's more of us than there is them," she told an audience of educators in 1974.

She remained an incontrovertible champion of her husband. "Review Malcolm—and realize what a mistake it was to have him killed," she commanded students. She continued to insist that the news media had bemired his message with "sensationalism, distortions, and mass hysteria." Unlike some elements of the Black Power generation, however, she borrowed from his latter-day anti-imperialism rather than his cruder down-with-"whitey" rhetoric. "And just what is blackness?" she challenged African-American audiences. "Many people define it as the extent to which you hate whites. But that's not true, not true at all."

The widow's increasingly centrist message baffled some nationalists. Many blacks and whites expected her to become a mute emblem of martyrdom or a bearer of her husband's sword. Mrs. Malcolm X was an entirely different creature. She was decidedly feminine. She was well spoken. She had energy and poise. But she lacked the minister's charisma and scalding indictment. "Betty was never a revolutionary," Sonia Sanchez later said.

As a speaker, the widow in those years could also be quite dull. Her talk at the National Association for the Education of Young Children's 1974 convention was disjointed and textbookish. Her topic was the community's responsibility to children. Her thesis was that a grassroots approach that recognized diversity and encompassed the church and home would enhance early childhood education more dramatically than state bureaucracy. But the audience must have felt like it was enduring an excruciating graduate-school lecture:

> Communities are successful or stable to the degree that they are concerned with the level of their effectiveness with the population that they are supposed to serve. Communities influence and vary in degrees. Now the state society (when I say state society or modern society or whatever, I don't necessarily mean the individual or the community but the state society, and this certainly is debatable) does not serve to a great degree the security needs. No large scale organization can really meet the psychic demands of individuals because, by its very nature, it is too large, too complex and too bureaucratic and all together too aloof from the gut meaning or community meaning which a lot of us live by.

At times Betty seemed out of touch. Her 1970 lecture before an overflow crowd at Wayne State was surprisingly low-key. Mourning students had donned armbands and the school had suspended classes in honor of two black students killed in a recent uprising at Jackson State College. Yet the widow made only passing reference to the incident. Days before her April 1974 speech at Simpson College in Indianola, Iowa, black undergrads took over the student center, protesting campus racism and other injustices. But during her address, Betty did not deviate from her standard discourse on the black woman's role.

Perhaps bitterness was the most glaring flaw of the widow's public persona. Sometimes the target of her indignation was clear. During a 1971 talk, a young woman in the audience confessed that she had problems understanding Black Islam. The girl's intentions may have been innocent, but Betty raked her over the coals:

> Problems understanding the Nation of Islam? Do you know any Black Muslims? Do they have a Black Muslim mosque in this vicinity? They do? Why don't you go there and find out? You attended? Well, then I think you should rephrase your question. You want to know what I have to say about them, isn't that right? Malcolm was put out of the movement because of some things he found out. Period. [The girl asked her to expound.] No, I don't think I will at this point. At this particular point I don't. If you don't already know. And I thought everybody knew [applause]. And if you don't know you kinda back in your homework [laughter and applause]. I was told there are maybe five or six Black Muslims in the audience. Maybe they'll raise their hands and I think they'll tell you.

Betty's resentment sometimes seemed as indiscriminate. During her early years on the circuit, audiences often left her lectures bewildered. "I'd come into places and people would say, 'Oh, Sister Betty was here,'" Sanchez later recalled. "And they'd say, 'Oh my goodness, that woman. What's *wrong* with her?' And you had to remind them that this was a woman who had lost a husband, shot right before her eyes."

———

The widowhood of martyrdom is a knife that cut both ways. We demand impossible virtue from a living symbol of sainthood. "I would like for the brothers and sisters to treat me like a person rather than as some kind of institution," Betty told *Ebony* in 1969. And yet from the wives of warriors we expect combat. "Betty was very conscious politi-cally—as Betty," James Smalls later said. "Many people missed how conscious she was because they kept viewing her as Malcolm's wife and not as Sister Betty." The mind-set rankled the widow. She insisted that she was an element rather than an "extension" of her husband, and accused blacks who expected her to be Malcolmesque of internalizing white notions of black homogeneity. "I have my own feelings about strength," she said. "It doesn't mean that I don't love as he loved."

In truth, she was still discovering the minister. "Since Malcolm died I have been exposed to a lot of elements," she said in 1969. "I was somewhat sheltered for eight years…and now I find it amazing the way he lived." The cult of Malcolm complicated the discovery, for though leftists agreed on his heroism, his meaning was another matter. In 1969, the mostly white academic senate at the University of California–Santa Cruz approved a proposal to name one of the school's seven colleges for Malcolm. The senate was acquiescing to an interra-cial student appeal, but Black Panthers in California scoffed at the "nonviolent guerrillas" behind the petition.

"Brother Malcolm stated many times that we should keep the white man out of our meetings," *The Black Panther* editorialized. "But here, whitey and the Negroes are sitting together planning a school in the name of Brother Malcolm." The commentary recalled the minis-ter's preaching that nonviolent revolution was a hoax, concluding that it would be "a cold blow" if the UC–Santa Cruz name change went through. The FBI, of course, was neutral. It duly monitored both the Panthers and the UC radicals as enemies of the establishment.

At times the grappling over Malcolm's legacy entangled Betty. Her struggles to define her public identity only confused matters. In August 1971 she registered to vote, consummating her transition from radicalism to civic duty. Her registration was in sync with her husband's wish for blacks to cast ballots in the name of self-determination. The minister, who had accused both political parties of exploiting blacks, might have preferred that she sign up as an independent, but few blacks would have quarreled with her registration as a Democrat, the party that had held the race's allegiance for decades.

Many were aghast, however, when she turned up at a ritzy black Republican fundraiser in Washington, D.C., the summer before President Nixon's 1972 reelection (and just three months after the leftward black agenda conference in Gary). The one hundred–dollars-a-plate banquet drew two thousand blacks and yielded two hundred thousand dollars for the incumbent's war chest. The Republican Party was hoping to woo blacks, only 12 percent of whom had backed Nixon in 1968. Most of the guests that evening were not Republican, and some complained that invitations to the affair—which announced not a rally for the president but an evening of "getting ourselves together"—had been misleading. Betty herself later told friends that she had not known in advance that the event was partisan.

She did not leave, though. Malcolm had pilloried society blacks who thought themselves refined because they orbited Washington power circles. Yet that evening his wife enjoyed a fancy supper, a dais seat next to actor and ex-football star Jim Brown, and a performance by her high-school heartthrob, singer Billy Eckstine. The presence of these and other black dignitaries was especially significant because African-Americans that year had threatened to bolt the Democratic Party if it did not include a "Black Bill of Rights" in its national platform. This didn't keep the audience from squirming when a Baptist minister during the fundraiser's benediction compared Nixon to Christ. Nor did it deter the Black United Front, a local black nationalist group that picketed the affair.

Though Betty was not a Nixon fan, she refused to beg pardon for her cameo with the Republicans. She had aligned with progressive and radical causes and figures in recent years, but she had sweltered too long under Black Islam to submit to rigid ideology. Never again, she said, would she "go off the deep end." Nor would she squeeze herself into the mold the Black Left cast for her. "There was pressure on Betty not to scandalize Malcolm," Robert Haggins, the minister's long-time photographer, later remembered. But the woman who had at times defied her domineering husband now refused to bow to his spiritual heirs.

She insisted on inner and outer self-definition, eschewing the audacious Afro many soul sisters of the day favored. She arrayed herself in African garments from time to time, but never as credentials of her blackness. "A conservative-looking person can be just as dedicated to making positive contributions as the person who goes around dressed in long, flowing African robes," she said. Though she was evolving as a political being, her self-hood was intact. Still, she could not escape her responsibility to the struggle. "I'm a very private person who is often compelled to become public," she said.

That public role could be enormously rewarding, especially after her husband's lionization by young blacks and intellectuals. By 1970, his autobiography had entered its eighteenth printing, selling more than one million copies and cropping up on high-school and college syllabi nationwide. Betty rejected his messianic legend. "There is nothing mysterious about him," she said. "He treated people as he wanted to be treated, and practiced what he preached." Yet it pleased her that he had become a keystone of black consciousness. Men and women on the street now greeted her reverently as "Sister Betty," and brick-and-mortar tributes bearing his name began to appear.

Malcolm X Liberation University opened in the fall of 1969 in Durham, North Carolina. The school, which evolved from a black student uprising at nearby Duke University and later expanded to Greensboro, featured biomedics and engineering programs and a Pan-African orientation. Chicago's Malcolm X College, however, was Betty's darling. The local college system, under pressure from the black community, had renamed the former Crane College after her husband.

She had attended the 1969 ceremony in which the name change was announced, having received a secret invitation from an administrator.

Students and city officials had gathered in a local church for the event. As the chancellor of the city college system looked on in near-horror, the incoming president had declared that Crane would thereafter be known as Malcolm X College, a name the students had quietly chosen in a vote weeks earlier. When she heard the announcement, Betty leapt from her chair and begun applauding wildly. "And the students, of course, went crazy," one observer remembered.

For a time, the honor was inauspicious. The Malcolm X College campus oozed West Side blight, and layers of graffiti blanketed the walls. "Pictures and words," the widow later remembered, "in case you didn't understand what you was looking at." Students dozed in the corridors. Police escorted scared white professors to class. Betty was mortified. "What in the name of goodness is this?" she demanded. Then the school's president, pro-black powerhouse Charles Hurst, helped whip the student body into shape and won state and other funds for a new $26 million campus. When Betty revisited the junior college in 1971 (as an honored guest with Angela Davis's father), she found a gleaming bulwark rearing from the ghetto. Four thousand students had entered the institution. (Black Panther Leader Fred Hampton enrolled shortly before his death in a police shootout.)Malcolm X College barred no applicant for lacking a high-school diploma.

Hurst himself was a dropout who had bootlegged spirits before catapulting himself into academia and earning a doctorate. Now, with his rippling dashikis and Black Power fist pendant dancing upon his chest, he reigned over a kingdom that coursed with its namesake's passion for self-determination. Betty beamed at the Malcolm portraits cluttering the halls and the red, black, and green pennant that flittered out front (MXC having become the nation's first public institution to fly black liberation colors). "That Chicago would be the hub of what Malcolm is all about is catching a lot of people by surprise," she later said, alluding to the city's status as the home of Nation of Islam headquarters. She embraced Hurst and his staff's mission and agreed to serve as the school's consultant, returning in 1972 to address its graduating class along with Floyd McKissick, who'd radicalized CORE in the late

1960s. "They're doing fantastic things to the minds of young people there," she said of MXC.

————

It was the minds of her own young people, however, that most concerned Betty. Though she was mounting podiums twice a month by the early 1970s, she poured her energy overwhelmingly into her children. No matter how often she intersected the spheres of black liberation, or how many nominal titles she accrued, single motherhood was the most powerful force behind the woman she was becoming, and her proudest achievement would always be her girls.

She wanted their lives to be a love affair with blackness, from its past to its possibilities. She enrolled them in weekend black history courses and stocked the house with African art. She clucked at suburban blacks who fretted when their kids began wrestling with questions of racial pride and solidarity. No, she would arm her girls against the white arrogance she encountered during her treks across the country. "They used to say that the black man has no history worth mentioning, no humanity worth defending," she told a visitor in 1971. "That's a fallacy. Blacks *do* have a history they should be proud of and a humanity with a value all its own."

Her focus on black history mirrored the rise of a nationalist black middle class. Traditionally, bourgeois blacks internalized white values and pursued integration. By the late 1960s, more and more privileged blacks were espousing racial self-determination. These professionals tended to see their destiny as inseparably linked to that of the world's black and brown. They were more willing to embrace African heritage and stress their cultural distinctiveness than their predecessors had been.

Of course, Malcolm had also dreamed of his daughters growing up with a firm sense of identity, and it was his vision that most inspired their black studies regimen. Betty exposed them to the caravan of black dignitaries that passed through the home. There were visits from such socially aware artists as soul legend Curtis Mayfield,

James Baldwin, Nikki Giovanni, Novella Nelson, and actress and R&B singer Melba Moore. Jesse Jackson's Afro and swagger made him the girls' favorite. They convulsed with giggles whenever the hip cats and cool mommas stopped by. "Come on over and dance for them," Betty would command one of her daughters. "My baby can dance!"

Sometimes the grown-ups talked soberly over coffee or tea. The children would hide in the hallway and collect scraps of discussions from the sons and daughters of black consciousness. "We were all in drama, so we imitated everyone once they left," Gamilah later recalled. The black-heritage lessons, formal and overheard, emboldened the girls. At the mostly white St. Joseph's Montessori School in Mount Vernon, one of the children interrupted a flustered teacher to advise her class that, "Columbus didn't discover anything." The Shabazz brood soon acquired a playground mystique as the Revolutionary's Daughters.

The girls were no more revolutionary than any other black kids from the suburbs. Yet Betty quietly imbued them with a soft nationalism. She told newsmen that she saw only black husbands in their futures. Though Malcolm had recanted his attack on miscegenation in his final days, the widow told *Look* in 1969 that there were more than enough honorable men within the race for her daughters to choose from when the time came. But she also taught the children to shun dogma. No people or creed, she warned, should dictate their conscience.

"I brought them up, actually, as world people," she later said. "Wherever they are, they belong." She dreamed of them traveling abroad, especially to those regions of Africa and the Middle East that Malcolm had toured on his final sojourns. She wanted them to see Asia and the West Indies. "They should know Grenada, the island where Malcolm's mother was born," she said. She hoped racial awareness would empower them to be and do with self-assurance. "I am confident that that is the way Malcolm would have wanted it," she said.

She never drilled Negritude into their hearts. "I grew up cross-cultural," Attallah later said. "In my house, there were many accents.

My taste buds were not formed on American food. The family background was African, Caribbean, Arabic, and Native American.... Instead of feeling one-fourth of something, I felt 400 percent." To enrich and occupy the girls, the widow enrolled them in piano and dance lessons (African and ballet). Some of the children studied theater or French. Others took up violin, clarinet, soccer, and track. There were days when they left for school before six A.M. and got home after eight in the evening.

The swirl of activities was necessary. Betty had to get the older girls out of the house so she could concentrate on the twins, or whoever needed her attention. At times, the rigorous schedule wore the children out. But the widow was a stern taskmaster who tolerated no excuses. She believed that regimenting her daughters' lives would ensure their success, and she pushed them hard. College was a must. "You weren't jack if you didn't have a college degree," Gamilah would remember. The widow told one of the girls in the eighth grade that she was going to major in math. There was no discussion. "I guess she was planting a root in all of us," Gamilah said.

The girls balanced the pursuits with precautions. For years there were no sleepovers, and Betty said where, when, and how they played. She insisted that there were enough bodies in the house and on the block for their entertainment. The strictures could be stifling, but the widow meant to mold her daughters. "They will not, as I did, have to have a baby to learn to share or to give," she said. "They will not only be able to take care of themselves, but will be able to make a contribution in the community or to the human family."

She exulted in their achievements. When Ilyasah crocheted a vibrantly colored vest, Betty bragged about her gifted nine-year-old. She made no apologies for the children's strict upbringing. She remembered the despair of the months after the assassination and swore that they would never experience such helplessness. What she wanted for her children she wanted for herself: the right to live with dignity.

Betty nurtured her daughters' bodies as well as their minds. She created trail mix with raisins and almonds. She fixed tuna fish sandwiches with shredded carrots and homemade wheat bread. She made yogurt, grew bean sprouts, and baked "sweet potato" pie with white potatoes or butternut squash. There were no pungent odors when she cooked her oxtail, and her salmon cakes were divine. She prepared everything the girls drank in a juicer because she wished them to have "the natural sugar." She concocted a purplish potion of beets, apples, and carrots, and told the girls it would "bathe" their cells.

The children sensed that their diet was different. Their friends let them sip soda just to watch their eyes water and see them choke. (Betty also forbade her daughters to chew gum, though she popped Doublemint gum like a pancake-house waitress.) What they may not have suspected was that Black Islam inspired the meals as much as their mother's nutritional training. They inhaled the chicken, fish, and lamb dishes and the occasional lean cut of beef, and endured the vegetables and grains. "We ate Wheatina like it was grits," Gamilah recalled.

Betty was determined to feed their spirits, too. Allah had delivered her in the early years of her widowhood. "Without prayer I would have gone mad," she told Muslim friends. She had discovered the power of prayer watching Malcolm kneel on his braided rug, then seeing him rise renewed. Now she was determined to bequeath the faith and raise her daughters according to her vision of the *Sunna* (the proper way of life). "She didn't want them to feel that it was Islam that killed their father," a Muslim crony later said. The children recognized the Lord's supremacy. They ate no pork. (Betty fired one of her housekeepers on the spot after she came home one evening and found a ham in the oven.) They celebrated Ramadan, the ninth month of the Muslim calendar in which believers fast, abstain, commune with family, and contemplate God.

"We follow the Islamic jurisprudence," the widow said. Recognizing that the children were growing up in a largely Christian environment, she also compromised. Come December, she would set a poinsettia on the marble coffee table or hang a stocking by the fireplace. (A Qur'an was on permanent display nearby.) The girls knew not to open Aunt Ruth's "Christmas" gifts until after Ramadan's closing feast. (Though one year they bored what they thought were discreet holes in the bottom of the boxes, pulled out the toys, then tried to conceal the crime with masking tape.) At the end of the holy month, Betty would drive to a Mount Vernon warehouse store and buy discount handbags or other cheap gifts in sets of six. She did not send the children to Muslim schools—another compromise. And she brought them to some of the Christian functions she occasionally attended.

Betty moved so easily in Christian spheres that the depth of her religious observance was often unclear to outsiders. Though she had often donned some sort of headwear in the years since her husband's death, she continued to eschew the traditional, draping headpieces common to Muslim women in the Nation and the Middle East. This inspired murmurs in some of New York's orthodox circles. Betty's motive for shunning the *khimar* was simple; she did not want to look like a Black Muslim. There are devout Muslim women both in the West and the East who choose not to shroud their hair. The Qur'an decrees only that women dress modestly. Betty was no schoolmarm. "She knew she looked good," Novella Nelson remembered. The widow shunned wispy miniskirts, plunging necklines, and painted-on pants, though some fundamentalists frowned at the knit dresses that hugged her figure.

She avoided traveling alone, in keeping with the traditional etiquette of a Muslim woman. In the 1980s and '90s, her disbursements of cash to relatives and friends revealed both her generosity and her commitment to the Islamic pillar of almsgiving. As for her devotion to the five daily prayers required of the faithful, "That's between her and Allah," one of her Muslim associates later said.

Betty's desire to teach her children the faith was clear. Not long after the family moved to Mount Vernon, she asked K. Ahmad Tawfiq to start tutoring the girls in Arabic and Islamic studies. Malcolm had been fond of Tawfiq, imam of New York's black orthodox Mosque of Islamic Brotherhood. He arrived at the Shabazz home every Wednesday with lessons about the Qur'an and ancient African history, sometimes delighting the girls with pet frogs and other fanciful gifts. The fulcrum of the family's faith, however, was the Islamic Center at 72nd and Riverside. Betty took the girls to its Sunday services from the time they were old enough to understand the goings-on. They rarely attended *juma* (the conventional Friday services), but Sunday worship was compulsory. "There was no getting mad about that," Gamilah later said.

The Center served an international congregation. In its converted brownstone mosque, the Shabazz daughters mingled with African, Arab, and American believers of all colors. The girls joined the other children for Arabic and Islamic lessons on Sunday mornings. In the afternoon they lined up for prayer, assembling behind the women (who in turn queued behind the men). After the prostrations, Betty would hand out the girls' allowance and head to a nearby coffee shop to peruse the Sunday newspaper while they bounded into nearby stores for illicit candy and adventure.

Though the widow was a regular at the Islamic Center, she was an atypical Muslim woman by most measures. She was outspoken and could be jarringly blunt when she thought a parishioner was violating her privacy or overstepping his or her bounds. She believed in Muslim women supporting and even yielding to their husbands, but she felt strongly that they should be well educated. (In Islam, the prayers of the learned are more valuable than those of the unschooled.) She rejected the notion that women should be unyieldingly docile as a matter of piety, an idea that many Muslim men of all colors and backgrounds embrace. "She had definite thoughts about the role of women and the practice of Islam that she would share if she cared enough about you," remembered A'aliyah Abdul Karim, a fellow parishioner.

Betty could be understated and gracious. When she met other believers, she crossed her hands over her chest and said, "Salaam" ("Peace"). She belonged to that growing school of Muslim womanhood that refuses to equate Qur'anic edicts of feminine modesty and virtue with submission to patriarchy. She was reticent about her personal affairs at the mosque. (Some of her friends swore she was more herself around the faithful, while others insisted that she was more guarded.) Yet she moved with bright, dynamic, liberated Muslim women.

These women faced the triple jeopardy of their black, Muslim womanhood with flair. Some of them organized Muslim fashion shows that stressed vibrant patterns and colors over drab, traditional garb. ("Modesty in Motion from Ocean to Ocean" was their slogan.) Others led organizations that dealt with issues affecting Muslim women in New York and around the world. Betty worshipped and socialized with these women for years. Some of them thought her mysterious or bourgeois and wondered about her "cool" spells. Her career and widening social circles separated her from many of them by the late 1970s or early 1980s. Still, her children knew them eternally as "aunts."

The Muslim cohorts understood that the widow wore Islam in her heart and not on her head. They accepted her singleness within a faith circle that frowns upon unmarried women, and they shared her contention that the orthodox community had failed to properly recognize or appreciate Malcolm before or after his martyrdom. "We should have been more assiduous about teaching the children about el-Hajj Malik, about the struggle and the whole human rights battle," Karim later said.

The Shabazz daughters could not truly appreciate who their father was politically because Betty never told them. "I taught them about him by being disciplined and strict," she later said. "My children think my persona is me when actually it is their father's." They grew up among his relics. Many of the well-thumbed volumes in the family library had been his. His hat and suitcase sat in a closet. One found souvenirs from his travels in various nooks, and his bespectacled face peered owlishly from portraits on the walls. Still, the girls reached their teens with little understanding of Malcolm as one of the century's prescient revolutionaries. "They had no clue," one of their playmates later said.

In time, they realized that Betty was a symbol for people throughout the world. They were curious about her trips abroad and sensitive to the manner in which outsiders approached her. They watched her cache of dashikis, African headdresses, foreign currency, books, gifts, and mementos from friends and admirers grow. Meanwhile they clung to the vestiges of Daddy they had always known—the stories and the proud sense that he had been utterly devoted to his people. Attallah, who had the clearest memory of him, was her sisters' ligament to their father. She and Betty still spoke of him as if he had just gone out for a newspaper, Ilyasah later said.

Yet Attallah could not talk about Malcolm the warrior, and Betty wouldn't. "In my father's absence, my mother nurtured and protected the significance and value of her husband's endless devotion to human rights," the eldest daughter later said. But though youngsters across the country were plunging into his autobiography, the widow never discussed the book with her children. Attallah was a teenager before she realized that she was more intimately linked to the characters in her father's memoirs than to those in *The Swiss Family Robinson*. Old friends would reminisce about him during visits, transfixing his daughters with tales of his razor wit and charm or his boundless energy. The girls were hungry for ballads and parables and anecdotes, and they never tired of listening to their father's character witnesses. Still, the narratives seemed biblically ancient and distant from their reality.

"I grew up largely unaware of that other world of Black America in which children study no music and attend deteriorating public schools and live in cramped apartments in violent neighborhoods," Ilyasah later said. "My mother neither went out of her way to show us this world nor to keep us from seeing it." In fact, Betty consciously shielded her children from the pain, chaos, and fury of Malcolm's memory. That she neglected for years to take them to nearby Ferncliff Cemetery was no casual oversight. (Attallah was eighteen before she saw her father's grave.) The widow, whose psychological bond to the black bourgeoisie had never died, was returning to the strivings of that class. "They were trying to give us an education," Jean Owensby, the girls' running mate, later said of Betty and the black parents of Mount Vernon Heights. "That was their revolution."

The Shabazz girls began seeing shadows of another revolution, the one to which they were betrothed by blood. They had long been aware of their power to ruffle grown-ups. Attallah was only seven or eight when, not knowing the words, she stood mutely through the Pledge of Allegiance. Yet her silence became an act of sedition in the minds of her white teachers. This pattern of forced awareness continued as the children got older. They learned from the outside in, from a world that was largely white, that they were of radical stock. And they grew conscious of the ghost in their veins.

It was not just Qubilah's fierce intellect or Attallah's gesticulations or Gamilah's defiance. The girls were inescapably Malcolm's daughters, and he manifested in endless subtleties. Malikah's fantasies that he was not dead but living undercover somewhere may have been harmless enough. The real danger flared when Attallah and Qubilah found their mother's stashed copy of his autobiography ("There was nothing on those pages I didn't witness," the eldest later said) or when Gamilah started writing poetry.

The verses throbbed with blood and angst and an inimitable voice. The incipient militancy horrified Betty. "They will kill you for what you write," she warned the child, banning the compositions. Yet her daughters had inherited Malcolm's compulsion to question. "I can remember saying to my mother, 'I want to save the world,'" Gamilah later said. "I remember the look on her face. It was sadness."

The heroic aspirations themselves did not disturb the widow; it was the youthful rebellion that she found unsettling. She hoped to raise conscientious citizens, not race spokeswomen or revolutionaries. She wished for her children the quiet, conventional success she wanted for herself. "I am not a leader," she often said. "I am a follower. All I have to do is look and see what [leadership] did to Malcolm." She taught her daughters that they contained an extraordinary essence, a spiritual wealth that outsiders would try to loot. She also imparted a sense of betrayal.

She suspected that cocooning the girls from their patrimony would be impossible, for she knew they would ultimately discover the injustices Malcolm had fought. She hoped to forestall the encounter, but it was a doomed cause. Gamilah was only seven when she wandered into the

family library and found an illustrated history of the Civil Rights movement. "And there was this one full page of the hosing down of the people and another where a cop was letting a German shepherd eat this
man's stomach out," she later said. "And I changed after that. I couldn't
be a kid when all this is going on."

———

Betty struggled to ensconce her daughters in middle-classdom even
as they flashed with Malcolm's curiosity and willfulness. Giving the
girls a privileged life had not been easy. Quarterly royalty checks from
Malcolm's autobiography provided the annual equivalent of a salary.
The 1972 movie, copyright payments, and other projects padded her
income. But clothing, housing, feeding, entertaining, and educating six
princesses can deplete a small fortune.

The widow had lived frugally on Malcolm's ministerial allowance.
In his absence she grew even thriftier. "How could I have six kids and
go to graduate school and every other month they were going to fore-
close on the house and my kids was in school and the car note and the
food and the this and the that and the other, " she later said. "How
could I do that if I didn't have some of his wisdom?" She rarely complained to friends about finances (though in late-night phone conversations with Novella Nelson, she wondered aloud how she was going
to feed all those girls). Her kids were not aware of the lean times; they
may not have wondered about those early months in which they ate
oatmeal and little else. Betty and Medgar Evers's widow, Myrlie Evers-
Williams, later swapped stories about how they made do. "You would
cook those neckbones in your peas or your beans or your greens and
then you would take them and put sauce on them," Evers-Williams
recalled. "It was never as easy as the public thought."

Betty's burden grew as her daughters reached adolescence. Phone
bills of five hundred dollars were not uncommon. Black revolutionaries and dignitaries occasionally sent her cash. Still, the girls' private
schools and extracurricular pursuits drained her bank account. In the
early years, she coped by clipping coupons, dressing the children in

hand-me-downs, and frequenting a local diner. Sometimes scarcity forced her into feats of heroism. The girls' elementary school often held potlucks, but the widow was stretched too thin to buy extra groceries. She peered dismally into her bare cupboards the night before one of the parties. It was almost daybreak before she invented a cheese puffs recipe and filled several cookie tins with the treats.

"If she was on TV or in the *Jet* magazine sayin', 'Oh, we ain't got no money,' I'm sure millions would have come in," Dick Gregory later said. Betty was too proud and private for such display, and charity was less necessary as time passed. As her older daughters approached puberty, her personal savings, lecture fees, the trust funds established after the assassination, and other cash sources collectively were sufficient to support the children's entrée to the ranks of the black elite. She had always enrolled them in the best private schools, sacrificing to offer them a superior education. As her financial picture brightened, she immersed them in the culture of the privileged. They attended charm school (where they learned to walk while balancing books on their heads) and expensive summer camps in Vermont. And they joined Jack & Jill.

A social club for the children of the black bourgeoisie, Jack & Jill began in the 1930s as a playgroup for the kids of well-to-do black women. Decades later, the organization boasted dozens of chapters nationwide. Only mothers hold membership in the by-invitation-only society, whose aims are community service, education, and social uplift. Some blacks consider the group an elitist clique for color-conscious social climbers. Betty hoped to introduce her children to an upwardly mobile black crowd. Soon they were sipping hot cocoa on ice-skating and ski retreats and appearing at fundraisers. "When I saw the girls and their mother laughing and playing at tennis parties, backyard cookouts, and semiformal dances, it was hard to remember this was the family of a martyred rebel," former neighbor Lawrence Graham later said.

Like many parents, Betty wanted her kids to have all that she had as a child and more. (Jack & Jill was similar in many ways to the Del Sprites, the exclusive high-school sorority she had joined in Detroit.) In the youth group, the Shabazz girls mingled with the college-bound sons and daughters of prosperous blacks who stressed education and achievement. The club's weekend outings allowed them to escape the racial isolation they endured at their white schools. The local Jack & Jill chapter sponsored occasional service projects, and the widow liked its emphasis on black heritage and pride.

Jack & Jill was vital to the Shabazz girls' development, Ilyasah later said, because it "reinforced the role of education and excellence in the black family" and exposed her and her sisters to black success stories. It was also a safe harbor. "Even though some of us whispered about the celebrity of the Shabazz family," a Jack & Jill member from the children's chapter later recalled, "for the most part they were just another group of kids in our play group." The girls remained active in the organization throughout their childhood. But as Attallah got older, she began questioning the group's relevance. Its aristocratic flavor turned Gamilah off. "They were oblivious to real human struggle," she later said of her Jack & Jill peers.

Despite the later tremors of dissent, Betty continued to envelop the girls in society. She sent Attallah and Qubilah to the United Nations International School (UNIS) in Manhattan, an exclusive academy for the children of ambassadors and the well heeled. The younger girls also attended prep schools, including a Lutheran grade school in Mount Vernon and the all-girls Masters School in Dobbs Ferry, New York. Betty wanted the best education for her daughters, even if that meant lily-white campuses. She hoped the advantages she offered them would soften the sting of Malcolm's absence. "Sometimes you may overcompensate," Evers-Williams later said. "You may try to do too much to make up for that horror."

Yet the children continued to face the fear and confusion that had always clouded their father's image. One of their playmate's parents once asked them earnestly if their family had trained to kill their enemies. UNIS officials braced for an onslaught of militancy after thirteen-year-old Attallah enrolled. "Instead I walked in wearing my lime-green dress, my opaque stockings, my patent leather shoes, and carrying my little patent leather pocketbook," she later said. "I was also exceedingly quiet for the whole semester."

Some black nationalists would grumble in later years that Betty had drenched her daughters in privilege and cocooned them from the minister's political legacy. The widow felt she owed no one an explanation of how she raised her daughters. She did not believe she was straying from her husband's path by offering the children comfort and opportunity. Though Malcolm had been a champion of the dispossessed, he had never settled his family in the ghetto. At the time of his death, he and Betty had been house shopping in an integrated and decidedly middle-class neighborhood. (Attallah later suggested that both her parents had aspired to move to Westchester County.)

The widow knew that the minister had wanted his girls to better themselves. In raising them, she blended her dreams and his inspiration. Just as her churchly foster parents had once shrouded her from the ugliness of race, she struggled to shield her daughters from the torment of the past. If the cost of security was the children's superficial knowledge of their radical heritage, so be it. "We call people Uncle Toms because they didn't run toward the sword," Attallah later said, "but they stayed alive so we could be here."

Coretta Scott King stayed alive, too. On the evening of Thursday, April 4, 1968, not long after she had returned from Easter-dress shopping with her daughter Yolanda, she got the call she had been dreading for more than a decade. "Doc just got shot," said Jesse Jackson, then a young aide to Dr. Martin Luther King Jr. An assassin's bullet had struck King as he stood on a second-floor balcony at the Lorraine Motel in Memphis, Tennessee. (He had arrived in Memphis the day before to organize support for striking garbage workers amid his Poor People's Campaign.) The shot had ripped through the thirty-nine-year-old rights leader's jaw and neck, severing his spinal cord.

Coretta answered the phone numbly over the next few minutes as the details trickled in. Reports of the shooting flickered across the television set. Her four children (ages five to twelve) were asking what it all meant. The eldest already knew. "Don't tell me! Don't tell me!" cried Yolanda as she ran from the room. Coretta rushed to the airport, hoping to catch the next flight to Memphis, but Atlanta's mayor ushered her soberly into a lounge. "Mrs. King," he said, "I have been asked to tell you that Dr. King is dead." Grief-stricken, Coretta hurried home to see about the children. Yolanda was asking whether she should hate the killer. Seven-year-old Dexter was wondering when Daddy would be back.

With whatever portion of her consciousness anguish had not submerged, she wondered how she would explain to her children that Daddy was dead. Meanwhile, a world away in suburban New York, Betty relived the heartache as she sat paralyzed before her television, watching news bulletins. Attallah bounded into the house from school and discovered her thus. "I watched my mother very carefully that day," she later remembered. "I never let my eyes off her, because I was and am in love with her."

The Shabazz household reeled with love and war in those adventuresome years. Betty in time became the mom of the block. She shuttled the neighborhood kids to the park and let them gorge on her homemade, whole-wheat buns. She called them "Precious." (One of the local girls was heartbroken years later when the widow dropped the pet name and began addressing her as "Jean.") To the Shabazz daughters, every woman on their street was "Auntie" or "Grandma." They grew lean and strong romping in the cul-de-sac or the nearby woods. Life was an escapade, a mystery they unlocked together as a confederation of girlhood. Theirs was a Nancy Drew world in which the villains would get their comeuppance and they, the sisters six, would emerge unbeaten.

In the meantime, they amused themselves. Attallah, who discovered theater in the second grade, was the center of their revelry. She had a thousand skits, including a solo fistfight that sent her sisters into paroxysms. She would stage some sort of provocation. There would be a shove or an insult. Soon she would escalate to blows, catching herself with roundhouses to the jaw and yanking herself by the hair. Finally she would deliver the decisive stroke and collapse in a shuddering death. The production roused the girls for mosque on many a Sunday.

These and other mornings meant a factory line of cereal bowls on the dining table and hot combs on the stove. The younger girls wore braids, which Betty was forever greasing and parting and plaiting and coiling around their scalps over whimpers and howls. (She forbade them to grow Afros. Legend held that one of the older children had not cared for hers properly, and her hair had fallen out in clumps.) Breakfast brought a stampede of wiry bodies from the nether regions of the house. The girls smashed into one another and fell apart and ran and jumped and quarreled. Most days they reconciled in time for school or cartoons.

The children invented dozens of singing groups and worshipped the Jackson Five. They were always in the living room crooning and caterwauling. Yet for all the gaiety, there was a lingering pain. It was most visible in Attallah, with her bouts of melancholy, and Qubilah, who was brooding and withdrawn. Each daughter felt it and looked to Betty for solace. Gamilah slept with her mother when she was small, using her behind for a pillow. "My first recollection of me was me crying in the backyard 'cause I had to wait for the swing," she wrote in a poem twenty-five years later. "My Momma comforted me gently whispering sweetly you can rock in my arms my baby."

The girls learned to hold onto the widow's arms and legs and spirit, relying on her for sustenance of heart, mind, and body. They could also drive her mad. "We were creative—too creative," Gamilah later said. "Raising all these smart kids, the average mischief isn't gonna happen. We had to do it whole-heartedly." Sometimes the kitchen was the crime scene. The girls almost burned down the house once trying to cook dinner. On another occasion, they baked pies. One child held a stool while another rummaged through the pantry shelves. They mixed the "batter" and shoved it into the oven. After the concoction inflated like a basketball, they pulled it out and slathered it with sugar-water "icing." Then they reached for the canned blueberry filling. By the time Betty got home, the kitchen was awash with flour and goo.

The children were well mannered around their mother, who suffered no foolishness. But when she got into her blue Oldsmobile and took off, they became roguish tree nymphs. Everything they were forbidden to do, they did. They strayed from the block and played tag in the woods and put off their chores. One careworn housekeeper or another was always running behind them. Aunt Ruth Summerford, who spent countless days at the Shabazz home during the girls' childhood, did not spare the switch. Still, the children always managed to steal away for rambles in the grove. Gamilah liked to do so in the nude. Neighbors would call her mother: "Betty, she's at it again." When the widow glanced out the bathroom window, the child's clothes would be strewn in a pile and she would be up in a tree.

The girls often organized the games that they and their mates played in the cul-de-sac. The neighborhood kids knew to keep an eye on the corner. When the widow's car rounded the bend, there would be a wild dispersal of bodies. The accomplices would fly across the street as the daughters vaulted the steps leading to the house and whipped out their notebooks. When Betty sauntered in, the inquisition began. Where's the homework? Had everyone had supper? Were the chores done? She would sleuth out the day's mischief and dole out punishment. Attallah called it the "P." ("Yeah, I'm on the 'P' again this week," she often told her playmates.)

As the daughters reached adolescence, the stakes increased. Jimmying the lock on the telephones with a bobby pin was a favorite routine. One sister would be blathering on the inside phone while another talked on the kitchen line. A third would station herself near the window, peering out the parted venetian blinds. As soon as the widow pulled into the parking lot, the blinds went click, the gossips hung up, the locks snapped shut, and the girls tore up the stairs. "I'm surprised she didn't start talking to herself, dealing with all of us," Gamilah later said.

Then Attallah discovered boys. The development blindsided Betty. Before she knew it, even Ilyasah was giggling and acting womanish. The widow started monitoring the sanitary napkins in the closet, making sure they disappeared at a steady rate. After she banned dating, the older girls simply snuck out. The newspaper boy and the man who mowed the lawn suddenly seemed ripe with possibility. Betty lectured about not running off into the woods with the boys. Not until the twins were teenagers did she permit formal dates. With so many girls hitting puberty in dizzying succession, boys were just too great a menace. "The house must have given off female hormones for miles," Gamilah later said.

Even with the help of the housekeepers and Aunt Ruth, the children frazzled Betty. She tried to be the nurturing mother and stern father, but simply being sole parent to six was more draining than she could have imagined. "I was not reared to take care of myself, let alone six little girls," she later said. She paired the children off, assigning a younger sibling to each older daughter. Attallah, the surrogate mother, knew to mind her sisters and remember the emergency phone numbers while Betty was away. Betty was stunned to discover that love, sharing, and sacrifice were not enough, that what her daughters demanded was greater than the sum of those essentials.

Her flurry of civic activities only deepened the strain. She joined the board of the Westchester Women's Service League. She headed the Mount Vernon Day Care Center PTA, a post that evolved into a board membership and then the presidency of the influential Westchester Day Care Council, which oversaw the county's childcare services. With the appointment came her first office, in nearby White Plains.

After an alarming number of unwed Mount Vernon girls got pregnant, the widow agreed to run a city program for expectant mothers. She taught health classes twice a week, stressing prenatal care while coaching the young women toward their high-school diplomas. Meanwhile she saw to her ambassadorial duties. In the summer of 1969, she toured five African nations with fourteen other black educators on a Rockefeller Foundation grant. (Ruth Summerford kept the girls while she was away.) During the study tour, she visited government and religious schools and "indigenous teachers" in Ghana and Nigeria, two of the lands that had mesmerized Malcolm five years before. Betty was equally spellbound, witnessing firsthand the bond between Africa and African-America that her husband had so passionately preached.

She came home bubbling about the "profound respect" the children she had met showed for their elders, a trait she found sorely lacking in America's youth. Africa's paradoxes depressed her. "I don't understand how a place can be so rich and so poor," she told *Newsweek*. "It brings to mind some of our neighborhoods—complete exploitation." Between the girls and her travels, lectures, and other obligations, the widow barely slept. Yet she could not bring herself to drop any of the duties. The volunteer work fulfilled her. It was exhilarating to feel genuinely qualified, to possess value that was not merely derived. Besides, she was settling an old debt. "To show my appreciation for my being able to deal with the death of Malcolm," she later said, "I have a responsibility to give a little to God."

The children thought she ought to give to the groove, too. They tried to teach her their dances, but she was as stiff as the gleaming hair she set nightly. That she was simply too beat to do the hustle was a reality they would not grasp for years. Betty needed time to recuperate from the pressures of single parenthood and concentrate on forging her career. She began sending the girls away for weeks or more on end, first to elite New England summer camps, then to upscale, largely white boarding schools nearby. They also sampled the black urban world their father had championed, spending the better part of many summers in North Philadelphia.

Betty had occasionally taken them to visit her birth father, Juju, and his wife, Madeline, in Philadelphia before the assassination. Now she dropped the children off for longer stays. They got to know their Uncles Stanley, Shelman, and John (Betty's much younger half-brothers). They played stickball in the street outside Juju's rowhouse and frolicked in sprawling Fairmont Park. The girls were unaccustomed to city life. In the gang-war years, they could not understand why they had to stay indoors. Once, when Shelmon took them for a trolley ride, they did not hop off behind him at the designated stop, and he had to run the car down to retrieve them. They experienced a more Southern brand of discipline in Philadelphia, for Juju swore by the belt. "He still had that stroke," Shelman later recalled.

—

Betty missed the girls while they were away, but at times she was lonely even while their giggles echoed through the house. She longed for Malcolm and the comfort of surrender, for the enveloping warmth of belonging to somebody. Though she had arrived at social affairs with various escorts in her early widowhood, she had not seriously considered remarrying. "I can't even think about marriage because to marry would be admitting that Malcolm is really dead, and although I know he's gone, I don't want the break to be so final," she once said.

She thought even a serious relationship unlikely. The girls, she said, occupied "99 percent" of her time. Besides, she felt too damaged for romance. Her artist clique urged her to remarry to ease the grief, loneliness, and financial burdens. She just laughed. No one seemed to understand the force of Malcolm's lingering presence. For her, he was *there*, and his ghost drove off suitors. The saintliness of public widowhood and Betty's suspicion of those who hazarded advances made her no more approachable. For all her fierce independence, she also feared Black America's disapproval. "People don't want me to have a boyfriend," she once told Amina Baraka jokingly. Friends, strangers, and journalists were forever asking the widow if she was going to get hitched again. She allowed only a dim possibility in the distant future.

For a time, she said "no" so violently that people wondered what had gone wrong between her and Malcolm. She may actually have declined at least one formal proposal early in her widowhood. A colleague later confronted her with the rumor that Muammar el-Qadaffi, leader of the Islamic state of Libya, had extended his hand to her as an act of chivalry in the lean years. "Could be," Betty replied with typical coyness. "But I'm not about being part of the harem."

"My biggest fight is being alone," Betty once confessed. She kidded about the predicament. "Say Rev, why don't the fellas flirt with me?" she asked a comrade. He pondered this for a moment. "I think you got this atmosphere about you that says, 'Look, but don't touch!'" he replied. Sometimes she could not laugh away the solitude. When the children were asleep or away, when she could not ring her female friends because the phone would wake their husbands, loneliness clasped her like a noose. "I wouldn't wish her life on anybody," Gamilah later said. "Is being married to my father seven years enough to carry you for the rest of your life?"

There were gentlemen callers, of course. One even managed to win her heart. Eventually, she broke it off. No doubt there were many complications, but it did not help that he started smoking pot. Always a fetching and shapely woman, the widow began gaining weight. Food was a fleeting solace. Yet nothing could soothe her a few years later when the man returned. He marched up to the front porch, rang the bell, and started pacing nervously. Betty was horrified. She thought she had gotten fat. "I'm rushing to leave," she shouted, then began crying softly. The visitor stood on the porch for a few minutes, staring at the door. Finally he whispered, "Okay, Betty," and left.

Chapter Fourteen

"DR. SHABAZZ"

—

"I don't want to make somebody else. I want to make myself."
—"Sula" (of Toni Morrison's *Sula*)

Betty in the early years of her widowhood metabolized more pain than she could have imagined. She gave herself to her daughters, cutting them a path in life beyond that of "victim." She struggled to personify her husband's memory, stepping into a public role snarled in the chaos of murder and martyrdom. She discovered service as self-therapy. As she traveled the country and ventured overseas, she began to confront Malcolm's meaning, to accept his notice that though the oppressed are not to blame for their oppression, they alone are responsible for their freedom. "People ask me, 'How were you able to be so strong?'" she later said. "I wasn't strong. I was weak. I cried and I cried. But I knew that when I finished crying, I would have to get up and go on with my life."

Doing so required no small evolution. Her first triumph had been to remain intact. "You talk about a woman who fought for her dignity," Amina Baraka later said. "She was determined not to be dragged down. She was determined not to become the stereotype." But the memory of defenselessness never dimmed. Her sense of dependency—on the efforts of the Concerned Mothers; on the generosity of comrades and strangers; on royalties, trust funds, and lecture fees—hovered over the feat of her survival. Though money was no longer as desperate a crisis, she needed a passage to economic security. She also wanted respectability and an identity beyond widow or mother. So in the fall of 1969, she drove forty minutes south to Jersey City State College (now New Jersey City University) and enrolled to finish the bachelor's degree she had abandoned fifteen years before for the promise of New York and a nursing career.

She carried a full load at Jersey City, making As and Bs in math, public health, and safety classes, and finishing her B.A. in a year with relative anonymity. "It's so peaceful," she told a reporter. "Nobody bothers me." She did the course work for a master's in health administration in two years, though she never completed her thesis on sickle cell anemia. That she earned an advanced degree as a full-time student is phenomenal, considering that she was simultaneously rounding the lecture circuit, upholding many of her parochial service duties, and steering her elder daughters through adolescence.

Though her social life withered, Betty welcomed the rigor. She had struggled all her adult life—first to become the dutiful Mrs. Malcolm X, then to transcend the Widow Shabazz. In returning to school, she hung both mantles at yesterday's doorsill. She talked about becoming a college professor. She hoped, as a model for her children, to embody Malcolm's adage that "education is our passport to the future, for tomorrow belongs to the people who prepare for it today." She dreamed about a diploma, the parchment that Malcolm had sometimes flouted in debates as a shingle for the white man's Negro—and yet privately coveted. A brooding day or two after the forty-seventh anniversary of her husband's birth, she telephoned Dr. Norma Jean Anderson at the University of Massachusetts–Amherst and announced that she wanted a doctorate. "Come," Anderson said, "let's talk."

———

Anderson was an associate dean for student affairs at Amherst, then one of few blacks to hold such a title at a major university. She had built a reputation for recruiting minorities and was a staunch advocate for students of color in higher education at a time when liberal financial aid and new opportunities were swelling the school's population of black

Ph.D. candidates. She had attracted many nontraditional students, and had also had some experience dealing with public figures (she was supervising Bill and Camille Cosby's graduate work at the time). Somebody had thought her a good contact for Betty and had passed along her name.

Not long after Betty's call in May 1972, the two women sat down and plotted a course to the widow's terminal degree. "She had a void to fill and a contribution to make," Anderson later remembered. They decided that she would spend three days per week in Amherst. She would arrive on Monday and leave Wednesday evening, attending classes during the day and spending her nights at a hotel. The unorthodox schedule did not daunt Betty. Anderson helped arrange for financial aid, and Betty became a student again. She chose to pursue an Ed.D. with a specialty in higher education administration and curriculum development, finally resolving the struggle between her passion for education and her love of the health sciences.

During the next three years, she rose early at the start of each week and cranked up the Oldsmobile for the two-and-a-half hour pilgrimage to Amherst. She was a bright if weary student. Her classmates and professors knew who she was. No one made much of a fuss, perhaps because she seemed so ordinary. Her luminous skin and eyes seemed to intrigue the men more than the historical mantle she wore. She talked and laughed with a few of the suitors who reminded her that she was lovely, but nobody presented much of a distraction.

She was hungry for conversation, though, and she and Anderson soon became confidantes. Anderson could not think of a woman of such stature as her mentee. What she found most divine about Betty, however, was her nonchalance. The widow was fiercely private about her daughters and the horrors of her past. Yet her presence was mild, and she and the dean relished lighthearted lunches and conversation about the promise of lush life. "We shared wisdom," Anderson later said. "We talked about spirituality." They also discussed where they were headed and whence they had come. There were times when Betty seemed immune to melancholy. Anderson admired her determination to dwell in the present and marveled at the luster that she had preserved through tragedy.

Betty shared her dreams for herself and her daughters. She told the dean that she wanted them to forgive the world for their father's death. She wanted them to live fully and richly, without vendetta. Though she had no delusion that she herself was a leader, she wanted the chance to contribute to a good fight—one that was distinctly hers. Her love for Malcolm had not ebbed. Sometimes she darkened when reminiscing about him, but the recollections were more often sugary. She would mention something he had tucked under the mattress for her or that she had whispered at his collar. She dealt with the grief by staying busy; work, she said, kept her sane. She had found that the university offered refuge from the trials of parenting six.

Her absence was hard on the girls. Betty took comfort in the fact that they were in elite schools and presumably less likely to go astray during her trips to Amherst (though at times they resented the parochial education). She was always on the phone with them, dispatching long-distance solace or guidance. The children had the best caretakers in the sturdy and straight-talking Aunt Ruth and in the chain of housekeepers. Sometimes they ate and spent the night at the home of a surrogate aunt across the street. But there were frantic moments when ten-year-old Gamilah wondered if the forces that had robbed her of a father were not wrenching her mother away, too. Years later, she remembered running down the footpath from summer camp toward the widow. "And she just looked kind of like gray," the fourth child recalled, "like she hadn't slept or she was sick or something. And that's when things started changing."

Betty tried to soften the transition. She maintained the battery of long-distance calls from Amherst. Sometimes she drove to campus, attended class, got right back into her car, and headed home. Before her Monday-morning departures, there were tender rituals. She would arrange an outing, or spend hours washing, brushing, and braiding the girls' hair. The bustling schedule of dance, theatre, and music classes kept them occupied after school, and Attallah, now in her mid-teens, took on more responsibility in the care of her siblings. But the children realized that Betty, their matriarch and metronome, had another master. And this obligation, besides slicing in half their time with her, seemed to be corroding her spirit. "Why does she always look tired? Why doesn't she want to play with us anymore?" wondered the younger children. Only the older ones sensed the weight of her mission. "We knew she was grieving and that she was working very hard—we were just too little to realize how much of either," Attallah later said. The daughters would not understand the depths of their mother's labors and sacrifice until well into womanhood. All they knew at the time was that she was always buried in books and spirals of papers.

Wednesday was reunion night. The widow would trudge through the door and welcome the onslaught of hugs with a weary smile. But an odd lethargy had replaced her strut. When studying, she often hushed the girls with stern looks or shipped them across the street to the neighbors. She was a destined soul who never forgot that the seemingly infinite work was for the children's sake as much as her own. She was mindful of their vulnerabilities. "She had a sixth sense that was incredible," Gamilah later remembered. But having lost their father, the girls now considered the dreadful possibility that they were losing some portion of their mother. In their own time, each would mourn the vanishing of the block mom who had once chaperoned expeditions to the park.

In those years, Betty did not sleep so much as black out when the opportunity presented itself. For all the rigors of single parenthood and her studies, she remained committed to several of the local organizations that had shaped her transition from housebound wife to graduate student. She directed Westchester County's Community Action Group (a service outfit) for a year and sat on the board of College Careers (a foundation for disadvantaged youngsters) while seeing to her duties with the Day Care Council of Westchester. Her desire to serve the community had deepened, as had her need for sisterhood. Hoping to fulfill both, she joined the New York Alumnae Chapter of Delta Sigma Theta in April 1974.

Founded at Howard University in 1913, Delta Sigma Theta, like other black fraternities and sororities, had played an integral role in the struggle for racial justice and opportunity in the twentieth century. One of the most distinguished African-American women's organizations, Delta counted in its ranks such dignitaries as National Council of Negro Women President Dorothy Height, U.S. Ambassador Patricia Roberts Harris, and Shirley Chisholm, the first black congresswoman. Malcolm comrade Fannie Lou Hamer and Betty allies Ruby Dee and Nikki Giovanni were among the activists who would accept honorary Delta memberships. Mrs. Malcolm X, who had yet to rise to such eminence, longed instead to become a full-fledged member (with voting privileges). Novella Nelson backed her decision. "Join it," she told her friend, "because then you'll truly get to know the sisters."

Nelson, herself a Delta, thought the sorority's black professional network would empower the widow as she finished her education and ventured into the career world. Betty, who had dreamed of Delta since her days as a Del Sprite in Detroit, needed little convincing. With the blessing of a past national president of the organization whom she had befriended, she made the call. Mary Redd was the "soror" who called back. The prospect of pledging Malcolm's wife left the social worker cotton-mouthed. "I was as nervous as I could be," she later said. The widow was no more composed as she prepared to address Redd, who would be her dean of pledges. The two stumbled through their first conversation, and Betty thereafter became a "pyramid"—a Delta pledge. She and Redd, who would become a dear friend, spoke regularly during the six-week initiation. The widow wanted to know exactly what she was in for. "Big Sister," she asked, "what's going to happen to me?"

Whatever happened, Betty was proud to have pledged, and in later years boasted at Delta conventions about having "crossed the burning sands." She remained active in the sorority throughout her later years, appearing at social affairs and helping support service initiatives aimed at addressing the educational and health needs of black children. In December 1980, she became a charter member of the organization's North Manhattan Alumnae Chapter, an achievement she was especially proud of. She loved Delta and was both a natural and a novelty in its circles. Sorors often approached her with awe and caution, their heads full of the media-manufactured Malcolm. Some of the sisters expected corollary ferocity from his widow. Many were surprised (and more than a few were relieved) when they discovered, instead, Betty. She, of course, wanted what many of them had—career success. The indigence of sudden widowhood was a circumstance that she wished to leave far behind. "I will never be caught in that position again," she told Redd.

It was this sense of purpose that inspired the forty-year-old widow's trip to Addis Ababa, Ethiopia, in February 1975 to attend the twenty-fourth Ordinary Session of the Organization of African Unity's Council of Ministers. She was to be an informal observer at the gathering of the OAU, which thirty-two of the continent's independent states had formed in 1963 to harness Africa's human and natural resources. The OAU represented a profound attempt at post-colonial African solidarity. In spirit, it was a monument to Pan-Africanism, which envisions a potent, united Africa in which the destinies of all Africans and African descendants converge. It was the assembled statesmen of the OAU to whom Malcolm in 1964 had appealed for help in bringing the U.S. before the World Court, and it was the OAU that had inspired his Organization of Afro-American Unity, also formed that year.

When Mrs. Malcolm X arrived for her own encounter with the OAU, it encompassed forty-two sovereign nations representing more than four hundred million citizens. Her status as a martyr's widow—a martyr who, more than any other figure, had widened the lens through which Black America and Black Africa viewed one another—won her audiences with several ambassadors and government ministers, some of whom had received Malcolm during his epic tours of the continent.

Betty had come to Ethiopia more as a student than a dignitary. She intended to use the data she collected at the one-week summit to finish her doctorate. She conducted interviews with more than three dozen delegates at the conference and with the OAU's executive secretary in New York. She analyzed documents outlining agreements between the

OAU and other international bodies, including the Arab League and the United Nations. She scrutinized the OAU's initiatives in educational development and drought relief. In the spring of 1975, she hunkered down to write her dissertation—"Organization of African Unity (Organisation de L'Unité Africane): Its Role in Education."

It was a sweeping topic, but the University of Massachusetts School of Education finally accepted Betty's proposal. In choosing to examine the OAU, she was confronting a subject largely foreign to her. Her access to top African dignitaries that February had enthralled her nonetheless. She had returned to the United States impassioned, eager to share her insights on the organization that had so engrossed her husband. Writing the dissertation would prove to be one of the great trials of her academic life. She was forever grateful to the advisors and mentors who buoyed her when "dismay set in" that she could not see it through. She persevered, as she always had. And in the summer of 1975—through despair, tears, sleep deprivation, and oaths hurled upward in the night—she finished.

The treatise was remarkable not for what it said, but for what it symbolized. Betty was not a gifted writer or theorist. She devoted most of the dissertation to a tedious description of the OAU's composition and structure. But the work was a measure of the intellectual distance she had traveled since her insular days as housewife. The widow touched upon some of the principles of Pan-Africanism and African socialism (including universal health care and education) that her husband had shuffled and reshuffled during his final struggles for ideological clarity. Betty wrote of the former philosophy that it "rejects both white racialism and black chauvinism. It stands for racial, political, and cultural co-existence on the basis of absolute equality and respect for human personality. Its vision stretches beyond the limited frontiers of the nation-state."

She sidestepped the debate over whether the OAU should function as a loose alliance of sovereign nations or as a kind of "United States of Africa," declaring that the continent's indigenous occupants should determine Africa's future rather than its former colonial masters or its sons and daughters in the Diaspora. She did submit, however, that Africa should be one "with regard to independence, leadership, and fraternity." The government ministers she had interviewed in Addis Ababa had clearly impressed her, as did the aims and design of the OAU itself. She was optimistic—perhaps romantically so—about the group's prospects for developing the continent. Her praise of its efforts to protect human rights and propel developing countries toward self-sufficiency largely ignored its weaknesses. (Ethnic strife, coups, border disputes, dependency on superpowers, a meager budget, the economic vestiges of colonialism, and deep ideological fissures had enfeebled the organization from the start.)

Instead Betty fixed on the dream of African unity and its implications for advancing university-level education on the continent, just as Malcolm had fixed on the dream of African/Afro-American solidarity and its power to deliver the Dark World. The widow was not irredeemably Pollyannaish. She acknowledged that "colonization and exploitation have left the continent mutilated." Still, the OAU parlay had filled her with hope for the new Africa, searing in her mind the image of Africans planning Africa for the Africans. "Some were Muslim, some were Christian, some were Hindu, and some believed in the indigenous religions," she later said. "There was a time when they would not have spoken to someone from a different religious, tribal, or educational level. But now these leaders sat together in the same room, at the same conference table, improving the quality of life of their people."

Intent on improving the quality of her own life, Betty successfully defended her dissertation that July. The morning of her appearance before the doctoral committee found her sick with self-doubt. She telephoned one of her advisors (who, as she later noted, happened to be white) and announced that she could not go through with it. "Oh, yes you can!" came the reply. Thus "Sister Betty," whom an unwed mother had turned over to a kindly older couple, who had married a revolutionary and witnessed her own gruesome transition to widowhood, who was unbeaten as single mother and survivor, between 1965 and 1975 rose from desperation to doctor. The children were there for graduation, hollering and carrying on. The widow beamed, confident that she would no longer be a captive of the past. She believed that Malcolm, who had dreamed of returning to school, would have been proud. "We need to be the first ones in the classroom and the last ones to leave," the minister had told a friend in his last days. "I want you to buy a Bible and a dictionary, and we're going to school."

Betty's return to the classroom the following year was more complex than the one Malcolm had envisioned. She had held part-time positions while completing her Ed.D., teaching remedial reading at Westchester Community College and childhood health care at a local high school. Overall, her professional experience was sketchy. Her task now was to land a job worthy of her education. Yet precisely how one did so was a mystery to her. She had never circulated a résumé or hunted for a job. She knew nothing of applications or interviews. What she knew was people. Her allies included figures of the black establishment and the grassroots. With a boost from both camps, she found herself by the fall of 1976 at Medgar Evers College.

Then composed of a few ragged buildings near black Bedford Stuyvesant and a neighborhood of Hasidic Jews, Medgar Evers College was a miniscule urban campus in the Crown Heights section of Central Brooklyn. Its 2,500 students made it the runt of the City University of New York (CUNY) system's eighteen schools. Some of its faculty, staff, and students called it the CUNY "stepchild" because of the abuse they felt the college had received from its city and state overseers during its short history. Medgar Evers College was born of struggle in 1969, as Betty was emerging in earnest on the public scene. CUNY officials had chartered the school after the cry for equal access to higher education in Brooklyn—one of the largest black communities in the Western Hemisphere—intensified with the Black Power ethos. The Medgar Evers College battle belonged to a larger black and Puerto Rican crusade for greater minority presence at the City University, which had traditionally served waves of white immigrants and native New Yorkers while neglecting many of the underprepared students of color facing shoddy high schools and poverty in the city's boroughs.

Fed up with the inequity, black and brown students finally paralyzed Harlem's City College with clamorous protests. From the maelstrom, a transfigured City University had emerged. Some of its campuses continued to draw mostly from white, middle-class neighborhoods, but system-wide reforms, including an "open admissions" policy and a massive remedial education program, increased the racial diversity of the schools and attracted new tides of needy students. Medgar Evers College pupils had been overwhelmingly black (90 percent), working class, and adult (age twenty-six on average) from the start. What truly distinguished the college, however, was its largely black-female faculty, and its 75 percent female student body. Medgar Evers reflected black Brooklyn. Its flavor was international (nearly half of the students were of Caribbean, Latin American, or African origin) and maternal (two-thirds of the women were mothers, many of them single heads of household).

The school's identity as a place where struggling black women and single mothers strove, a launching pad for the folk Malcolm had championed, would win Betty's devotion. "This is what's real," she later told friends. She had distant ties to Medgar Evers College long before it became her home, for many of the activists who for years had lobbied CUNY's rulers to establish the college were spiritual descendants of Malcolm. Some of them, including Malcolm historian and disciple Preston Wilcox, served on the school's community council, a permanent body with an advisory role. Nationalists such as former Brooklyn CORE president Sonny Carson, who sat on the search committee to select Medgar Evers College's first president, had even talked about renaming the college in Malcolm's honor. Betty agreed that it would be a fine gesture, but according to Carson, CUNY officials scuttled the idea.

The compromise was a college christened Medgar Evers College, after the slain NAACP field secretary. Yet Carson's crowd never retreated fully on the question of a Malcolm tribute. As early as 1967, he and his brethren at the School of Common Sense had received Betty as a first lady of militant struggle at rallies organized in her husband's memory. "We said, 'Would you please come to the street?'"

Carson later remembered. His group had helped raise funds for her and the children in the early years after the assassination. Once the nationalists learned that the widow had completed her doctorate and needed a job, they demanded that Medgar Evers College find a place for her. "Of course there was opposition from the general administration," Carson later said, speaking of some CUNY officials and faculty members. "Most of the academicians, they resented Malcolm's widow being there because it linked the school to us, and they didn't want to do too much with us."

Betty also had mainstream support. Acting out of allegiance for a martyr who was winning the late affection of some of the black elite, and out of respect for a widow who was much easier to endorse openly in life, New York City Clerk David Dinkins, an influential Democrat who later became the city's first black mayor, put in a good word with the proper bureaucrats. "I think Medgar Evers was lucky to have her and would have given her a job no matter what," he later said. Betty's name began circling the halls of the college, which had begun classes in 1971. She formally approached the school's administrators in late 1975. Dr. Richard Trent, its first president, took to the idea of having Mrs. Malcolm X on board, and ordered Dr. Hilda Richards, chair of the school's health sciences division, to make it so.

"She was rather shy," Richards later remembered. The prospect of teaching at the college excited the soft-spoken widow, but she needed stewarding through the application process. She had nursing credentials, but no consistent experience as a working nurse. She had a doctorate, but no solid professional background. Though the résumé she handed Richards brimmed with ambassadorial exploits, the document itself was in disarray. Richards had it retyped. She talked to Betty about her experiences, gleaning from the narrative the expertise that would qualify the widow for a faculty position. "Someone asked could we get someone more qualified," Richards later said. "My answer was, 'Yes, but we're going to hire her.' This was the rare opportunity we had to support our own."

Over the mumbling of a handful of faculty members who thought the appointment political, Medgar Evers College in January 1976 hired

Dr. Betty Shabazz as an associate professor of health sciences with a concentration in nursing. Her salary was an unremarkable $18,430. Her arrival was hardly more extraordinary. She peeked around the door of the school's health sciences office one morning and said, "Good morning." She seemed agreeably mild. Though she held herself with care, her new colleagues sensed that she was one of them—a woman looking to serve the neglected and explore her field. "Why did she want to come to Medgar Evers?" Dr. Bertie Gilmore, an instructor in the nursing program, later said. "That's the question people wanted to know. And she answered it almost immediately. She, too, was concerned about the plight of her people….She could empathize with people struggling to take care of their family and meet ends."

The health sciences division was another attraction for the widow. When Betty arrived, it consisted mainly of a core physical education course and a nursing program that had been accredited only two years before. Administrators hoped to develop a more comprehensive allied health discipline to offer students curricular diversity and produce graduates who could better serve the dire health needs of Central Brooklyn and the inner city. Betty had embraced the mandate to create such a degree-granting program. Yet in the end she was able only to design and teach health administration classes. She was unaccustomed to writing curriculum, negotiating rigid City University and state bureaucracy, and dealing with students who strained under a welter of academic deficiencies. "She thought that if you really want something done, all you need to do is talk to the right people," Gilmore later said. "Well, that didn't work."

Betty had discovered the embattled soul of Medgar Evers College, an institution "in diligent search of itself," as the *New York Times* later proposed. The school would have had a tough enough task offering hard-pressed students remedial courses and a solid liberal arts education without the burden of paltry budgets and drafty buildings (including a converted furniture warehouse). But Medgar Evers also faced crises of identity—it was a senior college that offered both associate and baccalaureate degrees—and survival. City University's overseers threatened to close the school in 1976 after a fiscal crunch forced the system to impose tuition, ending the open-admissions policy. Medgar Evers College faculty and students struck back, launching a fierce lobbying campaign that flared into a takeover of a CUNY office. That September, as Betty began teaching in the health sciences division, the school downgraded to a community college, losing funding and resources and gaining a deep sense of persecution at the hands of its mostly white overseers. The City University was itself already confronting a contentious salary discrimination lawsuit filed on behalf of a host of its female professors and otherwise wrangling with the politics of affirmative action and redress.

However sharply the ship was lilting, Betty was happy to be on board. City University's faculty included such distinguished Malcolmites as John Henrik Clarke. Its student population made it one of the world's most valuable institutions of higher learning for blacks and minorities. The pupils at Medgar Evers College were Malcolm's traditional constituents. There in the heart of Brooklyn, beside African hair-braiding boutiques, the projects, and the sacred grounds of what had once been Ebbets Field (where the fleet Jackie Robinson had burst into baseball), Betty discovered an oasis, a wellspring of colleagues, mentors, girlfriends, rivals, and confidantes. Over the years, as her profile rose, she would wave off job offers from other institutions, many of them better known. "At Medgar Evers they cherished the ground that she walked on," Gamilah later said. "For them, she *was* that mother on the block."

Some of the Medgar Evers College faculty got the early misimpression that Mrs. Malcolm X was demure. What they took for the softness of Muslim femininity was in fact caution, a quality that the widow stored in the wells of her heart. Medgar Evers College was overwhelmingly black, but Betty knew how unkind black could be, and for a time walked gingerly among her colleagues. As the months passed, she lowered her guard, though not all her suspicions. That President Trent was fond of her inspired some comfort, and it did not hurt that many of the professors and staff treated her like the Holy Mother. (Though Malcolm's vindication in the black establishment had only just begun, he was already a near deity in the halls of Medgar Evers College.)

Betty enjoyed a certain deference throughout her twenty-one years at the institution, but her air of immortality began dissipating soon after she arrived. Her newness to professorial life and the professional world demanded humility. When it grew clear that she was there to teach and learn rather than to reign, she found that most of her health sciences peers welcomed her. She identified those she could talk to in confidence and those she would have to steer clear of. Yet almost everyone she encountered at the school understood that she wished to be somebody in her own right. She acknowledged that "Mrs. Malcolm X" had at times been her visa. "You know what your strength is," she told one administrator. "This is something that I have."

She had not asked for the identity. Yet it was her karma, and she was learning to use what fate had dealt to accomplish what she willed. "Betty wasn't a person who evoked sympathy," a professor in the division later said. The women at Medgar Evers wondered how a woman could absorb so much misery. They marveled at her stamina and carriage, and at the way she swept across campus, shaping every room she entered.

Betty was free in her dignity. She dragged coworkers into Delancy Street shops for bargain hunts and hoarded free department store samples in her junky office. (Single motherhood had made her both pennywise and cheap.) When she drafted a colleague for lunch, there was no rushing the meals or the luxurious conversation, which invariably revolved around the private life of the day's conscript. Her chats were infamously epic. "I'm going to Betty's office," a colleague would tell her secretary. "Come knock on the door after an hour."

The widow enjoyed diplomatic immunity at Medgar Evers College. She would pinch a colleague's straining skirt and crinkle her nose. "Oh God, Girl. Look how you spreading." Anyone else would have wound up on their behind; Betty got away with it. She was health conscious, but with a tremendous appetite. On good days, she sent a coworker to a natural-foods store nearby for carrot or broccoli juice. On the best days, they binged on chicken wings. Betty was twice the size she had been when she married Malcolm. Still, her gorgeous, thick hair was always impeccable, and she scolded other faculty members when their makeup was amiss, or when they showed up in scuffed sneakers: "How you going to please your man lookin' like *that?*"

She fished for compliments passionately. "Lookin' good today, honey?" she would ask male colleagues. "You lookin' good, Sister Betty," they chorused. The widow talked fast and walked fearlessly. She was a font of sensibility and sound advice. "Girl, maybe you need to leave that man," she would counsel a young woman in the corridor. To her peers she was a sisterly meddler. "You still with that guy?" she would, not unkindly, ask a coworker whose beau was in prison. To her pupils, she was a phenomenon. Many of them struggled financially to stay in school, and some days, with a mother's discretion, she handed extra lunches to needy students. "Malcolm was the poor people's hero," she reminded colleagues. Her far-flung travels informed her conversations with international students, and she was the idol of matriculating moms.

She became the caretaker who counseled a fellow professor after a miscarriage, who unwound scarves from her neck and draped them around the shoulders of a colleague she adored. But you never saw the whole Betty. She often repelled those who drew too close. "Eventually she would mistreat you," one of her many secretaries said, "and you would leave." The widow suffered no fools. She could be brusque and uncouth when it suited her needs. "If she liked you, she liked you," a colleague remembered. "And boy, if she didn't like you…" Those who heard Betty cuss like a sailor had either incurred her wrath or become her friend.

She wore Malcolm's memory like a shawl that swept the feet of passersby. "Everything she said about him made you smile," one woman remembered. She was always humanizing the minister, reminiscing about what he liked to eat or how he would crush the children with hugs when he got home, or simply producing nuggets of his wisdom when she felt it was appropriate. "My husband says find the good and celebrate it," she would proclaim. She wanted him represented well and often. One of Medgar Evers College's Black History Month celebrations failed to honor him. "What happened to the brother?" she asked its coordinator. Dr. Safiya Bandele sometimes yanked the martyr's scholarly looking portrait off the widow's office wall and pretended to kiss it. "And she would like jump over the table to knock me out," the women's studies professor later recalled. "I said, 'Ooh, you wanna call me the B-word, right?'" Betty would lunge: "Leave my husband alone!" Bandele would parry: "The man is dead." Betty would settle back into her seat. "No, he's not."

The widow loved Medgar Evers College's mission to uplift blacks, particularly the black underclass, and she was happy to do her part. Like many of her colleagues, she spent much of the late 1970s developing programs, sitting on committees, and grappling with the question of how the self-described "college for developing people" could best serve the sons and daughters of the African Diaspora in Brooklyn. She was a "guest" speaker during Medgar Evers College programs on women and the black family, and in 1979 helped plan the college's Malcolm X lecture series. The rest of her time she devoted to teaching general health education classes, including a course on the evils of alcohol, tobacco, and drugs. She enjoyed the exchange with students, but she tended to be disorganized, and she struggled to master the rhythm of grading papers and lecturing.

President Trent decided in 1980 that she would be more valuable to the college in a purely administrative role (she was already overseeing the health sciences department) and promoted her generously that September to Director of Institutional Advancement. A year later, she was tenured at a salary of $23,093. Trent guessed that the widow could best use her talents and connections raising funds for Medgar Evers College, and that she would not regret leaving the classroom. He was right. Betty's widowhood had afforded her some ambassadorial experience. Although her disposition was hardly suited for true diplomacy, the art of emptying pockets requires both finesse and bluntness—qualities that she possessed in bundles. By the mid-1980s, she had become a mighty booster for the college.

She found her niche in administration. She enjoyed the prestige and prerogatives of the office, and the broad scope of the work. She spent her early mornings sipping coffee, sifting through the cataract of mail on her desk and planning her day, which often included meetings and phone calls on behalf of the college president and royal duties as Mrs. Malcolm X. She was content in Trent's cabinet. Yet there were tensions.

Her colleagues had long since accepted her humanness, with all its elegance and acerbity, but students were awestruck. They idolized her as their hero's mate and at times almost swooned in her presence. She clashed with that iconic identity in her early years at the college. Students were always bursting with questions about Malcolm. Betty's responses were usually polite but brief. At times she was sharp. She appreciated the love, but even awe can aggravate. She rarely mustered the spirited reception her admirers expected. Many Muslim students felt entitled to special access, which the widow could not always provide in those hectic times. "She was never allowed to have her privacy unless she was adamant about demanding it," a colleague later said. "I can understand why she insisted on having people at arm's length."

There were also pressures within the faculty and administration. Some felt that Trent had favored Betty, catapulting her into one of the college's top offices in the time most of her peers took to earn tenure. Before the widow gained momentum in her new role, there were fleeting whispers that she was not raising enough money. Trent had given her free reign to travel and lecture abroad, and some of her colleagues grumbled that she was representing Malcolm the man more assiduously than Medgar the institution.

In time, deeper strains surfaced. Medgar Evers College was a fountainhead of black protest whose infancy had been as turbulent as its origin. Only a year after Trent's arrival in 1971, students and faculty had staged a failed coup, denouncing the firing of several professors who had challenged the president's leadership. Uprisings flared over the next few years as student demands for black studies, a day-care center, decent facilities, and the retention of activist faculty went unfulfilled. By the time CUNY trustees stripped the college of its four-year status in 1976, many of Medgar Evers College's malcontents had begun to think of Trent as the handmaid of a hostile power structure. The school did not mellow with time. When New York Mayor Ed Koch, whose policies many blacks and Latinos decried during his three terms in office, later visited the campus, a small but noisy throng of students trailed him through the halls and stairwells chanting "Get racist Koch out of black Brooklyn!"

If black nationalism was the heart of Medgar Evers College, feminism was its pulse. Contemporary black feminism flowered during the 1970s with the deepening of black women's self-awareness. It was then that many black women began openly confronting the patriarchy of the Civil Rights, Black Nationalism, and Black Power movements. They rejected the misogyny that had inspired Black Muslims to define women as property, that had informed Stokely Carmichael's remark that "the only position for women in SNCC is prone," and that had entitled cultural nationalists to glorify submissiveness as the birthright of black womanhood. Often suspicious of the mainstream women's movement, which they saw as rife with the dominant culture's racism, black female writers, scholars, activists, and politicians began openly challenging the institutions of their oppression.

The fusion of pro-black and pro-women politics shaped the personal and professional identities of many Medgar Evers College women. "I was conscious of black at one time, and only black," remembered Dr. Zala Chandler, then the school's tutorial coordinator. "And then I started to recognize that even in this picture of blackness, women were consistently left out. I began to develop a feminist consciousness that complemented my black consciousness." Betty had moderate outlooks on both. She was a firm believer in women's independence, single motherhood having thrust the condition upon her. Yet her style was more coy than confrontational. "She would always remind me that you catch more flies with honey than vinegar," Bandele later said. "Sometimes I would come out of my woman's bag. And she'd say, 'That's not necessary. You have to be strategic to get what you want.' I'd say, 'Yes, but I'm not the flirty type. You do that.'"

Some Medgar Evers College women were disappointed that the widow was not outwardly political. They thought she was too accommodating to the Trent administration, whose policies they considered sexist and conservative. Yet they admired the role she had played as Malcolm's wife. They marveled at her strength in rearing her daughters in his absence and earning her doctorate. They learned from her, too. She taught them to be methodical, tactful, and persistent. She warned them to avoid the psychological swirl of turbulent souls and never to "let those men diminish you."

Other lessons they found less palatable. "You need to really be careful because you out there and you think you got your troops, but you turn around and your troops aren't there," she told Chandler, then an exuberant activist. The widow's caution to her insurgent peers was subtle but sincere. She urged them to consider their families before they plunged into struggle. She assured them that martyrdom was not as glorious as they imagined, reminding them that the masses had forgotten many of the women and men who had perished on their behalf. Her colleagues recognized that her mission was not to overturn society, but to seek reform through education. Most accepted this and embraced her as a sister among sisters who was reachable in many ways and untouchable in others. So it was until the Revolution of 1982.

Its veterans remember it as a battle for the soul of Medgar Evers College, but the uprising generated such turmoil that one administrator dubbed it the "De-Revolution." Long-smoldering grievances finally ignited that spring when Trent refused to appear at a biennial student government assembly in which the school's president traditionally addresses the student body. Angry faculty and students had tried fruitlessly to meet with him to discuss issues they considered crucial to the college's survival and growth. First among their complaints was the lack of child care at the institution, a resource that an independent commission of educators had identified as critical if Medgar Evers was to adequately serve its large population of single mothers.

Students and faculty also charged the Trent administration with mismanaging funds, fomenting hostility between the institution and the surrounding community, neglecting crumbling facilities, and stifling academic freedom.

Trent's disclosure in the *Village Voice* that he did not believe in black studies—another student and faculty demand—kindled the discontent. ("In a random sample of 10 students," the *Voice's* profile of the school reported, "none knew who Medgar Evers was.") Medgar Evers College students launched a two-week "strike" in March, issuing a list of demands. In the separate faculty and student votes that followed, a large majority of the college community supported resolutions censuring Trent. Students and professors formed a coalition to oust the president and remake the school in the spirit of Medgar Evers the man, a resurrection they said would end hiring discrimination and sexual harassment and promote a new sense of self-determination on campus.

The campaign took a decisive turn in April when students began what would become a 110-day occupation of Trent's office, which they converted into a childcare center. They named the makeshift day-care and command post after Ella Baker, SNCC's matriarch. The coalition renewed its call for the president's ouster, defying CUNY efforts to end the sit-in. By the summer, the affair had burgeoned. Representative Chisholm; grassroots groups such as the Sisterhood of Black Single Mothers; and scores of Brooklyn educators, clergy, activists, and shopkeepers backed the students. The Center for Constitutional Rights provided legal counsel. *Amsterdam News* and *New York Times* editorials backed the coalition's main demands. With President Reagan's extreme conservatism dominating national politics, the uprising at Medgar Evers College had come to represent the black woman's struggle for opportunity, educational justice, and dignity.

For Betty, it was a debacle. Trent stayed off campus during the early weeks of the takeover, trying vainly to drive students and faculty back to class. For days he refused to talk to reporters, instead deputizing Betty as his spokeswoman. She was less than ecstatic about the job. "This was indeed a hot potato," remembered Dr. Andrée Nicola McLaughlin, then a dean at the college and one of the coalition leaders. The widow's office phone trilled with journalists seeking the administration's response to the crisis. Betty announced that she would field all inquiries, then said she was too busy to discuss the matter. "Dr. Shabazz is not in," she told one caller in exasperation.

"There was a lot of pressure on her," McLaughlin later said. "People wanted to gain access to the flashpoints of controversy, and Trent would not avail himself to the public." The internal strain on the widow was even more trying than the media assault. A powerful bond had developed between the students and faculty. They believed in the righteousness of their struggle and shared the perils of defiance, risking suspension, pink slips, and even arrest. Betty was clearly on the administration's side, and thus an outsider to the sisterhood. "Wasn't no fence-sitting," a veteran of the upheaval later recalled. Behind the barracks, there was mixed response to the widow's role. Some protestors thought she had betrayed "The Cause" (and, by extension, her husband's ideals) by trying to salvage Trent's credibility. Others felt that the president had put her in a tough spot by thrusting the unsavory duty upon her.

In the end, the depth of Betty's conflict was unclear. Whatever sympathies she may have had for the coalition, she still had a mortgage and children to support. She was unwilling to forfeit her promising career and had no desire to fling herself into a crusade that some administrators and professors feared was degenerating into chaos. "Protest takes a lot of thought, concentration, discipline, and tenacity," she told *Essence* that October. "It encourages acceptance of responsibility and commitment to oneself and society....We shouldn't jump emotionally into protest....I remember Malcolm said, 'One must always consider seriously a process.'"

Betty told a colleague during the Medgar upheaval that it pained her to see black students and faculty warring with black administrators while "the boys downtown" (CUNY's white overseers) sat back and laughed. But her loyalty to Trent, her old advocate, remained firm. Her role in the shakeup finally collided with her historical identity when members of the coalition unfurled a Malcolm X poster in the school's corridors. Betty flared. "Don't be parading my husband around in this context!" she said. "That's your husband," somebody replied, "but he belongs to us, too." Betty was not going to debate the point.

Late that summer, after months of strife, Trent resigned and the sit-in ended. Slowly, painstakingly, Medgar Evers College healed. City University trustees appointed an interim president, who appeared with Betty and other administrators at a media conference at the school. The event was designed as a show of harmony and solidarity. But when the acting president referred to the widow, a chorus of boos rose from a few members of the coalition scattered in the audience. Betty recoiled. Before any of the assembled officials could react, she leapt to her feet, unleashed a volley of expletives, and fled the room in tears.

The interim president was mortified. He wanted to ask for Betty's resignation, but coalition leaders told him to think again. "We understood the problematic position she had been put in by the original president," McLaughlin later said. "We knew the motives for removing her weren't sound. And she was Malcolm's *wife!*" Betty kept her job, and the beleaguered campus continued to recover. By the time a new president arrived a year later, the widow had made peace with Medgar Evers College. In coming years, she found fulfillment in her career and earned the respect of students, professors, and staff. "Sometimes you disagree with your mother and your grandmother, and then you live long enough and you see their wisdom," Chandler later said. "If I had my druthers, I would have had a different persona for Betty Shabazz. She'd have been standing right there next to Malcolm with a big old Afro and her fist in the air. But there's more to our struggle than a fist in the air and an Afro."

That much grew clear shortly after the troubles of 1982, when Medgar Evers College opened a women's center, a resource Betty vocally defended. "Hey, it's necessary," she said. "Women have special needs because we have the special responsibility of child rearing." The widow became a kind of godmother to the center, whose staff handled welfare issues, made immigration referrals, and counseled survivors of abusive relationships. Work of that sort had intrigued Betty since her pre-Malcolm days. She liked the center's international focus, which meshed with her concern for the plight of women around the world. In later years, she often popped in during counseling sessions to offer pragmatic guidance and wisdom.

"Betty was about women and a college degree," Bandele, the center's director, later said. "That was her message: be economically independent." The widow's other watchword was persistence. "Don't give up," she told young women again and again. She was always looking to mend relationships, though she once urged a battered Muslim student to leave her boyfriend, dismissing the ambiguous advice the girl had gotten from an imam. "You shouldn't be hurt," Betty said firmly. "The Qur'an does not sanction that." A future Medgar president would discover the power of the widow's counsel when he encountered an alumna of the college—a single mother of four who had climbed from welfare to a career—about town one day. The woman told Dr. Edison Jackson that without the personal ministry of "Dr. Betty," she would not have graduated. "That was one of the greatest testimonies," Jackson later reflected. "Betty had planted a seed that fell on fertile ground and reproduced."

In 1984, the widow assumed the title she would hold at the school until her death: Director of Institutional Advancement and Public Affairs. She took on an array of duties, orchestrating Senior Awards Day and the annual lecture series, serving on the college's community council, and awarding to nursing students the Malcolm X Scholarships she created. Her mission was to empower and inspire students, as her regular lectures at the school revealed.

Still it was her informal role as Mrs. Malcolm X that earned her title an annex. Betty became Medgar Evers College's "cultural attaché," a diplomat who moved in disparate and cosmopolitan circles, who represented the institution at home and abroad. She held court at Medgar Evers College, mingling with Australian so-called Aborigine women and receiving an international delegation of schoolchildren who visited the campus in the early 1980s to plant a tree in Malcolm's honor. The latter event touched her through the years. "My little tree sure is growing!" she often twittered.

She was a formidable advocate for the school. "Blacks pay taxes like others pay taxes and they want their fair share of all of the resources," she proclaimed in 1986, as Medgar Evers College students lobbied state senators for senior-college status. The widow also became a symbolic member of the City University's troupe of black nationalist scholars. "She held her own at Medgar Evers," Dr. Leonard Jeffries, chair of City College's Black Studies Department, later said. "We held it at City College. Dr. [John Henrik] Clarke held it at Hunter. We interacted as an academic family." Betty prospected boldly on behalf of Medgar Evers College, tapping the political and financial resources of such influential comrades as Harlem congressman Charles Rangel and former assemblyman and Manhattan borough president Percy Sutton.

Her fundraising style would become local legend. The school was once five thousand dollars short on funds for an awards ceremony. The shortfall never fazed Betty. She grabbed the phone and cooed or cajoled. Minutes later, she sauntered over to a fellow administrator's office and pounded on the door. "Hey, Sweets!" she hollered. "We got ten thousand dollars!" As Betty's profile rose in the 1980s, so did that of the college. The woman and the institution evolved together, each shaping the other. "She was comfortable in her dual role as an emissary for Malcolm and an emissary for Medgar," Bandele remembered. A student-affairs counselor at the school agreed. "Betty for us was a soul sister and a colleague," she said.

Chapter Fifteen

JOURNEY TO RESPECTABILITY

"I do not weep at the world—I am too busy sharpening my oyster knife."
—Zora Neale Hurston

Betty served an array of mostly provincial groups and projects in the latter 1970s. She presided over a Westchester County foundation designed to help needy kids go to college. She oversaw community service for the United Way of Westchester. She labored on behalf of the American Educational Research Association and the African American Institute. The work sprang from a sense of duty to redeem children and the black family as well as empathy for society's cast-offs. (She could never forget that she had spent her early widowhood in exile from polite society.) She also needed to feel like she was complementing Malcolm's unfinished mission. She called it "walking in his footsteps."

Her friends understood that the labor was redemptive. Some of them fussed about her sleep deficit or muttered about her mad pace. "Betty was driven, driven, driven!" remembered one confidante. When they were old enough to know that such velocity was destructive, her daughters protested, too. The widow just smiled. "I have to be busy," she said. In interviews she pronounced herself a "workaholic" and complained cheerily that there weren't enough hours in the day. Most of her comrades quit grousing about her whiplash schedule until it became a crisis years later. One or two never stopped needling her. Only a few realized that the volunteering was compulsive. "That's Betty," they told themselves as she continued to cram her days with tasks.

As the widow's activities grew more cosmopolitan, her civic life quickened and broadened, affording her greater visibility. Though there were the typical lectures and appearances as Mrs. Malcolm X, she performed other high-caliber tasks with equal legitimacy as Dr. Shabazz. She sat on a U.S. Department of Health advisory committee on family planning. She cohosted a television series on black alternative schools with her journalist friend Gil Noble, interviewing teachers, administrators, parents, and students for New York's black news and public-affairs program *Like It Is*. After the Senate's only black member, Edward Brooke of Massachusetts, lost a re-election campaign, she joined baseball great Hank Aaron and other prominent blacks on a committee to draft Muhammad Ali for a senatorial bid.

By the early 1980s, her growing stature and multiplying relationships with black luminaries were opening doors. In 1983, she began hosting her own talk program, "A Forum for Women," on New York's WBLS-FM. "Render unto Caesar what is Caesar's and unto God what is God's," Betty intoned at the beginning of each show, quoting the Bible unabashedly (her allegiance to Allah notwithstanding). She interviewed authors, politicians, activists, and celebrities on the program, which she had designed for young women who were "trying to find their way." In the winter of 1984, she toiled on behalf of established women as well, hosting the National Council of Negro Women's forty-first annual convention in New York. Her friendship with Dorothy Height, NCNW president since 1957, helped win her the prestigious assignment.

Yet Betty's dimensionality, her identity as a woman of conscience and not merely an emblem, manifested most profoundly in her overseas work. Within this arena, she was a vocal defender of women's dignity. International audiences continued to receive her as a dignitary in reverence of Malcolm. Though she did not think this role shallow, she never functioned as "The Widow" at world conferences. It was rather her mature, independent advocacy that distinguished her presence in Nairobi, Kenya, during Forum '85, an unofficial assembly of women from a bouquet of nations and cultures. Black women flocked to the summit, which unfolded as the official United Nations Women's Conference was underway in Nairobi.

Betty joined a distinguished lineup of unofficial delegates, including the seventy-three-year-old Height, Angela Davis, Coretta Scott King, and feminists Betty Friedan and Bella Abzug, in appealing for the drafting of an antiapartheid resolution at the UN conference. She and the other leaders had spent hours discussing the ties between racism and sexism, deliberating the evils of militarization, and preaching solidarity with Nicaraguan and Palestinian refugees during a series of workshops. The topic that most engaged black women at the summit was South Africa's barbarous system of racial separation. At Forum '85, South African women delivered stark testimonies of life under white rule. "The homelands are tribal death cells," said one. "The lands are not fertile and there are only hungry women and children with no health facilities to speak of."

Many of the unofficial attendees pledged solidarity with the South Africans. The official United States delegation to the UN conference, however, had only reluctantly agreed to talk about apartheid, and only did so provided that the discussion "reflect unique concerns of women." Maureen Reagan, daughter of President Ronald Reagan, whose administration sanctioned a policy of "constructive engagement" with South Africa, ultimately condemned apartheid during a speech at the summit, calling the system "abhorrent to the government and the people of the United States." But to many of the women at Forum '85, the First Daughter's stance was duplicitous. "She assumed the posture that, like Zionism and apartheid, racism—and indeed the halting of the nuclear-arms race—are not 'authentic' women's issues," Davis later said.

Few could know better than Betty the "authenticity" of the colored woman's struggle, or how the intersection of race and gender shapes the lives of women around the globe. She would continue to speak to this reality on the international scene. Simply sharing the company of Davis and Height, a Marxist insurgent and a Civil Rights matriarch who represented divergent but salient traditions of struggle, was a personal triumph for the widow. She had once been a housewife who waited anxiously at home while her husband traversed Africa. She was now a conscientious world traveler returning to the continent to do the work of "peace, equality, and development"—the themes of the UN conference. Betty had actually arrived in Nairobi that January— six months before Forum '85 and the official women's summit—to meet with Kenyan leaders from the fields of health, economics, and education as a member of an advance team of black educators and specialists from the United States. As the widow discussed maternal health, child care, and women's emancipation with local and international leaders that winter and summer, she modestly but meaningfully extended the dialogue between African-America and Africa that Malcolm had elevated two decades before.

Betty performed her domestic diplomacy with equal grace in those evolutionary years. She was among the dignitaries who gathered in New York's Mother AME Zion Church for the 1976 funeral of Paul Robeson, the legendary performer whose bold activism on behalf of the Dark World Malcolm had admired.

The widow also found time for personal enlightenment and sheer pleasure. The 1975 spring European couture import show in Manhattan had nothing to do with Malcolm or Black America's well-being. Yet Betty was there, grinning at the edge of a catwalk that flittered with Dior suits and Givenchy evening dresses.

This was the era in which Betty joined a bowling league and a gourmet-cooking club of black professional women. She began working on a book about Haiti that she never completed. She shopped like newlyweds make love. She fried fish. She danced ably and unashamed when she and a girlfriend stole off to a nightclub, and she drained a cocktail or two by the end of the night. Self-contained and graceful on daises, she could be a Roman Candle in casual quarters. Those she trusted discovered this, especially as she effloresced in the early and mid-1980s. The men and women who caught her doing the "Electric Slide" at a dinner party or "telling lies and cracking on folks" with an assemblywoman at a summit of black and Latino legislators glimpsed the dimensions of her humanity (and "insanity" as one friend recalled.) "She was riotous," remembered Howard Dodson, director of Harlem's venerable Schomburg Center for Research in Black Culture. "Just crazy-ass funny."

Betty's *joie de vivre* startled those who expected to encounter the public "Widow" in private. Economist and columnist Julianne Malveaux once found herself beside Betty in a poolside lounge chair, and began a sputtering obeisance. "Child," Betty said amiably, "you had better get over all that." The widow had a bawdy sense of humor and a wicked, spontaneous laugh. "If you can choose between being happy and being sad, why is it people choose to be sad?" Malcolm had often asked her. In his absence, she had finally learned that happiness was something you chased like a madwoman. "I just didn't have time to dwell in anger, to deal in something that doesn't have any returns," she once declared. "If there was any love between us, it is stronger than any other force." Fifteen or twenty years into a tragic widowhood, she had come to symbolize the capacity of the human spirit. "I have managed—and a lot of people never really thought I would—I have managed to live without Malcolm," she said.

She was conscious of her ongoing metamorphosis, and she was satisfied with the evolving Dr. Shabazz, a woman infinitely more hopeful and vocal than the one who had commuted to Amherst in her slain husband's Oldsmobile. "I've changed because situations have changed and change was necessary," she said. She treasured her identity. "No one can take it away from me," she told the *Los Angeles Times*. "[Though] I rather appreciate the fact that people will connect me with my husband." In time, the Betty who had functioned as a memento of Malcolm began to evaporate, and Betty as her own force took shape. "She ceased to be Malcolm's wife," Dick Gregory later said. "You were too busy thinking about her as Betty Shabazz."

Black men and women of all stations found the transition heroic, and slowly, modestly, the Dr. Shabazz icon was born. James Campbell, the OAAU man whom Malcolm had asked the night before the assassination to stay in touch with Betty, returned to the United States in

1982 after a decade in Tanzania and was stunned to encounter the self-conceived widow. "She had grown tremendously in her outlook," he later said. What most struck the Malcolmite was her flight from the veil, a departure whose evidence lay more in her deportment than in her bared swath of hair. Dr. Shabazz was far more divergent than the Sister Betty that Campbell remembered. This was a woman who had escaped the stereotype of Muslim womanhood, who described herself as "more spiritual than religious" and believed that one ought to obey the Qur'an rather than Muslim patriarchy.

Betty had not become a "leader." She was more a dignitary than a spokeswoman with a platform and constituency. Nor was she an ideologue. Yet those who dismissed her as apolitical missed what Malcolm had known all along: that the frontier of human-rights struggle is vaster than the defense of the masses from tyranny. "It is important that we understand the significance of race, of class, and of ideologies," the widow said. "But let's face it, we have people in this country who don't have enough money to pay rent, who don't have food to eat, who can't afford to get proper health care." Malcolm's quest was the liberation of the multitude; Betty hoped to help people liberate themselves. "I'm not as committed, dedicated, or knowledgeable as my husband about this type of leadership," she said. "But I am as selfless."

The widow's generosity and elegance dazzled her comrades. "Very frankly, I think she has walked on water," Percy Sutton told the *Amsterdam News*. "She's one of the most remarkable people I have ever met." Betty glided into conversations, flattering or disarming effortlessly and without pretension. She was old-fashioned. She believed that "a right-thinking adult is better than money." She urged children and young adults to recognize the wealth of their parents' wisdom and to listen for the lessons of their experience. Yet she had a powerful sense of her own majesty. She liked underlings and equals to wait upon her, though she wanted nobody underfoot. At times she arrived at glitzy functions without invitation and dared anyone at the door to eyeball her. "Is Maya Angelou in there?" she would say as she strutted on through. "Well, I'm her guest."

She often insisted on her formal title, even among peers. When Amiri and Amina Baraka, whom she had known for years as comrades in the struggle, introduced her to their son with great flourish as "Malcolm X's wife," she demurred: "Dr. Shabazz, if you please." Amina decided later that the widow was not standing on ceremony, but demanding some acknowledgement of her journey, some recognition of the identity she had carved out of the ether. "At the same time one would have to say that being Malcolm's wife ain't such a big put down," Amiri told Betty. "You're still Dr. Betty Shabazz, but you was Malcolm's *wife*."

Betty sparred with friends on this and other points. Yet she cherished friendship as one of the forces that had enabled her survival. Her sense of loyalty was powerful and complex, a product of the betrayal that had marked her and Malcolm's saga. So she came swiftly to the aid of suffering comrades. Noble once produced an impolitic series for his television show that raised the ire of New York's Jewish community and almost cost him his job. "And a lot of middle-class black people did not come to my defense," he later said. "Betty did. She called. She came by. She said, 'What do you want me to do?' And that meant a lot. In offering herself, she was bringing all her artillery."

The widow extended this loyalty to many who had shown her kindness during her misery. Elinor Sinnette, a former member of the Committee of Concerned Mothers, was at a formal affair with her husband in the late 1970s when she was suddenly engulfed in bosoms. "We hadn't seen Betty for years, hadn't thought about her," Sinnette later said. Yet it was Betty (in a fleshier form than Sinnette remembered) who hustled across the dance floor and enveloped her. "I'm so glad to see you, dear friend," the widow said. "I will never forget what you did for me."

Yet for every soul the widow embraced, she held several marathon grudges. "You never knew when Dr. Betty took a slight," her publicist later said. She would abruptly stop talking to a neighbor or associate, often for what they considered a trivial bruise to her sensitivities. These wintry spells could last six months or six years. One of the most baffling involved Alex Haley, her old confidant.

"For Pete's sake," he wrote in a jovial 1982 letter, "how many <u>years</u> since we've exchanged so much as a hello note!" One of the forces behind the lapse was the widow's belief that the writer had been remiss in fulfilling a promise. Before his 1976 release of *Roots*, Haley announced at a New York book affair that he intended to sign his half of the royalties from *The Autobiography of Malcolm X* over to the widow. *Roots* was a massive success, and later spawned a historic television movie. Yet Haley hit stormy financial seas in the following years, embroiled in lawsuits with his publisher and authors who claimed he had plagiarized portions of their work. It was as late as 1980 before he was able to begin transferring his share of *The Autobiography* earnings. The widow was slow to forgive the delay, which she considered a breach of faith.

Betty could express disapproval subtly. (James Smalls once appeared with a younger woman at a program the widow had summoned him to. For an hour, Betty uttered not a word to the woman. Finally she turned and said, "You know, you are a cute little girl." Smalls reddened. "I knew that was to tell me, 'What are you doing with this young thing?'" he later recalled.) When affronted, however, the widow unleashed. "She would eat you alive, Jack!" Howard Dodson said. "You didn't want Betty to put them eyes on you." Harlem activist Elombe Brath echoed the sentiment. "If you mess with Betty and she confront you, man, she ain't comin' with no Islamic diplomacy," he said. "She'd get street on you in a second."

That forbidding persona collided with the gracious image. Though Betty's occasional gruffness cowed colleagues, associates, and assistants who held her in awe, some refused to accept the thrashings and even struck back. Herman Fulton, her secretary of twelve years, discovered early in his tenure that the widow seemed only to respect those who could draw blood, figuratively if not literally. Neither Fulton nor Betty would acknowledge their shared affection, and each cursed the other mercilessly as a matter of course.

Betty excommunicated or drew into her inner circles the men and women who resisted her onslaught. There was no formal reconciliation with friends she had lambasted; the charm simply returned when the vexation passed. Her dearest friends understood that much of the wrath was affected. She had not been born strong; she had become so. She had entered the 1980s wearing the '60s and '70s like a suit of armor. "Betty had no naïveté," Angelou later said. "You couldn't see who was an insider or an outsider." The widow was always on the watch for those who would exploit or betray. She found that refinement could not always expose the villains. "Girl, where did you learn to curse like that?" Angelou once asked. Betty said the menacing phone calls of the 1960s had revealed the talent. "I get profane and my enemies run," she told Smalls. "My friends stick around to see what's wrong."

There was compassion beneath the stern veneer. "I know she didn't take any mess from anybody, there was no doubt," Amina later said. "But her heart was so huge, you could feel it pulsating. She had a dire need to love and be loved." The widow's comrades discovered the vulnerability she tried to hide. "There were times when she would call me," Noble said, "and just by the way she spoke I could tell that she needed me to show up somewhere, even if she had laid me out the day before." Her close friends were few, partly because of her distrust and volatility. An obsession with privacy also kept her intimate circles small, though her outer social rings continued to widen.

She made hundreds of casual friends over the years. But within her inner circles lay revelations that her confidants would never share—revelations about Malcolm, her daughters, and her childhood. She could be eerily secretive even with dear friends, and like her late husband, she compartmentalized relationships.

Indeed, the widow was more circumspect than Malcolm. It was years before Mary Redd could recite the names of the Shabazz daughters, though she and Betty often discussed them. (The widow would refer to "Daughter Number Three" or "the twins.") Some of her girlfriends asked questions about her past that went unanswered for years, even after the women earned their way into her heart. They learned to keep certain queries to themselves and simply to listen when she phoned to unload, often between midnight and dawn.

Betty grew even more guarded as her profile rose. She was less tolerant of interviews. "I'm not serviced by them, and I don't seek them," she said. Amina Baraka thought she understood. "The media is always describing you as somebody you don't even know," she said. Yet the widow's view of reporters and writers—the "devils," white and black, that had so often distorted Malcolm—seemed especially cynical. She mastered the art of sealing off her personal life. "She got in her Fort Knox vault," Fulton later said. She refused to give journalists her date of birth. Inquiries about her love life drew a blank stare. She was convinced that the dozens of biographers and researchers that approached her over the years had ulterior motives. A Malcolmite and archivist well known among Harlem's nationalist crowd once asked her if she had any "indictable evidence" of Louis Farrakhan's involvement in her husband's death. She never spoke to him again.

Marge Battle, one of Betty's secretaries, saw the widow's severity as self-preservation. In the early 1980s, Battle watched a cavalcade of visitors march into Betty's office to capitalize on the Shabazz legacy. "There are people who want to run up to you and pinch off little pieces of the strength that you have done who knows what to gather about yourself," Battle later said. "And the next thing you know you're left bare and shivering in the wind." Even those callers who were not seeking the widow's endorsement or presence at this or that affair seemed to demand of her some sort of exhibition. Battle marveled at black strangers who expected Betty to receive them like family, whether or not they had an appointment.

Resisting the intrusions was draining. The widow, stoic and invincible before the public, sometimes unburdened among friends. She began attending upstate New York retreats of the National Black Holistic Society, a group formed to revive a holistic philosophy of black life. "She was able to bathe in the serenity and the kindness and love of the people who came," remembered poet and publisher Haki Madhubuti, one of the Society members.

The serenity of romance was more elusive. Suitors of the 1980s found Malcolm's ghost as daunting as admirers of the 1970s had. Some of them lasted no more than a couple dates with the widow. There were other barriers to love. Betty's daughters panicked throughout their teens at the idea of their mother remarrying. "They did not even want her to date," a friend remembered. Attallah started warming to the prospect in later years. "You know, if you ever marry again, I'm gonna give you away," she told her mother. "We'll break tradition."

There was little need for her daughter's courage. Betty enjoyed the attention of men and joked about finding a good one. Yet she told *Ebony* in 1984 that she was not sure she wanted to remarry. The following year she told *Essence* unequivocally that she had no desire to return to the altar. Some of her friends believed she was searching for a soul mate. She found the idea laughable. "Please," she told a colleague. "Who am I gonna marry after Malcolm?" Privately, though, she continued to discuss the possibility of remarriage. "Now, Betty, I think you and that fellow could get along," a friend sometimes said. "Girl, don't be telling me that," the widow would reply. "Now you know ain't nobody gonna marry me. I'm strong willed."

Betty was not going to surrender to spinsterhood. She pin-curled her hair nightly. She nurtured a passion for Ferragamo pumps and knit dresses. She was notoriously monochromatic. "Girl, you can't keep on wearing black," a friend told her, "because death is too close to us." The widow relished her femininity and struggled to slim down. "When you gon' help me lose this weight?" she would ask Gregory. "That ain't weight, that's gas, girl," he replied. "Cook the beans a little bit!" Ultimately, her comrades forgave her frailties, not because she was Mrs. Malcolm X but because she was Betty.

———

The widow's increasingly independent public identity helped propel her to respectability between the mid-1970s and 1980s. She had assumed first-lady status among her husband's spiritual heirs after the assassination, serving as a visible but retiring presence at Malcolm memorials. At the beckoning of the Black Panthers and student unions, she had ventured onto the lecture circuit in the late 1960s, becoming the minister's torchbearer for the new generation. As a surrogate to his image, she had nominally represented nationalism, Pan-Africanism, and the burgeoning black cultural movement. She had articulated some of his rudimentary principles, preaching self-determination (and, to a lesser degree, self-defense) in her own moderate style.

By the mid-to-late 1970s, however, the widow was operating largely apolitically, and her stature within the black establishment and the political mainstream—traditional targets of Malcolm's harangue— was growing. She had accumulated community-service and citizenship awards from the City of Mount Vernon and Westchester County. She also won less parochial accolades, becoming an honorary citizen of Tucson, Arizona, in 1975. A cultural center in Massachusetts was later named in her honor. Her widening recognition drew invitations to join corporate boards, and she accepted directorships of the Kenwood Foods Corporation and the *Amsterdam News*. Meanwhile her affiliation with black bourgeois organizations deepened. She was a visible participant in NCNW affairs and became a functional member of the NAACP and Urban League, traveling to their conventions and receptions with or without special invitation. (She later became an official NAACP life member).

In a sense, Betty's rising status in the black establishment was a sign of the times, for the nationalists that had seized the race's consciousness in the late 1960s and early 1970s lost ground to the integrationists in the ensuing years. As one black scholar observed, "a full account of the decline of black nationalism would assume encyclopedic proportions." Yet the dirty tricks and outright assault of J. Edgar Hoover's FBI and police forces on the Black Panthers and other groups, deep ideological feuds, a failure to understand the significance of black class stratification, and the sharp increase in the number of black elected officials—who overwhelmingly sacrificed self-determination for participation in the political process—all the nationalist ethos.

To some extent, mellowing figures like Muhammad Ali embodied the phenomenon. "You can't stay mad at your wife too long," Ali, who had begun promoting automobile accessories on television, told the *New York Times* in 1980. "The Vietnam War, that's over. Watergate, President Kennedy's assassination, that's history. People forget." Some of Betty's allies underwent a similar adaptation. Nikki Giovanni (of the widow's old artist crowd) had written "*Nigger can you kill?*" in a memorable 1968 poem. But the birth of her son in the 1970s softened her rhetoric and rearranged her priorities. "To protect Tommy there's no question I'd give away my life," she said in an interview. "I just can't imagine living without him. But I can live without the revolution, without world socialism, women's lib."

Betty's rise within the black bourgeoisie was more personal than political. She wanted respectability. She wanted the prestige and mobility within the black elite that she had at times enjoyed among Malcolm's heirs. With her career flourishing and her royal duties widening, her social circles began to gentrify. Her old friendships with black dignitaries and her ties to an array of civic groups spawned more relationships with influential black intellectuals, politicians, entertainers, and businesspeople. These professionals became the widow's allies and peers, though some of them represented the embrace of integration and accommodation of the power structure that Malcolm had assailed.

The elites were nonetheless delighted to have Mrs. Malcolm X in their midst (though some smiled at her flashes of indecorum). "A lot of the bourgeois clung to Betty out of a sense of guilt, a sense of having ignored her husband," said Noble, whose own relationship with the widow hastened his recovery from the "embarrassment and humiliation" of having once dismissed the minister as a demagogue. Betty was coming to understand that Malcolm's masculinity and message had empowered a broad spectrum of blacks, whether or not they explicitly agreed with him. Whatever the depth of her inner resentment, she was charitable to the late admirers, so long as they did not try to pass themselves off as her husband's running buddies. "She grinned—'Isn't it funny you come around now?'" Noble remembered. "But she was very tolerant of that."

Her nationalist friends were not. They tended to see the socialites who fawned over Malcolm's widow as phonies who "pimped off what the forcefulness of his struggle produced," as Amiri Baraka would propose. "I listen to people talk about how much they loved Malcolm," Sonia Sanchez later said. "I think, 'Mm-hmm, yeah.' People were scared of Malcolm. You found yourself alone if you started listening to that man."

One found oneself threadbare, as well, for the minister had forsworn wealth in pursuit of black freedom. Yet by the 1980s, Betty was authentically upper–middle class. She invested a large portion of her savings into Percy Sutton's Inner City Broadcasting Corporation, quietly becoming its second largest stockholder and joining celebrities Roberta Flack and Billy Taylor on its board.

Her corporate forays mirrored that of other black protest widows, including Margaret Young (wife of Urban League executive Whitney Young), who in the early 1970s joined the board of Philip Morris, Inc., the multinational cigarette maker. Betty's visibility was far greater, of course, and Malcolm's radical legacy complicated her passage to the mainstream. But the widow did not heed (nor even hear) the dissonance. Some of her allies thought the black elite were exploiting her for political expediency or personal comfort, validating their "blackness" with her friendship. Yet Betty was precisely where she wished to be.

She had not abandoned black liberation. Even her most gilded circles were linked to civil rights, albeit the integrationist struggle that sought equal opportunity to compete with whites, rather than a self-governed black nation or structural redistribution of wealth. Her mobility within the ranks of the privileged was less an effect of social climbing than the evidence of her influence. She was becoming a "mover," and she embraced other movers who succeeded in their careers and remained committed to the "Cause," however defined. Many of her "sisterfriends" were well-known activists deeply engaged in social-justice work. Her less-prominent comrades were professionals whose social awareness manifested in philanthropy and membership in civic and political organizations, fraternities, sororities, or church associations.

Some who observed the widow's rather cynical view of radicalism decided that she had grown disenchanted with black nationalism. Some thought her desire to win respectability for Malcolm had driven her into the establishment. They guessed that she was looking to extend the minister's audience beyond now marginal nationalist spheres. Others believed she was returning to pre-Malcolm sensibilities, that his primary constituents had limited utility for her, that she had developed stock in becoming a celebrity of the mainstream, rather than the fringe. Each of these theories contained strands of truth. Betty knew that many of her husband's most ardent disciples had failed to contribute meaningfully to her survival. She bristled with sarcasm when she recalled a program at the Harlem Apollo in which a Black Power guard had escorted her ceremoniously onto the stage and flanked her at parade rest, only to abandon her in the lobby after the affair. "I had to walk four blocks to my car, through all them drug-infested side streets," she told a friend. On the other hand, she continued to find support, whatever its motives, among unlikely castes and colors.

There is ample evidence that the widow was ambivalent about the Black Left. Clearly she wished to universalize Malcolm. Her ability to ignore the past when it suited her purposes was well known to friends. But the social whirl and political strivings of well-heeled blacks also represented a significant part of her evolving identity and vision of success. Her growing stature in these circles reflected the rise of her personality over the persona some of her husband's inheritors had projected upon her. Was Dr. Shabazz's journey to respectability a return to her roots?" an interviewer later asked one of her close friends. "A return to her roots?" the woman echoed. "I'm not sure she ever left."

That Betty was a pragmatist who believed in reforming the system from within was hardly news to her allies. This was the woman who had once urged Malcolm X College President Charles Hurst to befriend Chicago's Mayor Daley and focus on the administration of the school rather than agitating for community control and a solution to what he saw as "the total problem of being black in the United States." Yet many blacks were unaware of Betty's movements until her star began to rise in the 1980s and early 1990s. Some were startled in 1975 when President Ford appointed her to the American Revolution Bicentennial Council. The widow joined Angelou, Haley, and more than twenty other appointees on the prestigious committee, which funded and oversaw projects in connection with the nation's two hundredth anniversary.

During a summer 1976 press conference near the White House, Betty chided blacks who argued that the bicentennial was no cause for jubilee. "Celebrations are not always joyous," she said. The widow insisted that her people had contributed too much to their homeland to ignore its milestones. "Our ancestors who fought honorably for the freedom of America should not be forgotten," she said. Moments later, the media event ended and she took her place at a conference table within the Capitol. When Senator Edward Brooke entered the room, he hustled past fifty or so dignitaries to embrace her warmly. Then the committee went into session. The order of business that most intrigued Betty was an ambassador's request for funds to help build a memorial to Ralph Bunche, Nobel laureate, former undersecretary to the United Nations, and one of the many black moderates with whom Malcolm had clashed.

Somebody mentioned that Betty's ongoing support would be invaluable to the memorial effort. "Certainly," the widow said with a smile, "I'll be glad to help." The head of the Bicentennial Administration that day called Betty "one of the most dynamic people who have come and put their shoulder to the big wheel without any compensation." The widow was flattered. Later, when her name appeared among those of luminaries chosen to sign a scroll to be buried that year and disinterred in 2076, she was humbled. "What's really important is what Afro-Americans feel about themselves…that's what can make the Bicentennial so important for blacks," she told reporters. "We must constantly cultivate those qualities that demand change and freedom from oppression, regardless of what form it takes. And what better way than by telling the truth and having blacks participate in that truth in the Bicentennial."

That sort of reasoning resonated with the black middle-class, but it antagonized Malcolm's grassroots. Some of these ideologues ignored Betty's flirtations with the "ruling class" out of respect for their martyr. But her increasingly bourgeois profile inspired greater unease as the years passed. The widow did not seem ideologically invested in her husband's memory. Her lack of an openly defiant sensibility troubled Malcolmites who imagined that she was betraying their hero by dragging his name into quarters they believed he had condemned.

The disenchantment was mutual. Betty felt that those who professed love for her husband should back her unconditionally, even if her ambassadorship meant a dais seat at the Congressional Black Caucus weekend, an affair that had grown so corporate by 1977 that one Civil Rights veteran dubbed it the "Mascot Nigger Convention." "And that's when the brothers say, 'Well, Sister Betty, we don't give a hoot,'" remembered Dr. James Turner, head of Africana Studies at Cornell University and an old friend of the widow's. "That's the kind of bourgeois antics that only serves a small group and creates the illusion of power."

The widow never lost sight of the radical tradition her husband represented, and had no intention of betraying it. "She didn't have the deep consciousness that you would have wanted her to have," Professor Leonard Jeffries later said. What Betty had was a kind of reflected consciousness. The cost of Malcolm's brazenness had shaped her as much as his commitment to struggle. So *all* her movements—even social ascent—were strategic. "She never recovered from the terror of the FBI and the government, and in the back of her mind she knew that it could possibly reoccur unless she had access to the circles that would prevent them from ever bothering her again," a Medgar Evers College colleague said.

The Shabazz daughters knew stealth was crucial to their mother's methodology. She taught them composure. Tact and timing, she said, were everything. "If you keep running up to the door and say, 'Open the door!' they're not going to open the door," she told them. "But if you ring the bell and say, 'Excuse me, do you think this door could be opened at some point?' chances are, you get the door opened. Then, once you're inside…." In time, the men and women who worked and socialized with Betty also recognized her strategies. They discovered that her unwillingness to antagonize the power structure did not dim her devotion to the dispossessed. They learned that whether counseling the homeless or inner-city kids during the appearances she too frequently consented to, the widow believed her responsibility to Malcolm's people was accessibility. "It was almost a humility," the Schomburg Center's Howard Dodson later said of her deportment among the masses, "a sensitivity that was really quite remarkable."

By the 1980s, some Malcolmites had accepted that they could not seek in Betty a reincarnation of Malcolm. They adjusted to her personality and idiosyncrasies or simply agreed to disagree with her lifestyle. They understood that she was functioning outside her husband's pale and no longer flinched when her face appeared in decidedly un-Malcolmesque contexts. "So Malcolm's widow was a guest at their dinners," Sonny Carson later said. "That's not important to us. What's important to us is that Betty was Betty. Whenever she stood among white folks she represented us."

Her friends believed she was wise not to try to fashion herself after Malcolm. They insisted that she could make her greatest personal contribution as "Dr. Shabazz" in whatever circles she moved. "Was it that she had fallen back in love with the 'la-dee-das,' or was she trying to bring them around, trying to recruit people into giving back to the struggle that had created a lot of comfort and wealth for the black bourgeoisie?" Noble later asked. Some of Betty's allies tried to politicize the widow. Others ignored or accepted her contradictions. "I never would engage her," Sanchez recalled. "I just thought that she had had enough pain. Sometimes you look at people and you recognize that they have had enough pain in their lifetime."

———

Pain was a common element in the lives of the Movement widows—the wives of Medgar Evers, Malcolm X, and Martin Luther King Jr. So was grit. As Betty was rearing her children, toiling through school, and establishing her career in the 1970s and early 1980s, Myrlie Evers was following a similar script. She moved her daughter and two sons—the eldest of whom was nine at the time of Medgar Evers's death—to lily-white Claremont, California, in 1964, a year after the assassination. She enrolled at Pomona College and finished her bachelor's degree. In the following years, she found success as a college administrator, an ad executive, and a director of consumer affairs for the Atlantic Richfield Company.

Meanwhile she maintained a public profile. She traveled to college campuses to lecture about Civil Rights and women's empowerment. She participated in NAACP and other fundraisers, became a contributing editor for the *Ladies' Home Journal,* and endorsed political candidates who upheld the ideals for which her husband had fought. (Her own 1970 congressional bid was unsuccessful.) She accepted posthumous laurels for Evers and attended occasional commemorations in his honor. But over time the public memory of the man dimmed, diffusing into the tumult of the 1960s and the celebrity of King's martyrdom. In the early 1980s, Myrlie herself listened to some of her husband's speeches and realized with dismay that his voice did not sound the way she remembered it. "There is no vehicle for keeping his name alive," she told the *Washington Post.* "We will be exploring a foundation, a scholarship fund, a stamp, a commemorative coin, a way to keep his memory alive."

America's memory of the martyred NAACP field secretary may have waned, but his presence lingered in Myrlie's mind as starkly as the scene of his assassination. The terror of discovering his bloody form on the carport never fully dissipated. When she learned of Malcolm's murder, the trauma resurfaced. "I remember being in the driveway of my home in California when I heard the news," she later said. "I felt these claws of pain that just rip you apart." She became a "distant admirer" of Betty then, and of Coretta Scott King after Martin Luther King Jr.'s 1968 slaying. She felt a special kinship with Betty, who had also watched her husband die in the presence of her children. "At least she was spared seeing it," Myrlie later said of Coretta. "We literally got our husbands' blood on us."

It was not until Betty began her career, however, that her relationship with Mrs. Evers flowered. Though the two had met here and there, their first meaningful discussions were about Betty's presence at Medgar Evers College. "We talked about her willingness to come work there, and she was Malcolm's wife," Myrlie remembered. "To me, she didn't have to do that. That didn't have to be the place she chose." The pair began speaking over the telephone and looking forward to face-to-face encounters. They found that they genuinely liked each other. Myrlie had a touch of irreverence and a robust independence. "I was *not* always the quiet, long-suffering little woman behind the great man," she later declared. "I was *not* the always hopeful, always strong single mother. I was *not* always nice and forgiving, compliant and ladylike."

Betty could relate. In later years, she helped rename a street near Medgar Evers College in honor of the freedom fighter and was responsible for the school's conferring an honorary doctorate upon Myrlie Evers. She updated Mrs. Evers regularly on the college's goings-on, and summoned her to campus for strategic appearances. The pair talked about the disparity between their public images and their private selves, about the absence of a male figure in their children's lives and the contrast with Coretta Scott King's kids, who "at least had Martin's followers." Betty urged Myrlie to date, brushing aside the notion that Movement widows were doomed to spinsterhood, or to accept the hand of some potentate. "Step on out there, kid," she told her friend. "You're just getting older and uglier every day." (In 1976, at the age of forty-three, Myrlie married a fifty-eight-year-old union organizer and became Mrs. Evers-Williams.) The widows laughed more than they commiserated. "Absolutely no envy existed between us," Myrlie later said. "She could have seen me as competition. But that was not Betty."

It was different with Coretta Scott King. The news media and Civil Rights establishment projected Mrs. King as the maximum Civil Rights widow after Martin's assassination. She rose to this station instantly and elegantly, in the nostalgic style of Jackie Kennedy. In the ensuing years, she positioned herself as the surviving voice of her husband's political philosophy. She lectured about integration and nonviolence (principles that in abstraction were palatable to the American mainstream) and, to a far lesser degree, civic disobedience and direct action—King's protest tactics. She was a respected, articulate presence at poverty, pride, and womanpower conferences. She accepted honors on King's behalf, including the Medal of Freedom from President Carter. She campaigned for black congressional candidates and white liberals and lent her visibility to various causes of the poor and disenfranchised.

She devoted her most assiduous labors, however, to perpetuating her husband's image. She set out to "institutionalize the dream," but not by leading demonstrations or working on behalf of the Southern Christian Leadership Conference, which King had cofounded. Instead, with "stern dignity and coldly resolute intention," she poured her fund-raising prowess into the creation of the thirty-five-thousand-square-foot King Center. She assumed the presidency of the multimillion-dollar memorial complex in downtown Atlanta and ran the kingdom like a monarch. She also oversaw the crusade for a national holiday in King's honor, a vision that Congress fulfilled in 1983. The victory in the long battle for the holiday signified not only America's reverence for the Civil Rights martyr, but the almost hallowed moral authority Coretta now wielded. "It's like sitting down with Mother Theresa," a conservative Republican legislator once said after leaving a meeting with the widow.

But Coretta's eminence (and King's long shadow) spawned a quiet rivalry with Betty. The two widows operated in the late 1960s and 1970s like emissaries of distant lands. Blacks and white liberals who accepted nonviolent, integrationist struggle hailed Mrs. King, while Afro-Americans who believed in militant resistance to white supremacy elevated Betty. The notion that King and Malcolm X had stood at irreconcilable poles of these philosophies influenced the widows' early relationship. Despite the distinctiveness of their prime constituencies, however, Betty's and Coretta's larger audiences overlapped. Many of Malcolm's spiritual heirs admired King's courage and sincerity (though they questioned the wisdom of his tactics) and many of King's devotees respected Malcolm's pitiless diagnosis (though they shied away from his prescriptions).

Coretta Scott King acknowledged in her 1969 autobiography that the two leaders had held each other in high regard. "I know that, though he never said so publicly, Malcolm X had deep respect for Martin," she wrote. "He recognized that Martin was unique, not alone in talent or eloquence, but in fearlessness and courage. Malcolm admired manhood and he knew how supremely Martin exemplified it." King had expressed his "deep affection" for Malcolm in the telegram he sent Betty after Malcolm's slaying. Coretta Scott King later testified that Malcolm's death had profoundly affected her. "Perhaps that was because I had just met him, and perhaps it was because I had begun to understand him better," she said. "Martin and I had reassessed our feelings toward him. We realized that since he had been to Mecca and had broken with Elijah Muhammad, he was moving away from hatred toward internationalism and against exploitation."

Still, unease muted the spirit of reconciliation as Coretta Scott King and Betty began meeting on platforms in the early 1970s, most notably at the 1972 National Black Political Convention conference in Gary, Indiana. They understood the need for a sisterly front. "I think the fact that we were there [in Gary] together at least presented some semblance of unity," Mrs. King later said. The public cordiality, however, did not quickly become friendship. "They had agreed to coexist," said an executive aide who worked closely with both women for years. One obstacle to genuine camaraderie was the disparity of the widows' experiences. "When Martin died I felt almost like I was embraced by the whole world, and 240,000 people came to Atlanta for the funeral," Coretta acknowledged years later. "Betty didn't have that." Nor did Betty have the power to hasten her husband's rise as an American deity. "The world wanted me to be perceived as being alone," Betty later said. "I wouldn't get the kind of media support and governmental and organizational support that perhaps [Mrs. King] received."

Black America rarely acknowledges such vagaries. Eager to hoist the unity banner, black leaders portrayed the Movement widows as kindred spirits. During a Washington banquet, the 1974 Congressional Black Caucus honored Betty, Myrlie Evers-Williams, Coretta Scott King, and Margaret Young for embodying "the finest in black womanhood." Over the years, Betty and Evers-Williams answered several other summons to appear with Coretta Scott King as a sort of sacred triumvirate. At these affairs, the press and attending dignitaries often orbited about Mrs. King, leaving the other members of the "trio" standing alone. Betty and Evers-Williams chuckled about the favoritism. "Coretta was unaware of it," Evers-Williams later said. But inwardly, Betty resented Mrs. King, and began aggressively campaigning to be present wherever she was scheduled to appear. In

Betty's mind there was a quiet competition, a sense that Malcolm should be recognized whenever and wherever King was honored. But inequities glared even when the women shared podiums, for beside Mrs. King's entourage of speechwriters and aides, Betty seemed naked. "Coretta be pulling out her speech, and Betty be there with a napkin trying to jot down points," one activist recalled.

As the Movement widows got to know one another, they discovered that their styles and personalities were no less different. While Scott King rarely offered public remembrances of the private Martin Luther King Jr., Evers-Williams grew increasingly candid about life with Medgar Evers. "The more I talked about Medgar the more release and relief I would feel," she later said. Yet Betty seldom spoke directly to Myrlie or her other confidantes about the pain of losing Malcolm. While Mrs. King continued to preach integration and nonviolent social reform, Betty did not interpret her husband's political views or argue for their continued currency. Scott King's career revolved around Martin Luther King Jr.'s legacy. Betty's professional path was more independent. Mrs. King was consummately dignified and restrained. ("You won't see Coretta King boogaloo," a politician friend once said.) On the other end of the spectrum was soulful and free-spirited Betty, with Evers-Williams somewhere in between.

Ultimately, however, the widows found strength in commonality. They were all strong willed, stubborn survivors forever damaged by the loss of their world-shaking men. They all carved paths to financial security. They all wrangled with the challenges of single motherhood. They all struggled to stand on their own, to dwell in the present while fighting demons from the past. And they all became custodians of their husband's legacies. It would be years before they began to genuinely regard themselves as "a society of three," before Mrs. Malcolm X and Mrs. King's emerging partnership became a redemptive force for Black America. But Betty acknowledged a sisterhood before the politicians and news media had even proclaimed a trinity. In 1969, she spoke of the "common burden of all black women since the white man brought us here, sold our children, destroyed our men—Mrs. King, Mrs. Evers, and myself are no exceptions."

Chapter Sixteen

REPERCUSSION

"Sometimes you have to recognize who put Christ on the cross.
Sometimes you have to call a Pharisee a Pharisee."
—Milton Henry (Malcolm comrade)

In time Betty realized that she must join the labors of Malcolm's memorialists to revive his name. This did not occur to her in the late 1960s or early 1970s, when his legend seemed moored in African-America. Back then, the minister's image and preachings were everywhere the restive generation was. He was to Black Arts and Black Power what Marcus Garvey had been to the Harlem Renaissance—the flame of the resistance. The occasion of Malcolm's birthday in the time of the Panthers was cause for rallies outside Newark City Hall, and black collegians asked themselves, "What would Malcolm have done?" the way Christians did of their messiah. The minister's message suffered some misuse at the hands of idolaters and pretenders, yet he lived in the black politics, the black economics, the black esthetic. In those days, Malcolm *was* the culture.

But even saints can slip from the scene. By the late 1970s, the Cult of Malcolm was battered and aging. Some of the leftists who were not in exile or in jail had retreated into establishment politics, universities, or corporate America. Others were running cultural centers or otherwise working in the community, often without their old sense of purpose. The movement had so transfigured that the meaning of black capitalism was more hotly discussed than Malcolm's classic "ballots or bullets" ultimatum. Even some of the institutions that invoked his spirit were dead or dwindling. North Carolina's Malcolm X Liberation University had folded, and Malcolm-King College of Harlem was fighting for survival.

The cultural apparatus of black self-determination was crumbling, and dimming Malcolm's legend as it went. Internationally he remained a potent symbol of resistance to imperialism. (Children at a guerrilla-run elementary school in Eritrea demanded "Who killed Malcolm X?" of a touring American journalist in 1977.) He fared less auspiciously in his own land. (Ferncliff Cemetery received so few visitors that his gravesite sprouted weeds.)

Yet there remained an army of ideologues who lived by Malcolm's words. Much of their efforts were invisible to White America. Yet the hardcore SNCC, CORE, and Panther veterans, the militant clergy and the Marxists, the activist-scholars and the artist-intellectuals, the Afrocentrists and the sidewalk vendors and the neighborhood griots all played in the commemorative symphony. Through the 1970s and early 1980s, ghetto peddlers bootlegged cassettes of Malcolm speeches and hawked Malcolm buttons and posters. Streets, schools, parks, and cultural centers in black neighborhoods took his name. A modest parade of pilgrims continued their annual sojourn to his grave, and documentaries such as El Hajj Malik became favorites at community programs.

A handful of Harlemites printed "By Any Means Necessary" T-shirts, plastered Malcolm's ashen image across the front, and unloaded them in the street. "We sold thousands but we gave away thousands more," James Smalls later said. The Republic of New Africa and other leftist and student groups sponsored forums featuring the reminiscences of Malcolm comrades. The minister's recorded voice, hauntingly granular and familiar, like that of a big brother from whom one has been too long separated, echoed in speeches and memorials across urban America. In Omaha, Nebraska, the Malcolm X Memorial Foundation won recognition of its hero's birthplace in the National Register of Historic Places. The Organization of Afro-American Unity, which had become a commemorative body under Ella Collins, called for ritual drumming on the minister's birthday.

The Malcolm X Cultural Education Center in southeast Washington began sponsoring an annual Malcolm X Day. Four thousand weekenders turned out in 1978, when the special guest was ex-Panther leader Bobby Seale. In 1981, almost eighteen thousand joined the family affair, which featured funk bands, voter registration, and impromptu workshops on "black-on-black crime" and police brutality. "When we honor Malcolm, we honor ourselves," an organizer said. "On this day we declare peace." In 1978, throngs of Harlemites made their way to the local YMCA on the martyr's birthday and paid a dollar to hear the poetry of Yusef Iman, Jayne Cortez, and Amiri Baraka. In February 1979—the fourteenth anniversary of the assassination—Sonia Sanchez was among the headliners at a memorial in the drafty and dilapidated Audubon Ballroom courtesy of the Afrikan Peoples Party and the National Task Force for Cointelpro Litigation and Research.

———

Betty was involved in the efforts to keep Malcolm's flame aglow—and she wasn't. She took part in the sense that she appeared and made remarks at dozens of memorials. Many Malcolm scions invited her to their February and May affairs. "We could commune with him vis-à-vis her," activist Elombe Brath remembered. She would decide where to go based on her schedule, tradition, and the merits of the program and sponsors. She was always grateful for recognition of the minister. Yet one never forgot that she was simultaneously raising a half-dozen teenagers and building a career. In those years, Malcolm memorials still generated bald hostility within and beyond black neighborhoods, and the widow's first concern was her daughters' well-being. "I'm sure that she knew we were keeping his legacy alive," Sanchez later said. What the widow did not seem to grasp was the profundity of her husband's imprint on a generation.

She performed her commemorative duties, nevertheless. On the tenth anniversary of Malcolm's death, she returned to Harlem's I.S. School 201, the campus that had long battled the board of education

over the question of community control. There was the customary
black-pride dance and music, and remarks by Percy Sutton and historian Dr. Yosef ben-Jochannan (Dr. Ben). Betty presented five
Malcolm X Awards for service and dedication to black liberation that
evening. She decorated activists again in 1979 when a Black Unity
Awards ceremony at Boys and Girls High in Brooklyn fell among her
memorial week appearances. On this occasion, the widow honored
Queen Mother Moore and a fourteen-year-old boy who had rescued a
young Latina from a vicious beating at the hands of a band of white
youths.

May 1981 brought a grander affair, the Washington Malcolm X Day
Celebration that drew close to eighteen thousand. Betty got into a
chauffeured car with her friend Laura Ross Brown and cruised to the
affair, whose dignitaries included Reverend Ben Chavis, spokesman for
the National Black Independent Political Party. Betty spent much of the
afternoon sidestepping reporters, practically ducking behind Brown's
skirt. Finally the newsmen cornered her. "I don't know what Malcolm
would say today because if he was alive a lot of the things going on today
wouldn't be going on," she said. "I feel very sad that he isn't here today
because we have a lot of young people who are precipitously going from
crisis to crisis."

In 1985, it was the widow's turn to accept a garland at a Malcolm
event. That May, the Committee to Honor Black Heroes presented her
with a Malcolm X Achievement Award during a Bedford-Stuyvesant
ceremony. She was powerfully moved. But when she came to the
microphone, it was to scold those who lamented her husband's absence
while ignoring his example. "We should no longer believe in the
leader-flock syndrome," she declared.

Whether Betty was at a memorial, conference, forum, or lecture,
her mission was to guard Malcolm's legacy and humanize his memory.
She wanted to lift him from the "street corner" she felt the news media
had consigned him to. She wanted the world to see him as a statesman
whose murder was injustice rather than as some rabble-rouser who had
perished in a Negro blood feud. Finally, dangerously, she wanted his
name associated with nonviolence; not in the tactical, Gandhian

sense, but in the sense that he had hurt no one. "When people think of him, they think of violence," she said. "But when you examine his life, you cannot find one thread of violence—or one death—connected to him while he lived. He said he believed in humanity, but would spend his time working with those who were denied their humanity— blacks—and for that he was branded a separatist."

The widow was fiercely protective and proprietary in all matters Malcolm. She thought this posture necessary, and to some extent it was. The cultural memory of Malcolm had fragmented like shards in a kaleidoscope. By the early 1980s, little more than slogans remained. "Martin Luther I-Have-A-Dream King and Malcolm By-Any-Means-Necessary X," journalist and OAAU man Peter Bailey later said. "That's all they knew." There was the sense among young blacks that Malcolm had told off the white man, but they were scarcely less inclined than their fairer countrymen to accept the authority of the *Washington Post* that the minister had been "a violence-prone radical" best known for "urging blacks to commit violence against whites."

Betty understood this. Her solution was to make herself a one-woman militia for Malcolm's image, and to attack anyone—enemy or ally—who she even dreamed had besmirched his name. "As great as Malcolm, Marcus Garvey, and Paul Robeson were," Leonard Jeffries once said at a Chicago conference, "we're blessed in this period because we have the knowledge of computers." Betty later ambushed the black studies professor in the hallway. "Len Jeffries," she said, "don't you ever say that Malcolm didn't know anything. He knew everything!" Smalls drew a similar rebuke years later when he discussed Malcolm and Collins's relationship at length on a radio program. Afterward, producers advised him that a Mrs. Shabazz was on the line. "Don't you ever mention my husband's name and don't mention me, when you talkin about that Ella!" Betty roared.

Of course, the widow's real quarrel was not with Malcolm lovers, but defamatory outsiders. A less-than-flattering portrayal of Malcolm in a 1978 television dramatization of King's life infuriated her. The NBC series had also roiled Civil Rights captains and King comrades who protested that the small-screen King came off weak-willed and cowardly. Betty was more concerned with the depiction of her own man. She complained that the film painted him as a "senseless grinning hyperphrenic whose total philosophy was based on hate," and announced her intentions to sue NBC. In celebrating King, it was not necessary to "disparage and defame the memories of other leaders," she said.

Betty wished for Malcolm all the glory and ceremony America lavished upon King. It chafed her to hear King's accomplishments sung without mention of her husband. Condemning the Vietnam War, denouncing international exploitation, globalizing African-American struggle—Malcolm had done all this and more before King, she reminded friends. After the passage of the King holiday under Reagan's administration, she began pondering a national tribute for Malcolm. She imagined a monument with class, something that would help universalize his appeal and garner the respectability she felt he deserved. In 1985, it struck her—she would get her guy a stamp.

Egypt had been the first to create a Malcolm X postal stamp, which it released shortly after the assassination. Years later, an Egyptian professor arrived at Medgar Evers College and told Betty about the commemorative token. It was then that she had her epiphany. The ideal tribute? A U.S. postal stamp honoring her husband. "This is what I want for Malcolm," she told a colleague. "Are you crazy?" the woman said. "Do you think the government..." But Betty wasn't listening; she had already begun to plot. (The fact that a postal inspector had been among the lawmen that honeycombed Betty and Malcolm's first Queens flat with bullets back in 1958 did not dim her resolve.) In 1984, the Islamic Republic of Iran issued its own Malcolm stamp commemorating the "Universal Day of Struggle against Race Discrimination." Betty was encouraged. She mentioned her idea to Laura Ross Brown one day as the two overlooked the Potomac River from the balcony of the developer's Alexandria, Virginia, apartment. "How can we get the brother a stamp?" the widow asked. They decided that she would telephone Ronald Dellums of Oakland, California, a senior black congressman she was friendly with, and see what he could do.

———

Though no more than a few friends knew about Betty's stamp fantasy, the ambition reflected an attitude that had been marinating for years. "Betty felt that Malcolm should be afforded a much loftier position in the Civil Rights movement," Baraka would recall. But Malcolm had never been a Civil Rights leader. He had in fact spent a great deal of energy attacking the Civil Rights enterprise, which argued that blacks and whites together must redeem America and pry open her doors so that all her citizens might enjoy her promise. Martin's career had been the most eloquent expression of this philosophy. Malcolm, on the other hand, had begun from the premise that the system was innately rotten. During his dash over the landscape of revolutionary ideology, he had called upon the oppressed to withdraw physically and spiritually from the system, to dismantle the system, to wrest power from the system and rule themselves.

Betty never pondered such matters when it came to Malcolm. She loved him as wife, and believed he was worthy of the widespread adulation the King holiday symbolized. The fact of the holiday seemed to more impress her than the irony that a right-wing politician like Reagan could now recall King as an innocuous minister of goodwill and brotherhood. Such hollow nostalgia, a Harvard scholar later noted, helped create "a comforting icon out of the career of a political iconoclast." Yet as far as Betty was concerned, Malcolm was as universal as King. Her lectures never patently diluted the minister. She simply rounded off his edges, speaking in parochial terms of his vision of justice rather than his dark prophesies of bloodshed (which in the 1960s had very nearly come true). "She knew what she wanted to promote," Evers-Williams later declared. "It made no difference what anybody else said." Betty did not want Malcolm decaffeinated, either. "One time she called me at the last minute to fly out to Howard [University] for some little Negro stuff," Baraka recalled. "Because she wanted somebody to say what Malcolm really represented, despite these niggers trying to cover it with their cobwebs of ignorance and duplicity."

One glimpsed all the widow's curatorial impulses—the desire to demilitarize Malcolm while preserving his potency, to humanize yet immortalize, to elucidate and vindicate—during yet another Howard affair. The year was 1979. The occasion was the culminating Malcolm X Week address. The sponsor was a consortium of student organizations at the historically black Washington school. Betty had come to talk about Malcolm, but she also interwove her own message of education and self-help. The nationalism that had rung in her speeches a decade before had faded. She was shy and regal as she stood before the hushed auditorium that February. The talk she delivered after an effervescent host wound up his introduction—"she's *beautiful*, brothers and sisters"—exemplified both her trusteeship of Malcolm and the moderate pragmatism that had become her hallmark.

Oppression is not incidental but orchestrated, she said; so the minister is less misunderstood than misrepresented. She spoke of the international "fury" over his platform, of America's deceit in branding him "the messiah of violence." She declared quite candidly that however idolized and reviled, Malcolm was about the business of revolution. "And believe me," she said, "it is a revolution to get blacks to love one another." She began skewering myths. She dismissed the notion that Malcolm was maniacal or malevolent, that he had somehow created the racial malice to which he held a scorching lantern, that he despised all Christians and not merely the architects of the African slave trade. "His father was a Baptist minister," she reminded the audience. "And my parents were Methodists."

She discussed Malcolm's Third World consciousness, quoting him in the present tense: "He says, 'When we realize how large this earth is and how many different people are on it and how closely they resemble us, we recognize that alliances are possible.'" She upheld his position on self-defense. "People immediately said violence and guns," she said, but one must consider all possible strategies to achieve a goal. "Growing your own food—isn't that defending yourself?" she asked with a bashful smile. Establishing black banks, cultivating black doctors, nurses, and engineers—wasn't that self-preservation? The minister had preached survival and community control. Those who heard "bloodshed" must themselves have been violent.

Yet true self-determination meant renouncing more than the oppressor's definitions, she said. One must also reject low expectations. She denounced ghetto schools that labeled youngsters uneducable and scolded blacks who bought such rubbish. "Somebody said to me today, 'You know, the white man is really something, he just keeps us from doing a whole lot of things,'" she said. "But we don't need the white man to teach our children how to read and write." She recalled that the Civil Rights establishment had resisted Malcolm's efforts to convert the struggle to a human rights crusade. "But at the moment, human rights are heralded as a panacea for ills around the world," she said. Alas, vindication could not revivify. Some "programmed" blacks had cheered when a coup d'état toppled Kwame Nkrumah's government. Now Ghanaians were struggling to rekindle the Redeemer's legacy. "'Cause gone are the glorious hotels," the widow said. "Gone is the high life. They don't do the high life with the same strut." Regrets abound. "But the spirit of Osagyefo is long gone."

What should young blacks do now? Don't waste classroom time, Betty said. And don't waste yourself on a cheap high. "They did it in our parents' and grandparents' day on the limb of a tree," she said. Now annihilation lay at the end of a needle or pipe. "One of my daughters the other day said, 'Oh, Mommy, that's the joint,'" she recalled. "And I don't hit them, but I wanted to take my shoe off. Because when you say, 'That's the joint,' you mean it's together, it's good, it's hip, it's the best." Yet pot is carcinogenic and causes chromosomal and neurological damage, the widow warned. She reminisced about a time when blacks kept friends and family off dope by all means. "But what I hear now is brother got brother turning on and sister got sister turning on, and even some parents got children turning on," she lamented. The oppression has been systematic, she said. The work of liberation, she said, must be as systematic. "What we are going to have to do is rely on ourselves and be brother and sister, one to the other."

———

Memorializing Malcolm was Betty's joy and burden. Every February and May, the posters, books, and tapes resurfaced. The ancient photographs reappeared, waking painful memories. Every February and May, Malcolm's words hurtled like shrapnel, piercing her again. The widow preferred to recall her husband in the company of dear friends—on her terms and in her space. In those fleeting moments, she reanimated Malcolm more powerfully than any memorial could. She said that if he had lived she would have kept having babies. She said he was well prepared and that he worked hard to remain so. "You know," she added wistfully, "I always listened to him." She talked about the minister when the spirit moved her. But never with Dick Gregory. The activist-comedian didn't talk Malcolm with Betty for the same reason that he didn't talk King with Coretta Scott King. "She knew King and I knew King," he said of the latter widow. "What is there to talk about? She have to explain to people who Martin was. She don't have to explain it to me."

———

Betty's attitude toward the merchandising of her husband reflected her style of guardianship. "Malcolm, to what surely would have been his own astonishment, had become a commercially tradable image," a biographer wrote in the 1970s. Most of the paraphernalia in those years were trivial—bumper stickers and greeting cards. Little was licensed, so Betty hardly profited at all. She expressly permitted a few assorted novelties, but many of the products were sold from makeshift stands on ghetto sidewalks and were beyond her control. The Malcolm industry—both its legitimate and underground sectors—entered the 1980s modestly. In 1982, for instance, an amateur artist asked Alex Haley for permission to render a quote from Malcolm's autobiography in calligraphy and market it as a poster. Haley consented, advising the woman that she must also seek approval from Betty, the copyright coholder.

Based on the testimony of Attallah, the widow's response was likely favorable. The eldest daughter later said that:

> In the early days—the sixties, seventies, and eighties, before my father's likeness had become a licensed commodity—my mother didn't mind the bootlegged T-shirts, cassette tapes, and framed photos being sold at various events around the country during his birthday, Black History Month, and the like. In those years she felt it was one of the pulses that kept Malcolm alive on campuses, in community centers, and on cultural occasions. As a mother and educator, she was comforted by the thought that such remembrances would enable young people to have an opportunity to be exposed to her husband, ask questions, learn, and achieve. Pass it on! When people commented on the exploitation, she'd generously reply, "It's love that's making them do this for my husband." On the other hand, if the intentions of the merchant were not honorable, you'd better believe that she'd be heading in their direction to inform them of their malfeasance and impropriety.

There were times when Betty's approach to the market seemed rather laissez–faire indeed. She understood that the poor and oppressed clutch idols so that they can draw themselves from their beds each morning. In the early 1980s, as hip-hop was crystallizing, she gave serious thought to a young man's request to stylize Malcolm's motto in a demo "scratch" tape. He offered a demonstration, toting his boom box into the widow's office. "Buh-buh-buh-buh-buh by any means," went the mix, "buh-buh-buh-buh-buh-buh by any means necessary." As the years passed, however, Betty grew more particular about ownership. She once discovered that *Like It Is* host Gil Noble had been independently selling tapes of a Malcolm documentary he had produced for his television program. When she confronted him, he explained that he was only charging the nominal fee necessary to recoup the cost of warehousing the tapes, and that his purpose was not profit but education. The widow had assumed that he was hustling, but he brooked her suspicions. "She would let nobody mess with her husband," Noble later said. "And you don't see that too often."

———

The grassroots kept Malcolm's name alive in the street. Pathfinder, the socialist press, kept his words in print. Through the years, playwrights and theater companies also sought to conjure his spirit onstage. *Message to the Grassroots*, a play, opened in England in the late 1960s. The Afro-American Studio of Harlem performed *El Hajj Malik—The Dramatic Life and Death of Malcolm X* off Broadway in 1970. The more ambitious productions appeared in the 1980s. *When the Chickens Came Home to Roost*, a taut and edgy one-act play, opened in 1981 to bright reviews. Set in Elijah Muhammad's office in 1963 (just as that nasty business of the elder's escapades with young secretaries was coming to a boil), *Chickens* showed the disintegration of Malcolm and Muhammad's bond. During two scenes, Malcolm (deftly played by a young Denzel Washington) gingerly questioned Muhammad about his transgressions as the pixieish character swiveled between flattery and hostility. "This ain't no democracy—it's the Nation of Allah," the old man exclaimed during a tindery moment.

Four years later, *X* the opera arrived. It was a family affair; a young black composer had created the libretto with his cousin and brother. Actor Avery Brooks was the baritone Malcolm, while tap sensation Savion Glover, then a gradeschooler, played the childhood Malcolm. *X*, which closely followed the narrative of the autobiography, joined the New York City Opera repertoire in 1986 after opening in Philadelphia. Its cast included a Betty character bathed in the duteous light that would characterize future portrayals of the first lady. (Ella Collins, in the person of a commanding mezzo-soprano, was among the other depicted figures.) Though she carped on the libretto privately (and publicly in a later program held at City College), Betty liked the fact that *X* acknowledged her. "You would think that there was no Betty in Malcolm's life," she told Myrlie Evers-Williams after seeing an earlier stage production. "How the hell you think we got them kids?"

Her attendance with almost three thousand other spectators of the opera's world premiere in New York offered her a foretaste of a new media Malcolm. His image had transmogrified in his two-decade absence. No one could doubt that his passage to sainthood was transcending the nationalist realm. (Corporate support for X came from such mainstream sources as Westinghouse Electric and Xerox.) Those who overheard the widow's prudently worded comments at the premiere might have sensed that she welcomed the transition. "New York is an ethnic town where different ethnic groups are developing a respect, a tolerance for other ethnic groups," she said. "I do hope this continues." (Also in the audience was filmmaker Spike Lee, who had lately risen to the rank of celebrity on the success of *She's Gotta Have It*.)

By the mid 1980s, Betty was arriving at a fuller understanding of her husband's true meaning. "The legacy of this man—it hit her one day," Sonia Sanchez later said. The ardor of each Malcolm tribute seemed to startle the widow anew; the grander the tribute, the deeper her sense of vindication. She would not live to see the 1999 release of the U.S. Malcolm X postal stamp, the ultimate symbol of Malcolm's transmutation. ("Them white folks finally found a way to lick Malcolm," Gregory later quipped. "If Betty was alive when it came out, I would have had 'bout five hundred dollars worth of them stamps on me, and I would have handed them to her and said, 'Here's your new quilt.'") But the widow's vision of glory for the minister never blurred. "One day," she told Evers-Williams, "one day they will know who my husband was."

Among the triumphs of the time was a little-noticed name change in Brooklyn. In the spring of 1985, a Bedford-Stuyvesant community board voted to rename Reid Street "Malcolm X Boulevard." Residents of the historic black neighborhood had pushed for the change. Reid had been a white farmer who owned land in their area during the early 1800s. Malcolm had been a black prince who replaced a piece of their collective soul. There was some dissent among neighbors. One church worried that the name change would chill redevelopment efforts in the troubled community. Yet hundreds turned out to support the proposal at a board meeting in which Betty spoke simply and elegantly of the minister's fearlessness in confronting a corrupt and powerful system. Brooklyn Nationalist Sonny Carson picked the widow up for a drive some days later. "C'mon, I'll take you to see something," he said. He drove her over to the newly minted Malcolm X Boulevard. As the shiny street sign came into view, Betty buried her head and wept.

—◆—

Betty wanted a profound monument for Malcolm; for her daughters she wanted prosperity and spiritual health. "Our mother kept our home strictly private," Attallah later said, "and she kept a very low profile, which immensely helped us." Betty sheltered the girls even more vigilantly as her stature rose. By design, most of her ambassadorial appearances were solo acts. She ushered her brood to occasional programs and events. The daughters knew their public role called for reticence. "My mother will kill me if we say anything political," Attallah told reporters during royal outings of her late teens.

Betty saw herself as a "sergeant" with a rowdy battalion. As her daughters approached womanhood, she linked each with close girlfriends she admired, arranging internships and apprenticeships. "This is going to be your second mom," she told one of the twins upon introducing her to a confidante. The widow spared no energy or expense in fashioning her mademoiselles. "She was consumed with trying to situate the girls," a comrade later said. Though she had become a woman of affairs, the knowledge that six souls relied utterly on her remained her most powerful motive. "If you want to do something for me, help my children," she often said. "But, honey, let me tell you about them first!"

She taught her daughters that economic and emotional independence began with education. She taught them that black women, particularly Shabazzes, must overexcel to survive. The lessons became liturgy. "You did your homework," Ilyasah later said. "You did what you were supposed to do because you couldn't give an excuse." For all her austerity, Betty was always bailing the girls out of fixes. One of her friends discovered this lioness instinct over a bit of gossip. The widow was chatting with a Mount Vernon day-care colleague one afternoon when the woman mentioned a local mother who had vigorously defended her son, a murder convict. "She wasn't trying to help him before he got in trouble," the woman said, expecting an "amen" from Betty. "Now look," the widow snapped, "today you want to be on your high horse. But if your child was in trouble, you'd do just what that mother is doing. You'd lie, you'd steal, you'd do whatever it took to try to help your son. So don't you dare tell me about what this mother should or shouldn't be doing."

Betty's guardianship seemed to pay off. By the late 1970s, the Shabazz daughters, from the adolescent twins to the elder teenagers, had grown into beautiful and talented young women. Attallah enrolled at nearby Briarcliffe College with plans to major in international law. Qubilah, the brainiest of the lot, went off to Princeton. Though she dreamed of attending Spelman, the prestigious black women's college in Atlanta, Ilyasah enrolled at the State University of New York's New Paltz campus at her mother's behest. Gamilah (a theater arts major), Malikah (architecture), and Malaak (biochemistry) also attended schools in the area or region. Betty wanted her girls arrayed about her. After "eighteen years of scrimping, sacrificing, counseling, and mothering," as Haley described her struggle, she was not ready to release them to the world.

Attallah set out anyway, becoming a stage actress during her twenties. She dreamed of playing Josephine Baker, but took less glamorous roles in children's plays and area productions. "I would also like to write a play or script about my mother, Betty Shabazz, who's one of those strong, dynamic black women who have made a serious contribution to her family and to the community at large," she told *Essence*. In 1979, she met Martin Luther King Jr.'s eldest daughter, Yolanda, an actress three years her senior, during an interview for *Ebony*. Curiosity drew the two into rambling conversations. Once they overcame the jitters of facing an icon's daughter and their unease as children of men widely thought to be natural enemies, they became fast friends. They formed Nucleus, an eight-member theater troupe, and performed plays of self-realization and faith before schoolchildren across the country.

Willowy and regal like her father, Attallah became a public figure in the style of her mother. She spoke to mixed crowds about Malcolm (as Dad rather than revolutionary) while covering topics such as tolerance, faith, and pride. So uncanny had her resemblance to the minister grown that Haley, her godfather, called her Little Red (Big Red having been one of Malcolm's street monikers). The daughter never lost that elastic grin and T-square posture. "Even the enigmatic, elusive quality is Malcolm," Haley thought. Attallah liked the comparison, but sought singularity. "I think I would have been a humanitarian even if I weren't Malcolm X's daughter," she said. "But perhaps some of my characteristics are inherited from my father and my mother, who has also had a great influence on my life. She is my role model for women." Attallah was becoming the public face of the Shabazz daughters. (In 1983, *Ebony* named her among the "Fifty Young Leaders of the Future.") Her siblings were no less bright or artistic. "They're outgoing, healthy, and without bitterness," Betty boasted.

Even rebellious Gamilah, who continued writing defiant poetry in college, began a new age of endearment with her mother. The fourth daughter came home on an academic break and discovered that Betty had loosened up. The two even indulged in girl talk. "Me, I was always open," Gamilah later said. "I'm kind of a shocker. She'd go, 'Oooh, God. No—I can't, I can't.'" But when Gamilah returned to campus, the answering machine would impart all the wonders of sex and romance that the widow could not divulge face-to-face. "She didn't have to be my father anymore," Gamilah said.

Betty's brigade seemed to have come through without casualties. "She's made a tremendous contribution to African-American people to have raised six women so successfully," a New York City deputy mayor told the *Amsterdam News*. Even the widow's old nemesis agreed. "There is no doubt in my mind that they will [become leaders] in time," Ella Collins said of her nieces, "unless they become discouraged by the negativeness they see." But Betty had failed to sufficiently arm her daughters with a narrative of her and Malcolm's experience. Her suppression of the past had laid bare the young women she struggled to shelter, and they left the sanctuary of Mount Vernon ill equipped to claim their birthright.

Some of their angst was typical of an icon's offspring. Attallah was in her early twenties when the Panamanian government invited her to judge the Miss Panama pageant. Dreaming of sun-drenched leisure, she flung a beach hat and swimsuit into a bag. When she arrived in the tropical republic, officials greeted her as a diplomat and plunked her onto a dais to deliver a speech. The burden of her heritage had never been heavier. "Everyone had dressed me in glasses, a mustache, and a goatee," she imagined. The King children also collided with expectations. As a fifteen-year-old, Yolanda King caused a rumpus in Atlanta when she played a prostitute in *The Owl and the Pussycat*. At Smith College she faced a new dilemma. "Kids in my era were more militant and closer in terms of tactics to Malcolm," she later recalled. "I didn't even know Malcolm and I didn't understand Daddy, so here I was trying to defend something I thought I knew about but really didn't."

The militancy of Malcolm's legacy increased the Shabazz daughters' burden. While some white students shunned Qubilah at Princeton, some black students resented her. They misinterpreted her shy dignity as apparent disinterest in the battle for the school to divest its stock holdings in South Africa, then under apartheid rule. Similar pressures seemed to toughen Attallah. She created a strong public persona, taking possession of her personal Malcolm (in her mother's tradition) and painting him as a sentimental, boyishly gentle father and husband who had openly bared his emotions around his wife and children. Meanwhile she rejected definition by both his detractors and devotees:

> I can't think of looking at the [Gary] Hart kids and assuming they're all going to be footloose. But people see me and assume that because of my father I'm going to be politically so left that I have a tilt in my walk. Or that I wouldn't like white people, which is not what I was brought up to believe. Or that my hair is braided to make a statement instead of as a convenience. Or that I'm on the quiet side because I'm too serious as opposed to shy.

Some of Attallah's siblings lacked her durability and wilted under the judgment of others. Blacks at SUNY–New Paltz wanted Ilyasah to be a spokeswoman. The third daughter struggled merely to be a biology major. "Look," she said, "my hair's permed, OK?" Qubilah, the most sensitive of the sisters, had an even tougher time shouldering the Shabazz name. She dropped out of Princeton after two semesters and moved to Paris, where she studied and worked as a translator. Unable to find her footing, she drifted through small jobs and rooming houses. Eventually she met an Algerian man and had a son. She named him Malcolm.

Little Malcolm was not Betty's first grandchild. Attallah had a daughter in high school. The baby had threatened the widow's dream of her girls' idyllic passage to womanhood. She was deeply disappointed, having been born out of wedlock herself. She provided for her granddaughter until Attallah left home, but she rarely talked about the pregnancy among close friends, and told some acquaintances in later years that the girl had been adopted. She hoped to hide what she considered family blemishes. Resolving them, however, only got harder. The daughters that she had so painstakingly crafted started running into trouble. There was the natural pubescent anguish as well as deeper afflictions. Their heritage amplified both. "Whether you say they're like everybody else or not, they're not like everybody else, and people don't treat them like everybody else," Amina Baraka later said. "Any failure that they may have, it's somehow a conscious failure, like they're trying to hurt the black community." The cruelty of strangers and allies who discovered the daughters' human flaws caused tremendous strain. At times there was a sense of betrayal. *How could you be ordinary?* The girls learned as they matured that American celebrity is an industry, and each chose to embrace or resist commodification.

There were also pressures within the family. Betty's strictures were at times overwhelming. She was controlling, a genius of the guilt trip. Sometimes it seemed to Gamilah that she was "so hell-bent on education that nothing else mattered." Even the widow's eminence could oppress. "In some respects, Betty's triumph over the obstacles, her successes, actually added to the pressure on the children," a family friend later said. "They ended up having to deal with two icons."

The widow continued trying to shield her daughters from the more painful legacies of the original family icon. "Malcolm felt that blacks should know who their family is," she once told an interviewer, speaking of her husband's influence on Haley's *Roots*. Yet she isolated her girls from the minister's blood brothers and sisters in the Midwest. She eschewed her in-laws long after they had left the Nation of Islam and put the ugly affairs of the 1960s behind them, expressing regret for joining Black Islam's denunciation of the minister in those desperate days. They had become professionals and were quietly leading mainstream lives. But Betty shunned them. She rarely talked about them among friends, and with the notable exception of the eldest brother, Wilfred, talked *to* them even less frequently. "Betty knew Ella was keeping track of her and Ella knew Betty was keeping track of her," a comrade later recalled. The relationship went no further.

Attallah would nevertheless come to believe that "the past cannot be totally discarded as efforts are made toward a more hopeful future," as the widow herself had pronounced. As a teenager, the eldest daughter defied her mother by visiting Malcolm's brothers and sisters in Detroit. Her paternal aunts and uncles found her hungry for knowledge about their side of the family. "And so we were glad to have her with us," Wilfred, who became a spokesman for a local nonprofit, later said. While in Detroit, Attallah also met Malcolm's mother. The minister's siblings had rescued Louisa Little from a Michigan asylum in the 1960s, and the wearied but proud matriarch was now living with one of her daughters. Attallah bathed in the wisdom of her grandmother's eyes. "She is a remarkable West Indian lady who's led a fantastic life," she later said.

Betty was understandably reluctant to forgive the betrayal of the Malcolm siblings who had denounced the minister before and after his death and shunned his funeral. Her unwillingness to expose her daughters to certain family members on her own side was rather more mysterious. The girls knew their grandpa Juju (her birth father) and their Philadelphia uncles (her half-brothers). But they knew almost nothing of their three maternal aunts—Betty's half-sisters and the younger daughters of her biological mother, Ollie—living in Michigan and Texas. The widow was determined to protect her daughters from the pain of her childhood. Yet they inevitably felt the reverberations. Years later, at Ollie's funeral, Betty became hysterical with grief. "She hadn't seen this woman in years," Gamilah later remembered. "[She] loved Helen Malloy as her own. And she fell apart at the funeral and said, 'That's my *mother!* That's my *mother!*'"

Still, the widow never stopped quarantining the past. In a sense, "Don't look back" had been her credo long before it became the last commandment of her doomed husband. Consciously or otherwise, she was bequeathing the philosophy to her children. She was angry with Attallah for visiting Malcolm's siblings, a challenge to her authority that shook her relationship with the firstborn. There were intervals of estrangement with the other girls, as well. By age fourteen, Gamilah was growing increasingly difficult to handle. Betty temporarily sent her to stay with an OAAU organizer in Philadelphia with whom she had kept in touch. The family was going through a rough time, and she wanted the child to attend an equestrian camp in the area. Gamilah became even more unmanageable in Philadelphia, and begged to come home. But the widow could handle no more. "Raising the children became a real problem for her," the OAAU veteran later said. "It was more than she was cut out for, more than anybody could have been cut out for."

Gamilah started running away from home in later years, fleeing her mother's demands as she chased her father's meaning. (The fourth daughter always believed that it was Malcolm who saw her through those bumps with the street. "I walked out of situations where I could have been dead more than ten times over," she later said. "And if it wasn't for something guiding me...") The mutinies troubled Betty, but it was her daughters' later falterings that tormented her. Attallah dropped out of Briarcliffe College in 1977 after the Westchester

County private school became a campus of Pace University. (She later told reporters that she could not afford the tuition hike.) She held a series of jobs, including stints as a Con Edison customer-service rep, a cleaning woman, and a beauty-school instructor. She was poised, resourceful, and well spoken. Yet like most of her sisters, she was slow to find her niche, and Betty mourned the dying of her dream of advanced degrees for the girls. "They weren't making the kind of progress in life she wanted them to," a friend later said.

The pressure of being sole parent to six began taking a visible toll. Publicly the widow refused to discuss her daughters, saying only that some were in college while others had graduated. At times she tacitly acknowledged her burdens. "I'm part of the statistical class of single parents," she told one reporter. "I have to deal with all those areas that cause concerns and difficulties for single parents." She seemed unable or unwilling to acknowledge how deeply her lifestyle and the trauma of the past had affected her daughters. She told friends that the girls tended to fall for men's machinations because they lacked a father figure. Yet they had also inherited her distrust of would-be supporters, a trait as debilitating as it was necessary. Betty had returned to school and reinvented herself largely for her daughters, but the strain of her absence and the strivings of the last decade had severely disrupted the family.

She had always balanced the duties of motherhood and widowhood. Now she struggled to reconcile her daughters' defiance. "I tell you, she tried hard with those children," a girlfriend later said. The widow continued to cushion the girls as they ventured into the world. But even as she funded airy apartments, she withheld what they may have needed most: frank conversations about heritage and identity, about Malcolm and February 21, 1965. Her bloodline was thinning; she lost Juju in the autumn of 1986 to complications arising from a colon cancer–related operation. Yet she was too used to fleeing the past to transfer the history that might have helped her daughters better understand their spiritual inheritance.

History disrupted their lives, anyway. Qubilah still talked about the firebomb attack, though an era had passed since that dreadful night.

Attallah stiffened whenever she bumped into members of the Nation. She was seventeen or eighteen when the grief flared anew. She visited her father's grave for the first time, hoping for an intimate moment, but found a busload of admirers paying their respects. In those years, she and her sisters could no more fathom Betty and Malcolm than any teenager fathoms her parents. "But once I'd left school, I was working on my own, living away from this wonderful woman, this mother, this father as well, this...mommy," Attallah later said. "And as you grow older, you realize how young thirty-nine is. I don't remember if it was his birthday or his memorial day, but a day came when I realized he's dead. I never knew till then how much the void nauseated me."

The past intruded on Betty, too. After fifteen years as a backdrop for her nightmares, the Audubon Ballroom lurched back into her waking world. City officials were talking about redeveloping the gaudy Washington Heights palace where Malcolm had fallen in a fusillade. New York had owned the long-abandoned dance hall since the mid-1970s. The Jazz Age relic had deteriorated faster than its brown and black neighborhood, which had seen better days but still boasted sturdy houses and bustling stores. Through the years, the Audubon had squatted on a wedge between Broadway, St. Nicholas, 165th, and 166th, growing plywood skin and gaping through the sockets of its splintered windows at the thriving Columbia-Presbyterian Medical Center across the street, where surgeons had once reached into the minister's wasted chest to knead his heart. The ballroom now had the feel of a mausoleum. Within its rickety walls, the once-turquoise drapes were blanching and the scarred floors were rotting away. Its façade still bore a fanciful terra cotta scene of a ship slicing through choppy seas, a mermaid slinking from its prow. The mermaid, however, had lost her right arm.

Prospectors eyed the property with no less avarice, and by the early 1980s the city was mulling several construction proposals. The most aggressive belonged to Columbia University, which hoped to build a space-age medical-research center on the site. The city liked the bid, but neither Mayor Koch's administration nor the university wished to take on Malcolm's ghost. Knowing the Audubon's history and the sanctity of Malcolm's martyrdom, Columbia arranged a meeting with Betty and sent Larry Dais, its debonair black community-affairs representative, to convey its vision for a research complex that would explore such advances as gene splicing, spray bandages, and microelectric limbs. The widow listened to the pitch, studying Dais carefully. "She wanted to know was this a *black* man," he later said. Though the ballroom was sacrosanct to the black liberation movement, it was not formally an historic site. Only Betty had the clout to snarl Columbia's plans. The widow was dispassionate but firm when she finally spoke. Whoever wound up inhabiting the Audubon should somehow serve her husband's legacy, she told Dais. Then she leaned toward him. "If it was up to me," she said, "I'd never walk into that place again."

Betty withheld her blessing for the project for some time. She knew the black community would have much to say on the matter of the dance hall's fate and that Harlem traditionally viewed Columbia as a hostile neighbor. When it grew clear that the university was gathering momentum, she played her hand. She saw Malcolm as a humanitarian, she said, and she wished the Audubon to stand as a living memorial to his ideals. She proposed that the school endow a million-dollar fund to support annual scholarships for black medical students. In return for the award, the scholars would serve health-care centers in poor communities of color. Columbia agreed, and the Malcolm X Medical Scholarship was born. One of the first memorials that sprang entirely from Betty's head, the scholarship was an example of her mainstream strategies for honoring a man who had terrified the mainstream. The widow began communing with the scholars during annual reaffirmation sessions. "Every time I meet them there's nothing we talk about except the need for them to go beyond the call of duty to see that blacks get the best quality of care," she later said.

Meanwhile Columbia sealed the Audubon deal. The university had hoped to renovate the theater and dance hall that comprised the building, but it soon decided that it would do better to raze the decrepit edifice and surrounding properties, which it also owned. Betty could not bear the thought of setting foot in the ballroom. Still, the idea of the place disintegrating under a wrecking ball troubled her. Whether Columbia would destroy the dance hall or incorporate it into its new development, now conceived as an industrial research park, remained unclear until 1985, when the school began moving on demolition plans. Adamant about the university honoring its commitment to the scholarship, the widow also began quietly appealing for the Audubon's preservation. "Evil happened in it," she told the *Times*, "but I don't think it is evil."

Betty's efforts to save the scene of her grisliest memories caused her some unease. The ghosts of the 1960s began looming long before the Audubon affair, though. In 1970, as the widow was commuting to Jersey City to earn her master's degree, an undercover cop revealed from the witness stand during the Panther 21 trial that he had infiltrated Malcolm's cadre in the mid-60s. Gene Roberts, who served as one of the minister's bodyguards on the day of the assassination, had appeared to give the mortally wounded leader mouth-to-mouth resuscitation minutes after the shooting. A widely circulated photo had captured him bowed over Malcolm's body. He never testified during the martyr's trial and did not "come out from under" as an agent provocateur until the indictment of the Black Panther partisans on fantastic conspiracy charges.

Roberts's confession that he had been spying on Malcolm at the time of the slaying fueled speculation that police had been part of the cabal. Suspicion intensified in the mid- and late 1970s when bales of secret documents emancipated from government files exposed the depths to which the FBI, CIA, and other intelligence groups had gone in the 1960s and early 1970s to monitor and repress black protest. As ominous details of the FBI's "Cointelpro" program emerged, including J. Edgar Hoover's decree that the Bureau would seek to "prevent the rise of a 'messiah' who could unify, and electrify, the militant black nationalist movement," Jesse Jackson and other black leaders renewed accusations that Uncle Sam had figured prominently in the deaths of Malcolm, King, and Panther leader Fred Hampton. Revelations that the FBI had bugged King's telephones and connived to smear his reputation and disrupt his work ultimately led Coretta Scott King to seek reparations from the government.

Betty kept a low profile as the Bureau released sheaves of papers cataloguing its twelve-year campaign to neutralize her husband. Scholars, journalists, and Malcolmites in later years would pore exhaustively over the unclassified records, which exposed an obsessive surveillance of Malcolm and a repertoire of deception and dirty tricks. Based on new evidence that the agency had knowledge of impending threats to the minister's life, some students of the files would conclude that the FBI had been guilty of malignant neglect and even criminal connivance in his murder. His widow never strayed from her position that the government had facilitated the assassins. Yet she showed an enduring disinterest in the files and avoided discussing them publicly. "A number of people have gotten that information," she said of the documents many years later. "The names and some other information have been blocked out. But I have not requested it, don't want it, don't feel that the majority of it is true."

Betty knew that the intelligence community had waged war on Malcolm. No shameful trail of federal papers, however, would drive her to public pronouncements about state conspiracy. She had buried the intrigue of assassination with the 1966 conviction of three Black Muslims for her husband's murder and had spent the intervening years insulating herself and her daughters. This again proved a failing strategy. In late 1977, the long-closed homicide case resurfaced. Talmadge Hayer (now known as Mujahid Halim), the sole confessed killer, in a sworn statement declared that Thomas 15X Johnson (now Khalil Islam) and Norman 3X Butler (Muhammad Abd al-Aziz), both of whom had also spent the last thirteen years in prison for the slaying, were innocent. Hayer had tried to exonerate the two in 1966, but he now provided detailed descriptions of the crime and named his alleged confederates. Though he claimed not to have known who handed down the death order, he said four Muslim brothers—a functionary and three parishioners from the Nation's Newark Mosque—had joined him in carrying out the execution as vengeance for Malcolm's heresies against Muhammad. "There was no money paid to me for my part in this," he added, reversing his original testimony. "I thought I was fighting for truth and right."

The radical civil-liberties attorney William Kunstler agreed to take the story to court. Hayer's new account of the crime jibed with multiple eyewitness reports and the prevailing opinion of detectives that more than three assailants had felled Malcolm. The theory that Jersey Muslims were in fact the killers also seemed to resolve a blaring anomaly: how the minister's security force could have allowed Johnson and Butler, both known Fruit of Islam legionnaires from the Harlem mosque, to steal into the Audubon audience on that infamous day. But a judge refused to reopen the case, holding that Hayer's oath did not constitute worthy grounds. Kunstler presented the convict's affidavit to the Congressional Black Caucus. Betty, however, did not want the case reviewed. The Caucus, whose members had personal ties to the widow, respected her wishes.

Hayer had finally talked—had told the tale that it was indeed a Black Muslim execution squad that gunned down Malcolm—because Muhammad had left the scene. The Messenger, who for four decades had convinced a worshipful segment of his race that he had learned the universe's truths at the feet of Allah and who had bestowed upon Malcolm the eclectic dogma that the minister converted into an inimitable witness for black liberation, passed unto the ancestors on February 25, 1975. The seventy-seven-year-old mystic's death was a shuddering blow to his Nation, but the Original People pressed on, as they always had. The kingdom had hemorrhaged after Malcolm's assassination, and there had been prophecies of its doom. Yet Black Islam had gradually found new believers and legitimacy within African-America. It found new estate, too. Despite notorious mismanagement and staggering debts, the Muslim empire by the 1970s included schools in forty-six cities, restaurants, stores, a bank, a publishing company that printed the country's largest circulating black newspaper, and fifteen thousand acres of farmland in three states.

The Nation had gentrified and mellowed. Its hierarchs started crowing less about white devils. Even its monarch tempered his rhetoric. "The slavemaster is no longer hindering us—we're hindering ourselves," Muhammad proclaimed the year before his death. "The slavemaster has given you all he could give you. He gave you freedom. Now get something for yourself." Louis Farrakhan, the Malcolm protégé who as Louis X had once declared the minister "worthy of death," succeeded Malcolm both as head of the New York mosque and as the sect's national spokesman, achieving a manner of respectability among Harlem's civic crowd.

But there was trouble in paradise. A series of bloody feuds in the early 1970s plunged the sect into chaos. In 1971, Muhammad son-in-law and Fruit of Islam chief Raymond Sharrieff was shot and wounded near the *Muhammad Speaks* office. Two members of a dissident Muslim faction were murdered three months later in apparent retribution for the attack. The following year, New York police who claimed they were answering a detective's distress call burst into the Nation's Harlem temple and scuffled with its parishioners. The skirmish swelled into a riot as more than one thousand blacks massed outside the temple, igniting a police cruiser and pelting white policemen with rocks and bottles. Farrakhan vaulted atop a parked car to quell the uprising, urging the throng to "just be cool" and earning the applause of the *Times*, which hailed his "dependability in Harlem."

Yet some of the most grotesque chapters in the Nation's history lay ahead. In January 1973, a Black Muslim posse surged into the home of Hamaas Abdul Khaalis, a Hanafi Muslim leader who had denounced Muhammad as a charlatan. The enforcers massacred seven members of Khaalis's family, including three infants. Four months later, another squad from the ranks of Black Islam killed Malcolm X Foundation helmsman Hakim Jamal in his Boston home. Jamal, who in 1967 escorted Betty to a Malcolm memorial in San Francisco, had also openly condemned Muhammad. The Muslim butchery dragged into that autumn of 1973, when a pair of black men assassinated James Shabazz, minister of the Nation's Newark mosque. In the following weeks, two congregants from the mosque died of gunshot wounds, and the beheaded bodies of a couple more former members were discovered in a park. While only a fraction of the overwhelmingly peaceable Original People were entangled in the gruesome affairs, the sect showed a lingering proclivity to deal less than civilly with splinter congregations and dissidents, many of whom echoed old charges that Black Islam had grown insulated, financially corrupt, and narrowly sectarian.

Muhammad's son Wallace (later Warith) agreed. The former Malcolm confidant's objections to the Nation's doctrinal and moral impurities had twice culminated in his banishment. He had returned to the fold and served at Muhammad's side. Yet when Muhammad passed, he assumed the throne and began transforming his inherited kingdom. He counseled the Muslim faithful (then estimated to number between twenty-five thousand and two hundred fifty thousand) to honor the American flag and vote in public elections. He disbanded the notoriously thuggish Fruit of Islam guard and set about dismantling the empire's businesses and holdings. He reformed the ministry, slashing salaries and forbidding decadence. He formally abandoned the "white devils" designation, the doctrine of innate white evil and the color ban on membership. Most significantly, he refashioned the sect in accord with traditional Sunni Islam, renaming it the World Community of al-Islam in the West and establishing the Qur'an and the ancient Prophet Muhammad as exclusive authorities of the creed. He recognized Fard simply as the Nation's founder (rather than as Allah incarnate) and Elijah Muhammad as its patriarch (rather than divine prophet).

Many of the believers were unable to make the dizzying transition from separatist sect to fundamentalist communion, and membership eroded in the following years. Among the disenchanted was the velvet-mouthed Farrakhan, who chafed under the Wallace reformation until 1977, when he broke with the prodigal to rebuild the Nation upon Muhammad's orthodoxy. The forty-four-year-old Farrakhan proclaimed himself the spiritual heir to Muhammad and began organizing fellow dissidents around the original kingdom's dogma. "We have to ask ourselves what we are going to do about where we are," he told one audience. "If we don't, then tomorrow, while we're singing the lullaby of integration, we will find ourselves dead under the heels of racism." Farrakhan's Nation had won a moderate following by the early 1980s. The evangelist's charisma and spellbinding oratories enraptured his loyalists, though he had achieved nowhere near the national prominence of his erstwhile idol Malcolm. Wallace, on the other hand, seemed more concerned with propelling his own congregation toward Eastern Islam—and with restoring Muslim regard for Malcolm. Already the heir had renamed the Harlem mosque "Malcolm Shabazz Temple Number Seven."

The original Temple Number Seven—the one that had erupted in flames after Malcolm's murder—had in 1964 and early 1965 boiled with enmity for the apostate. In February 1976, it fell to Farrakhan, who had yet to bolt Wallace's régime, to explain the dramatic rededication. The new recognition of Malcolm did not signal a break from the old policies of Black Islam, the spokesman said. Nor had the sect rehabilitated the martyr's name. Rather, the "Honorable Wallace D. Muhammad" was seeking balance. Farrakhan stressed that the Original People still considered Malcolm guilty of sins against Allah. "He knew where the Nation should go and would ultimately go," Farrakhan said, "but as a leader he lacked the patience to wait for the development of the minds of the followers." The spokesman nevertheless acknowledged "the great work that Malcolm X did when he was among the Nation of Islam."

Betty was unimpressed. It hardly dazzled her that the mosque where assistant ministers once wished for the destruction of her husband had been reborn as Harlem's most visible monument to him. Nor did she seem dazzled by the Wallace reformation or the fact that some of his sweeping policies mirrored the amendments that Malcolm himself had urged. She had not spoken to Wallace since the assassination, had not forgiven him for returning to the kingdom from exile before the minister's body was in the ground. Now the widow turned an indifferent eye on both the revamped and restored sects of Islam. Books and news reports of the late 1970s and early 1980s that sought to unravel the mysteries of Malcolm's assassination (including a 1981 airing of 60 Minutes that explored the possibility that Butler and Johnson had been falsely accused) seemed to leave her similarly disaffected. Speculating journalists and experts could not resurrect her man. Besides, she had too many obligations to the living to indulge in exhumations.

Malcolm's ghost visited her nonetheless. She would sometimes murmur wandering soliloquies in what one friend believed was a pidgin Arabic. "She didn't want you to know anything, but she had to get it out of her," the sister said. Occasionally the widow would talk in what another confidante described as riddles. "Eventually you will understand," Betty told her. Myrlie Evers-Williams understood better than most. "There were times I would see the tears swell up, and there were times when she would squeeze my hand," she later recalled. The spells were scarce and fleeting, and the Shabazz composure always snapped back into place. At times the pain surged. "Malcolm, how could you have left me?" the widow would exclaim.

Betty told friends that she had always known that a death squad would come for the minister. She remembered that awful certainty. She talked about how she and Malcolm had feared for the children. She remembered the threatening calls that had so enraged him. She struggled to swallow the acid, to reconcile her commitment to serve blacks with her fury that blacks themselves had pulled the trigger. "Betty knew her husband had got killed," Elombe Brath later said, "and nobody really did that much about it. Didn't nobody really took nobody out for it."

Then there was the eternal issue of the assassins' identities. She swore that the Muslims had slaughtered her husband. Her more ideological comrades felt that the state had played rather a larger role. Some of them debated her on the point. "The Nation and them didn't do that," Baraka told her again and again, with as much tact as he could muster. Though she yielded slightly on the matter much later, Betty for years would hear none of the conspiracy theories. She believed fiercely that Muslims had been the architects of the plot and not merely its instruments. "What could the Nation do to make it up?" somebody once asked her at a public affair. "Bring my husband back," she said, and walked away.

The particular target of her malice was Farrakhan. Elijah Muhammad had passed into the hereafter, but Farrakhan was alive and well and wielding the power that Malcolm had nurtured so generously within him. The widow often recalled her husband's tutelage of the former Boston minister. She talked about "bringing that boy into our home"—about Farrakhan's pilgrimages to their place in Queens to learn from Malcolm the mysteries of Islam and black nationhood. She remembered that the kid cleric would occasionally sleep in the basement between coaching sessions. She said he was "like a son," and recalled that she often cooked for him before Malcolm gave him cash for the journey home. She said that after Malcolm decided to quit the sect, she had listened in on a gloomy phone conversation between him and Farrakhan. "I can't join you," she remembered the younger man saying mournfully. "I love you, but I can't do that." She recalled the venom Farrakhan had spurted at Malcolm in later weeks and months, and never stopped thinking of the damnation as a betrayal in the family. Though he had always denied personal complicity, it was her unrelenting conviction that Farrakhan was directly linked to her husband's death.

Her friends tried to soften her hatred. "Farrakhan and them didn't do that," Baraka repeated. "And I'm not no lover of Farrakhan or no Nation, because I was with Malcolm." Another friend urged her to forgive Farrakhan for her own good and that of her progeny. "Look, this has got to stop," the sister told her. "For the sake of the children and the next generation." Betty was unmoved. She watched during Muhammad's last years as Farrakhan filled the role her husband had held. "I don't know why Muhammad would try to make another Malcolm," she said. She watched as Farrakhan—who had once written that, "only those who wish to be led to hell, or to their doom, will follow Malcolm"—split with the flock and established an offshoot congregation.

Then came 1984 and Jesse Jackson's presidential bid. The campaign inspired Farrakhan to break from Muhammad's abstentious approach to organized politics. He registered to vote, volunteered the Fruit of Islam for Jackson's security detail, and began stumping for the candidate. The apostle's incendiary rhetoric drew the sort of attention that Jackson might have preferred to forgo. Matters worsened when a black *Washington Post* reporter overheard and printed Jackson's offhand remark about "Hymietown," a disparaging reference to Jews. In a broadcast from Chicago shortly afterward, Farrakhan called the journalist a traitor and suggested that his followers would punish the man with death. Amid the media firestorm that followed, the public learned that Farrakhan had also referred to Hitler as "a great man." Farrakhan argued that he had meant "wickedly great" as Jackson struggled both to distance himself from the provocateur and retain his increasingly significant support.

The affair had already elevated Farrakhan to national stature. On a nationwide tour the following year, the fiery orator lectured to vast and rapturous black audiences, including a crowd of twenty-five thousand in New York's Madison Square Garden. Black moderates fretted about his seemingly abrupt rise. "When it comes to intergroup relations [Farrakhan's rhetoric] has been extremely harmful," Coretta Scott King said during a Washington press conference that September, "and I regret very much that this has been the case, because he is such a great orator and can be very influential."

Coretta Scott King was not the sole black protest widow lamenting Farrakhan. Betty had generally dodged the news media in the first half of the 1980s, but she granted several interviews in 1985, the twentieth anniversary of Malcolm's death. One of the last was with Gabe Pressman of WNBC-TV New York early that November. Betty had agreed to appear on Pressman's Sunday show, *News Forum,* to memorialize Malcolm and deliver niceties on behalf of her ally David Dinkins, who would rise that winter from city clerk to Manhattan Borough president. In light of Farrakhan's recent exposure, however, Pressman during the program asked her about the Muslim chief. The widow, whose "praise the good" motto practically everyone around her knew, who had mastered the art of repression and for two decades had refrained from publicly uttering Farrakhan's name, finally spoke her mind.

Farrakhan was an "opportunist" who created disarray and who had hurt Jackson's run for the White House, she said. She wondered why the firebrand did not spend less time baiting Jews and instead address ongoing crises in South Africa, Mozambique, and Angola. She acknowledged that Malcolm had recruited him to Black Islam, but she insisted that the younger man "was not a close associate," and noted that he had in fact cawed for Malcolm's death. It was out. Mrs. Malcolm X had told the world what she thought of the spiritual leader of Allah's revived kingdom. "I regret the day I ever had the unfortunate opportunity to meet him," she said.

Chapter Seventeen

CELEBRITY

—

"I shall come back to you."
—Marcus Garvey

By the 1980s, Betty counted a constellation of distinguished blacks among her friends. Her prestige as a bourgeois sister who spoke simply and moderately for progressive causes eclipsed her reputation for irascibility. She was drifting quietly into New York's policy circles, endorsing David Dinkins's mayoral bid by offering hosannas from this or that lectern. ("It is of great moment to say that one is supported by Dr. Betty Shabazz," the politician later declared.) Her international diplomacy, ties to black civic groups, and public bearing broadened her influence. "She was the most accessible of the women who inherited the mantle of grace and struggle after the deaths of their husbands," recalled Temple University Afrocentrist Molefi Asante, who met the widow in 1989 on the speaker's rostrum at a black health retreat in upstate New York. "She gave off an air of quiet confidence without all of the affectations. There were no pretensions, and that's why we loved her."

Some of the love Betty received almost universally was derivative and always would be. Yet the strangers who welcomed her "with greetings usually reserved for a dear aunt," as one reporter noted, were embracing an evolving icon as much as a legacy. Now in her early fifties, the widow had become a fixture at New York's Black and Latino Caucus gatherings and the National Council of Negro Women's Black Family Reunions. At Medgar Evers College, she sashayed the halls calling out to her dears. She landed beside former congresswoman Shirley Chisholm on a short list of candidates for the school's presidency, but waved off the nomination. "At this point in my life, I don't need any headaches," she said. (Compton College President Edison Jackson got the job in 1989 and proclaimed the widow Medgar's "cultural attaché.")

Among the highlights of the decade for Betty was her inclusion in *I Dream a World*. The 1989 book, Pulitzer Prize–winner Brian Lanker's pageant of seventy-five of the planet's most illustrious black women, affirmed her presence in a sisterhood of strength and arrayed her earthy portrait alongside black-and-white photographs of such heroines as actress Ruby Dee, activist Angela Davis, and Rosa Parks, mother of the Civil Rights movement. Unlike Parks, however, the widow's power had long since transcended symbolism. This much grew clear one winter afternoon when an armed black man and woman forced Gamilah into a car on West 60th Street in Manhattan and robbed her of jewelry and credit cards before releasing her on Amsterdam Avenue. The shaken but unharmed twenty-three-year-old called her mother. Within minutes, a fleet of squad cars careened onto the block, painting the scene in blaring blue and red. Gamilah later discovered that Betty had called a prominent judge, who had in turn rung the nearest precinct. It was a sign both of Betty's standing and the changing of eras that the New York constabulary that had once regarded Malcolm as an enemy of the state now treated his survivors like state ministers. The widow spent the weekend after the robbery at Gamilah's house. "And we slept in the same bed just like when I was little," the fourth daughter remembered.

Betty's eminence was the fruit of her strategies, her dignity, and her negotiation of astonishingly brutal terrain. What elevated her most abruptly, however, was Malcolm's "Second Coming." The rebirth began with the minister's partisans, who had been faithfully memorializing him since he fell. The passage of the King holiday intensified their crusade for a rediscovery of the militant. Black schoolchildren began confronting Malcolm as they studied King. In many black neighborhoods, commemorations evolved around the King holiday in January and Malcolm's memorial day in February, bracketing a time of remembrance for the struggle's most sacred ancestors.

By the mid-1980s, Harlem nationalists were lobbying to rename the local Lenox Avenue in Malcolm's honor. The sometimes-rancorous effort followed the birth of the Bedford-Stuyvesant Malcolm X Boulevard that had moved Betty to tears. There was some squabbling among ideological allies over whether the latest petition should instead be for an "El-Hajj Malik El-Shabazz Boulevard." Still, the disunited front managed to press city council into approving the tribute. On May 4, 1987, Betty, Rev. Al Sharpton, and other dignitaries looked on as Mayor Koch, who had initially resisted the renaming campaign, signed into law a bill proclaiming Lenox Avenue from West 111th to West 145th "Malcolm X Boulevard." The rechristened strip of Lenox, where Malcolm had skulked as a hustler and strode as an evangelist, was a rousing triumph for Black New York.

Yet the Malcolm resurgence throbbed most powerfully in the hip-hop soul. The socially conscious rhymes of rap pioneers like Grandmaster Flash and the Furious Five evolved into the searing lyrics of radical emcees by 1987. Malcolm's voice, preachings, and philosophy began resounding in defiant hip-hop anthems. Though much of the nationalism and Muslim dogma streamed into rap from the tongues of "Five Percenters," members of one of the Nation's dissident factions, Malcolm's outrage and pride appealed broadly to the liberationist spirit of hip-hop, which had boiled out of New York ghettos in the late 1970s. Soon crews and wordsmiths like Boogie Down Productions, X-Clan, Poor Righteous Teachers, Gangstarr, Paris, Brand Nubian, and Public Enemy (whose 1987 "Bring the Noise" featured Malcolm's sonorous voice proclaiming "No sell out!") were sampling and invoking the martyr.

Meanwhile the black-brown, hip-hop generation embraced his image. Kids sported buttons and leather medallions embossed with his face and T-shirts emblazoned with his slogans. Guys on the street exclaimed, "That shit was *Malcolm*," to express authenticity, integrity, desirability, and blackness. Sales of the minister's autobiography and printed speeches rocketed. In the summer of 1989, when Spike Lee's racially charged *Do the Right Thing* arrived in theaters, one could hear audiences murmuring "amen" as a Malcolmism materialized on screen. Blacks were seizing Malcolm's spirit amid devastating inner-city poverty, a crack-cocaine epidemic, and the swelling specters of AIDS and rekindled racism. The liberal mainstream, which had once limned Malcolm as a "bearded Negro advocate of violence" and "radical fanatic," also began recasting him as a revolutionary hero. Even the *Boston Globe* editorial page hailed him as "a prophet" and exulted that his reputation had "survived the calumnies of those who hated and feared him."

Not everyone was as eulogistic. By 1992, white columnist Colman McCarthy was scolding Malcolm's "prettifiers"—including Betty—and recalling the minister as "a second-rate mind spouting a third-rate agenda." Writing in the *Washington Post*, McCarthy insisted that Malcolm, who "lacked a political base or even the know-how to establish one," had inflamed racial ills and urged blacks to violence as a consequence of intellectual deformity. "He could have learned the power of nonviolent resistance from his contemporary Martin Luther King, Jr.," McCarthy sneered, "but, lazy of mind, he preferred snideness and ridicule to study." Among the black dissenters from Malcolm's pop-culture cult were Carl Rowan (who had famously dismissed Malcolm as a crackpot after the assassination and now made not dissimilar comments) and former Supreme Court Justice Thurgood Marshall, who questioned the gravity of the minister's accomplishments.

Yet the most damaging dispraise came in the form of a "white" book—political scientist Bruce Perry's *Malcolm: The Life of a Man Who Changed Black America*. Released in 1991, the exhaustively researched and weirdly speculative biography sought to disprove central elements of Malcolm's autobiography and identified not racism but Freudian forces and a self-destructive impulses as the motives behind the revolutionary's adult life and militancy. Perry refuted Malcolm's account of his father's death at the hands of white racists and argued that the 1965 Valentine's Day firebombing of the Shabazz home was the desperate act of the minister himself. Most appallingly for the devotees of a martyr who had come to embody black manhood and masculinity (notions traditionally wedded to heterosexuality), Perry also portrayed Malcolm as having engaged in homosexual sex during his young adulthood.

Malcolm's apostles were building monuments long before his deconstructionists arrived. As hip-hop was appropriating the minister in the latter 1980s, a coterie of scholars, writers, and nationalists—the original "children of Malcolm"—were gathering to amplify his memory. Black intellectuals and veteran Malcolmites organized a series of parleys around his life and legacy. Disparate Malcolm groups federated as the Malcolm X Commemoration Commission and called on Black America to recognize his May 19 birthday as a "people's holiday." In 1990, the twenty-fifth anniversary of the assassination, the Commission sponsored a flurry of events. The cerebral culmination of the revival was "Malcolm X: Radical Tradition and a Legacy of Struggle," a New York conference that assembled a spectrum of nationalists, Pan-Africanists, feminists, Marxists, and black theologians that November. But the Year of Malcolm had climaxed emotionally back in February during a massive tribute at Abyssinian Baptist Church, which in a bygone era was among the worship houses that had refused to host Malcolm's last rites.

Betty played her traditional role in the commemorations, offering remarks at Brooklyn memorials; reminiscing in workshops during Malcolmite summits at Hunter College; stretching with a girlish smile during a street ceremony to touch an oversized bust of her husband on the chin. She peered radiantly over Mayor Koch's shoulder as he ordained Malcolm X Boulevard, kissing and hugging him afterward. The embrace scandalized black nationalists, who had no love for Koch. But Gamilah was tickled. "I called my mother the day I saw her picture in the paper staring down at Koch," she later remembered. "The look on her face was that soft smile, like, 'Hmmph! Can I *hear* Malcolm X Boulevard?'"

Betty befriended Koch and was an occasional guest at Gracie Mansion, the mayor's residence. The relationship was strategic, whatever genuine fondness developed between the two. Ennobling Malcolm was high on the widow's agenda, an agenda that alliances with power brokers like Koch helped propel. (By the same token, it never hurt for a politician whose name stoked the ire of black and brown constituents to appear publicly with Malcolm's old lady.) But Betty was not a catalyst in the creation of Malcolm X Boulevard. That credit belongs to Harlem's New Afrikan People's Organization and other grassroots camps that crusaded for the change.

The widow's guardianship never waned. She was furious when the Perry biography appeared and joined Malcolm's devotees and blood brothers in denouncing the work, which, despite copious endnotes and reviews in distinguished publications, relied heavily on unnamed sources and often drew damning conclusions from scant evidence. One black writer dismissed the book as "a white man's psycho-social, sexual mythology…a negation of Malcolm's family, his background, and his aspirations." Betty, who had uniformly refused to cooperate with Perry and other biographers, was no more forgiving. "That man has problems," she said of Perry. "I am not going to waste my time dealing with him and his twenty years of research." Part of what incensed the widow was the book's accurate revelation that she had not been the first woman Malcolm considered marrying—"Malcolm kind of rebounded to Betty," the artfully conjectural Perry said in one interview—and that their marriage had been troubled. "Well, typically the widow is the custodian of the myth," the author later told CNN, recognizing Betty's stake in shrouding "the fact that [Malcolm] did not confide in her, and the fact that it was a very, very difficult marriage with little if any intimacy; little if any closeness; and a great deal of stress on both sides."

Betty had a growing sense of Malcolm's significance and the severity of his distortion in the mainstream. She knew the world did not know *her* man. Yet she had not translated her desire to elucidate him into a definite program. She was still embroiled in inner conflict between Malcolm the global figure and Malcolm the husband who had stranded her with a swarm of children. There were hints that she imagined herself in a more substantial role. As early as 1987, she embraced an evolving plan to institutionalize the minister's memory. A coalition of black intellectuals had fashioned themselves into a Malcolm X Work Group and begun talking about launching a Malik Shabazz Institute that would centralize the martyr's documents, host annual conferences, and otherwise sustain his legacy.

They envisioned not a tourist destination (what Atlanta's King Center had become), but a powerful, multipurpose foundation in the spirit of Jimmy Carter's presidential library. Betty liked the idea that she would be the institute's nominal head, with an office and personal secretary in whatever edifice it occupied. But her ambivalence toward the task of taking formal command of Malcolm's memory continued to frustrate black scholars. "Yeah, alright, we'll talk about it later," she said whenever Cornell University's James Turner prodded her to begin collecting the minister's scattered papers for research purposes. The widow raged privately against Perry and others she considered derogators. Yet she was only loosely tied to the efforts of academics and activists to promote an authentic, radicalizing image of her husband.

A few transcendent minutes with Winnie Mandela helped change that. To black South Africans, Winnie was "Mother of the Nation," the wife of Nelson Mandela—jailed leader of the outlawed African National Congress—and symbol of regal defiance to the apartheid regime. Winnie, whose original Xhosa name "Nomzamo" means "trials," had risen from barefoot beginnings among the peasants of the Pondoland hills to become South Africa's first black medical social worker. She had married Nelson, then a dashing lawyer and ANC organizer, on June 14, 1958—exactly five months after Malcolm had wed the former Betty Dean Sanders. Winnie had seen Nelson only sporadically and clandestinely over the next few years, as he went underground to deliver the ANC's message to fervent audiences and revolutionary leaders throughout South Africa and across the continent. The apartheid government had captured the insurgent, and in 1964 sentenced him to life imprisonment on charges of plotting to overthrow white rule.

During the years that followed, the state had tried to crack Winnie's devotion to her husband and the struggle. She had weathered bannings and internal exile, jail, house arrest, harassment, detention without trial, and even assassination attempts with fierce courage. Nelson Mandela had routinely rejected government offers of freedom on condition that he forsake his politics and renounce armed struggle. He had become a legend—the focus of international sympathy in the fight against apartheid. Meanwhile Winnie had raised their two daughters, borne the banner of Black South Africa, and evolved into a revered matriarch of Joan of Arc proportions. Her story captivated the black masses and at once matched and clashed with Betty's. Both women were bright and fetching students of healing who had wed electrifying nationalists several years their senior. Each had endured awesome hardship at her husband's side. Each had heard her man condemned as a terrorist and seen him wrenched away. Both had labored on, struggling to rear children and stay true to the cause while resisting the treachery of the state and dubious allies.

Controversy had bruised both. Winnie had found herself submerged in scandal in the latter 1980s and had drawn rebukes from ANC leaders and Nelson Mandela himself after praising burning-tire executions of suspected police agents and collaborators, building a sleek "presidential mansion" in shabby Soweto, and forming a band of young toughs—the so-called Mandela United Football Club—that township residents and black leaders accused of beatings, kidnappings, and the murder of at least one black youth who refused to support an ANC operation. Tales of Winnie's erratic behavior and corruption damaged her stature, to the South African government's delight. Yet she and Nelson Mandela remained inextricably linked as icons of the militant battle for black freedom and self-determination. Winnie knew well that she had "married the struggle, the liberation of my people." Unlike Betty, once a cloistered housewife whose frustration with her husband's lifestyle had sometimes flared before his apostles, Winnie had served as a spiritual comrade-in-arms to Nelson, dealing inwardly with much of her wrath and anguish. Her role in the movement had steeled her, nurturing in her a commitment comparable to his.

Mrs. Malcolm X idolized her. In a sense, Winnie represented the partner she might have become had Malcolm lived (and had the two reconciled). "She is a very spiritual person, she is a very clear and refreshing kind of woman, and she's a very soft woman," the widow later said of Mrs. Mandela, "but she exhibits real strength when she raises her hand." Betty revered Nelson Mandela, too, not only because Malcolm had admired him or because she saw glimmers of her husband in the ANC champion's indomitable aura, but because Nelson dwelled in that portion of her heart that would always belong to nationalism and Pan-Africanism. In a time of wealthy, compromising race spokesmen, he fulfilled the criteria of "validity and reliability" that had been her litmus test of leadership since Malcolm. The widow would align herself with Mr. Mandela, defending his refusal to renounce armed struggle before apartheid fell. "The man is not into terrorism," she declared. "What he is saying is they can't die anymore. We need to redefine and reinterpret what violence is. If someone knocks the heck out of you, you have the responsibility to get him off you by any means necessary."

Despite her adulation of the ANC's first couple, Betty had not met Winnie during her trips to southern Africa, though she had glimpsed the matriarch on an excursion to Namibia (an experience that brought her to tears) not long before the Mandelas' historic visit to America in the summer of 1990. South African President F. W. de Klerk had released Nelson from prison that spring. The seventy-one-year-old emerged silver-headed and rawboned, having spent twenty-seven years in confinement—much of it at hard labor. He strode like a warrior-king into the embrace of Winnie and South Africa's masses, his presence and militancy undiminished. "Our march to freedom is irreversible," he proclaimed as he prepared for talks with the government that would lead to a new constitution and the dismantling of apartheid. Nelson's liberation exhilarated Betty. She was elated when she learned that he and Winnie would call on Harlem during a whirlwind U.S. tour designed to raise funds and support for the ANC cause. The widow joined the welcoming committee early that summer, eager to help America's black Mecca receive Africa's lion.

Precisely how this encounter should happen had already sparked debate. Government officials and national black leaders would orchestrate the Mandelas' trek through eight U.S. cities in eleven days. The wishes of grassroots activists, black moderates, and federal authorities collided on the question of the Harlem visit. Harlemites had fought simply to get their village on the ANC leader's itinerary. Their success had brought a rush of black establishmentarians who envisioned a celebrity-laden, corporate gala (though U.S. corporate investment in South Africa had long buttressed apartheid). Nationalists who saw Nelson Mandela as a beacon of militant struggle hoped for a more ideological affair spotlighting the evils of apartheid and the plight of political prisoners (a fitting theme, they reasoned, since Mr. Mandela's stature was largely a product of his nearly three decades behind bars). Some of the ideologues viewed Betty, whose focus was on winning maximum publicity for the Mandelas, as a confederate of the Mayor Dinkins clique they feared was stealing their thunder. "We got bumrushed," activist Sam Anderson later grumbled. "Their vision was Mandela the Star, the Martin Luther King for Africa." The State Department was also in the mix, opposing plans to host the Mandelas in African Square, the heart of Harlem where Adam Clayton Powell, Martin Luther King, and Malcolm had held forth.

On June 21, the Mandela motorcade trundled into Harlem, and contention melted in jubilee. Winnie and Nelson Mandela took their places on the platform that Thursday night before a cheering crowd of thousands. Behind them, among the crush of dignitaries, was Betty, who had once ventured into the ferment of African Square only with her husband's permission. Now she sat racing with adrenaline, the flowers she was to hand Winnie Mandela clutched against her body. Activist Elombe Brath came forward to introduce the widow, who would introduce Winnie Mandela. Brath was all nerves, and Betty strained to hear when he turned to her and whispered something raspy. She took the microphone with practiced formality and drew a breath. Winnie Mandela, her heroine, stood regally on the opposite side of the lectern. "I was told to introduce myself," said the widow. "But I'm sure most of you know that I am Betty Shabazz, or Mrs. Malcolm X."

Upon learning the identity of the sturdy woman at her side, Winnie Mandela let out a spontaneous "Oh!" and reached across the lectern to grab Betty, pulling her into a smothering embrace. The widow stood limply for a heartbeat, her head nestled against Winnie's bosom. Winnie released her, only to clasp her in another frantic squeeze. Betty struggled to staunch the tears, swiping at a face from which all composure had drained. The crowd thundered as Winnie looked on with sisterly affection. Emotion had overcome the famed Shabazz poise. Betty managed to utter a few more words. "Time is short," she said. "Time is very short. And I would like to stand right here and cry for a thousand years. But I cannot. Let me just say, we applaud your indisputable human spirit. To show our love to you and our appreciation, these flowers are being presented to one of the greatest women among us—Mrs. Nelson Mandela."

Winnie accepted the bouquet and the microphone. "Amandla!" ("Power!") she cried. The Mother of South Africa spoke earnestly and powerfully. It was a great honor, she said, "to stand here in the capital of a revolution throughout the world." She proclaimed Harlem the "Soweto of America," and thanked black Americans for standing with their South African brethren. "We followed closely your own struggle against the injustice of racial discrimination and economic inequality," she said. "We continue to be inspired by your indomitable fighting spirit." She called on de Klerk to honor his pledge to negotiate in good faith for a new South Africa. And if negotiations collapsed, she told the throngs, "I want to know that you will be there with us when we go back to the bush and fight the white man!" The rally, having climaxed, drew quickly to its keynote. Dinkins called for stronger economic sanctions against apartheid. Congressman Charles Rangel promised Harlem's continued solidarity in the fight. Finally Nelson Mandela's voice echoed across 125th

Street. Betty may not even have registered the words. She was still swabbing at her eyes as she stood in the background propped against the diminutive Brath, who tipped his head toward hers in gentle support.

—

The widow reunited with Mr. Mandela in 1993 at an extraordinary assemblage of black dignitaries. Randall Robinson, head of the lobbying group TransAfrica; ousted Haitian President Jean-Bertrand Aristide; Dinkins; Jesse Jackson; and a host of African and Caribbean ministers and ambassadors gathered in a Washington church that January amid the pomp of Bill Clinton's inauguration to discuss the crisis of Haitian boat refugees and support the ANC's upcoming election battle. During the program, Jackson introduced Betty from the pulpit. As she strode down the aisle of Metropolitan Baptist, onlookers rose in ovation. Witnessing the largely Christian salute to a Muslim widow from whom the black bourgeoisie had once recoiled, a black woman turned to her companion somewhere in the sanctuary. "My God," she said, "don't things change?"

Betty joined Aristide and others that evening in denouncing Clinton's decision to uphold President George Bush's policy of rejecting Haitian refugees, though she also exalted Clinton's election as an end to the Bush era. "If it is a new day...if our morale is up...we must help in the governing, in the management and this administration," she said. "We can no longer sit back and blame one person." She later enjoyed a light moment with Nelson Mandela, with whom she had failed to gain an audience during a recent trip to South Africa (though she had received a kind note from Mrs. Mandela). "I'm giving you this check even though I didn't get a chance to see you in your homeland," she told Mandela with a wicked smile, placing five thousand dollars in the collection pot for the ANC. "Well, you should have tried harder," the elder said, grinning. "No," the widow returned, "you should have told your people to get me through the door." And the two shared an easy laugh.

Some portion of an old resistance left Betty during the 1990 Winnie Mandela encounter. To the widow, Mrs. Mandela was the ultimate revolutionary and always would be. She found Winnie's strength and wholeness of spirit overpowering. The cathartic embrace had electrified Harlem. For Betty it had also been an intense reminder of Malcolm's meaning to the Dark World. After the hug, thought Harlem Malcolmite Preston Wilcox, the widow became "a participant rather than merely a spectator in our struggle." She had already grown more diligent in her memorial role. The sheer magnitude of the Abyssinian Church tribute that February had stunned her. An overflow crowd had gorged the church, and C-SPAN had broadcast the program, which included a procession down Malcolm X Boulevard and a Schomburg Center reception. Attallah had approached members of the Commemoration Commission at the event to thank them for helping to engineer the revival. "For the first time my mother has begun to bring out family heirlooms," she said.

Meeting Winnie Mandela only further unfurled the widow's sails and broadened her consciousness. She became an architect of Abyssinian's magnificent annual Malcolm memorials. She raised funds prodigiously for the Malcolm X Medical Scholars. She strew her commemorative lectures between ever more distant points. (Her May 1991 itinerary included Washington, Chicago, Des Moines, and Madison.) She informally adopted Malcolm Shabazz schools across the country (including several in tough cities like Newark, New Jersey), making ambassadorial visits, sponsoring supplies, and even rewriting curricula. "If it was too radical, she walked away," her publicist later remembered. Her attitude toward some of her husband's biographers—whom she had once treated universally like lepers—grew more solicitous. In the mid 1980s, she had looked askance at James H. Cone, a distinguished black theologian who was completing a comparative study of Malcolm and King. "She was concerned that her husband was going to play second fiddle," he recalled. Now she encouraged the author (having sensed that he was at least as partial to Malcolm as King) and even phoned him occasionally at Union Theological Seminary and invited him to lunch.

She began functioning at public affairs more as Malcolmite than honored guest, and turned up at some of the disciples' programs of her own volition. University of Toledo Professor Abdul Alkalimat, convenor of "Radical Tradition and a Legacy of Struggle," formally invited her to address the summit's opening session. While she might have been content in the past to simply perch on the dais and deliver parochial remarks, the Betty who took the podium that November was forthright and finished, an ever more sophisticated emissary for Malcolm. Alice Windom, a member of the American expatriate colony that had received Malcolm in Ghana; C. Eric Lincoln, the esteemed scholar who had penned *The Black Muslims in America*; and Abdulrahman Mohamed Babu, the Tanzanian revolutionary whom Malcolm had befriended, were among the Malcolmites who congregated for the affair, the first Malcolm retrospective of such scope and breadth.

The widow's remarks at the occasion reflected its auspiciousness. She seemed to realize that this was her chance to reconnect with the discipleship. Though she had warred with several of the assembled women and men during the last quarter century, she took time to thank several who had helped her along the way. She recognized Alex Haley, saying that she did not know what she would have done without his friendship. (The gesture was timely; he died fifteen months later.) Then she started talking Malcolm. "Malcolm was a visionary," she said. "Visionaries always get in trouble, don't they? We can dream dreams...no, no, no...wish I could have found another word." She paused, her throaty chuckle punctuating the allusion to King's famous speech. "We can have visions and understand where we need to be," she continued, "and when we try to get there, find that we run up against all sorts of blocks....I am delighted that I met Malcolm, that I was married to Malcolm. I don't know where I would be at this point in my thinking. I see people around the world, and the only thing I say is, 'Thank God I met Malcolm.'"

Just as Betty was becoming a powerful flag bearer for her late husband, she again found herself embroiled in hostilities with the grassroots. In 1990, a coalition of students, activists, and preservationists
escalated efforts to save the Audubon Ballroom, which Columbia
University was preparing to raze to build a twenty-five million–dollar
biotechnology research park amid the densely peopled black and
Latino neighborhood of Washington Heights. Columbia eventually
agreed to conserve a portion of the original Audubon for a Malcolm
tribute, a proposal that Betty, after some deliberation, endorsed as
"appropriate." But some members of the coalition, which wanted the
whole ballroom spared and considered the demolition plan a racist act
of desecration, suggested that Columbia had bought her support by creating the Malcolm X Medical Scholarship. They accused her of joining the ranks of "big-name blacks" whom they believed the city and
school had recruited to quell public outcry in the name of development
and high-tech jobs. Aggravating the matter were charges of environmental racism—one Columbia official described the level of likely biological hazard from the prospective biotechnology lab as "not very
high"—and the university's severe alienation from its black neighbors.

The widow argued that while the movement to save the Audubon
had only surfaced in recent months, at least half a dozen black students
from needy families had become Malcolm X Scholars in recent years
and were providing health care in poor neighborhoods. For her,
empowering "living and breathing" beneficiaries of her husband's
legacy was more worthwhile than fighting for an atrophying eyesore.
Even as the debate seethed, young do-nothings shot dice in the shadows of the Audubon's graffiti-caked hulk. Yet blight did not diminish
the sacredness of the place, where dark splotches of Malcolm's blood
still stained the stage. (As preservationists noted, King's death site, the
Lorraine Hotel in Memphis, had become a protected landmark.) In
early 1993, activists and college students massed outside the rat-ridden
dance hall with a megaphone. "Save the Audubon!" an emcee yelled.

"By any means necessary!" the crowd hollered. But the biotech park was a done deal. After much tug-of-war with city agencies and politicians (most notably Manhattan Borough President Ruth Messinger), Columbia had agreed to preserve a still larger chunk of the ballroom interior for a significant tribute to Malcolm. Two months before the Audubon street demonstration, Mayor Dinkins had named Betty cochair of a commission that would plan the 6,500-square-foot facility. "I'm delighted that this memorial has finally taken place for Malcolm, who believed that all human beings should have a right to dignity, options, and opportunity," the widow announced at a media conference.

———

The Audubon affair pitted the old Betty, who had at times clashed with the Black Left, against the new Betty, who was growing more engaged as a Malcolm memorialist. Still, Amiri Baraka later recalled, the widow's rapport with her husband's spiritual heirs was taking on promising political dimensions when she "ran into the whole Spike Lee warp." A confluence of forces trained the floodlights on Mr. and Mrs. Malcolm X in the late 1980s and early 1990s. But it was the motion picture and its accompanying hype that inaugurated the minister as pop star and launched his widow into the atmosphere of celebrity. The movie itself took more than two decades to arrive. Betty was involved in its genesis—producer Marvin Worth had optioned the film rights from her and Haley in 1967. She had consulted for and helped promote Warner Brothers' 1972 Malcolm documentary, the project that proceeded the dramatic script James Baldwin had deserted in the late 1960s. In the intervening years, the notion of a big-screen Malcolm had receded from her consciousness. Worth's dream of dramatizing the minister never died. For years he shopped for writers, directors, and studios, but Malcolm's story stubbornly resisted the passage to cinema.

In the early 1980s, comedian Richard Pryor's bid for the lead role dead-ended in another shelved script. David Bradley, black author of the novel *A Chaneysville Incident*, later had a go at a script of his own.

The draft interested comedian Eddie Murphy (who offered to play Haley), but yielded no deals. Bradley later concluded that Hollywood executives "didn't keep firing writers because the scripts were wrong. They kept firing writers because the story was wrong." The feature had taken on a quixotic aura by the late 1980s, when Worth paired white director Norman Jewison with Pulitzer Prize–winning playwright Charles Fuller to produce yet another script. Worth considered Betty's goodwill vital to the project. (He later told Spike Lee that he needed Fuller's "black credibility" to win her favor.) But the Fuller effort bore no fruit. Meanwhile Lee, whose popularity had peaked with *Do the Right Thing*, began proclaiming before the media that "only a black man" could make a legitimate Malcolm movie.

Though there was brisk debate on the matter, Jewison ultimately yielded to Lee, who took over the project in late 1990 and launched something of a guerrilla war to realize his vision. The filmmaker wanted a three-hour plus epic at a cost exceeding thirty-three million dollars. Warner Brothers wanted just over two hours at less than twenty million dollars. Lee wrangled bitterly with the production house over money and scope. After he overspent his budget, a lineup of black luminaries (including Bill Cosby, Oprah Winfrey, Janet Jackson, Michael Jordan, and Magic Johnson) forked over a generous sum in "bailout" cash. Lee continued shooting, with Oscar-winning actor Denzel Washington (who a decade before had portrayed Malcolm on stage with the Negro Ensemble Company) in the title role and ingenue Angela Basset as Betty.

All the while, the real-life Betty drifted closer to the production. If Lee was grappling with the magnitude of Malcolm's life and legend, he was also reckoning with the whims of the minister's widow. The thirty-five-year-old director had anticipated some static from Betty. (Someone had told him that the matriarch, after reading a much-earlier script, had flung her supper at its author.) But he was unprepared for Mrs. Malcolm X's volatility. "One day she would be all lovey-dovey— 'Oh, I love you, Spike'—and the next day I'd be nothing but a cursed-out bum," he later said. Betty's early approach to the project was aloofness; she agreed to serve as a consultant but offered little input and ignored requests for the minister's clothes, photos, and documents. Yet as the first day of filming neared, she grew more concerned about the picture and began asking to see a script.

Lee resisted as long as he could before handing her the scene book in late 1991. His instincts were right. "She hated the script—hated it," he remembered. "She said it was the worst piece of shit she'd ever read in her life." What riled the widow most was the portrayal of her and Malcolm's relationship. The Lee screenplay, which the filmmaker had adapted from the script Baldwin and writer Arnold Perl had produced, depicted Betty as a loving and dutiful wife who clashed with her husband over his myopia about the Nation's corruption and souring feelings toward him, as well as his relative indigence among the Muslim hierarchs. Yet the widow told Lee adamantly that she and Malcolm never bickered. "There was never any tension about money?" the filmmaker later asked rhetorically. "Was this some kind of Disney, Merrie Melodies, Archie and Betty life they led?"

More Lee-Betty rancor lay ahead, but the widow was the least of the filmmaker's troubles. Long before the cameras rolled, Malcolmites pounced on the project. Amiri Baraka charged that Lee did not have the ideological integrity to pull off a biopic of the martyr. He and other black nationalists and intellectuals feared that the young director would focus too heavily on Malcolm's "Detroit Red" years, diminishing the minister's gravitas as a global human-rights warrior who underwent a series of profound ideological and personal evolutions. Some black critics argued that Lee's films burlesqued militant characters. Malcolm purists worried about the dilution of their man. At a summer 1991 rally in Harlem, Baraka delivered an open letter to Lee bearing the signatures of prominent activists and warning against any defilement of the minister. "We will not let Malcolm X's life be trashed to make middle-class Negroes sleep easier," Baraka proclaimed.

The furor grew in the following months. A broad segment of Black America had come to embrace Malcolm as the ultimate symbol of liberation, and nobody wants their idol tampered with. "Probably no scriptwriter alive could write a script that would satisfy the diverse groups who feel an ownership of Malcolm," Haley once observed. For his part, Lee argued that he had a right as an artist to pursue his vision. "Malcolm belongs to everyone and everyone is entitled to their own interpretation," he said. The filmmaker, who had conducted interviews with several of Malcolm's siblings, former lieutenants, and confidants, insisted that he had done his homework, that his intentions were honorable, and that he himself was an heir to Malcolm's philosophies. "I read Malcolm's autobiography in junior high school," he said. "It changed my life. To me, the veil was lifted." But Lee and Baraka continued to spar in a nasty public feud.

Betty stayed out of the fray, as was her wont. She had publicly supported the movie. She was overseas when filming began, so her "consulting" had not included personal coaching sessions with Bassett. But she appeared at the summer 1992 press conference in which Lee announced the celebrity bailout of the production. She understood the widespread anxiety over Hollywood's treatment of her husband, having weathered years of efforts to smear his name. "People who really knew Malcolm, who understand the thrust and the importance of his leadership, have a right to question anyone who's doing anything on [him]," she said. "And I'm talking about a lot of young people who have invested a lot over the years and feel that they have something to say about how Malcolm is presented." She was equally sympathetic to Attallah's qualms about the upcoming film. "What you need to understand is she has a right to be upset with the way people view her father," the widow said of her eldest daughter. "For the longest time, we were his audience and his cheerleaders—myself and the girls."

Still, Betty was not about to shun the picture. She recognized that Lee, Hollywood's notoriously outspoken black bard, was one of woefully few filmmakers of color with the clout to produce a Malcolm picture of any magnitude. She realized that her husband had been a work in progress as a man and a moving target as a martyr, and she rejected the notion that his legacy was the exclusive domain of any ideology. What placed her most squarely behind the movie, however, was the hope that it would achieve in three-plus hours what she had consciously sought for Malcolm through the last quarter century: vindication. Betty wanted Malcolm's name painted in the sky, and Lee happened to be holding the palette. "Yes, Malcolm was a very complex person," she said, "but that should not present any obstacles. I think I understand what Mr. Baraka is talking about. It should be a balanced film."

Her assurance was of little comfort to Lee's detractors. She seemed determined to walk the line between the filmmaker and the nationalists without dismissing the movie. "She tried to deal with Spike and I even-handedly," Baraka later recalled. Yet the widow was never so political that one forgot her fierce commitment to working with whomever she pleased, and her forbearance toward Lee continued to rankle Malcolm's guardians. As the movie controversy was heating up in 1991, Baraka asked if she had read the script. She confessed that she hadn't. "How could you *not* read the script?" he asked incredulously. (This was shortly before she harangued the screenplay out of Lee's hands, erupted at its Malcolm-Betty sketches, then dispatched to the filmmaker her written exhortations. "I said what was true, what was not true," she later recalled.) When the widow appeared on the set of the film, she irked Dick Gregory, too. "I'm on the radio talking 'bout this movie ain't gon' do nothing but destroy Malcolm," he remembered. "And she was like 'Ohhhh, *Gregory!*' But you know, she never came to me and said, 'Y'all stop doin' that.'"

~

The battle for Malcolm was a battle to determine Black America's ideological future. Traditional nationalists, elated that Malcolm had resurfaced amid the reigns of Presidents Reagan and Bush, considered it their duty to rescue Malcolm from commercialism and salvage his radi-calizing properties. Other blacks welcomed the widening embrace of the minister, both because they hoped his message of pride would empower a new generation and because his mainstream appeal jibed with their bourgeois nationalist sensibilities. Betty belonged to the latter camp; she promoted a Malcolm whose legacy was universal and whose strength all could access. But her personal and political ties to the activists who had declared their misgivings about the film, including Roy Innis of the Congress of Racial Equality and Ron Daniels, cochair of the Malcolm X Commemoration Commission, drove her to offer conciliatory statements after ignoring months of controversy.

Ignoring the Malcolm franchise was more difficult. The martyr had proven his commercial appeal among black and white radicals in the late 1960s and early 1970s, and among rap's original and crossover audiences in the latter 1980s. But he did not become a growth industry until the Lee hagiography. In late 1990, the filmmaker designed a promotional silver-on-black "X" baseball cap and began selling it in his retail stores. The caps became a craze after basketball star Michael Jordan wore one during a television interview. Soon practically everyone—from inner-city bloods to suburban mall-crawlers to President Bill Clinton—seemed to be donning the hat, and a blizzard of "X" T-shirts, pendants, jackets, and jerseys struck American sidewalks.

Some Malcolmites grumbled that the commodification was blasphemous. But so long as the paraphernalia were tasteful, Betty was not bothered in the least. "The young people wearing the 'X' may not know everything about Malcolm," she said, "but they know he was for them. They're making a statement. If they want to wear a piece of Malcolm memorabilia, why not? They want to feel spiritually connected." The widow likened that connection to the solace her husband's fur hat had provided her after the assassination. Yet by 1991, the merchandising had ballooned to absurd proportions. There were "X" medallions, bookmarks, basketballs, refrigerator magnets, beach towels, air fresheners, posters, calendars, duffel bags, postcards, coffee mugs, sunglasses, bow ties, neckties, buttons, belts, running shorts, wristwatches, sneakers, boots, board games, and, infamously, potato chips (courtesy of a black company). One astute critic coined a slogan for the market: "*Buy* any means necessary."

The commercialism engulfing Malcolm's image reawakened some of the sensitivities of the early 1970s, when the counterculture had idealized the hero, pasting his image on bumpers. Now the stakes were much higher. Betty knew symbolism had great spiritual value in the lives of the oppressed. She knew, too, that the exploitation had gotten way out of hand. "I woke up one morning totally nonplussed and thought, 'This is abuse in the broadest, deepest, and wildest sense," she later recalled.

"If I don't sleep, eat, or anything else, this is going to end.'" In early 1992, she hired Curtis Management Group of Indianapolis, a white firm that represented the estates of James Dean, Jesse Owens, Satchel Paige, and Babe Ruth. Between 1992 and 1993, the company licensed 350 to four hundred Malcolm products (from educational flashcards to $2,500 gold rings) representing estimated profits of one hundred million dollars, of which roughly 5 percent went to Betty in fees.

———

Betty was not the first black protest widow to draw a legal cordon around her husband's life and legacy. Coretta Scott King had developed a reputation for rigidly enforcing her copyright of everything Martin. The King Center exacted lofty fees from an array of enterprises that sought the use of the leader's image, recorded voice, or works. By the early nineties, Coretta's ironhanded dominion of the estate was chafing some of her husband's Civil Rights comrades and admirers. A series of highly publicized court battles amplified the issue. The King family sued USA Today for publishing the full text of "I Have a Dream" without paying fees; Boston University for refusing to relinquish control of the personal papers Martin had donated to the school (his alma mater); and the producers of "Eyes on the Prize," the award-winning public television series on the Civil Rights movement, for failing to surrender royalties from the documentary's video sales.

Coretta ultimately gained tremendous control over her husband's legacy—and franchise. While the King Center vended exclusive mementos ("The Dream Lives" sweatshirts were brisk sellers), the estate sold King's likeness and oratories to commercial, artistic, and educational ventures, including books and Michael Jackson videos. "Accurate and appropriate" were the estate's watchwords; it rejected proposals for King floormats and knives. Few blacks openly begrudged the King-family revenues, much of which benefited the Center. King had lived and died modestly. If his only real bequest—his name, words, and renown—generated profit, should not his long-suffering widow and children benefit? Yet Mrs. King's stern proprietorship may have dimmed the presence of her husband's image on the American scene and fueled the notion that she had strayed from his focus on the plight of the poor and oppressed. Her eminence continued to ebb in later years as the family increasingly permitted commercial representations of King that lacked clearly redeeming educational or social elements.

Whatever Betty may have thought of Coretta's model of guardianship, her oversight of Malcolm's estate did not seem vastly different in intent. Some of her friends would suggest that her approach was somehow less mercenary, or that it was her lawyers who drove her to stringently exercise her copyright in the era of the movie. Nobody accused her of trading on her husband's name. But Betty had sought out Curtis Management, not vice versa. Whether or not she consciously followed Coretta's lead, her move to control the Malcolmania represented the evolution of her capitalist, proprietary, and protective impulses. As the Schomburg Center's Howard Dodson later acknowledged, Betty wished Malcolm to belong to her in the sense that Martin belonged to Coretta. "Except Malcolm was already sort of out of the box," he said.

The widow's grip on "X" nevertheless narrowed and bleached the field of those the brand enriched. Large manufacturers and retailers such as JCPenney and Montgomery Ward could afford the rights. Yet the little merchants, including independent black peddlers whose cheap Malcolm wares had helped maintain the minister's popularity, often became casualties. They grumbled about efforts to capture Malcolm's image, protesting that he was *their* martyr, after all. The copyright enforcement "short-circuited Malcolm's mass popular appeal as a motif of liberation," Molefi Asante, father of Afrocentricity, later said. Dodson disagreed. "Who has the right to exploit Malcolm?" he asked. "[Betty's detractors] are ticked because she's saying she has the exclusive right." Actually, Curtis Management said it for her. "Dr. Shabazz does feel an obligation to the public that his message be carried on," Mark Roesler, the company's chief executive, told the press, "but how she commercially exploits that is only her decision."

The decision to litigate was more likely the firm's. Betty launched two major copyright-infringement lawsuits in 1992. That fall, a week after unauthorized "X" caps and T-shirts cropped up at a Las Vegas clothing convention, she and Curtis Management filed suit in the city, listing as defendants more than a dozen apparel vendors. The widow almost simultaneously instituted proceedings against the late Haley's estate, which under the authority of the author's brother had sold the original manuscript of Malcolm's autobiography at auction for one hundred thousand dollars without remitting Betty's half of the proceeds (she owned the copyright with Haley). The manuscript, which bore Malcolm and Haley's edits in red and green ink and contained working drafts of three chapters omitted from the published book, had turned up among the author's affairs after his death that February.

The court action that most roiled some Malcolmites came the year before, when the widow sued Abdul Alkalimat and Writers & Readers, the small, black-owned house that had published his *Malcolm X for Beginners*. The suit, filed jointly with Pathfinder Press in Manhattan federal court, held that the book for young adults quoted large portions of Malcolm's writings without permission. (Pathfinder had bought the rights to many of the minister's speeches years earlier and continued to pay Betty modest royalties from sales of its Malcolm books.) Attorneys settled the dispute out of court, but Alkalimat was incensed. The Chicago scholar had been memorializing Malcolm for a quarter century. He had convened "Radical Tradition and a Legacy of Struggle" only months before the lawsuit. He had known Betty for years and had even dined with her in celebration the night Lenox Avenue became Malcolm X Boulevard.

His belief that white socialists at Pathfinder had exploited her standing as widow to protect their bottom line curtailed whatever lasting resentment he might have felt. (Pathfinder called the suggestion preposterous, noting that it had circulated the minister's speeches even when he was commonly regarded as a pariah and sales were moderate to trickling.) Alkalimat knew that Betty was only trying to maintain the sovereignty of the Malcolm estate and "make sure that the family got a fair share of the dough," he later said. The two soon reconciled publicly. Yet some Malcolm disciples were disgusted that the widow had sided with a white publisher against a black press and an activist-intellectual comrade. Betty was having none of it. She insisted that Alkalimat and Writers & Readers could have spared everyone grief simply by seeking her signature from the jump. "I'm the one being exploited," she said.

The question at the root of the quarrel—*Who owns Malcolm and whose purposes should he serve?*—resurfaced weeks before the film's release when newspapers revealed that a staunch conservative with ties to the South African regime stood to profit handsomely from licensing of the martyr's merchandise. First the *Indianapolis Star*, then New York's *Newsday*, reported in late 1992 that Beurt SerVaas, a seventy-three-year-old Indianapolis businessman, headed a private company whose subsidiaries included Curtis Management. According to *Newsday*, SerVaas had met repeatedly with South African officials in the 1970s and expressed willingness to invest in *The Citizen*, a state-sponsored newspaper designed to counter hostility toward the South African government in the international press. SerVaas was a former publisher of the *Saturday Evening Post*, which maintained only one foreign bureau—in Cape Town—and ran editorials sympathetic to South Africa's rulers. Years earlier, during World War II, he had served as an agent of the OSS, a precursor to the CIA.

SerVaas denied any involvement with the South African government, and told *Newsday* that it was thanks to Curtis Management that the Shabazz family was "realizing the monies that are justly owed to them." But his connection to Malcolm's estate appalled black ideologues. "It's like the Ku Klux Klan being in charge of the distribution of material about Dr. Martin Luther King," an American Committee on Africa official declared. Betty cohort Elombe Brath, whose Patrice Lumumba Coalition had helped organize the cultural boycott of the apartheid regime, said he was sure the widow had not suspected that a shadow overhung her Curtis arrangement. Still, he said, "She should have checked. You don't get caught like that." Betty answered the charge with indignation. "I resent someone asking me about SerVaas," she snipped. "I hired Mr. Roesler and Curtis Management to help put an end to the exploitation of me and my children. I know nothing of Mr. SerVaas." In truth, an *Indianapolis Star* reporter had advised her of SerVaas's background weeks earlier. Asked whether she had since rethought the Curtis deal, she replied, "I'm with a company headed by Mr. Roesler. Beurt SerVaas went to South Africa."

Entanglement with South African politics was another circumstance Betty and Coretta Scott King shared. The latter widow had traveled to the racially torn country in 1986 to convince white officials and anti-apartheid forces to renew talks. But she cancelled appointments with President P.W. Botha and Zulu Chief Buthelezi, who many blacks spurned for his cooperation with Botha, after Winnie Mandela and Reverend Allan Boesak announced that they would not meet with her if she saw the two men. Boesak, head of the World Alliance of Reformed Churches, had taken Mrs. King to task for scheduling the Botha visit, declaring that for her to break bread with a figure whose hands were "dripping with the blood of our children" would be unforgivable. Botha accused Boesak and Mrs. Mandela of betraying the spirit of negotiation. Caught in crossfire, Coretta had hastily issued a statement saying that she had come to South Africa "in a Christ-like spirit to gather additional information about the human sufferings here and the need to have a dialogue with as many South Africans as possible."

Yet Betty's South Africa scandal seemed more personally damaging than that of her counterpart, largely because Malcolm is more intimately tied to African liberation struggle than Martin. Brath could see that the widow was wounded when she pulled him into her car for some straight talk shortly after the *Newsday* article appeared. "You gonna join with our enemies now," she growled, referring to his comments on the SerVaas affair. "Now, you know better than that," Brath replied. Gradually the conversation warmed, and the pair began reminiscing about Harlem's past. Brath brought up Malcolm's relationship with fellow Garveyite and "Buy Black" czar Carlos Cooks, who had passed away in 1966. Malcolm and Cooks's missions had converged, though their ministries never had. "Why couldn't they get together?" the widow asked pensively. "If they could only have got together."

———

Betty and Spike Lee got together, but only in the eleventh hour. Even after their spat over the script subsided, the two tussled over marketing rights. Lee's merchandising company had moved tides of "X" gear (including $375 leather jackets) through his pricey gift shops without cutting Betty in on profits. The widow mulled a lawsuit but knew that the action would cast a pall over the upcoming hagiography. Instead she let Curtis Management tighten the screws. "We've given him deadlines," Roesler said of Lee, "but we're running out of patience." The face-off was growing increasingly awkward for Betty and Lee, both of whom were invested (spiritually and otherwise) in the film, by the time they finally banged out a contract. On November 17, a day before the movie opened, the filmmaker inked the deal, handing over licensing fees and a portion of the retail action.

Then *Malcolm X* was upon the world. The film fixated on Malcolm's street-hustling era, painted his discipleship to Elijah, and skimmed over his post-Nation voyages and awakenings. Denzel Washington was magnificent, channeling Malcolm (and reciting many of his actual pronouncements) in scene after riveting scene. Malcolm's crackling exchanges with a devoted and elegantly seductive Betty were among the brilliant sequences of the epic, which the *Washington Post* hailed as "an engrossing mosaic of history, myth, and sheer conjecture." But the film was profoundly flawed. Lee canvassed Detroit Red's romps with white girls far more fastidiously than Malik Shabazz's Dark World diplomacy. The distortion (and the screenplay's other inaccuracies and omissions) enshrined Malcolm as cultural icon without meaningfully reviving the nationalist, Pan-Africanist, and international ambassador who had linked Black America and Africa and godfathered a legacy of radical struggle.

Betty left an upstate New York fasting retreat the afternoon of the premiere with a supply of apple, beet, and carrot juice for the drive to Manhattan. What she craved was a glass of wine. She told herself that she could handle this. She did her deep-breathing exercises. Nothing worked. "I was going to see my husband and I wouldn't be able to bring him home," she later said. The evening was a swirl of anxiety and anticipation. Finally she arrived at the premiere. Dianna Ross, Bobby Brown, Stevie Wonder, Whitney Houston, and Madonna traipsed across the red carpet. Yet Betty had eyes for only one star. "My girls and I, we're going to see my husband," she said, "and Denzel is he tonight." Minutes later she was sitting in the theater marveling at Bassett's portrayal of a young Muslim woman whose shimmering confidence enthralled Malcolm—a woman the widow did not recognize. ("She went straight to the bull's-eye," Betty later said of Bassett's character, chuckling at the idea that the minister would have succumbed to so forthright a woman.) Then the harrowing scenes rolled. Betty felt her composure crumbling. Her hands began drifting over her head. Ilyasah caught them and coaxed them south. "It's all right, honey," the third Shabazz daughter cooed, "I'm here."

Serious Malcolmites lambasted the movie. Former OAAU man Herman Ferguson groused that Lee's Malcolm had wound up an accommodationist. "First they assassinated the messenger," he said, "now they're attempting to assassinate the message." To John Henrik Clarke, the inattention to the minister's bond with Kwame Nkrumah and other Third World revolutionaries was tantamount to making lemonade without lemons. "You have sweet water," the elder said, "but you can't call it lemonade." Still, box-office registers were singing, as were black notables from Reverend Al Sharpton to Bobby Seale. "Spike Lee has made a great contribution to history," Jesse Jackson said, though he worried that mythology was clouding Malcolm's meaning.

If Betty had similar concerns, she swallowed them. No movie could capture Malcolm, she said, but she called the Lee effort an "excellent introduction." She dismissed charges that frivolity drenched the picture's early sequences. (Malcolmites took particular exception to the scene in which their young hero rinses the lye from his scalp in a toilet bowl after undergoing a hair-straightening conk.) "Malcolm was such a serious subject that one might welcome a little lightheartedness," she said, recalling that satire had been central to her husband's pedagogy. She acknowledged that *Malcolm X* was a silhouette. "What can you show in three hours?" she asked. Yet she generally avoided appraising the film during interviews.

Even this temperate stance—*Malcolm X* as appetizer—vexed some of the movie's detractors, including some of Malcolm's siblings, who saw the martyr's commodification as wholesale betrayal. Ella Collins was among those who charged Lee with profiteering. Now a seventy-seven-year-old diabetic and double amputee living in a nursing home, she revived her ancient feud with Betty by questioning the widow's grasp of her late husband's politics. Betty "doesn't know enough about Malcolm to consult on anything," Collins said. "She would go to certain places and hear him speak. But her activities were very limited. She was having babies." ("I don't have any respect for that lady," Betty shot back.) Months before the picture's release, several of Malcolm's other siblings had also expressed to Lee their misgivings about the widow's association with the project.

Betty paid the rumblings no mind. She was caught in the reverie. Her Malcolm was back, and suddenly he was beloved. She had always sworn by the African proverb that says, "Call an ancestor's name every day and he shall live forever." Now the minister's presence enveloped her. Wedged in Manhattan traffic one afternoon before the film premiere, she spotted a man in "X" regalia. "I like your shirt," she shouted, flashing a thumbs-up. "Thank you, Sister," the man replied with a grin. Betty ignored the symbolism-versus-substance debate that had embroiled the film. One of her allies thought that the picture's flaws "ripped and tore at her." But the widow had never fashioned herself as a custodian of her husband's ideological purity and felt no obligation to distance herself from the *Malcolm X* spectacle, even as it slathered Malcolm across superficial canvases.

Betty had worried that the movie would unearth her and the minister's domestic warfare or portray him "like some wimp." She was

unhappy that the finished product lacked scenes of the family man frolicking with his wife and kids, the benign figure she and her eldest
daughters had so industriously promoted. But she was willing to abide
more grievous historical flaws in exchange for the respectability and
wealth *Malcolm X* would generate for her family and the glory it would
lavish upon Malcolm. She endured the frivolities of hero worship for a
similar return. "So what? So what? So what? SO WHAT?" she said of
the orgy of "X" merchandise, insisting that the fashion craze would
steer youngsters toward a deeper knowledge of her husband. "No one
gets a book and starts at the last chapter," she said.

In the end, she was right. Despite its failings, *Malcolm X* revived
Malcolm more powerfully than a thousand street ceremonies, and
wove threads of his political thought into the orthodoxy of a new generation. This was Betty's Year of Malcolm, and no one who knew her
story could blame her for basking. She had sworn long ago that the
world would someday celebrate him. Myrlie Evers-Williams phoned
the morning of the premiere to remind her of that pledge. "This is the
day!" Myrlie announced. "I told you," Betty said quietly. "And someday they will recognize Medgar."

The news media courted Betty amorously in the age of *Malcolm X*.
By early fall 1992, several months worth of interview requests cluttered
her docket. Just a decade earlier she had been a relative unknown
beyond the ranks of nationalism and the black intelligentsia. Now she
was appearing on *Oprah*. Hours after the film's world premiere, the
weary but exultant widow regaled an audience at Harvard, where her
husband had transfixed law students thirty-one years before. She was
not outwardly bitter that the society that had once reviled him and
shunned his wife now celebrated him and fawned over her. In the
climbing years of her career, when schoolchildren saw his name and
said "Malcolm Ten" or addressed her as "Mrs. Ex-es," she had striven to
hold herself like a first lady. She had always believed that his message
was just and that it would endure. "They say yesterday's philosophy is

today's common sense," she said. She loved young people, and she was pleased that they had helped resurrect Malcolm. "Whatever spell the older generation held Malcolm under," she said, "the younger generation has broken it."

Betty traveled throughout the U.S. and as far abroad as Germany (where backcountry kids were costuming themselves in "X" gear) to talk Malcolm. She fancied herself an interpreter of his, though she tended to drain him of his righteous indignation and howling rebuke. Her Malcolm was not an outraged apostle; he was a statesman, a spokesman for universal dignity. He "knew his self-worth and was hoping that people would get a sense of their own self-worth," she said. "But when he came home, I saw a warm human being—not in spite of his day's work, but inclusive of his day's work." Betty's Malcolm was the comfortable American icon that even Supreme Court Justice Clarence Thomas tacked to his chest. (Attallah championed the same sweet character, declaring that her dad's "any means" slogan "can include reading books and studying hard.") But the widow drew the line at Dan Quayle, the conservative vice president who professed in the age of Rodney King (the black motorist whose LAPD beating had flung back the sheets on the American race dilemma) that he was mining Malcolm's autobiography for insights into racial discord.

Betty's centrist politics and widow's inviolability led the media and black gatekeepers to project her as a spokeswoman. She sat on a May 1993 race-relations panel with Public Enemy's Chuck D. (an original hip-hop Malcolmite) and columnist William F. Buckley Jr. in Hartford, Connecticut, and took exception to Buckley's remark that the root of the Los Angeles street rebellions was not a white jury's acquittal of the Rodney King sluggers, but a "sense of frustration, the principal agent of which is the plight of the one-parent family." Yet she was loath to blame white racism for black woes. While she acknowledged the omnipresence of white supremacy and discussed its ills in sophisticated global and historical terms, her mantra was "we are where we are because of us." She recognized that racial wounds had begun to heal in the years since her husband's death, and insisted that to say otherwise was inappropriate.

The halls of liberal black leadership agreed, and rewarded both her public advocacy and the symbolism of her survival. In 1990, the New York Urban League, whose philosophies her husband had scorned, presented her with the Frederick Douglass Award, its highest honor. The following year, Congressman Rangel and Reverend Sharpton joined a throng of Harlemites in declaring Malcolm X Boulevard "drug-free" as a tribute to the widow. "We changed the name of this street to Malcolm X," Sharpton said, "and now we must change the game to Malcolm X." In 1993, the National Congress of Negro Women honored her during President Clinton's inauguration at a breakfast ceremony at the Washington Marriott. Still, nothing beat the 1992 *Essence* Awards. That summer, the premier black women's magazine paid homage to Betty and several other inimitable women (including Debbie Allen, Maya Angelou, and Gladys Knight) in New York's Madison Square Garden. During the ceremony, the widow clutched Angelou's hand involuntarily under the dais table. She was struggling to keep her composure when her daughters appeared onstage for a poignant tribute. "She almost broke my hand," Angelou later recalled.

The veneration for Betty marked a shift in black consciousness. In the late 1980s and early 1990s, the widow's stature climbed on the crest of a bourgeois or "soft" nationalism that stressed cultural distinctiveness while embracing mainstream standards of success. As Harvard Black Studies Professor Henry Louis Gates has observed, both confidence and resignation shaped this rough consensus; while the Civil Rights movement's economic gains had inspired confidence, blacks also resigned themselves to the reality that Martin Luther King Jr.'s dream of a color-blind society was just that—a dream. Enter Malcolm. "The rigorous separatism associated with the name Malcolm X is not part of that consensus," Gates said, "but his hopes that black Americans would assume a larger role in shaping their own destiny surely are." Mrs. Malcolm X, inexorably middle class yet eternally wedded to nationalism, was an ideal heroine for the times.

Meanwhile, King's star was fading and with it Coretta Scott King's. The black masses still revered the apostle of nonviolence, but corporate acceptability had bled him of his post-Nobel radicalism. As Gates noted, "It has been convenient to airbrush out…his antiwar political protests; his interest in democratic socialism; his recognition that the battle for equality was passing from the realm of Civil Rights to that of economic justice." Another writer put it more plainly, noting that in modern black orthodox theory, "Malcolm played the heavy to Martin Luther King's softy." Of course, this narrow view of Malcolm almost invariably overlooked the militant's acknowledgement of the brotherhood of man. "Malcolm may have adopted the stance of transracial humanism toward the end of his life," Gates said, "but most people—not the least the political heirs he had decided to disinherit—felt free to ignore such vagaries." The scholar concluded that the complexities of both leaders defied American iconography: "Simplify, simplify—that is the imperative of the hero industry."

The changing fortunes of black martyrdom and public widowhood did not hurt Betty and Coretta's relationship. Now that the two commanded roughly commensurate clout and cash, Betty's resentment waned and their bond actually deepened. They began actively supporting one another's personal and professional causes. Betty joined a celebration of mass at a Chicago church during the 1992 King holiday, speaking of self-determination during a ceremony in which altar boys paraded up the aisle hoisting a portrait of King. She teamed up with Coretta that summer at a "Stop the Violence" forum in Los Angeles, lending the moral force of widowhood to the pacifist efforts of Civil Rights leaders, students, and members of the "Bloods" and "Crips" street gangs. She occasionally made state visits to the King Center, and Coretta faithfully answered her summonses to Medgar Evers College.

The pair forged a genuine friendship—something their husbands may privately have longed for. They exchanged girlfriend talk and Mother's Day bouquets. In September 1995, Coretta sent Betty, her one-time rival, a letter so gracious and heartfelt that the latter widow glowingly passed it around her circle of friends. "I have written you many mental notes and letters since that wonderful weekend we spent together in Brooklyn...." Mrs. King said, reminiscing about a recent Medgar Evers College commencement. "I shall always treasure the memory of these occasions. The time we spend together is always so meaningful. We are truly sisters and kindred spirits. I can't thank you enough for your Mother's Day remembrance. You are so very kind. May God always bless you abundantly....I am finally enclosing the hand cream which I promised you. Sorry it took so long. Lots of love, Sisterly Yours, Coretta." The rapprochement was as healing for the widows as it was for the African-American soul. A prominent Black Arts movement figure later saw the two huddling warmly somewhere and was momentarily stricken. "Goddamn," he thought, "that's power."

—

Betty may never have fully accepted fame. Her friends knew her as a reluctant public figure who surrendered to the role largely out of a sense of obligation to her husband and the masses that idolized him. "I loved him," she explained, "and he loved the people." Having no choice but to play the celebrity game, she learned to play it well. She became a skillful speaker—never spectacular, but polished in her cadence and imposing in her dramatic pauses. She grew equally agile in the informal politics of her civic affairs, discovering that black luminaries do best when they stick to the center and tilt left or right as circumstances dictate. "She understood how you had to meander around landmines," a friend later said. As in the case of Coretta, the Civil Rights leadership had often called her to serve as an emblem of its causes. Now she shrewdly used her relationships with the same leaders for access and mobility.

She was naturally outspoken, but often refrained from speaking out. She had learned the wisdom of watching and waiting, of allowing newcomers to reveal their intentions and establish their credibility. If they did not, she would gently discredit them, peeling away pretense. "Quite frankly, those white folk always try and figure out how they're going to run something," Dodson later said. "And Betty would just cut through the bullshit. Her position was unchallengeable." The widow began to enjoy her celebrity. Whether she was endorsing a rootsy congressional candidate from Brooklyn or talking about single motherhood at a Delta Sigma Theta conference in the Bahamas, she savored her influence and the deference she received. She started opening up, abandoning her old stoicism for a more human persona.

In February 1992, she uncloseted more of her history than she would have dreamed of airing only a few years before. During a candid, three-hour interview with *Essence* (in which an editor found her "by turns charming and coquettish, prickly and demanding"), she acknowledged that her husband had been as tyrannical as he was tender, and that she had left him three times because he refused to let her work outside the home. In her previous accounts of an idyllic marriage, Malcolm's old lieutenants (who recalled their leader's domestic life as deeply strained) had discovered her proclivity for make-believe. But the widow's *Essence* piece, a genuine unbosoming, revealed new maturity and a budding sense of security. Betty was getting more comfortable with herself, and it showed. "There are those who would expect me to be more political than I am," she said. "There are those who would expect me to be more religious than I am....Whatever it is I am today, I am what I need to be."

Some of this self-possession flowed from her world ambassadorship. She traveled abroad regularly for women's summits and other affairs, visiting Asia, Europe, and the Caribbean on missions of education and goodwill. Like Malcolm, she found no encounter more enriching than the African embrace. In the early 1990s, she mingled with dignitaries and commoners in Kenya, South Africa, Zimbabwe, Uganda, and Ghana, usually traveling alone or with a single aide. Sometimes she was a state guest. More often she moved as a member of a delegation, working with nongovernmental groups in international caucuses. Whether touring a South African squatter's camp before the historic elections or running workshops about women and communications at a 1990 women's conference in

Nairobi, she brought to Africa her wisdom about women's empowerment, poverty, human rights, and development. And she left with
widened vistas.

African audiences expected of her a political fundamentalism
that she had never possessed, but they unfailingly received her like a
queen mother. To postcolonial nations, many of which had gained
independence through armed struggle, Malcolm was the maximum
symbol of liberation. Their fight had not been for Christian principle
or integration, but land, which the minister had recognized as the
singular object of revolution. Black Africa's rulers and citizenry were
accordingly moved to meet the widow, who they regarded as a symbol of the integrity of their struggle. In South Africa and Kenya, her
presence moved former political prisoners and revolutionaries to
tears. They told her that they had smuggled her husband's speeches
into the colonial prisons, that he had kept them hungry for freedom.
Betty never tired of such testimony, which she accepted with humility and pride. She often sent the devotees sets of Malcolm books
upon returning to the United States.

Stateside, the widow's growing confidence with herself, the minister,
and his faithful manifested in a powerfully nurturing public presence.
She had discovered her purpose as a custodian of martyrdom, and it was
to heal. She was among the leaders who worked to help ease tensions
between blacks and Jews in Brooklyn's Crown Heights, a neighborhood
that had howled with racial violence in 1991. When Washington Mayor
Marion Barry was caught using cocaine, Betty reminded his detractors of
his Civil Rights résumé. "As a young person, he was very productive, and
we must never forget that," she told an Urban League conference. "We
shouldn't support drug use. But look at what drove him to drug use. We
have to not criticize, but investigate, offer support, analyze, and encourage people to stay on the right path."

In 1993, she visited heavyweight boxer Mike Tyson behind bars.
The former champion had a reputation for recklessness outside the
ring and was serving a six-year sentence for allegedly raping a young
Miss Black America contestant. But he had come to Islam in a
medium-security prison near Indianapolis, and the widow stopped in

to encourage his reeducation. She and Tyson prayed in Arabic and discussed his journey to Allah. "I am as pleased and proud of his development as any mother or professor would be," she later said in a statement, insisting that Tyson was "dealing with education in a way that he has never had the opportunity before," and that he belonged in a "non-punitive learning-teaching environment." Later that year, she attended a Chicago tribute to Wallace Muhammad (now Warith Deen Mohammad) who had renamed and recast his father's congregation in Islamic orthodoxy. She had not seen the prodigal son since 1965. Now she praised his stewardship of American Muslims and his devotion to the One Lord of the Worlds.

Betty's generosity of spirit also spilled from her pocketbook. She was always wiring money to extended family and friends. (Her secretary spent many a wintry afternoon trudging through the snow to the Western Union.) She was famous for handing out one hundred–dollar bills in South Africa and for relieving down-and-out friends without bruising their egos. During one conversation with an old comrade who was in a bind, she abruptly asked him to move her double-parked car. While he was gone, she slipped five hundred dollars in his eyeglasses case. Though she knew virtually every black luminary, she never mistook celebrity for wealth. Dick Gregory, who for a time had trouble making ends meet, once ran into her in an airport. "Baby, you okay?" she asked him. "You alright? You need anything? You're going to Africa, take this." Gregory parried. "Betty, don't be puttin' no dollars in my pocket," he said. The widow gave without need. On one pilgrimage to Saks Fifth Avenue with Zerrie Campbell, the first female president of Malcolm X College, her companion admired a faux alligator-skin overnight bag. Betty later had her driver buy the bag and drop it off at Campbell's hotel. When the Chicago administrator opened it, a medley of perfumes tumbled out. Earlier, the two had dined at a chic Manhattan restaurant that always seated the widow at its corner table. "We just sat there and drank wine, ate portabella mushrooms, and gossiped until times got better," Campbell later said.

Betty's growing influence continued to win recognition. She accepted invitations to join the Skinner Farm Leadership Retreat, a biannual gathering of national black leaders (known internally as "the Family") who meet quietly to discuss the state of the race, and Links, Inc., an elite social-service organization for well-heeled black women. She maintained a grueling speaking schedule and caught no more than four or five hours of sleep a night. Her datebook was dark with scribbled appointments and obligations. Teaching was her elixir, her way of cleansing her soul. But she was exhausted. She checked into hotels just to escape the telephone. She took dear friends to her appearances, and signaled to them when she was ready to be rescued from the bustle. Sometimes her confidantes said "enough," and forbade her to book another event. Only rarely did she obey. "I work until I can't see," she told *Essence*. "Then I go home at night and the only thing I can think of is eating and sleeping. And I get up the next morning and watch the news, do some reading, and take a long, long bath—a nice bubble bath—get dressed up, put on my nice cologne, get my briefcase, and I'm back at work. Long hours again. And I am happy."

Chapter Eighteen

MOTHER'S DAY

———

"When you cross the black woman you have struck a rock."
—Traditional South African adage

Betty shored up her international résumé in her early sixties. In September 1995, she was among the civilian emissaries who mingled with delegates from 185 countries—thirty thousand attendees in all—at the United Nations Fourth World Conference for Women in Beijing, China. "How can you call yourself a leader of women and you don't want to go?" she scolded a girlfriend before jetting off to Beijing, where she phoned in ebullient accounts of the proceedings to her radio audience back home. On another excursion, she helped open Ghana's Nkrumah Memorial amid renewed veneration for the revolutionary. (Ironically, she was filling in for Louis Farrakhan, who had originally been scheduled to speak for Black America at the event.) She attended a more glorious inauguration at a Malcolm X Park ribbon cutting in Uganda. A makeshift fence and a queue of soldiers corralled the ceremony. When Betty spotted schoolchildren straining for a glimpse, she marched over, yanked a fence post, and waded into the throngs. "There were thousands of people who just wanted to touch this woman," an onlooker remembered.

As with the Mandela encounter a few years before, some of the widow's finest foreign diplomacy occurred on American soil. In October 1995, she helped host Ghanaian President Jerry Rawlings and his wife during their visit to New York to celebrate the United

Nations's fiftieth anniversary. "It was touching seeing the regard in which you are held by your people, and especially the youth," Rawlings later said in a thank-you note. "We were grateful to have been associated with you during the remarkable week, and I am convinced your martyred husband would have been pleased to see the role model you have become for the Woman of African descent....Let me reiterate what Osagyefo Dr. Kwame Nkrumah himself told you a long time ago: You will always have a home in Ghana." Also that autumn, a correspondent for the Chinese newspaper *World Journal* interviewed Betty in Mount Vernon. "Before closing our talks," he recalled in the profile, "she cited an idiom of the black people: a young tree, although bent under hardship, can grow straight and strong." The journalist offered another metaphor for his subject's life: "I thought of the traditional way of the Chinese farmers, who tread down upon or roll over with the stone the wheat seedlings so that they may grow strong."

Betty's public persona had grown strong indeed. She was everywhere Black New York was, everywhere black phenomenal women were, everywhere black dignity was exalted. She joined her friend C. Delores Tucker and other extraordinary women at National Political Congress of Black Women (NPCBW) affairs honoring achievement and decrying gangsta rap. She backed the causes and political campaigns of allies such as Reverend Al Sharpton. She collected an honorary doctorate from Pennsylvania's historically black Lincoln University. ("I wish you power that equals your intelligence and your strengths," she told the graduates. "I wish you success that equals your talent and your determination. And I wish you faith.") She attended power summits with Princeton Professor Cornel West, Reverend Jesse Jackson, and short-lived NAACP Director Ben Chavis. She showed up at more modest affairs, too, celebrating with a black woman who had opened several McDonald's restaurants in Harlem and huddling in a ring of women for a reading of the folklore slave mothers had once whispered to their children. "Everywhere I'd go, I'd see her," former New York Mayor David Dinkins remembered. "The black leadership groups for AIDS, anything at the Schomburg Center, the NAACP, the Urban League meetings. She's always there."

The widow's philanthropy was as profuse as her presence. She gave thousands of dollars to black organizations and often donated her $5,200 speaker's fee to educational foundations. She was forever brow-beating comrades into contributing to this or that scholarship fund. Her style of leadership was low-key, but she kept a court of well-placed pro-fessionals who were happy to do her bidding when summoned. Thirty years after she had watched cowards slaughter her husband, Betty seemed utterly in control. There were few pockets of African-America in which she was not immediately recognized. She felt genuinely respected and appreciated. She sidestepped controversy. She prayed. She fasted. She even shed a few pounds.

She was always jotting healthy recipes for fish or chicken into her notebooks and leaving herself stern reminders: "No starch....Less oil....1/4 the butter." She joked about her proportions. (One reporter thought her face collapsed in "a composition of brown dumplings" when she laughed.) But her skin was still as lush as any landscape. She never ventured into the world unless fully made-up, her hair whipped and glossy. She moved with that sinuous cool peculiar to large black women, and no longer felt duty-bound to resist when the spirits swept her onto the dance floor. (At Congressional Black Caucus receptions, she did the Electric Slide as recklessly as if she were in her own living room.) Her "Forum for Women" radio guests saw her perch before the microphone at WLIB's Park Avenue studio, adjust her headset without mussing her hair, then start undulating when the engineer cued her theme song, Whitney Houston's "I'm Every Woman."

To many, Betty's grandeur was her commonness. "Me and the lim-ousine driver, that was her man," Dick Gregory remembered. "She just loved this old, wild, crazy nigger. When he was in New York he'd get me and we'd call her. 'Betty, what you doin'? What time you get out of school? We gon' come get you and act da fool.'" The widow made peace with her idiosyncrasies, letting her tardiness reach scandalous dimensions. When she struck up a conversation with singer Ida McBeth in a Kansas City restaurant bathroom, she was already nearly thirty minutes late for a November 1995 speech before a roomful of Links. (She was now the organization's National Chairwoman for International Trends.) "Ooh girl, what kind of makeup do you use?" she asked the woman as event organizers hammered on the door. Sensational entrances were Betty's calling card. When gathering for retreats, members of the Black Holistic Society would form a circle and pray before unpacking. But the widow was invariably late. The others would stall. "And then here comes this woman, screaming, 'I'm here! I'm here!'" one man recalled. "When she arrived, it was as if our circle was complete, as if we were all really complete."

Betty herself seemed complete in those days. She soared when she might have wallowed. Malcolm had smashed into her life and left with a thunderclap, but the reverberations had grown eloquent with the passage of years. He was "my greatest teacher," the widow told an audience in Milton, Massachusetts. In January 1996, she flew to San Diego to launch the $7.3 million Malcolm X Library, and marveled that the fountain at its entrance bore one of her favorite Malcolmisms: "I have often reflected upon the new vistas that reading opened to me. As I see it today, the ability to read awoke inside me some long-dormant craving to be mentally alive." She loved the ecumenical flavor of the opening ceremony, which included an invocation in English and Spanish by a Roman Catholic nun, African drumming, the presentation of colors by a spit-and-polish Boy Scout, the singing of the Black National Anthem, and a Muslim benediction in Arabic. "This is a great day," she told the crowd. "It could have been a prison that they built in your neighborhood."

The widow even transcended ribbon cuttings. In April 1996, she clashed with Edwin Meese, who had been attorney general under Ronald Reagan, in two hours of fierce debate on affirmative action. During the forum at the University of St. Thomas in St. Paul, Minnesota, students hollered "All right, sister!" as she drubbed Meese and hailed affirmative action as a first step toward reparations for slavery. Betty was honing her political voice. Some of her friends believed she was starting to confront the hypocrisies of the power structure her husband had scourged. "She became very forceful in terms of speaking her heart and speaking her experience and having more direct influence on people," Amiri Baraka said. Others thought the evolution was inward. "One saw a maturation, an acceptance of what had happened to her in life," Sonia Sanchez said. "She finally settled into the reality of who she was and who Malcolm was, and the love and adulation people felt for him, and that she was intertwined with that." Almost everyone agreed that the widow was gaining clarity and that the trauma of the 1960s seemed to be fading. Said a friend, "The ghost of that affair wasn't hanging over her as much."

———

Coretta Scott King and Myrlie Evers-Williams saw Betty's spirit billow. After an annual celebration at the King Center in Atlanta, the latter two widows stole away from the crowd for fifteen minutes of joy. "Girl, do you think I'm losing weight?" Betty asked breezily. "My hips the same size?" The pair cackled about their new harvest of wrinkles. "Honey, we gonna have a facelift?" one woman asked. "Oh, no," the other replied, "we don't do that sort of thing." The Movement widows were now calling each other "sister" and meaning it. They chatted late at night between planes and trains, and talked about getting away together for some much-needed girlfriend time. They also began intersecting more meaningfully and often.

In the fall of 1995, they cochaired a crusade to register one million black female voters by the 1996 presidential election and joined Rosa Parks at the head table of a NPCBW brunch honoring the "mothers of the Civil Rights movement." At the brunch, thirty-two-year-old Ilyasah, thirty-nine-year-old Yolanda King, and forty-one-year-old Reena Evers saluted their mothers before one thousand black women in a Washington hotel ballroom. Mrs. King could not recall having ever seen Betty weep. Then Ilyasah started to speak. "I never could explain death to her," a teary Betty told the audience after her third daughter's testimonial. By the end of the evening, the ballroom was awash in sentiment. "My sisters Betty and Coretta, we have been through so much together," Myrlie said. "It is difficult to talk about this....We call it putting up a front." Coretta's voice splintered when she finally spoke. "Myrlie said we don't cry in public; we had to be strong so others could be strong," she said. "We are crying because we feel a sense of fullness, and we thank God that He brought us to this day."

Myrlie and Coretta may not have glimpsed Betty's more disquieting faces. Despite the shower of accolades, the wealth of relationships, and the brash pleasure she took from life, Mrs. Malcolm X was still thrashing at phobias. She had never seemed more invincible. Yet it was precisely when she was most in her element that the old haunts resurfaced. Even as she found professional symmetry and personal satisfaction, she was becoming the tragic parable she had defied. Even in the era of her belated celebrity, she was weaving through the valley traveled by so many anonymous black women, women who fought uncertainty and heartache every day. Those who glimpsed her streaks of quiet desperation sensed that her suffering was far from over. She let a few of these confidants inside her barricades, but only so far. Betty was a survivor, and the survival tools she knew best were secrecy and fury.

"She could go *off!*" her longtime secretary remembered. "Her eyes would change colors: 'Vengeance is mine!'" The widow continued to reward those who touched her graces and breathe fire on those who took liberties. Sometimes she blistered a hapless soul over the phone, slammed down the receiver, then smiled sweetly at her publicist: "I did that for effect." But the severity that had once been a shield seemed to have fused with her persona. In lashing out against threats real and imagined, she often wound up damaging herself. "It was just society that made her such a hard shell," Gamilah later said in an interview. Did she have an alternative? "Not in the seventies," the daughter said. "Not in the eighties. In the nineties she did. And she started changing."

Betty's two or three closest friends saw a softer soul. She kept her relationships with these women strictly separate for twenty-five or more years, and did not freely share all her vulnerabilities even with them. Yet they knew enough to understand her, and to be the big sisters she needed. When she had to rest body and soul, one of these friends would pick her up and pop in a favorite CD, and the two would sing, "You don't have to be a supermodel." "Next thing I know, girlfriend is asleep," Mary Redd remembered. The widow often seemed weightless when she ran with Redd or another of her "girls." She shopped, ate good dinners, and took in plays or Roberta Flack concerts.

Still, Betty shuttered burdens within. Her comrades and colleagues knew not to pry into her childhood, the affairs of her daughters, or 1965. They knew that she was living behind the veil. They grew accustomed to her evasiveness and wariness, to never being exactly certain what she was thinking at any given moment. She was still sequestering herself in hotels, sometimes using the alias "Malik Shinaz." (She had briefly called herself "Malikah" or "queen"—the name she gave one of the twins—in the first groping months after the assassination.) She forbade her assistants to disclose where and when she was traveling. She avoided discussing sensitive or personal matters over the telephone. She was notoriously difficult to reach and scrupulous about who got her rosters of phone numbers. Her allies knew better than to share such information casually. "Even if one of her daughters called, I'd say, 'Okay, I'll get back to you,'" one confidant remembered. "Then I'd call Betty and say, 'How do you want me to handle this?'"

From a distance, the circumspection seemed healthy. "There was a great sense of what lay in the world that could take her life or the lives of her children at any time," her publicist said. Yet the depth of the suspicion, however legitimate, proved devastating. The widow was constantly questioning why this or that character had entered her life. Some thought she was too busy testing the loyalties and intentions of others to complete her own circle of emotions. "She could have used some serious counseling on that," a friend said. But Betty, who had trained as a psychiatric nurse, refused to see a therapist. To her that was "telling other folks your business." She understood the ruinous irony of the black community's stigma against counseling. She knew that those who have caught the most hell need the most help. She was nonetheless convinced that the peril of disclosure outweighed the promise of relief, and that she could ultimately heal herself.

So she continued surreptitiously taping phone conversations with dubious allies and publicly aligning herself with figures she privately maligned as "barracudas." She relished her celebrity even as her desire for anonymity deepened and the pains she took to cloister herself increased. While she sought refuge from the treachery of the past, she worked closely with various state and federal agencies of government—the historical source, she believed, of some of her misery. Her ties to black elected officials and politicos propelled her into Washington power spheres. By 1996, the Democratic National Committee was regularly faxing her "speaking points," and her name made the guest list for President Clinton's White House teas. Yet she never stopped believing or at least behaving as though her phone was tapped. She never forgot the executive branch's ploys to surveil, destabilize, neutralize, defame, and even, she thought, facilitate assassination.

Her double consciousness alternately amused and annoyed her nationalist friends, who had no qualms about identifying the state as the enemy. On one visit to Ghana with an American delegation of Pan-Africanists, the local U.S. Mission invited her to a Fourth of July jubilee. She asked Harlem activist Elombe Brath to accompany her. "I said, 'Betty, shit, I can't do it—I ain't a citizen," Brath recalled. "She got mad and went off by herself. She felt obligated because of who she was. But shit, I wasn't doing that!" The lines between the system and the struggle had been blurring for more than a quarter century; Betty was not the only black protest figure whose navigation of the two occasionally caused herself and others unease. Indeed, some of her conflicts as a privileged black woman with marginally nationalist sensibilities reflected the classic black-intellectual dilemma. Yet the trauma and intrigue of Malcolm's death widened the gap between the public and private Betty. She paid dearly for the disparity. In some ways, her daughters did, too.

—◆—

Betty never stopped shepherding or shielding her children, but her relationships with several of the young women continued to fray. Three of the daughters—Attallah, Qubilah, and Gamilah—were now single mothers, a condition that Betty had not been anxious for them to experience. (Gamilah's brief marriage had ended in divorce, and she was raising her preadolescent son, Malik, on her own.) The Shabazz women were service-minded. Now in her mid-thirties, Attallah had founded Prism, a nonprofit company designed to foster multicultural harmony. Malikah had formed a mentorship group—the fleeting National Organization of African Students in America. Meanwhile, thirty-year-old Gamilah's career as a conscious rapper had dwindled after a dalliance with a major record company. (The rap-star ambition did not thrill Betty, though Gamilah laced her rhymes with her father's words.) The daughters' sense of social responsibility had not driven them to finish college. With the exception of Ilyasah, who had completed school and was working for the City of Mount Vernon, they were still bumping between jobs and passions, struggling to reconcile the two. To the widow, this was "drifting."

Betty feared that she had spoiled her children into restlessness and rebellion, but continued to rescue them from the hot water they occasionally waded into. (Her intervention may have helped Malikah escape with a mere $250 fine in the summer of 1995 after authorities accused the twenty-nine-year-old of buying herself clothing and luggage with the credit card of a Utah man whose house she was tending. According to her lawyer, Malikah thought she had permission to use the card while the man was on vacation.) Betty's demands further strained her relationship with her daughters. She did not want them to work run-of-the-mill, nine-to-fives, or even apply for Social Security numbers. (Her distrust of the system had led her to shelter them from federal identity.) She hoped they would instead earn advanced degrees and lead quiet, professional lives. When they spurned her counsel, Betty sometimes punished them as she did her underlings—with long spells of frosty silence or shriveling rebukes: "Daddy would turn over in his grave!" Her severity had long repelled imposters. At times it had a similar effect on her beloved.

———

Friction with her daughters bruised the widow's heart; the death of her foster mother crushed it. On September 13, 1994, three weeks shy of her ninety-sixth birthday, Helen Malloy, who had persuaded Betty's biological mom to surrender her firstborn daughter and then lavished the child with love, went home to the Lord. Rosa Parks was among the guests at the memorial service in Detroit's Bethel AME. The loss of her "Ma' dear," her last remaining guardian, shook Betty. But for the widow, grief was hardly an exotic emotion. She had been mourning for three decades. And though pressing forward had grown easier, glancing backward had not. She no longer dreamed of the spray of bullets or heard the clap of Malcolm's skull against the stage. What haunted her still was his collapse, the Christ-like gesture in which his reflexes had cast his arms, his flagging jaw and rolling eyes, his almost serene descent through the wooden chairs behind him.

Betty was still in pain, the sort of pain that could erupt like a sheet of flame, as it had a couple years earlier during a University of Cincinnati lecture. She had discussed colonialism and Third World development that evening, and was wrapping up with the grand-motherly caution that everyone your color isn't your kind. "I've seen a lot of black people who have taken money and sold their people down the river," she said. "So I'm not so into that only black people can do good. Because my husband [died at] the hands of an assassin. Regardless of how he was motivated, [the assassin's] hands were black." She paused. Her palms had floated upward involuntarily. Her eyes shut and her head drooped. She had not meant to close this way, but suddenly the years were spooling, and she was once again hustling the kids into a smarmy Uptown dance hall to see their daddy speak. Twelve seconds melted in churning silence. Finally Betty spoke. "May God bless all of us," she said. She then turned and left.

Though the widow may never have fully dealt with Malcolm's death, she began to see the full implications of the seemingly allied forces behind his murder. "I'm sure those discussions and sometimes loud arguments we had [about the depth of government complicity] weighed on her," Amina Baraka later said. Betty's own experience broadened her vision, too. While she needed no enlightenment on the subject of black betrayal, her social ascent had also exposed her to the hypocrisy of the ruling class. She had seen firsthand how ruthlessly power preserves itself, and she had discovered how deeply Malcolm threatened the status quo. Still, she was never going to forgive the triggermen or the Muslims she believed had given the command.

One of those triggermen was now practically a neighbor. Talmadge Hayer (a.k.a. Mujahid Halim), the single confirmed assassin among the three Muslims that had gone to prison for Malcolm's slaying, had become the last of the trio to gain his freedom. (The state had already paroled the pair of alleged accomplices he swore never set foot in the Audubon on that bloody Sunday.) The man who had emptied a .45 into the minister's twitching body was working at a homeless shelter on a desolate island in Manhattan's East River and living quietly with his wife in a suburb less than a mile from Betty's home. He had become an imam of orthodox Islam behind bars, expressing regret for Malcolm's assassination and declaring that, "Time has told that a lot of things he said were true." The minister's older brother Wilfred accepted Hayer's self-portrayal as a pawn of the Malcolm hate industry, an industry whose captains had included hierarchs of the Nation and the federal government. "It's just that I don't hold him responsible for the killing," Wilfred told an interviewer. "He was responsible for pulling the trigger, but there were others more responsible than him for killing Malcolm."

Betty was still convinced that Black Muslim authorities had issued the order, and that Louis Farrakhan had been a chief agent of the plot. She was not alone. The question of Farrakhan's role in the slaying had bedeviled the Nation of Islam helmsman for years. After Betty denounced Farrakhan as an "opportunist" in 1985, television journalist Gil Noble had called on the Muslim captain to confess that his blustering damnation had helped seal Malcolm's doom. "He didn't pull the trigger, but he knows that he's got a lip," Noble said during a speech at New York's City College. "Everybody knows that the man's got a lip, and he knows the impact that he had." Noble's remarks reflected the ambivalence of black nationalists who embraced Farrakhan's militancy (and conservative stances on morality and family values) but had misgivings about his possible link to the assassination. "Many people in positions of power understand that schizophrenia we have about Farrakhan," Noble said.

On the subject of Malcolm, Farrakhan had proven himself equally inconsistent. He had variously cast his erstwhile "big brother" as a barefaced Judas or misguided apostate—and in either scenario, as a man who got what was coming to him. But before pro-Malcolm audiences, he sounded more harmonious chords. Though he continued to deny any direct involvement in the assassination, he acknowledged that he had fueled the climate of violence in which the assassins struck. He never pardoned Malcolm's desertion or blasphemy of Elijah Muhammad, yet he said in a 1991 interview with Spike Lee that he had "loved Malcolm much more than words are able to describe," and called the martyr's life "the most exemplary of the century." Speaking of his own vituperations of Malcolm in a later interview, however, he declared that, "Nothing that I wrote or said yesterday do I disagree with today."

The Malcolm question did not fetter Farrakhan. After the Black Muslim membership boom of the mid-1980s, Muhammad's self-proclaimed heir flourished. He made prosperous diplomatic forays into the Muslim World. In the United States, his lectures drew tens of thousands of blacks. Radio and television broadcasts, audiotapes and videotapes, and the Nation's organ, the *Final Call*, delivered his scathing message of separatism and self-determination to the inner cities. The teeth-gnashing he inspired among mainstream Civil

Rights leaders and whites only bolstered his image as an unbridled warrior. "No, you are not supposed to like or understand Mr. Farrakhan," one black columnist wrote. "If you did, he would be no better than the sellout gatekeeping 'kneegros' that you trot out to parrot your concerns."

Most blacks who heeded Farrakhan's rhetoric did not join his troops or even accept his total program. But his challenge to White America resonated with the masses, as did the Nation's ability to rehabilitate lost souls. Still, his grotesque attacks on American and international Jewry continued to draw rebukes and alienate even fervent black nationalists. Since the mid-1980s Jesse Jackson hullabaloo in which Farrakhan had notoriously proclaimed Hitler "great" and Judaism a "dirty religion," many of the provocateur's speeches had coursed with condemnations of Jews as manipulators of Hollywood and the media, masters of the slave trade, leeches of the black community, and corrupters of their faith. Farrakhan melded religious hostility and righteous ire about the economic and political dominion of some Jews (among other ethnicities) over blacks with the sort of bitter, xenophobic invectives with which white supremacists had long assailed the African world.

Farrakhan later made conciliatory gestures, declaring that he wished to mend black-Jewish relations and giving a violin benefit conspicuously featuring a concerto by Jewish composer Felix Mendelssohn. He also made overtures to the black establishment that had long shunned him, striking a more temperate pitch in a bid for national legitimacy. In 1993, having been barred from the thirtieth anniversary commemoration of the 1963 March on Washington, he accepted an invitation to a Congressional Black Caucus weekend forum in which the Nation, the NAACP, and other black organizations proclaimed a "Sacred Covenant," and pledged to never again allow outside forces to divide them. The following year, at the beckoning of the NAACP's Ben Chavis, he attended a two-day National African-American Leadership Summit that drew a cortege of leading race women and men.

Yet Farrakhan's rapprochement with black leaders began disintegrating in late 1993 after his national spokesman, Khalid Muhammad, spewed venom in a speech at a small New Jersey college, smearing Jews (as "bloodsuckers of the black nation" and "hook-nosed...imposters"), the Pope (as a "no-good cracker"), and others. The oration drew a riptide of black and white scorn. Farrakhan stood by Khalid's "truths," but after some prevarication denounced his phrasing. He later demoted Khalid, declaring that "I had to rebuke him because I want him to be the great statesman he was born to be." Farrakhan continued to ride the windstorm of controversy, emerging as a powerful rhetorician with grassroots appeal. Yet his narcissism and duplicity estranged black activists of all creeds. And the mystery of his entanglement with Malcolm's murder was an abscess that continued to fester in Black America.

The abscess began oozing in 1993. That February, on the twenty-eighth anniversary of the assassination, Farrakhan delivered a three-hour bombast titled "The Honorable Elijah Muhammad & Malcolm X: Twenty-Eight Years Later—What Really Happened?" before an audience of nine thousand at the Savior's Day convention in Chicago. The sermon exalted Muhammad as the fount of Malcolm's wisdom and influence. "You've got to give credit to the teacher," Farrakhan said. But in a gust of impenitence, the cleric appeared to acknowledge the sect's responsibility for the death of its errant son. "Did you teach Malcolm?" Farrakhan asked White America rhetorically, his blood rising. "Did you clean up Malcolm? Was Malcolm your traitor or ours? And if we dealt with him like a nation deals with a traitor, what the *hell* business is it of yours?"

The declaration became the bombshell of *Brother Minister: The Assassination of Malcolm X*, an awkwardly eloquent documentary (from a black-white directing duo) that presented evidence of both Black Muslim and FBI complicity in the murder. Betty entered 1994 dodging such matters, as she had for years. She refused to comment on reports that Farrakhan had visited the Nation's Newark mosque—the home temple of the Muslims Hayer had fingered as the true assassins—shortly before the slaying. Instead she busied herself preaching racial harmony in stark contrast to Farrakhan's gospel. (Hours after the March 1 shooting of four

Hasidic Jews in New York, she made an appeal for tolerance alongside a Brooklyn rabbi during a talk at Brandeis University in Massachusetts.) But her loathing of the firebrand and his faithful had not waned.

"Years ago there were people that decided they wanted to kill my husband," she said sarcastically during the Brandeis address. "I see them every day now and they want to hug me. They want to say that they are sorry." Days later, innuendo gave way to indictment. During an interview with WNBC-TV, which had broadcast Betty's denouncement of Farrakhan nine years before, veteran *News Forum* host Gabe Pressman showed the widow a portion of the unreleased *Brother Minister* featuring Farrakhan's year-old rant against Malcolm. Betty was cool while viewing the clip, but her eyes flashed. When Pressman asked if she believed Farrakhan had anything to do with the assassination, her response seemed almost blasé in its controlled wrath. "Of course, yes," she said. "Yes. I mean, it was a matter of…it was a badge of honor. I mean, nobody kept it a secret. It was, it was, a badge of honor. Everybody talked about it."

The widow mentioned that at a black power conference in Atlanta "a couple of years" after the murder, she had heard Farrakhan talk about Malcolm "like he was the worst person on Earth." She also volunteered her opinion that the Black Muslim chief lacked "strong loyalties to anything or anyone except himself." But it was the "badge of honor" pronouncement—Betty's first public indictment of Farrakhan as an accessory to her husband's slaying—that sparked a firestorm. "Widow Pins Malcolm X Murder on Farrakhan" the *New York Post* trumpeted that Saturday, a day before the *News Forum* interview aired. A flurry of print and broadcast stories followed.

The Nation responded swiftly. Farrakhan knew better than to strike back at the revered widow of Black America's "shining prince." His aides instead suggested publicly (as they had nine years before) that Pressman, on behalf of a larger Jewish conspiracy, had invited Betty on the show to undermine the Nation's leader. "It is the evil motivations of the wicked Anti-Defamation League and other Jewish organizations who have launched this attack against Louis Farrakhan because they want to stop the rise of black unity," a Black Muslim minister said.

Insisting that the media had exploited an anguished widow for its sinister purposes, the sect filed a fruitless defamation suit against the *Post*. A week and a half after Betty's charge, Farrakhan appeared on ABC's *20/20*, declaring that Malcolm "would be so much more valuable to us alive" and seeming to commiserate with the widow. "Betty Shabazz never said that Farrakhan was a plotter in the death of Malcolm," he said. "But she said that Farrakhan helped to create the atmosphere. And that I can agree with."

A few Farrakhan sympathizers took a more suspicious view of Betty's accusation, suggesting that it was politically convenient for the widow to implicate a black insurgent instead of fingering the CIA, FBI, or New York City police. "Why is it of sudden interest to white people if Betty Shabazz thinks Mr. Farrakhan had something to do with her husband's murder?" a black columnist demanded. "The real question is, why did it take thirty years to ask the question? I am sure she knows this curiosity does not come from some new-found love of Malcolm X on the part of Mr. Farrakhan's critics." For days, reporters rang the widow's home and work phones. She refused to elaborate on—or recant—her comments. "I have every right to say something about my husband, and I will," she said. "They [the Nation] have used my husband as its agenda for years."

She insisted that her position on the assassination had remained steadfast for three decades, but called for a new investigation. "It was five individuals," she said in her first espousal of the quintet theory of assassins. "Two of them got away." (She still clung to the belief that all three men that had done time for the deed had been righteously condemned.) Meanwhile, five prominent black Boston-area ministers denounced Farrakhan as a hypocrite for preaching against black-on-black violence while failing to condemn the fratricide linked to his own organization. "For thirty years there have been whispers," said one cleric, "but no one has stood on the wall and demanded that Minister Farrakhan answer the question."

The *enfant terrible* of black leadership was through answering questions; he had graduated to playing victim. "You are looking at the most vilified black man in the history of America," he said in a speech, declaring that Satanic forces were conspiring "to use a dead man against the only living Black American who can't be bought." Betty had plunged back into the quiet work for which she was known, though the depth of her antipathy for the Nation's leader was clear. She and Farrakhan intersected twice in the weeks after the hubbub. That June, during a closed session of the National African-American Leadership Summit in Baltimore, she found herself seated at a large round table just a few degrees from the provocateur. (Columbia University Black Studies Professor Manning Marable, who sat between the two, recalled the experience as one of the "most striking" of the three-day gathering.)

The summit's organizers had hoped to provide a cordial setting in which an array of black leaders could commune. Differences with Farrakhan and the controversial Chavis had driven off traditional figures such as Coretta Scott King, but Betty had always supported the idea of a united black front (one of her husband's foremost principles). And though her proximity to Farrakhan made for an awkward scene, her presence at the politically leftward event was significant. Days later, she again ran into the Black Muslim commander at the Washington funeral of Reverend Tom Skinner, who with his wife Barbara had founded the leadership retreats that had in recent years drawn Betty to the Skinner's farm in Tracy's Landing, Maryland. This time, the widow was no more than a couple of pews from her nemesis. Again the two icons steered clear of each other, each savvy and shrewd, each personifying kindred yet violently clashing outlooks and histories. But irony was even then narrowing the divide. Within a year, they would come face to face in an encounter that salved the race's soul and tore the widow's.

It was trouble with Qubilah that began their alliance. Like her big sister, Qubilah had glittering memories of her father. She had always known Betty as the disciplinarian and Malcolm as the mush. She was only four when he died, yet his pride and hilarity had already marked her consciousness. She remembered his thistly whiskers, too. He used to chase her around the house, trying to rake her with his beard. He would dip her finger into his morning coffee. "He almost had me convinced that I was made of brown sugar," she later told an interviewer. She would wait up until the early morning for him to return from work, then delight in his habit of polishing off half-gallon buckets of ice cream. He often fed her imaginary food while she blissfully pretend-chewed. Her pronunciation of "Sugar Shack," a hip dance at the time, cracked him up. "I used to call it 'Shuggy Sha,'" she recalled.

The grim memories were no less powerful. For Qubilah, the night of the firebomb had begun with a stick of Bazooka Joe gum from Daddy's secretary. When the minister spotted his second daughter smacking away, he hooked an index finger into her mouth and pulled out the wad. (He believed chewing gum contained pork fat.) Qubilah, who had been straining to blow a bubble, had a fit. "I punched him as hard as I could in his stomach," she said. "He laughed." This further enraged the child, who marched off to bed in cast-off pajamas. Atallah and two-year-old Ilyasah slumbered nearby. "I remember thinking I can't wait until I was grown up," Qubilah said. Then there was the clunk of a Molotov cocktail against the side of the house. "When I woke up, I saw flames coming through the windows," she said. "I'd never seen this before….It started getting real hot." She bolted upright and shrieked for her father. In an instant, he was pounding down the stairs. "There were flames coming through the hallway and from the library," she said. "We went out the back door. It was February and freezing cold, and my feet were cold because I had torn a hole in my footsies. I remember he was standing outside and holding a rifle. He was ready to fire back. He wouldn't pick me up."

What happened a week later Qubilah hardly ever discussed in later years, but the din of her dad's shooting would ricochet through her life. It resounded in the essay she scrawled for her mother as an eight-year-old: "Malcolm X was a brave leader….His black preachings were in everybody's heart….He dyed [sic], but his black beautiful soul…." It echoed through her solitude at a Lutheran grade school and at Manhattan's elite United Nations International School, where classmates remembered her sitting alone near a stairwell and sneaking a flask of liquor into class. ("How shall I say goodbye to my friends?" she wrote in the school's 1977 yearbook. "I'll sing my song, then depart... hoping they will see the agony burning through me.") The bedlam of gunfire haunted her at Princeton, where she attended two fall semesters but never meshed with the black cliques. She was "kind of a phantom, a loner," a black professor recalled. Qubilah had another explanation for her isolation. "I didn't arrive on campus with combat boots and a beret, and I didn't speak Swahili," she said.

She had always been the most brilliant and shy Shabazz. She was articulate and unusually philosophical, and after attending Quaker-run camps in Vermont, converted to the faith at age eleven. Some took her introspection for serenity. Others sensed that she was seeking. (As a small child, she once wandered into a neighbor's driveway and asked, "Do you know who my father was?") By the time she dropped out of Princeton and moved to Paris "on a lark," her godfather Gordon Parks had seen glimmers of a fragile soul. "I would get a smile out of her, but rarely laughter," the photographer and playwright remembered. "I think she was a lonely woman. But what she believed in, she did, and it didn't matter what her mother or anyone else thought."

While studying at the prestigious Sorbonne and working as a language tutor and translator, Qubilah spoke out against anti-Semitism and the prejudice she saw displayed toward Iranians. She "associated with people who were at the lowest rung" because she wished to help them, Percy Sutton recalled. But she also began unraveling, placing rambling calls to former high-school classmates in the middle of the night and complaining that people were after her. ("I'm not your classic schizophrenic," she later told a confidant, "but I do kind of go from one self to another.") She met an Algerian Muslim and soon after, at age twenty-four, had a son. According to one of Betty's friends, it was the widow's idea to name the child Malcolm.

Qubilah and the Algerian soon parted ways. "She won't talk about him," Parks later said. "I think probably it was a mistake in her life." Baby

Malcolm was a few months old when his mother brought him back to the United States. They settled briefly in Los Angeles before moving again to New York in 1986, where Qubilah got a telemarketing job. Over the next few years, the beautiful and well-spoken young woman hopped with her son from one dingy apartment to another in a string of seedy neighborhoods. She waitressed for a Bay Area Denny's, sold advertising for a civil-service worker's directory in New York, then landed in Philadelphia, where her step-grandmother (Juju Sandlin's widow) and uncles lived. Associates said that Qubliah continued to refuse her mother's money, although Qubilah later claimed that Betty had long withheld financial support. By 1992, she was hopscotching between three apartments and her grandmother's North Philadelphia home. At one place, the relative of a landlord was always letting Little Malcolm in because Qubilah was away. At another, the child slept in the living room while his mother worked downtown at an International House of Pancakes.

Though Qubilah was constantly broke, she managed to briefly enroll her son in private school. She drank, though, sometimes heavily, and a family debate whirled over how best to care for the boy, who had periodically stayed with his grandmother and at least one aunt in New York. Over the next year and a half, Qubilah lived with friends at several Manhattan addresses, then in a number of rented rooms in an upper Riverside Drive apartment building in Harlem that she later described as a "crack den." (Qubilah later denied, in an interview with me, ever having exposed her son to unsavory people.) Qubilah's proofreader job at a law firm barely kept her afloat, and she was having trouble with her eight-year-old son, who ran away at least once. Meanwhile, Spike Lee's film was bathing Betty and the other daughters in fame. Qubilah accompanied her mother to the film premiere, but the two were not often on good terms. Qubilah was too gypsy-spirited to tolerate regimentation. There were other struggles. The widow agonized over her daughter's transience, but Qubilah spurned intervention. "I am comfortable in my own skin," she said. In my interview with Qubilah, she claimed that her relationship with Betty was highly strained, and said that Betty tried to take custody of Little Malcolm to punish her for leaving the family as a young woman.

Qubliah also struggled with her father. "Never, never, never—Qubilah never talked about her father," an associate remembered. Many wondered why not. "I just don't like it," Qubilah said. She made occasional, low-key appearances, collecting an award on her mother's behalf, and later speaking at the University of Minnesota at the invitation of black students. But she would not generally volunteer who her father was, preferring sincerity to celebrity or politics. The teller at a check-cashing place once asked if she was any relation to Malcolm X. "Yeah," she replied.

She had read her father's autobiography several times and could passionately defend his ideals when necessary. It made her crazy when people invoked his name as a metaphor for violence. "If the privileged classes had been subjected to the indignities my race and other races were subjected to, they'd be just as angry," she later said. Yet her father roamed an inner frontier that she could not easily explore. "I was always angry he left me behind," she said. "My rationale was if he were a simple store clerk, he would still be here."

Neighbors and friends knew Qubilah as poet, aspiring writer, and a sweet and unassuming spirit. She never maligned anyone, and she never talked about Farrakhan. Still, she was painfully aware of the bad blood between the Muslim chief and her mother. Unbeknownst to the Shabazz family, Betty's March 1994 "badge of honor" accusation had jolted her. Already teetering emotionally, Qubilah began obsessing about Farrakhan, a figure whose name in the Shabazz household had been as rank and unspoken as a family secret. Qubilah, now thirty-three, had Farrakhan on the brain late that spring when she reached out to Michael Fitzpatrick, a former United Nations International School (UNIS) classmate whom she had been fond of as an adolescent, but had not spoken to since 1980. "During the conversation," Qubilah later told the FBI, "I jokingly asked Fitzpatrick if he would kill Louis Farrakhan. I suggested it…because I knew he was capable of doing it."

She knew because Fitzpatrick had always been roguish. Even at UNIS, he was confrontational, a "pasty-faced, curly-haired fellow in overalls," a swaggering prankster with felonious charm who sold switchblades from his locker and fired guns off the school's roof. "He was *the* scary guy in the class," one former student recalled. While still a teenager, Fitzpatrick, son of a Jewish businesswoman and an Irish-American labor organizer, joined the right-wing Jewish Defense League (JDL), and in 1976 pled guilty to conspiracy charges in the bombing of a Russian-language bookstore in Manhattan. He turned government informer soon after, and later collected ten thousand dollars from the FBI to infiltrate a JDL splinter group and testify against two of its members, who were eventually convicted of a 1978 attempt to bomb an Egyptian tourist office in New York.

Fitzpatrick vanished into the witness-protection program, moving to Minneapolis under an assumed identity. By 1980, he was married and back in New York, living on the Upper West Side and, by his account, "laying rails for the Communist Workers Party." (Though others claimed that he was spying on its Revolutionary Youth League for the feds.) The following year, Albany, New York, cops arrested him in connection with a protest against a South African rugby team, and discovered tear gas, clubs, a bayonet, a hunting knife, and a metal pipe in the trunk of his Buick. The weapons-possession charges were ultimately dismissed and the court records sealed. (Lawyers for Qubilah later suggested that Fitzpatrick intended to use the arsenal to implicate fellow demonstrators on behalf of the FBI.)

In the mid 1980s, Fitzpatrick—divorced, boozing, and strung out on cocaine—returned to Minneapolis. He haunted "recovery circles" and an anarchist collective's bookstore, where he talked of Molotov cocktails and tried to draw members of the collective into drug dealing and a bizarre scheme to attack an election polling place with bags of human feces. Some of the anarchists later insisted that he was trying to set them up for arrest. "He's a Svengali—very penetrating, very persuasive," a former colleague said. "He's the best kind of con man out there. He makes you believe whatever you want to think that he is." A woman who met Fitzpatrick around 1987 thought him one of the better-dressed addicts she had ever encountered. "I figured him for either a coke dealer or a car salesman," she later said.

A strapping man with a Grim Reaper tattoo on his left arm and a dragon on his right, Fitzpatrick was into hand-rolled cigars, gold jewelry, leather jackets, fast cars, and gaming tables, and he mentioned now and then that he had gone to school with Malcolm X's daughter. He was married a second time, for eight months, in 1991. He worked for several gold and rare-coin dealers, then filed for bankruptcy in 1993. He left one job on especially bad terms after leaking customer names to competitors and claiming to be in the witness-protection program "for killing a mafioso." The following month, police found him and others in an apartment strewn with crack pipes. He admitted to flushing cocaine down the toilet.

By early 1994, he was drying out in Alcoholics Anonymous and holding down a lucrative new job. But he was still facing drug charges when he telephoned Qubilah—whom he had not spoken to in fourteen years—just before Memorial Day. (He later claimed that he was returning the call she had placed to his mother.) Whether or not he believed Qubilah was serious about doing away with Farrakhan, he reported the conversation to an FBI contact in Atlanta days later. Meanwhile, he and Qubilah exchanged phone calls in what she was coming to regard as a courtship. Within weeks, she was infatuated. "He plays a good game," she later said. "I had a tendency to get real whiny, and he'd always coo. He was very affectionate. I fell in love with him over the telephone. My friends thought it was total insanity."

Qubilah and Fitzpatrick talked regularly by phone in June and early July. He "asked me if I was serious about killing Farrakhan," she later said in her FBI statement. "I told him I wanted Farrakhan dead but would feel guilty if someone else was involved and got caught." By mid July, Fitzpatrick spoke of nothing but Farrakhan. Qubilah had no inkling that her old high-school chum was setting her up, seeking on behalf of the FBI to "recapture" her intent to avenge her father. Eventually the bureau promised him forty-five thousand dollars for his cooperation in the case. (He may also have hoped to win leniency on the drug charges.) Fitzpatrick began secretly recording his talks with Qubilah on July 27.

According to government transcripts, she said in several calls over the next two days that the thought of killing Farrakhan—"a slimy pig"—had long been an obsession and that she was grateful that Fitzpatrick would undertake "something that should have been done thirty years ago." Fitzpatrick told her that he loathed Farrakhan as "an enemy to my people," and that the leader's death would be righteous. "I think this shit is great...." he said. "I think it's karma."

Qubilah believed her mother had endangered herself by condemning Farrakhan. "I do think that eventually he's going to, in a very slick way, have her killed," she told Fitzpatrick during a conversation in late June 1994. The two talked details of the assassination scheme, discussing nightscopes and silencers and death after Friday prayer service. Fitzpatrick mentioned that a friend who owed him a favor might be able to get him a deal on "a professional." Qubilah said she had little money, but Fitzpatrick urged her to wire him at least one thousand dollars for immediate expenses. "I just want to make sure you want me to proceed on this," he said.

The conversation continued:

> Qubilah: "Michael, how could I not want you to? I mean
> really, ask yourself, how could I not want you to?"
> Fitzpatrick: "Right, well understand, because this is something I want to make [sure] isn't just idle chatter."
> Qubilah: "Michael, I have a lot at stake. I lost my father
> and I'm risking losing my mother."

Later, Fitzpatrick seemed to steel himself. "I'm just going to proceed," he said. "I'm just going to fucking set this shit up. It sounds like I should prepare myself for the ugly, you know, the big ugly."

Amid the ugly talk, Qubilah dreamed of a love affair. She began telling neighbors in Harlem that Fitzpatrick had proposed marriage. She told Fitzpatrick that her ten-year-old son resented the fact that his friends "have mothers and fathers and he doesn't. So he feels that he's undeserving." Government transcripts show that Fitzpatrick gained her confidence by letting the boy refer to him as "my dad," then lied to her about going to Chicago to scout out Farrakhan's security. (According to Sutton, Little Malcolm urged his mom to marry Fitzpatrick after the informer promised him that he would have his own bedroom when they moved into a house.) Fitzpatrick reported in August that the murder plot was "workable." Qubilah confessed that she was still "nervous about the whole thing." She worried about the scrutiny her family would face, and about the likelihood that Farrakhan's followers would blame Jews for the slaying. Fitzpatrick assured her that investigators would only target Jewish militants, and reiterated that "I really need to get some money from you." Days later, Qubilah apologized, saying that problems in New York were distracting her from the scheme. "I don't handle pressure or stress very well," she said. Again Fitzpatrick cooed. "If you want a friend," he told her, "I'm there for you."

—

The following month, at Fitzpatrick's encouragement, Qubilah left her sixty-dollar-a-week Harlem apartment and moved to Minneapolis, where she hoped to find decent work, child care, and medical treatment for her son's hyperactivity. When she and Little Malcolm arrived in St. Paul by train, Fitzpatrick picked them up in an FBI-owned car and booked them into a room at a Holiday Inn that the FBI had wired for video surveillance. Bureau agents were in a nearby room. With Fitzpatrick doing most of the talking while steering Qubilah toward a hidden camera, the two discussed the murder plot for forty-five minutes. He said the hit would happen in a month or so, and that it would be easy. "The longer you wait...the more iffy I will feel about it," she said. He said his credit card was maxed out. She handed him $250. Fitzpatrick left the motel and returned to his St. Paul apartment. Qubilah and her son spent several nights in a cheap motel, then moved into a one-room apartment in a working-class neighborhood on the edge of downtown Minneapolis. She borrowed a few dollars from a new friend, applied for welfare, and began hunting for a job.

Minneapolis was not the watershed she had hoped for, but life there was bearable for a time. Within weeks, she was receiving food stamps plus four hundred dollars a month in public assistance. She found a modest job and started cashing weekly payroll checks of $100 to $150. She enrolled Little Malcolm in a Montessori school. She spoke knowingly about black history and Arab-black relations with neighbors and acquaintances, who found her quiet and exceedingly private. Her landlord later remembered her as respectful and intelligent. "She has a beautiful, bright son," he said. Qubilah spent hours sipping Turkish coffee by a windowside table at a nearby coffee shop.

Whatever serenity she might have found soon dissolved. Little Malcolm had begun a pattern of bizarre behavior at school. Late that November, at the request of officials who suspected neglect, police removed the boy from his mother's apartment and took him to a children's home. The nursing staff at the home noted his injuries, which he said resulted from skirmishes with his mom. Qubilah denied harming her son but said she wanted him hospitalized and maintained that he was suffering from psychosis. (He had spent time at a Minneapolis medical center sometime earlier, but doctors determined that he needed no medication. According to a report, he told authorities that he wanted to live with an aunt in New York.) Days later, Little Malcolm changed his story, telling a county child-protection worker that his mother had not laid a hand on him in Minnesota. "He is very bright, but has and is being treated for mental problems," the worker said in a report. Authorities labeled the abuse case "unfounded," and after a short stay with Betty and other family in New York, the boy returned to his mother.

Little Malcolm was not Qubilah's only problem. She had tried frantically to reach Fitzpatrick as her son pinwheeled out of control. For weeks she had called his apartment, but his roommates told her repeatedly that he had moved out and that they did not know where he was living. What they did not tell her is that they had kicked him out because of his drug habit and general creepiness. (He had bragged to them about his violent past and his array of guns, which included a Glock 9-millimeter semiautomatic with a thirty- or forty-round clip.) Fitzpatrick finally phoned Qubilah in late October and twice in early November. "Everything is set up," he said. She told him that she was "leery," that she was "afraid to have any involvement in it at this point."

She stressed that she was not giving him "the go ahead" until she had had time to think. As the result of talking to his former roommates, she asked if he was a government informant. He assured her that he was not.

By early December, Qubilah later told the FBI, she wanted to call off the assassination plan, but she could not reach Fitzpatrick. She sought solace from the bottle, as she had in the past. A few days before Christmas, she gave a short interview to a local television station that was filming a documentary on check-cashing services. Producers did not know who she was, but later remembered her because she gave a janitor twenty dollars, and because her breath reeked of liquor. "I was born on Christmas Day and I always have, like, lousy presents," she told the camera crew after handing the janitor the cash. "I always like being Santa Claus on Christmastime, so I decided that starting December 1, for the whole month, I'm just gonna make myself happy, and this makes me happy."

The happiness soon withered. Days before her thirty-fourth birthday, Qubilah got a visit from the FBI, an agency that had notoriously harassed her father, and that her family always believed had had something to do with his death. Shaking, Qubilah asked the pair of agents in her apartment whether this was about her son. Not wanting her to know Fitzpatrick's true role, they told her that they had uncovered her murder-for-hire plot during an investigation of the coin industry. Qubilah composed herself over cigarettes and soda while the agents played portions of her and Fitzpatrick's taped conversations. Then she signed a four-page statement drafted by the agents, acknowledging that the $250 she had given Fitzpatrick was "in furtherance of the scheme to murder Farrakhan." She told the agents that she had figured Fitzpatrick for dead and feared that he might kill her for squealing if he was not. It was around New Year's Eve when she learned for sure that the man she had once hoped would whisk her away to a new life was an informer.

Betty was shattered. When she learned in late December or early January that her nomadic daughter, the delicate soul whose wanderings tormented her, had gotten tangled in a freakish plot to assassinate Farrakhan, something within her collapsed. "It was like a doom set over her," one of her best friends later recalled. But as had so often been the case, Betty could not buckle. She and her old ally Sutton planned a course of action amid rumors that Qubilah was facing imminent federal indictment. They called upon Harlem Congressman Charles Rangel, who sent an open letter to U.S. Attorney General Janet Reno. The missive may ultimately have landed on the president's desk, but according to Sutton, neither Reno nor the Clinton Administration—which the widow had lavished with praise since 1992—would intervene with Minnesota authorities. On Thursday, January 12, Qubilah was arrested on charges that she had conspired to kill her father's protégé-turned–bitter rival.

The indictment, which listed nine counts of using telephones and crossing state lines to arrange the assassination, hit like a comet. *Newsweek* tagged the Qubilah case "an improbably lurid sequel" to the Malcolm whodunnit. Betty proclaimed the affair not just improbable but evil, insisting that her daughter had been framed. "It is unfortunate that anyone would do that to a young woman," she told the press. "And it says how quick people are and how they will do anything to get their political ends." A less calculated statement revealed the panic that had engulfed the widow. "That's what they've done to my daughter because she did not have a father—Farrakhan and all these people, they did all of that," she exclaimed bitterly.

Betty was not present in the federal courthouse in Minneapolis for Qubilah's brief appearance (in gray pants, a purple sweater, and neatly braided hair) before a magistrate, who released the young woman on a $10,000 uninsured bond. Instead she busied herself rounding up a mighty team of lawyers to supplement the public defender the court had appointed. She may have been hoping to strike a balance she had sought in the past, coming quietly to a daughter's aid while maintaining a business-as-usual front. "She didn't need to do this….Someone else was behind this," she told a television news crew in a Tallahassee airport hours after the indictment. The following day she appeared at a symposium for teachers in Atlanta and refused to discuss the case with reporters.

Everyone else was talking. Betty's comrades rushed in to defend Qubilah's character—and her mother's. Sutton called the accused an ideal young lady. "Dr. Shabazz has raised her daughters to be outstanding women," he said. Dick Gregory echoed the thought. "If she had planted this kind of bitterness in the children, it would have emerged in all the close conversations we've had over the years," he said. *New York Amsterdam News* publisher Wilbert Tatum described the widow's second child as temperate and thoughtful. "It's not that she doesn't have fire, she does; but she has common sense," he said. Hazel Dukes, president of the NAACP's New York State chapter and one of Betty's closest sorors, concurred. "I can't believe outright this kid initiated a plot," she said. "I saw her grow up. I hope we can clear the air, that this won't be a news story forever."

Qubilah's family and friends gasped at the dimensions of the crime that the docile woman in cornrow braids stood accused of. She faced a shuddering ninety years in prison and more than two million dollars in fines. "None of my sisters are capable of something like this," said Malaak, the "younger" twin. Meanwhile, African-America rippled with suspicion. Malcolm's slaying was still resonant in the hearts of many blacks, and hardly anyone professed faith that the FBI was handling the daughter with more integrity than it had the father. Some said the Bureau was seeking to rekindle the blood feud between Malcolmites and Black Muslims that it had fomented decades earlier. Others said the federal government was hoping to sully Malcolm's name while sabotaging Farrakhan's contemporary black nationalism. Many wondered whether it was mere coincidence that the government had announced its case against Qubilah days before Martin Luther King Jr.'s birthday, and more than a few suggested that the indictment was an effort to derail a march of one million black men on Washington, D.C., that Farrakhan and other leaders were planning for that October.

Some blacks were slower to cry conspiracy. J. Edgar Hoover, they reasoned, was long dead. Who stood to profit from the framing of a brittle young woman? "There's no need to drive a wedge into black America," one black columnist observed. "It's anything but solid now anyway." Still, the notion that odious government forces were again at work struck a chord with an overwhelming population of blacks. The rough consensus spanned the boardroom, the barbershop, and the spectrum of black leadership. Conrad Worrill of the National Black United Front looked askance at the case, as did Reverend Calvin Butts of Abyssinian Baptist Church. Tatum berated the "cynical" attempt to destroy black-Jewish cooperation. A talk-show host in Atlanta proposed that a headline reading "Malcolm X's Daughter Charged in Plot to Kill George Bush" would be more plausible than the one heralding the Farrakhan scheme, since the former president had once headed the CIA.

"I am not a conspiracist by nature, but when we look at the wretched history of the FBI and the massive campaign of undermining and devaluing black leaders, you don't need to be a conspiracy theorist," said black studies scholar Michael Eric Dyson, who noted the "riveting" irony that an organization that had done so much to besmirch black leadership stood poised to protect the most reviled figure in contemporary black culture. Recognizing that the Qubilah case was churning up the ancient bitterness of the Malcolm-Nation schism, however, black leaders began privately spurring Betty and Farrakhan toward détente. "I sent a letter immediately saying, 'Y'all, this ain't going nowhere—y'all should declare a truce, a unity at this moment,'" Amiri Baraka remembered. The week of Qubilah's arrest, a delegation of activists met with Farrakhan and urged him to respond compassionately. He needed little convincing. Though the FBI had briefed the Muslim chief about the brewing assassination plot months earlier, he announced through a spokesperson when the case went public that his heart went out to the Shabazz family.

Then, five days after the indictment, the leader scored a coup for both his image and Qubilah's cause. Speaking before two thousand at his elegant Mosque Maryam on Chicago's South Side, he described Qubilah as "a child I knew and held in my arms as a baby." She "is a child...who grieves over the loss of her father," he said. "It is easy to send a trained set-up artist to manipulate her emotions and make her a tool in a diabolical scheme...to divide black people." Farrakhan insisted that the news media had seized the story in an effort to set him up for imprisonment or assassination because he was "becoming the voice of Black America." He again swore his innocence in Malcolm's death. If the government had entrapped Qubilah, he said, blacks should demand her release.

Betty accepted the gambit. She hardly had a choice with Qubilah facing years behind bars. Still, Farrakhan's support seemed genuinely to astonish her. "I was totally surprised with the extent of his humanity, and the understanding my daughter had nothing to do with this," she later told reporters outside a St. Paul courthouse. The widow had arrived in the Twin Cities with Sutton on the day of Farrakhan's oratory. She came laden with artillery, having recruited the radical Civil Rights attorney William Kunstler, two Washington lawyers, and a private investigator to Qubilah's defense team. (Kunstler, who delighted in his notoriety as "the most hated lawyer in America," was the same attorney who had presented Talmadge Hayer's affidavit to the courts and then the Congressional Black Caucus in the 1970s in an attempt to reopen the Malcolm murder case.)

Betty also brought the weaponry of her presence. Due to a defense-team mix-up, she missed the January 18 arraignment of her daughter, who wore a black shawl over her head and softly pled not guilty. The mishap rattled the already distraught widow. "Nobody picked me up!" she yelled at the lawyers in the lobby of the federal building. "Why did you do me like that? That's my daughter!" Moments later she drew the veil of composure over her shoulders for an all-defense-counsel hearing at the district court. Draped in a black knit outfit and a gold necklace with a peaceful Arabic inscription, she stood powerfully beside the mousy defendant. Even with a phalanx of attorneys fanning about her, she cut the most imposing figure in the court as she delivered an impassioned monologue before the justice.

She said she had reared her children without hatred, insisting that a "skilled manipulator" had lured Qubilah into trouble. She declared that she was behind her daughter "all the way" and vowed that there would be an acquittal "when the dust settles." Betty would stand sturdy throughout the Minnesota nightmare, bearing the strain without a husband to crumple against, as she so often had. She called friends and unburdened two or three times a day during the pretrial hearings. When an old comrade from Chicago showed up unexpectedly, the tears welled. Yet in court she was the indomitable matriarch, the woman who Sutton privately called "drill sergeant," who sat scrawling notes on a legal pad and helped conduct the choir of defense lawyers. "I want my daughter finished with this," she said.

In the end there would be no trial. The government dropped the murder-conspiracy charges on May 1. In return, Qubilah agreed to undergo psychiatric, drug, and alcohol treatment; complete a two-year probation; acknowledge that her original FBI confession was "substantially true"; accept responsibility for her part in the assassination plan; and concede that the Bureau and the U.S. Attorney's Office had "acted in good faith." It was a happy outcome for the widow and her besieged daughter, who nuzzled each other affectionately after the deal was struck. "I'm relieved that it's over," Qubilah said as she left the courthouse for the last time.

But it had been a harrowing spring. With a flourish of legal motions, the defense team had dueled an equally resolute federal prosecutor amid a media carnival. Kunstler, Sutton, and company had blasted the government's case as outrageous, "despicable" entrapment, and Fitzpatrick—its singular witness—as a "vile and evil seducer." Qubilah, they submitted, was guilty only of "a thought crime." Meanwhile, the prosecution had faced the unsavory, even embarrassing task of arguing that the faltering young lady (a figure Parks called "naïve, almost saintly") had willfully orchestrated murder and consummated the act with $250—an absurdly low sum for a contracted murder.

A government lawyer had sought in preliminary hearings to portray the defendant as "obsessed" with killing Farrakhan. Yet his main evidence—a videotape and several audio recordings that the informer had collected without supervision—seemed tainted and inconclusive. Fitzpatrick dominated the taped conversations. Though Qubilah spoke bluntly of assassination, she backpedaled toward the end, despite the scheming reassurances of the man she regarded more as a beau than a collaborator. Fitzpatrick himself was troublesome for the prosecution. As the media unearthed the informer's sordid past, Kunstler's team had launched a withering attack on his character, promising to "show the world what a sorry excuse for a human being he really is." Agents provocateur are by nature slippery. ("Swans don't swim in sewers," the old adage goes.) Yet as *Time* observed, "there may not be many government informants more rough-edged than Fitzpatrick." The witness's credibility further eroded when he admitted on the stand to "living off the government," and acknowledged that he had already pocketed thirty-four thousand dollars for his role in the Shabazz case. Fitzpatrick claimed that he had agreed to inform on Qubilah for the peace of his conscience, but of all the characters in the fishy affair, he wound up smelling the worst.

His disgrace did not ease what Betty called Qubilah's "deepest hurt." After the indictment, the young woman had shut herself in her Minneapolis apartment, ducking journalists, skipping trips to the grocery store, and shedding twenty pounds. The sudden publicity was anathema to a woman who had always shunned not just the limelight, but voter registration cards and driver's licenses. Little Malcolm had headed back east to stay with family, gloomily telling Sutton, "I got my mother in trouble." Qubilah had sunk into depression. "I was no longer the mother to my son," she later said. "The life I was living was not a life." On court days she sat in her gray suit, her fingertips crimping her lips. Her suffering wrenched Betty. "It's my daughter; I can't," the normally unflinching widow told reporters who asked for her thoughts as she left a hearing that March. Yet even through the plea bargain the senior Shabazz had opposed any acknowledgement of guilt by her second eldest. "To use a young girl like that is unconscionable," she said of Fitzpatrick and the FBI.

Betty's worst fears had crystallized in Minneapolis. She had struggled most of her life to shelter her children—both from the world's evil and her own bitterness and suspicions. When viewed through the most cynical lens, the Qubilah matter seemed to have proven her double failure.

But she fought that notion throughout the proceedings, objecting to suggestions that she had fed her daughters "a steady diet to dislike Farrakhan." She upheld her public obligations between court hearings, traveling to Massachusetts in late February to deliver a talk on education, affirmative action, and the status of blacks and women. She performed her maternal duties even more assiduously. "If it were not for my mother, I don't think I would have held up at all," Qubilah later said. "She absorbed a lot of the pain for me." For the widow, those days in court were pure misery.

Without Farrakhan's grace, they would almost certainly have been worse. Betty warmly praised the minister's "patience and generosity" and acknowledged his "kindness in wanting to help my daughter and not for one minute believing" the charges. She had far from forgiven him, but she knew that his gallantry had dimmed the prosecution's flame and very likely spared Qubilah serious jail time. There had been other blessings amid the ordeal. The widow had received supportive letters from as far away as Australia and South Africa. Later that year, the U.S. Embassy of Saudi Arabia, the nation whose ruler had opened his kingdom to her thirty years before, sent her a letter of concern and a $2,112 check under her Malik Shinaz alias. "Thank you for your inquiry," she wrote back. "I am well and living in Mount Vernon, New York. May the God who controls the universe be merciful as we continue to pray and learn the lessons of life."

Closer to home, the outpouring had included two late January rallies on her family's behalf. The first was an evocative gathering of Movement daughters. During the Schomburg Center program, Betty had dabbed her eyes and glowed as Bernice King, Reena Evers, and the daughters of Sutton, Baraka, Jesse Jackson, Alice Walker (author of *The Color Purple*), and former Atlanta Mayor Andrew Young expressed their "profound belief" in the Shabazz clan and hailed the widow as "the perfect example of calm." Days later, Coretta Scott King had joined a battalion of black luminaries in another show of unity. "Unable to discredit [Malcolm] in life, those who would disparage his legacy now seek to stigmatize his family and undermine their effort to promote his teachings," Coretta had declared in the sanctuary of Manhattan's Riverside

Church. "We are here today to say this will not work, and we will stand in unshakable solidarity with Qubilah's family."

The groundswell, especially from black women, was a testament to the Shabazz pedigree. "They have touched royalty; they have touched a family that is sacred to us," one Brooklyn pastor said. Betty and her daughters had also come to represent the survival of black women and families through thirty turbulent years of freedom quest, white conservative backlash, and decaying communities and leadership. Qubilah's widely publicized struggles with alcohol, single motherhood, and emotional ills touched many women of color, as did the widow's passionate labors to protect her child in the absence of a father. Black women of all stations empathized with Betty. They knew that she had once been threadbare, with seven lives to weave from darkness. They knew the trauma of the black woman's burden—to stay strong and silent through crises. So they rallied in the spirit of their foremothers, who a century before had formed clubs to resist the treachery of Southern white men who routinely cast them as unchaste. "Time and again," Princeton History Professor Nell Painter said, "black women have come together, just as we see with Malcolm's daughter, to defend our honor."

Qubilah began anew that May. She moved to San Antonio and prepared to start work as a writer for a radio station Sutton's family owned. She checked into a three-month treatment program that featured psychological and chemical-dependency evaluations, vowing that she was "going to make the best of my stay." The following month, she sent her mother a short letter that brimmed with rejuvenation. She said a recent trip to run errands in Minneapolis had been "horrid" because she had arrived amid a heat wave and wound up with a rash and a tremendous headache. She mentioned that she had paid a few bills and visited her orthodontist, who had inserted a second wire on her front teeth. She was upbeat about the fact that she had gotten the manager at her new San Antonio place to install a washer-dryer—a "big relief," since she would no longer have to cart a suitcase to the

Laundromat like "a homeless person." She mentioned that her plants were doing well. "Josephine and Hilda [her cats] should be arriving from Minneapolis on Sunday or Monday," she added. "We're going to have a chicken liver feast to celebrate." But her son would not be there. He was now living with Betty in New York. "Please have Malcolm give me a call," Qubilah wrote. "Tell him that I love him and miss him. Let him know that he'll be visiting his mother in August."

In a sense, the widow started over, too. Many of her old habits lingered. If anything, the Minneapolis nightmare deepened her circumspection. "You have to watch what you say to your brother," she told an audience at a Malcolm tribute that May. "You have to watch what you say to your sister because you never know, it might be their job." Yet the episode also reminded her of the state's treachery and clarified her truest loyalties. It was a tough lesson. She would spill into the summer emotionally and physically spent, but there was something that she had to do before she could rest. There was a sacrifice she had to make, an offering in return for the happy outcome of the Qubilah affair. Days after the announcement of the settlement, she gathered her comrades and courage and dipped into Harlem for "A New Beginning."

Haki Madhubuti helped set it up. The Chicago writer and publisher, a friend of the widow's since the 1970s, had rung Farrakhan hours after the news about Qubilah's arrest broke back in January. "I hope you're not buying this," he said. The minister had assured him that he was not and had asked him to pass a message along to Betty. "Tell her that I'm going to do right here," he said. "Whatever I can do to help, I will." Madhubuti had arrived at the federal courthouse in Minneapolis shortly after. "What are you doing here?" the widow had asked him, visibly moved. "Where else would I be?" Madhubuti replied. Later, at the defense-team headquarters, the two had shared an intimate talk. Betty was distraught over the plight of her second daughter. "We just got to protect her as much as we can," Madhubuti said. Then he brought up his conversation with Farrakhan.

Betty knew that the two had history. After Farrakhan had bolted the Wallace Muhammad reformation in the mid 1970s, Madhubuti had gotten the virtually flockless minister audiences with Chicago's black nationalists and had helped him reestablish the Nation's base in the city. In return, Farrakhan had promised a more activist, progressive brand of Islam. The widow understood that his and Farrakhan's was a "movement association." She never criticized the partnership, though she did warn Madhubuti to watch his back. ("Be careful," she said, "he's a snake!") The two men had split over ideological differences shortly after and had not been friendly since. (Madhubuti believed Farrakhan had gone back on his word, restoring the Muslim kingdom to the insular "family religion-business" it had become under Elijah Muhammad.) Yet Madhubuti now found himself conveying Farrakhan's goodwill. "Do you want me to tell him anything?" Madhubuti asked Betty. She was silent for a moment. "Just tell him 'thank you,'" she said quietly.

Madhubuti returned to Chicago a couple days later and phoned Farrakhan. No one had a clue how the murder-for-hire case would turn out. A long, costly trial seemed likely, though the defense team was working *pro bono*. "You think we can raise some money?" Farrakhan asked. Madhubuti said he wasn't sure, and took the offer back to Betty. He told her that Farrakhan had requested a face-to-face talk, and that the Muslim chief envisioned a fund-raiser on Qubilah's behalf. "Let me think about it," the widow said. Madhubuti urged her to consent. "For your children and his children and the children of the struggle," he said, "it might be something you need to seriously consider." The next day she agreed to a private meeting. She believed that the FBI had planted an infiltrator in Qubilah's life to revive an ideological (if not physical) black civil war, and she was genuinely grateful to Farrakhan for refusing to go for the ruse.

If they were to meet, however, it would be on her terms. She wanted the talk to happen in a secure New York City spot—somewhere she would feel safe. Madhubuti and Farrakhan's aides decided on LaGuardia Airport. Early one April morning, Betty's driver ferried her over to the Queens landmark. The meeting was to happen around 10 or 11 A.M. Yet Madhubuti's plane—originally scheduled to land at 8 A.M.—was delayed. Betty began frantically calling his home phone every fifteen minutes. Only her chauffeur was with her, and Farrakhan and his people were to arrive any moment. Finally Madhubuti touched down and hustled over to the airport's Holiday Inn. He found Betty in the restaurant lounge having tea. One of the minister's sidemen had tried to approach her, but she did not want to be bothered. "I was just getting ready to go home," she told Madhubuti. Then she repeated the ground rules. "I don't want to embrace anybody," she said. "I just want to talk."

Madhubuti left the widow and rendezvoused with Farrakhan, his wife Khadijah, and top Nation officials in the US Air private lounge. "Don't try to embrace her," Madhubuti cautioned the minister. "Don't even try to shake her hand. She's willing to listen, but she's not going to make a decision." Minutes later, Madhubuti squired Betty into the room. She took a seat across from Farrakhan and the discussion began. There was no mention of Malcolm, though the unspoken history charged the air. The topic at hand was the expense of Qubilah's case and what could be done about it. Farrakhan pledged the Nation's help. Everyone agreed that a fund-raiser at the Apollo would be the best strategy. Madhubuti's concern was the money. "I felt that the Nation of Islam owed reparations to the Shabazz family," he later said. The widow, however, was preoccupied with principle. She told Madhubuti that she still didn't trust Farrakhan. "Neither do I," he replied. "But what alternative do we have?"

The night before the benefit, Betty began phoning her people. "I gotta do this," she told one man, speaking of the event. "But I don't want to be by myself." Later she rang a dear friend. "She said, 'You be at the Apollo Theatre at such and such time,'" the woman remembered. "I said, 'What? What am I going to wear?'" Few of Betty's confidants were surprised to get the call a few hours before the affair. Nor did they wonder why she did not care to talk about the impending encounter. She did declare emphatically, however, that she did not want her daughters to attend and that she did not wish to shake Farrakhan's hand. Sutton, Maya Angelou, and almost everyone else she loved and respected had encouraged her to meet the Muslim chief publicly. Now she just wanted to get it over with. "Tonight you really have to try and find space in your heart," a friend told her.

She arrived at the Apollo early in the afternoon on Saturday, May 6 with Sutton, Madhubuti, and a small band of her friends. She waited backstage as the hours slipped by. "I do not want to embrace this man," she told Madhubuti. "You've got to see that that does not happen." Finally the seats began to fill out front. A standing-room only crowd of 1,400 gathered, trickling past the grim men and gowned women handling pat-downs at the door. Tickets had gone for fifteen dollars to one hundred dollars, and an adjacent theatre brimmed with spectators who paid ten dollars to watch the event on screen. Satellite hookups would beam the proceedings to thousands more in mosques, churches, and auditoriums around the country. The air hummed with expectation. As the program got underway, the crowd rejoiced at the mere mention of the evening's two stars. Outside, hundreds of onlookers clotted a cordoned-off strip of 125th Street. Vendors peddled T-shirts as entertainers from jazz great Lionel Hampton to singer Johnny Gill to rapper Doug E. Fresh arrived. Ben Chavis and Rangel were also among the parade of luminaries. The scene behind the theater's curtain was less festive. Betty kept her distance when Farrakhan entered the backroom with his entourage, greeting him only with a few crisp words. "I thank you for what you have done," she said.

Later, the splendor of the black oral tradition resounded onstage. Reverend Butts offered a stirring prayer, hailing the gathering as proof that "a people united can never be defeated." A medley of hip-hop artists rapped a tribute to unity. Sonia Sanchez invoked the African ancestors in a poem and praised the widow and the minister for "showing our young brothers and sisters we know how to walk in dignity." Activist C. Vernon Mason proclaimed the irony that everyone had winked at all night: that Uncle Sam, in his mischievousness, had unwittingly linked two long-estranged black icons. "When I practiced law, I never thanked the government for a conspiracy," Mason said. "But FBI, thank you for this!" The euphoria was catching and the spirit of triumph and reconciliation cathartic. Practically everyone in the place seemed to believe.

The notable exception was Betty, who roosted in a balcony with Mrs. Farrakhan, surveying the revival below and looking as though she wanted to be anywhere but there. At 11:30 P.M., amid tumultuous applause, she finally descended to the podium. There she spoke not of conspiracy or forgiveness, but of Malcolm. After the emotional reminiscences, she said that she was delighted to "have this opportunity this day. This is a wonderful Mother's Day gift." (The holiday was a week away.) She then thanked her daughter's defense team. "Finally," she said, "I would like to thank Mr. Louis Farrakhan, you know him as Minister Farrakhan, for his original gentle words of assurance for my daughter and myself and her sisters. As he said, 'We will have to help Brother Malcolm's family.' I like the way he said that, and I hope that he continues to see my husband as 'Brother Malcolm.'" Minutes later, event organizers tried subtly to curtail her rambling remarks. (Their satellite time had almost elapsed, and the Muslim helmsman had yet to speak.) She spoke on. "Minister Farrakhan, may the God of our forefathers forever guide you on your journey," she said in closing. "May your conceptual framework keep broadening."

It was after midnight when the Nation of Islam leader took the stage. During his speech, he would compare the evening to the rapprochement of Germans and Jews; white and black South Africans; Israelis and Palestinians; and Protestants and Catholics in Northern Ireland. He would chide those who had scorned his and Betty's détente, and apologize to the widow for "hurt and offense created by words and deeds." While conceding that unscrupulous forces had manipulated his "zeal and love," he would again deny personal involvement in Malcolm's death. Before striding over to the microphone to exalt the occasion as a first step toward "total reconciliation," however, he veered toward Betty. Madhubuti managed to inject himself halfway between the two, so what began as an attempt at a hug became a limp, awkward handshake. The widow smiled slightly and dropped her head as she offered her hand. Farrakhan never saw her eyes.

At the end of the grueling evening, as much as $250,000 had been raised toward Qubilah's counseling and the care of her son. Several audience members had given one thousand–dollar checks, including *60 Minutes* newsman Mike Wallace. A few hardcore Malcolmites sneered at the benefit from afar. "I wouldn't be above asking some curious questions myself," said John Henrik Clarke. "Is the hunter now in bed with the hunted?" Charles Kenyatta, who had become a Baptist minister since his era as a Malcolm lieutenant, was characteristically more blunt. "It's disgusting," he said of the Apollo reunion. "It's all designed to bring respectability to Farrakhan." Yet most blacks who attended the affair seemed delighted that recent events had cast the Nation's captain as an elegant statesman. "For those of us who love Dr. Shabazz, who love Farrakhan, who love Malcolm X, we no longer have to choose sides," one man exulted as he left the theater.

Betty would maintain a respectful if cool relationship with Farrakhan. Her dialogue with him and his top men continued for a time, if only to finalize cash transfers and other details of the arrangement. That October she would join him and hundreds of thousands at the Million Man March in Washington, D.C., briefly mounting the platform on the Capitol steps to good-naturedly remind the sea of men that women represent 70 percent of the planet's poverty, and do most of the work. ("Malcolm would have wanted me to be here," she told a girlfriend.) It appeared to many that when it came to hoisting the unity banner, Betty had learned to submerge her bitterness. "She was aware of the Machiavellian Treatise—if you can separate them, you can rule them," Angelou later said. Yet almost everyone who knew the widow understood that the Apollo handshake had been less a genuine fence mending than a mother's Faustian bargain to save her daughter's skin. "Solidarity Reigns!" the *Amsterdam News* bugled. But a discerning columnist at a newspaper across town got the scoop. For Betty, wrote E. R. Shipp of the *Daily News*, May 6, 1995 "was not unity day or reconciliation day or forgiveness day. It was Mother's Day."

Chapter Nineteen

STARTING OVER

—————

"I saw the image of my grandmother lying helplessly
upon her bed and there were yellow flames in her black hair."
—Richard Wright, *Black Boy*

Betty almost died in the winter of 1995–96. She had never devoted much energy to her own well-being, having spent most of her life as den mother to six and queen mother to many. She rarely saw doctors, and the only medical procedures she regularly underwent were colonic irrigations. Over time, the frenetic schedule and chronic self-neglect took their toll, and she contracted an aggressive infection, the details of which she would keep even from many of her close friends. She struggled to preserve her aura of invincibility. Yet when the widow returned from Beijing and the World Conference for Women in the autumn of 1995, her confidante Laura Ross Brown knew at a glance that she was in serious trouble.

The two met in the ladies room after a Links executive council meeting. Betty was moving slower than a gnat in chowder. She was hunched over and had gained weight. "I know your face as well as I know my own," Brown told her, "and you're sick. You have to go home and go to bed." The sixty-one-year-old widow managed a grin. "My other friends think I look good," she said. "They're lying to you," Brown replied. Later that December, Betty returned from a White House function totally bushed and phoned Brown. Her friend ordered her to stay home from work the next day. "I was just adamant," Brown later recalled. That Monday the widow spent a few hours at the office, but went home early in a weary fog and took to bed.

She later called another friend, Columbia University administrator Larry Dais, to say that she was gravely ill and that she was not going to see a doctor. "She just didn't sound right," Dais remembered. He and Ilyasah drove to the hotel where she was staying. Determined not to go to the hospital, Betty refused to answer the door. Dais pleaded and cajoled. He told her that he had some important papers for her to sign (a ploy Ilyasah thought especially unkind). The widow would not or could not budge. She told her visitors that she was resting, and, still worried, they left.

Ilyasah returned to the hotel the next day. Betty's voice floated through the door, but she did not appear. Eventually she stopped responding altogether. After knocking wildly for several minutes, the frantic daughter called the police, who quickly arrived and forced open the door. They found the widow in bed, fully dressed but almost comatose. An ambulance rushed her to Westchester Medical Center. She was severely dehydrated and suffering from exhaustion and the ravages of an infection, which had spread unchecked throughout her body. For days she drifted in and out of trances as doctors replenished her intravenously and battled the disease. She had always told friends that she wanted to die peacefully in her sleep. Now it seemed quite possible that she would get her wish.

In the end, though, she recovered. She left the hospital after a five-week stay and moved in for a time with Ilyasah, with whom she had remained close. She had been fiercely secretive throughout the ordeal. She checked into the hospital under an alias and later forbade her publicist to tell anyone that she was ill. She refused to inform many of her friends and at least one of her daughters that she was at Westchester Medical. Yet the coterie that visited her in the hospital, including Percy Sutton and Medgar Evers College President Edison Jackson, saw her vulnerability more starkly than ever before. One day the widow awoke from a feverish stupor to find her confidante Mary Redd by her side. "You've been here all this time?" she asked incredulously. "You did this for me?" Redd smiled. "I had to make sure that you'd be around," she said as the widow drifted off.

Mingling with the faces hovering over Betty's bed was one that fluttered beneath her consciousness. In her deepest trances, she later told Jackson, Malcolm came to her. She was overjoyed to see her beloved. Death clearly had not decaffeinated him, for he was the same stern authoritarian who had left her three decades before. He told her firmly that it was not her time. She was not going to die, he said, so she might as well turn around and head back. She could not believe it. All these years she had pined for him, and here he was forbidding her to join him. "I was so mad," she later said. "I wanted to go with him."

———

Betty made a spiritual leap after the illness. To some of her friends, she seemed more awake, more aware of her mortality. Others thought she softened. "Some of the sharpness was taken," Redd recalled. Friends hoped that the widow's new temperance would slow her down. They scolded her nearly suicidal disregard for her health and warned her to simplify. In her last days at the hospital, she vowed that she would. She promised to pare down the business travel and pay attention to herself for a change. "She was going to rest more," Brown said. "She was going to have fun vacations. We were going to go back to the Bahamas." The widow even agreed to see a therapist, finally acknowledging that some unspoken compulsion was fueling her often reckless pace.

The reformation did not last. Betty never sought counseling, and by fall 1996 she was again hurtling between bookings. She evaluated the Million Man March on a Congressional Black Caucus Foundation panel, cochaired a New York Urban League awards dinner, keynoted a memorial for the black man slain by a white mob in New York City's Howard Beach, attended a national black leadership summit, condemned educational inequity alongside NAACP officials, and preached diversity at the University of South Dakota. Meanwhile she raised diabetes awareness on her radio program; mentored students at her adopted schools; made an ambassadorial trip to her mother-in-law's native Grenada; memorialized Commerce Secretary Ronald Brown and the Congo's revolutionary martyr Patrice Lumumba; and kept her routine February and May engagements.

One of the forces sucking her back into the centrifuge was her expanding relationship with the Democratic Party and the White House. She was a vocal presence on President Clinton's 1996 African-American reelection campaign committee. She believed in the Democrats' mission and basked in the glamour of the president's inaugural affairs. Early in Clinton's second term, in a syndicated column widely published in black newspapers, she praised what she saw as his efforts to soften welfare reform's impact on the poor. (He later drew sharp criticism from the Left for gutting the government dole.)

A need to resist also drove her back to the breakneck lifestyle. This "power of standing up" was a bequest of her husband, she explained in an open April 1997 letter to Rosa Parks. "I remain steadfast in my admiration of both of you [Parks and Malcolm] and my own personal commitment to ensure that injustice is always met with resistance," she told the Civil Rights matron. "I have learned from the lives of two history-makers, even as I write my own."

Yet the widow's pace was again draining her. And though illness had thawed her disposition, her sense of urgency deepened. "She got a focus after that scare," Dais remembered. "She realized that today could be it, tomorrow could be it." Even as her public life surged, Betty inwardly recoiled from the glare. "There were just so many forces pulling on her," Dais said. "Always a spotlight, always somebody waiting to say 'I told you so.'" The widow continued to seek shelter in her relationships. "My friend says I have to leave because I have another appointment right now," she sometimes told event organizers before fleeing with a cohort for a one-on-one breakfast. She still phoned friends at 2 A.M. to gossip and giggle, but the search for sanctuary was wearing her down. "There was something in the last two years, like she was tired," her friend Ruth Clark said. "It was almost as if she was ready to go and be with Malcolm."

She could not go far with a rootless adolescent on her hands. Despite the glut of engagements and appearances, it was her grandson that most frazzled her in those days. Little Malcolm had been living with her since his mother's indictment on murder-for-hire charges. He had become the widow's legal ward as part of Qubilah's May 1995 plea bargain. The move from Minneapolis did not immediately jar the ten-year-old child. He was used to an ambulant lifestyle in which he switched schools and cities more often than he did his sneakers. And he had often stayed with his grandmother and aunts in the past as his mother struggled to right herself. Still, his keen young mind was boiling with trouble when he arrived in suburban New York.

In truth, the angst had always been there. Once, as a three-year-old, he had set his shoes on fire. His preschool teachers had cooed over him when he snuggled against them with almost desperate neediness, and an incredible smile made him popular with the first-grade crowd. But he seemed lonely and was often hungry and unkempt. In the third grade, he brought a knife to school. At around the same age, he became deluded and was briefly hospitalized. The wars with his mother escalated in the tempestuous years that followed. He loved her dearly, but resented her alcoholism and roaming, habits that dragged him into the domains of prostitutes and crackheads. At one tenement, he wandered by an open doorway and spotted a nude woman lying spread-eagle on a bed, a sight that repulsed him and worried Qubilah.

Through all the turmoil, he hungered for a father. He was said to have known his birth father, but the two had had little contact. In grade school, he called school-bus drivers and male teachers "Dad" before they gently corrected him. When his mother fell for a meaty fellow she nicknamed "Fitz," he was elated. "You're my Michael," he told the informer in a conversation taped for the FBI. "How's that Malcolm?" Fitzpatrick asked. "You're my dad," the boy replied. A mortified Qubilah took the phone and apologized, but Fitzpatrick shushed her. "Sounds like he wants a dad," he said. "You know what I mean?

Like a normal kid who wants a dad. That's all." Little Malcolm later composed a ditty about Fitzpatrick. He grinned from New York to Minneapolis when he and his mother moved to be near the beguiler. Months later, when Qubilah was arrested for murder conspiracy, the child's already stormy world imploded.

His grandmother would also struggle to recover from the Fitzpatrick affair. She hinted at her anguish among friends. "You never know what will happen with your children," she told the Reverend Al Sharpton. "You never can forget, Al, these children are not growing up normally. We put a lot of pressure and crises on them that they didn't ask for." Privately she wept over Qubilah and blamed herself for the young woman's woes, but she had always been the family's Rock of Gibraltar. When the time came to take in Little Malcolm, she did so gamely, hoping to shield and steady him while Qubilah collected herself and underwent drug treatment in San Antonio. In some ways, the boy's plight mirrored his grandfather's calamitous childhood and evoked memories of Betty's own partition from her birth mother at roughly the same age. ("I guess that's why she never legally separated Qubilah and Malcolm," Gamilah later said. "She had some issues from way back when.") So the widow pruned her schedule, decorated a room in her airy apartment, and again assumed the duties of motherhood.

All seemed well for a while. Betty showered the child with gifts, hoping to comfort him and compensate for the upheaval in his life. She bought him computers and clothes and enrolled him in prep school. The two delighted in each other. He called her "Mama Betty" and teased her endlessly. She joshed him back, relishing his youthful verve. Little Malcolm was charming and bright. (Qubilah later boasted that he had skipped two grades.) He loved to read, spoke some French and Arabic, and pronounced words like an urbane grown-up. He dreamed of becoming a lawyer or barber. His grandmother often accompanied him on taxi rides to the opulent Chapel School, a Lutheran academy in the nearby suburb of Bronxville. Though his grades were erratic, his teachers agreed that he had huge potential, and Betty waited breathlessly for him to flourish. "He's going to make me proud," she said.

Yet he still blistered with rage and confusion. "You could tell he needed a man's touch," Mount Vernon Mayor Ernest Davis remembered. He needed serious professional attention, too. The widow was more inclined to apply her old formula of firm guidance and TLC. (Qubilah would tell police that her son was schizophrenic, and that she was reluctant to let her mother and sisters care for him because they refused to accept the depth of his illness.) Betty was no more capable of acknowledging the trauma rippling through the Shabazz bloodline than she had been as a young, single mom. She was as strict with her grandson as she had been with her daughters, and though Little Malcolm yearned for a stable environment, he chafed under the discipline. He wanted a young, spry mom who could race after him. At times he taunted the widow, fussing at her for collapsing into her chair instead of cruising the mall with him. As his resentment deepened, he grew unruly, talking back to adults and acting up. He wanted to return to his mother, who complained that she missed him. Betty finally surrendered. In December 1996, she sent the eleven-year-old off to Texas, praying that he and Qubilah could make a fresh start.

Meanwhile, the widow plotted a fresh start of her own. She was on the verge of a transition that she had mulled for years, and the heart of her plan was the Audubon Ballroom. In 1995, after a decade of tussling between city agencies, politicians, Malcolmites, preservationists, and Columbia University, the once-moldering building was reborn as a glinting, six-story bulwark of gray aluminum and green glass. The sleek new structure, an installation in what would become Columbia's five-building, twenty-eight million–dollar biotechnology park, symbolized the compromise struck between forces that viewed the site as a womb for high-tech development and those who wished to preserve Malcolm's death place in pristine form. The Washington Heights landmark was now a complex that housed laboratories, a city health clinic, a coffee bar, a Chemical Bank branch, and a Barnes & Noble bookstore. Two-thirds of the original Audubon shell had been preserved. A seven million–dollar restoration project fed by city and state funds had also spared 40 percent of the interior hall in which Malcolm had fallen. Layered in white sheetrock, its walls awaited the furnishing of a proposed memorial and museum.

Gabriel Koren was shaping a life-size bronze statue of the martyr for the ballroom's ground-floor lobby. Another artist, Daniel Galvez, was painting an imposing, thirteen-by-sixty-three-foot mural of Malcolm's life on the east wall of the dance hall's second floor. (Workers had long since removed the wooden stage that had drunk a lethal volume of the minister's blood.) The transfigured Audubon seemed a sweet marriage of science and history. That October, Columbia's first Malcolm X Scholar (then one of the program's sixteen alumni) joined Governor George Pataki in opening the complex's biotechnology center, whose tenants would include a tissue-engineering firm that specialized in growing human skin for the treatment of burn victims.

But by 1996, plans for the second-floor Malcolm memorial had stalled. The city claimed that it had fulfilled its promise to renovate the ballroom and provide raw space for the tribute. The memorial's advisory commission (formed under Mayor Dinkins) contended that Mayor Rudy Giuliani's office was reneging on the prior administration's vow to cover operating costs. "We felt like we were being jerked around," remembered Howard Dodson, cochair of the commission.

For Betty this was especially unsettling. Though the Audubon still conjured grim memories, she had found herself immersed in the development of its memorial. She scrutinized designs for all phases of the project. She visited Koren's studio while the sculptor was refining Malcolm's likeness and delivered a blunt critique. ("No, his lips weren't like that. And what you got on his head?") She attended planning meetings and conspired with commission members to wring more memorial cash from tight-fisted city officials. "She would have been a great poker player," recalled Michael Mowatt-Wynn of the Harlem-Heights Historical Society. "She would look you straight in the eye and negotiate hard." The widow finally decided that she should see what she was fighting for. In January 1997, after shunning the site for thirty-two years, she swallowed hard, shut her eyes, and walked back into the ballroom.

She had expected a rending flashback, but once she collected herself and stilled her heart, she liked what she saw. She entered the building not through the original 166th Street entrance (the threshold Malcolm's gurney had crossed on his journey to eternity) but a majestic Broadway Avenue doorway. Upstairs she encountered the vacant memorial space, including a hall with glassy floors and gleaming walls (the restored portion of the ballroom). During her private tour of the unfinished facility, visions of a human-rights center devoted to her husband's principles unfurled before her. She had long dreamed of such an establishment, which she imagined would host international conferences and teach policy makers and the public about a range of rights issues, with a focus on women and children. She hoped to serve as the titular head of a Malcolm X Educational Foundation that would help oversee the center, occupying an office in the Audubon and working with Columbia and the Historical Society, the memorial's operating body.

The foundation had evolved in her mind for years. In many ways it represented the next phase of her growth as a Malcolm memorialist and educator. She had talked seriously about forming such an organization with several of her husband's apostles in the 1980s. Now that the ballroom offered a possible home, the foundation became a near obsession. She began recruiting a half-dozen of her most trusted comrades for a board. She wanted to incorporate, but not before she had done her homework. To ensure credibility and institutional support, she wanted Columbia to play a key role. She hoped the foundation would fuse her legacy and Malcolm's and anchor her advocacy in coming years. She looked forward to retiring from Medgar Evers College, where she had spent the last two decades forging a career and an identity. Now the foundation would be her livelihood. "This," she told friends, "is where I'm going to make my mark."

For Betty, the foundation meant control. In thirty-two years, she had weathered more distortion and derision of her husband and more exploitation of her widowhood than she cared to recall. Malcolm had died largely alone, and she and the girls had survived with few resources or eminent benefactors. A parade of characters had since tried to take possession of the minister, often claiming loyalties that never existed. Betty would have no more of it. Maybe the old scars began to bleed. Maybe her tolerance finally ran dry. Whatever the case, she became more standoffish around the phonies in the end. Where were they when Malcolm needed them, when he could not even get a funeral in a black church? "They didn't want to *touch* him," she hissed in a bitter moment.

There was something even deeper. The foundation and even the disillusionment were part of a larger shift, a desire to have a normal life, to start over. Betty wanted freedom. She wanted peace and quiet. She was tired of having to be so profoundly secretive about her whereabouts. She was tired of bearing her daughters' burdens. She promised herself that she would treat them like young women and let them be self-sufficient. Her illness had convinced her that she needed to take stock, to clarify or reaffirm relationships. She talked about buying a condominium somewhere, about hiring some workers to fix up her place in Roxbury. For half a lifetime she had been in emotional flight. Now she was ready to plant her feet. "I'm going to get out of Mount Vernon," she told Mayor Davis. "I don't want my kids to know where I am. I can just disappear and get lost. 'Cause you never know, child. You could be dead tomorrow."

———

Betty escaped in the summer of 1996. After dreaming of a retreat for more than a year, she, Coretta Scott King, and Myrlie Evers-Williams met at a Florida spa for a few balmy days of revelry. The trip would be an antidote. "We were all under such tremendous pressure," Myrlie later remembered. They invited Maya Angelou, who had encouraged the vacation. She turned them down. "I'm nobody's widow," she said. "Besides, not one of you knows how to make a decent drink." The trio had gotten a grant with the help of a well-placed black woman in Coca-Cola's Atlanta office ("none of us were wealthy,"

Myrlie later said) and had laid the ground rules. No conversation about the cause or the legacies, and no discussing the late husbands. The Movement widows pledged to drop their veils.

And for a while they did. Myrlie arrived first. By the time the other two showed up, she had already had a powerful massage. They discovered her in the spa's exercise and sauna wing, droopy-eyed and weaving. "I know you don't drink," Betty said, "so you can't be drunk. But honey, what has happened to *you?*" Myrlie chuckled. "The same thing that's about to happen to the two of you," she said. Coretta looked a little unsure, but Betty could hardly wait. After the massages, the three met for a meal at the resort's restaurant. When the fashionably puny portions were brought before them, they fell silent. Betty, an epicurean, called for seconds. "Honey, I know I need to lose some weight," she said. "But this is ridiculous. I want some *food!*"

Later, the trio set out on a walk with several of the spa's guests. When they realized that the others had done five miles for their one, they decided to try aerobics instead. They returned to their rooms and climbed into their grungy clothes. Coretta emerged with immaculate makeup and hair, dignified as always. Betty and Myrlie pulled on baseball caps. Myrlie flipped hers around backward. "It was just something to rebel against, you know, the image," she later said. The widows headed for their private class. "What can you teach us, honey?" Betty asked the aerobics/dance instructor. "We want to learn some of the new ones." Mrs. Malcolm X launched into a giddy rendition of the Achy Breaky, beckoning to "Retta" to join her. Myrlie just marveled. "Betty…I can't capture this in words…." she later said. "It's the way she moved when she talked. She was very seldom still. There was a fluidness to her, a self-assuredness, an 'I am woman!' A sex mama, too."

That evening the three watched a televised basketball game in Coretta's suite, with Betty explaining the action. Eventually the conversation turned to their thirteen daughters and sons. Would they be alright? Were they marred for life? "We all agreed that we had done the best we really could," Evers-Williams later said. The widows further broke their promise by talking Medgar, Martin, and Malcolm. They talked about sharing them with the world; about belonging to a highly unusual personality, brilliant and obsessed; about a too-fleeting union with someone who inspired not only you, but everyone else—inspired to love, to excel, to be human. They sat on Mrs. King's bed in that fancy spa and remembered the soaring sense of being alive when every moment counts.

The serenity Betty found in Florida eluded her second eldest in Texas. Qubilah's San Antonio beginnings had been promising. She had settled into her production and promotions job at KSJL-96.1 FM in the fall of 1995. She had sought anonymity, taking the pseudonym Karen Taylor and plunging into her work. But her old demons soon resurfaced. That October, police responding to a neighbor's call encountered a drunk and reeling Qubilah. She told them that she was considering suicide and that she had tried to take her own life in the past. They carried her to a psychiatric hospital. She would be hospitalized at least three more times in coming months.

Then a man entered the picture. In December 1996, Qubilah appeared at a company Christmas party on the arm of a tall stranger. She introduced Theodore Turner as her husband. Never a splashy dresser, she wore an elegant black cocktail dress and a sexy hairdo that night. "Wow," said a coworker, "what a difference a man makes." Qubilah had married Turner that month, though she told police weeks earlier that he had choked her and slammed her against a wall in a jealous rage. According to Texas corrections authorities, the thirty-eight-year-old meat salesman was also a repeat burglar sentenced in 1992 to twenty-five years in prison and paroled in 1995. Despite their problems, Qubilah believed she and her new husband could raise Little Malcolm. Days after they were wed, she flew to New York to retrieve the boy. (It is unclear how much Betty knew about her daughter's new husband or the couple's turbulent relationship.)

Turner and Malcolm hit it off. When the Little Rock, Arkansas, native arrived at San Antonio Airport to pick up his new wife and stepson, he found Qubilah pushing a slim twelve-year-old in a wheelchair.

Qubilah told him that he would have to lift the crippled child into the car. Moments later he discovered that the two had played a practical joke on him. "He wanted to see if I had the strength to carry him," Turner later said of the boy. Little Malcolm was elated to be back in Texas, with a mom, a dad, and a room of his own. The seventh-grader enrolled at the two hundred–student Redeemer Lutheran School and joined the basketball team. He was on the second string and played mostly garage-style ball. Turner, who Little Malcolm said had played in college, came to a few games anyway. During one match, the lanky child hit a three-pointer in his stepdad's presence and swelled with pride. Turner helped Little Malcolm polish his dribbling and passing skills and brought him along on his door-to-door rounds.

Meanwhile, the meat salesman's marriage was spoiling. In January 1997, Qubilah told police that he had pushed her from a slow-moving car and threatened to shoot her. By the end of the month, the couple had split up. Little Malcolm, whom teachers had found mannerly and bright, began to self-destruct. His grades plummeted and he started skipping school. When school officials asked about his chronic absences, he blamed stomachaches or claimed that he had overslept and missed the bus. Qubilah promised to straighten him out, but did not always know where he went when he played hooky.

Then the scuffles got ugly. On February 26, Qubilah told police that her son had attacked her and that she wanted him committed to a mental hospital. She said he had stopped taking his medicine. The boy told police that he was angry because Qubilah had been drinking and would not drive him to school. Officers carried him to a psychiatric unit. After a short stay, he returned to his mother. The following month he transferred to a public middle school, where he seemed withdrawn and unhappy. In April, he called police and said that he and his mother had gotten into another argument. Qubilah told the responding officer that she and the child were fighting again and that she was considering placing him in foster care. She worried that he was running with young toughs from a neighborhood gang.

Days later, Betty said "enough." To Qubilah's apparent relief, the widow again sent for her grandson. She had decided that this time the boy would live with her permanently. In late April, she asked officials at the Chapel School, which Little Malcolm had attended before leaving for San Antonio, to readmit him. The academy's headmaster was dubious. "It is my strong opinion that he should have an academic assessment...tutorial help sought—a plan for Malcolm—BEFORE just plunking him down in a classroom to continue his erratic ways [original emphasis]," he wrote in a letter forwarded to Betty.

The widow seemed confident in her decision to raise her grandson, who arrived from San Antonio just past midnight on April 26 and walked groggily into LaGuardia Airport. His shoulders were stooped. He thought Mama Betty would be mad, but she enveloped him with a hug when they met in baggage claim. The two walked to the car arm in arm, and he nodded off against her on the ride to her new place, a posh co-op in a leafy neighborhood of Yonkers (north of Manhattan).

———

There is some ambiguity about the widow's emotional condition in those last days. Her long-time secretary believed she was dangerously frayed. He watched her piston across campus at Medgar Evers College, her pull-cart of papers skittering behind her, money sometimes falling from her purse, and suspected that she was coming undone. To others, she had never seemed mellower or less fearful of the past. She was in good health and humor when she phoned friends to fund-raise for scholarships and books on behalf of Medgar Evers College students, and was eagerly awaiting a second retreat with Myrlie Evers-Williams and Coretta Scott King in June. "She was managing herself quite well," said James Turner, head of Africana Studies at Cornell University. "She was not in any crisis. All her expectations were before her." Whatever the depth of Betty's self-possession, her close friends realized that she was bone-tired and that Little Malcolm's return was a burden that would test even the matriarch's durability.

She and the boy had some good times. That May, the two celebrated her sixty-third birthday at a favorite restaurant. Larry Dais joined them, bringing a gift of coconut cake. He had meant for her to carry it home, but she insisted they eat it right away. A waiter started to take it into the kitchen to slice it. "No, no, no," Betty protested, "you cut it right here."

Still, most days were taut and somber. Late that month, the widow asked Angelou to prepare a meal for her because she was too tired to cook for herself. She hung out with Ruth Clark one evening but showed no hint of her normal vivacity. "There were a lot of things that were unanswered in my mind that she told me that night," Clark later recalled. "This conversation that we had, it appeared to me that she knew she wasn't going to be here that long. I was stunned, some of the things that she said—some things I will never say."

Malcolm's birthday offered a reprieve. On May 19, one of New York City's black radio stations played the martyr's speeches throughout the afternoon. Betty flagged a cab and told the driver to tune in and keep the meter running. She shut her eyes and bumped around Manhattan, listening to her husband rap. That evening, before attending memorials in New Jersey and Harlem, she granted WBAI-FM an interview. One of the station's program hosts mentioned that Malcolm would have been seventy-two. "Oh my God!" The widow squealed. "I can't believe it. I can't believe it….My mother thought he was too old for me….When you say seventy-two, I say, 'Ooh, yeah, she had a point there.'…I am delighted that I had the opportunity to share part of his life, because he was a great guy. Thank you Mr. Bernard White and Ms. Amy Goodman. It's been a pleasure talking about the guy that I love so much!"

The day was only an intermission from Little Malcolm's troubles. Betty agonized over her grandson, who had grown more turbulent during his stay in San Antonio and now began running away from home. On Saturday, May 31, the widow asked Dodson to save her and the boy tickets for a John Henrik Clarke tribute the following afternoon at the Schomburg Center. "I'm too old to be raising children," she said during the conversation. "I don't have the energy at this stage of my life. It is taking too much." The next day, Mayor Davis spotted her walking near some restaurants in downtown Mount Vernon. She was deep in thought. Little Malcolm, who was trailing her by ten paces, seemed

equally pensive. He had willingly returned to New York and his grandmother's care, but again he had found himself missing his mother and
friends in San Antonio. Days earlier he had told a playmate how cool
Texas was. "Do you think if I get into enough trouble they'll send me
back?" he asked.

———

James Smalls got the call at six in the morning on June 1, 1997.
"What happened to Sister Betty?" a friend from Detroit asked. Smalls
had no idea, but said he would call Leonard Jeffries. Surely the scholar
could dispel this rumor that the widow had met some tragedy. Jeffries
had heard nothing. By 7 A.M., Ruth Clark knew. Somebody telephoned
her to say that Betty had been badly hurt in a fire. "No way," Clark said.
"No way. I just spoke to her a couple days ago." Minutes later,
Reverend Richard Dixon, the widow's old Mount Vernon friend, called
Davis. "I heard that Betty Shabazz is dead," he said weakly. Dodson
learned the truth via voicemail that afternoon. Before the Clarke gala,
he had checked around for the widow, wondering where she was.
Attallah already knew. She had gotten the news around noon from an
airline employee in Los Angeles International, where she had just
stepped off a flight. The young man nodded at her as she hustled to
baggage claim. "How's your mom?" he asked. "Fine, thank you," she
answered routinely. "Is she going to pull through?" the man asked.
Attallah's eyes caught his. "Pull through?" she echoed.

Hours earlier, the streets of Brooklyn and Harlem had hummed
with reports that Betty was clinging to life, a victim of arson. Medgar
Evers College photographer Brother Akeem, who years before had
coaxed the camera-wary widow into posing for the school newspaper
by promising to capture her loveliness, heard that she had been
attacked and went nearly berserk with rage. Like many Malcolm devotees, he instantly suspected conspiracy. "People was really angry and
mad and upset," he later remembered. "That something could happen
to Dr. Shabazz, that somebody might have done that...." For an hour
or two it looked like the talk about some evil befalling Mrs. Malcolm

X in racially troubled Yonkers might provoke a street response from that less-restrained quarter of Black New York that considered her its Madonna. The fiery Reverend Sharpton, whose core audience is necessarily skeptical of the news media and the police, suggested at midday that Betty might have been the victim of a hate crime. But before long, amid a flurry of television and radio bulletins, America discovered that the culprit was kin.

Police had found Little Malcolm wandering barefoot and bewildered through Mount Vernon just before daybreak, his clothes reeking of gasoline. He had been knocking on doors and asking for an ambulance. He complained that he was not feeling well. When police arrived, he could not tell them his name or address. "My house is on fire and I ran out," he said. An ambulance delivered him to a Mount Vernon hospital, where he was examined and released to detectives. Still dazed and frightened, he told them that he had burned Mama Betty's place because he was unhappy living with her. According to officers, he said he believed his grandmother's death would hasten his return to San Antonio. Percy Sutton and others who talked to the boy later that morning would reject the officers' account of the alleged confession. They said Little Malcolm was despondent, and that he told them between sobs that he never meant to harm the widow.

But he had harmed her—and horrifically. Investigators later determined that sometime Saturday evening, Malcolm had gotten hold of some gasoline and doused a hallway near Betty's room. Hours later, he struck a match. At about 1:40 Sunday morning, shortly before he was seen rambling around a nearby neighborhood, firefighters had been summoned to the widow's three-bedroom apartment complex. There they had discovered her crumpled in a windowless hallway outside the sixth-floor condominium. Moments earlier, she had awakened to flames and the stench of lathering smoke, as she had on a Valentine's Day thirty-two years before, when the Molotov cocktails rained. She had sprung from her bed, and in what some investigators later suspected was an attempt to snuff the fire and save the grandson she believed was still inside, had raced toward a small blaze in the corridor outside her bedroom. The flames had devoured her nylon nightgown and engulfed her. She was delirious by the time neighbors came to her aid, swaddling her in a sheet. She kept mumbling something through grimaces and groans as ambulance attendants arrived and began working to stabilize her for the trip to Jacobi Medical Center in the Bronx. "My grandson," she said over and over. "My grandson is in there."

He was not, of course, but Betty paid an unspeakable price for the moments she must have spent lunging through the noxious clouds in search of him. The fuel-stoked flames had burned ferociously, charring virtually the entire expanse of the silken skin her husband had once cherished. Her lips and nose were gone. Her eyes were sealed, her lungs singed. So ghastly were her wounds that even doctors at Jacobi's burn unit—specialists who routinely deal with the most gruesome injuries— might have winced. When Ilyasah arrived at the hospital around 3 o'clock that morning, she scarcely recognized the woman who lay before her. "I couldn't stay in the room and see her like that," she later remembered.

Soon the rest of the daughters were at their mother's bedside. (Qubilah flew in from San Antonio that Monday and headed straight to the hospital to keep a tearful vigil with her sisters.) They spoke lovingly to her, fighting the urge to collapse in wailing misery. The widow, who had been conscious and somewhat responsive on arrival at Jacobi, was able to acknowledge them by moving her jaw, legs, and feet. She was heavily sedated, and appeared almost comatose. Her daughters learned that it would be a miracle if she survived. It would be mercy, they suspected, if she did not.

Amazingly, she lingered for three weeks, clasped in a quarrel between life and death. Dr. Bruce Greenstein, director of Jacobi's burn unit, would fall in love with her for the way she fought. There was no reason to believe that the sixty-three-year-old widow would last more than a few days, or even forty-eight hours. She was blanketed with third-degree burns, which penetrate the skin's underlying tissue. Recovering from the trauma of such injuries is difficult enough, but severe burns can continue to wreak havoc on the body. Plasma, blood cells, and water leak at a frightful rate, depleting the bloodstream of fluid and starving the kidneys, heart, and lungs. In the case of such hemorrhaging, doctors seek to bathe a patient's organs and replenish nutrients—the medical equivalent of trying to keep a sieve full. Add the stress of sheer agony (ten thousand times the pain of a scalded finger) and the imminent threat of infection and lethal pneumonia, and one begins to understand why serious burns can be more deadly than gunshot wounds.

The Shabazz daughters asked Greenstein and his team to treat Betty's injuries as aggressively as possible. The widow underwent five skin-graft operations in seven days, an excruciating but essential chain of procedures. Surgeons excised portions of dead tissue from her body and replaced them with sheets of temporary, artificial skin designed to help regenerate her dermal layer. (In a bitter irony, the human skin being experimentally grown and tested for safety in one of the Audubon complex's laboratories was unusable for patients with burns as grievous as Betty's.) Her tolerance of the surgeries astonished doctors, who she managed to communicate with through subtle movements. "Dr. Shabazz is an incredibly strong person," Greenstein said.

Betty's strength was no revelation to the dignitaries and less-eminent figures streaming into Jacobi. What stopped their hearts was the depth of her misfortune. How could tragedy have again visited this woman? The question tormented the ambassadors, celebrities, and political figures massing at the hospital, a procession that included former Mayors Ed Koch and Dinkins and the current Mayor Giuliani, Sutton, Sharpton, Evers-Williams, the Reverend Jesse Jackson, boxing promoter Don King, and an emissary of Minister Farrakhan. Maya Angelou and Mrs. King wept during the journey from Atlanta to pray over their fallen sister. Betty could respond to callers only by moving a leg. Some who briefly entered her room in sterile gear (to prevent infection) felt a profound calm. "When people are spiritually connected, there is a response without words," Coretta said.

Visiting friends wore ribbons of lavender (Betty's favorite color) and awaited updates from members of the Shabazz family, who huddled upstairs near the widow's room. Meanwhile, an anonymous throng of admirers congregated in the hospital lobby. "She's just like the rest of us," a fifty-one-year-old laborer told a stranger, explaining that he himself was rearing two grandchildren because his daughter was hooked on cocaine. A landscape of bouquets and a healing wish from President Clinton were among the other expressions of concern. Comedian Dick Gregory tried to buoy the daughters with funny stories. Like many, he believed Betty—whose resilience seemed long ago to have entered the realm of imperishability—could pull through. "You can never underestimate the strength of her spiritual power," Sharpton said, "and we believe that God will have mercy on her." Dinkins was clutching hope, too. But Sutton seemed to brace himself. "There's little that you can say except to remind people you have to celebrate a life well lived," he declared.

The widow's half-hug with death would have been awful enough without the sickening thought that a relative was to blame. Some Shabazz comrades remained unconvinced that Little Malcolm had deliberately torched his grandmother's apartment. That the stricken but likable boy could perform an act of such savagery was beyond their comprehension. For several hours after firefighters had snuffed the blaze, local and federal authorities had apparently operated under the same premise. The possibility that a would-be assassin was at large had even momentarily drawn the FBI's attention. Yet by the afternoon of the fire, police had taken the grandson into custody under preliminary delinquency charges, convinced that Little Malcolm was their arsonist.

The skinny, well-groomed child cowered when Sutton visited him in Westchester Psychiatric Hospital, where he was briefly admitted that Sunday before being shuttled to a juvenile detention center. "He covered his head and acted like he was sleeping so that the world would go away," said Sutton, who would serve as the boy's lawyer. "He's frightened, he's sorry, and he did not believe what had happened." The next day, the child was escorted into Westchester County Family Court in a billowing sweatshirt, jeans, and sandals. He seemed distant during the brief appearance, nervously drumming his fingers and appearing to mouth words as Sutton addressed the court. A judge asked the child to identify himself. "Malcolm," he replied. At another hearing that week, Qubilah dabbed her son's face with a crumpled tissue. He flinched then relented, allowing her to stroke his cheek.

News of the widow's catastrophe shook sympathizers across the country, though many had only a dim knowledge of her past. The shockwaves registered in foreign lands where Malcolm was longer established as a universal hero and where his widow was a less obscure figure in the public consciousness. (After the fire, the *Amsterdam News* got calls from journalists in Africa, Asia, Europe, South America, Australia, Canada, and the Caribbean.) But Betty belongs most poignantly to the lore of New York City, and as she tarried between worlds, it was the sympathy of New Yorkers that seemed most visceral. Local radio stations received a chorus of kind wishes for the widow. Christians and Muslims gathered at uptown worship houses, murmuring that "only prayer can help Sister Betty through this."

Then came the blood drives. The week after the blaze, hundreds queued up to donate a pint to the widow, who needed regular transfusions of plasma and white cells. (The collected blood was earmarked for Jacobi.) The crowd outside Carver Federal Savings Bank, which hosted a drive in the basement of a branch near 125th and Malcolm X Boulevard, was thick with the sons and daughters of Harlem. There were also donors of various creeds and colors from beyond the black cultural mainland. Word of mouth lengthened the file of volunteers, who fanned themselves with medical forms while attendants painted their arms with antiseptic. Each donor signed a card or scrawled a note to be delivered to the Shabazz family. "I gave blood to you because of the blood your husband lost," one donor wrote.

The deeply sedated widow may not have fully comprehended the outpouring, but her daughters linked hands outside Jacobi to acknowledge the support and appeal for continued prayers. "We have not been a family who has ever asked for anything ourselves," Attallah said, stifling sobs. "Our father did not….He was a doer. Our mother wouldn't have. She's a giver. But we…are requesting your continued prayers, because she does need it." A fund to help cover Betty's treatment swelled with donations. A battalion of men arrayed themselves before the hospital for a Father's Day rally, standing by Mrs. Malcolm X, they said, as proxies for her husband.

In the second week of the ordeal, the widow began to succumb. She had fought hard. Entwined with tubes and breathing through a hole in her neck, she had tried valorously to write messages to family members. Doctors believed she could hear and understand what loved ones uttered in her ear. "Rest," some whispered, "go well." Aisha Al-Adawiya read aloud from a Qur'an and played soothing music for her old friend. At times, the widow seemed serene, almost angelic. Yet some of the men and women keeping vigil believed that she was hanging on for a reason. "She has something to say," Clark told Sutton. "She is not leaving until she says it."

At the end, after the prayers and fasting and weeping, the daughters surrounded their mother. In the past twenty-two days, they had learned more about the woman—about the silhouette of her fears and rhapsodies, about the spectrum of her allegiances and loyalties, about the caliber of her courage and the arc of her spirit—than they had in twenty-two years. Even amid the torment, they churned with love and rage. Sutton would report that Little Malcolm had only wished to scare his Mama Betty, that he believed she would dial 911 from the safety of her bedroom as the apartment hallway burned harmlessly. But just at that moment, as the Shabazz sisters watched their only remaining parent dwindle, the explanations rang hollow. "It's not going to lessen the blow," Malikah, one of the twins, later said. "It's not that I stopped loving him, but he has to deal with whatever comes his way, and our job is to make sure he deals with it….His ultimate forgiveness will have to come from God, not us or the judge."

God's pardon may have found Little Malcolm in Lenox, Massachusetts, where the twelve-year-old was sentenced to eighteen months in a home for emotionally troubled children after pleading guilty to the juvenile equivalent of second-degree manslaughter and arson. Psychiatrists would confirm that he was profoundly disturbed, portraying him as schizophrenic with psychotic episodes. Yet he was of sufficiently sound mind and character to apologize for his grandmother's demise in conversations with family and friends, and in a private letter he wrote to the widow. "I loved Mama Betty, and Mama Betty loved me," he told Sutton. The Shabazz clan later joined surrogate aunts and uncles in praying that the man-child would rise from cataclysmic beginnings, as had his grandfather, to become as staunchly loyal to truth and freedom as Malcolm X had. They believe that Betty's last wish, the message she labored to deliver, was "Take care of the boy."

In the mid-afternoon of June 23, 1997, when the widow finally laid down her burden, her daughters and comrades did not feel brave. They felt diminished. Nonetheless true to her inherited aristocracy, Attallah squared herself before the press. "Our mother has made a transition...." she said. "My father lived strong; my mother did honorably....She is very mighty where she is. She is boundless where she is. She is strong where she is. She will have her eye on you." Moments later, a City College official broke into a jog on 125th Street. He had gotten word of Mrs. Malcolm X's passing, and did not feel right keeping it to himself. He darted among the collision of stores, telling faces familiar and strange that she was gone. Smiles withered. Laughter ceased. The man ran on and on, unspooling a ribbon of gloom. Overhead the marquee of the Apollo Theatre offered a salute: "We Love You, We Miss You, Dr. Betty Shabazz."

Epilogue

HOMEGOING

—

"And my soul and your soul will meet in
de day when I lay dis body down."
—Negro Spiritual

Two days after the widow's death, before surrendering her to immortality, the Shabazz daughters arranged themselves before her again. They had come to Harlem's Unity Funeral Home—which had hosted Malcolm's wake thirty-two years earlier—for the ceremonial cleansing. In Islam, loved ones prepare their dead for the journey beyond with elegant ritual. So there in the stillness of Unity's dim chambers, under the eye of Aisha Al-Adawiya, the young women washed their mother. They bathed her in oils, anointed her with scents, swathed her in the traditional cloth, and blanketed her in a snowy shroud. "It was beautiful, absolutely beautiful," Al-Adawiya later said. The daughters offered Allah their petitions and praise. Then, their task complete, they left the home to ready themselves for the next feat of bravery.

Meanwhile Betty's body, which Islamic law had spared the indignity of autopsy, lay cradled in a closed casket. The copper box sprouted a canopy of wreaths and bouquets later that afternoon, as a somber parade of mourners shuffled past. Some of the visitors—including a caravan of black women, young and old—kneeled briefly in the waking room before trudging onward. Outside, the lines coiled around the corner of Frederick Douglass Boulevard and 126th Street. The ornery Harlem sun blasted the necks of those who had come to honor Mrs. Malcolm X.

Many of the women wore ornate church hats, head wraps, or cascading dreadlocks. Others doddered along with canes or steered baby strollers toward the funeral chapel. The subway disgorged more and more workers and retirees whom Betty had somehow touched. Among the several thousand who queued up for two or more hours that Wednesday and Thursday in late June 1997 were Reverends Jackson and Sharpton, Sonia Sanchez, soul singer James Brown, and author Toni Morrison. But it was the subway crowd, the everyday folks, who sanctified the vigil.

The following day, the believers took over. During a spare funeral service at the Islamic Cultural Center on Manhattan's Upper East Side, hundreds chanted the prayer for the dead. "Our Sister Betty Shabazz died by burning," Imam Mohammad Salem Agwa said during the rites. "May Allah forgive the person who did that." Afterward the bereaved filed out of the hall and the Shabazz daughters emerged to stand barefoot beside the coffin, their heads veiled. Finally the cortege left for Ferncliff Cemetery, Westchester County. Onlookers huddled behind barricades, watching Mrs. Malcolm X vanish into the uptown snarl. She was buried that afternoon in the Hartsdale graveyard, directly above her husband's plot. During the private ceremony, the daughters wept as incense wafted and earth tumbled onto their mother's coffin. "I remember the day she got married, the day her husband was slaughtered," Percy Sutton said, "and I will always remember this day, too."

That Sunday, more than two thousand mourners packed the soaring Riverside Church in Manhattan for an ecumenical memorial service. The ceremony drew an eclectic congregation of politicians, artists, clergy, celebrities, and other luminaries. Barely a sprinkling of personages had braved Malcolm's obsequies three decades before. But the current and former New York City mayors; New York Governor George Pataki; Reps. Maxine Waters, Charles Rangel, Eleanor Holmes Norton, and Carolyn B. Maloney; Labor Secretary Alexis Herman; Coretta Scott King and Myrlie Evers-Williams; Maya Angelou, Ossie Davis, and Ruby Dee all crammed into Riverside's glorious sanctuary to bid his widow farewell. Elsewhere in the cathedral, several hundred admirers watched the proceedings on a closed-circuit television, and a legion gathered on the sidewalk outside to listen to the speeches over a loudspeaker.

Christian and Muslim clergy offered prayers. Herman read a letter from President Clinton that proclaimed Betty "a true heroine, a fine role model, and a valued friend." Later, the Shabazz daughters ascended to the pulpit and gathered behind the microphone. As her sisters struggled to keep their composure, Attallah asked the audience to picture Malcolm extending an amber arm to Betty and summoning her with the words, "Come on, Brown Sugar." In their eulogy, Dee and Davis also imagined a reunion: "Go well, Sister Betty; your journey ends, and Malcolm steps from the shadows to greet his much beloved fresh from yesterday's deep and pain-filled river. And Malcolm will embrace you, and kiss you, and whisper in your ear. 'Well done, Betty.'" Of all the speakers, only Angelou mentioned the boy whose grisly deed had authored the occasion. "God created him," she said of Little Malcolm, "but we made him."

Later that summer, the twelve-year-old began serving his eighteen-month sentence at Hillcrest Center, a Lenox, Massachusetts, psychiatric institute that specializes in juvenile arsonists. The metamorphosis his grandmother had once awaited seemed to begin almost immediately. By September, he had grown two inches and learned to play the drums. He was elected class secretary at the residence, which was home to sixty boys and girls with serious behavioral illnesses. He told his lawyers proudly that he had even begun working in the cafeteria, and they reported that he was receiving no psychiatric medication. (The adolescent's therapy at Hillcrest consisted of weekly individual and group session, though some health professionals argued that such treatment was insufficient for a patient as deeply disturbed as Little Malcolm.)

He was back in trouble before long. After serving out his sentence at Hillcrest, he was transferred in 1999 to a center in Yonkers, New York, that has had success treating firestarters. The then fourteen-year-old child began running away from the place, fleeing through a window on one occasion. He also repeatedly escaped another Westchester County group home in which he was subsequently enrolled, once by hopping a fence and catching a taxi cab. A family-court judge tacked a year onto his sentence for the breakouts and sent him to a more secure facility. Additional violations led to more extensions. The boy's brilliance continued to dazzle case workers, therapists, and other adults. He became a computer wizard and talked about going to college.

Yet in early 2002, after his release from a detention center, he was arrested in Middletown, New York (sixty miles north of New York City), in connection with a burglary and assault. Police charged him and another seventeen-year-old with robbing a teenage boy of one hundred dollars, roughing him up and threatening him with a gun, then traveling to his home in Wallkill, New York, and stealing more cash before attacking him again. Malcolm X had counted the indignity of prison among his own sordid beginnings. Now the martyr's grandson was shuttled to a jailhouse to await hearings. Four-and-a-half years earlier, as her nephew was beginning his confinement at Hillcrest, Ilyasah said in an interview that she felt Betty's spirit urging her and her sisters to look after the boy. "We have to focus on Malcolm; we have to make sure that he will be well, that he doesn't lose the rest of his childhood," the second daughter said. "My mother didn't want him to grow up in the system."

The torment of Betty's passing still ripples through the lives of the Shabazz daughters. Each has found ways to cope. At times, Ilyasah imagines that her mother has let herself into her place in Mount Vernon and will be waiting for her when she gets home. Gamilah pictures the widow resting on a porch, calling to her and her sisters to "Go 'head, baby." Malikah, however, has a material reminder of her mother. Betty discovered shortly before she died that the thirty-two-year-old twin was pregnant. Despite the widow's earlier efforts to spare her daughters the trials of single motherhood, she supported Malikah's decision to have the baby on her own. Betty would never hold her new granddaughter, yet the child would hold part of her. In January 1998, Malikah gave birth to a little girl. She named her Bettih Bahiyah.

NOTES

INTRODUCTION: A MIRACLE IN THE DESERT

ix *"Black women have just argued"*: Lanker, Brian and Barbara Summers, eds. *I Dream A World; Portraits of Black Women Who Changed America.* New York: Stewart, Tabori & Chang, 1999, 104.

ix *Hajar the Egyptian hunts for water*: Narrative is largely drawn from the traditional Muslim parable of Hajar. Ali, Yusuf Abdullah. *The Meaning of the Holy Qur'an.* Beltsville: Amana Publications, 1989, 65. In the Bible, Hagar is a slave rather than a wife of Prophet Abraham, who is recognized by Muslims, Christians and Jews. See Genesis 16:7-8: "And the angel of the Lord found her by a fountain of water in the wilderness, by the fountain in the way to Shur. And he said, Hagar, Sarai's maid, whence camest thou? And whither wilt thou go?"

ix *The water of Zamzam is cool*: Aisha al-Adawiya Interview, May 31, 1999.

x *"The Amen to a very long prayer"*: "Mrs. Malcolm X Pens Us A Note." *New York Amsterdam News,* April 10, 1965.

x *"My mother was on the real side"*: Gamilah Shabazz Interview.

xi *Mrs. Malcolm X's durability*: President Edison O. Jackson bestowed on her the title of "Director of Institutional Advancement and Public Affairs and Cultural Attaché"; Aisha al-Adawiya Interview.

xi *"It is always in you"*: Maya Angelou Interview, September 9, 1999.

xi *"Performing surgery on a family member"*: Gil Noble Interview.

xii *"I ain't bringin' no dirt"*: Dick Gregory Interview, July 30, 1999.

xii *"World that a paranoid might dream of"*: Peter Goldman Interview, April 21, 1999.

xii *"Want nobody to know"*: Herman Fulton Interview.

xii *"The simplicity they yearned for"*: Attallah Shabazz Interview, March 26, 1999.

xii *"There's too much pain"*: Sister Cybil Clarke Interview.

xiii *"Those who know ain't talkin'"*: Sister Khadiyyah Interview, February 13, 2000.

xiii *"Her life defies clarity of diagnosis"*: Gil Noble Interview, April 8, 1999.

xiii *Betty's bottled-up suffering*: Robert Little June 23, 1997 letter to Shabazz nieces. (Courtesy of Gamilah Shabazz).

xiii *Widow occasionally talked in riddles*: Mary Redd Interview, May 20, 1999.

xiii *Mumbling a kind of "gibberish"*: Ruth Clark Interview, April 14, 1999.

xiv *"Swamps do not create mosquitoes"*: Dick Gregory Interview.

xiv *"That she survived at all is miraculous"*: Maya Angelou Interview.

xiv *"Back into the grave"*: Sister Jean Reynolds Interview, February 13, 2000.

xv *She was queenly and eruptive*: Gil Noble Interview.

xv *Cuss like twenty men*: Maya Angelou, Interview.

xv *"That lady had the prettiest eyes"*: James Smalls Interview March 19, 2000.

xv *"Her femininity just oozed"*: Myrlie Evers-Williams Interview.

xv *"The sister did not play"*: James Smalls Interview.

xv *Royalty never weeps in the streets*: Sarah Wellington quoting Betty Shabazz in "The True Malcolm X Speaks." Library Distributors of America, 1997.

xv   "A *tireless traveler and resolute voice*": Niara Sudarkasa quoted in "Betty Shabazz and Harris Wofford Honored at Lincoln University's 1995 Commencement." *Lincoln University Newsletter* 8, no. 8 (June 1995): 1.

xv   A "*rocksteady*" *homegirl*: Juollie Carroll Interview, March 31, 1999.

xv   "*A flawed, lovely human being*": Annette Hutchins Interview, May 14, 2000.

xv   "*Amongst the spirit of women*": Attallah Shabazz Interview.

xvi *Betty in her final weeks*: Herman Fulton Interview.

xvi "*I'm tired of being strong*": Howard Dodson Interview, April 16, 1999.

xvi "*She was in flight*": Herman Fulton Interview.

xvii "*Mothers of the Civil Rights Movement*": Laughinghouse, Amy. "Mothers of the Civil Rights Movement." *Upscale*, May 1997, 38.

xvii *During the shoot*: Myrlie Evers-Williams Interview, August 30, 1999.

xvii *Unraveling in his last frazzled days*: Goldman, Peter. *The Death and Life of Malcolm X*. Chicago: Illini Books, 1979, 3.

xvii "*It was rough, but I made it*": "Dr. Betty Shabazz's Final Words." *Democracy Now*. Pacifica Radio, May 19, 1997.

Chapter 1: A Brass Valentine

1   "*Very seldom did I think of myself*": Edwards, Audrey and Susan L. Taylor. "Loving and Losing Malcolm." *Essence*, February 1992, 51.

1   *Those mannish hands*: Gamilah Shabazz Interview, January 15, 2000.

1   *Oldest steel-rod man in the country*: Stanley Sandlin Interview, December 5, 2000; Shelmon Sandlin, Jr. Interview, January 13, 2001; Not-for-attribution Telephone Interview, January 15, 2001.

2   *Pinehurst, a miniscule town*: Papers of the Vianna Historical Society, courtesy of Melanie Sangster.

2   *Pinehurst native, born May 28, 1934*: Betty Shabazz Tuskegee University transcript; Betty Shabazz Northern High School transcript.

3   *The origins of Helen Lowe*: Helen Malloy Obituary in program for memorial service, held September 22, 1994 at Bethel A.M.E. Church, Detroit. (Courtesy of Bentley Historical Library, Ann Arbor, MI).

3   "*I told him I wasn't ready*": Cohen, Ann and Monroe Walker. "Her goal: Black solidarity." *Detroit News*. (Undated. Courtesy of Bentley Historical Library).

3   *Repair shop on Detroit's Chene Street*: Booker T. Washington Trade Association Directory, Detroit, 1935; Malloy's Shoe Service flyer c. 1950.

3   *Hastings Street in the Brewster Project*: Booker T. Washington Trade Association Business Exhibit Program, Detroit 1948.

3   *The place was a collision of Negroes*: Sugrue, Thomas J. *The Origins of the Urban Crisis*. Princeton: Princeton University Press, 1996, 36; Moon, Elaine Latzman, ed. *Untold Tales, Unsung Heroes*. Detroit: Wayne State University Press, 1994, 274.

4   "*I wanted to be a man*": Ibid, 27.

4   *New hell in the North*: Sugrue, Thomas J. *The Origins of the Urban Crisis*. Princeton: Princeton University Press, 1996, 22, 29.

4   "*Motto and brand*": Malloy's Shoe Service coupon. (Courtesy of Burton Historical Collection, Detroit).

4   *A stalwart deliverywoman*: Jacqueline Gay Interview, March 21, 2001.

4   *Yellow house at 313 Hague Street*: Shabazz, Betty. "From the Detroit Riot to the Malcolm Summit." *Ebony*, November 1995, 63.

4   *Life for most Negro Detroiters was so tattered*: Moon, Elaine Latzman, ed. *Untold Tales, Unsung Heroes*. Detroit: Wayne State University Press, 1994, 113; Sixteenth Census of the United States, 1940:

The Labor Force, III, 612-613.

5 *"Dignity and worthiness of productive labor"*: "Tuskegee Institute-Its Origin and Development", Tuskegee Institute Division of Public Relations, May 31, 1950. (Courtesy of Bentley Historical Library).

5 *Shoemaking, machinery, and foundry work*: L. D. Malloy Tuskegee Institute transcripts, 1911 to 1918 (Courtesy of Tuskegee University); Helen Malloy audiocassette, Helen Malloy Papers, Burton Historical Collection, Detroit.

5 *"That chair has four legs!"*: Ibid.

5 *"There every time the doors opened"*: Suesetta MacCree Interview, February 13, 2001.

6 *"Bethel people married Bethel people"*: Ibid.

6 *"It was church or nothing"*: Jacqueline Gay Interview.

6 *Mighty challenge to lethargy*: "One Hundred Years at Bethel Detroit." Bethel A.M.E. Church, 1941 (Pamphlet. Courtesy of Burton Historical Collection].

6 *Band of free black Methodists*: Ibid.

6 *Under the pastorate of William H. Peck*: Moon, Elaine Latzman, ed. *Untold Tales, Unsung Heroes.* Detroit: Wayne State University Press, 1994, 84.

6 *Bethel helped clothe and feed*: Thomas, Richard W. *Life for Us is What we Make It; Building black community in Detroit, 1915-1945.* Indianapolis: Indiana University Press, 1992, 146; Sugrue, Thomas J. *The Origins of the Urban Crisis.* Princeton: Princeton University Press, 1996, 177-178.

6 *Magnet for visiting blacks*: Suesetta MacCree Interview; Lydia Hibbert Interview.

6 *She would die a Methodist*: Lanker, Brian and Barbara Summers, ed. *I Dream A World; Portraits of Black Women Who Changed America.* New York: Stewart, Tabori & Chang, 1989, 104.

6 *"She hadn't been treated right"*: Lydia Hibbert Interview.

7 *Betty simply showed up*: Suesetta MacCree Interview.

7 *"The Malloys looked after the needy"*: "Helen Malloy Receives Humanitarian Award." June 9, 1979. (Publication unknown. Courtesy of Burton Historical Collection).

7 *Ollie Mae raised Betty*: Not-for-attribution Telephone Interview, January 15, 2001.

7 *Betty was about nine when*: Helen Malloy audiocassette, Helen Malloy Papers, Burton Historical Collection.

7 *"She got attached to us"*: Ibid.

8 *Betty's mother was "mean"*: Cohen, Ann and Monroe Walker. "Her goal: Black solidarity." *Detroit News.* (Undated. Courtesy of Bentley Historical Library).

8 *"You are not going to take her"*: Helen Malloy audiocassette, Helen Malloy Papers, Burton Historical Collection.

8 *In the Malloys' custody*: Gamilah Shabazz Interview.

8 *They would love her*: Shabazz, Betty S. 1975. *Organization of African Unity: Its Role in Education.* Ph.D. dissertation, University of Massachusetts, Amherst. (Quote is taken from dedication page).

8 *"The white man's ice is colder"*: Lydia Hibbert Interview.

9 *Housewives League of Detroit*: Papers of the Booker T. Washington Trade Association Collection and the National Housewives' League of America Collection (Courtesy of Bentley Historical Library); Papers of the Housewives' League of Detroit Collection (Courtesy of Burton Historical Collection).

9 *Helen Malloy would serve the League*: Cohen, Ann and Monroe Walker. "Her goal: Black solidarity." *Detroit News.* (Undated. Courtesy of Bentley Historical Library).

9 *Boycotts of white shops*: Minority Business Newsletter, published by Michigan Office of Minority Business enterprises, 1959. (Courtesy of Burton Historical Collection).

9 *Battle on behalf of Pure Gold Syrup*: Charleston, Lula. "Housewives Pioneered in Black Business Patronage." *Michigan Chronicle*, June 7, 1980.

10 *"People would shut the door in our faces"*: Cohen, Ann and Monroe Walker. "Her goal: Black solidarity." *Detroit News*. (Undated. Courtesy of Bentley Historical Library).

10 *"It was an educational experience"*: Evans, Akosua Barthwell. "Merchants Survived with Housewives' Aid." In McGehee, Scott and Susan Watson, eds. *Blacks in Detroit*. Detroit: Detroit Free Press, 1980, 65.

10 *"I ain't going to no black doctor!"*: Ibid. Lydia Hibbert Interview.

10 Helen Malloy worked *"like a madwoman"*: Evans, Akosua Barthwell. "Merchants Survived with Housewives' Aid." In McGehee, Scott and Susan Watson, eds. *Blacks in Detroit*. Detroit: Detroit Free Press, 1980, 65.

10 *Thousands of dollars into black businesses:* Ibid.

10 *A great believer in prayer:* Montemurri, Patricia. "Activist Taught the Bible to Generations." *Detroit Free Press*, September 21, 1994.

10 *"Did not know how to say no"*: Ibid.

11 *First doses of black history*: Housewives' League of Detroit Fannie B. Peck Day Business Queen poster, 1951 in papers of Housewives' League of Detroit, Burton Historical Collection.

11 *National Council of Negro Women and NAACP*: Directory of the National Housewives' League of America, Inc. 1971-74 in Papers of the National Housewives' League of America Collection, Bentley Historical Library.

11 *Malcolm had taught her far more*: Norma Johnson Interview, June 22, 1999.

11 *"When I say that she just goes ape!"*: From the transcript of the "Haley Book Interview with Betty Shabazz" conducted by Anne Romaine, January 27, 1989, Medgar Evers College, Brooklyn, New York. (Courtesy of Special Collections, Hoskins Library, the University of Tennessee at Knoxville).

11 *"I'm talking about understanding one's self"*: Ibid.

12 *"The class interests of the black bourgeoisie"*: Thomas, Richard W. *Life for Us is What we Make It; Building black community in Detroit, 1915-1945*. Indianapolis: Indiana University Press, 1992, 146; Sugrue, Thomas J. *The Origins of the Urban Crisis*. Princeton: Princeton University Press, 1996, 215.

12 *Betty's teenage years*: Shabazz, Betty. "From the Detroit Riot to the Malcolm Summit." *Ebony*, November 1995, 63.

12 *Arkansas bumpkin become entrepreneur*: Ibid.

12 *She knew nothing of Islam and black separatism*: Hitsky, Barbara. "A Prediction: Explosive Future for Our Children." *Detroit News*, May 21, 1970.

13 *"Typical lil' African-American girl"*: Shabazz, Betty. "From the Detroit Riot to the Malcolm Summit." *Ebony*, November 1995, 63.

13 *The Malloys pampered her*: "Betty Shabazz," *Biography Today*, April 1998, 86.

13 *"Pick a week out of my life"*: Edwards, Audrey and Susan L. Taylor. "Loving and Losing Malcolm." *Essence*, February 1992, 52.

13 *Hard-timer named Malcolm Little*: X, Malcolm as told to Alex Haley. *The Autobiography of Malcolm X*. New York: Ballantine Books, 1993, 194.

13 *Malcolm swam an "ocean of blackness"*: Haley, Alex and X, Malcolm. *The Autobiography of Malcolm X*. New York: Ballantine, 1993, 192.

13 *His childhood was poor and calamitous*: Franklin, John Hope. From Slavery to Freedom. New York: Alfred A. Knopf, Inc., 1980, 354-356; Fredrickson, George M. *Black Liberation*. New York: Oxford University Press, 1995, 138-139.

14 *"A very happy child until he was six"*: Foley, Eileen. "Our Children Hold the Key to a Future Free of Killings, Malcolm's Widow Says." *Philadelphia Inquirer*, May 24, 1972; *Chicago Daily News*, May 22, 1972.

14 *A boy's relationship with his mother and sisters*: Ibid.

15 *From the ashes rose Malcolm X*: See in general: Haley, Alex and X, Malcolm. *The Autobiography of Malcolm X*. New York: Ballantine, 1993.

16 *Muhammad was born Elijah Poole*: See in general: Evanzz, Karl. *The Messenger*. New York: Pantheon Books, 1999.

16 *Complete confidence in Elijah Muhammad*: Lincoln, C. Eric. *The Black Muslims in America*. Trenton: Africa World Press, 1994, 90.

17 *Muhammad was "the meaning"*: Lomax, Louis E. *When the Word is Given*. Westport: Greenwood Press. 1963, 90.

17 *Malcolm absolutely worshipped the elder*: Haley, Alex and X, Malcolm. *The Autobiography of Malcolm X*. New York: Ballantine, 1993, 216.

17 *"Elijah had Malcolm by the throat"*: Charles Kenyatta Interview.

17 *"Not a very ethnic kind of upbringing"*: Shabazz, Betty. "From the Detroit Riot to the Malcolm Summit." *Ebony*, November 1995, 62; "Dr. Betty Shabazz's Final Words." *Democracy Now*. Pacifica Radio, May 19, 1997.

17 *Fraternized with a few whites*: Johnnie Fairchild Interview.

17 *"Small instances of direct racial hostility"*: Shabazz, Betty. "From the Detroit Riot to the Malcolm Summit." *Ebony*, November 1995, 63.

17 *"Plant some dread disease"*: Johnnie Fairchild Interview.

17 *Overt discrimination in downtown restaurants*: Ibid.

17 *"White tenants in our white community"*: Thomas, Richard W. *Life for Us is What we Make It; Building Black Community in Detroit, 1915-1945*. Indianapolis: Indiana University Press, 1992, 146; Sugrue, Thomas J. *The Origins of the Urban Crisis*. Princeton: Princeton University Press, 1996, 73-74.

17 *The ensuing melee was "ungodly"*: Shabazz, Betty. "From the Detroit Riot to the Malcolm Summit." *Ebony*, November 1995, 64.

18 *Police had killed seventeen blacks*: Ibid, 29; Thomas, Richard W. *Life for Us is What we Make It; Building Black Community in Detroit, 1915-1945*. Indianapolis: Indiana University Press, 1992, 167.

18 *One survivor later remembered the carnage*: Moon, Elaine Latzman, ed. *Untold Tales, Unsung Heroes*. Detroit: Wayne State University Press, 1994, 84.

18 *Detroit was a racial minefield*: Johnnie Fairchild Interview.

18 *"We just sort of regarded ourselves as human"*: Johnnie Fairchild Interview.

18 *"We knew what we had to do"*: Vernice Williams Interview.

18 *High branded you an "E-Light"*: Ibid.

19 *"Rough, harsh, uneven, and too dark skin"*: Thomas, Richard W. *Life for Us is What we Make It; Building Black Community in Detroit, 1915-1945*. Indianapolis: Indiana University Press, 1992, 194.

19 *Betty's earth-brown complexion*: Herman Fulton Interview.

19 *"Black is beautiful"*: Abdullah Abdur Razzaq Interview; Perry, Bruce. *Malcolm; The Life of A Man Who Changed Black America*. Barrytown: Station Hill, 1991, 171.

19 *She did not especially stand out*: Johnnie Fairchild Interview.

19 *That each alien encounter was the start of a love affair*: Brown, Jamie Foster, ed. *Betty Shabazz; A Sisterfriend's Tribute in Words and Pictures*. New York: Simon & Schuster, 1998, 42.

20 *Betty had rhythm*: "The Viking," semi-annual yearbook of Northern High School, Detroit, January 1952, 41. (Courtesy of Burton Historical Collection).

20 *"Girl, you can strut!"*: Brown, Jamie Foster, ed. *Betty Shabazz; A Sisterfriend's Tribute in Words and Pictures*. New York: Simon & Schuster, 1998, 42.

20 *"She was always the lady"* Vernice Williams Interview.

20 *Never gave their families trouble* Gamilah Shabazz Interview.

20 *At the height of Betty's rascality*: Brown, Jamie Foster, ed. *Betty Shabazz; A Sisterfriend's Tribute in Words*

and Pictures. New York: Simon & Schuster, 1998, 42.

21 She wasn't particularly newsy: Suesetta MacCree Interview.

21 Belonged to the Del Sprites: Vernice Williams Interview; Carol Sayers Puryear Interview: Hon. Teola Hunter Interview; Bernice F. Morton Interview; Sylvia Jackson-Muthlab Interview.

21 Attend Mr. Malloy's alma mater: From the transcript of the "Haley Book Interview with Betty Shabazz" conducted by Anne Romaine, January 27, 1989, Medgar Evers College, Brooklyn, New York. (Courtesy of Special Collections, Hoskins Library, the University of Tennessee at Knoxville).

22 "You'd think I was her real mother!": Helen Malloy audiocassette, Helen Malloy Papers, Burton Historical Collection.

22 The foster parent who had rocked her through measles: From the transcript of the "Haley Book Interview with Betty Shabazz" conducted by Anne Romaine, January 27, 1989, Medgar Evers College, Brooklyn, New York. (Courtesy of Special Collections, Hoskins Library, the University of Tennessee at Knoxville).

22 Always known how to comport herself: Lanker, Brian and Barbara Summers, ed. I Dream A World; Portraits of Black Women Who Changed America. New York: Stewart, Tabori & Chang, 1989, 104.

22 "Was trying to tell me in ten words or less about racism": Ibid.

CHAPTER 2: A VELVET GLOVE

23 "The world was black and controlled by blacks": Cora Eaves Braynon Interview, April 3, 2001.

23 Tuskegee on a five-year plan: Ibid.

24 "She thought we were able to pay her way": Helen Malloy audiocassette, Helen Malloy Papers, Burton Historical Collection.

24 A Tuskegee education was costly: 1952-1953 tuition for out-of-state student based upon the Tuskegee University fee sheets, courtesy of the Business and Fiscal Affairs Office, Tuskegee University.

24 Leaned on one of his old friends : Helen Malloy audiocassette, Helen Malloy Papers, Burton Historical Collection.

24 She seemed neat and pleasant: Miles McAfee Interview.

24 Pageboy hairstyle and quick grin: Mary Redd Interview, May 20, 1999.

24 "She was never loud": Elizabeth P. Fox Interview, April 1, 2001.

24 Her first love: Miles McAfee Interview.

24 Tall and "kind of reddish": Cora Eaves Braynon Interview.

24 She was also stunning: Maya Angelou Interview, September 9, 1999.

25 Every black woman was entitled to seven veterans: Elizabeth P. Fox Interview.

25 Tuskegee had a backwoods feel: Ibid.

25 "Daddy King": Maxine Prince Johnson Interview.

25 Women sat on the right of the sanctuary, men on the left: Maxine Prince Johnson Interview, April 3, 2001.

25 She could not afford frequent trips home: Miles McAfee Interview.

25 Home of a girlhood friend's sister: Suesetta MacCree Interview, February 13, 2001.

25 Golden few that would ennoble the race: Cora Eaves Braynon Interview.

26 "We were happy amongst ourselves": Miles McAfee Interview.

26 Cloistered serenity was fleeting: Cora Eaves Braynon Interview.

26 "We were not ready to go to war": Miles McAfee Interview.

26 Bigotry was immaterial: Cora Eaves Braynon Interview.

26 Town tested aura of invulnerability: Elizabeth P. Fox Interview.

26 "If you're just quiet it will go away": From the transcript of the "Haley Book Interview with Betty Shabazz" conducted by Anne Romaine, January 27, 1989, Medgar Evers College, Brooklyn, New

York. (Courtesy of Special Collections, Hoskins Library, the University of Tennessee at Knoxville); Lanker, Brian and Barbara Summers, ed. *I Dream A World; Portraits of Black Women Who Changed America.* New York: Stewart, Tabori & Chang, 1999, 104.; Jones, Marsha. "Betty Shabazz." *About…Time*, January 1993, 14.

26 *Saw no outright racial violence*: 1952 and 1953 Tuskegee Report, Tuskegee Clippings File (courtesy of Alabama State Department of Archives and History).

26 *Tapestry of segregation and discrimination*: Ibid.

26 *Drifted through her classes*: Ibid.

27 *One A at Tuskegee*: Betty Sanders Tuskegee Institute transcript (courtesy of Tuskegee University Office of the Registrar).

27 *Another romance at Tuskegee*: Edwards, Audrey and Susan L. Taylor. "Loving and Losing Malcolm." *Essence*, February 1992, 52.

27 *Front desk of campus hospital*: John A. Andrew Clinical Society program (courtesy of Tuskegee University Archives).

27 *Betty pondered a nursing career*: Ibid.

27 *Harvey's voice like a screwdriver*: Cora Eaves Braynon Interview.

27 *"Iron fist in a velvet glove"*: Elizabeth P. Fox Interview.

27 *First dean of the School of Nursing*: Carnegie, Mary Elizabeth. *The Path We Tread; Blacks in Nursing, 1854-1984.* Philadelphia: J. B. Lippincott, 1994, 82.

28 *Integrate the Alabama Nurses' Association*: Ibid, 83.

28 *"I wasn't welcome"*: Elizabeth P. Fox Interview.

28 *"When you're white, you're 'Miss'; when you're black, you're 'Nurse'"*: Ibid.

28 *"You didn't see any unattractive nurses from Tuskegee"*: Ibid.

28 *Three-year school in Brooklyn*: Edwards, Audrey and Susan L. Taylor. "Loving and Losing Malcolm." *Essence*, February 1992, 52.

28 *"Don't let the grass grow under your feet"*: Elizabeth P. Fox Interview.

28 *"New York is the place that my husband loved"*: "The Sister's Been Doing Her Homework" Pacifica Tape Library audiocassette of Betty Shabazz' 1971 speech at McClymonds High School in Berkeley, CA. (courtesy of Rutgers University Music Library).

28 *Come fully to womanhood*: Abdullah Abdur Razzaq Interview, April 15, 2000.

29 *Malcolm swooped onto the campus*: Norma Johnson Interview, June 22, 1999.

29 *An eighth-grade dropout*: Lincoln, C. Eric. *The Black Muslims In America.* Trenton: Africa World Press, 1994, 190.

29 *Regretted having missed out on college*: Robert Haggins Interview.

29 *Betty's education was genteel and strict*: Shabazz, Betty. "From the Detroit Riot to the Malcolm Summit." *Ebony*, November 1995, 64.

30 *Begun by Booker T. Washington*: Tuskegee Institute—Its Origin and Development." Pamphlet prepared by Tuskegee Institute Division of Public Relations, May 31, 1950. (Courtesy of Bentley Historical Library, University of Michigan).

30 *"Cast down your bucket"*: Washington, Booker T. *Up From Slavery.* New York: Penguin Books, 1986, 219.

30 *"Advance the cause of Negro education"*: "Tuskegee Institute—Its Origin and Development." Pamphlet prepared by Tuskegee Institute Division of Public Relations, May 31, 1950. (Courtesy of Bentley Historical Library, University of Michigan).

31 *"The turning point in my life and racial consciousness"*: Shabazz, Betty. "From the Detroit Riot to the Malcolm Summit." *Ebony*, November 1995, 63.

31 *Brooklyn State College School of Nursing*: Norma Johnson Interview.

31 *Rustic Alabama*: Elizabeth P. Fox Interview.

31 *Searching for roots*: Ruth Summerford Interview.

31 *Betty's bond with New York*: Ibid.

32 *Jitterbugging with men*: Ibid.

32 *"She wore Malcolm's mantle with dignity and grace"*: Leonard Jeffries Interview, April 8, 2000.

32 *"She didn't live a life commensurate with Malcolm's"*: Yosef ben-Jochannan Interview, February 5, 2001.

32 *Betty's fourth daughter tell a story*: Gamilah Shabazz Interview.

33 *"The assassination of Malcolm"*: Ahmed Osman Interview, January 29, 2001.

33 *"Bookstores sell racial books almost exclusively"*: Opotowsky, Stan. "Harlem." *New York Post*, March 3, 1958.

33 *Killens saw the community as a plantation*: Angelou, Maya. *The Heart of a Woman*. New York: Bantam Books, 1982, 34.

33 *Harlem a "rebuke to the north"*: "Lehman Calls Harlem A Rebuke to the North." *New York Post*, June 4, 1956.

33 *"Despite Harlem's decay*: Opotowsky, Stan. "Harlem." *New York Post*, March 3, 1958.

34 *Some Negroes shunned the stepladder evangelists*: ben-Jochannan, Yosef A. A. *Africa; Mother of Western Civilization*. Baltimore: Black Classic Press, 1971, 2.

34 *As James Baldwin noticed*: Baldwin, James. *The Fire Next Time*. New York: Vintage Books, 1993, 49.

34 *Malcolm peddled his street gospel*: Goldman, Peter. *The Death and Life of Malcolm X*. Chicago: University of Illinois Press, 1973, 54.

34 *Paroled into Elijah Muhammad's embrace*: Ibid., 51.

34 *Join unto your own*: Abdullah Abdur Razzaq Interview; Charles Kenyatta Interview, August 13, 1999.

34 *Had Betty dawdled at Lenox Avenue*: Abdullah Abdur Razzaq Interview; Charles Kenyatta Interview; Muhammad, Elijah. *Message to the Blackman in America*. Chicago: Muhammad Mosque of Islam No. 2, 1965, 58.

34 *The Honorable Elijah Muhammad teaches us*: Haley, Alex and X, Malcolm. *The Autobiography of Malcolm X*. New York: Ballantine, 1993, 225.

35 *"We wanted to do something to help others"*: Ruth Summerford Interview.

35 *Nursing was a coveted profession for a black woman*: Ibid.

35 *Montefiore Hospital in the hardscrabble Bronx*: Ibid.

35 *Black nurses got the tough assignments*: Ibid.

35 *White male patients take liberties with Negro attendants*: Ibid.

35 *"Up South"*: Cone, James H. *Martin & Malcolm & America; A Dream or a Nightmare*. Maryknoll: Orbis Books, 1997, 89.

35 *Malcolm introduced her to the word "racism"*: Edwards, Audrey and Susan L. Taylor. "Loving and Losing Malcolm." *Essence*, February 1992, 54.

36 *"Only a stone would not have had a race consciousness in Detroit"*: Maya Angelou Interview.

36 *Betty needed a break from cafeteria food*: "Betty Shabazz Remembers Malcolm." *Like It Is*. WABC-TV, May 19, 1991; Lanker, Brian and Barbara Summers, ed. *I Dream A World; Portraits of Black Women Who Changed America*. New York: Stewart, Tabori & Chang, 1999, 104.

36 *Friday night dinner party*: Edwards, Audrey and Susan L. Taylor. "Loving and Losing Malcolm." *Essence*, February 1992, 52.

36 *Betty never tasted anything so delicious*: Ibid; Jean Reynolds and Sis. Khadiyyah Interview, February 13, 2000.

36 *Temple Seven lecture*: Edwards, Audrey and Susan L. Taylor. "Loving and Losing Malcolm." *Essence*, February 1992, 52.

37 *Betty left the lecture dizzy*: Lanker, Brian and Barbara Summers, ed. *I Dream A World; Portraits of Black Women Who Changed America*. New York: Stewart, Tabori & Chang, 1999, 104.

37 *"He's very disciplined, he's good looking"*: Edwards, Audrey and Susan L. Taylor. "Loving and Losing

Malcolm." *Essence*, February 1992, 52.

37 *Many of the faithful were sobered-up cons*: Lincoln, C. Eric. *The Black Muslims In America*. Trenton: Africa World Press, 1994, 23.

37 *"Wake up to society's kick in the teeth"*: Ibid, 47.

37 *"The minister is here!"*: Edwards, Audrey and Susan L. Taylor. "Loving and Losing Malcolm." *Essence*, February 1992, 54.

37 *Rangy man hustling up*: Ibid.

38 *I was mesmerized*: Sonia Sanchez Interview.

38 *He in my time was the Christ*: Jean Reynolds Interview.

39 *"She was wrapped in his love"*: Myrlie Evers Williams Interview, August 30, 1999.

39 *"He was going someplace much more important"*: Edwards, Audrey and Susan L. Taylor. "Loving and Losing Malcolm." *Essence*, February 1992, 54.

39 *"This man is totally malnourished!"*: Ibid.

40 *"No one could see what I saw"*: Ibid.

40 *His augustness captured her*: Edwards, Audrey and Susan L. Taylor. "Loving and Losing Malcolm." *Essence*, February 1992, 54.

40 *Circle of standby Muslim and Christian counselors*: Herman Fulton Interview.

40 *Malcolm preached that first night*: Ibid.

40 *The minister won her heart*: Edwards, Audrey and Susan L. Taylor. "Loving and Losing Malcolm." *Essence*, February 1992, 54.

CHAPTER 3: LEAVING THE GRAVE

41 *"There isn't a Negro in America who hasn't been trampled on!"*: Lincoln, C. Eric. *The Black Muslims In America*. Trenton: Africa World Press, 1994, 67.

41 *"Your brother was fine!"*: Laura Ross Brown Interview, June 11, 1999.

41 *"My reaction was akin to respect"*: Clarke, John Henrik, ed. *Malcolm X; The Man and his Times*. Trenton: Africa World Press, 1990, 132.

42 *Some took his formal pleasure for shyness*: Ibid.

42 *"It wasn't a concert smile"*: Percy Sutton Interview, September 21, 2000.

42 *During her second visit*: Edwards, Audrey and Susan L. Taylor. "Loving and Losing Malcolm." *Essence*, February 1992, 54.

42 *"Will you be back?"*: Ibid.

42 *"Are you going to the temple?"*: Ibid.

42 *"They thought it was my fault"*: Ibid.

42 *"Malcolm reassured me"*: Mills, David. "The Resurrection of Malcolm X." *Washington Post*. February 25, 1990, F6.

43 *"A different perspective"*: Ibid.

43 *"He met you on your ground"*: Abdullah Abdur Razzaq Interview, April 16, 2000.

43 *"My parents would kill me"*: Edwards, Audrey and Susan L. Taylor. "Loving and Losing Malcolm." *Essence*, February 1992, 52.

43 *"Them Moo-slims"*: Ruth Summerford Interview, January 16, 2000.

43 *He brimmed with "worldly maturity"*: McFadden, Robert D. "Betty Shabazz, A Rights Voice, Dies of Burns," *New York Times*, June 25, 1997, D20.

43 *Fearsome combat for the minister's attention*: Osman Karriem Interview, June 25, 1999.

43 *Share Malcolm with his admirers*: Edwards, Audrey and Susan L. Taylor. "Loving and Losing Malcolm." *Essence*, February 1992, 54.

43 *"She was never a hanger-on"*: Percy Sutton Interview, September 21, 2000.

43 *"Malcolm was everything a man could be"*: Jean Reynolds Interview, February 13, 2000.

44 *"He was shining like silver"*: Abdullah Abdur Razzaq Interview.

44 *"Ready to kill the first cracker"*: Charles Kenyatta Interview, August 13, 1999.

44 *"It was like a movie audition"*: Osman Karriem Interview.

44 Baiting the minister: Ibid.

45 *"Hope he noticed you"*: Laura Ross Brown Interview.

45 Marrying Brother Minister: Edwards, Audrey and Susan L. Taylor. "Loving and Losing Malcolm." *Essence*, February 1992, 54.

45 *"Marriage had no interest for me"*: Haley, Alex and X, Malcolm. *The Autobiography of Malcolm X*. New York: Ballantine, 1993, 230.

45 Sermon's rough on women: Abdullah Abdur Razzaq Interview.

45 *"Layin' in the cut"*: Charles Kenyatta Interview.

45 *"Weakness was a woman's 'true nature'"*: Ibid; Haley, Alex and X, Malcolm. *The Autobiography of Malcolm X*. New York: Ballantine, 1993, 230.

45 Slavery robbed the Negro man: Geracimos, Ann. "Introducing Mrs. Malcolm X." *Herald Tribune*, June 30, 1963.

46 When you hear Charlie McCarthy speak: Lomax, Louis E. *When the Word is Given*. Westport: Greenwood Press, 1963, 81.

46 *"Walked the banana boat"*: Sister Khadiyyah Interview, February 13, 2000.

46 Malcolm *"would attack anything"*: Karriem Interview.

46 *"Tricky, deceitful, untrustworthy flesh"*: Haley, Alex and X, Malcolm. *The Autobiography of Malcolm X*. New York: Ballantine, 1993, 230.

46 *"Hatred and contempt toward women"*: Hooks, Bell. *Ain't I A Woman*. Boston: South End Press, 1981, 109.

46 *"Threshold of feminism"*: Cone, James H. *Martin and Malcolm and America*. Maryknoll: Orbis Books, 1991, 274.

47 *"No nation can rise higher than its women"*: Geracimos, Ann. "Introducing Mrs. Malcolm X." *Herald Tribune*, June 30, 1963.

47 *"Mother tongue, mother culture"*: Abdullah Abdur Razzaq Interview.

47 Mankind's first nurse and teacher: Muhammad, Elijah. *Message to the Blackman in America*. Chicago: Muhammad Mosque of Islam No. 2, 1965, 59.

47 Restoring the black woman's honor: Ibid, 58-60.

47 *"Educate a woman, educate a family"*: Shabazz, Betty. "The Legacy of My Husband." *Ebony*, June 1969, 180.

47 *"Backbone of civilization"*: Geracimos, Ann. "Introducing Mrs. Malcolm X." *Herald Tribune*, June 30, 1963.

47 *"A man should never be ashamed to say"*: Abdullah Abdur Razzaq Interview.

47 Against violating their wives' rights: Les Brown Interview, March 12, 2000.

48 The woman herself was the jewel: Abdullah Abdur Razzaq Interview.

48 *"looking for a 'producer'"*; Ibid.

48 Educating and civilizing the children: Abdullah Abdur Razzaq Interview.

48 In MGT: Eissien-Udom, E. U. *Black Nationalism*. Chicago: University of Chicago Press, 1962, 89.

48 *"Restore femininity to women"*: Geracimos, Ann. "Introducing Mrs. Malcolm X." *Herald Tribune*, June 30, 1963.

48 *"The sisters wasn't going for that"*: Ibid.

49 *"There's a rooster in the hen house"*: Sister Khadiyyah Interview.

49 *"She did not forget her place"*: Ibid.

49 Malcolm was towing the Nation: Edwards, Audrey and Susan L. Taylor. "Loving and Losing Malcolm." *Essence*, February 1992, 54.

49 *"I knew I wanted him"*: Shabazz, Betty. "Living With Malcolm." *Emerge*, February 1990, 26.

49 *Seek her out at temple affairs*: Edwards, Audrey and Susan L. Taylor. "Loving and Losing Malcolm." *Essence*, February 1992, 54.

50 *Grown up largely without his biological parents*: Haley, Alex and X, Malcolm. *The Autobiography of Malcolm X*. New York: Ballantine, 1993, 10.

50 *The movement was Malcolm's mistress*: Charles Kenyatta Interview.

50 *The minister encouraged marriage*: Abdullah Abdur Razzaq Interview.

50 *Developed a singular self-restraint*: Goldman, Peter. *The Death and Life of Malcolm X*. Chicago: Illini Books, 1979, 20.

50 *"Just noticed" Betty*: Haley, Alex and X, Malcolm. *The Autobiography of Malcolm X*. New York: Ballantine, 1993, 231.

51 *Malcolm had taken the surname Shabazz*: Lincoln, C. Eric. *The Black Muslims In America*. Trenton: Africa World Press, 1994, 105.

51 *Betty's formal conversion*: Ibid, 119.

51 *Lengthen their gowns*: Ruth Summerford Interview.

51 *"He had a crush on this lady"*: Percy Sutton Interview.

51 *"I guess being in New York was expensive"*: Suesetta MacCree Interview, February 13, 2001.

51 *"Maybe it was their discipline"*: Ruth Summerford Interview.

51 *Utterly proselytized by Malcolm*: Laura Ross Brown Interview.

52 *She was a Muslim*: Shabazz, Betty. "From the Detroit Riot to the Malcolm Summit." *Ebony*, November 1995, 64.

52 *Loss of her soul*: Shabazz, Betty. "Living with Malcolm." *Emerge*, February 1990, 26.

52 *"Gone Moo-slim"*: Lydia Hibbert Interview.

52 *Threatened to quit paying*: Haley, Alex and X, Malcolm. *The Autobiography of Malcolm X*. New York: Ballantine, 1993, 233.

52 *"A man being a man"*: Laura Ross Brown Interview.

52 *"My folks' philosophy was everybody for themselves"*: Shabazz, Betty. "Living with Malcolm." *Emerge*, February 1990, 26.

53 *Need for liberation struggle*: From the transcript of the "Haley Book Interview with Betty Shabazz" conducted by Anne Romaine, January 27, 1989, Medgar Evers College, Brooklyn, New York. (Courtesy of Special Collections, Hoskins Library, the University of Tennessee at Knoxville).

53 *Awareness had flared in the South*: Franklin, V.P. *Black Self-Determination*. New York: Lawrence Hill Books, 1992, 211.

53 *She might have studied Gandhi*: Ibid.

53 *1955 lynching of Emmett Till*: Williams, Juan. *Eyes on the Prize*. New York: Viking, 1987, 41-43.

54 *"Elijah Muhammad is very significant"*: "The Black Supremacists," *Time*, August 10, 1959, 25.

54 *"Most people can't deal with reality"*: Lanker, Brian and Barbara Summers, ed. *I Dream A World; Portraits of Black Women Who Changed America*. New York: Stewart, Tabori & Chang, 1999, 104.

54 *Transformation from parochialism to globalism*: Edwards, Audrey and Susan L. Taylor. "Loving and Losing Malcolm." *Essence*, February 1992, 104; Shabazz, Betty. "Remembering...Malcolm." *Essence*, February 1987, 61.

54 *"Hanging on to Islam"*: Haley, Alex and X, Malcolm. *The Autobiography of Malcolm X*. New York: Ballantine, 1993, 233.

54 *"Islam the true religion of our fore parents"*: Evanzz, Karl. *The Judas Factor*. New York: Thunder's Mouth Press, 1992, 47.

55 *Allah's chosen people*: Lincoln, C. Eric. *The Black Muslims In America*. Trenton: Africa World Press, 1994, 72.

55 *According to Black Islam*: Ibid, 72-75.

55 *Silk peddler named Master Fard*: Ibid, 11-17.

55 *Scour Christianity and intergationism from her mind*: Frady, Marshall. "The Children of Malcolm." *The New Yorker*, October 12, 1992, 68.

55 *"Christian beliefs under the Muslim dress"*: Sara Mitchell Interview, December 18, 2000.

55 *Muslims wanted their bit of earth*: Ibid, 22-23.

56 *God "a Negro"*: Henry McNeal Turner Papers: "Autobiography."

56 *"A better life than I have had"*: Geracimos, Ann. "Introducing Mrs. Malcolm X." *Herald Tribune*, June 30, 1963.

56 *Minister subsidized Betty*: Cohen, Ann and Walker, Monroe. "Her Goal: Black Solidarity." *Detroit News*, 4A.

56 *Inability to share her new exotic life*: Haley, Alex and X, Malcolm. *The Autobiography of Malcolm X*. New York: Ballantine, 1993, 233; "Betty Shabazz Remembers Malcolm." *Like It Is*. WABC-TV, May 19, 1991.

56 *"Was like Jackie Kennedy"*: Lydia Hibbert Interview.

57 *"A lot of time wasted"*: "Betty Shabazz Remembers Malcolm." *Like It Is*. WABC-TV, May 19, 1991.

57 *Teaching women's health and basic hygiene*: Sister Khadiyyah Interview.

57 *"Fine, Brother Minister"*: Haley, Alex and X, Malcolm. *The Autobiography of Malcolm X*. New York: Ballantine, 1993, 231-232.

57 *The visitors studied speech*: Geracimos, Ann. "Introducing Mrs. Malcolm X." *Herald Tribune*, June 30, 1963; Sister Khadiyyah Interview.

57 *"She was in that clique"*: Sister Khadiyyah Interview.

57 *"The pervasiveness of the middle-class spirit"*: Eddien-Uedom, E. U. *Black Nationalism*. Chicago: University of Chicago Press, 1962, 104.

58 *Petty jealousies and suspicions*: Sister Khadiyyah Interview.

58 *"You don't come talkin' 'bout where you came from"*: Charles Kenyatta Interview.

58 *"No woman was noticeable"*: Ibid.

58 *Against the "middle class"*: Muhammad, Elijah. *Message to the Blackman in America*. Chicago: Muhammad Mosque of Islam No. 2, 1965, xxiv.

58 *"Whole new way of living and learning"*: "Betty Shabazz Remembers Malcolm." *Like It Is*. WABC-TV, May 19, 1991.

59 *Eating to lice*: Geracimos, Ann. "Introducing Mrs. Malcolm X." *Herald Tribune*, June 30, 1963; Sister Khadiyyah Interview.

59 *"We were looking like angels"*: Sister Khadiyyah Interview.

59 *"Food is your cosmetics"*: Geracimos, Ann. "Introducing Mrs. Malcolm X." *Herald Tribune*, June 30, 1963.

59 *"She refused to look anything but beautiful"*: Brown, Jamie Foster, ed. *Betty Shabazz; A Sisterfriend's Tribute in Words and Pictures*. New York: Simon & Schuster, 1998, 38.

59 *Submit fully to Allah*: "Betty Shabazz Remembers Malcolm." *Like It Is*. WABC-TV, May 19, 1991.

59 *Respect each other's "true natures"*: Abdullah Abdur Razzaq Interview; Charles Kenyatta Interview.

60 *FBI had begun monitoring him*: Goldman, Peter. *The Death and Life of Malcolm X*. Chicago: Illini Books, 1979, 62-63; Carson, Clayborn. *Malcolm X; The FBI File*. New York: Carroll & Graf, 1991, 95.

60 *Harlemites materialized*: Goldman, Peter. *The Death and Life of Malcolm X*. Chicago: Illini Books, 1979, 55-59.

61 *In October 1957, he was hospitalized*: Carson, Clayborn. *Malcolm X; The FBI File*. New York: Carroll & Graf, 1991, 62.

61 *"He was all-giving"*: Jones, Marsha. "A Woman's View." *About...Time*, January 1993, 14.

61 *Never consent to an arranged marriage*: Collins, Rodnell P. with Bailey, Peter. *Seventh Child*. Secaucus:

Carol, 1998, 96.

61 *"I had even convinced myself"*: Haley, Alex and X, Malcolm. *The Autobiography of Malcolm X.* New York: Ballantine, 1993, 232.

62 *He did not have much time*: Ibid.

62 *"Persistently and correctly"*: Shabazz, Betty. "From the Detroit Riot to the Malcolm Summit." *Ebony,* November 1995, 64.

62 *Pondering Sister Betty X*: Haley, Alex and X, Malcolm. *The Autobiography of Malcolm X.* New York: Ballantine, 1993, 233.

62 *Match her and the minister*: Norma Johnson Interview.

62 *"Just friends"*: Clarke, John Henrik, ed. *Malcolm X; The Man and his Times.* Trenton: Africa World Press, 1990, 133.

62 *"Just plain jealous"*: Edwards, Audrey and Susan L. Taylor. "Loving and Losing Malcolm." *Essence,* February 1992, 104.

63 *She smiled back*: Ibid.

63 *Serious partying planned*: Frady, Marshall. "The Children of Malcolm." *The New Yorker,* October 12, 1992, 70.

63 *"Wedding dress all ready"*: Clarke, John Henrik, ed. *Malcolm X; The Man and his Times.* Trenton: Africa World Press, 1990, 132.

63 *"Fickle-hearted"*: Frady, Marshall. "The Children of Malcolm." *The New Yorker,* October 12, 1992, 69.

63 *"You can't play with this guy"*: Ibid.

63 *Mulling a proposal*: Frady, Marshall. "The Children of Malcolm." *The New Yorker,* October 12, 1992, 69.

64 *"Something you never kid about"*: Clarke, John Henrik, ed. *Malcolm X; The Man and his Times.* Trenton: Africa World Press, 1990, 133.

64 *"You're going to do what?"*: Osman Karriem Interview.

65 *"Authority to deal with them"*: Haley, Alex and X, Malcolm. *The Autobiography of Malcolm X.* New York: Ballantine, 1993, 232-233; Osman Karriem Interview.

65 *"Always talking about the minister"*: Edwards, Audrey and Susan L. Taylor. "Loving and Losing Malcolm." *Essence,* February 1992, 104.

65 *"Marry my brother?"*: Ibid.

65 *Though he later reflected*: Biographer Eugene Victor Wolfenstein later noted that Malcolm described his courtship "in a self-mocking, ironical tone that reflects both his eventual acceptance of Betty's role in his life and the residual perseverance of his old [misogynistic] attitudes." (Wolfenstein, Eugene Victor. *The Victims of Democracy; Malcolm X and the Black Revolution.* Los Angeles: University of California Press, 1994, 264).

66 *"In-laws were outlaws"*: Haley, Alex and X, Malcolm. *The Autobiography of Malcolm X.* New York: Ballantine, 1993, 233-234.

66 *"The one thing I won't do is argue"*: Ibid, 230, 233.

66 *"Marriage was a responsibility"*: Clarke, John Henrik, ed. *Malcolm X; The Man and his Times.* Trenton: Africa World Press, 1990, 133-134.

66 *"That was far from the case"*: Charles Kenyatta Interview.

66 *"Allah's greatest blessings"*: Carson, Clayborn. *Malcolm X; The FBI File.* New York: Carroll & Graf, 1991, 142.

67 *Bound for matrimony*: Yosef ben-Jochannan Interview, February 5, 2001.

67 *"Get lost!"*: Haley, Alex and X, Malcolm. *The Autobiography of Malcolm X.* New York: Ballantine, 1993, 234.

67 *House guest of Elijah Muhammad*: Ibid.

67 *"You left my husband in the Nation"*: Aisha Al-Adawiya Interview, April 14, 1999.

68 "There is no God but thee": Lincoln, C. Eric. The Black Muslims In America. Trenton: Africa World Press, 1994, 106.

68 The man who came into the room: Baldwin, James. The Fire Next Time. New York: Vintage, 1993, 63.

68 "Elijah wanted me for himself": Norma Johnson Interview, June 22, 1999.

68 "The Old Man had eyes for Betty": Charles Kenyatta Interview.

68 "A very serious sterp": Evanzz, Karl. The Judas Factor: The Plot to Kill Malcolm X. New York: Thunder's Mouth Press, 1992, 73.

69 "A fine sister": Haley, Alex and X, Malcolm. The Autobiography of Malcolm X. New York: Ballantine, 1993, 234.

69 "Meant to be this way": Vivian, Octavia. Corett.a. Philadelphia: Fortress Press, 1970, 34.

69 "I guess he got lonely": Knebel, Fletcher. "A Visit with the Widow of Malcolm X." Look, March 4, 1969, 75.

69 Destined to be with Malcolm: Trescott, Jacqueline. "Betty Shabazz, Recalling the Life Behind the Image." The Washington Post, November 18, 1992, C-3.

69 "If I were in his life": Shabazz, Betty. "Living with Malcolm." Emerge, February 1990, 26.

69 Pasty and hungry-looking: Edwards, Audrey and Susan L. Taylor. "Loving and Losing Malcolm." Essence, February 1992, 54.

69 "I was willing to try": Jones, Marsha. "A Woman's View." About...Time, January 1993, 14.

69 Filling station pay phone: Haley, Alex and X, Malcolm. The Autobiography of Malcolm X. New York: Ballantine, 1993, 233.

69 "Are you ready to make that move?": Edwards, Audrey and Susan L. Taylor. "Loving and Losing Malcolm." Essence, February 1992, 104.

70 Betty screamed: Shabazz, Betty. "Remembering Malcolm X." Essence, February 1987, 61.

70 "Betty screamed again: Laura Ross Brown Interview.

CHAPTER 4: WINDOWS OF THE HEART

71 "None of us knew Malcolm": Dick Gregory Interview, July 30, 1999.

71 "At least they acted that way": Haley, Alex and X, Malcolm. The Autobiography of Malcolm X. New York: Ballantine, 1993, 235.

71 Resembled a broker: "Betty Shabazz Remembers Malcolm." Like It Is. WABC-TV, May 19, 1991.

72 "Him for a son-in-law": Edwards, Audrey and Susan L. Taylor. "Loving and Losing Malcolm." Essence, February 1992, 104.

72 Soon Betty, too, was sobbing: Ibid.

72 Islam's dietary prohibitions: "Betty Shabazz Remembers Malcolm." Like It Is. WABC-TV, May 19, 1991.

72 "He got cold feet": Helen Malloy audiocassette, Helen Malloy Papers, Burton Historical Collection.

72 Not wanted Betty to get married: Cohen, Ann and Walker, Monroe. "Her Goal: Black Solidarity." Detroit News, 4A.

72 "Betty told me to come": Ibid.

72 "Very powerful and interesting to people": Ibid.

73 "It's not that Mom couldn't sing": Gamilah Shabazz Interview, January 15, 2000.

73 "Fussed over who did the most": Mary Redd Interview, May 20, 1999.

73 "I'm not sure Juju expected this": Stanley Sandlin Interview, December 5, 2000.

73 Betty appeared in Muslim garb: Shelmon Sandlin, Jr. Interview, January 13, 2001.

73 She was to be married within hours: Edwards, Audrey and Susan L. Taylor. "Loving and Losing Malcolm." Essence, February 1992, 104.

74 "Drive fast!": Ibid.

74 "The sun could not set": Ibid, 104, 107.

74 She would embrace the world: From the transcript of the "Haley Book Interview with Betty Shabazz"

conducted by Anne Romaine, January 27, 1989, Medgar Evers College, Brooklyn, New York. (Courtesy of Special Collections, Hoskins Library, the University of Tennessee at Knoxville).

74 *A justice of the peace*: Haley, Alex and X, Malcolm. *The Autobiography of Malcolm X.* New York: Ballantine, 1993, 235.

74 *"All of the Hollywood stuff!"*: Ibid, 236.

74 *Pressed her lips to his cheek*: Edwards, Audrey and Susan L. Taylor. "Loving and Losing Malcolm." *Essence*, February 1992, 107.

75 *"A hotel room is just so large"*: Ibid.

75 *The couple worshipped that Sunday*: Haley, Alex and X, Malcolm. *The Autobiography of Malcolm X.* New York: Ballantine, 1993, 236.

75 *"I didn't even know he was courting"*: Jean Reynolds Interview, February 13, 2000.

75 *"Malcolm X Wed"*: "Malcolm's Wed, It's a Surprise." *New York Amsterdam News*, January 25, 1958, 14.

76 *"You had to marry who they picked"*: Sister Khadiyyah Interview, February 13, 2000.

76 *"Big stars only came to big stars"*: Charles Kenyatta Interview, August 13, 1999.

76 *"Told Malcolm to stand on his head"*: Abdullah Abdur Razzaq Interview, April 16, 2000.

76 *Not even Ella Collins*: Haley, Alex and X, Malcolm. *The Autobiography of Malcolm X.* New York: Ballantine, 1993, 231.

76 *"I wasn't concerned with anything"*: Jean Reynolds Interview.

76 *"She stood her ground"*: Sister Khadiyyah Interview.

76 *"Walk by the wayside"*: Ruth Summerford Interview.

77 *With the juggernaut temple's number-one man*: Charles Kenyatta Interview.

77 *"You can't take care of no family"*: Sister Khadiyyah Interview.

77 *"I married him because I loved him"*: Jones, Marsha. "A Woman's View." *About...Time*, January 1993, 14.

77 *Betty would acknowledge no such calculation*: Trescott, Jacqueline. "Betty Shabazz, Recalling the Life Behind the Image." The Washington Post, November 18, 1992, C-3.

77 *"He loved his parents"*: Lanker, Brian and Barbara Summers, ed. *I Dream A World; Portraits of Black Women Who Changed America.* New York: Stewart, Tabori & Chang, 1999, 104.

77 *"She's the only woman"*: Haley, Alex and X, Malcolm. *The Autobiography of Malcolm X.* New York: Ballantine, 1993, 237.

77 *Myopia of his Black Muslim years*: Decaro, Louis A. Jr. *On the Side of my People.* New York: NYU Press, 1996, 3.

77 *"All she's put up with"*: Haley, Alex and X, Malcolm. *The Autobiography of Malcolm X.* New York: Ballantine, 1993, 428.

78 *"Full-time job"*: Ibid, 237.

78 *"Betty does this, so she understands me"*: Ibid.

78 *"The greatest thing in my life"*: Shabazz, Betty. "The Legacy of My Husband." *Ebony*, June 1969, 82.

78 *"God and truth"*: Betty Shabazz Papers (Courtesy of Gamilah Shabazz).

78 *"How powerful a man"*: Charles Kenyatta Interview.

79 *"I knew she was a strong woman"*: Percy Sutton Interview.

79 *Brandishing her marriage certificate*: Ruth Summerford Interview.

79 *"I was always holding back"*: Trescott, Jacqueline. "Betty Shabazz, Recalling the Life Behind the Image." The Washington Post, November 18, 1992, C-1.

79 *First great challenge would be the kitchen*: From the transcript of the "Haley Book Interview with Betty Shabazz" conducted by Anne Romaine, January 27, 1989, Medgar Evers College, Brooklyn, New York. (Courtesy of Special Collections, Hoskins Library, the University of Tennessee at Knoxville).

79 *The minister needed proper nourishment*: Shabazz, Betty. "The Legacy of My Husband." *Ebony*, June 1969, 176.

80 *"Preoccupied with keeping the brother healthy"*: Safiya Bandele Interview, April 1, 1999.

80 *"Back to the old routine"*: Shabazz, Betty. "The Legacy of My Husband." *Ebony*, June 1969, 176, 178.

80 *Malcolm's nutrition deficiency disappeared*: Ibid.

80 *"I'll cook in a minute"*: Clarke, John Henrik, ed. *Malcolm X; The Man and his Times*. Trenton: Africa World Press, 1990, 135.

80 *Fawned over cinnamon apple pie*: From the transcript of the "Haley Book Interview with Betty Shabazz" conducted by Anne Romaine, January 27, 1989, Medgar Evers College, Brooklyn, New York. (Courtesy of Special Collections, Hoskins Library, the University of Tennessee at Knoxville).

81 *"I was just...wow!"*: Gil Noble Interview, April 8, 1999.

81 *"But he loved ice cream"*: "Betty Shabazz Remembers Malcolm." *Like It Is*. WABC-TV, May 19, 1991.

81 *"Oh man, Betty!"*: Halima Toure Interview, August 4, 1999.

81 *"His breadth of commitment"*: Shabazz, Betty. "Remembering...Malcolm X." *Essence*, February 1987, 61.

81 *"He was informally educated"*: "Betty Shabazz Remembers Malcolm." *Like It Is*. WABC-TV, May 19, 1991.

81 *"Benefit their own"*: Abdullah Abdur Razzaq Interview; Muhammad, Elijah. *Message to the Blackman in America*. Chicago: Muhammad Mosque of Islam No. 2, 1965, 39.

81 *"Anything by or about black people"*: Shabazz, Betty. "The Legacy of My Husband." *Ebony*, June 1969, 178.

82 *"Forever compensating" for his crooked years*: Edwards, Audrey and Susan L. Taylor. "Loving and Losing Malcolm." *Essence*, February 1992, 109.

82 *"Willing to give his life"*: Claude Lewis Interview, March 28, 1999.

82 *You don't be in a house"*: Abdullah Abdur Razzaq Interview.

82 *"You didn't meet with Sister Betty"*: Yosef ben-Jochannan Interview, February 5, 2001.

82 *"You don't have tea with a Muslim's wife"*: Haley, Alex and X, Malcolm. *The Autobiography of Malcolm X*. New York: Ballantine, 1993, 336.

83 *Trouble picturing him as a family man*: Hines, Bea L. "Widow Pushes Malcolm's Work—But Her Way." *Reuters*, February 20, 1971.

83 *"He was really a balanced person"*: "Betty Shabazz Remembers Malcolm X." *Like It Is*. WABC-TV, May 19, 1991; Shabazz, Betty. "Remembering...Malcolm." *Essence*, February 1987, 61.

83 *Tenderness "that every woman looks for"*: Clarke, John Henrik, ed. *Malcolm X; The Man and his Times*. Trenton: Africa World Press, 1990, 135.

83 *"Opened the windows of my mind and heart"*: Shabazz, Betty S. 1975. *Organization of African Unity: Its Role in Education*. Ph.D. dissertation, University of Massachusetts, Amherst. (Quote is taken from dedication page).

83 *Returned from trips bearing gifts*: Shabazz, Betty. "Remembering...Malcolm X." *Essence*, February 1987, 61.

83 *A new hiding place every time*: Clarke, John Henrik, ed. *Malcolm X; The Man and his Times*. Trenton: Africa World Press, 1990, 135.

84 *"Yesterday was Valentine's Day"*: Shabazz, Betty. "Remembering...Malcolm X." *Essence*, February 1987, 61.

84 *Chance to unwind with her man*: Shabazz, Betty. "The Legacy of My Husband." *Ebony*, June 1969, 178.

84 *Extraordinary love affair*: Hopkins, Ellen. "Their Father's Daughters." *Rolling Stone*, November 30, 1989, 84.

85 *"Apple Brown Betty"*: Shabazz, Betty. "The Legacy of My Husband." *Ebony*, June 1969, 178.

85 A crash course in "the male": From the transcript of the "Haley Book Interview with Betty Shabazz" conducted by Anne Romaine, January 27, 1989, Medgar Evers College, Brooklyn, New York. (Courtesy of Special Collections, Hoskins Library, the University of Tennessee at Knoxville).

85 Torrid footnote about his prowess: Mary Redd Interview; Laura Ross Brown Interview.

85 "He was my lover": "Betty Shabazz Remembers Malcolm X." Like It Is. WABC-TV, May 19, 1991.

85 How sublimely beautiful he made her feel: Edwards, Audrey and Susan L. Taylor. "Loving and Losing Malcolm." Essence, February 1992, 109.

85 "He just liked me": Ibid.

85 "Loved me for me": Shabazz, Betty. "Remembering...Malcolm X." Essence, February 1987, 61.

85 "His sweetheart, his baby": Myrlie Evers-Williams Interview, August 30, 1999.

85 Widow's love affair: Gamilah Shabazz Interview.

86 "She loved him very much": Percy Sutton Interview.

86 "Hard to fathom": Shabazz, Betty. "Remembering...Malcolm X." Essence, February 1987, 61.

86 "Apprehensive about marriage": Clarke, John Henrik, ed. Malcolm X; The Man and his Times. Trenton: Africa World Press, 1990, 135.

86 "Greatest urge is to be men": Haley, Alex and X, Malcolm. The Autobiography of Malcolm X. New York: Ballantine, 1993, 95.

86 Malcolm warmed to his spousal role: Edwards, Audrey and Susan L. Taylor. "Loving and Losing Malcolm." Essence, February 1992, 107.

86 "Telephoning his Betty": Gallen, David, ed. Malcolm X; As They Knew Him. New York: Ballantine Books, 1992, 296.

86 "What's all this?": Ibid.

86 Malcolm took love seriously: Shabazz, Betty. "Remembering...Malcolm X." Essence, February 1987, 61.

86 Expectations of a good wife: Clarke, John Henrik, ed. Malcolm X; The Man and his Times. Trenton: Africa World Press, 1990, 134.

86 "Understanding of my shortcomings": Ibid. 135; Cain, Joy Duckett. "A Conversation with Dr. Betty Shabazz." Essence, February 1985, 12; Shabazz, Betty. "Remembering...Malcolm X." Essence, February 1987, 61.

87 "You doing all the listening": Clarke, John Henrik, ed. Malcolm X; The Man and his Times. Trenton: Africa World Press, 1990, 135.

87 Trust and communication came naturally: Edwards, Audrey and Susan L. Taylor. "Loving and Losing Malcolm." Essence, February 1992, 107.

87 "I preferred to listen to him": Shabazz, Betty. "Remembering...Malcolm X." Essence, February 1987, 61.

87 "I had it once": Ibid.

87 "Knew him as a wife": Abdullah Abdur Razzaq Interview; Dick Gregory Interview.

88 Spat that briefly turned ugly: Myrlie Evers-Williams Interview.

CHAPTER 5: SINEWS OF INDEPENDENCE

89 "No nation can gain": Frances Ellen Watkins Harper, "Woman's Political Future," in May Wright Sewall, ed. World's Congress of Representative Women. Chicago: Rand McNally, 1894: 433-437.

89 "You have to let go of Malcolm": Maya Angelou Interview, September 29, 1999.

89 "Family to the whole congregation": Jean Reynolds Interview, February 13, 2000.

90 "He was always on the go": Charles Kenyatta Interview, August 13, 1999; Shabazz, Betty. "Remembering...Malcolm X." Essence, February 1987, 61.

90 "A man who could speak up for his race": Whitten, Leslie H. New York Journal-American. February 27, 1966, 14-L.

90 Yearning for someone "to cuddle with": James Smalls Interview, March 19, 2000.

90 "I know she likes to be with her husband": Haley, Alex and X, Malcolm. The Autobiography of Malcolm

X. New York: Ballantine, 1993, 237.

90 *Malcolm was less than affectionate*: Safiya Bandele Interview, April 1, 1999.

90 *Dime novel romance*: Collins, Rodnell P. with Bailey, Peter. *Seventh Child*. Secaucus: Carol, 1998, 95.

90 *"I want that"*: Safiya Bandele Interview.

90 *"At least I have my TV"*: Charles Kenyatta Interview.

91 *She had subscribed to a way of life*: Ibid.

91 *Acquired a new asceticism*: Shabazz, Betty. "The Legacy of My Husband." *Ebony*, June 1969, 180.

91 *"Proud of the way she carried herself"*: "Sonji: 'I Will Fight To Hold My Husband.'" *Philadelphia Afro American*, July 3, 1965, 1.

92 *"Wouldn't even say 'hell'"*: Goldman, Peter. *The Death and Life of Malcolm X*. Chicago: Illini Books, 1979, 83.

92 *"Clothed in words"*: Charles Kenyatta Interview.

92 *"I drive by my watch"*: Haley, Alex and X, Malcolm. *The Autobiography of Malcolm X*. New York: Ballantine, 1993, 196.

92 *Betty's tardiness*: Gil Noble Interview, April 8, 1999.

92 *The movement had saved his life*: Charles Kenyatta Interview.

92 *His approach to his work*: Clarke, John Henrik, ed. *Malcolm X; The Man and his Times*. Trenton: Africa World Press, 1990, 138.

92 *Counseled the Muslim brothers*: Charles Kenyatta Interview.

92 *"Wouldn't recommend that"*: "Betty Shabazz Remembers Malcolm X." *Like It Is*. WABC-TV, May 19, 1991.

92 *"Malcolm was a little too strict"*: Edwards, Audrey and Susan L. Taylor. "Loving and Losing Malcolm." *Essence*, February 1992, 107.

92 *"I was moving into his space"*: "Betty Shabazz Remembers Malcolm X." *Like It Is*. WABC-TV, May 19, 1991.

92 *"Just to be with him"*: Ibid.

93 *"My husband is brighter"*: From the transcript of the "Haley Book Interview with Betty Shabazz" conducted by Anne Romaine, January 27, 1989, Medgar Evers College, Brooklyn, New York. (Courtesy of Special Collections, Hoskins Library, the University of Tennessee at Knoxville).

93 *Was not "worshipful"*: Gil Noble Interview.

93 *"Thorough indoctrination"*: Shabazz, Betty. "The Legacy of My Husband." *Ebony*, June 1969, 176.

93 *"A lot of Malcolm"*: Jones, Marsha. "A Woman's View." *About…Time*, January 1993, 14.

93 *A devoted helpmate*: Claude Lewis Interview, March 28, 1999; Haley, Alex and X, Malcolm. *The Autobiography of Malcolm X*. New York: Ballantine, 1993, 403.

93 *His "burnin'" uniform*: Haley, Alex and X, Malcolm. *The Autobiography of Malcolm X*. New York: Ballantine, 1993, 196.

93 *"Charm the spots"*: James Smalls Interview.

94 *All the Chicago theocrats*: Goldman, Peter. *The Death and Life of Malcolm X*. Chicago: Illini Books, 1979, 60.

94 *"Made sure we didn't leave the table"*: Karim, Benjamin with Gallen, David and Skutches, Peter. *Remembering Malcolm*. New York: Ballantine, 1992, 62.

94 *"I handled it"*: "Betty Shabazz Remembers Malcolm." *Like It Is*. WABC-TV, May 19, 1991.

94 *"a 50/50 basis"*: Smith, Corinne. "Black Women Get a Shot in the Arm." *Detroit News*, February 25, 1971, 4C.

95 *"This woman's grammar was hooked up!"*: Ibid.

95 *"Home life into the street"*: Maya Angelou Interview.

95 *"Girl, do you talk like that"*: Edwards, Audrey and Susan L. Taylor. "Loving and Losing Malcolm." *Essence*, February 1992, 107.

95 *"She was very polite"*: Claude Lewis Interview.

95 *"The way a queen might"*: Geracimos, Ann. "Introducing Mrs. Malcolm X." *Herald Tribune*, June 30, 1963.

95 *"A general silence that is unnerving"*: Lomax, Louis E. *When the Word is Given*. Westport: Greenwood Press, 1963, 70.

95 *"A woman who speaks loudly"*: Moses, Edwin. "Wallace Muhammad Says Women Not Forbidden to 'Make-up.'" *Mr. Muhammad Speaks*, (Special Edition) 1961, 7.

96 *"violate the trust"*: Shabazz, Betty. "Remembering…Malcolm X." *Essence*, February 1987, 61.

96 *She was one of four women*: Haley, Alex and X, Malcolm. *The Autobiography of Malcolm X*. New York: Ballantine, 1993, 237.

96 *"I don't know who the four"*: "Dr. Betty Shabazz's Final Words." Interview with Bernard White and Amy Goodman, Pacifica Radio, WBAI, New York City, May 19, 1997.

96 *"You can never fully trust"* Haley, Alex and X, Malcolm. *The Autobiography of Malcolm X*. New York: Ballantine, 1993, 396.

96 *"Our women have been there"*: Claude Lewis Interview.

96 *"Stand up and fight like men"*: Wood, Joe. "Looking for Malcolm." *Village Voice*, May 29, 1990, 43.

97 *"She sought to be the helpmate"*: Percy Sutton Interview, September 21, 2000.

97 *"All of us try in some ways"*: Geracimos, Ann. "Introducing Mrs. Malcolm X." *Herald Tribune*, June 30, 1963.

97 *"Attracted to the male"*: Haley, Alex and X, Malcolm. *The Autobiography of Malcolm X*. New York: Ballantine, 1993, 96.

97 *"Let your women keep silence in the churches"*: From 1 Corinthians 14:34 in the Holy Bible, King James Version.

98 *Like a man possessed*: Evers, Myrlie with Peters, William. *For Us, the Living*. Garden City: Doubleday, 1967, 272.

98 *Betty would reminisce fondly*: Clarke, John Henrik, ed. *Malcolm X; The Man and his Times*. Trenton: Africa World Press, 1990, 134.

98 *"She knew her place"*: Claude Lewis Interview.

98 *Officially, Muslim ministers*: Karim, Benjamin with Gallen, David and Skutches, Peter. *Remembering Malcolm*. New York: Ballantine, 1992, 64.

98 *"This is men's business"*: Claude Lewis Interview.

98 *"I was a good Muslim wife"*: "Betty Shabazz Remembers Malcolm." *Like It Is*. WABC-TV, May 19, 1991.

99 *"She didn't just say 'Good evening'"*: James Smalls Interview.

99 *"Sister Betty was not different"*: Percy Sutton Interview.

99 *"She was very well read"*: Ibid.

99 *"You had to be top cotton"*: Charles Kenyatta Interview.

99 *The opinion she expressed around company*: Percy Sutton Interview; Claude Lewis Interview; Abdullah Abdur Razzaq Interview.

100 *"I shared Malcolm"*: Edwards, Audrey and Susan L. Taylor. "Loving and Losing Malcolm." *Essence*, February 1992, 107.

100 *"He didn't even want me to have women friends"*: Ibid.

100 *Succumb to her "womanish nature"*: Ibid.

100 *"When you return from out of town"*: Abdullah Abdur Razzaq Interview.

100 *Malcolm wanted nothing competing*: Edwards, Audrey and Susan L. Taylor. "Loving and Losing Malcolm." *Essence*, February 1992, 109.

100 *Occasionally she invited her cousin*: Ruth Summerford Interview, January 16, 2000.

100 *"I was not accessible to a great number"*: From the transcript of the "Haley Book Interview with Betty

Shabazz" conducted by Anne Romaine, January 27, 1989, Medgar Evers College, Brooklyn, New York. (Courtesy of Special Collections, Hoskins Library, the University of Tennessee at Knoxville).

101 *Smirked at the portraits of Muhammad*: Suesetta MacCree Interview, February 13, 2001.

101 *"I could send someone to get you"*: Ibid.

101 *"We didn't get into a whole lot"*: Ruth Summerford Interview.

101 *"In my home I didn't discuss that"*: Percy Sutton Interview.

101 *"Loving my husband was leaving them"*: Trescott, Jacqueline. "Betty Shabazz, Recalling the Life Behind the Image." The Washington Post, November 18, 1992, C-3.

101 *"You want to do what?"*: Edwards, Audrey and Susan L. Taylor. "Loving and Losing Malcolm." *Essence*, February 1992, 109.

102 *"Where are you going?"*: Kareemah Abdul Karim Interview, August 5, 1999.

102 *Malcolm "did not believe that a woman's role"*: Shabazz, Betty. "The Legacy of My Husband." *Ebony*, June 1969, 180.

102 *"He wouldn't even entertain the idea"*: Edwards, Audrey and Susan L. Taylor. "Loving and Losing Malcolm." *Essence*, February 1992, 109.

102 *"Biologically and aesthetically"*: Reddick, L. D. *Crusader without Violence; A Biography of Martin Luther King, Jr.* New York: Harper, 1959, 5.

102 *"She saw my being relegated"*: Trescott, Jacqueline. "Betty Shabazz, Recalling the Life Behind the Image." The Washington Post, November 18, 1992, C-3.

102 *The state of New York had issued*: Betty Shabazz New York State Nurse's License, January 14, 1958; Geracimos, Ann. "Introducing Mrs. Malcolm X." *Herald Tribune*, June 30, 1963.

102 *"An educated woman...can't resist"*: Haley, Alex and X, Malcolm. *The Autobiography of Malcolm X.* New York: Ballantine, 1993, 4.

103 *"Sat, moved, talked, did everything"*: Ibid, 34.

103 *"Mellow thunder"*: Dyson, Michael Eric. *Making Malcolm.* New York: Oxford University Press, 1995, 141.

103 *Her protests were subtle but "continuous"*: Abdullah Abdur Razzaq Interview.

103 *"Just didn't go in the home"*: Laura Ross Brown Interview.

103 *"Without having to be rude"*: Maya Angelou Interview.

104 *"When he came down on you"*: Abdullah Abdur Razzaq Interview; Charles Kenyatta Interview; Claude Lewis Interview.

104 *"I'm sure it's the same with you"*: Claude Lewis Interview.

104 *"Betty was out at MGT"*: Brown, Jamie Foster, ed. *Betty Shabazz; A Sisterfriend's Tribute in Words and Pictures.* New York: Simon & Schuster, 1998, 40.

104 *"He would really get into showin'"*: Ibid.

104 *Betty came in from the kitchen*: Karim, Benjamin with Gallen, David and Skutches, Peter. *Remembering Malcolm.* New York: Ballantine, 1992, 63-64.

105 *"The religiosity of the Nation"*: Sister Cybil Clarke Interview.

105 *"But there were flashbacks"*: Gil Noble Interview.

105 *The constraints, zealotry, and other tensions*: Edwards, Audrey and Susan L. Taylor. "Loving and Losing Malcolm." *Essence*, February 1992, 109.

[unclear] Trescott, Jacqueline. "Betty Shabazz, Recalling the Life Behind the Image." The Washington Post, November 18, 1992, C-3.

105 *"When you get tired of people"*: Ruth Summerford Interview.

105 *"I don't have a job where I can"*: Laura Ross Brown Interview.

106 *"Each time I left he found me"*: Edwards, Audrey and Susan L. Taylor. "Loving and Losing Malcolm." *Essence*, February 1992, 109.

106   "Girl, every time I came back": Myrlie Evers-Williams Interview.

106   "I knew the brother meant it!": Laura Ross Brown Interview.

106   He allowed his wife: Edwards, Audrey and Susan L. Taylor. "Loving and Losing Malcolm." Essence, February 1992, 109.

106   "And sister.": Trescott, Jacqueline. "Betty Shabazz, Recalling the Life Behind the Image." The Washington Post, November 18, 1992, C-3.

106   "In that movement": Trescott, Jacqueline. "Betty Shabazz, Recalling the Life Behind the Image." The Washington Post, November 18, 1992, C-3.

106   "I was stable": Hall, Terri. "For Betty Shabazz, Life is Full Again." Mount Vernon Daily Argus, March 5, 1977.

106   In later years, she acknowledged: Cain, Joy Duckett. "A Conversation with Dr. Betty Shabazz." Essence, February 1985, 12.

106   "I just wanted love": Edwards, Audrey and Susan L. Taylor. "Loving and Losing Malcolm." Essence, February 1992, 110.

107   In the seemingly authentic: March 25, 1959 Malcolm X Letter to Elijah Muhammad (Courtesy of Moments in Time, Washingtonville, New York).

108   Betty embarked on her most enduring: Attallah Shabazz Interview, March 26, 1999.

109   It was motherhood that kept Betty home: Clarke, John Henrik, ed. Malcolm X; The Man and his Times. Trenton: Africa World Press, 1990, 137.

109   Took to pampering her: Ibid.

109   Quoted Qur'anic passages: Shabazz, Betty. "The Legacy of My Husband." Ebony, June 1969, 180.

109   He talked temple minutiae: Karim, Benjamin with Gallen, David and Skutches, Peter. Remembering Malcolm. New York: Ballantine, 1992, 175-176.

109   "It looked like somebody had taken Malcolm": Wilfred Little Interview with Bernard White and Amy Goodman, Pacifica Radio, WBAI, New York City, June 24, 1997.

109   But her reward had come: Clarke, John Henrik, ed. Malcolm X; The Man and his Times. Trenton: Africa World Press, 1990, 137.

110   "The gentleness he showed": Ibid., 136.

110   At the time, though, Betty's strongest emotion: Ibid.

110   Malcolm expounded upon the essential nutrients: Ibid., 73.

110   "One of the happiest times of my life": Hall, Terri. "For Betty Shabazz, Life is Full Again." Mount Vernon Daily Argus, March 5, 1977.

110   "I was Malcolm's choice": Trescott, Jacqueline. "Betty Shabazz, Recalling the Life Behind the Image." The Washington Post, November 18, 1992, C-1.

110   "A good Muslim woman and wife": Haley, Alex and X, Malcolm. The Autobiography of Malcolm X. New York: Ballantine, 1993, 237.

110   "She's there for me": Claude Lewis Interview.

111   "You are present when you are away": Haley, Alex and X, Malcolm. The Autobiography of Malcolm X. New York: Ballantine, 1993, 237.

111   "What's in her head": Yuri Kochiama Interview.

111   "Everything she does is for me?": Norma Johnson Interview.

111   "She didn't want to be a regular sister": Charles Kenyatta Interview; Abdullah Abdur Razzaq Interview.

111   She had an attitude: Gallen, David, ed. Malcolm X; As They Knew Him. New York: Ballantine, 1992, 14.

111   "Betty was Betty, right or wrong": Charles Kenyatta Interview; Sister Khadiyyah Interview.

111   "How close they could get": Mary Redd Interview.

111   "Bring you and the family this pie": Gamilah Shabazz Interview.

112   *"I know you love my husband"*: Sister Khadiyyah Interview.

112   *"We went to war with that brother"*: Ibid.; Jean Reynolds Interview.

112   *One morning...two white detectives*: "3 Moslems Seized as Police Fighters." *New York Amsterdam News*, May 24, 1958, 21; "Moslems Await 'D-Day' in New York Court." *Pittsburgh Courier*, May 24, 1958, 7; "Moslems Freed, Cry For Arrest of Cops." *Pittsburgh Courier*, March 28, 1959, 3.

113   *"Wasn't moving fast enough"*: Carson, Clayborne. *Malcolm X: The FBI File*. New York: Carroll & Graf, 1991, 189.

114   *Betty and Malcolm's home*: Ibid.

114   *The Muslim outcry escalated*: Ibid.

CHAPTER 6: A PERILOUS ORBIT

117   *"It's much easier to fight"*: From the transcript of the "Haley Book Interview with Betty Shabazz" conducted by Anne Romaine, January 27, 1989, Medgar Evers College, Brooklyn, New York. (Courtesy of Special Collections, Hoskins Library, the University of Tennessee at Knoxville).

117   *Sugar killed him*: Helen Malloy audiocassette, Helen Malloy Papers, Burton Historical Collection.

117   *"Blue-eyed Willies"*: Carson, Clayborne. *Malcolm X: The FBI File*. New York: Carroll & Graf, 1991, 148.

118   *"When the brother started out"*: Charles Kenyatta Interview.

118   *"There were others striving"*: Ibid.

119   *I charge the white man"*: Lomax, Louis. *To Kill A Black Man*. Los Angeles: Holloway House, 1968, 66.

119   *The Christian religion has failed*: Ibid, 69.

119   *The white press instantly descended"*: "The Black Supremacists." *Time*, August 10, 1959, 24-25.

120   *The African finds it difficult*: X, Malcolm. "Africa Eyes Us." *Amsterdam News*, August 22, 1959.

121   *"She does know how to cook"*: From the transcript of the "Haley Book Interview with Betty Shabazz" conducted by Anne Romaine, January 27, 1989, Medgar Evers College, Brooklyn, New York. (Courtesy of Special Collections, Hoskins Library, the University of Tennessee at Knoxville).

121   *"It's much easier to fight"*: From the transcript of the "Haley Book Interview with Betty Shabazz" conducted by Anne Romaine, January 27, 1989, Medgar Evers College, Brooklyn, New York. (Courtesy of Special Collections, Hoskins Library, the University of Tennessee at Knoxville).

121   *"An integrated cup of coffee"*: Bird, Robert S. "Muslim Aim: Rid Harlem of Dope, Vice." *New York Herald Times*. June 24, 1963.

122   *"He was so cool with this"*: Robert Haggins Interview.

122   *"I guess my feeling was"*: Clarke, John Henrik, ed. *Malcolm X; The Man and his Times*. Trenton: Africa World Press, 1990, 138; Trescott, Jacqueline. "Betty Shabazz, Recalling the Life Behind the Image." The Washington Post, November 18, 1992, C-3.

122   *"Betty would put down the phone"*: Haley, Alex and X, Malcolm. *The Autobiography of Malcolm X*. New York: Ballantine, 1993, 244.

123   *Season their homemade vegetable soup*: "Household Hints." *Muhammad Speaks*, April 1962, 22; "'Inner Beauty' as Reflected in Personality Key to True Beauty." *Muhammad Speaks*, September 15, 1962, 17.

123   *Men and women of science"*: "Women's News and Notes." *Muhammad Speaks*, December 30, 1962, 16; "Nursing Supervisor, Mother Still Finds Time for Study." *Muhammad Speaks*, March 4, 1963, 16; Deanar, Tynetta. "Women In Islam." *Muhammad Speaks*, March 18, 1963, 17.

124   *"He should have been a foreign policy advisor"*: "Dr. Betty Shabazz's Final Words." Interview with Bernard White and Amy Goodman, Pacifica Radio, WBAI, New York City, May 19, 1997.

124   *"Daddy's home!"*: Hopkins, Ellen. "Their Fathers' Daughters." *Rolling Stone*, November 30, 1989, 82.

124   *"Whenever Daddy was home"*: Hopkins, Ellen. "Their Fathers' Daughters." *Rolling Stone*, November

30, 1989, 82; Strickland, William. "Malcolm X, Make It Plain." New York: Penguin, 1995, 124; Clarke, John Henrik, ed. *Malcolm X; The Man and his Times*. Trenton: Africa World Press, 1990, 134.

124 *"His presence was so very calming"*: Gallen, David, ed. *Malcolm X; As They Knew Him*. New York: Ballantine Books, 1996, 274.

124 *His confused toddlers*: Clarke, John Henrik, ed. *Malcolm X; The Man and His Times*. Trenton: Africa World Press, 1990, 135.

125 *"An even grander parent"*: Hopkins, Ellen. "Their Fathers' Daughters." *Rolling Stone*, November 30, 1989, 82.

125 *"You don't have to do this"*: "Betty Shabazz Remembers Malcolm." *Like It Is*. WABC-TV, May 19, 1991.

125 *"In terms of quality"*: Clarke, John Henrik, ed. *Malcolm X; The Man and His Times*. Trenton: Africa World Press, 1990, 134.

125 *Tender little talks*: "Talk with Mrs. Malcolm X!" *New York Amsterdam News*, March 13, 1965, 4.

125 *"My mother set the rhythm"*: Strickland, William. "Malcolm X, Make It Plain." New York: Penguin, 1995, 125.

125 *Were it not for racism's stronghold*: Gallen, David, ed. *Malcolm X; As They Knew Him*. New York: Ballantine Books, 1996, 13.

125 *"God had allowed us to create"*: Shabazz, Betty. "The Legacy of My Husband." *Ebony*, June 1969, 176; Edwards, Audrey and Susan L. Taylor. "Loving and Losing Malcolm." *Essence*, February 1992, 109.

125 *"Other people will spoil your children"*: Shabazz, Betty. "The Legacy of My Husband." *Ebony*, June 1969, 176.

126 *"You were never a bad girl"*: Finke, Nikki. "A Certain Peacefulness." *Los Angeles Times*, January 8, 1989.

126 *"He saw in her a lot of traits"*: Clarke, John Henrik, ed. *Malcolm X; The Man and His Times*. Trenton: Africa World Press, 1990, 136.

126 *"Early years as quaint and "wholesome"*: Hopkins, Ellen. "Their Fathers' Daughters." *Rolling Stone*, November 30, 1989, 82-84.

126 *Remember their heritage*: Booker, James. "Exclusive Interview! Talk With Mrs. Malcolm X!" *New York Amsterdam News*, March 13, 1965, 4.

126 *Never marry outside their race or faith*: Geracimos, Ann. "Introducing Mrs. Malcolm X." *Herald Tribune*, June 30, 1963.

127 *"When I went to school"*: Hopkins, Ellen. "Their Fathers' Daughters." *Rolling Stone*, November 30, 1989, 84.

127 *Determined not to shelter their daughter*: Ibid, 82.

127 *"The black woman has the chief responsibility"*: Ibid., 84; Shabazz, Betty. "The Legacy of My Husband." *Ebony*, June 1969, 180.

127 *A cherubic Attallah appeared*: "Culture and Worship in the Muslim Home." *Mr. Muhammad Speaks*, September 1960, 6; "Natural Beauties." *Muhammad Speaks*, Sept. 15, 1962, 4.

127 *Father's attention much more finite*: Haley, Alex and X, Malcolm. *The Autobiography of Malcolm X*. New York: Ballantine, 1993, 237.

127 *"I wanted a son for him"*: Clarke, John Henrik, ed. *Malcolm X; The Man and His Times*. Trenton: Africa World Press, 1990, 136.

128 *"Never be the aggressor"*: Lincoln, C. Eric. *The Black Muslims in America*. Trenton: Africa World Press, 1994, 3.

128 *Prince's eloquence eclipsed their king's*: Casey, Phil. "Crowd Appears, Elijah Doesn't at Muslim Rally." *Washington Post*, June 26, 1961, A3.

129 *"Blacks are still knocking"*: Lincoln, C. Eric. *The Black Muslims in America*. Trenton: Africa World

Press, 1994, 19.

129 *It is not a case of integration*: Fox, Jack V. "Communism Believed to Be the Least of Many Factors Behind Riot at UN." *Philadelphia Evening Bulletin*, February 28, 1961.

129 *Now you have twenty million black people*: Clarke, John Henrik, ed. *Malcolm X; The Man and His Times*. Trenton: Africa World Press, 1990, 153-154.

130 *"If my work won't let me be"*: Haley, Alex and X, Malcolm. *The Autobiography of Malcolm X*. New York: Ballantine, 1993, 272.

131 *Described Muhammad and Malcolm as "dramatic personalities"*: Leaks, Sylvester. "World Outlook of Ruby Dee." *Muhammad Speaks*, October 11, 1963, 21.

131 *"He realized the potential"*: Clarke, John Henrik, ed. *Malcolm X; The Man and His Times*. Trenton: Africa World Press, 1990, 139.

131 *"Woman who cries all the time"*: Haley, Alex and X, Malcolm. *The Autobiography of Malcolm X*. New York: Ballantine, 1993, 396.

131 *"I have a wife who understands"*: Ibid, 397.

132 *"Sometimes you have to exaggerate"*: Frady, Marshall. "The Children of Malcolm." *The New Yorker*, October 12, 1992, 79.

132 *"He left me on the floor"*: Sonia Sanchez Interview, August 10, 1999.

133 *"So many didn't know him"*: Sylvia Woods Interview, September 20, 2000.

133 *"He used to say that people"*: Shabazz, Betty. "The Legacy of My Husband." *Ebony*, June 1969, 180; Jones, Marsha. "A Woman's View." *About…Time*, January 1993, 14.

133 *a "chump"*: Lomax, Louis. *When the Word is Given*. Westport: Greenwood Press, 1963, 74.

133 *"turn the other cheek"*: Clarke, John Henrik, ed. *Malcolm X; The Man and his Times*. Trenton: Africa World Press, 1990, 136.

133 *nothing but a barbiturate* Walker, Wyatt Tee. "Nothing But A Man." *Negro Digest*, August 1965, 31.

133 *"For years Malcolm said"*: Charles Kenyatta Interview.

134 *"Coffee with a cracker"*: Williams, Juan. *Eyes on the Prize*. New York: Viking, 1987.

134 *"You're right, absolutely right"*: Lanker, Brian and Barbara Summers, ed. *I Dream A World; Portraits of Black Women Who Changed America*. New York: Stewart, Tabori & Chang, 1999, 104.

134 *"The guy was so strong"*: Frady, Marshall. "The Children of Malcolm." *The New Yorker*, October 12, 1992, 79.

135 *Death a justifiable* homicide: *Washington Post*, April 29, 1962, 3A; *Los Angeles Times*, May 15, 1962.

135 *"Hold fast to Islam"*: Goldman, Peter. *The Death and Life of Malcolm X*. University of Illinois Press, 1979, 99.

136 *Mosque's survivors faced assault charges*: *Muhammad Speaks*, July, 1962; "Los Angeles Hearing Set Stage For Explosive Trial of Muslim Police Victims." *Muhammad Speaks*, December 30, 1962, 2.

136 *Patrice Lumumba was dead*: *Muhammad Speaks*, March 13, 1964, 9.

136 *Nasser had sent for Lumumba's twenty-nine-year-old* widow: Muhammad *Speaks*, July 17, 1964, 19.

136 *By June 1963, Medgar Evers was dead*: Evers, Myrlie and Peters, William. *For Us, the Living*. New York: Doubleday, 273-274.

137 *I come to you tonight with a broken heart*: Ibid, 302-303, 310.

CHAPTER 7: FORESIGHT

139 *"Imagine how you would feel"*: Baldwin, James. *The Fire Next Time*. New York: Vintage International, 1993, 9.

139 *"I thought his heart would pop"*: Abdullah Abdur Razzaq Interview, March 27, 1999; Sister Khadiyyah Interview.

140 *"Who likes the first lady?"*: Ibid.

140 *"Tryin' her level best"*: Charles Kenyatta Interview.

140 *She would bear Malcolm no sons*: Ibid.

140 *"He loved the children"*: Edwards, Audrey and Susan L. Taylor. "Loving and Losing Malcolm." *Essence*, February 1992, 109.

140 *"Do you love me or my money?"*: Shabazz, Betty. "Remembering...Malcolm X." *Essence*, February 1987, 61.

141 *"Trapped by material possessions"*: Essien-Udom, E. U. *Black Nationalism*. Chicago: University of Chicago Press, 1962.

141 *"No use for schemes"*: Shabazz, Betty. "The Legacy of My Husband." *Ebony*, June 1969, 180.

141 *"Practically nothing of his own"*: Clarke, John Henrik, ed. *Malcolm X; The Man and His Times*. Trenton: Africa World Press, 1990, 138.

141 *"A higher calling"*: Charles Kenyatta Interview.

141 *"No, sir, deal Holy Apostle"*: Clarke, John Henrik, ed. *Malcolm X; The Man and His Times*. Trenton: Africa World Press, 1990, 138.

141 *"Islam is mathematics"*: Essien-Udom, E. U. *Black Nationalism*. Chicago: The University of Chicago Press, 1962, 202.

142 *But Betty did the math*: Abdullah Abdur Razzaq Interview.

142 *By 1960, Muhammad and his Nation controlled*: Evanzz, Karl. *The Rise and Fall of Elijah Muhammad*. New York: Pantheon Books, 1999, 173; Goldman, Peter. *The Death and Life of Malcolm X*. University of Illinois Press, 1979, 83.

142 *"the money was big"*: Charles Kenyatta Interview.

142 *"Tell it like it is"*: Goldman, Peter. *The Death and Life of Malcolm X*. University of Illinois Press, 1979, 82.

142 *"In any community"*: Charles Kenyatta Interview.

142 *"Brother, what's your problem?"*: Ibid.

143 *The sect's "creeping capitalism"*: Goldman, Peter. *The Death and Life of Malcolm X*. University of Illinois Press, 1979, 109.

143 *Black Islam was the solution*: Haley, Alex and X, Malcolm. *The Autobiography of Malcolm X*. New York: Ballantine, 1993, 202.

143 *Cloud a "noble vision"*: "Betty Shabazz Remembers Malcolm." *Like It Is*. WABC-TV, May 19, 1991.

143 *"In his moment"*: Charles Kenyatta Interview.

144 *"Every woman would have liked"*: Abdullah Abdur Razzaq Interview.

144 *He referred to Betty only as "your wife"*: Ibid.

144 *"You and her were not equals"*: Ibid.

144 *"You can't live off the crumbs"*: Sister Khadiyyah Interview.

144 *"We need to have some money"*: Norma Johnson Interview.

145 *Allah would provide*: Poston, Ted. "Widow Talks of Her Life with Malcolm." *New York Post*, February 23, 1965, 2.

145 *"We nearly broke up"*: Haley, 297.

145 *"A wife who would sacrifice her life"*: Haley, Alex and X, Malcolm. *The Autobiography of Malcolm X*. New York: Ballantine, 1993, 297.

145 *The debate smoldered on*: Norma Johnson Interview.

145 *Declined to move his family to the capital*: Handler, M. S. "Malcolm X Starting Drive in Washington," *New York Times*, May 10, 1963, 1.

145 *"Sometimes he was so damned perceptive"*: Abdullah Abdur Razzaq Interview.

145 *"Quick picking up" talents*: Haley, 241.

146 *"When I was in prison"*: Strickland, William. *Malcolm X, Make It Plain*. New York: Penguin, 1995, 126.

146 *"Not a romantic but a realist"*: Shabazz, Betty. "The Legacy of My Husband." *Ebony*, June 1969, 175.

146 *"He had got to a place"*: Charles Kenyatta Interview.

146 *Rockwell had attended Muslim rallies*: "TV Spotlight on Malcolm X and Muslims." *New York Herald Tribune*, June 5, 1963.

148 *"President Kennedy did not send troops"*: Handler, M. S. "Malcolm X Scores Kennedy." *New York Times*, May 17, 1963.

148 *"The real mood of the black masses"*: "Harlem is Bracing for Muslim Rally," *New York Amsterdam News*, June 29, 1963, 2.

148 *Internal caucus of black leaders*: "Malcolm X Calls for Negro Unity." *New York Amsterdam News*, August 10, 1963.

148 *"What is this so-called Negro revolution?"*: Allegander, Bill. "Blood Must Be Shed." *Philadelphia Tribune*, November 19, 1963, 4.

149 *"Some wanted to take their pistols"*: Herman Fergusson Interview.

149 *"Malcolm submitted"*: Decaro, Louis A, Jr. *On the Side of My People*. New York: New York University Press, 1996, 185.

150 *"Broke her neck coming over to speak"*: Jean Reynolds Interview.

150 *"They were frightened"*: Percy Sutton Interview.

150 *World tugged Malcolm away*: Charles Kenyatta Interview.

150 *A web of relationships*: Breitman, George. *Malcolm X Speaks*. New York: Grove Weidenfeld, 1990, 12.

151 *He sampled their societies*: Goldman, Peter. *The Death and Life of Malcolm X*. University of Illinois Press, 1979, 82.

151 *"He was smokin'"*: Charles Kenyatta Interview.

151 *"She wanted to meet all of Malcolm's contacts"*: Ibid; Herman Fergusson Interview.

152 *"Malcolm accepted Cassius"*: Hauser, Thomas. *Muhammad Ali*. New York: Touchstone, 1992, 97-98.

152 *"Did not have an intimate relationship"*: From the transcript of the "Haley Book Interview with Betty Shabazz" conducted by Anne Romaine, January 27, 1989, Medgar Evers College, Brooklyn, New York. (Courtesy of Special Collections, Hoskins Library, the University of Tennessee at Knoxville).

152 *"Some contagious quality"*: Haley, Alex and X, Malcolm. *The Autobiography of Malcolm X*. New York: Ballantine, 1993, 310; Hauser, Thomas. *Muhammad Ali*. New York: Touchstone, 1992, 97-98.

152 *An interview with Malcolm for Playboy*: Haley, Alex. *Playboy*, May, 1963.

152 *Commissioned to write Malcolm's life*: Haley, Alex and X, Malcolm. *The Autobiography of Malcolm X*. New York: Ballantine, 1993, 394.

152 *"A man of the world"*: From the transcript of the "Haley Book Interview with Betty Shabazz" conducted by Anne Romaine, January 27, 1989, Medgar Evers College, Brooklyn, New York. (Courtesy of Special Collections, Hoskins Library, The Uiversity of Tennessee at Knoxville). Haley, Alex and X, Malcolm. The Autobiography of Malcolm X. New York: Ballantine, 1993, 345.

CHAPTER 8: REVELATIONS

163 *"I never had a moment's question"*: Haley, Alex and X, Malcolm. *The Autobiography of Malcolm X*. New York: Ballantine, 1993, 345.

163 *"I don't think he had given up"*: Abdullah Abur Razzaq Interview.

163 *"a great deal of stress"*: Edwards, Audrey and Susan L. Taylor. "Loving and Losing Malcolm." *Essence*, February 1992, 109.

163 *"I'd rather be dead"*: Evanzz, Karl. *The Judas Factor*. New York: Thunder's Mouth Press, 1992, 168.

163 *his known foes*: Goldman, Peter. *The Death and Life of Malcolm X*. University of Illinois Press, 1979, 125.

163 *"put out that fire"*: Charles Kenyatta Interview.

163 *Betty continued to worship*: Clarke, John Henrik, ed. *Malcolm X; The Man and his Times*. Trenton:

Africa World Press, 1990, 140.

164 *"Knowing his temperament"*: Haley, Alex and X, Malcolm. *The Autobiography of Malcolm X*. New York: Ballantine, 1993, 414.

164 *"But I already submitted"*: Lomax, Louis E. *To Kill A Black Man*. Los Angeles: Holloway House, 1968, 134.

164 *the minister tossed them out*: Evanzz, Karl. *The Messenger; The rise and fall of Elijah Muhammad*. New York: Panheon, 1999, 281; Clarke, John Henrik, ed. *Malcolm X; The Man and his Times*. Trenton: Africa World Press, 1990, 182-204.

164 *"A lot of money"*: Shabazz, Betty. "Living With Malcolm." *Emerge*, February 1990, 26.

164 *Dear Holy Apostle himself*: Haley, Alex and X, Malcolm. *The Autobiography of Malcolm X*. New York: Ballantine, 1993, 309.

164 *"He was being punished"*: Edwards, Audrey and Susan L. Taylor. "Loving and Losing Malcolm." *Essence*, February 1992, 110.

164 *"I was going downhill"*: Haley, Alex and X, Malcolm. *The Autobiography of Malcolm X*. New York: Ballantine, 1993, 413.

165 *"willing to do his bidding"*: Clarke, John Henrik, ed. *Malcolm X; The Man and his Times*. Trenton: Africa World Press, 1990, 140.

165 *the couple's first vacation*: Strickland, William. *Malcolm X, Make It Plain*. New York: Penguin, 1995, 168.

165 *"if he had horns"*: Plimpton, George. "Miami Notebook: Cassius Clay and Malcolm X." *Harper's Magazine*, June 1964, 54-61.

165 *switch him off and on*: Lomax, Louis E. *To Kill A Black Man*. Los Angeles: Holloway House, 1968, 127.

166 *"an inseparable, beautiful marriage"*: Haley, Alex and X, Malcolm. *The Autobiography of Malcolm X*. New York: Ballantine, 1993, 311.

166 *"some black Svengali"*: Goldman, Peter. *The Death and Life of Malcolm X*. University of Illinois Press, 1979, 127.

166 *"David slew Goliath"*: Hauser, Thomas. *Muhammad Ali; His Life and Times*. New York: Touchstone, 1991, 100.

166 *Malcolm was ringside*: Ibid.

166 *"Mr. Muhammad will destroy him"*: Massaquoi, Hans J. "Mystery of Malcolm X." *Ebony*, September 1964, 42.

166 *"Malcolm believed the white press"*: "Cassius (Muhammad Ali) Speaks Out On Malcolm X." *New York Amsterdam News*, January 16, 1965, 1.

167 *"I haven't done anything,"*: Hauser, Thomas. *Muhammad Ali; His life and times*. New York: Touchstone, 1991, 110.

167 *Ali would become*: Ibid 488-490.

167 *would accuse Herbert and the sect*: Ibid 130-135.

167 *"their own narrow definition"*: Ibid 110.

167 *"if Muhammad Ali had stuck with Malcolm"*: Collins, Rodnell P. *Seventh Child; A family memoir of Malcolm X*. Secaucus, NJ: Birch Lane Press, 1998, 157.

167 *"A great number of young people"*: Hauser, Thomas. *Muhammad Ali; His life and times*. New York: Touchstone, 1991, 110-111.

167 *At the Chicago convention*: Muhammad, Elijah. "Our Day Is Near At Hand." *Muhammad Speaks*, March 13, 1964, 3.

167 *spilled onto the pages*: "Malcolm X's Role Dividing Muslims." *New York Times*, February 26, 1964.

167 *the first direct order*: Haley, Alex and X, Malcolm. *The Autobiography of Malcolm X*. New York: Ballantine, 1993, 315.

168 *"Hating me"*: Ibid, 306.

168 *"an imposter on the phone"*: Claude Lewis Interview.

168 *"he had a fit"*: Charles Kenyatta Interview.

168 *"will have to be judged"*: "Nationalist Pleads For Malcolm X." *New York Amsterdam News*, February 29, 1964.

169 *"psychological divorce"*: Haley, Alex and X, Malcolm. *The Autobiography of Malcolm X.* New York: Ballantine, 1993, 311.

169 *"Betty said nothing"*: Ibid, 312.

169 *Betty never doubted*: Shabazz, Betty. "The Legacy of My Husband." *Ebony*, June 1969, 176.

169 *"the Old Man ain't gonna let you"*: Charles Kenyatta Interview.

169 *"It never stopped him"*: Clarke, John Henrik, ed. *Malcolm X; The Man and His Times.* Trenton: Africa World Press, 1990, 140.

169 *Betty left out*: Lomax, Louis E. *To Kill A Black Man.* Los Angeles: Holloway House, 1968, 129.

169 *only his wife*: Haley, Alex and X, Malcolm. *The Autobiography of Malcolm X.* New York: Ballantine, 1993, 312.

169 *the bitter conversations*: Clarke, John Henrik, ed. *Malcolm X; The Man and His Times.* Trenton: Africa World Press, 1990, 140.

169 *incredible, torturous betrayal*: "Betty Shabazz Remembers Malcolm." *Like It Is.* WABC-TV, May 19, 1991.

170 *"I am prepared to cooperate"*: Handler, M.S. "Malcolm X Splits With Muhammad." *New York Times*, March 9, 1964.

171 *himself as an evangelist*: Griffin, Junius. "Malcolm X Plans Muslim Crusade." *New York Times*, April 3, 1964.

171 *"The Nation had paid the gas"*: Abdullah Abur Razzaq Interview.

171 *Days after the split*: Booker, James. "Malcolm X: 'Why I Quit and What I Plan Next.'" *New York Amsterdam News*, March 14, 1964, 51.

171 *"The final cord"*: Clarke, John Henrik, ed. *Malcolm X; The Man and his Times.* Trenton: Africa World Press, 1990, 142.

171 *"never dreamed"*: "Muhammad Rejects Force In Black Muslim Campaign." *The Philadelphia Evening Bulletin*, March 10, 1964.

171 *"There is no weeping"*: Samuels, Gertrude. "Feud Within the Black Muslims." *The New York Times Magazine*, March 22, 1964, 106.

172 *Muslim Mosque had siphoned*: Freudenheim, Milton. "Malcolm X Building Own Force in New York." *New York Herald News.* Undated. Freudenheim, Milton.

172 *"Whenever a brother"*: Crawford, Marc. "The Ominous Malcolm X Exits from the Muslims." *Life*, March 20, 1964, 40.

172 *"a rooster stop crowing"*: Samuels, Gertrude. "Feud Within the Black Muslims." *The New York Times Magazine*, March 22, 1964, 104.

172 *"twisting the white man's tail"*: Haley, Alex and X, Malcolm. *The Autobiography of Malcolm X.* New York: Ballantine, 1993, 466.

172 *reciting passages to reporters*: Freudenheim, Milton. "Malcolm X Building Own Force in New York." *New York Herald News.* Undated.

172 *a political party or an army*: Griffin, Junius. "Malcolm X Plans Muslim Crusade." *New York Times*, April 3, 1964.

172 *"uncontrollable elements"*: Booker, James. "Malcolm X Ignores Brother." *New York Amsterdam News*, April 4, 1964, 2.

172 *"We can't awaken"*: Freudenheim, Milton. "Malcolm X Building Own Force in New York." *New York Herald News.* Undated.

172 *"his Texas cotton patch"*: Handler, M.S. "Malcolm X Splits With Muhammad." *New York Times*, March

9, 1964.

173   *"Now you're going to get investigated"*: Cone, James H. *Martin & Malcolm & America*. Maryknoll: Orbis Books, 1991.

173   *"We do not know"*: Samuels, Gertrude. "Feud Within the Black Muslims." *The New York Times Magazine*, March 22, 1964, 107.

173   *"ultimately suicidal"*: "Rights Leaders Are Angered By Malcolm X Warning." *The Evening Bulletin*, March 13, 1964.

173   *"dark night of social disruption"*: Crawford, Marc. "The Ominous Malcolm X Exits from the Muslims." *Life*, March 20, 1964, 41.

173   *"A lot of people"*: Powledge, Fred. "Negroes Ponder Malcolm's Move." *New York Times*, March 15, 1964.

174   *"the tax dollars"*: Freudenheim, Milton. "Malcolm X Building Own Force in New York." *New York Herald News*. Undated.

174   *lectures before white college students*: Handler, M.S. "Malcolm X Splits With Muhammad." *New York Times*, March 9, 1964.

174   *"I haven't met any"*: Griffin, Junius. "Malcolm X Plans Muslim Crusade." *New York Times*, April 3, 1964.

174   *"let him stop exploiting"*: Breitman, George, ed. *Malcolm X Speaks*. New York: Grove, 1966, 25.

174   *Reporters fixed*: "Brother Malcolm: His Theme Now is Violence," *U.S. News & World Report*, March 30, 1964, 38.

174   *"When people would say 'violence'"*: From the transcript of the "Haley Book Interview with Betty Shabazz" conducted by Anne Romaine, January 27, 1989, Medgar Evers College, Brooklyn, New York. (Courtesy of Special Collections, Hoskins Library, the University of Tennessee at Knoxville).

174   *"as I live and breathe"*: Ibid.

174   *"the way I understood him"*: Edwards, Audrey and Susan L. Taylor. "Loving and Losing Malcolm." *Essence*, February 1992, 110.

174   *"I was there"*: "Betty Shabazz Remembers Malcolm." *Like It Is*. WABC-TV, May 19, 1991.

174   *"support his life mission"*: Ibid.

175   *he was not kidding*: Ibid, 109.

175   *"very, very vicious"*: Ibid.

175   *"black, white, green, or blue"*: Freudenheim, Milton. "Malcolm X Building Own Force in New York." *New York Herald News*. Undated.

175   *The Nation blamed Malcolm*: Poston, Ted. "Malcolm and the Muslims." *New York Post Daily Magazine*, February 22, 1965.

175   *Muhammad Speaks ran a cartoon*: "Malcolm Exposed by Brother." *Muhammad Speaks*, April 10, 1964, 3.

175   *he dismissed it publicly*: Booker, James. "Malcolm X Ignores Brother." *New York Amsterdam News*, April 4, 1964, 1.

175   *Her poise was unraveling*: Haley, Alex and X, Malcolm. *The Autobiography of Malcolm X*. New York: Ballantine, 1993, 416.

175   *"How is it possible"*: Ibid, 415.

176   *a dispassionate letter*: Booker, James. "Seek to Evict Malcolm X From Home In Queens." *New York Amsterdam News*, April 18, 1964, 1.

176   *"all she's put up with"*: Haley, Alex and X, Malcolm. *The Autobiography of Malcolm X*. New York: Ballantine, 1993, 428.

176   *not frightened for himself*: Ibid, 419.

177   *"the continuity and the image"*: Strickland, William. *Malcolm X, Make It Plain*. New York: Penguin,

1995, 173.

177 *"places we couldn't go"*: Hopkins, Ellen. "Their Fathers' Daughters." *Rolling Stone*, November 30, 1989, 84.

177 *"certain unanswered questions"*: Clarke, John Henrik, ed. *Malcolm X; The Man and his Times*. Trenton: Africa World Press, 1990, 140.

177 *In the weeks following*: Decaro, Louis A. *On the Side of My People; A religious life of Malcolm X*. New York: New York University, 1996, 200.

178 *Betty's resentment of the sibling*: Sarah Mitchell Interview.

178 *"Why, he can't even move"*: Perry, Bruce. *Malcolm; The Life of a Man Who Changed Black America*. New York: Station Hill, 1991, 319.

178 *"That second letter"*: Ahmed Osman Interview, January 29, 2001.

178 *Perhaps Betty*: Geracimos, Ann. "Introducing Mrs. Malcolm X." *New York Herald Tribune*, June 30, 1963.

178 *In the meantime*: Carson, Clayborne. *Malcolm X; The FBI file*. New York: Carroll & Graf, 1991, 266, 286; Haley, Alex and X, Malcolm. *The Autobiography of Malcolm X*. New York: Ballantine, 1993, xvi.

179 *On the plane to Jeddah*: Haley, Alex and X, Malcolm. *The Autobiography of Malcolm X*. New York: Ballantine, 1993, 341.

179 *That very morning*: Ibid, 340.

180 *"the men acted as if"*: Ibid, 341.

180 *what Betty would think*: Ibid, 344.

180 *"please phone my wife"*: April 25, 1964 Malcolm X letter to Alex Haley (courtesy of Gregory J. Reed).

180 *he had cabled her regularly*: Haley, Alex and X, Malcolm. *The Autobiography of Malcolm X*. New York: Ballantine, 1993, 237.

180 *"I could always expect a call"*: Poston, Ted. "Widow Talks of Her Life With Malcolm." *New York Post*, February 23, 1965, 2.

181 *"She hated me with a passion"*: Charles Kenyatta Interview.

181 *"a particular aversion to me"*: Abdullah Abur Razzaq Interview.

181 *"She was very pleased"*: Percy Sutton Interview.

182 *"Where is he now?"*: Strickland, William. *Malcolm X, Make It Plain*. New York: Penguin, 1995, 180.

182 *"The more he traveled"*: Ibid, 183.

182 *Black Muslim dissidents*: "Anti-White gang of 400 is Reported in Harlem." *New York Times*, May 6, 1964.

182 *Unaware of the absurd allegations*: Handler, M. S. "Malcolm X Pleased By Whites' Attitude on Trip to Mecca." *New York Times*, May 8, 1964, 1.

182 *Witnessing this*: Ibid.

183 *"an entire nation now lost"*: Goldman, Peter. *The Death and Life of Malcolm X*. University of Illinois Press, 1979, 169.

183 *"His attitude and ideas changed"*: Poston, Ted. "Widow Talks of Her Life with Malcolm." *New York Post*, February 23, 1965, 2.

183 *"Malcolm didn't hate whites"*: Knebel, Fletcher. "A Visit with the Widow of Malcolm X." *Look*, March 4, 1969, 75.

184 *one of the few figures who realized*: Jamal, Hakim A. *From the Dead Level*. New York: Random House, 1971, 216.

184 *telephone friendship*: Wilson, Gertrude. Mrs. Malcolm X—"A Friend Of Mine." *New York Amsterdam News*, February 27, 1965.

184 *bandied the notion*: Juanita Poitier Interview, July 31, 2000.

184 *portrayed his new philosophy*: Haley, Alex and X, Malcolm. *The Autobiography of Malcolm X*. New York:

Ballantine, 1993, 345.

184 *"Whatever Malcolm did"*: Clarke, John Henrik, ed. *Malcolm X; The Man and his Times*. Trenton: Africa World Press, 1990, 143.

184 *"A lot of people said"*: Jones, Marsha. "A Woman's View." *About…Time*, January 1993, *14*.

184 *"freedom for oppressed people"*: Clarke, John Henrik, ed. *Malcolm X; The Man and his Times*. Trenton: Africa World Press, 1990, 141.

185 *She attributed much*: Ibid.

185 *proposing a united front*: "Malcolm X Woos 2 Rights Leaders." *New York Times*, May 19, 1964.

185 *Having become a Sunni Muslim*: Shabazz, Betty. "The Legacy of My Husband." *Ebony*, June 1969, *180*.

185 *reciting Islamic prayers*: Haley, Alex and X, Malcolm. *The Autobiography of Malcolm X*. New York: Ballantine, 1993, 198.

186 *"He just signed his death warrant"*: Juanita Poitier Interview.

186 *"He metamorphosed"*: Maya Angelou Interview.

186 *Betty and the children never strayed far*: Angelou, Maya. *All God's Children Need Traveling Shoes*. New York: Random House, 1986, 139.

186 *The minister told the expatriates*: Angelou, Maya. *All God's Children Need Traveling Shoes*. New York: Random House, 1986, 131.

187 *Africans, he charged*: "My Next Move—Malcolm X an Exclusive Interview." *New York Amsterdam News*, May 30, 1964.

187 *as an informal ambassador*: "Malcolm Rejects Race Separation." *New York Times*, May 24, 1964.

187 *it was the greatest honor*: Haley, Alex and X, Malcolm. *The Autobiography of Malcolm X*. New York: Ballantine, 1993, 363.

187 *In letters home*: "Real Malcolm X." *New York Amsterdam News*, March 20, 1965; Booker, James. "Is Mecca Trip Changing Malcolm?" *New York Amsterdam News*, May 23, 1964, 14.

188 *she would deftly interpret*: "Betty Shabazz Remembers Malcolm." *Like It Is*. WABC-TV, May 19, 1991.

188 *a new communiqué*: Poston, Ted. "Widow Talks of Her Life With Malcolm." *New York Post*, February 23, 1965, 2.

188 *"I knew"*: Lewis, X. "Rips Malcolm's Treachery, Defection." *Muhammad Speaks*, May 8, 1964.

188 *She was jubilant*: Haley, Alex and X, Malcolm. *The Autobiography of Malcolm X*. New York: Ballantine, 1993, 419.

189 *"He looked brand new"*: Strickland, William. *Malcolm X, Make It Plain*. New York: Penguin, 1995, 183.

189 *Two hours later*: Haley, Alex and X, Malcolm. *The Autobiography of Malcolm X*. New York: Ballantine, 1993, 419.

189 *That evening at the Hotel Theresa*: Ibid, 420.

189 *"No longer do I subscribe"*: "Malcolm Rejects Race Separation." *New York Times*, May 24, 1964.

190 *"If whites want to help"*: "My Next Move—Malcolm X an Exclusive Interview." *New York Amsterdam News*, May 30, 1964.

190 *"perhaps we need some blood brothers"*: Breitman, George. *Malcolm X Speaks*. New York: Grove Weidenfeld, 1990, 65-66.

190 *He said his travels*: "My Next Move—Malcolm X an Exclusive Interview." *New York Amsterdam News*, May 30, 1964; Matthews, Les. "Malcolm X Questions LBJ." *New York Amsterdam News*, March 30, 1964; "Malcolm X Objective—African Aid for Negroes." *New York Herald Tribune*, May 22, 1964.

190 *"22 million American Negroes"*: "Malcolm Rejects Race Separation." *New York Times*, May 24, 1964.

191 *"It was primarily a non-white problem"*: Clarke, John Henrik, ed. *Malcolm X; The Man and his Times*. Trenton: Africa World Press, 1990, 141.

191 *"It's the same old Malcolm"*: X, Louis. "Fall of a Minister." *Muhammad Speaks*, June 5, 1964.

191 *"had been intelligent enough"*: Clarke, John Henrik, ed. *Malcolm X; The Man and his Times*. Trenton: Africa World Press, 1990, 142.

191 *Malcolm had not wanted*: "My Next Move—Malcolm X an Exclusive Interview." *New York Amsterdam News*, May 30, 1964.

192 *Within hours*: World Telegram, June 18, 1964.

192 *wreathed by his men*: Blackman, M.C. "8 Guards, 32 Police for Malcolm." *New York Herald Tribune*, June 16, 1964.

192 *"they was going to testify"*: Charles Kenyatta Interview.

192 *"I told her the difficulties"*: Percy Sutton Interview.

192 *The defense had to prove*: Goldman, Peter. *The Death and Life of Malcolm X*. University of Illinois Press, 1979, 191.

192 *Betty always insisted*: Frady, Marshall. "The Children of Malcolm." *New Yorker*, October 12, 1992, 75.

193 *"The judge really favored"*: Percy Sutton Interview.

193 *another counterpunch*: Cahill, Edith J. and Erwin Savelson. "Malcolm X: Man Marked for Death." *New York World Telegram*, 1.

193 *The outburst did not shift*: "Another Month For Malcolm X" *New York Herald Tribune*. June 17, 1964.

193 *He finally ordered the eviction*: "Order Eviction of Malcolm X," *New York Amsterdam News*, September 5, 1964, 1.

193 *As their case had begun to unravel*: Ibid.

193 *"Muhammad was nobody"*: Blackman, M.C. "8 Guards, 32 Police for Malcolm." *New York Herald Tribune*, June 16, 1964.

193 *"I'm not disturbed"*: Percy Sutton Interview.

CHAPTER 9: THE DEATH CARD

195 *"The vigilance extends to his home"*: Cahill, Edith J. and Erwin Savelson. "Malcolm X: Man Marked for Death." *New York World Telegram*, 1.

196 *"Get in the restaurant!"*: Goldman, Peter. *The Death and Life of Malcolm X*. University of Illinois Press, 1979, 199; Carroll, Maurice C. "The Near-Battle of Black Muslims." *New York Herald Tribune*, June 18, 1964.

196 *"I've gotten all the publicity"*: Carroll, Maurice C. "The Near-Battle of Black Muslims." *New York Herald Tribune*, June 18, 1964.

196 *"There was a time bomb"*: James Campbell Interview, March 27, 2002.

197 *"It was a terror-filled time"*: Safiya Bandele Interview.

197 *Betty had had to vaccinate*: Perry, Bruce. *Malcolm; The Life of a Man Who Changed Black America*. New York: Station Hill, 1991, 235.

197 *The procedure was legitimate*: Ruth Summerford Interview.

197 *There was a soft exchange*: Massaquoi, Hans J. "Mystery of Malcolm X." *Ebony*, September 1964, 40.

198 *"We don't have to kill him"*: "Malcolm X to Elijah: Let's End the Fighting." *New York Post*, June 26, 1964.

198 *A dream organization to align Africa and African-America*: Herman Ferguson Interview, February 12, 2000.

198 *Its base, however, was pure Malcolm*: Breitman, George, ed. *By Any Means Necessary*. New York: Pathfinder, 1970, 55-90.

198 *"There is some person who wants to be what I am"*: Goldman, Peter. *The Death and Life of Malcolm X*. University of Illinois Press, 1979, 202.

199 *"If it were not for the Messenger"*: Shabazz, John. "Muslim Minister Writes to Malcolm." *Muhammad Speaks*, July 3, 1964.

199 *"Two-legged dogs"*: Massaquoi, Hans J. "Mystery of Malcolm X." *Ebony*, September 1964, 39.

199 *The Mississippi Freedom Summer had opened with bombings:* Williams, Juan. *Eyes on the Prize.* New York: Viking, 1987, 238.

199 *Amicably observe an NAACP convention: New York Times,* June 28, 1964, 1.

200 *The elder had fathered four children: Washington Post,* July 4, 1964, 5.

200 *His "talking stick" at the ready: New York Daily News,* February 15, 1965, 5.

200 *"If you're in the middle of the Atlantic":* "Betty Shabazz Remembers Malcolm." *Like It Is.* WABC-TV, May 19, 1991.

200 *"Just give him this message":* Evanzz, Karl. *The Judas Factor.* New York: Thunder's Mouth Press, 1992, 240.

200 *"It was constant":* Muriel Feelings Interview, April 6, 2000.

201 *"Sometimes we would say something threatening":* Evanzz, Karl. *The Messenger; The rise and fall of Elijah Muhammad.* New York: Panheon, 1999, 294.

201 *"Curse that phone until they hung up":* Maya Angelou Interview.

201 *"Honey, come on over here":* Hopkins, Ellen. "Their Fathers' Daughters." *Rolling Stone,* November 30, 1989, 84.

201 *"Someone tried to kill their father":* Shabazz, Betty. "The Legacy of My Husband." *Ebony,* June 1969, 176.

201 *Orderly and "semi-suburban":* Muriel Feelings Interview.

202 *"Her concern was not just in losing him":* Percy Sutton Interview.

202 *"I couldn't bring myself to listen":* Clarke, John Henrik, ed. *Malcolm X; The Man and His Times.* Trenton: Africa World Press, 1990, 124.

202 *"It's evaporated. I don't know where!":* Haley, Alex and X, Malcolm. *The Autobiography of Malcolm X.* New York: Ballantine, 1993, 427.

202 *Battles "material as well as spiritual":* Decaro, Louis A. *On the Side of My People; A Religious Life of Malcolm X.* New York: New York University, 1996, 239.

202 *"She saw her husband being destroyed":* Herman Ferguson Interview.

203 *The importance of giving freedom to the woman: By Any Means Necessary.* New York: Pathfinder, 1992, 202.

204 *The secular OAAU partly to transcend patriarchy:* Herman Ferguson Interview.

204 *"Malcolm valued women's opinions":* Maya Angelou Interview.

204 *"A woman's role should be determined":* Shabazz, Betty. "The Legacy of My Husband." *Ebony,* June 1969, 180.

204 *"Be an intelligent human being":* Breitman, George, ed. *Malcolm X Speaks.* New York: Grove Weidenfeld, 1990, 135.

204 *Malcolm would not hear of it:* Martin Luther King also had, "all through his life, an ambivalent attitude toward the role of women," his wife Coretta later recalled. King viewed women as intellectual equals of men, but saw *his* wife exclusively as "a homemaker and a mother for his children." (King, Coretta Scott. *My Life with Martin Luther King, Jr.* New york: Holt, Rinehart & Winston, 1969, 60, 91).

204 *"She longed to participate in the movement":* Sara Mitchell Interview.

204 *Offering children and adult one-hour Saturday classes:* Bailey, Peter. "Education: Liberation School." *OAAU Newsletter,* August 3, 1964, 5.

205 *"I can't even go to the store":* Muriel Feelings Interview.

205 *"haley didn't get any big secrets":* From the transcript of the "Haley Book Interview with Betty Shabazz" conducted by Anne Romaine, January 27, 1989, Medgar Evers College, Brooklyn, New York. (Courtesy of Special Collections, Hoskins Library, the University of Tennessee at Knoxville).

205 *"He told bad things about himself":* Decaro, Louis A. *On the Side of My People; A Religious Life of Malcolm X.* New York: New York University, 1996, 251.

206 *"Safe passages"from the minister's dictations*: From the transcript of the "Haley Book Interview with Betty Shabazz" conducted by Anne Romaine, January 27, 1989, Medgar Evers College, Brooklyn, New York. (Courtesy of Special Collections, Hoskins Library, the University of Tennessee at Knoxville).

206 *"Everybody's talking to her"*: Yuri Kochiama Interview.

206 *"She felt a responsibility to be brave"*: Muriel Feelings Interview.

206 *"She had to play the traditional role"*: Ibid.

207 *"He knew how charming, how slick Elijah was"*: Charles Kenyatta Interview.

207 *"He wanted her to stay home"*: Sara Mitchell Interview.

207 *"Anything that Betty wants please get it"*: Abduallah Abdur Razzaq Interview.

207 *"Just call me brother"*: Sara Mitchell Interview.

207 *Self-sacrificing impulse and devotion*: Booker, James. "Malcolm Died Broke." *New York Amsterdam News*, February 27, 1965, 2.

208 A *"benign jealousy" over Malcolm*: Muriel Feelings Interview.

208 *"There were rumors and counter-rumors"*: Herman Ferguson Interview.

208 *"There was a culture of confusion"*: James Campbell Interview; Charles Kenyatta Interview.

209 *Ask the minister himself*: According to biographer Bruce Perry, Malcolm was miffed when he returned from overseas and discovered that Betty had been showing up at his Hotel Theresa office to "check on things." (Perry, Bruce. *Malcolm; The Life of A Man Who Changed Black America*; New York, Station Hill Press, 1991, 319).

209 *"Keep my mouth shut"*: Abdullah Abdur Razzaq Interview.

209 *"Few women who weren't in love with my husband"*: Muriel Feelings Interview; Sara Mitchell Interview; Abdullah Abdur Razzaq Interview.

209 *She could hear him reject the admirers*: Muriel Feelings Interview.

209 *"They paid money to some ladies"*: "Dr. Betty Shabazz's Final Words." Interview with Bernard White and Amy Goodman, Pacifica Radio, WBAI, New York City, May 19, 1997.

210 *"He only spoke of his wife"*: "Lawyer Says Malcolm Was Poisoned." *New York Amsterdam News*, March 13, 1965.

210 *She wrote back that very day*: "Betty Shabazz Remembers Malcolm." *Like It Is*. WABC-TV, May 19, 1991.

210 *"Sometimes you have to watch what you say to men"*: Sara Mitchell Interview; Muriel Feelings Interview.

210 *"Our problems are your problems"*: Handler, M. S. "Malcolm X Seeks U.N. Negro Debate." *New York Times*, August 13, 1964.

211 *Rejected the bill as a "rubber check"*: "Rights Bill Hit By Malcolm X." *Philadelphia Inquirer*, June 20, 1964.

211 *The conference "relieved and delighted" him*: Clarke, John Henrik, ed. *Malcolm X; The Man and His Times*. Trenton: Africa World Press, 1990, 300-301.

212 *Political strategies Malcolm had championed*: "Malcolm X Claims Role In Attacks on U.S. at UN." *New York Times*, January 2, 1965.

212 *The minister and his d"terrorist" loyalists' hatred*: Bartlett, Charles. "Malcolm X, An Angry Extremist." *The Evening Star*, July 28, 1964.

212 *"Malcolm had no business in Africa"*: Lanker, Brian and Barbara Summers, ed. *I Dream A World; Portraits of Black Women Who Changed America*. New York: Stewart, Tabori & Chang, 1999, 84; Handler, M. S. "Malcolm X Seeks U.N. Negro Debate." *New York Times*, August 13, 1964.

213 *Malcolm's crusade was both legal and noble*: "Betty Shabazz Remembers Malcolm." *Like It Is*. WABC-TV, May 19, 1991.

213 *Doctors pumped his stomach*: Muriel Feelings Interview.

213 *The minister worried:* Donations and the largesse of the states Malcolm visited apparently enabled the tour.

213 *I'm trying to weigh everthing objectively:* September 22, 1964, Malcolm X letter to M. S. Handler (Alex Haley papers, courtesy of Schomburg Center for Research in Black Culture, New York).

214 *"We shared a conern about his safety":* Collins, Rodnell P. *Seventh Child; A Family Memoir of Malcolm X.* Secaucus, NJ: Birch Lane Press, 1998, 177.

214 *"Malcolm is worthy of death":* X, Louis. "Boston Minister Tells of Malcolm—Muhammad's Biggest Hypocrite." *Muhammad Speaks,* December 4, 1964, 11.

214 *"She remained firm in the faith":* Lomax, Louis E. *To Kill A Black Man.* Los Angeles: Holloway House, 1968, 200.

215 *"The impression that I'm jiving":* Herman, David. "Malcolm X's Last Meeting." *The Militant,* March 1, 1965, 2.

215 *"They all wanted to jump him":* Charles Kenyatta Interview.

215 *"Put you on a cross!":* Robert Haggins Interview.

215 *"Malcolm could never hide":* Davis, Ossie and Ruby Dee. *In This Life Together.* New York: William Morrow, 1998, 308.

215 *"Bring Betty and the chilren":* Goldman, Peter. *The Death and Life of Malcolm X.* University of Illinois Press, 1979, 220.

215 *"They were crazy about him":* Claude Lewis Interview; Sara Mitchell Interview.

215 *He was prepared for the worst:* Mayfield, Julian. "Malcolm X: 1925-1965." *The African Review,* May 1965, 8.

216 *"Malcolm wanted to die":* Herman Ferguson Interview; Charles Kenyatta Interview; Abdllah Abdur Razzaq Interview.

216 *Take a breather from the struggle:* Collins, Rodnell P. *Seventh Child; A Family Memoir of Malcolm X.* Secaucus, NJ: Birch Lane Press, 1998, 180.

216 *"It was another universe":* Maya Angelou Interview.

216 *"We are addicted to America":* Collins, Rodnell P. *Seventh Child; A Family Memoir of Malcolm X.* Secaucus, NJ: Birch Lane Press, 1998, 184.

217 *They were unable to reconcile:* James Smalls Interview, March 19, 2000.

217 *"Malcolm had no friends":* Charles Kenyatta Interview.

217 *"She was a loyal soldier":* Percy Sutton Interview; Claude Lewis Interview.

217 *"The only person I'd trust with my life":* David, Gallen, ed. *Malcolm X; As They Knew Him.* New York: Ballantine Books, 1992, 271.

217 *"This one will be the boy!":* Haley, Alex and X, Malcolm. *The Autobiography of Malcolm X.* New York: Ballantine, 1993, 431.

218 *"He was always trying to pacify her":* Sara Mitchell Interview.

218 *"But it was his law":* Charles Kenyatta Interview; Abdullah Abdur Razzaq Interview; Lomax, Louis E. *To Kill A Black Man.* Los Angeles: Holloway House, 1968, 182.

218 *"He was going to get it":* Clarke, John Henrik, ed. *Malcolm X; The Man and His Times.* Trenton: Africa World Press, 1990, 142.

219 *"Don't look back and don't cry":* Edwards, Audrey and Susan L. Taylor. "Loving and Losing Malcolm." *Essence,* February 1992, 110.

219 *"I just closed my eyes":* Clarke, John Henrik, ed. *Malcolm X; The Man and His Times.* Trenton: Africa World Press, 1990, 124.

219 *"He knew he was to be martyred":* Ahmed Osman Interview.

219 *"No man will want you with all these children":* Norma Johnson Interview.

219 *"Somebody's going to do something":* Claude Lewis Interview.

219 *Malcolm compiled a list:* Parks, Gordon. *Voices in the Mirror.* New York: Doubleday, 1990, 235; Lomax TKABM, 229.

219 *"Running my husband all over the country"*: Hauser, Thomas. *Muhammad Ali; His Life and Times.* New York: Touchstone, 1991, 110.

220 *"He learned some things the governement did not want"*: Knebel, Fletcher. "A Visit with the Widow of Malcolm X." *Look*, March 4, 1969, 74.

220 To *"even the score" with white aggressors*: Wilkins, Roy. "Mau Mau Idea Will Sputter and Die." *The Evening Bulletin*, January 6, 1964.

220 *"I had planned to visit him in jail"*: King, Coretta Scott. *My Life With Martin Luther King, Jr.* New York: Holt, Rinehart and Winston, 1969, 255-256.

221 *Bodyguards and police kept him cordoned*: "Malcolm X Starts Campaign; Police Outnumber Audience." *Philadelphia Inquirer*, January 15, 1965.

221 *Stop frisking spectators at the door*: Herman Ferguson Interview.

221 *"I feel like I'm on a tightrope"*: Mitchell, Sara. *Shepherd of Black Sheep.* Macon: Sarah Mitchell, 1981, 19.

222 *"The French government is worth less than a penny"*: "Malcolm X Barred By French Security." *New York Times*, February 10, 1965.

222 *"Powerful forces were beginning to move against him"*: Clarke, John Henrik, ed. *Malcolm X; The Man and His Times.* Trenton: Africa World Press, 1990, 142.

222 *"I've been making a serious mistake"*: Herman Ferguson Interview.

222 *She was having a nervous breakdown*: Evanzz, Karl. *The Messenger; The Rise and Fall of Elijah Muhammad.* New York: Panheon, 1999, 318.

223 *Again, Macolm bounded into the house*: Knebel, Fletcher. "A Visit with the Widow of Malcolm X." *Look*, March 4, 1969, 77.

223 *Our home was burning down aound us*: Haley, Alex and X, Malcolm. *The Autobiography of Malcolm X.* New York: Ballantine, 1993, 3.

223 *"I learned how great his strength was"*: Edwards, Audrey and Susan L. Taylor. "Loving and Losing Malcolm." *Essence*, February 1992, 109.

223 *"My mother's like that, too"*: Hopkins, Ellen. "Their Fathers' Daughters." *Rolling Stone*, November 30, 1989, 84.

223 *"Imagine anybody being that cruel"*: Edwards, Audrey and Susan L. Taylor. "Loving and Losing Malcolm." *Essence*, February 1992, 109.

224 *Malcolm thought it was the Muslims too*: Goldman, Peter. *The Death and Life of Malcolm X.* University of Illinois Press, 1979, 263.

224 *"Because my wife understands"*: Breitman, George, ed. *Malcolm X Speaks.* New York: Grove Weidenfeld, 1990, 158.

224 *"I have no compassion or mercy or forgiveness"*: "Malcolm Accuses Muslims of Blaze; They Point to Him." *New York Times*, February 16, 1965.

225 *"We knew it didn't belong there"*: Evanzz, Karl. *The Judas Factor.* New York: Thunder's Mouth Press, 1992, 292.

225 *Charged Black Islam with the firebombing*: "Bottle of Gasoline Found on a Dresser in Malcolm X Home." *New York Times*, February 17, 1965.

225 *"We have money tied up here"*: "Malcolm X, Family Flee Fire Bomb Attack on Home." *New York Herald Tribune*, February 15, 1965.

225 *Powerless to grant any further stays*: Abdullah Abdur Razzaq Interview.

225 *He took Betty house shopping*: Haley, Alex and X, Malcolm. *The Autobiography of Malcolm X.* New York: Ballantine, 1993, 437.

225 *Draw up a will*: Goldman, Peter. *The Death and Life of Malcolm X.* University of Illinois Press, 1979, 265.

226 *"We'll all be together"*: Haley, Alex and X, Malcolm. *The Autobiography of Malcolm X.* New York:

Ballantine, 1993, 437.

226 *"Every time I look at her she gets pregnant!"*: James Campbell Interview.

226 *"Of course it won't!"*: Ibid, 439.

226 *"It was a very warm conversation"*: "Malcolm X" Warner Brothers documentary, Marvin Worth Productions, 1972.

226 *"Wake up, brother"*: Morrison, Allan. "Who Killed Malcolm X?" *Ebony*, October 1965, 135.

227 *"It was still an exciting adventure"*: Strickland, William. *Malcolm X, Make It Plain*. New York: Penguin, 1995, 203.

227 *"We were seated near the front"*: Edwards, Audrey and Susan L. Taylor. "Loving and Losing Malcolm." *Essence*, February 1992, 110.

227 With the exception of two uniformed officers: Goldman, Peter. *The Death and Life of Malcolm X*. University of Illinois Press, 1979, 269.

228 *"Y'all poppin' game!"*: Charles Kenyatta Interview.

228 *"Why haven't you told me he wasn't coming?"*: Abdullah Abdur Razzaq Interview.

229 *"He died of a broken heart"*: Goldman, Peter. *The Death and Life of Malcolm X*. University of Illinois Press, 1979, 273; Haley, Alex and X, Malcolm. *The Autobiography of Malcolm X*. New York: Ballantine, 1993, 442; Sara Mitchell Interview.

229 *"No one else in there they'd be shooting at"*: Frady, Marshall. "The Children of Malcolm." *New Yorker*, October 12, 1992, 78.

229 *"If he would only fall"*: Herman Ferguson Interview.

229 *"They never actually saw it"*: Ibid.

229 *"Like they were posing for a picture"*: Herman Ferguson Interview.

230 *"Are they going to kill everyone?"*: Goldman, Peter. *The Death and Life of Malcolm X*. University of Illinois Press, 1979, 274.

230 Reuben Francis shot one of the gunmen: Ibid, 274-276.

230 Six or seven of his disciples surrounded him: Kihss, Peter. "Malcolm X Shot to Death at Rally Here." *New York Times*, February 22, 1965, 10.

231 *"You gonna blow up his lungs"*: Sister Khadiyyah Interview.

231 *"He can't see you like this!"*: Ibid.

231 *"Interested in getting papers out of his pocket"*: Murray, David and Ralph Blumenfeld. "Cops Seek Muslim Link in Killing." *New York Post*, February 22, 1965.

231 *"He's gone! And I'm pregnant!"*: Clarke, John Henrik, ed. *Malcolm X; The Man and his Times*. Trenton: Africa World Press, 1990, 96.

231 She stood there numbly, feeding the infant: Muriel Feelings Interview; Yuri Kochiama Interview.

231 *"Suddenly I feel too old"*: Hopkins, Ellen. "Their Fathers' Daughters." *Rolling Stone*, November 30, 1989, 84.

231 The police got Malcolm onto a stretcher: Mitchell, Sara. "I Remember Malcolm X…" *Georgia Informer*, March 1990, 4.

232 *"I had to be strong for her"*: Jean Reynolds Interview.

232 Betty had wept hysterically: "I Saw the Killing from the 12th Row." *Afro-American*, February 27, 1965, 10.

232 *"Malcolm X is dead"*: Todd, George. "Geo, Todd and Malcolm X." *New York Amsterdam News*, February 27, 1965, 2.

232 *"They took his heart out"*: Sister Khadiyyah Interview.

233 The club's annual dance: Kihss, Peter. "Malcolm X Shot to Death at Rally Here." *New York Times*, February 22, 1965, 10.

233 *"The niggers did it, Lomax"*: Lomax, Louis E. *To Kill A Black Man*. Los Angeles: Holloway House, 1968, 248.

CHAPTER 10: AFTER THE WINTER

235 "[The black woman] had nothing": Morrison, Toni. "What the Black Woman Thinks About Women's Lib." New York Times Magazine, August 22, 1971, 63.

236 "He's just upset about your father": Ibid.

238 "The whole room was a wailing woman": Neal, Larry. "New Space/The Growth of Black Consciousness in the Sixties." in Floyd B. Barbour, ed. The Black Seventies.. Boston: Porter Sargent, 1970, 26.

238 "What are we gonna do": "Follower of Fallen Chief Fear-Stricken." The Philadelphia Tribune, February 23, 1965, 2.

238 The onyx ring inscribed with "Allah": Karim, Benjamin. Remembering Malcolm. New York: Ballantine, 197.

238 "The best year of my life": Goldman, Peter. The Death and Life of Malcolm X. University of Illinois Press, 1979, 270; Clarke 97, 105.

238 "I'll tell you this": Montgomery, Paul. "Harlem is Quiet as News Spreads." New York Times, February 22, 1965, 11.

238 The noose that finally claimed Malcolm: Gregory, Dick. Up From Nigger. New York: Stein and Day, 1976, 84-85.

238 But all was quiet: Ibid.

236 "Don't forget to teach": Wilson, Gertrude. "Mrs. Malcolm X—A Friend of Mine." New York Amsterdam News, February 27, 1965, 37.

236 "They've taken him away": Wilson, Gertrude. "Mrs. Malcolm X—A Friend of Mine." New York Amsterdam News, February 27, 1965, 37.

237 "Is Daddy coming back": Parks, Gordon. "The Violent End of A Man Called Malcolm X." Life, March 5, 1965, 30.

237 Ella Collins eyed her sister-in-law: Collins, Rodnell. Seventh Child. New York: Birch Lane Press, 186.

237 Only pretending to be dead: Finke, Nikki. "A Certain Peacefulness." Los Angeles Times, January 8, 1989.

237 "Dear Daddy, I love you": Haley, Alex and X, Malcolm. The Autobiography of Malcolm X. New York: Ballantine, 1993, 447.

237 "I hope you get your wish": Parks, Gordon. "The Violent End of A Man Called Malcolm X." Life, March 5, 1965, 30.

238 Would take his life: Parks, Gordon. Voices in the Mirror. New York: Doubleday, 1990, 234-235.

238 "Thank you for coming": Wilson, Gertrude. "Mrs. Malcolm X—A Friend of Mine." New York Amsterdam News, February 27, 1965, 37.

239 Clamored for her attention: Kihss, Peter. "Malcolm X Shot to Death at Rally Here." New York Times, February 22, 1965, 10.

240 Await his widow: Goldman, Peter. The Death and Life of Malcolm X. University of Illinois Press, 1979, 287.

240 Betty almost crumpled: Collins, Rodnell. Seventh Child. New York: Birch Lane Press, 186.

240 "You'll have to talk to my attorney": Michaelson, Judy and Carl J. Pelleck. "The Widow's Ordeal—Identifying His Body." New York Post, February 22, 1965, 2.

240 Talmage Hayer lay writhing: Talese, Gay. "Man Beaten by Crowd Refuses to Talk." New York Times, February 22, 1965, 10.

241 Hayer was not talking: Goldman, Peter. The Death and Life of Malcolm X. University of Illinois Press, 1979, 288.

241 Investigators now had names: Kihss, Peter. "Malcolm X Shot to Death at Rally Here." New York Times, February 22, 1965, 10.

241 Black protest generals rushed to condemn: Robinson, Douglas. "Rights Leaders Decry 'Violence.'" New York Times, February 22, 1965, 11.

242 *"We are not afraid"*: Moore, Michael. "Muhammad Under Guard; Fear Reprisal." *New York Post*, February 22, 1965, 2.

243 *A cloak of hysteria had descended*: Guard Malcolm's Bier." *New York Post*, February 23, 1965, 2.

243 *"They wanted to execute him"*: Abdullah Abdur Razzaq Interview.

243 *Tensions mounted on Tuesday*: Ibid; Gross, Kenneth and Ralph Blumenfeld. "Blast Wrecks Muslim HQ Here." *New York Post*, February 23, 1965, 3.

243 *"You could find very few"*: Strickland, William. *Malcolm X, Make It Plain*. New York: Penguin, 1995, 211.

244 *"I took the Greyhound"*: Ahmed Osman Interview.

244 *Abomination to Islam*: Haley, Alex and X, Malcolm. *The Autobiography of Malcolm X*. New York: Ballantine, 1993, 447-448.

244 *Malcolm's last rites were kosher*: "Watch Kept In New York and Chicago." *Evening Star*, February 23, 1965; Jaaber, Heshaam. *The Final Chapter...I Buried Malcolm X*. Jersey City, NJ: New Mind Productions, 1992, 69.

245 *Refuse the burden of laying him down*: "15 Harlem Protestant Churches Vetoed X Rites," *Afro American*, March 6, 1965.

245 *It would have to do*: Haley, Alex and X, Malcolm. *The Autobiography of Malcolm X*. New York: Ballantine, 1993, 450.

245 *"I founded Faith Temple"*: "Bishop Defies Threat to Church and Home Over Malcolm X Funeral." *Philadelphia Tribune*, March 6, 1965, 2.

246 *"They can contact my husband's lawyer"*: Poston, Ted. "Widow Talks of Her Life with Malcolm." *New York Post*. February 23, 1965, 2.

247 *"I saw that boy speak"*: Nadle, Marlene. "Burying Malcolm X." Village Voice, March 4, 1965; *New York Herald Tribune*, February 27, 1965; "He Made Us All Feel Alive." *The Militant*, March 1, 1965, 4.

247 *"She handles herself beautifully"*: Haley, Alex and X, Malcolm. *The Autobiography of Malcolm X*. New York: Ballantine, 1993, 449-450; DeCaro, Louis A. *On the Side of My People*. New York: New York University, 1996, 290; Poston, Ted. "New Clue Bared On Malcolm." *New York Post*, February 26, 1965, 3.

247 *"The most portentous event"*: Haley, Alex and X, Malcolm. *The Autobiography of Malcolm X*. New York: Ballantine, 1993, 450-451.

247 *"If you're looking for some reading"*: Hicks, James. "Another Angle; Malcolm X." *New York Amsterdam News*, February 27, 1965, 9.

247 *"Even his sharpest critics"*: "The Murder of Malcolm X." *New York Post*, February 22, 1965, 18.

248 *"A socialist weekly"*: Smith, W. G. "Who Killed Malcolm X?" *The Spark*, February 26, 1965, 1.

248 *"A political killing with international implications"*: Goldman, Peter. *The Death and Life of Malcolm X*. University of Illinois Press, 1979, 300.

248 *"It is because of you"*: "He Made Us All Feel Alive." *The Militant*, March 1, 1965, 4.

248 *"The true rebel leader"*: Mayfield, Julian. "Malcolm X: 1925-1965." *The African Review*, May 1965, 9.

248 *"The violence of the world"*: He Made Us All Feel Alive." *The Militant*, March 1, 1965, 4.

248 *Newspapers around the world*: Ibid.

248 *"A thorn in the side"*: "China Reds Say Malcolm X Was Slain by 'Imperialists.' *New York Times*, February 25, 1965, 18.

248 *"There was concern"*: Kihss, Peter. "Hunt for Killers in Malcolm Case 'On Right Track'." *New York Times*, February 25, 1965, 1.

248 *Cannonade of less flattering words*: Warren, Robert Penn. "Malcolm X: Mission and Meaning." *The American Literary Anthology*. New York: Random House, 1969.

248 *"He belonged to the past"*: Young, Whitney. "To Be Equal." *Afro American*, March 6, 1965, 17.

249 *"His own overwhelming talent"*: "Death of a Desperado." *Newsweek*, March 8, 1965, 25.

249 *"His heart filled with hate"*: Gregory, John Michael. "Malcolm X Viewed Death as Path to Martyrdom." *Philadelphia Daily News*, February 23, 1965.

249 *"However deep his dedication"*: "Malcolm X." *The Evening Star*, February 24, 1965.

249 *"They were afraid to match him"*: Booker, James. "Talk With Mrs. Malcolm X!" *New York Amsterdam News*, March 13, 1965, 4.

249 Liberals *"are opposed to assassination"*: "Malcolm X." *Spartacist*, May-June, 1965.

249 *"We did not want to kill Malcolm"*: Goldman, Peter. *The Death and Life of Malcolm X*. University of Illinois Press, 1979, 301; "Chicago—Malcolm's Brothers Pass Up Funeral." *New York Herald Tribune*, February 27, 1965; Haley, 457.

250 *Philbert and Wilfred's final repudiation*: Evanzz, Karl. *The Messenger*. New York: Pantheon Books, 1999, 325.

250 *Schizophrenic funeral*: Nadle, Marlene. "Burying Malcolm X." *Village Voice*, March 4, 1965, 1; Ahmed Osman Interview.

251 *Malcolm was thus swaddled*: Ibid.

251 *"The press was trying to strip him"*: Goldman, Peter. *The Death and Life of Malcolm X*. University of Illinois Press, 1979, 302-303; Ahmed Osman Interview.

251 *Muslims are not to weep*: Jaaber, Heshaam. *The Final Chapter...I Buried Malcolm X*. Jersey City, NJ: New Mind Productions, 1992, 52-53; Ahmed Osman Interview.

251 *Shoppers stayed away*: *New York Herald Tribune*, February 27, 1965.

251 *"Steady, Eddie!"*: "Steady, Eddie!" *New York Amsterdam News*, February 27, 1965, 1.

252 *"It looked like a town under siege"*: Ahmed Osman Interview.

252 *"It was fourteen degrees out"*: Goldman, Peter. *The Death and Life of Malcolm X*. University of Illinois Press, 1979, 302.

252 *A thousand mourners crammed*: Nadle, Marlene. "Burying Malcolm X." *Village Voice*, March 4, 1965, 10.

253 *Phenomenally beautiful and terribly alone*: Alpern, David M. "1,000 Mourners Bid Malcolm X Sorrowful Adieu." *Afro American*, March 6, 1965, 2; Foley, Eileen. "Our Children Hold the Key to a Future Free of Killings, Malcolm's Widow Says." *Philadelphia Inquirer*, May 24, 1972; Frady, Marshall. "The Children of Malcolm." *New Yorker*, October 12, 1992, 78; Herman Ferguson Interview.

253 *"I was a man with whom nobody"*: Davis, Ossie and Ruby Dee. *In This Life Together*. New York: William Morrow, 1998, 311.

253 *"The death of Malcolm X"*: Haley, Alex and X, Malcolm. *The Autobiography of Malcolm X*. New York: Ballantine, 1993, 461.

253 *Consecrated his remains*: Halstead, Fred. "He Would Not Bow His Head to Any Tyrant." *The Militant*, March 8, 1965, 1, 5.

254 *Here, at this final hour*: Haley, Alex and X, Malcolm. *The Autobiography of Malcolm X*. New York: Ballantine, 1993, 461-462.

254 *Finally she broke*: Nadle, Marlene. "Burying Malcolm X." *Village Voice*, March 4, 1965, 10.

254 *"I was genuinely impressed"*: Booker, James. "Talk With Mrs. Malcolm X!" *New York Amsterdam News*, March 13, 1965, 4.

255 *More than 25,000 onlookers*: Queen, Bob. "Threats Fade at Funeral." *Philadelphia Afro-American*, March 6, 1965, 7.

255 *EL-HAJJ MALIK EL-SHABAZZ*: Goldman, Peter. *The Death and Life of Malcolm X*. University of Illinois Press, 1979, 303.

255 *"We'll bury him first"*: Ibid; "Thousands Attend Rites for Malcolm X." *Sunday Star*, February 28, 1965, B-4; Alpern, David M. "1,000 Mourners Bid Malcolm X Sorrowful Adieu." *Afro American*, March 6, 1965, 1.

255 *Betty did not sleep:* L and L 110.

256 *"He tried to impress on his children":* Booker, James. "Talk With Mrs. Malcolm X!" *New York Amsterdam News,* March 13, 1965, 4.

256 *The police had been advertising:* Kihss, Peter. "Hunt for Killers in Malcolm Case 'On Right Track'." *New York Times,* February 25, 1965, 1.

256 *"I ain't seen nothing":* Goldman, Peter. *The Death and Life of Malcolm X.* University of Illinois Press, 1979, 290.

256 *Butler was already facing charges:* Ibid, 299; "Return Indictments in Malcolm Murder." *Afro American,* March 20, 1965, 1.

257 *Oozing hostility:* Poston, Ted. "New Clue Bared On Malcolm." *New York Post,* February 26, 1965, 3; Gross, Kenneth and Ralph Blumenfeld. "Blast Wrecks Muslim HQ Here." *New York Post,* February 23, 1965, 3.

257 *She told the officer:* March 1, 1965 New York Police Department Supplementary Complaint Report filed by Officer James Rushin; Goldman, Peter. *The Death and Life of Malcolm X.* University of Illinois Press, 1979, 296.

257 *And no, she knew nothing :* March 1, 1965 New York Police Department Supplementary Complaint Report filed by Officer James Rustin. [New York City Municipal Archives].

257 *The interview lasted no more:* Goldman, Peter. *The Death and Life of Malcolm X.* University of Illinois Press, 1979, 296.

257 *Earlier, on March 3:* "Return Indictments in Malcolm Murder." *Afro American,* March 20, 1965, 1.

257 *"It is my understanding":* Kihss, Peter. "Widow of Malcolm X Speaks With Police About His Slaying." *New York Times,* March 2, 1965.

259 *"Well, it goes back to":* Transcript of Betty Shabazz Grand Jury Testimony, New York City, March 9, 1965. [New York City Municipal Archives].

259 *"So there we were":* Haley, Alex and X, Malcolm. *The Autobiography of Malcolm X.* New York: Ballantine, 1993, 11.

259 *"I didn't know how":* Cain, Joy Duckett. "Dr. Betty Shabazz." *Essence,* February 1985, 12.

259 *When his autobiography entered:* Montgomery, Paul L. "Malcolm X A Harlem Idol on Eve of Murder Trial." *New York Times,* December 6, 1965, 46.

259 *"My father left us his legacy":* Gamilah Shabazz Interview.

260 *The black protest's miscreant:* Kihss, Peter. "Hunt for Killers in Malcolm Case 'On Right Track.'" *New York Times,* February, 25, 1965, 1.

260 *The Organization of Afro American Unity:* Kihss, Peter. "Hunt for Killers in Malcolm Case 'On Right Track'." *New York Times,* February 25, 1965, 1.

260 *"They ain't even payin'":* Abdullah Abdur Razzaq Interview.

260 *"We had no money":* Sonia Sanchez Interview, August 10, 1999.

260 *Hours after the assassination:* "An Appeal for the Family." *New York Post,* February 22, 1965, 3.

261 *"There were people who admired":* Poston, Ted. "Widow Talks of Her Life with Malcolm." *New York Post.* February 23, 1965, 2.

261 *"Restored manhood to the Negro":* Kihss, Peter. "Hunt for Killers in Malcolm Case 'On Right Track.'" *New York Times,* February 25, 1965, 1.

261 *"The Negro community owes a debt":* "Trust Fund For Malcolm's Kids," *New York Amsterdam News,* February 27, 1965, 1.

261 *"Misunderstanding and possible violence":* "Church Says It Did Not Refuse Malcolm." *New York Amsterdam News,* March 6, 1965, 2.

262 *"It is something we did":* Ruby Dee Interview, July 7, 2000.

262 *"When people helped President Kennedy's wife":* Kihss, Peter. "Widow of Malcolm X Speaks With Police About His Slaying." *New York Times,* March 2, 1965; "Trust Fund For Malcolm's Kids," *New York*

Amsterdam News, February 27, 1965, 1.

262 *The fund surpassed $4,000*: "Mrs. Malcolm X Fund Now at $4,000." *New York Amsterdam News*, March 6, 1965, 2.; "Malcolm X Fund Grows To $5,200." *New York Amsterdam News*, March 13, 1965.

262 *It topped $6,000 days later*: "Malcolm X Widow Gets $500 Gift." *New York Amsterdam News*, March 20, 1965.

262 *"It would be ideal"*: Juanita Poitier Interview; "Malcolm's Widow Getting More Aid," *New York Amsterdam News*, June 26, 1965, 28.

262 *Students against Social Injustice*: "N.Y. Folk Sing to Aid Family of Malcolm X." *The Militant*, April 12, 1965.

263 *The circle of fifteen women*: "Malcolm's Widow Getting More Aid," *New York Amsterdam News*, June 26, 1965, 28.

263 *By July, chanteuse Lena Horne*: "Festival for Mrs. Malcolm X." *New York Amsterdam News*, July 24, 1965, 12.

263 *"At the time the family"*: Juanita Poitier Interview; Metcalfe, Ralph, Jr. "How Blacks Remember Malcolm X." *Jet*, May 20, 1971, 27.

263 *"Jazz potpourri"*: "In Aid of Mrs. Malcolm X." *New York Herald Tribune*, August 8, 1965, 27.

264 *At the end of the night*: "Aid Mrs. Malcolm X Buy New Home." *New York Amsterdam News*, August 9, 1965; "Widow of Malcolm X May Buy Home Here," (Mount Vernon, NY) *Daily Argus*, August 9, 1965, 1; "In Aid of Mrs. Malcolm X." *New York Herald Tribune*, August 8, 1965, 27.

264 *"Even in circles that don't"*: Montgomery, Paul L. "Malcolm X a Harlem Idol on Eve of Murder Trial." *New York Times*, December 6, 1965, 46.

265 *"It's wonderful"*: Martin, Mylas. "Jazz Benefit for Mrs. Malcolm X." August 9, 1965, *New York Herald Tribune*, 7.

265 *"A lot of black people"*: From the transcript of the "Haley Book Interview with Betty Shabazz" conducted by Anne Romaine, January 27, 1989, Medgar Evers College, Brooklyn, New York. (Courtesy of Special Collections, Hoskins Library, the University of Tennessee at Knoxville).

265 *"Money wasn't like it is"*: Sister Cybil Interview, June 6, 2000.

265 *"Buy milk for Malcolm's babies"*: "For Malcolm's Babies," *Village Voice*, May 29, 1990, 45.

266 *More than a smattering of white*: Ring, Harry. "Interview With James Shabazz." *The Militant*. March 8, 1965, 3; Krebs, Albin."A Break in Malcolm Case? 2 Brought in at Midnight." *New York Herald Tribune*, February 26, 1965, 2.

266 *Malcolm's lieutenants had refused*: Abdullah Abdur Razzaq Interview; Metcalfe, Ralph, Jr. "How Blacks Remember Malcolm X." *Jet*, May 20, 1971, 27.

266 *"Had it not been for some"*: From the transcript of the "Haley Book Interview with Betty Shabazz" conducted by Anne Romaine, January 27, 1989, Medgar Evers College, Brooklyn, New York. (Courtesy of Special Collections, Hoskins Library, the University of Tennessee at Knoxville).

266 *She and the children would stay*: Edwards, Audrey and Susan L. Taylor. "Loving and Losing Malcolm." *Essence*, February 1992, 110.

266 *"Everybody met Betty"*: Dr. Ben Interview, February 5, 2001.

266 *"You know where Betty is?"*: Sonia Sanchez Interview, August 10, 1999.

267 *"When Malcolm was hit"*: Haki Madhubuti Interview, June 2, 2000.

267 *"We wanted to offer our help"*: Sonia Sanchez Interview.

267 *"I began to lament the fact"*: Amiri Baraka Interview, July 19, 1999.

267 *"Nobody abandoned her"*: Sara Mitchell Interview.

267 *"We got closer to her"*: Muriel Feelings Interview.

267 *"I remember trying"*: Sister Khadiyyah Interview; Herman Ferguson Interview.

268 *"There was so much fear"*: Herman Ferguson Interview.

268 *"I lived for weeks"*: Karim, Benjamin. Remembering Malcolm. New York: Ballantine Books, 1992, 200.

269 *"She was a grieving widow"*: Abdullah Abdur Razzaq Interview.

269 *The command appalled the brothers*: Collins, Rodnell P. *Seventh Child*. Secaucus, NJ: Birch Lane Press, 1998, 184.

269 *Betty soon realized*: June 11, 1965 John Henrik Clarke letter to Lynne C. Shifflett [from John Henrik ClarkePapers, courtesy of the Schomburg Center].

269 *"She said the first thing"*: Gamilah Shabazz Interview, January 15, 2000.

269 *"She grew up overnight"*: Sister Khadiyyah Interview.

269 *"Men are predators"*: Abdullah Abdur Razzaq Interview.

270 *"The classes moved in"*: Charles Kenyatta Interview; Herman Ferguson Interview.

270 *"Betty wasn't an easy person"*: Juanita Poitier Interview; Sara Mitchell Interview.

270 *But Betty had no real political agenda*: Ferguson Interview.

270 *Ella Collins proclaimed herself*: Krebs, Albin. "A Break in Malcolm Case? 2 Brought in at Midnight." *New York Herald Tribune*, February 26, 1965, 2.

270 *"We will carry out my brother's program"*: "Malcolm X's Sister Takes Charge of the OAAU." *Philadelphia Afro-American*, March 20, 1965, 2.

271 *To the bewilderment of some*: Kihss, Peter. "Malcolm X's Sister Takes Over; Says She Fears New Violence." *New York Times*, March 16, 1965, 33; "Malcolm's Widow In Mecca." *New York Amsterdam News*, April 3, 1965, 50.

271 *"I called a meeting"*: Abdullah Abdur Razzaq Interview.

271 *"They say his infant"*: Hunt, Frank. "Malcolm X Still Lives," *Afro-American Magazine*, February 19, 1966, 1.

271 *She had already announced*: "Malcolm X Followers Plan Memorial Fete." *Afro-American*, May 15, 1965, 7; "Mrs. X Is Back Has No Plans." *New York Amsterdam News*, May 8, 1965, 1; "Memorial Meeting for Malcolm X" flier [courtesy of Schomburg Center].

271 *Making her first public address*: "40th Birthday of Malcolm X." *Afro-American*, June 5, 1965; "Malcolm X Day" Flier [courtesy of Shomburg Center].

272 *"Ruthlessly dominating leader"*: James Smalls Interview, March 19, 2000.

272 *"I think of all the work"*: Montgomery, Paul. "Malcolm X a Harlem Idol on Eve of Murder Trial." *New York Times*, December 6, 1965, 46.

272 *She responded enthusiastically*: Merit Publishers, *Malcolm X Speaks* press release, 1965 [courtesy of Schomburg Center].

272 *Louis Lomax had approached the widow*: Collins, Rodnell P. *Seventh Child; A family memoir of Malcolm X*. Secaucus, NJ: Birch Lane Press, 1998, 202.

273 *"Tools and fools"*: Ibid, 197.

273 *Militant Labor Forum*: Goldman, Peter. *The Death and Life of Malcolm X*. University of Illinois Press, 1979, 162.

273 *"Betty was strong-willed"*: Steve Clarke Interview, January 23, 2001.

273 *"I lose track with them"*: Dr. Ben Interview.

274 *"If we had had more family unity"*: Collins, Rodnell P. *Seventh Child; A family memoir of Malcolm X*. Secaucus, NJ: Birch Lane Press, 1998, 198-199.

CHAPTER 11: BAHIYAH

275 *"Betty, you'll have to speak"*: Juanita Poitier Interview, July 31, 2000.

275 *"I lost faith in a lot"*: Jones, Marsha. "Betty Shabazz." *About…Time*, January 1993, 15.

275 *"She was in turmoil"*: Dr. Ben Interview.

275 *In the days after the assassination*: Worthy, William. "Indonesians Mourn Malcolm X's Death."

Philadelphia Afro-American, March 13, 1965, 1; Haley, Alex and X, Malcolm. *The Autobiography of Malcolm* X. New York: Ballantine, 1993, 455.

276 *"They say death was too good"*: Chuck Stone Interview; Amiri Baraka Interview; Campbell, Roy H. "Carrying On For Malcolm X." *Philadelphia Inquirer Daily Magazine*, May 12, 1988, F1.

276 *"Sometimes she would curse"*: Ferguson Interview; Not-for-attribution Interview.

276 *"The brothers didn't know"*: Alice Mitchell Interview; Muriel Feelings Interview.

276 *"All of them niggers"*: Sister Khadiyyah Interview.

277 *The Malcolmites were unconvinced*: Evanzz, Karl. *The Judas Factor*. New York: Thunder's Mouth Press, 1992, 315.

277 *After he revealed*: Parks, Gordon. *Voices in the Mirror*. New York: Doubleday, 1990, 235.

277 *"It was my security blanket"*: "Dr. Betty Shabazz's Final Words." Interview with Bernard White and Amy Goodman, Pacifica Radio, WBAI, New York City, May 19, 1997; Jones, Marsha. "Betty Shabazz." *About…Time*, January 1993, 15.

277 *I said, "Betty, they want to talk"*: Juanita Poitier Interview.

278 *"She was not aware"*: Sister Cybil Interview; Amiri Baraka Interview.

278 *"I could be someplace"*: From the transcript of the "Haley Book Interview with Betty Shabazz" conducted by Anne Romaine, January 27, 1989, Medgar Evers College, Brooklyn, New York. (Courtesy of Special Collections, Hoskins Library, the University of Tennessee at Knoxville).

278 *"What I thought best"*: Ahmed Osman Interview; Juanita Poitier Interview; "Malcolm's Widow In Mecca." *New York Amsterdam News*, April 3, 1965, 50.

280 *Dual role was a happy burden*: Ahmed Osman Interview.

280 *Among the luminaries*: Ibid; Jaaber, Heshaam. *The Final Chapter…I Buried Malcolm X*. Jersey City, NJ: New Mind Productions, 1992, 52-53; Lang, Jeffrey. *Struggling to Surrender*. Beltsville, Maryland: Amana Publications, 1994, 186.

280 *Allah had certainly chosen*: Rauf-Abdul, Muhammad. "Pilgrimage to Mecca." *National Geographic*, November 1978, 581-601; Pickthall, M. M. *The Life of the Prophet Muhammad*. Beltsville, Maryland: Amana Publications, 1998, 10.

282 *He meant for her to survive*: Rauf-Abdul, Muhammad. "Pilgrimage to Mecca." *National Geographic*, November 1978, 581-601; Ahmed Osman Interview.

282 *"This ancient city"*: "Mrs. Malcolm X Pens Us A Note." *New York Amsterdam News*, April 10, 1065, 2.

282 *"Why can't we have a little comfort"*: Sara Mitchell Interview; Shabazz, Ilyasah. *Growing Up* X. New York: Ballantine Books, 2002.

283 *"I stopped focusing"*: Edwards, Audrey and Susan L. Taylor. "Loving and Losing Malcolm." *Essence*, February 1992, 110.

283 *She reflected upon her children*: Campbell, Roy H. "Carrying On For Malcolm X." *Philadelphia Inquirer Magazine*, May 12, 1988, F1.

283 *"You and your children"*: Ahmed Osman Interview.

283 *"I knew, after the pilgrimage"*: Ibid; Cain, Joy Duckett. "Dr. Betty Shabazz." *Essence*, February 1985, 12.

283 *"My new name"*: April 1965 postcard from Betty Shabazz to Claude Lewis [courtesy of Claude Lewis]; Undated postcard from Betty Shabazz to Alex Haley [courtesy of Schomburg Center, Alex Haley Papers].

284 *As President Johnson signed*: Williams, Juan. *Eyes on the Prize*. New York: Viking, 1987, 285-285; King, Martin Luther. *Where Do We Go From Here; Chaos or Community?* Boston: Beacon Press, 1967, 2.

284 *"I wanted to move"*: Frady, Marshall. "The Children of Malcolm." *New Yorker*, October 12, 1992, 78.

284 *"I was terribly disillusioned"*: Pauley, Gay. "Martyr's Widow Decries Rule By Brute Force," *Philadelphia*

Daily News, May 20, 1972.

285 By *September the Shabazz children*: "Aid Mrs. Malcolm X Buy New Home." *New York Amsterdam News*, August 9, 1965.

285 *Whispers of other cash sources*: Charles Kenyatta Interview; Lomax, Louis. *To Kill A Black Man*. Los Angeles: Holloway House, 1968, 180-181; Perry, Bruce. *Malcolm; The Life of a Man who Changed Black America*. New York: Station Hill, 1991, 508.

285 *It remains unclear*: Sara Mitchell Interview; Robert Haggins Interview; Collins, 195.

285 *Malcolm did not want her to remarry*: Norma Johnson Interview, June 22, 1999.

286 *"I couldn't handle one"*: "Dr. Betty Shabazz's Final Words." Interview with Bernard White and Amy Goodman, Pacifica Radio, WBAI, New York City, May 19, 1997.

286 *"I said to Juanita"*: Ibid.

287 *It was a rare surfacing*: Hunt, Frank. "Malcolm X Still Lives." *The Afro-American Magazine*, February 19, 1966, 1; Montgomery, Paul. "Malcolm X a Harlem Idol on Eve of Murder Trial." *New York Times*, December 6, 1965, 46.

287 *Face his accused killers*: Montgomery, Paul. "Malcolm X a Harlem Idol on Eve of Murder Trial." *New York Times*, December 6, 1965, 46.

287 *It was the twenty-sixth day*: Hunt, Frank. "Malcolm X Still Lives." *The Afro-American Magazine*, February 19, 1966, 1.

288 *"They killed my husband!"*: Goldman, Peter. *The Death and Life of Malcolm X*. University of Illinois Press, 1979, 333-335.

288 *The People's case was firm*: "Who Issued the Orders." *Newsweek*, March 21, 1966.

288 *Yes, he had done it*: Charles Kenyatta Interview; Sullivan, James W. "Admits Killing Malcolm X." *Herald Tribune*, March 1, 1966.

289 *Hayer claimed her had met*: Ibid.

289 *And so, it seemed*: Goldman, Peter. *The Death and Life of Malcolm X*. University of Illinois Press, 1979, 373.

290 *All of this may or may not have happened*: Ibid, 361.

290 *Each of the disciples*: Charles Kenyatta Interview; Abdullah Abdur Razzaq Interview; Robert Haggins Interview, July 6, 1999.

291 *"The more I keep thinking"*: Haley, Alex and X, Malcolm. *The Autobiography of Malcolm X*. New York: Ballantine, 1993, 438.

291 *Malcolm said from the beginning*: "Dr. Betty Shabazz's Final Words." Interview with Bernard White and Amy Goodman, Pacifica Radio, WBAI, New York City, May 19, 1997.

291 *"Betty Shabazz knows"*: Abdullah Abdur Razzaq Interview.

291 *"To her, all of them"*: Sara Mitchell Interview.

292 *"No words can express"*: February 25, 1965 Yuri Kochiama letter to Betty Shabazz and July 12, 1967 Shabazz letter to Kochiama [courtesy of Yuri Kochiama].

CHAPTER 12: RECONSTRUCTION

293 *A train of mourners trudged*: Gustaitis, Rasa. "Who Mourns Malcolm X?" *New York Herald Tribune*, February 21, 1966; "75 March to Mark Malcolm's Death," *New York Times*, February 21, 1966; Rice, William. "A Year Later, Only 75 In Parade for Malcolm X," *New York Daily News*, February 21, 1966, 24.

294 *"When Betty moved there"*: Ruth Summerford Interview, January 12, 2001; Jean Owensby Interview, April 23, 1999.

295 *"The Mount Vernon NAACP"*: "Negro Group Marches To City Hall, Presents Housing, School Requests." (Mount Vernon) *Daily Argus*, August 21, 1965, 1; "Integration Bid Renewed by NAACP," (Mount Vernon) *Daily Argus*, September 3, 1965, 2.; Robinson, Patricia. "School Integration: Westchester Style." *Liberator*, September 1966, 8-10.

295 *"The first people who reached out"*: Graham, Lawrence Otis. "From Outcast to Heroine." *U.S. News & World Report*, June 16, 1997, 60; Norma Johnson Interview, June 22, 2000.

295 *"What kind of name"*: Ibid.

296 *The widow later recalled*: Pauley, Gay. "Martyr's Widow Decries Rule By Brute Force," *Philadelphia Daily News*, May 20, 1972.

296 *"When we did put the pictures up"*: Shabazz, Betty. "The Legacy of My Husband." *Ebony*, June 1969, 176.

296 *"Something terrible had happened"*: Knebel, Fletcher. "A Visit with the Widow of Malcolm X." *Look*, March 4, 1969, 74.

297 *"After a while"*: Hopkins, Ellen. "Their Fathers' Daughters." *Rolling Stone*, November 30, 1989, 120.

297 *Malcolm X was a brave leader*: Shabazz, Betty. "The Legacy of My Husband." *Ebony*, June 1969, 176.

297 *"I always knew that, OK"*: Corey, Mary and M. Dion Thompson. "The Content of Their Character." *Baltimore Sun*, March 29, 1998.

297 *"I felt kind of misty"*: Shabazz, Betty. "The Legacy of My Husband." *Ebony*, June 1969, 176.

297 *She hid her copy*: Corey, Mary and M. Dion Thompson. "The Content of Their Character." *Baltimore Sun*, March 29, 1998.

297 *"He was there"*: Gamilah Shabazz Interview, January 15, 2000.

298 *"There is an African proverb"*: Ruth Summerford Interview; Hopkins, Ellen. "Their Fathers' Daughters." *Rolling Stone*, November 30, 1989, 120; Tamu, Ewe. "Betty Shabazz: 27 Years, the Stillness of Death." *Morena*, February 1993, 5.

298 *"When he was hurting"*: Peterman, Peggy. "A Second Voice." *St. Petersburg Times*, March 10, 1989, 1D

298 *"Regardless of what she says"*: From the transcript of the "Haley Book Interview with Betty Shabazz" conducted by Anne Romaine, January 27, 1989, Medgar Evers College, Brooklyn, New York. (Courtesy of Special Collections, Hoskins Library, the University of Tennessee at Knoxville).

298 *"I can stress the happy times"*: Shabazz, Betty. "The Legacy of My Husband." *Ebony*, June 1969, 176.

299 *Single parenthood exhausted Betty*: Ibid, 182.

299 *"the mop and bucket"*: Gilliam, Dorothy. "Reuniting the Positives." *Washington Post*, September 12, 1988, D3.

300 *"You've got to talk"*: From the transcript of the "Haley Book Interview with Betty Shabazz" conducted by Anne Romaine, January 27, 1989, Medgar Evers College, Brooklyn, New York. (Courtesy of Special Collections, Hoskins Library, the University of Tennessee at Knoxville).

300 *"It was nothing for her"*: Jean Owensby Interview, April 23, 1999; Ruth Summerford Interview.

300 *"We thought she was talking"*: Gamilah Shabazz Interview.

300 *"She was a Trojan"*: Rev. Richard Dixon Interview, February 8, 2001.

301 *"But we'd duck"*: Ibid.

301 *The FBI kept a keen eye*: Blackstock, Nelson. *COINTELPRO: The FBI's Secret War on Political Freedom.* New York: Vintage Books, 1976.

301 *"You must remember"*: Sharrieff, Raymond. "The Devil Uses Malcolm." *Muhammad Speaks*, June 4, 1971.

301 *There is no evidence*: FBI Malcolm X Files, New York, February 1963.

302 *"Get away from me!"*: James Smalls Interview, March 19, 2000.

302 *"I made an unrealistic decision"*: Lanker, Brian and Barbara Summers, ed. *I Dream A World; Portraits of Black Women Who Changed America.* New York: Stewart, Tabori & Chang, 1999, 104.

303 *A six-man chorale sang*: Johnson, Thomas A. "Mourners Mark 'Malcolm X Day.'" *New York Times*, May 20, 1966; Caldwell, Earl. "Angry Anthems in the Rain—'Malcolm X Day' Is Marked." *New York Post*, May 20, 1966, 8.

304 *"There was at that time"*: Herman Ferguson Interview, February 12, 2000.

304 *"She needed to get away"*: Hall, Terri. "For Betty Shabazz, Life Is Full Again." (Mount Vernon) *Daily Argus*, March 5, 1977.

305 *"She had an easy way"*: Dorothy Pleas Interview, February 23, 2002.

305 *Betty empathized with the housewives*: Ibid.

306 *"I was ready to die"*: Seale, Bobby. *Seize the Time*. New York: Random House, 1968, 3.

306 *"washed my hands"*: Cleaver, Eldridge. *Soul on Ice*. New York: Dell Publishing, 1992, 70.

306 *Only twenty people came*: "20 Gather to Listen to Voice of Malcolm X." *Washington Post*, June 18, 1967.

306 *The widow gleamed with anticipation*: Fayer, Steve and Henry Hampton with Sarah Flynn. *Voices of Freedom*. New York: Bantam Books, 1990, 365; Newton, Huey. *Revolutionary Suicide*. New York: Writers and Readers, 1995, 130-131; Seale, Bobby. *Seize the Time*. New York: Random House, 1968, 125; Cleaver, Eldridge. *Post-Prison Writings and Speeches*. New York: Random House, 1969, 23-36; "Frightening 'Army' Hits the Airport." *San Francisco Chronicle*, February 22, 1967, 1, 6.

309 *"No one will tell us"*: Johnson, Thomas A. "March in Harlem Honors Malcolm." *New York Times*, February 23, 1967, 26.

310 *The occasion turned ugly*: "30 Arrested in Chicago Melee at Service Honoring Malcolm X." *New York Times*, May 22, 1967, 26.

310 *As his icon grew*: Buder, Leonard. "Donovan Yields on I.S. 201 Event." *New York Times*, February 21, 1968; "The Beatification of Malcolm X." *Time*, March 1, 1968, 16.

311 *Cooper crowd got carried away*: Fraser, Gerald C. "Malcolm X Memorial Services and Protest Mark Date of Death." *New York Times*, February 22, 1969, 22.

311 *"Some people invoke Malcolm's name"*: Shabazz, Betty. "The Legacy of My Husband." *Ebony*, June 1969, 180.

311 *"We enjoyed her company"*: Grace Killens Interview, November 20, 2000.

312 *"Glad to see the brothers"*: January 19, 1968 Larry Neal letter to "Brother George" (Larry Neal Papers, courtesy of Schomburg Center, New York).

312 *"I didn't keep up"*: Sister Khaddiyah Interview.

312 *"Do you know many"*: Maya Angelou Interview, September 22, 1999.

313 *Her new freedoms*: Elinor Sinnette Interview, April 1, 2002.

313 *"She didn't have to be the martyr's wife"*: Novella Nelson Interview, March 5, 2002.

314 *Worth signed Arnold Perl*: Kempner, Aviva. "Marvin Worth's 25 Years on 'Malcolm X.'" *Washington Jewish Week*, December 24, 1992, 17.

314 *Betty was a consultant*: Canby, Vincent. "Two Studios Plan Malcolm X Films." *New York Times*, March 9, 1968, 23; FBI Malcolm X Files, March 26, 1968; Collins, Rodnell. *Seventh Child*. Secaucus, Birch Lane Press, 1998, 204.

315 *Baldwin was not the only*: Baldwin, James. *No Name in the Street*. New York: The Dial Press, 1972, 11.

315 *"would have liked"*: Peters, Art. "Here's a Surprise: Hollywood Has Done Right by Malcolm X." *Philadelphia Inquirer*, May 30, 1972, 31.

315 *"as a hero"*: West, Hollie I. "'Malcolm X': Manhood." *Washington Post*, May 22, 1972, B1; Cocks, Jay. "Historical Primer."

315 *"For Warner Bros."*: *Time*, June 12, 1972.

315 *With newsreel footage*: Foley, Eileen. "Our Children Hold the Key to a Future Free of Killings, Malcolm's Widow Says." *Philadelphia Inquirer*, May 24, 1972; Cosby, John Jr. "Letter to James Earl Jones." *The Liberator*, June 1969, 18-19; "Malcolm's Birthday Is Observed Here With Visit to Grave." *New York Times*, May 20, 1972, 17; "Film On Malcolm X To Open Next Week." (Mount Vernon) *Daily Argus*, May 18, 1972; West, Hollie I. "'Malcolm X': Manhood." *Washington Post*, May 22, 1972, B6.

316 *Collins and other students*: Foley, Eileen. "Our Children Hold the Key to a Future Free of Killings, Malcolm's Widow Says." *Philadelphia Inquirer*, May 24, 1972; Sara Mitchell Interview, December 18, 2000; Baldwin, James. *No Name in the Street*. New York: The Dial Press, 1972, 11; "Malcolm's Birthday Is Observed Here With Visit to Grave." *New York Times*, May 20, 1972, 17.

316 *Whether or not the widow*: Imari Obadele Interview, March 27, 2002.

317 *"Most of the people who"*: Metcalfe, Ralph Jr. "How Blacks Remember Malcolm X." *Jet*, May 20, 1971, 27.

317 *Clark sent her*: January 13, 1969 Betty Shabazz letter to John Henrik Clarke; October 30, 1968 John Henrik Clarke letter to Betty Shabazz (John Henrik Clarke papers, courtesy of Schomburg Center, New York).

317 *The anthology appeared in 1969*: Clarke, John Henrik, ed. *Malcolm X; the Man and His Times*. Trenton: Africa World Press, 1990, 132-143.

318 *"She could be almost flirty"*: Peter Goldman Interview, April 21, 1999.

318 *Betty was more forthcoming*: Knebel, Fletcher. "A Visit With the Widow of Malcolm X." *Look*, March 4, 1969, 74-81.

320 *The article finally appeared*: Shabazz, Betty. "The Legacy of My Husband." *Ebony*, June 1969, 172-182.

321 *"Live off my husband's reputation"*: Richard Dixon Interview, February 8, 2001.

321 *"We don't want Black History"*: "Sister Betty Shabazz." *Forum*, May 1971, 9.

322 *She felt a further sense of duty*: Campbell, Roy H. "Carrying On For Malcolm X." *Philadelphia Inquirer Magazine*, May 12, 1988, F1.

322 *"Role of Black Women"*: Betty Shabazz Curriculum Vitae (courtesy of Medgar Evers College, New York).

322 *"Black Americans want the same"*: Morehead State University Press Release (Courtesy of Morehead State University); Hitsky, Barbara.

322 *"Until there is peace"*: "A Prediction: Explosive Future For Our Children," *Detroit News*, May 21, 1970, 1C.

322 *She trumpeted woman power*: Foley, Eileen. "Our Children Hold the Key to a Future Free of Killings, Malcolm's Widow Says." *Philadelphia Inquirer*, May 24, 1972; Smith, Corinne. "Black Women Get a Shot in the Arm." *Detroit News*, February 25, 1971; Ward, Hiley, H. "Was Malcolm X a Saint of God?" *Detroit Free Press*, February 15, 1969, 10A; Shackelford, Snadra. "Shabazz Sees No End to Black Woman's Struggle." (Appleton) *Post Crescent*, April 15, 1975, 1C.

323 *"Malcolm didn't preach violence"*: "Where Are They Now?" *Newsweek*, November 3, 1969; Ward, Hiley H.

323 *"My goodness"*: "Was Malcolm X a Saint of God?" *Detroit Free Press*, February 15, 1969, 10A.

323 *"so many problems"*: Hitsky, Barbara. "A Prediction: Explosive Future For Our Children," *Detroit News*, May 21, 1970, 1C.

323 *"We the students of Malcolm X High"*: Shabazz, Betty. "The Legacy of My Husband, Malcolm X." *Ebony*, June 1969, 175.

324 *"Most of the white students"*: Shackelford, Sandra. "Shabazz Sees No End to Black Woman's Struggle." (Appleton) *Post Crescent*, April 15, 1975.

324 *"A righteous black man"*: Wyse, Iris. "McClymonds New Principal." *Black Panther*, January 4, 1969, 5.

324 *East Bay was not ready for Betty*: "The Sister's Been Doing Her Homework." Pacifica Tape Library recording of Betty Shabazz's May 18, 1971 speech at McClymonds High School, Berkeley, California; Davis, Angela. *Angela Davis; An Autobiography*. New York: Random House, 1974.

CHAPTER 13: HUMANIST

327 *Betty's speeches*: Hitsky, Barbara. "A Prediction: Explosive Future For Our Children," *Detroit News*, May 21, 1970, 1C.; Van Wert, Robert. "Malcolm X Widow: No Progress." (Mount Vernon) *Daily Argus*, August 31, 1971.

327 *She embraced radicalism*: Herman Ferguson Interview; "Militants Seeking Black Government." *New York Times*, March 28, 1968, 50; Thompson, Walt. "What's Left of the Black Left?" *Ramparts*, June 1972, 47; FBI Malcolm X Files, May 1971.

328 *Obligations of single parenthood*: Hitsky, Barbara. "A Prediction: Explosive Future For Our Children," *Detroit News*, May 21, 1970, 1C.

328 *"a piece of this land"*: Ward, Hiley H. "Was Malcolm X a Saint of God?" *Detroit Free Press*, February 15, 1969, 10A.

328 *In a 1971 talk*: "The Sister's Been Doing Her Homework." Pacifica Tape Library recording of Betty Shabazz's May 18, 1971 speech at McClymonds High School, Berkeley, California.

329 *"It's 'nation time'"*: Blatchford, Frank and Angela Parker. "Hatcher, Jesse in Policy Split." *Chicago Tribune*, March 12, 1972, 1-2.

329 *"Some people say it failed"*: Fayer, Steve and Henry Hampton with Sarah Flynn. *Voices of Freedom*. New York: Bantam Books, 1990, 565-581.

329 *She became a trustee*: "Minutes of the 34th Annual Meeting," National Housewives League of America, July 11-14, 1971. (Courtesy of Bentley Historical Library, Ann Arbor, Michigan).

329 *Bill Russell also assumed*: "Black Coach Gets Office in PUSH." *Washington Post*, January 21, 1973, A20.

329 *Betty and other dignitaries*: Herman, Edith. "PUSH Seeks Black Economic Power." *Chicago Tribune*, July 26, 1973, 8.

330 *"We're supposed to share the riches"*: "Where Are They Now?" *Newsweek*.

330 *She condemned an attempt*: November 3, 1969; "Gov. Wallace Vows He Won't Quit." *Chicago Today*, May 16, 1972, 2; Foley, Eileen. "Our Children Hold the Key to a Future Free of Killings, Malcolm's Widow Says." *Philadelphia Inquirer*, May 24, 1972.

330 *"We now spend billions"*: Pauley, Gay. "Martyr's Widow Decries Rule By Brute Force." *Philadelphia Daily News*, May 20, 1972.

330 *"if their thing is war"*: 1974 National Association for the Education of the Young Child Conference booklet (courtesy NAEYC).

330 *An incontrovertible champion*: Ward, Hiley H. "Was Malcolm X a Saint of God?" *Detroit Free Press*, February 15, 1969, 10A; Hitsky, Barbara. "A Prediction: Explosive Future For Our Children," *Detroit News*, May 21, 1970, 1C.

331 *"Betty was never a revolutionary"*: Sonia Sanchez Interview, August 10, 1999.

331 *Communities are successful or stable*: 1974 National Association for the Education of the Young Child Conference booklet [courtesy NAEYC].

332 *At times Betty seemed*: "Malcolm X's Widow To Lead S.C. Black Awareness Week." *Simpsonian*, April 18, 1974, 1; Hitsky, Barbara. "A Prediction: Explosive Future For Our Children," *Detroit News*, May 21, 1970, 1C.

332 *"Problems understanding the Nation"*: "The Sister's Been Doing Her Homework." Pacifica Tape Library recording of Betty Shabazz's May 18, 1971 speech at McClymonds High School, Berkeley, California.

332 *"I'd come into places"*: Sonia Sanchez Interview.

333 *"I would like"*: Shabazz, Betty. "The Legacy of My Husband." *Ebony*, June 1969, 182; James Smalls Interview.

333 *"I have my own feelings"*: Hines, Bea L. "Widow Pushes Malcolm's Work—But Her Way." *Reuters News Service*. February 20, 1971.

333 *She was still discovering the minister*: Ward, Hiley H. "Was Malcolm X a Saint of God?" *Detroit Free Press*, February 15, 1969, 10A; "Militants: St. Malcolm X." *Newsweek*, March 3, 1969, 27.

333 *"Brother Malcolm stated"*: "Brother Malcolm Lives On." *The Black Panther*, September 14, 1968, 5.

334 *She registered to vote*: Betty Shabazz August 13, 1971 voter registration application (courtesy of Westchester County, New York Board of Elections).

334 *Banquet drew two thousand*: Delaney, Paul. "Black Parlays in Capital Hail Nixon and Thurmond." *New York Times*, June 12, 1972, 30; Booker, Simeon. "Blacks Raise $200,000 To Reelect Nixon." *Jet*, June 1972.

335   *"go off the deep end"*: Knebel, Fletcher. "A Visit with the Widow of Malcolm X." *Look*, March 4, 1969, 75.

335   *"There was pressure on Betty"*: Robert Haggins Interview, July 6, 1999.

335   *She insisted*: Novella Nelson Interview.

335   *"A conservative-looking person"*: Hines, Bea L. "Widow Pushes Malcolm's Work—But Her Way." *Reuters Newswire*, February, 20, 1971.

335   *"I'm a very private person"*: Van Wert, Robert Jr. "Malcolm Widow: No Progress." (Mount Vernon) *Daily Argus*, August 31, 1971, 1.

335   *That public role*: Hoffman, Nicholas Von. "Malcolm Lives." *Washington Post*, December 1, 1969, C4; "Books: Malcolm X: History as Hope." *Time*, February 23, 1970, 88; Ward, Hiley H. "Was Malcolm X a Saint of God?" *Detroit Free Press*, February 15, 1969, 10A; "Where Are They Now?" *Newsweek*, November 3, 1969.

335   *Malcolm X Liberation University opened*: Davis, Willie E. "Malcolm X Liberation University." *SOBU Newsletter*, February 6, 1971, 10; Stone, Donald. "MXLU Speaks." *Rhythm*, winter 1970, 14; "Monument to Blackness." *Newsweek*, August 2, 1971, 46-47; "Intellectual Black Power." *Time*, August 16, 1971, 50; "Songs, Jazz Mark Malcolm Graduation." *Chicago Tribune*, June 8, 1972, 12; "The Sister's Been Doing Her Homework." Pacifica Tape Library recording of Betty Shabazz's May 18, 1971 speech at McClymonds High School, Berkeley, California; Pinkney, Alphonso. *Red, Black, and Green*. New York: Cambridge University Press, 1976, 191.

337   *She wanted their lives*: Van Wert, Robert Jr. "Malcolm Widow: No Progress." (Mount Vernon) *Daily Argus*, August 31, 1971, 14.

337   *Black Power ethos*: Wilcox, Preston. "Black Interests Come First." *New Generation*, Fall, 1967, 20.

338   *"We were all in drama"*: Gamilah Shabazz Interview.

338   *The girls were no more revolutionary*: Knebel, Fletcher. "A Visit with the Widow of Malcolm X." *Look*, March 4, 1969, 79; Cain, Joy Duckett. "Dr. Betty Shabazz." *Essence*, February 1985, 12; Shabazz, Betty. "The Legacy of My Husband." *Ebony*, June 1969, 182.

339   *"I grew up cross-cultural"*: Christon, Lawrence. "Going Her Way." *Los Angeles Times Calendar*, March 1, 1992, 84.

339   *"You weren't jack"*: Gamilah Shabazz Interview.

339   *The girls balanced the pursuits*: Legacy, 182; Corey, Mary and M. Dion Thompson. "Following the Light." *Baltimore Sun*, March 29, 1998; Foley, Eileen. "Our Children Hold the Key to a Future Free of Killings, Malcolm's Widow Says." *Philadelphia Inquirer*, May 24, 1972.

339   *She exulted in their achievements*: Amina Baraka Interview.

340   *Betty nurtured her daughters' bodies*: Knebel, Fletcher. "A Visit with the Widow of Malcolm X." *Look*, March 4, 1969, 74.

340   *"We follow the Islamic jurisprudence"*: "Where Are They Now?" *Newsweek*, November 3, 1969, 16.

341   *"She knew she looked good"*: Novella Nelson Interview.

341   *Betty's desire to teach her children*: Gamilah Shabazz Interview; A'aliyah Abdul Karim Interview, June 25, 1999; Kareemah Abdul Karim Interview, August 5, 1999; Aisha Al-Adawiya Interview, April 13, 1999; Halima Toure Interview, August 4, 1999.

344   *Betty was a symbol*: Messud, Claire. "No Disrespect to the Widow." *The Guardian* (London), March 1, 1993, 11; Jean Owensby Interview; Shabazz, Ilyasah with Kim McLarin. *Growing Up X*. New York: Ballantine Books, 2002.

344   *Yet Attallah could not*: X, Malcolm with Alex Haley. *The Autobiography of Malcolm X*. New York; Ballantine Books, 2000, xi; Hopkins, Ellen. "Their Fathers' Daughters." *Rolling Stone*, November 30, 1989, 120.

344   *"I grew up"*: Ibid.

345 *"There was nothing on those pages"*: Corey, Mary and M. Dion Thompson. "Following the Light." *Baltimore Sun*, March 29, 1998.

345 *"I am not a leader"*: Freedland, Jonathan. "America's Black Widows." *The Guardian* (London), February 13, 1995, T7.

345 *"I changed after that"*: Gamilah Shabazz Interview.

346 *Betty struggled*: Laughinghouse, Amy. "Mothers of the Civil Rights Movement." *Upscale*, May 1997, 39; "Dr. Betty Shabazz's Final Words." Interview with Bernard White and Amy Goodman, Pacifica Radio, WBAI, New York City, May 19, 1997.

347 *"If she was on TV"*: Milton Henry Interview, April 4, 2002; Gamilah Shabazz Interview; Dick Gregory Interview, July 30, 1999.

347 *"When I saw the girls"*: Graham, Lawrence Otis. *Our Kind of People*. New York: HarperCollins, 1999, 14; Graham, Lawrence Otis. "From Outcast to Heroine." *U.S. News & World Report*, June 16, 1997, 60.

348 *"They were oblivious"*: Gamilah Shabazz Interview; Graham, Lawrence Otis. *Our Kind of People*. New York: HarperCollins, 1999, 28, 40.

348 *"Sometimes you may overcompensate"*: Myrlie Evers-Williams Interview.

348 *"Instead I walked in"*: Bailey, Peter A. "The Ties That Bind." *Essence*, January 1982, 107.

349 *"We call people Uncle Toms"*: Peterman, Peggy. "A Second Voice." *St. Petersburg Times*, March 10, 1989, 1D.

349 *Coretta Scott King stayed alive*: King, Coretta Scott. *My Life With Martin Luther King, Jr.* New York: Holt, Rinehart and Winston, 1969, 317-318; Caldwell, Earl. "Martin Luther King Is Slain in Memphis; A White Is Suspected; Johnson Urges Calm." *New York Times*, April 5, 1968, 1.

350 *"I watched my mother"*: Hopkins, Ellen. "Their Fathers' Daughters." *Rolling Stone*, November 30, 1989, 120.

351 *"My first recollection of me"*: From "Light Sacred Candle...Momma," a poem by Gamilah Shabazz, 1994. (Courtesy of Gamilah Shabazz).

351 *"We were creative"*: Gamilah Shabazz Interview; Jean Owensby Interview.

353 *Her flurry of civic activities*: Laughinghouse, Amy. "Mothers of the Civil Rights Movement." *Upscale*, May 1997, 39; White, Joyce. "Motherhood." *Essence*, May 1979, 88.

353 *She saw to her ambassadorial duties*: Hall, Terri. "For Betty Shabazz, Life Is Full Again." (Mount Vernon) *Daily Argus*, March 5, 1977; Foley, Eileen. "Our Children Hold the Key to a Future Free of Killings, Malcolm's Widow Says." *Philadelphia Inquirer*, May 24, 1972.

354 *She came home bubbling*: "Malcolm X's Widow Returns From Africa," (Mount Vernon) *Daily Argus*, August 9, 1969, 2; "Where Are They Now?" *Newsweek*, November 3, 1969, 16; From the transcript of the "Haley Book Interview with Betty Shabazz" conducted by Anne Romaine, January 27, 1989, Medgar Evers College, Brooklyn, New York. (Courtesy of Special Collections, Hoskins Library, the University of Tennessee at Knoxville).

355 *"He still had that stroke"*: Shelmon Sandlin Interview, January 13, 2001; Stanley Sandlin Interview, December 5, 2000.

355 *Betty missed the girls*: Zala Chandler Interview, July 3, 1999; "Mrs. Medgar Evers—A New Life but Bitter Memories Linger." *New York Times*, March 26, 1970; Smith, Corinne. "Black Women Get a Shot in the Arm." *Detroit News*, February 25, 1971, 4C; Amina Baraka Interview; Richard Dixon Interview; Shabazz, Betty. "The Legacy of My Husband." *Ebony*, June 1969, 182.

356 *"I wouldn't wish her life"*: Gamilah Shabazz Interview.

CHAPTER 14: "DR. SHABAZZ"

357 *"I don't want to make somebody"*: Morrison, Toni. *Sula*. New York: Alfred A. Knopf, 1974, 92.

357 *"People ask me"*: Teresa Lori. "Malcolm X's Widow: 'Go Change Things.'" *St. Louis Post-Dispatch*, January 29, 1993, 4C.

357 *"You talk about a woman"*: Amina Baraka Interview, July 19, 1999.

358 *So in the fall of 1969*: Betty Shabazz Curriculum Vitae [Courtesy of Medgar Evers College]; Interview with New Jersey City University Registrar's Office, November 16, 2000.

358 *"It's so peaceful"*: Foley, Eileen. "Our Children Hold the Key to a Future Free of Killings, Malcolm's Widow Says." *Philadelphia Inquirer*, May 24, 1972.

358 *"Education is our passport"*: Breitman, George, ed. *By Any Means Necessary*. New York: Pathfinder, 1998, 68.

358 *"let's talk"*: Norma Jean Anderson Interview, April 11, 2002.

358 *Anderson was an associate dean*: Norma Jean Anderson Interview.

360 *Her absence was hard on the girls*: Gamilah Shabazz Interview, January 15, 2000; Jean Owensby Interview, April 23, 1999; Shabazz, Ilyasah. *Growing Up X*. New York: Ballantine Books, 2002; Laughinghouse, Amy. "Mothers of the Civil Rights Movement." *Upscale*, May 1997, 39; Haley, Alex. "Alex Haley Remembers Malcolm X." *Essence*, November 1983, 122.

361 *Founded at Howard University*: Canady, Hortense. "Black Women Leaders: The Case of Delta Sigma Theta." *Urban League Review*, Summer 1985, 92-95.

362 *"Join it"*: Novella Nelson Interview, March 5, 2002.

362 *The two stumbled*: Mary Redd Interview, May 20, 1999.

363 *This sense of purpose*: Shabazz, Betty S. 1975. *Organization of African Unity: Its Role in Education*. Ph.D. dissertation, University of Massachusetts, Amherst; Meyers, David B. "Intraregional Conflict Management by the Organization of African Unity." *International Organization*, Summer 1974, 345-373; Jones, Marsha. "Betty Shabazz." *about…time*, January 1993, 16.

365 *Betty successfully defended her dissertation*: Norma Johnson Interview, July 22, 1999; Robert Haggins Interview, July 6, 1999.

366 *Then composed of a few ragged buildings*: Betty Shabazz Curriculum Vitae [Courtesy of Medgar Evers College]; Traub, James. "The Importance of City College to Black America." *The Journal of Blacks in higher Education*, Autumn 1994, 56-60; "Pulling Up the Welcome Mat for Black Students at the City University of New York." *The Journal of Blacks in Higher Education*, Summer 1998, 79-80; "CUNY/Medgar Evers College." *Village Voice*, January 13-19, 1982, 68; Chandler, Zala and Andrée Nicola McLaughlin. "Urban Politics in the Higher Education of Black Women: A Case Study." in Bookman, Ann and Sandra Morgan, eds. *Women and the Politics of Empowerment*. Philadelphia: Temple University Press, 1988, 182-183; Chandler, Zala and Andrée Nicola McLaughlin. "Black Women on the Frontline: Unfinished Business of the Sixties." *Radical Teacher*, 1984.

367 *Carson's crowd never fully retreated*: Sonny Carson Interview, March 12, 2000.

368 *Mainstream support*: David Dinkins Interview, May 7, 2002.

368 *"She was rather shy"*: Hilda Richards Interview, July 30, 1999.

368 *Over the mumbling*: Betty Shabazz Curriculum Vitae [Courtesy of Medgar Evers College]; Norma Johnson Interview.

369 *"Why did she"*: Bertie Gilmore Interview, April 30, 1999; Joyce Canady Interview, April 30, 1999.

369 *The embattled soul*: Chandler, Zala and Andrée Nicola McLaughlin. "Urban Politics in the Higher Education of Black Women: A Case Study." in Bookman, Ann and Sandra Morgan, eds. *Women and the Politics of Empowerment*. Philadelphia: Temple University Press, 1988, 183; "CUNY's Helpers in a Women's Class-Action Suit." *New York Times*, June 19, 1980, A-22.

369 *"At Medgar Evers"*: Gamilah Shabazz Interview.

370 *Some of the Medgar Evers faculty*: Dorris Withers Interview, March 31, 1999; Norma Johnson Interview, June 22, 2000; Juollie Carroll Interview, March 31, 1999; Zala Chandler Interview, June 13, 1999; Herman Fulton Interview, July 30, 2000; Safiya Bandele Interview, April 1, 1999.

373 *President Trent decided*: Chandler, Zala and Andrée Nicola McLaughlin. "Urban Politics in the Higher Education of Black Women: A Case Study." in Bookman, Ann and Sandra Morgan, eds.

Women and the Politics of Empowerment. Philadelphia: Temple University Press, 1988, 182; Marge Battle Interview; Doris Withers Interview; Norma Johnson Interview.

375 *"Get racist Koch out"*: "Protesters Heckle Koch at College in Brooklyn." *New York Times*, August 11, 1983, B6."

375 *Feminism was its pulse*: "A Black Feminist Statement." in Guy-Sheftall, Beverly, ed. *Words of Fire.* New York: The New Press, 1995, 232; Giddings, Paula. *When and Where I Enter.* New York: William Morrow & Company, 1984, 299-324.

375 *"I was conscious of black"*: Zala Chandler Interview; Safiyah Bandele Interview.

376 *Its veterans remember it*: Doris Withers Interview; "CUNY/Medgar Evers College." *Village Voice*, January 13-19, 1982, 68; Chandler, Zala and Andrée Nicola McLaughlin. "Urban Politics in the Higher Education of Black Women: A Case Study." in Bookman, Ann and Sandra Morgan, eds. *Women and the Politics of Empowerment.* Philadelphia: Temple University Press, 1988, 180-201; Rule, Sheila. "Medgar Evers College Protest Grows." *New York Times*, April 23, 1982, B3.

377 *For Betty, it was simply a debacle*: Andrée Nicola McLaughlin Interview. "Family Affair at Medgar Evers College." *New York Times*, April 28, 1982, A26; Doremus, Andrea. "Andrée Nicola-McLaughlin." *Ikon*, Spring/Summer 1984, 98-106.

378 *"Protest takes a lot of thought"*: Juollie Carroll Interview; "Our Style of Protest." *Essence*, October 1982, 136.

378 *It pained her*: Zala Chandler Interview.

379 *"We understood the problematic position"*: Andrée Nicola McLaughlin Interview.

379 *"Sometimes you disagree"*: Zala Chandler Interview.

380 *"Betty was about women"*: Safiya Bandele Interview.

380 *"the greatest testimonies"*: Edison Jackson Interview, March 31, 1999.

380 *"Blacks pay taxes"*: Torain, Martin. "Black College Claims Second-Class Treatment." *New York Metro*, June 4, 1986.

381 *"She held her own"*: Leonard Jeffries Interview, April 8, 2000.

381 *Her fundraising style*: Juollie Carroll Interview.

CHAPTER 15: JOURNEY TO RESPECTABILITY

383 *"I do not weep at the world"*: Hurston, Zora Neale. "How It Feels to be Colored Me." in Alice Walker, ed. *I Love Myself When I am Laughing.* New York: The Feminist Press, 1979, 153.

383 *Betty served an array*: Curriculum Vitae; Hall, Terri. "For Betty Shabazz, Life Is Full Again." (Mount Vernon) *Daily Argus*, March 5, 1977; "A Move to Draft Ali for U.S. Senate." *Sun Reporter*, August 16, 1979, 8; "First Ladies of the Struggle." *Ebony*, February 1984, 124; Laura Ross Brown Interview, June 11, 1999; Cain, Joy Duckett. "Dr. Betty Shabazz." *Essence*, February 1985, 12; Lanker, Brian. *I Dream A World.* New York: Stewart, Tabori & Chang, 1989, 104.

385 *"The homelands are tribal deaths"*: Gilliam, Dorothy. "Women Tell of life Under Apartheid." *Washington Post*, July 18, 1985, C3.

385 *Many of the unofficial attendees*: Hendrix, Kathleen. "Black Women Unite At Forum '85." *Los Angeles times*, July 17, 1985, 1; Davis, Angela. *Women, Culture & Politics.* New York: Random House, 1984, 109-115; *Delegate Magazine*, 1985, 286.

386 *She was among the dignitaries*: Hunter, Charlayne. "5,000 at Robeson's Funeral in Harlem." *New York Times*, January 28, 1976, 36.

386 *Betty's joie de vivre*: Laura Ross Brown Interview, June 11, 1999; Howard Dodson Interview, April 16, 1999; Malveaux, Julianne. "Loving Life; the Legacy of Betty Shabazz." *Black Issues in Higher Education*, July 24, 1997, 53; Kilday, Gregg. "Four Widows Who Dwell in the Present." *Los Angeles Times View*, September 27, 1974, 6; "First Ladies of the Struggle." *Ebony*, February 1984, 124.

387   *"I've changed because"*: Hall, Terri. "For Betty Shabazz, Life Is Full Again."(Mount Vernon) *Daily Argus*, March 5, 1977.

387   *"No one can"*: Cimons, Marlene. "Four Widows Who Dwell in the Present." *Los Angeles Times View*, September 27, 1974, 6-7.

387   *"She ceased to be"*: Dick Gregory Interview, July 30, 1999.

388   *"She had grown"*: James Campbell Interview, March, 27, 2002.

388   *"It is important"*: Cain, Joy Duckett. "Dr. Betty Shabazz." *Essence*, February 1985, 12.

388   *"I am as selfless"*: Valburn, Marjorie. "Dr. Betty Shabazz, Lady With Towering Strength." *New York Amsterdam News*, December 14, 1985, 22.

388   *Generosity and elegance dazzled her comrades*: "Dr. Betty Shabazz, Lady With Towering Strength." *New York Amsterdam News*, December 14, 1985, 4; Howard Dodson Interview.

389   *"Dr. Shabazz, if you please"*: Amiri and Amina Baraka Interview; July 19, 1999.

389   *"Betty did."*: Gil Noble Interview, May 5, 2000.

389   *"We hadn't seen Betty"*: Elinor Sinnette Interview, April 1, 2002.

389   *"You never knew"*: Jean Owensby Interview, April 23, 1999.

390   *"For Pete's sake"*: February 4, 1982 Alex Haley letter to Betty Shabazz, Alex Haley Papers (Courtesy of Schomburg Center for Research in Black Culture, New York).

390   *James Smalls once appeared*: Leonard Jeffries Interview, April 8, 2000.

390   *"She would eat you alive"*: Howard Dodson Interview.

390   *"If you mess with Betty"*: Elombe Brath Interview, April 8, 2000.

390   *Her secretary*: Herman Fulton Interview, July 30, 2000.

391   *"Betty had no naïveté"*: Maya Angelou Interview, September 29, 1999.

391   *"I get profane"*: James Smalls Interview, March 19, 2000.

391   *"I know she didn't take any mess"*: Amina Baraka Interview.

391   *"There were times"*: Gil Noble Interview.

391   *She made hundreds*: Mary Redd Interview, May 20, 1999.

391   *It was years*: Mary Redd Interview.

392   *"I'm not serviced"*: Amina Baraka Interview.

392   *"Fort Knox vault"*:Herman Fulton Interview.

392   *A Malcolmite and archivist*: Preston Wilcox Interview, March 1, 2002.

392   *"There are people who want to run"*: Marge Battle Interview, April 1, 1999.

392   *"She was able to bathe"*: Haki Madhubuti Interview, June 2, 2000.

392   *The serenity of romance*: "First Ladies of the Struggle." *Ebony*, February 1984, 124; Cain, Joy Duckett. "Dr. Betty Shabazz." *Essence*, February 1985, 12; Zala Chandler Interview, June 3, 1999; Brown, Jamie Foster, ed. *Betty Shabazz; A Sisterfriend's Tribute in Words and Pictures*. New York: Simon & Schuster, 1998, 93; Dick Gregory Interview.

393   *The widow's increasingly independent public identity*: Betty Shabazz Curriculum Vitae [Courtesy of Medgar Evers College]; "First Ladies of the Struggle." *Ebony*, February 1984, 124; "Dr. Betty Shabazz Is Our New President." *College Career News*, Summer 1978; James Turner Interview, May 13, 2002.

394   *"a full account"*: Marable, Manning. *Blackwater*. Dayton, Ohio: Black Praxis Press, 1981, 93-121.

394   *"You can't stay mad"*: Katz, Michael. "Ali: Ready, Willing, But Is He Able?" *New York Times*, September 29, 1980, C-1.

395   *"To protect Tommy"*: Wedemeyer, Dee. "Motherhood Mellows a Revolutionary." *Chicago Tribune*, March 12, 1972, 5-9.

395   *"A lot of the bourgeois clung to Betty"*: Gil Noble Interview.

395   *Her nationalist friends*: Amiri Baraka Interview; Sonia Sanchez Interview, August 10, 1999; Herman Fulton Interview; Slacum, Marcia A. "Fight for a Franchise." *Washington Post*, March 4, 1984, B-

1; Brown, Jamie Foster, ed. *Betty Shabazz; A Sisterfriend's Tribute in Words and Pictures.* New York: Simon & Schuster, 1998, 67.

396   *Her corporate forays:* "Bored of Directors?" *Black Times,* January 1973, 10; James H. Cone Interview, May 11, 1999.

397   *Pre-Malcolm sensibilities:* James Turner Interview; Gil Noble Interview; Mary Redd Interview.

397   *This was the woman:* Charles Hurst Interview, May 3, 2002.

397   *Some were startled:* McGriff, Sharon. "Maya Angelou Authors New Book." *Sun Reporter,* November 22, 1975, 13; Byrd, Earl. "Malcolm X's Wife: The Bicentennial Is for Blacks, Too." *Washington Star,* June 29, 1976, B1; Brodie, James Michael. "Carrying on Malcolm's Legacy." *Black Issues in Higher Education,* 22.

399   *The disenchantment was mutual:* Trescott, Jacqueline. "The Caucus and the Comic." *Washington Post,* September 26, 1977, B-1.

399   *"And that's when the brothers say":* James Turner Interview.

399   *She didn't have:* Leonard Jeffries Interview.

399   *So all her movements:* Molefi Asante Interview, March 31, 1999; Safiya Bandele Interview, April 1, 1999.

399   *The Shabazz daughters knew stealth:* "Dr. Betty Shabazz, Lady With Towering Strength." *New York Amsterdam News,* December 14, 1985, 4.

400   *"If you kept running":* Gamilah Shabazz Interview, January 15, 2000.

400   *"almost a humility":* Howard Dodson Interview.

400   *"So Malcolm's widow":* Sonny Carson Interview, March 12, 2000.

400   *"Was it that":* Gil Noble Interview.

400   *"I never would engage her":* Sonia Sanchez Interview.

400   *Myrlie Evers was following a similar script:* Evers-Williams, Myrlie. *Watch Me Fly.* New York: Little, Brown & Company, 1999; Conconi, Chuck. "Personalities." *Washington Post,* May 24, 1983, B3.

401   *His presence lingered in Myrlie's mind:* Evers-Williams, Myrlie. *Watch Me Fly.* New York: Little, Brown & Company, 1999, x, 81; Myrlie Evers-Williams Interview, August 30, 1999.

402   *Betty could relate:* Myrlie Evers-Williams Interview; "Myrlie Evers, First Civil Rights Widow, Weds Again." *Jet,* August 19, 1976, 14-15.

402   *It was different with Coretta:* Williams, Juan. "Coretta's Way." *Washington Post Magazine,* June 4, 1989, 14-19, 39, 40; Crouch Stanley. *Always In Pursuit.* New York: Pantheon Books, 1998, 100; Harris, Art. "Carrying on the Dream." *Washington Post,* January 19, 1986, K3.

403   *But Coretta's eminence:* James Turner Interview; King, Coretta Scott. *My Life With Martin Luther King, Jr.* New York: Holt, Rinehart & Winston, 1969, 261-262.

404   *Still, unease muted the spirit:* Fayer, Steve and Henry Hampton, eds., with Sarah Flynn. *Voices of Freedom; An Oral History of the Civil Rights Movement From the 1950s Through the 1980s.* New York: Bantam Books, 1990, 580; Not-for-attribution Interview; Pomerantz, Gary. "Malcolm's Widow Shabazz Has Long Awaited Recognition of '60s Leader." *Atlanta Journal-Constitution,* September 6, 1992, A1; Cimons, Marlene. "Four Widows Who Dwell in the Present." *Los Angeles Times View,* September 27, 1974, 1, 6-8; Myrlie Evers-Williams Interview; Abdul Alkalimat Interview, June 11, 2002.

405   *As the Movement widows got to know one another:* Myrlie Evers-Williams Interview; Harris, Art. "Carrying on the Dream." *Washington Post,* January 19, 1986, K5; Ward, Hiley H. "Was Malcolm X A Saint of God?" *Detroit Free Press,* February 15, 1969, 10A.

CHAPTER 16: REPERCUSSION

407   *"Sometimes you have to recognize":* Milton Henry Interview, April 4, 2002.

407   *Malcolm was the culture:* Fraser, Gerald C. "Ceremonies Held for Malcolm X." *New York Times,* May 20, 1971, 45.

407 *But even saints can slip*: "Launch Drive To Save Malcolm-King College." *New York Amsterdam News*, July 23, 1975, B1.

408 *Children at a guerrilla-run elementary school*: Randal, Jonathan C. "Eritrean's Long Struggle Also a War of Ideas." *Washington Post*, May 3, 1977, A10.

408 *An army of ideologues*: James Turner Interview, May 13, 2002;; Alexander, Bill. "Ten Years of Tribute to Malcolm." *Washington Post*, May 14, 1981, 1; Gil Noble Interview, May 5, 2000; Leonard Jeffries Interview, April 8, 2000 Elombe Brath Interview, April 8, 2000. ; Valburn, Marjorie. "Dr. Betty Shabazz, Lady With Towering Strength." *New York Amsterdam News*, December 14, 1985, 22. Marge Battle Interview, April 1, 1999.

408 *"We sold thousands"*: James Smalls Interview, March 19, 2000.

408 *Malcolm X Memorial Foundation*: AFRAM Newsprints Malcolm X Memorial Flyer File (courtesy of AFRAM Newsprints, Harlem, New York); "Omaha, Neb. Group Seeking Memorial Honoring Malcolm X." *Jet*, June 4, 1985, 5.

409 *Four thousand weekenders*: Morgan, Thomas. "Parks Packed on Sunny, Warm Day; Sunshine Swells Crowds on Malcolm X Day." *Washington Post*, May 22, 1978, C1.

409 *"We would commune with him"*: Elombe Brath Interview, April 8, 2000.

409 *"I'm sure that she knew"*: Sonia Sanchez Interview, August 10, 1999.

409 *She performed her commemorative duties*: "The East to Honor Malcolm X." *New York Amsterdam News*, February 15, 1975, 3; AFRAM Newsprints Malcolm X Memorial Flyer File (courtesy of AFRAM Newsprints, Harlem, NY).

410 *May 1981 brought a grander affair*: Alexander, Bill. "Ten Years of Tribute to Malcolm." *Washington Post*, May 14, 1981, 1; Browne, Zamgba J. "Widow, 2 Others Get Malcolm X Awards." *New York Amsterdam News*, May 25, 1985, 9.

411 *"When people think of him"*: Cimons, Marlene. "Four Widows Who Dwell in the Present." *Los Angeles Times View*, September 27, 1974, 7.

411 *"That's all they knew"*: Peter Bailey Interview, May 23, 2002.
"violence-prone radical": Sargent, Edward D. "Jesse Jackson; What He Can Do for Blacks, Financially."

411 *Washington Post*, May 6, 1985, F8.

411 *"He knew everything!"*: Leonard Jeffries Interview, April 8, 2000.

411 *Smalls drew a similar rebuke*; James Smalls Interview.

411 *The NBC series*: Wilkins, Roger. "'King' Disappoints NBC and Some Civil Rights Leaders." *New York Times*, February 16, 1978, C19; Shepard, Stephen. "Lay It On the Lion." *Bay State Banner*, March 23, 1978, 12.

412 *Betty wished for Malcolm*: Laura Ross Brown Interview, November 23, 1999; Safiyah Bandele Interview, April 1, 1999; Lee, Paul. "Their Malcolm X…And Ours." *Michigan Citizen*, January 3, 1999, 8.

413 *"Betty felt that Malcolm"*: Amiri Baraka Interview, July 19, 1999.

413 *"a comforting icon"*: Weiwsbrot, Robert. "Celebrating Dr. King's Birthday." *The New Republic*, January 30, 1984, 10.

413 *"It made no difference"*: Myrlie Evers-Williams Interview, August 30, 1999.

413 *"One time she called me"*: Amiri Baraka Interview, July 19, 1999.

414 *The year was 1979*: Videotape of Betty Shabazz February 28, 1979 speech at Howard University (courtesy of E. Ethelbert Miller and Howard University Resource Center).

416 *Memorializing Malcolm*: Mary Redd Interview, May 20, 1999; Hilda Richards Interview, July 30, 1999; Dick Gregory Interview, July 30, 1999.

416 *Betty's attitude towards the merchandising*: Goldman, Peter. *The Death and Life of Malcolm X*. Chicago: University of Illinois Press, 1979, 379.

416 *An amateur artist asked Alex Haley*: February 4, 1982 Alex Haley Letter to Jan Freeman, Alex Haley

Papers (courtesy of Schomburg Center for Research in Black Culture, New York). X, Malcolm with Haley, Alex. *The Autobiography of Malcolm X*. New York: Ballantine Books, 2000, xxi, xxii.

417 *There were times:* Marge Battle Interview; Gil Noble Interview.

418 *The grassroots kept Malcolm's name alive:* Breitman, George. *The Assassination of Malcolm X*. New York: Pathfinder Press, 1976, 128; *New York Times*, October 4, 1970, 5; Rich, Frank. "The Stage: Malcolm X and Elijah Muhammad." *New York Times*, July 15, 1981, C21; McLellan, Joseph. "'X': Opera as History." *Washington Post*, October 13, 1985, L1; Howard Dodson Interview, April 16, 1999; Myrlie Evers-Williams Interview.

419 *Also in the audience:* Fraser, C. Gerald. "A Committed Crowd Supports Premiere of 'X'." *New York Times*, September 29, 1986, C13.

419 *"The legacy of this man":* Sonia Sanchez Interview.

419 *"Them white folks":* Dick Gregory Interview.

419 *"One day":* Myrlie Evers-Williams Interview.

419 *Among the triumphs:* "Community Board Approves Street Name Change to Commemorate Malcolm X." *New York Metro*, April 2, 1985. Elombe Brath Interview.

420 *For her daughters:* Haley, Alex. "Alex Haley Remembers Malcolm." *Essence*, November 1983, 122; Byrd, Earl. "Malcolm X's Wife: The Bicentennial Is for Blacks, Too." *Washington Star*, June 29, 1976, B1; Brown, Jamie Foster, ed. *Betty Shabazz; A Sisterfriend's Tribute in Words and Pictures*. New York: Simon & Schuster, 1998, 45, 143; Laura Ross Brown Interview, November 23, 1999.

420 *She taught her daughters:* Laughinghouse, Amy. "Mothers of the Civil Rights Movement." *Upscale*, May 1997, 39; Dorothy Pleas Interview, February 8, 2001; Finke, Nikki. "A Certain Peacefulness." *Los Angeles Times Magazine*, January 8, 1989, 1; Haley, Alex. "Alex Haley Remembers Malcolm." *Essence*, November 1983, 122.

421 *"I would also like to write a play":* Bailey, Peter A. "The Ties That Bind." *Essence*, January 1982, 107.

421 *In 1979, she met:* Clayton, Dawn. "The Daughters of Malcolm X and Martin Luther King Team Up to Bring A Play of Hope to Kids." *People*, September 5, 1983, 99; Christon, Lawrence. "Going Her Way." *Los Angeles Times Calendar*, March 1, 1992, 84; Dove-Morse, Pheralyn. "Daughters of Slain Leaders Continue Their Fathers' Work." *National Leader*, March 3, 1983, 20; Trescott, Jacqueline. "Martin Luther King III." *Washington Post*, August 27, 1983, C1; Cain, Joy Duckett. "Dr. Betty Shabazz." *Essence*, February 1985, 12.

422 *Even rebellious Gamilah:* Gamilah Shabazz Interview, January 15, 2000.

422 *"She's made a tremendous":* Valburn, Marjorie. "Dr. Betty Shabazz, Lady With Towering Strength." *New York Amsterdam News*, December 14, 1985, 4.

422 *"unless they become discouraged":* Tarter, Margaret. "Malcolm X's Sister: His Mentor." *Bay State Banner*, February 17, 1977, 15.

423 *Some of their angst:* Bailey, Peter A. "The Ties That Bind." *Essence*, January 1982, 107; Clayton, Dawn. "The Daughters of Malcolm X and Martin Luther King Team Up to Bring A Play of Hope to Kids." *People*, September 5, 1983, 100.

423 *The militancy of Malcolm's:* Graham, Lawrence Otis. "From Outcast to Heroine." *U.S. News & World Report*, June 16, 1997, 60-61; Finke, Nikki. "A Certain Peacefulness." *Los Angeles Times Magazine*, January 8, 1989, 1.

424 *Some of Attallah's siblings:* Corey, Mary and M. Dion Thompson. "The Content of Their Character." *Baltimore Sun*, March 30, 1989; Lecayo, Richard. "The Troubles She's Seen." *Time*, June 16, 1997, 48.

424 *Little Malcolm was not:* Laura Ross Brown Interview; Amina Baraka Interview, July 19, 1999; Howard Dodson Interview.

425 *"Malcolm felt that blacks should know":* "Dr. Betty Shabazz's Final Words." Interview with Bernard White and Amy Goodman, Pacifica Radio, WBAI, New York City, May 19, 1997.

425 *"Betty knew Ella"*: James Smalls Interview.

425 *Attallah would nevertheless*: Hurst, Charles. *Passport to Freedom*. Hamden, CT: Linnet Books, 1972, 10; Sara Mitchell Interview, December 18, 2000; Bailey, Peter A. "The Ties That Bind." *Essence*, January 1982, 107.

426 *"She hadn't seen this woman in years"*: Gamilah Shabazz Interview.

426 *"Raising the children"*: Muriel Feelings Interview, April 6, 2000.

426 *"I walked out of situations"*: Gamilah Shabazz Interview.

426 *The mutinies*: Finke, Nikki. "A Certain Peacefulness." *Los Angeles Times Magazine*, January 8, 1989, 1; Christon, Lawrence. "Going Her Way." *Los Angeles Times Calendar*, March 1, 1992, 84; Valburn, Marjorie. "Dr. Betty Shabazz, Lady With Towering Strength." *New York Amsterdam News*, December 14, 1985, 4.

427 *She had always balanced*: Laura Ross Brown Interview; Ruth Summerford Interview, January 12, 2001; Shelmon Sandlin Interview, January 13, 2001; Clayton, Dawn. "The Daughters of Malcolm X and Martin Luther King Team Up to Bring A Play of Hope to Kids." *People*, September 5, 1983, 100; Corey, Mary and M. Dion Thompson. "The Content of Their Character." *Baltimore Sun*, March 30, 1989; Hopkins, Ellen. "Their Father's Daughters." *Rolling Stone*, November 30, 1989, 77.

428 *After fifteen years as a backdrop*: Haberman, Clyde. "City Discussing A Hotel Project on Site of Audubon Ballroom With Private Developers." *New York Times*, May 4, 1981, B3.

428 *The most aggressive*: "Columbia Is Buying Audubon Ballroom." *New York Times*, February 24, 1983, B9.

429 *"She wanted to know"*: Larry Dais Interview, June 8, 1999.

429 *Betty withheld her blessing*: Anderson, Susan Heller and David W. Dunlap. "Ballroom in Jeopardy." *New York Times*, September 11, 1985, B3; Anderson, Susan Heller and David W. Dunlap. "Endangered Ballroom." *New York Times*, October 11, 1985, B4; Anekwe, Simon. "Dr. Shabazz Not Consulted by Those Trying to Save Audubon." *New York Amsterdam News*, March 17, 1990, 5.

430 *Gene Roberts, who served as one*: Asbury, Edith Evans. "Detective Tells Panther Trial of His Attempt to Save Malcolm X." *New York Times*, December 8, 1970, 40.

430 *Suspicion intensified*: Carmody, Deirdre. "Blacks Plan Suit to Get FBI Files." *New York Times*, March 23, 1974, 61.

430 *As ominous details*: Smith, Baxter. "New Evidence of FBI 'Disruption' Program." *Black Scholar*, July-August 1975, 43-48.

431 *Coretta Scott King to seek reparations*: "Dr. King's Family Seeking Damages." *New York Times*, October 25, 1979, B15.

431 *Twelve-year campaign*: Anderson, Karl E. "Movie Scripts on Malcolm X Interested FBI." *Washington Post*, November 5, 1979, A10.

431 *"A number of people"*: "Dr. Betty Shabazz's Final Words." Interview with Bernard White and Amy Goodman, Pacifica Radio, WBAI, New York City, May 19, 1997.

431 *In late 1977, the long-closed homicide case*: Maitland, Leslie. "Malcolm X's Slayer Calls Two Innocent Though Convicted." *New York Times*, December 7, 1977, B4; "Federal Hearings Asked Into Malcolm X Murder." *New York Times*, April 30, 1979, D8; Goldman, Peter. "Who Killed Malcolm X?" *Newsweek*, May 7, 1979, 39; Laurino, Maria. "Who Were the Killers?" *Village Voice*, February 26, 1985, 28.

432 *Passed unto the ancestors*: "Elijah Muhammad Dead; Black Muslim Leader, 77." *New York Times*.February 26, 1975, 1.

433 *The Nation had gentrified*: Goldman, Peter. *The Death and Life of Malcolm X*. Chicago: University of Illinois Press, 1979, 397-394; De Angelis, Therese. *Louis Farrakhan*. Philadelphia: Chelsea House Publishers, 1998, 73-79.

433 *Some of the most grotesque chapters:* "Black Leader Slain By Boston Gunmen; Muslim Feud Hinted."
New York Times, May 3, 1973, 26; "Black Muslim Leader Shabazz Slain in Trap." *Chicago Tribune,*
September 5, 1973, 1; Delaney, Paul. "Internal Struggle Shakes Black Muslims." *New York Times,*
January 21, 1972, 1; Evanzz, Karl. *The Judas Factor.* New York: Thunder's Mouth Press, 1992, 317-
322.

434 *Muhammad's son Wallace:* Sheppard, Nathaniel Jr. "Nationalist Faction of Black Muslim Movement
Gains Strength." *New York Times,* March 8, 1982, A12; Goldman, Peter. *The Death and Life of
Malcolm X.* Chicago: University of Illinois Press, 1979, 434-435; Gardell, Mattias. *In the Name of
Elijah Muhammad.* Durham: Duke University Press, 1996, 119-143.

434 *Among the disenchanted:* Cummings, Judith. "Black Muslim Seeks to Change Movement." *New York
Times,* March 19, 1978, 37.

435 *Already the heir:* Hunter, Charlayne. "Black Muslim Temple Renamed for Malcolm X; Move Reflects
Acceptance of Slain Ex-Leader." *New York Times,* February 2, 1976, 1.

435 *"He knew where the Nation should go":* Hunter, Charlayne. "Black Muslim Temple Renamed for
Malcolm X; Move Reflects Acceptance of Slain Ex-Leader." *New York Times,* February 2, 1976,
1.

436 *Books and news reports:* Laurino, Maria. "Who Were the Killers?" *Village Voice,* February 26, 1985, 28.

436 *Malcolm's ghost visited her:* Ruth Clark Interview, April 14, 1999; Mary Redd Interview, May 20, 1999;
Myrlie Evers-Williams Interview; Hilda Richards Interview, July 30, 1999; Elombe Brath
Interview.

436 *She swore that the Muslims:* Amiri Baraka Interview; Elombe Brath Interview; Gil Noble Interview;
James Smalls Interview; Haki Madhubuti Interview, June 2, 2000.

437 *Her friends tried to soften:* Amiri Baraka Interview; Ruth Clark Interview; Alpern, David M. "The
Farrakhan Factor." *Newsweek,* May 7, 1984, 43; Milton Henry Interview.

438 *Jesse Jackson's presidential bid:* "Jesse Jackson's Controversial Ally." *U.S. News & World Report.* April
23, 1984, 13; "Bombshells From a Black Muslim." *U.S. News & World Report,* October 21, 1985,
10.

438 *"When it comes to intergroup relations":* "Coretta King Criticizes Farrakhan, Says Muslim Leader Has
Hurt Civil Rights Cause." *Los Angeles Times,* September 19, 1985, 14.

438 *She granted several interviews:* "Malcolm X's Widow Denounces Farrakhan." *New York Metro,*
November 3, 1985; "Widow of Malcolm X Condemns Farrakhan." *New York Times,* November 4,
1985, B7; Sinclair, Abiola. "Betty Shabazz Denounces Farrakhan." *New York Amsterdam News,*
November 16, 1985, 24.

CHAPTER 17: CELEBRITY

441 *"I shall come back to you":* Jacques, Amy, ed. *The Philosophy and Opinions of Marcus Garvey.* Dover,
Massachusetts: The Majority Press, 1986.

441 *"It is of great moment":* David Dinkins Interview, May 7, 2002.

441 *"She was the most accessible":* Molefi Asante Interview, March 31, 1999.

441 *"with greetings usually reserved":* Gilliam, Dorothy. "Reuniting the Positives." *Washington Post,*
September 12, 1988, D3.

442 *Short list of candidates:* Browne, Zamgba J. "4 Tapped for Presidency." *New York Amsterdam News,*
September 12, 1987, 4.

442 *Among the highlights:* Lanker, Brian, ed. *I Dream A World.* New York: Steward, Tabori & Chang, 1989.
Gamarekian, Barbara. "Show's Subjects Gather to Celebrae Sisterhood." *New York Times,*
February 9, 1989, C20.

442 *One winter afternoon:* "Man and Woman Rob Malcolm X's Daughter." *New York Times,* January 6,
1988, B3; Gamilah Shabazz Interview, January 15, 2000.

442 *The rebirth began*: Winerip, Michael. "Our Towns: Dr. King's Dream Lives On in East Orange." *New York Times*, January 19, 1986, 36; Browne, J. Zamgba. "Parades Mark Malcolm's Day." *New York Amsterdam News*, May 17, 1986, 4.

443 *Lobbying to rename*: Noel, Peter. "Name That Street Row Heating Up in Harlem." *New York Amsterdam News*, May 31, 1986, 3; *Big Red News*, May 16, 1987, 1.

443 *Most powerfully in the hip-hop soul*: Pareles, Jon. "'Radical Rap: Of Pride and Prejudice." *New York Times*, December 16, 1990, B1; Ahearn Charlie. "The Five Percent Solution." *Spin*, February 1991, 55-57, 76.

443 *The black-brown, hip-hop generation*: Fraser, Gerald. "The Voice of Malcolm X Has an Audience Again." *New York Times*, February 20, 1990, B3; Wood, Joe. "Looking for Malcolm." *Village Voice*, May 29, 1990, 42; Gillespie, Marcia Ann. "Malcolm's Journey from Troubling Prophet to Icon." *Emerge*.

444 *"a prophet"*: February 1990, 23; "Malcolm X's Unsilenced Voice." *Boston Globe*, February 21, 1990, 18.

444 *Not everyone was as eulogistic*: McCarthy, Colman. "Malcolm X's Ruinous Message." *Washington Post*, November 21, 1992, A25. Hoar, William P. "Malcolm X: Myth Versus Reality." *The New American*, November 30, 1992, 5-10; Frady, Marshall. "The Children of Malcolm." *New Yorker*, October 12, 1992, 81; Page, Clarence. "What Malcolm X Really Accomplished." *Washington Times*, November 25, 1992, G4.

444 *Most damaging dispraise*: Perry, Bruce. *Malcolm; The Life of a Man who Changed Black America*. New York: Station Hill Press, 1991.

445 *To recognize his May 19 birthday*: Chavis, Ben. "A Call for Malcolm X National Day." *New York Amsterdam News*, March 17, 1990, 15.

445 *Twenty-fifth anniversary*: Fraser, Gerald. "The Voice of Malcolm X Has an Audience Again." *New York Times*, February 20, 1990, B3; Daniels, Ron. "With Respect to Malcolm." *Essence*, February, 1990, 126.

445 *Betty played her traditional role*: *Big Red News*, May 24, 1986, 1; *Big Red News*, May 16, 1987, 1; Gamilah Shabazz Interview; Elombe Brath Interview April 8, 2000; Browne, J. Zamgba. "Parades Mark Malcolm's Day." *New York Amsterdam News*, May 17, 1986, 4.

446 *The widow's guardianship*: Herman Fulton Interview, July 30, 2000.

446 *"That man has problems"*: Boyd, Herb. "Family of Malcolm X Denounces White Author of New Book." *New York Amsterdam News*, November 30, 1991, 5.

446 *"Well, typically the widow"*: Transcript of November 18, 1992 CNN broadcast titled "Historical Place of Malcolm X Evaluated."

446 *Betty had a growing sense*: Abdul Alkalimat Interview, June 11, 2002.

447 *"Yeah, alright"*: James Turner Interview, May 13, 2002.

447 *Transcendent minutes with Winnie Mandela*: Benjamin, Anne, ed. *Part of My Soul Went with Him*. New York: W. W. Norton & Co., 1984; Harrison, Nancy. *Winnie Mandela*. London: Victor Gollanca, Ltd., 1985.

448 *Winnie had found herself submerged*: Reiss, Spencer. "Soweto's 'Winnie Problem.'" *Newsweek*, February 13, 1989, 35; "South Africa; Fallen Queen." *The Economist*, February 18, 1989, 40; Transcript of "Mandela: A New Standard of Leadership?" the July 29, 1990 taping of *Like It Is*, WABC-TV, New York; Reynolds, Barbara. "Mandela's Mission." *USA Today*, June 27, 1990, 11A.

449 *"Our march to freedom is irreversible"*: Transcript of "Mandela: A New Standard of Leadership?" the July 29, 1990 taping of *Like It Is*, WABC-TV, New York; Whitaker, Mark with Jeffrey Bartholet and Spencer Reiss. "Free!" *Newsweek*, February 19, 1990, 38.

450 *"We got bumrushed"*: Sam Anderson Interview, March 5, 2001.

450 *On June 21*: Sawyer, Jon. "Winnie Mandela Warns of War." *St. Louis Post-Dispatch*, June 22, 1990, 18A; Transcript of "Mandela: A New Standard of Leadership?" the July 29, 1990 taping of *Like It*

Is, WABC-TV, New York; "Mandela Through the Eyes of Harlem." Light-Action Production, Broadway Video,1990.

452 *The widow reunited*: Jackson, Derrick Z. "Helping the Oppressed." *Boston Globe*, January 24, 1993, 75; "Words of the Week." *Jet*, February 8, 1993, 40; Annette Hutchins Interview, May 14, 2000.

453 *An old resistance*: Preston Wilcox Interview, March 1, 2002; James Turner Interview.

453 *Unfurled the widow's sails*: "Widow Announces 20th Malcolm X Holiday Gala." *New York Amsterdam News*, April 13, 1991, 10.

453 *"If it was too radical"*: May 18, 1999 Jean Owensby letter to author.

453 *"She was concerned"*: James H. Cone Interview, May 11, 1999.

454 *Betty who took the podium*: Abdul Alkalimat Interview; Transcript of Betty Shabazz Speech, "Malcolm X: Radical Tradition and a Legacy of Struggle" Conference, November 1, 1990, New York (courtesy of Abdul Alkalimat).

455 *She found herself again embroiled*: Anekwe, Simon. "Dr. Shabazz Not Consulted by Those Trying to Save Audubon." *New York Amsterdam News*, March 17, 1990, 5; Muschamp, Herbert. "Architecture View; Once and Future Audubon." *New York Times*, August 23, 1992; Lawrence, Beverly Hall. "The Last Dance; Audubon Ballroom To Be Reborn as Biotech Center." *Newsday*, November 5, 1992, 89; Macintyre, Ben. "White Heroes Join Malcolm X Tribute." *The Times* (London), November 18, 1992; Carillo, Karen. "Coalition Charges Columbia U. with 'Environmental Racism.'" *New York Amsterdam News*, January 2, 1993, 1; Carillo, Karen. "Columbia U.'s Audubon Project Said to Enjoy Support From Prominent Blacks." *New York Amsterdam News*, April 10, 1993, 3.

456 *The movie itself*: Thompson, Anne. "Spike Lee Has Firm Handle on Slippery Malcolm X Story." *Toronto Star*, July 28, 1991, C1; "Black Celebs 'Bail Out' Director Spike Lee's 'Malcolm X' Film Project." *Jet*, June 8, 1992, 30; Seymour, Gene. "What Took So Long?" *Newsday*, November 15, 1992, 5; King, Susan. "Her 'American Dream'; Angela Bassett Says Playing the Mother of the Jacksons was Emotional and Uplifting." *Los Angeles Times TV Times*, November 15, 1992, 4; Lee, Spike with Ralph Wiley. *By Any Means Necessary*. New York: Hyperion, 1992, 9.

457 *Betty drifted closer*: Lee, Spike with Ralph Wiley. *By Any Means Necessary*. New York: Hyperion, 1992, 25, 33, 98.

458 *Malcolmites pounced on the project*: "The Battle for Malcolm X." *Newsweek*, August 26, 1991, 52-54; Seymour, Gene. "What Took So Long?" *Newsday*, November 15, 1992, 5; Rule, Sheila. "Film; Malcolm X: The Facts, the Fictions, the Film." *New York Times*, November 15, 1992.

459 *Betty stayed out of the fray*: Christon, Lawrence. "Going Her Way." *Los Angeles Times Calendar*, March 1, 1992, 5; Boyd, Herb. 'Dr. Betty Shabazz Expresses Views on Spike's Film About Her Husband." *New York Amsterdam News*, August 17, 1991, 3.

460 *"She tried to deal with Spike and I"*: Amiri Baraka Interview, July 19, 1999.

460 *"I said what was true"*: O'Donnell, Maureen. "Malcolm X's Widow Urges Blacks to Seek Self-Reliance." *Chicago Sun-Times*, January 20, 1992, 3.

460 *"I'm on the radio"*: Dick Gregory Interview, July 30, 1999.

461 *Ignoring the Malcolm franchise*: Carr, Jay. "Spike and Malcolm; X Marks the Spot Lee has Put Himself On." *Boston Globe*, November 15, 1992, 77; "X Marks the Hip." *People*, October 12, 1992, 87; Hanson, Paul. "Designers Hope Malcolm X Ring Appeals to Both Rich and Poor." *St. Petersburg Times*, December 11, 1992, 3B; "X as a Fashion Statement: 'It's More Than a Letter.'" *St. Petersburg Times*, November 19, 1992, 1E; Freeman, Gregory. "'X'-Ploitation Is Overwhelming Message of Man." *St. Louis Post-Dispatch*, November 17, 1992, 1C; Davis, Ed. "Finding the Good in 'X' Merchandising." *Pittsburgh Courier*, November 21, 1992, A7; Sullivan, R. Lee. "Spike Lee Versus Mrs. Malcolm X." *Forbes*, October 12, 1992, 136; Bock, James. "King's Heirs Battle to Protect His Legacy." *Baltimore Sun*, January 19, 1994, 14A.

462 *Coretta Scott King had developed a reputation*: "King's Heirs Battle to Protect His Legacy." *Baltimore Sun*, January 19, 1994, 1A.

463 *"sort of out of the box"*: Howard Dodson Interview, April 16, 1999.

463 *"Malcolm's mass popular appeal"*: Molefi Kete Asante Interview, March 31, 1999.

463 *"Dr. Shabazz does feel"*: Hackett, Larry. "The Selling of Malcolm X: $100 Million in Spinoffs at Stake." *The Gazette* (Montreal), November 17, 1992, B6.

464 *The decision to litigate*: "Betty Shabazz Sues Over 'X' Profiteering." *New York Amsterdam News*, October 3, 1992, 26; "Malcolm X's Widow Suing Over Use of Name, Image on Caps, Other Apparel." *Jet*, October 5, 1992, 36; "Chronicle; "Malcolm X's Wife Sues Haley Kin on Manuscript Sale." *Washington Post*, November 22, 1992; "Malcolm X's Widow Suing Haley Estate." *Los Angeles Times*, November 22, 1992, A24; Malcolm X's Widow Charges Copyright Infringement." *New York Times*, July 10, 1991, B4; Boyd, Herb. "Dispute over Malcolm X Book Pits Betty Shabazz Against Chicago-based Activist." *New York Amsterdam News*, July 20, 1991, 8.

465 *Newsday, reported*: Rothmyer, Karen. "Malcolm X Deal Angers Admirers." *Newsday*, November 6, 1992, 4.

466 *Entanglement with South African politics*: Clairborne, William. "King Meets With Boesak After Snub of Botha." *Washington Post*, September 11, 1986, A35; Schmemann, Serge. "Coretta King Cancels Botha Talk After Pressure By Apartheid Foes." *New York Times*, September 10, 1986, A1.

466 *Brath could see*: Elombe Brath Interview, April 8, 2000.

467 *Betty and Spike Lee got together*: Sullivan, R. Lee. "Spike Lee Versus Mrs. Malcolm X." *Forbes*, October 12, 1992, 136; Pendleton, Jennifer. "Malcolm X's Widow, Lee Sign Licensing Pact." *Variety*, November 23, 1992, 62.

467 *"an engrossing mosaic"*: Kempley, Rita. "Spike Lee's Epic on a Human Scale." *Washington Post*, November 18, 1992, C1.

468 *Betty left an upstate New York*: Trescott, Jacqueline. "The Many Faces of 'Malcolm X'; Betty Shabazz, Recalling the Life Behind the Image." *Washington Post*, November 19, 1992, C1; "Malcolm X's Wife Among Celebrity Throng for 'X' Opening." Transcript of November 17, 1992 CNN broadcast.

468 *To John Henrik Clarke*: Boyd, Herb. "Dr. John Henrik Clarke Helped Malcolm X Write the OAAU Charter." *New York Amsterdam* News, November 28, 1992, 8.

468 *As were black notables*: Newkirk, Pamela. "X: 28 Years After; 'First, Messenger; Now, Message.'" *Newsday*, February 21, 1993, 22; "Black Leaders Hold Differing Views on 'Malcolm X'." Transcript of November 25, 1992, CNN broadcast.

468 *She swallowed them*: Carr, Jay. "Spike and Malcolm; X Marks the Spot Lee has Put Himself On." *Boston Globe*, November 15, 1992, 77; Trescott, Jacqueline. "The Many Faces of 'Malcolm X'; Betty Shabazz, Recalling the Life Behind the Image." *Washington Post*, November 19, 1992, C1; Cunningham, Bill and Daniel Golden. "Malcolm, the Boston Years." *Boston Globe Magazine*, February 16, 1992, 19; Lee, Spike with Ralph Wiley. *By Any Means Necessary*. New York: Hyperion, 1992, 49.

469 *Betty paid the rumblings*: Pomerantz, Gary. "Malcolm's Widow Shabazz Has Long Awaited Recognition of '60s Leader." *Atlanta Journal-Constitution*, September 6, 1992, A1; Graham, Renee. "Keeping Her Husband's Message Alive." *Boston Globe*, November 18, 1992, 45; Abdul Alkalimat Interview; Williams, Jeannie. "An 'X' Opening that Opens Your Eyes." *USA Today*, November 18, 1992, 2D.

470 *"they will recognize Medgar"*: Myrlie Evers-Williams Interview, August 30, 1999.

470 *The news media courted Betty*: Pomerantz, Gary. "Malcolm's Widow Shabazz Has Long Awaited Recognition of '60s Leader." *Atlanta Journal-Constitution*, September 6, 1992, A1; Graham, Renee. "Keeping Her Husband's Message Alive." *Boston Globe*, November 18, 1992, 45; Nelson,

Jill. "Voice of Malcolm X Resounding in Song, Speeches and Celebrations." *Washington Post*, May 20, 1989, B7.

471 *Betty traveled*: Sterritt, David. "Behind the 'Malcolm X' Film: A Need to Set Things Straight." *Christian Science Monitor*, November 24, 1992, 1.

471 *The widow drew the line*: Roberts, Sam. "Metro Matters; Dan Quayle, Malcolm X and American Values." *New York Times*, June 15, 1992, B3.

471 *May 1993 race-relations panel*: Drury, Dave and Ellen Nakashima. "Can't We Get Along? Forum Seeks Answer." *Hartford Courant*, May 23, 1993, B1; Green, Rick. "School Entranced By Shabazz's Message; Malcolm X's Widow Offers Her Wisdom." *Hartford Courant*, February 20, 1993, B1.

472 *New York Urban League*: "Chronicle." *New York Times*, March 12, 1990, B9.

472 *"We changed the name"*: Butts, Carolyn A. "Harlem Honors Dr. Betty Shabazz, Declares Malcolm X Blvd. Drug Free." *New York Amsterdam News*, March 30, 1991, 3.

472 *During President Clinton's inauguration*: Murphy, Frances. "Inaugural Celebration Hits Washington by Storm." *Washington Afro-American*, January 23, 1993, A1.

472 *"She almost broke my hand"*: Maya Angelou Interview, September 29, 1999.

472 *"The rigorous separatism"*: Gates, Henry Louis. "Heroes, Inc." *New Yorker*, January 16, 1995, 6. Gates, Henry Louis and Hendrik Hertzberg. "Requiem; The Unexpected Legacy of Betty Shabazz." *New Yorker*, July 7, 1997, 4.

473 *"Malcolm played the heavy"*: Wood, Joe. "Looking For Malcolm." *Village Voice*, May 29, 1990, 43.

473 *Betty joined a celebration*: O'Donnell, Maureen. "Malcolm X's Widow Urges Blacks to Seek Self-Reliance." *Chicago Sun-Times*, January 20, 1992, 3.

473 *She teamed up with Coretta*: Pomerantz, Gary. "Work with L.A. Gangs Paying Off, King Says." *Atlanta Journal-Constitution*, June 27, 1992, D10.

473 *Coretta sent Betty*: September 1995 Coretta Scott King Letter to Betty Shabazz (courtesy of Gamilah Shabazz).

474 *"that's power"*: Amiri Baraka Interview.

474 *Her friends knew her*: Messud, Claire. "No Disrespect to the Widow." *The Guardian* (London), March 1, 1993, 11; Howard Dodson Interview; Larry Dais Interview, June 8, 1999.

475 *Candid, three-hour interview*: Edwards, Audrey. "The Fire This Time." *Essence*, October, 1997, 76. Edwards, Audrey and Susan L. Taylor. "Loving and Losing Malcolm." *Essence*, February 1992, 50; Mills, David. "The Resurrection of Malcolm X." *Washington Post*, February 25, 1990, F6.

475 *She traveled abroad regularly*: Annette Hutchins Interview, May 14, 2000.

476 *The widow's growing confidence*: Moore, Teresa. "Minority Workers Key to Economy, Black Leader Says." *Newsday*, July 30, 1990, 6; Goldman, Ari L. "Blacks and Jews Join Hands for a Brighter Future." *New York Times*, December 18, 1992, B1; Johnson, Jason B. "Brooklyn Rabbi, Malcolm X Widow Discuss Racial Peace." *Boston Herald*, March 2, 1994, 3.

476 *Mike Tyson behind bars*: "Betty Shabazz Visits Mike Tyson In Prison." *Jet*, April 15, 1993, 46; "Newsmakers; 'His Prayer Moved Me.'" *Houston Chronicle*, March 19, 1993, A2.

477 *She attended a Chicago tribute*: "Islamic Leader Mohammed Saluted." *Chicago Sun-Times*, May 2, 1993, 42.

477 *Betty's generosity of spirit*: Annette Hutchins Interview; Herman Fulton Interview; James Smalls Interview, March 19, 2000; Dick Gregory Interview; Zerrie Campbell Interview, July 2, 1992.

478 *Betty's growing influence*: Mary Redd Interview, May 20, 1999; Ruth Clark Interview, April 14, 1999; Edwards, Audrey and Susan L. Taylor. "Loving and Losing Malcolm." *Essence*, February 1992, 112.

CHAPTER 18: MOTHER'S DAY

478 *"When you cross the black woman"*: Harrison, Nancy. *Winnie Mandela*. London: Victor Gollancz, Ltd., 1985, 64.

479 *Betty shored up her international resume*: Tyler, Patrick E. "Hillary Clinton in Beijing as Women's Conference Opens." *New York Times*, September 5, 1995, A3; Laura Ross Brown Interview, June 11, 1999; Leonard Jeffries Interview, April 8, 2000; James Smalls Interview, March 19, 2000.

480 *"It was touching"*: President Jerry John Rawlings' November 22, 1995 letter to Betty Shabazz (courtesy of Jean Owensby).

480 *"Before closing our talks"*: Dr. Weiyan Meng's November 2, 1995 letter to Betty Shabazz (courtesy of Gamilah Shabazz).

480 *She joined her friend*: "Reorganized Black Women's Political Congress Takes on Racism, Sexism." *New York Amsterdam News*, October 9, 1993, 15.

480 *She backed the causes*: Browne, J. Zamgba. "Sharpton Assails Critics." *New York Amsterdam News*, June 11, 1994, 1. Burroughs, Todd. "John Henrik Clarke and the Reconstruction of the African Mind: Drums in the Global Village." *New York Amsterdam News*, February 11, 1995, 10.

480 *"I wish you power"*: Shabazz, Betty. "Commencement Address." in *Journal of African American Speeches*. Washington, D.C.: Bethune-DuBois Publications, 1997, 93.

480 *More modest affairs*: Connors, Cathy. "Carol Riley Expands her Restaurant Chain and a Community Pays Tribute." *New York Amsterdam News*, December 23, 1995, 20; "Local Ladies Recite, Wax Nostalgic with Author." *New York Amsterdam News*, November 4, 1995, 18.

481 *The widow's philanthropy*: Betty Shabazz Papers (courtesy of Gamilah Shabazz).

481 *She was always jotting*: Trescott, Jacqueline. "The Many Faces of 'Malcolm X'; Betty Shabazz, Recalling the Life Behind the Images." *Washington Post*, November 18, 1992, C1; Mary Redd Interview, May 20, 1999.

481 *"Me and the limousine driver"*: Dick Gregory Interview, July 30, 1999; Coleman, Christena. "Every Woman's Tragedy." *Daily News* (New York), June 5, 1997, 54.

482 *A conversation with singer Ida McBeth*: Hearne, Christopher, Jr. "Betty and Ida Become Bathroom Buddies; Malcolm X's Widow, KC Singer Share Magic Makeup Moments." *Kansas City Star*, November 16, 1995, E2.

482 *"And then here comes"*: Haygood Wil and Fred Kaplan. "For Shabazz, No Refuge from Legacy of Struggle." *Boston Globe*, June 8, 1997, A1.

482 *"my greatest teacher"*: Dowdy, Zachary R. "Shabazz to Curry Crowd: Prepare for the Future." *Boston Globe*, February 24, 1995, 28.

482 *In Jaunuary 1996*: Flynn, Pat. "Big Crowd Welcomes New Library Warmly." *San Diego Union-Tribune*, January 7, 1996, B1.

482 *In April 1996*: Smith, Matthew P. "Activist, Meese Debate Affirmative Action." *Pittsburgh Post-Gazette*, December 7, 1995, C5.

483 *"She became very forecful"*: Amiri Baraka Interview, June 19, 1999.

483 *"One saw a maturation"*: Sonia Sanchez Interview, August 10, 1999.

483 *"The ghost of that affair"*: James Turner Interview, May 13, 2002.

483 *The Movement widows were now calling*: Myrlie Evers-Williams Interview, August 30, 1999.

483 *In the fall of 1995*: Browne, J. Zamgba. "Women Launch Crusade." *New York Amsterdam News*, September 30, 1995, 14; Weinraub, Judith. "Delores Tucker, Gansta Buster; She's Playing Defense in Her Offensive Against Rap." *Washington Post*, November 29, 1995, C1; Harris, Hamil R. "Women of Sorrow and Strength; Widows of Civil Rights Leaders Are Honored at Power Brunch." *Washington Post*, September 25, 1995, D3.

484 *"She could go off!"*: Herman Fulton Interview, July 30, 2000.

484 *"I did that for effect"*: Jean Owensby Interview, April 23, 1999.

484 *"It was just society"*: Gamilah Shabazz Interview, January 15, 2000.

485 *A softer soul*: Mary Redd Interview; Laura Ross Brown Interview; James Turner Interview; Betty Shabazz Papers (courtesy of Gamilah Shabazz); Larry Dais Interview, June 8, 1999.

485 *From a distance*: Betty Shabazz Papers (courtesy of Gamilah Shabazz).

485 *"There was a great sense"*: Jean Owensby Interview.

485 *Some thought*: Laura Ross Brown Interview; Ruth Clark Interview, April 14, 1999; Herman Fulton Interview.

486 *"I ain't a citizen"*: Elombe Brath Interview, April 8, 2000.

487 *Betty never stopped shepherding*: Gamilah Shabazz Interview; Finke, Nikki. "A Certain Peacefulness." *Los Angeles Times Magazine*, January 8, 1989, 1; Powell, Kevin. "New Black Student Group Founded by Daughter of Malcolm X." *New York Amsterdam News*, November 9, 1991, 33; Mitchell, Rick. "X Roads; Malcolm X's Daughter Wants Music to be Accepted on its Own Merits." *Houston Chronicle*, November 27, 1992, 1; "Fine in a Shabazz Case." *New York Times*, June 15, 1995, A18.

488 *On September 13*: Helen Malloy Obituary in program for memorial service, held September 22, 1994 at Bethel A.M.E. Church, Detroit (courtesy of Bentley Historical Library, Ann Arbor, MI).

488 *Betty was still in pain*: Videotape of Betty Shabazz's February 6, 1992 speech at University of Cincinatti (courtesy of Gamilah Shabazz).

489 *"I'm sure"*: Amina Baraka Interview, June 19, 1999.

489 *One of those triggermen*: Churcher, Sharon. "I Pulled the Trigger on Malcolm X." *Weekly Journal*, March 11, 1993, 5.

490 *Betty was still convinced*: Noel, Peter. "Tell us about your role in Malcolm X's Murder." *New York Amsterdam News*, November 16, 1985, 1; Levinsohn, Florence Hamlish. *Looking for Farrakhan*. Chicago: Ivan R. Dee, 1997, 78.

490 *On the subject of Malcolm*: Lee, Spike. *By Any Means Necessary*. New York: Hyperion, 1992, 50-56; Barboza, Steven. *American Jihad*. New York: Doubleday, 1993, 146-147.

490 *The Malcolm question did not fetter Farrakhan*: Gardell, Mattias. *In the Name of Elijah Muhammad: Louis Farrakhan and the Nation of Islam*. Durham: Duke University Press, 1996, 119-143; Garfield, William F. Lowman. "Attacks on Farrakhan Measure his Success in Galvanizing Us." *Pittsburgh Post-Gazette*, April 13, 1994, B2; Madhubuti, Haki. *Claiming Earth*. Chicago: Third World Press, 1994, 74; Singh, Robert. *The Farrakhan Phenomenon*. Washington, D.C.: Georgetown University Press, 1997, 54-59; Haskins, Jim. *Louis Farrakhan and the Nation of Islam*. New York: Walker and Company, 1996, 107-110.

492 *A three-hour bombast*: O'Donnell, Maureen. "Farrakhan To Muslims: Honor Elijah Muhammad." *Chicago Sun-Times*, February 22, 1993, 10.

492 *The declaration became the bombshell*: "Brother Minister: the Assassination of El-Hajj Malik Shabazz." Jack Baxter and Jefri Alalmuhammed, X-Ceptional Productions, Inc., 1997.

493 *Hours after*: Johnson, Jason B. "Brooklyn Rabbi, Malcolm X Widow Discuss Racial Peace." *Boston Herald*, March 2, 1994, 3.

493 *Innuendo gave way to indictment*: "Widow of Malcolm X Suspects Farrakhan Had Role in Killing." *New York Times*, March 13, 1994, A33; Kellogg, Valerie. "Widow Rips Islam Leader; Role in Death of Malcolm X." *Newsday*, March 13, 1994, 4; Boyd, Herb. "Betty Shabazz Denies Charges of ADL Influence." *New York Amsterdam News*, March 19, 1994, 3.

493 *The Nation responded swiftly*: Boyd, Herb. "Betty Shabazz Denies Charges of ADL Influence." *New York Amsterdam News*, March 19, 1994, 3; "Farrakhan Admits Spreading Ideas That Led to Malcolm X's Slaying." *Los Angeles Times*, April 23, 1994, A4; Salaam, Yusef. "Women Writers Have Inspirational Evening at the Studio Museum." *New York Amsterdam News*, May 28, 1994, 29; Garfield, William F. Lowman. "Attacks on Farrakhan Measure His Success in Galvanizing Us." *Pittsburgh Post-Gazette*, April 13, 1994, B2; Frankel, Bruce. "Farrakhan Sues 'Post' Over Malcolm X Story/Widow Calls for Probe of 1965 Slaying." *USA Today*, March 16, 1994, 3A.

494   *She insisted that her position*: Frankel, Bruce. "Farrakhan Sues 'Post' Over Malcolm X Story/Widow Calls for Probe of 1965 Slaying." *USA Today*, March 16, 1994, 3A; Boyd, Herb. "Betty Shabazz Denies Charges of ADL Influence." *New York Amsterdam News*, March 19, 1994, 3.

494   *Playing victim*: Browne, J. Zamgba. "Farrakhan Says a Racist Plot Plans His Assassination." *New York Amsterdam News*, March 26, 1994, 33.

495   *"most striking"*: Marable, Manning. *Beyond Black & White*. New York: Verso, 1995, 163.

495   *The summit's organizers*: Boyd, Herb. "NAACP's Leadership Conference Elicited 500 Memberships Daily." *New York Amsterdam News*, June 25, 1994, 4.

495   *Days later*: Goodstein, Laurie. "Eclectic Extended Family Bids Farewell to Minister." *Washington Post*, June 25, 1994, C3.

495   *Trouble with Qubilah*: Furst, Randy. "Events Shattered Quiet Life Shabazz Would Prefer." *Minneapolis Star Tribune*, May 9, 1995, 1A; Farber, M. A. "In the Name of the Father." *Vanity Fair*, June 1995, 62-66; "Percy Sutton and Dr. Shabazz Discuss Qubilah's Case," *Like It Is*, WABC-TV, New York, May 7, 1995; Lee, Felicia R. "Much Black Skepticism on Charges of a Plot by Daughter of Malcolm X." *New York Times*, January 14, 1995, 8; Jordan, Gorge E. "A Low Profile in Minnesota." *Newsday*, January 14, 1995, A4; Bentley, Rosalind and Kimberly Hayes Taylor. "From New York to Minneapolis, Shabazz has Led a Quiet Life." *Minneapolis Star Tribune*, January 18, 1995, 12A; Duchschere, Kevin. "Daughters of Black Notables to Start Legal Fund for Shabazz." *Minneapolis Star-Tribune*, January 25, 1995, 11A; Sexton, Joe. "Daughter of Malcolm X: Dreams Turned to Dust." *New York Times*, January 22, 1995, 1.

499   *Neighbors and friends knew Qubilah*: Fainaru, Steve and Colum Lynch. "Charges Defy Image of Malcolm X Daughter." *Boston Globe*, January 15, 1995, 2; Farber, M. A. "In the Name of the Father." *Vanity Fair*, June 1995, 62, 65-66; Beals, Gregory, et al. "Back in the Line of Fire." *Newsweek*, January 23, 1995, 21; Lacayo, Richard. "Follow the Leader." *Time*, January 30, 1995, 51.

501   *By early 1994*: Furst, Randy. "Events Shattered Quiet Life Shabazz Would Prefer." *Minneapolis Star Tribune*, May 9, 1995, 1A; Farber, M. A. "In the Name of the Father." *Vanity Fair*, June 1995, 66, 68, 69; Herbert, Bob. "In America; Always the Violence." *New York Times*, June 9, 1997, A25.

503   *The following month*: Bentley, Rosalind and Kimberly Hayes Taylor. "From New York to Minneapolis, Shabazz has Led a Quiet Life." *Minneapolis Star-Tribune*, January 18, 1995, 12A; Braun, Stephen and Judy Pasternak. "Malcolm X's Daughter Held in Plot to Kill Farrakhan." *Los Angeles Times*, January 13, 1995, A1; Terry, Don. "Nation of Islam Says It Doubts Account of Assassination Plan." *New York Times*, January 14, 1995, 1; Ison, Chris and Paul McEnroe. "Roommates of Alleged Hit Man: Shabazz Calls Became Nuisance." *Minneapolis Star-Tribune*, January 17, 1995, 1A; Sexton, Joe. "Daughter of Malcolm X; Dreams Turned to Dust." *New York Times*, January 22, 1995, 1; Ison, Chris and Paul McEnroe. "FBI Transcripts Show Shabazz's Evolution; Apparently Willing Participant Grew Fearful as Plot Took Shape." *Minneapolis, Star-Tribune*, 6A; Ison, Chris and Paul McEnroe. "The Sad and Troubled Life of Qubilah Shabazz." *Minneapolis Star-Tribune*, January 22, 1995, 1A.

505   *Betty was shattered*: Russakoff, Dale. "'Climate of Tragedy' Clings to the Family of Malcolm X; As Betty Shabazz Fights for Life, Grandson Appears in Court." *Washington Post*, June 3, 1997, A3.

506   *A course of action*: "Percy Sutton and Dr. Shabazz Discuss Qubilah's Case," *Like It Is*, WABC-TV, New York, May 7, 1995.

506   *"an improbably lurid sequel"*: Beals, Gregory, et al. "Back in the Line of Fire." *Newsweek*, January 23, 1995, 21.

506   *Betty proclaimed the affair*: Terry, Don. "Daughter of Malcolm X Charged With Trying to Kill Farrakhan." *New York Times*, January 13, 1995, A1; Jones, Charisse. "Qubilah Shabazz: An 'Ideal Young Lady'." *New York Times*, January 13, 1995, A16; Perl, Peter. "Plot to Kill Farrakhan Is

Alleged; Malcolm X's Daughter Faces Federal Charges." *Washington Post*, January 13, 1995, A1; Jordan, George E. "A Low Profile in Minnesota." *Newsday*, January 14, 1995, A4.

507 *Everyone else was talking:* Ritter, John and Andrea Stone. "Charge Mingles With Bad Blood/30 Years Later, Another Claim of Conspiracy." *USA Today*, January 13, 1995, 3A; Lee, Felicia R. "Much Black Skepticism on Charges Of a Plot by Daughter of Malcolm X." *New York Times*, January 14, 1995, 8.

507 *Qubliah's family and friends gasped:* Lee, Felicia R. "Much Black Skepticism on Charges of a Plot by Daughter of Malcolm X." *New York Times*, January 14, 1995, 8.

507 *"None of my sisters":* Sinclair, Abiola. "Malaak Shabazz Speaks Out for Sis." *New York Amsterdam News*, January 28, 1995, 24.

507 *The FBI was handling the daughter:* Perl, Peter. "Ex-FBI Agent Says Informer Did Not Entrap Malcolm X Daughter." *Washington Post*, January 15, 1995, A6; Tatum, Wilbert A. "Ms. Shabazz, Minister Farrakhan and the FBI: Different Drummers." *New York Amsterdam News*, January 21, 1995, 12.

508 *Ancient bitterness:* Amiri Baraka Interview, June 19, 1999; Haki Madhubuti Interview, June 2, 2000.

508 *The leader scored a coup:* Walsh, Edward. "Farrakhan Says U.S. Concocted Plot Charge; Government Accused of Manipulating Shabazz." *Washington Post*, January 18, 1995, A3; Howlett, Debbie. "Farrakhan Accuses Federal Government in Plot." *USA Today*, January 18, 1995, 5A; Jordan, George E. "Farrakhan: Shabazz' Life May Be in Danger." *Newsday*, January 18, 1995, A19.

509 *Betty accepted the gambit:* Connors, Cathy. "'My Child Was Set Up, Entrapped'" Qubilah Shabazz Pleads Not Guilty To All Counts." *New York Amsterdam News*, January 21, 1995, 1; Perl, Peter. "Shabazz Pleads Not Guilty In Alleged Assassination Plot." *Washington Post*, January 19, 1995, A3; Terry, Don. "Malcolm X's Daughter Enters Not guilty Plea." *New York Times*, January 19, 1995, B10; Farber, M. A. "In the Name of the Father." *Vanity Fair*, June 1995, 69.

510 *The government dropped the murder-conspiracy charges:* Gladwell, Malcolm. "U.S., Shabazz Settle Farrakhan Murder Plot Case." *Washington Post*, May 2, 1995, A1; Terry, Don. "Both Sides in Shabazz Case Say Tapes Prove Their Point." *New York Times*, February 28, 1995, A17; Braun, Stephen. "Farrakhan Case Transcripts Sketch Malcolm X's Daughter." *Los Angeles Times*, February 28, 1995, A21; Groeneveld, Benno. "Shabazz Lawyers Say She's Accused of "Thought Crime." *Chicago Sun-Times*, March 9, 1995, 25; Furst, Randy. "Fitzpatrick: FBI promised $45,000 for Informant Work in Shabazz Case." *Minneapolis Star-Tribune*, March 24, 1995, 1A.

512 *Later that year:* January 4, 1996 Betty Shabazz letter to Embassy of Saudi Arabia. (Courtesy, Gamilah Shabazz).

512 *Closer to home:* Terry, Don. "Black 'Sisters' Support Daughter of Malcolm X." *New York Times*, January 26, 1995, A12; "King's Wife Backs Qubilah Shabazz." *Times-Picayune*, February 1, 1995, A4; Tanner, Adam. "Seeing Entrapment, Blacks Rally Behind Malcolm X's Daughter." *Christian Science Monitor*, February 3, 1965, 3; Greene, Leonard. "Malcolm X's Widow Still Mourns His Loss." *Boston Herald*, February 24, 1995, 8; White, Evelyn C. "Black Women Embrace Shabazz." *San Francisco Chronicle*, February 20, 1995, A1.

513 *A short letter:* June 23, 1995 Qubilah Shabazz Letter to Betty Shabazz (courtesy of Gamilah Shabazz).

514 *"You have to watch":* Andrews, Laura. "Malcolm X Tribute: A Day of Reflection." *New York Amsterdam News*, May 27, 1995, 27.

516 *Helped set it up:* Madhubuti, Haki. *Claiming Earth*. Chicago: Third World Press, 1994, 80-85; Haki Madhubuti Interview, June 2, 2000; "Percy Sutton and Dr. Shabazz Discuss Qubilah's Case," *Like It Is*, WABC-TV, New York, May 7, 1995.

516 *The night before the benefit:* Jones, Charisse. "Crowds Fill Apollo to Witness Shabazz and Farrakhan Meet." *New York Times*, May 7, 1995, 1; Gladwell, Malcolm. "Farrakhan Seeks End of Rift With Shabazz; Apologizes for 'Hurt' But Denies Involvement in Malcolm X Death." *Washington Post*, May 8, 1995, A1; Purnick, Joyce. "Metro Matters; An Unlikely Matchmaker for Shabazz and

Farrakhan." *New York Times*, May 8, 1995, B1; Henican, Ellis. "Strange Bedfellows on Stage at Apollo." *Newsday*, May 2, 1995, A4; Mary Redd Interview; Ruth Clark Interview.

519 *"It was Mother's Day."*: Shipp, E.R. "Apollo Get-Together Was About Qubilah." *Daily News*, May 17, 1995.

CHAPTER 19: STARTING OVER

521 *"I saw the iamge of my grandmother"*: Wright, Richard. *Black Boy*. New York: Harper & Row, 1945, 11.

521 *"I know your face"*: Laura Ross Brown Interview, June 11, 1999.

522 *"She just didn't sound right"*: Larry Dais Interview, June 8, 1999.

522 *"You've been here"*: Mary Redd Interview, May 20, 1999.

523 *Malcolm came to her*: Edison O. Jackson Interview, March 31, 1999.

523 *"Some of the sharpness"*: Mary Redd Interview.

523 *"rest more"*: Laura Ross Brown Interview.

523 *She evaluated the Million Man March*: Wright, James. "Loud Cheers for Clinton at CBCF." Washington *Afro-American*, September 21, 1996, A1.

523 *The reformation did not last*: "First Lady Hillary Clinton Keynotes NCNW Inaugural." Washington *Afro-American*, October 12, 1996, A1; "Two to Serve as Co-Chairs of Annual Frederick Douglass Awards Dinner." *New York Amsterdam News*, March 22, 1997, 4; Pryce, Vinette K. "10 Years After Howard Beach Assault, Recitals, Songs at Brooklyn Museum." *New York Amsterdam News*, December 7, 1996, 9; James, Wright. "Dr. Chavis, Min. Farrakhan Snubbed at New Black Leadership Meeting." *Washington Afro-American*, December 14, 1996, A1.

524 *A need to resist*: Shabazz, Betty. "Leaving Welfare." *Los Angeles Sentinel*, March 12, 1997, A6; Betty Shabazz Papers (courtesy of Gamilah Shabazz).

524 *"so many forces"*: Larry Dais Interview.

524 *"like she was tired"*: Ruth Clark Interview, April 14, 1999.

525 *Her grandson that most frazzled her*: Russakoff, Dale. "'Climate of Tragedy' Clings to the Family of Malcolm X; As Betty Shabazz Fights for Life, Grandson Appears in Court." *Washington Post*, June 3, 1997, A3; Gosselin, Peter G. "Malcolm X Widow Hurt in Fire; Kin Is Arrested." *Boston Globe*, June 2, 1997, A1; Morrison, Dan. "He's Frightened; Malcolm Shabazz Appears in Court with Percy Sutton." *Newsday*, June 3, 1997, A7; Morrison, Dan. "Malcolm: Fire Bid to Go Home; Tells Friend He Wanted to Return to Mom." *Newsday*, June 4, 1997, A4; Morrison, Dan and Monte R. Young. "Torn By Troubles; Legal and Personal Woes Follow Shabazz Family." *Newsday*, June 8, 1997, A7; Legal Fisher, Marc and Dale Russakoff. "A Legacy of Trauma." *Washington Post*, June 7, 1997, A1.

526 *His grandmother would also struggle*: Coleman, Trevor W. "A Mother's Struggle." *Emerge*, September 1997, 40-58.

526 *To take in Little Malcolm*: Rutenberg, Jim et al. "He Missed Mom, Got 'Stressed Out'." *Daily News*, June 3, 1997, 22; Hewitt, Bill et al. "Fisher, Marc and Dale Russakoff. "A Legacy of Trauma." *Washington Post*, June 7, 1997, A1; Russakoff, Dale. "'Climate of Tragedy' Clings to the Family of Malcolm X; As Betty Shabazz Fights for Life, Grandson Appears in Court." *Washington Post*, June 3, 1997, A3.

526 *"I guess that's why"*: Gamilah Shabazz Interview, January 15, 2000.

527 *"You could tell"*: Ernest Davis Interview, February 6, 2001.

527 *The once-moldering building was reborn*: Rozhon, Tracie. "Research Park rising on Site of Audubon Ballroom." *New York Times*, June 11, 1995; Unger, Michael. "Biotech Incubator Opens in the City; Center on Site Where Malcolm X Died." *Newsday*, October 17, 1995, A41.

528 *But by 1996*: Grant, Peter. "Rift Over Audubon Plan; City Vs. Panel on Funding for Malcolm X Memorial." *Daily News*, March 27, 1996, 50; Michael Mowatt-Wynn Interview, July 23, 1999.

529 *She liked what she saw*: Michael Mowatt-Wynn Interview; Larry Dais Interview; James Turner Interview, May 13, 2002; Sonny Carson Interview, March 12, 2000.

530 *"I'm going to get out"*: Ernest Davis Interview.

530 *Betty escaped in the summer*: Myrlie Evers-Williams Interview, August 30, 1999; Evers-Williams, Myrlie. *Watch Me Fly*. New York: Little, Brown & Co., 1999, 304; Brown, Jamie Foster. *Betty Shabazz; A Sisterfriends' Tribute in Words and Pictures*. New York: Simon & Schuster, 1998, 17-20.

532 *Eluded her second eldest in Texas*: Russakoff, Dale. "'Climate of Tragedy' Clings to the Family of Malcolm X; As Betty Shabazz Fights for Life, Grandson Appears in Court." *Washington Post*, June 3, 1997, A3; Morrison, Dan. "He's Frightened; Malcolm Shabazz Appears in Court with Percy Sutton." *Newsday*, June 3, 1997, A7; Rutenberg, Jim et al. "He Missed Mom, Got 'Stressed Out.'" *Daily News*, June 3, 1997, 22; Fisher, Marc and Dale Russakoff. "A Legacy of Trauma; This week's Near-Fatal Fire Is the Latest in a Lifetime of Tragedies that have Engulfed the Shabazz Family." *Washington Post*, June 7, 1997, A1; Yglesias, Linda. "At Center of Tragedy Is a Lost Boy Who Wanted Normal Life." *Daily News*, June 8, 1997, 7; Morrison, Dan and Monte R. Young. "Torn By Troubles; Legal and Personal Woes Follow Shabazz Family." *Newsday*, June 8, 1997, A7.

534 *"It is my strong opinion"*: April 30, 1997 Dick Rath letter to Paula Rosen, Betty Shabazz Papers (courtesy of Gamilah Shabazz).

534 *There is some ambiguity*: Herman Fulton Interview, July 30, 2000.

534 *"She was managing"*: James Turner Interview.

534 *A gift of coconut cake*: Larry Dais Interview.

535 *Late that month*: Maya Angelou Interview.

535 *"There were a lot of things"*: Ruth Clark Interview. James Smalls, March 14, 2000.

535 *Betty flagged a cab*: "Dr. Betty Shabazz's Final Words." Interview with Bernard White and Amy Goodman, Pacifica Radio, WBAI, New York City, May 19, 1997.

535 *"I'm too old"*: Howard Dodson Interview.

535 *Spotted her walking*: Ernest Davis Interview.

536 *"Do you think"*: Rutenberg, Jim et al. "He Missed Mom, Got 'Stressed Out.'" *Daily News*, June 3, 1997, 22.

536 *"What happened to Sister Betty?"*: James Smalls Interview, March 14, 2000.

536 *"No way"*: Ruth Clark Interview.

536 *"I heard"*: Ernest Davis Interview.

536 *Via voicemail*: Howard Dodson Interview.

536 *"How's your mom?"*: Shabazz, Attallah. "The Longest Prayer." *Essence*, October, 1997, 73.

536 *"People was really angry"*: Bro. Akeem Interview.

537 *The culprit was kin*: Gosselin, Peter G. "Malcolm X Widow Hurt in Fire; Kin Is Arrested." *Boston Globe*, June 2, 1997, A1.

537 *Police had found Little Malcolm*: Russakoff, Dale. "'Climate of Tragedy' Clings to the Family of Malcolm X; As Betty Shabazz Fights for Life, Grandson Appears in Court." *Washington Post*, June 3, 1997, A3; Gosselin, Peter. "Malcolm X Widow Hurt in Fire; Kin Is Arrested." *Boston Globe*, June 2, 1997, A1; Morrison, Dan. "He's Frightened; Malcolm Shabazz Appears in Court with Percy Sutton." *Newsday*, June 3, 1997, A7; Fitz-Gibbon, Jorge et al. "Malcolm X Grandson Sorrty; Psych Tests Ok'd in Shabazz Arson." *Daily News*, June 3, 1997, 7; Coleman, Trevor W. "A Mother's Struggle." *Emerge*, September 1997, 50; Percy Sutton Interview, September 21, 2000.

538 *Amazingly, she lingered*: Coleman, Chrisena, et al. "Malcolm X Widow Burned; Dr. Betty Didn't Give In." *Daily News*, June 2, 1997, 3; Cooke, Robert. "Doctors Focus on Infections." *Newsday*, June 3, 1997, A24; Scott, Janny. "Severity of Shabazz's Burns Hurt Her Chances to Survive." *New York Times*, June 3, 1997, B6; McPhee, Michele. "Friends Offering Prayers & Hope." *Daily News*, June 3, 1997, 7; Ramirez, Margaret. "Doctors Replace Shabazz Skin." *Newsday*, June 5, 1997, A6;

Dwyer, Jim. "New Life Now Growing Where Malcolm X Died." *Daily News*, June 5, 1997, 6; Fitz-Gibbon, Jorge and Jane Furse. "Family: Pray for Shabazz; Grandson Arraigned in Closed Courtroom." *Daily News*, June 7, 1997, 7; Dick Gregory Interview, July 30, 1999; Fitz-Gibbon, Jorge et al. "Malcolm X Grandson Sorry; Psych Tests Ok'd in Shabazz Arson." *Daily News*, June 3, 1997, 7; Bruni, Frank. "Mother Tries to Calm Son At Hearing on Shabazz Fire." *New York Times*, June 4, 1997, B2.

541 *Local radio stations*: Hinckley, David. "WLIB Callers Pray for Betty." *Daily News*, June 3, 1997, 76.

541 *Christians and Muslims gathered*: Dino, Hazell. "Ecumenical Prayer Service Held for Dr. Betty Shabazz." *New York Amsterdam News*, June 7, 1997, 11; Tatum, Wilbert A. "Betty Shabazz: Goodnight, Sweet Princess." *New York Amsterdam News*, June 28, 1997, 14.

541 *Then came the blood drives*: Gross, Jane. "Compelled by Shabazz's Situation, Hundreds Give Blood." *New York Times*, June 10, 1997, B3; Goldman, John J. "New Yorkers Open Hearts For Shabazz; Vigil: Scores Stream in to Give Blood As Widow of Malcolm X Fights for Life." *Los Angeles Times*, June 13, 1997, A1.

541 *Her daughters linked hands*: "Praying for Shabazz," *Newsday*, June 16, 1997, A18; Fitz-Gibbon, Jorge and Jane Furse. "Family: Pray for Shabazz; Grandson Arraigned in Closed Courtroom." *Daily News*, June 7, 1997, 7.

542 *"go well"*: Aisha Al-Adawiya Interview, May 31, 1999.

542 *"She has something to say"*: Ruth Clark Interview.

542 *At the end*: Coleman, Trevor W. "A Mother's Struggle." *Emerge*, September 1997, 58; Gamilah Shabazz Interview; Gross, Jane. "Experts Testify Shabazz Boy Is Psychotic." *New York Times*, July 30, 1997, B1; Williams, Monte. "Shabazz Youth Admits Setting The Fatal Fire." *New York Times*, July 11, 1997, A1; Ruth Clark Interview; Gross, Jane. "Lawyers for Malcolm Shabazz Say He Thrives in Treatment." *New York Times*, September 27, 1997, B5; Harden, Blaine and Dale Russakoff. "Betty Shabazz Dies of Burn Injuries; 3-Week Fight for Life Brought Wide Support for Malcolm X's Widow." *Washington Post*, June 24, 1997, A1; Sutton, Larry. "Fond Memories and Many Tears; Grim News Saddens Friends, Strangers." *Daily News*, June 24, 1997, 5.

EPILOGUE: HOMECOMING

545 *Two days after the widow's death*: Bruni, Frank. "Honoring Shabazz and 'Things That She Stood For.'" *New York Times*, June 26, 19997, B1; "Shabazz Daughters Prepare Her for Burial." *Newsday*, June 26, 1997, A5; Cauvin, Henri E. and Chrisena Coleman and Jere Hester. "Mournful Shabazz Farewell." *Daily News*, June 26, 1997, 4; Swarns, Rachel L. "At Funeral for Shabazz, Grief, Prayer and Respect." *New York Times*, June 28, 1997, A23; Coleman, Chrisena and James Rutenberg. "Final Farewell to Shabazz; Hailed as a Hero by Hundreds at E. Side Funeral." *Daily News*, June 28, 1997, 5. Bruni, Frank. "Stirred by Her Life, Thousands Attend Service for Shabazz." *New York Times*, June 30, 1997, A3.

547 *Twelve-year-old began serving*: Gross, Jane. "Lawyers for Malcolm Shabazz Say He Thrives in Treatment." *New York Times*, September 27, 1997, B5.

547 *Back in trouble*: McQuillan, Alice. "Shabazz Flees Detention." *Daily News*, July 29, 1999, 33.

548 *A year onto his sentence*: "Longer Term Ordered for Malcolm Shabazz." *New York Times*, August 4, 1999, B2.

548 *Yet in early 2002*: "Malcolm X Kin Arrested Again." *Newsday*, January 27, 2002, A14.

548 *"We have to focus on Malcolm"*: Williams, Monte. "A Shabazz Daughter Learns to Cope After Loss." *New York Times*, August 23, 1997, A28.

548 *The torment of Betty's passing*: Corey, Mary and M. Dion Thompson. "Following the Light." *Baltimore Sun*, March 29, 1998, 1A.

INDEX

ABOUT THE AUTHOR

Russell J. Rickford is the coauthor of *Spoken Soul*, about the expressive qualities of black vernacular, and he is a former *Philadelphia Inquirer* reporter. He graduated Magna Cum Laude from Howard University and studied under such black scholars as Molefi Kete Asante, Russell Adams, Charles Metz, and E. Ethelbert Miller. He was born in Guyana and currently lives in New York City, where he is a Ph.D. candidate in history at Columbia University.

DATE			

35.00   12-30-03

FREEPORT MEMORIAL LIBRARY

BAKER & TAYLOR